Anthology of Magazine Verse

&

Yearbook of American Poetry
1980 Edition

About the Editor...

Alan F. Pater edited the *Anthology of Magazine Verse* annually from 1935 through 1942; he also was editor and publisher of *The Poetry Digest* and *The Poet & The Critic* magazines.

ANTHOLOGY OF MAGAZINE VERSE

AND YEARBOOK OF AMERICAN POETRY

1980 EDITION

Edited by

ALAN F. PATER

Introduction by
WILLIAM H. PRITCHARD

BEVERLY HILLS
MONITOR BOOK COMPANY, INC.

FIRST ANNUAL EDITION

Printed in the United States of America

ISBN number: 0-917734-04-1

ISSN number: 0196-2221

The Anthology of Magazine Verse & Yearbook of American Poetry is published annually by Monitor Book Company, Inc., 195 South Beverly Drive, Beverly Hills, CA 90212.

Preface

Much of the world's finest and most prolific poetry has first appeared in periodical literature: poetry monthlies and quarterlies, general literary magazines, college journals, etc.

Regrettably, most of those publications have limited circulations, and once an issue has been read—and the next one arrives—it is filed away and rarely opened again. But the wealth of excellent work contained in their pages—by both talented, promising new poets and well-known, established writers—should be kept alive, distributed more widely and be readily available. That is the *raison d'etre* of the *Anthology of Magazine Verse*.

After William Stanley Braithwaite ended his much respected annual surveys of magazine poetry in 1929, there was a lamentable gap in the important business of selecting and preserving in book form the verse of the day. That pause was temporarily filled with the re-emergence of the *Anthology of Magazine Verse* in the mid-1930's through the early 1940's by the editor of this current volume, but World War II then interrupted the continuation of the series.

Now, this new series of annual collections is aimed at re-establishing the purpose and spirit of the Braithwaite books on a continuing basis, and thereby providing a yearly barometer of the trends of poetry in the United States and Canada.

An effort has been made to include poems of various lengths, forms and styles, as well as a multiplicity of subjects and geographical originations. And the spread of magazine sources chosen reflects these criteria.

It should be noted that the sources included in any given volume of the Anthology constitute only a portion of the total number of periodicals regularly received by the editor and considered for suitable material. Since the quality of the individual poem is the main criterion for acceptance, the specific magazines represented in each edition of the Anthology will necessarily vary from year to year.

Magazine poetry best represents the era in which it is written—it is current, abundant, as varied in style and content as the numberless journals in which it is published. Its topics are today's issues and events, as well as the perennial ones. New poets, who, because of the current realities of the book world, find it difficult to have their work published in hardcover, fortunately have an outlet in the increasing volume of magazines that print new and original poetry. It is from their ranks that the future major poets will emerge.

Also part of this volume is the *Yearbook of American Poetry*—the first and only annual gathering of factual material in this burgeoning field. The *Yearbook*'s directories, bibliographies and listings (to be updated with each succeeding edition) will provide a yearly record of information and reference material for the world of poetry—an area heretofore lacking a comprehensive information sourcebook of its own.

Together, the *Anthology of Magazine Verse and Yearbook of American Poetry* will, hopefully, be inspiring, stimulating, informative, and an accurate reflection of the state of the poetic form today.

Beverly Hills,
California   A.F.P.

Table of Contents

PART ONE

Anthology
of Magazine Verse

Introduction

by
WILLIAM H. PRITCHARD

*Professor of English, Amherst College; member of
editorial board,* The Hudson Review

Sixty-seven years ago, William Stanley Braithwaite published the first of his yearly collections titled *Anthology of Magazine Verse*. The 1913 volume was a slim one, under seventy pages of poems drawn from seven magazines, and was graced, naturally enough, with a good many names unfamiliar to us today: Ruth Guthrie Hardin and Ruth Comfort Mitchell; Robert Alden Sanborn and Tertius vanDyke. Its best poem may well be "The Field of Glory," by Edwin Arlington Robinson; its most famous one is surely "Trees," by Joyce Kilmer. There was as yet no Frost, no Amy Lowell, no Conrad Aiken or Wallace Stevens, though they were to appear in subsequent volumes of the anthology. But Braithwaite did not let any possible lack of individual poetic riches deter him from making large inspirational gestures toward Poetry generally. He dedicated the anthology

> *To the Poets of America*
> *Singing today*
> *The soul of their country*
> *Truth, beauty, brotherhood*
> *Their names are torches*

and began his introduction by calling poetry "one of the realities that persist":

> The facade and dome of palace and temple, the monuments
> of heroes and saints, crumble before the ruining
> breath of time, while the Psalms last. So when
> another year passes and we sum up our achievements,
> there is no achievement more vital in registering
> the soul of a people than its poetry.

Braithwaite appeared confident of his taste. He spoke of "a general high standard" found in magazine verse from the year just concluding; he praised certain long poems (not included) such as Henry van Dyke's "Daybreak in the Grand Cañon of Arizona" for breathing a "fine national spirit, full of reverence for the greatness with which the American destiny is symbolized in the natural grandeur of our country"; he saluted Vachel Lindsay, author of "General William Booth Enters Into Heaven" as "a man with a big vision." And he felt proud in calling attention to a poet named Mahlon Leonard Fisher who had written a sonnet, "November," which Braithwaite termed one of the three best sonnets ever written by an American poet (along with Longfellow's "Nature" and Lizette Woodworth Reese's "Tears"), and which began in a way that now sounds unpromising to our ears: "Hark you such sound as quivers?"

The present anthology (456 pages of poems) is more than six times as long as Braithwaite's and contains, as his did, a good many poets unfamiliar even to a reader like myself who claims to be somewhat conversant with contemporary verse. America is a large country, and Alan Pater, this volume's editor, has shown an unregional catholicity in being as willing to select from *Poetry Northwest* as *The American Scholar*, from *Nitty Gritty* as from *The Hudson Review*. This catholicity shows up also in the democratic gesture of arranging the poems alphabetically by author; nor does the editor make any discernible attempt to impress us with the importance of particular poets at the expense of other ones. It is up to the reader, as he makes his way about this book, to find the points where he wants to stop, check, reread. This is one of the pleasures and challenges of having so much to choose from what has already been chosen.

It makes also for some uncertainty, seven decades after Braithwaite's first anthology, about the question of how important poetry is to our society. I do not mean to attack once more the philistines, or deplore the erosion of the reading habit, or look fearfully at other media—though these are natural things to do. I mean to suggest that even in the academic community, if my own is typical, where one might expect to find a strong "minority culture" engaged in discussion and argument about contemporary literature, one hears relatively little talk about new poets and poetry. Whereas the literary non-specialist, or even a specialist member like an English teacher, would try to keep current with Bellow or Updike or Mailer, and perhaps follow with interest three or four novelists to his particular taste while sampling a variety of other new fiction, nothing comparable occurs with respect to new poetry. No one has ever assumed that only novelists were interested in reading new novels; but entertaining the assumption that only poets are interested in new poetry would not be so outrageous a thing to do.

I am speaking mainly from the evidence of the new books which get borrowed from the library, or from the subjects of conversations heard around me; and if such a situation is exceptional rather than common, I should be glad to be contradicted. But if it is not exceptional it still seems to me no cause for despair, especially since the fact of this large, strong, varied anthology of poems speaks for the vitality of the enterprise. Put simply, more American poets are writing more poems at a level which (leaving aside Braithwaite's "high standard," whatever that was) only a very exclusive sensibility indeed would condescend to. But reasons for suspecting that there is a connection between contemporary poetry's lack of a large reading audience, and the impressive amount of good writing found in this anthology of poems, are worth exploring. I should also like to suggest, with reference to a few examples, the kind of interest and confidence this poetry typically inspires.

Let us try on the notion, however simplified and exaggerated it is, that poets mainly write for other poets, whereas novelists hope to reach a wider audience, to reach that much yearned for "general reader." It might be thought then that to write for other poets is to identify your concerns as purely aesthetic, oriented toward style rather than substance, preoccupied with something called technique at the probable expense of something called life. Yet, as T.S. Eliot importantly reminds us, "We cannot say at what point 'technique' begins or where it ends." Analogously, who is to say where "poet" begins and ends? Is a poet someone with an obsession about ways of saying things? He is also, she is also—in Wordsworth's famous salute—" . . . endowed with more lively sensibility, more enthusiasm and tenderness, who has a greater knowledge of human nature and a more comprehensive soul . . . pleased with his own passions and volitions . . . delighting to contemplate similar volitions and passions as manifested in the goings-on of the universe." It is fine to think of the poet as a man speaking to men; but if, as I suspect, many contemporary poets feel their audience to be essentially made up of fellow practitioners, then the stakes are that much higher. How can one write so as to gratify so many lively sensibilities, such comprehensive souls?

Generalizing on the basis of the poems before us—a hazardous enough occupation—we could say that there are some things one need *not* do: one need not go in for extravagances of tone or diction; one need not go on at length about the conditions (usually bad) inside one's head; one need not affect a slam-bang way either of beginning or ending the poem so as to "grab" the reader. In fact, one need not sound especially "poetic":

> Above my daughter in the tree
> white spider lowers itself on a string,
> hangs like a blind eye that can establish
> only light or dark. What is between
> twelve and thirteen is unclear,
> a quiver of thrusts and halts.
> She is unsure herself
> except for the way it feels to swing
> her legs into space, or stretch

> like the hands of a clock and balance
> as if she were nothing, a negative print
> of a spider, a stopped moment.

Written by a poet I'd never heard of before (Marita Garin) and published in a magazine equally unknown to me (*National Forum*), "White Spider" in its modest, intelligent authority, in the subtlety of its movement, the delicacy and clarity of its perceptions, may stand as a small model for much of the good work done in this anthology. The "stopped moment," rendered with affection, surprise, admiration, is what many of these poems are concerned with. Gary Gildner remembers his father:

> Putting out the candles
> I think of winter, that quick
> dark time before dinner
> when he came upstairs after
> shaking the furnace alive,
> his cheek patched with soot,
> his overalls flecked with
> sawdust and snow,
> and called for his pillow,
> saying to wake him
> when everything was ready.

Just the thinking, the seeing of it, is enough. Sometimes the stopped moment is too much, as in Lowell Jaeger's "Poem For My Mother":

> . . . there I am in the driveway
> leaving, waving to you in the window;
>
> you with your apron your warm smile but nervous
> hands, your dance of weak knees
> and the broken look in your eye. But I wave
> you wave, maybe I honk and around the
>
> corner I curse, slam my fist on the
> dash, hating the way I hurt you . . .

Or it may be eerily, impersonally memorable, as Sam Hamill (in "The Wakening") sees his father trying to care for a coop full of dying chicks:

> All night his ears rang
> between the echoes of his heart
> with the sickly *cheep, cheep*
> of small white heads agape
> from twisted necks,
> beaks dropped open to ask
> what no one ever knows, refusing
> feed and drink as they died,
> twisted in the palm of his hand.

Each of the poems in which these familial remembrances occur is rhythmically distinct, attempting to realize its own pace by following the natural movements of a speaking voice. This is in part a consequence, it must be admitted, of a disinclination on the part of many poets writing today and represented here, to work with rhyme and strict stanzaic forms. They are inclined rather toward the calculatedly irregular. But it may also have something to do with a fear of poetic afflatus, the bardic note which in their different ways some of the best and some of the worst poems from the earlier part of this century were bent on achieving. In the words of Vern Rutsala's ruefully titled poem, "Less is More"; but the slogan can have its positive satisfactions. In "Among Friends," Greg Kuzma tells us he lives "no longer among mountains," is married and settled down, has a dog who makes "vast demands, which we take delight in indulging," and grows a garden in weather that is "durable and bright." The implication is that, really, it is possible to live someplace else than on the heights. Lou Lipsitz is sardonic (in "The Radical in the Alligator Shirt") about growing old and out of the 1960's ("I used to lead peace marches / but now I'm an assistant dean") and ends up rather sentimentally chopping at himself:

> I used to tell my students the truth
> but now I think that youth is a stage
>
> I used to distrust anyone over thirty
> but now I know why: they knew better.

Is less somehow more, or is it really less? The question remains open as William Matthews contemplates "An Airline Breakfast":

> The older I grow, the better
> I love what I can't see:
> the stars in the daytime,
> the idea of an omelet,
> the reasons I love what I love.
> It's what I can see I have to nudge
> myself to love, so wonderful
> is the imagination. Even this wretched
> and exhausted breakfast is OK

The "nudge" is what takes place again and again in poems that say what can be said, imaginatively, for living with less.

A reader like myself who first came to poetry thirty years ago, experiences another way in which what seems like less may just possibly be more. I refer to the fact that whether I admired or was indifferent to individual poems in this anthology, I felt for the most part as if I understood them. To someone raised on Oscar Williams's anthologies from the 1940's and 50's with their high quotient of allusive or cryptic or disjunctive or highly symbolical goings-on, it comes as a mild shock to encounter poem after contemporary poem that, without being simple-minded, expresses thoughts that can be followed. This expression is centrally achieved through syntax (though not centrally through rhyme or stanza) as it shapes the figure each poem makes. By comparison with the new poems of three or four decades ago, the poems of 1979 offer relatively little of the overwhelming; their voices are pitched lower, their tones more rueful and rooted. There is precious little reliance on what Philip Larkin once memorably referred to as "The Myth-Kitty." And Kingsley Amis's opining that "Nobody wants any more poems about foreign cities" may also have turned out to be true. At least the poems in this anthology keep away from Venice and Paris in favor of the likes of Marshalltown, Iowa, or Colstrip, Montana.

Obviously there is the danger that such self-limiting, self-aware performances will end up sounding a bit dry, simply not containing very much of the news that stays news Pound said poetry had to be to be any good. One of the ways a contemporary poem manages to arrest a subject, and a reader, is by making us pay attention to a voice that cannot be easily classified as either personal or impersonal, but seems to draw on responses from both realms. The opening stanza of James Richardson's "Dividing the House" is perfectly unostentatious, perfectly lucid:

> Eloquent as stuck drawers, we come out
> with everything, too late, too hard.
> Today no tears—we're praising
> self-sufficiency, the adaptation
> of higher animals to early loss.

Impersonal and cool, this is surely not self-display; yet it displays the speaker as very much himself. While an extremely personal elegy by Frederick Morgan, dedicated to his dead son, somehow speaks for a grief that is more than private, as in these lines:

> And yet, your eyes still burn with joy,
> Your body's splendor never fades
> sometimes I seek to follow you
> across the greenness, into the shade
> of that great forest in whose depths
> houses await and lives are lived,
> where you haste in gleeful search of me
> bearing a message I must have—

Individual human grief becomes a part of something larger, mythic if you will, but quietly discovered rather than heavily applied from without.

Not the least interesting thing about this anthology is the way it resists the idea of Major Poets. To be sure, we meet work by names whose contribution to American poetry has been a large one, extending over a long period of time—I am thinking of an Eberhart, a Kunitz, a Nemerov, a Stafford. And there are impressive individual contributions by poets whose reputations are not yet secured and whose work, we remind ourselves, deserves our further attention: William Dickey, Richmond Lattimore, David Wagoner, Judith Moffett, and the aforementioned James Richardson and Frederick Morgan. But the book by its very nature democratizes, makes us look at the individual poem and ask ourselves whether, in particular cases, in the particular instance, the way of using language is any larger, more "major" than as it appears in the poem of a writer we may never have heard of before. And in these terms one would be willing to assert that there is no better poem in the volume than one by a writer who I presume is as unknown to most readers as she was to me. Here is the first stanza of "Mid-Plains Tornado," by Linda Bierds:

> I've seen it drive straw straight through a fence post—
> sure as a needle in your arm—the straws all erect
> and rooted in the wood like quills.
> Think of teeth being drilled, that enamel and blood
> burning circles inside your cheek. That's like the fury.
> Only now it's quail and axles, the northeast bank
> of the Cedar River, every third cottonwood.

It continues with no loss or diminishment of energy until its end.

"Organized violence upon language" was one of the best ways in which Robert Frost characterized poetry; by means of such violence and such organization, the furies of a tornado are composed into grace and shapeliness, just for the stopped moment. As the grandeurs of a striptease artist are no less violently composed in William Jay Smith's "Epitaph of a Stripper," which will serve also as an epitaph for this introduction:

> Here lies the stripper stripped, disrobed for good;
> Death wholly bares what life but partly could.
> The house lights dim: each pointed star-tipped breast
> Invites complete approval east and west.

Index of Poets

Index of Translators

(Due to publishing deadline requirements, poems for the Anthology are selected from magazines with cover dates during the 12-month period ending October 31 of each year. Poems for this edition of the Anthology were selected from magazines with cover dates during the 12-months ending October 31, 1979)

ANTS

I stood in my mother's kitchen
staring at dead ants. At least
fifty littered the orange countertop,
grotesque little bodies twisted from the poison
sprayed from a can last night.
As I watched, two live ants
crawled from a crevice, their antennae
waving with curiosity and hope.
And I thought about my mother,
how all her life she has been
pushing back the things
that threaten to destroy,
and how in the end
they always find that crevice
that shows them the way
back to the air, to the light, to her.

Poets On   *Katharyn Machan Aal*

READING TODAY'S NEWSPAPER

Reading today's newspaper I weep.
It seems that man is at it again—
clubbing seals, killing whales, massacring dolphins,
shooting children on the highway to Tel Aviv,
firing the hills of Lebanon in mad, bloody revenge.
Why is it, facing death, we hold
the body of our dreams
barreltight over a waterfall of endless tears?

I look at a photograph of a mother seal
who has crawled over the skinned body of her pup
trying to protect it from the camera.
I feel like this:
I feel like a refugee from something inside myself
trying to defend
something that may already be dead.

The hand that cuffs the child,
the ear that refuses to listen,
the nose that turns upward,
the mouth that laughs, judges
& can find nothing to praise or affirm
but would drown all other voices—
is this too not terrorism?

Consider your own body.
Where does your breath come from?
From where comes your power to speak & move?
Listen to the steady rhythm of your heart.
Let power flow from your heart
heartening this heartless world.

This morning opens like a dry newspaper,
a vast desert
on which one tear glistens like dew.
I behold this tear as a mirror,
my spiritbreath for tomorrow.

Heart mirror, show me my face.
Heart mirror, sing for me the forgotten song.
Swell like a river, a mighty ocean
until we hear in ourselves again
the forgotten song of love.

City Miner   *Steve Abbott*

HUNTING WITH MY FATHER

When I was a boy we always did it this way:
I wake to the smell of coffee
and you are at the fire,
its flames mirrored in your glasses.
Buck, the Colonel's dog, sleeps on beneath the bunk house,

his old legs quivering with problems of their own.
The raw south Texas dawn is about to break
and at the camp we are quiet as we eat.
Three deer hang gutted from a live oak,
their long shapes still graceful.

Father and I will hunt this desert
as if our lives depend on it,
but the kill is not what draws us here.
Every morning we walk the long mesa,
slowly working the ravines overgrown with mesquite.
When we come to a water hole we will post for hours
watching the grey end of the afternoon.
Standing there, deep in the silence of animals,
my father is showing me the greater world
that I might find my resemblance in it.

Ploughshares   *Tom Absher*

POETRY WORKSHOP IN A REFORM SCHOOL

The only difference, I said,
is these locks talk out loud.

I brought incense and poems,
apples and a branch of autumn leaves.
These children have eaten the incense,
their mouths dyed green with expectation.
They have rolled up the leaves for smoking
and opened the apple, hoping for razors.
They have swallowed the images. They are
disappointed.

Poems scented with ashes have traveled
the veins of these children.
Here, any word is the same knife,
any word is a phony door.
The children with green faces
are sick of artful communion.
And I have come away peeled to the bone,
having given away all my weapons.

ASFA Poetry Quarterly   *Betty Adcock*

PROTECT ME

Protect me from the gloom dispensers,
The dry throats that rasp disaster,
Gargling with questionable minerals
And crunching antediluvian rock.
Their bony fingers
Strum the chords of doom too often

While I prefer the *Trout* by
Franz Seraph Peter Schubert.

Good morning to you,
Measles, mumps and other dark dimensions.
I heard of death before
And need no apocryphal licorice.
I also know of life.
I ate some apples in my days.
Jonathans, Winesaps, Shockleys, and
All devoid of worms.
I've heard the roosters cry,
I heard a hearty laugh performed.

The Christian Century   *Hans Adler*

DISILLUSIONMENT

I machine-gunned tourists
for the liberation
of Palestine.
I massacred Catholics
for the independence of Ireland.
I poisoned aborigines
in Amazon jungles
to make way
for housing developments
and progress.
I assassinated Sandino,
Jesus,
Marti.
I launched Carrero Blanco
on his ascension
to heaven.
I exterminated Mai-Lei
for the welfare of democracy.
Nothing has worked:
despite all my efforts
the world continues the same.

The Virginia Quarterly Review   *Claribel Alegria*
                              —*Translated by Darwin Flakoll*

AFTER LOVE

As you lie there in the shadows of the room,
like the silence that remains after making love,
I, from the depths of my half-sleep, rise lightly toward
your tender, cooling borders that still sweetly exist.
And with my hand I stroke the delicate outer boundary of
    your
        withdrawn life,

I feel the hushed, musical truth of your body that only a
      moment
            ago sang like a disordered fire.
And your half-sleep allows the clay—which lost its lasting
      form
            in the act of love,
which leapt up like a hungry, ragged flame—
to turn itself back again into the true body that remakes
      itself
            in its enclosure.
            Touching the warm edges of a lover's body—silky,
      unhurt,
delicately naked—we know that her life will go on.
Love is a momentary destruction, a combustion that
      threatens
the pure creature we love, the one who's wounded in our
      fire.
But after we've pulled away from her destroyed flames
and looked at her, we see clearly the new, re-formed life,
the quiet, warm life that called to us from the sweet surface
            of her body.

Here is love's perfect vessel, filled
and overflowing with its serene and glistening golden blood.
Here are the breasts, the belly, her rounded thigh, her foot
      below
and her shoulders above, her neck like a soft new feather,
her cheek not scorched, not burnt, but frank with its new
      rosy flush,
and her brow where the daily thought of our love makes its
      home
            and keeps watch with clear eyes.
And at the center, sealing her bright face which the yellow
      evening
            warms without a fuss,
lies her mouth, torn, pure in the light,
Modest entry to the storehouse of fire!
With these fingers that are afraid and aware, I stroke your
            delicate skin
while, with my mouth, I begin again to cover your cooling
      hair.

The Paris Review   *Vicente Aleixandre*
                                   —Translated by Lewis Hyde

LAPIDARY

      The line of the cut must be clean
      and your nerves have to hold.
      Forget what you had for breakfast. Keep
      Still. Grip the chisel. If your nails dig in
      near the love line, stop and pare them.
      Fit your back to the task.

Don't ask why. This is not the time.
Forget that you think you're losing
that old sure touch. Raise the mallet.
Prepare
to be soft and brutal. The line
of the cut must be loving,
and the tap as hard as your heart.
When you breathe again
your breath will blow the stone in two.

Poet Lore   *Bonnie L. Alexander*

ON A WEDNESDAY

sucking soup out of a spoon
(by candlelight, rain
hissing in the street), I hear
the cat at her bowl,
lapping,
refrigerator whirring,
alarm clock ticking,
hot air breathing out vents
when the thermostat clicks

and behind those,
the hum my cells share
with blurred atoms,
the boiling spin of stars
the yogi's om:

do not
listen too long to this
dissonant organ chord, or you
may go mad, into a frenzy
the pleasure is so great;

beware the orgasm of astronomer's sky,
nirvana, satori;
they may release you from responsibility
for this small planet,
fragile crumb,
speck of cosmic dust.

when
the first photos came back
of the blue and white marble
floating in darkness,
an Italian poet wrote O earth

what are you doing up there in heaven?

watching how this jewel rises
above the moon's horizon
we may learn that all the heaven there is

is here,
if we can bear it.

Contemporary Quarterly   *Jody Aliesan*

GREEN PASTURES

The boy who has crawled
through the barbed wire fence to chase his dog
lies down in green pastures. Off to the right
a cottage and an old stone barn
look serenely deserted. Is there a soul
that cannot be restored? A time on the planet
all bets are called off? I have seen such pastures
at the end of Korea, littered with bodies, the medics
fanning across them like a flock of butterflies
to opening flowers. There is a pasture
high in the Adirondacks Winslow Homer painted
with two stabs of light. The boy seems asleep
or trying to close his eyes so tightly he will enter
the mind of his dog. All bets off? What does it take
to convince you that the hills are not asleep,
and the boy is not dreaming? Turning back and forth
in a North Dakota pasture is a radar screen
looking out for the Russians. In a small bowl of hills
wires are strung above deep pasture grass
to catch the faintest traffic from the stars
parsecs away. It is hopeless
to ignore a world that did not pass away
despite our avowals. Sunrise. Sunset. The green
stems of grass that touch against the boy
seem to hold the wind in place. A tractor
ridden by the brushstroke of a man
has been weaving for hours
on the farmlands behind us. Surely it is time
to rest, to lie down in the green beneath the blue
and call it a day;
or if we cannot do that, call it something given
to us—like sleep and waking up and sometimes rain
standing in the air around us as we walk
gratefully through it and it parts a little while.

Poetry   *Dick Allen*

VERSE FOR VESTIGIALS

Sometimes a child is washed from that warm room
still webbed, or with a trace of gill or pouch.
The myriad lives remembered in the womb
may leave a mark. Though pulled up to a slouch
they tell us once we crawled, and had to reach;

we had to push, make do, compress and hide,
inch up a little farther on the beach,
try for a toehold on the mountainside;

we reached and so we walk, who might have flapped
or worse. We reached and gouged and grabbed and mucked
out of the mire. Our sphere is booby-trapped
(by walkers) and could even self-destruct;
but say it once for luck: at least we lope
along on twos.
        The markings are for hope.

Blue Unicorn   *Elizabeth Allen*

ON CORWEN ROAD

On Corwen Road
I met a maid
more fair than any known,
all zephyr soft and perfumed as
the sweetest briar blown.

She kissed me
lightly on the brow
and beckoned me to follow
across the road, beyond the wall
toward a distant hollow.

I rose and followed
swift as man
might follow any maid,
yet caught her not on grassy slope
not yet by leafy glade.

But then was stopped
beside a lake
to see her standing there,
breast deep—and shining like a gem,
transparent as the air.

For she was of the Tylwyth Teg
enchanting mortal eyes
and far too gossamer a thing
for such an oaf as I.

Yet shall I feel her
presence near
with every passing breeze
though 50 years and more
have passed
dry-sapping this older tree.

Poet Lore   *Jay Ames*

WHEN FATHER SLEPT

He led his five senses into dreams
confident nothing was too much to expect,
or capable of resisting his control.
One arm always remained behind
reaching out from sleep
above a pillow, or over
my mother's shoulder.
He could have told us the arm was a marker,
a flare sent up to remind the wakeful
he would return unchanged,
demanding the conquests of sleep
to follow him out.
But they never did.
Instead, they camped in legions
curled on the dreaming side of his arm
where one by one they became
the promises he made us.

Cedar Rock   *James Anderson*

HOPE

No sorrows or plagues popped
from Pandora's box, but hope.

Hope will marry you to a werewolf,
sell you stock in a circus of bears,
and swear with a straight face
that a pair of angels will dance
on your plot.

Hope will work you up
to the boiling point,
then turn off the gas,
stand you up for happy hour,
forget to mail the last page
of a love letter.
Hope will write wish after wish
in big block letters
all over your cartoon cloud.

Hope will tell you
that he is working late at the office
and that *he loves you, he loves you*
a thousand times. Hope will also tell you
that the Pope skis and a vixen
swings by its tail.
Hope will snap your will
like a bread stick.

Hope is an absolute prerequisite
when applying for a padded cell.
A pockmarked orderly will vow,
"Oh, I will let you out."

Hope is a sad-faced clown
in sneakers.

ASFA Poetry Quarterly   *Kenneth L. Anderson*

GOD IS HERE AGAIN

Days get shorter and
longer and shorter again,
but the nights are always
long for the bewildered
heart, and reason becomes
more irrelevant with time.

God is never near at
hand, and He is absent
both night and day,
always absent,
despite all
importunities.

Then comes the memory
of a kiss, the aroma of
an embrace, the soft
stare of a child, the
tender touch of a spring
evening, and God is
here again, and
all His angels.

The Literary Review   *Charles Angoff*

THE LIGHTHOUSE

("No light propitious shone"—Cowper)

Above the hidden rocks all night
I turn a golden eye
as from my solitary height
I sweep the blackened waves with light
warning the ships to fly.

Or if among the drops and swirl
of fog my beam is spread,
I signal with my horn, whose wail
calls like a voice behind the veil
to skirt the reefs ahead.

But sometimes in the mist that lifts
over the dim-lit foam,
a ship without a compass drifts.
It spies a beacon through the rifts
and thinks I guide it home.

It presses forward on the wave
despite my wailing horn
to find its harbor in a grave.
This is the ship I cannot save,
more doomed the more I warn.

The vessel shatters at my base
crushed to the rocky wall
and sinks beneath without a trace—
as if I lured it to the place
and drowned it with my call.

Poet Lore   *John Seller Anson*

PROVERBIAL

A wind is always blowing:
the windmills spin and spin.
The flame as it is glowing
widens and grows thin.
A rill is always flowing:
the millwheels spin and spin.
Whatever comes is going,
and what will be has been.

Blue Unicorn   *John Seller Anson*

THE RAVINE

I had watched these trees get gradually bigger,
Coming at me crookedly like veins in old hands.
So when I climbed down roots in their straggling shadow
It made me shiver, like going in swimming.
Leaves between walls smelled of wet by my face,
Where an overhung ledge was dripping on ferns
So they nodded like puppets. On blue clay close
To the water, I would see the sand bar with raccoon's
Footprints, and notice in the bank where current had cut it—
These shells of mussels, and oysters, and scallops,
Too deep in roots for somebody to have buried,
And in a wet clay shadow like a long time ago,
I realized the ocean must have hidden them there.
I had read about dinosaurs' times, when the water
Had been higher, and had heard it in a shell up to my ear.
But I didn't just stay in the damp, I cut out

A scallop shell still perfect and secret, closed up
With mud inside it, then climbed back up,
To see our town's plan simple in the distance,
Houses laid out like a child's wooden blocks,
And Christmas lights burning on our water tank already.
The ravine had reminded me of our boat turning over,
But now I had come back into light on my own.
Air tasted good when I breathed the cold sun.

Southern Poetry Review   *James Applewhite*

FOLLOWER

I follow October, that yogi
of leaf and light.
Or November, the precise moment
the last leaf falls.
I follow the tracks of rain
left in the night,
the drifts of spiders,
windprints across the river.

Of you, though, I mostly dream of
following: your body
that preserves the light
given to leaves
long sunk into the Earth,
your fingers' moons
that rake my back,
your soul weaving away
from me like a snake
to places I cannot follow.

The Michigan Quarterly Review   *Michael Arvey*

HUMILIATION REVISITED

Is this the gym? . . . Then this must be the wall
on which I scrawled a naughty word in chalk
when I was eight. It made the children laugh,
but Erma told Miss Beasley. She got mad
and whacked my hands until the blood showed through,
her mustache wiggling all the while she told
how I'd be sent to School for Wayward girls.
So after class I had to stay and scrub
my sin with suds, the teacher looking down.

That seems almost a century ago.
My books are on the children's reading list;
The school invited me to speak today.
Miss Beasley and her wooden rule are gone;

The wall is paneled now with oak veneer
and hides the plastered surface of my sin . . .
but standing here, remembering, I hurt.

Ball State University Forum   *Nova Trimble Ashley*

FOUR SPACIOUS SKIES

When I was small, this continent was mine.
Days when I felt expansive, I would
Spread the country all across the lawn
And lie on it, stomach on Kansas,
Toes dipped in the Gulf of Mexico,
Forehead pressed to the Canadian border.
Or I would straddle the phallic tip of Florida,
Stretching out my arms to stroke the coastlines,
Feeling for islands.
Wheat fields tickled me
And cities poked into my flesh like
Rocks under the picnic blanket.

Days when I was compact in my bravery,
The country grew, its edges reaching
To the corners of the neighborhood,
Until it took all afternoon to
Cross the tracks to Texas
Where the coyote of a hound dog
Bayed at the gas pumps and where
The ruffians leaned on the hitching posts,
Cursing, laughing, blowing at their beers.
I would pad through, red-skinned and moccasined,
Chewing on dried beef.

At twilight I would double back across
The plains and forests, gathering
America's bounty: feathers, nuts,
Labels, nuggets of glass.
I would pocket them and
Wade through the Missouri,
Hurl myself across the Appalachian fences,
Run the open highway of the drive
And fall into my own backyard,
Clutching Long Island.

New Collage Magazine   *Susan Astor*

DAME

That dog was always a dizzy blond:
Nearsighted,
Anxious to please,
Confused.

Every night she slept under the bed
Dreaming of open fields;
Every morning banged awake against a wooden sky.
Males found her irresistible:
They sniffed and paced for hours in the yard
Until she broke away and ran to them
Windblown, breathless as a star,
Posing for the mounts as for so many quick pictures.
She would return parched and exhausted,
Tail in a half smile.

She made odd mistakes for an animal:
Growled at her own reflection;
Fell unexpectedly into holes of her own digging.
Once she spent all afternoon confined by an imaginary leash.
Even when she died she was mixed up;
Nested in the kitchen, pacing herself for the pain,
Thinking she was in another labor.
She panted to a stop, still scatterbrained,
Misinterpreting the last rough spasm,
Waiting for pups.

The Black Warrior Journal   *Susan Astor*

A DELICATE IMPASSE

Now, my dear, we're getting down
to what you call "the nitty-gritty"
when you asked me why I bathe
but twice for each your seven.
And before you add another straw
to my poor mother's back,
I assure you this peculiar peeve
hatched full-grown
from my unruly mind—
no stain on my upbringing.
I shall be, then, quite blunt:
Those sheddings on the bottom of the tub,
as I bend to wash them down the drain,
strike me as somewhat less
than inexhaustible.
And so I am reminded,
each fall by hairy fall,
we come nearer to the night
when they will cease—& me.
For it's no use to argue
that cliche you have in store.
It is "next to," I agree;
where we differ is degree
& desirability.
Take me or not: alive,

with dust behind my ears,
& nearer godlessness.

Kansas Quarterly   *Kenneth John Atchity*

LOVE POEM

I want
to make a myth of you,
to postulate
the miraculous feats of your youth,
the dragons you slew
in countries beyond the place
where sea receives the sun.
I want a story
of you wandering like Ishmael
city to city, heart to heart.
I want you empty
like a finished god
surveying the world he knows
with wise scrutiny,
with scorn for the weak-at-heart.
I want you to be Ulysses
looking for one last escapade—
and I want to be
your final adventure.

Prism International   *Rosemary Aubert*

STILL LIFE

No longer a real thing,
no heart hangs in my chest.
I've lost my behind,
        my middle.
I'm a flatty:
        an old master,
            a cartoon.
Somehow I've strayed
into a drawing-room comedy,
        a carnival,
            silent flicks.
Through speech and spectacle
I see you.
I'm one of those faces
pressed against your glass,
        breathless,
            soundless.
I hold you with my eyes
like small flames licking
imitation logs; then

I know you are one of me:
a photograph of the real thing.

Kansas Quarterly   *Regina M. Austin*

IN A WORLD OF CHANGE

Exit the fond, the familiar. Enter the strange.
Time is defined
As the measure of change.

Future shock explodes the status quo.
The faster things change
The older we grow.

I hold the secret of eternal youth.
I cling to You,
O unchanging Truth.

The Lyric   *Joseph Awad*

DREAMING ABOUT FREEDOM

What I would be doing if I were out,
what kind of things would surround me, and
the people I would talk with, and touch?
It's been a long time—a woman's hair,
her breasts, the singing of her touch,
or crawling around the floor with children—
all take their place among the stars,
among Capricorn, the Twins and Venus.

I think I would probably go out at night
and breathe the fresh air, listen to the tinkles
of town glitter in the night; I would probably pause
by lawns, knowing how they understand
me, with their aromas, and flush out my wild
beautiful thoughts and feelings, like wild birds
so easily scared away by the sound of closing cages.

Rockbottom   *Jimmy Santiago Baca*

IN BETWEEN THE CURVE

In between the curve
of the main asphalt road
and the L-shaped dirt road,
cornering to join it
was left a little square of woods
we used to slip into and kiss;
children laughed,
we emerged red-faced, embarrassed
to walk past them.

Some days coming home, alone—
days when the sunlight
hit the leaves quietly,
the children were playing elsewhere,
and a single squirrel fled
from the one old house
at the tip of the road across
the dirt to the safety of the square

when the wood, like Merlin's,
masking the air
with the color of the sun
obliterated the pre-fab houses
lining the L
with a stream as its border
and a path that led down
into the center of its magic—

I slipped by myself into the woods
to gather mountain laurel
that no longer grew there
and walk the old longer paths
lined with bluetts and trickles
of water running through the leaves
and rocks into brown pools
to dally by the edge of the stream.

Ann Arbor Review   *Barbara Bacon*

THE DEFIANT ONE

He is all male.
You cannot think that snivelling death,
Wan-pale, germ-ridden, panting in its pain,
Would dare defy this man.
His cigarette, cocked jauntily,
Sits at mocking angle to his teeth.
His fingers flick disdainful ashes.
He has guffawed at life and toasted the reckless,
His rock-hard laughter tumbling down
The mountain of his ego,
And leered a thousand winks at female passersby.

Yet there is within him
A monster in the sea of his blood,
Its tentacles creeping his passageways,
Multiplying malignant cells,
Eating through his tissues like knowing yeast.
He who defied all law, subverted that of men,
Blasphemed the divine, will be torn down like Babel
By that last decree.

The Chaparral Poet   *Alice Morrey Bailey*

HERMIT

*"Civilization is the art of living in towns of such size
that everyone does not know everyone else."*
                                          —*Julian Jaynes*

*"I don't get along with people. I don't like their ways.
I just grow a garden and stay in these hills."*
                                          —*An Ozark Hermit*

1.
Afternoon deepening now, a dark animal growing
into its coat of sleep—
all around the house, the perfect garden, rows
of thick stalks, the colors of night gathering
just at the level of the trees;
here, a few tools dropped, lost feathers.
No sound.

Again, I have missed him,
my presence probably felt long before I arrived.
This is how it always is.
From where I stand, alone, a hundred cold paths
already spread away . . .
here they lead, each one, into the woods beyond,
his own vast community of shadows.

2.
Now, I kneel to the ground, knowing that
this place is his. That these clouds over
my head, whenever they have rained, have touched
the earth with his hands.

                 That these leaves,
now heavy on the branches, have turned daily
toward the sound of his voice. That
these stones must be the very loaves on which
he was fed as a child.

                 And now I realize
that I have begun to dig here with my own hands,
as if they too knew exactly what they sought.

The Chariton Review   *David Baker*

THE BLUE CHURCH

*(after "L'Eglise d'Auvers"
     by Van Gogh)*

The windows are deep blue
as the sky.
The woman who walks
down the left fork
of the road that branches
at the church door
is hunched like a cow.

Blue shadows spot the road.
The clock is faceless,
the bell tower silent
with blue wind
winding through the shutters.

The sky turns dark
on the horizon.
The woman who walks
toward the trees
sees the flowers go black
one by one,
and the orange tile
on the far barn
turn to sky.

Yankee   *Peter Balakian*

PREGNANT TEENAGER ON THE BEACH

From her pool in the muddy shallows
she squints sixty yards out
at the white blister of the sunning deck.
On the diving board
a girl her own age shrieks,
topples with a bronzed youth
into the green water.
Separately they rise, an arc of light
like a rapier between them.
Laughing,
their glances fence,

lock.

Before her, in water low as their knees,
a circle of mothers
tow children on inflated plastic ducks,
sprinkle the murky water
over their sun-burned thighs.
She looks into their eyes:
can they remember a night
when the stars rose like a host
in the spring sky?

She stares at her abdomen
where beneath the tight skin
a sea churns,
alive with that small fish
whose gills prepare for the barbed air.
A heavy wave pulls her to shore,
drops her among stones

and cracked shells.

The Mississippi Valley Review   *Mary Balazs*

THE LONG WORD

You spoke me.
Blowing me out
in a long word.
Your mouth formed
my syllables,
the tongue excited
to touch the taste
of newness.
You challenged
my angular bendings,
and perceived
the forked roots,
at times, accepting
the curve of my silences.
It might have been
enough.

It was not enough
to print parts of your
life in my flesh,
and lie the night
within me,
a smooth, narrow ribbon
wound through me,
binding up my soundless
sleep.
It was not enough
to explain
this tight meaning.

I smile,
knowing you are plumbing
library stacks,
dissatisfied with every
language,
puzzling through the jig-saws
of lost alphabets.
You will find me again,
believing
it is the first time,
and be able to finish
your poem.

The Malahat Review   *Deirdre Ballantyne*

FATHER OF THE VICTIM

"Rape?" he says.
"Bitch!" he says,
and his lips curl like peeled bark
around the spit-flaked word.

As the child-form huddles on a chair
his eyes slide up and down the curving flesh,
finger the shreds of cloth that hide its breasts.
His hand wipes flat across his mouth,
adjusts his fly.
"Bitch!" he says again,
and "Whore!"
The cop at the door unwraps a stick of gum.

Poet Lore   *Rae Ballard*

STORM WARNING

Why do I batten down my doors
When the lake, a lovely sheet of glass,
Reflects the bordering trees
    in waveless images?
And not a ripple moves the waiting grass.
I shush the hen and chickens to the shed
(so they'll be safe beneath
    their feathered bed)
And close the windows tight and scan
The clear, blue sky and shake my head
And feel an unaccustomed chill.
Why? I saw deep in our woodland lot
A seagull sitting on a little hill.

The Atlantic Advocate   *Alice Bardsley*

ABSENCE

(in honor of Bernice Ames)

Tall poles leaned like dust-bowl fences
from the wind the day you died
and rain blurred the desert highway,
the ribs of buttes behind me,
my windshield pocked with gravel.
A grit of salt and alkali
drained off dead oceans into air.
Thirst blew out of valleys
and starved hills where
the arrogant scratch their names.

There is no containing the names
of dead poets.
You cared for the breath
and light through each vein
of every leaf.

Leave us to our anger.
I will go back to your house

and the desert
carrying these words like water.

Yankee   *Jeannette Barnes*

OLD SOLDIERS HOME AT MARSHALLTOWN, IOWA

No movement on the hill: the old soldiers
are dying, dying into mushrooms they dream.
On the grounds near the rising river, the slow
phallic plants grow white and low. The days
swell, and no one stoops to the task at hand.

The old soldiers are dying, dying into the spring:
statues turn green with the grass. The tavern
at 13th and Summit echoes this green death
but there is no song of esprit de corps,
no body lying on the floor drunk on
a reverie of a Flander's field or Argonne.

Even the drugstore across from the gate
is as vacant as the eyes you sometimes see
at the dark windows on the hill. The years
have emptied Seberg's of more than wares.
Time was when Jean Seberg was a bedside name,
the darling of bored veterans and gossips in
this town, the star of Saturday matinees.

From the tavern stool, you listen to the whir
of the laundromat across the street washing
some lonely nurse's whites, spinning them free
of trenches, the soiled touch she's come to dread.
You know that you've got it wrong, dead wrong,
that life here is as vital as your organs.
But somewhere in your head the old soldiers
are dying, dying into the fullness of spring.

New Letters   *Jim Barnes*

BORGES

Old man from the North, immaculate liar,
your iron helmet and the deadened eyes
waken at dawn, and watch red spears take fire
and fade on Danish beaches. You despise
the lazy, learned man moving in gentle
amazement with a cane, who keeps a gold
watch in his coat so he can lose the mental
melee with time. You feel remorse for old
Jorge Luis Borges, outwitting God,
Persians, and the algebra of being. Both of
you hunt like madmen for a word. Your love
never shows, although it burns behind the sword

of iron and the cane. You are a fraud
and friend, a haunting light and lonely lord.

The American Scholar   *Willis Barnstone*

ON THE DEATH OF PARENTS

It has certainty, like the fall of a stone.

Studied before, it is almost weight,
but in its midst
mistake,
    a turn not,
    an advice not,
    a food not
        taken.

The look on the children's faces is all O,
the only scream they show.

    They listen
    to a father killed,
    a child
    not knowing,
    showing
    at school
    the day after,

and O, O is what they know.

Someday, my dear, in our prime,
or long after our fates are known,
and they caught unawares
or in full distant preparation,

    we shall pass,

and they shall rise up from this knowledge.

They shall rise up from this knowledge.

The Ontario Review   *Alfred Barson*

THE DEATH OF THE SAILOR'S WIFE

In her room she is
small and adrift
in the sea of antiseptic white.
At the end of the hall
relatives are tiny ships on nervous waters,
huddled around the warped and creaking
hospital couch.
Only doctors and nurses,
who ply the calm halls,
know the storm has passed
and all that remains is the

slow twirl of the lighthouse beacon
over the darkening waters.

Great Lakes Review   *Fred Barton*

STOPPED IN MEMPHIS

Rain's grey buckshot spatters the windshield
and the highway runs so deep we pull to the side,
taillights flashing. Other cars plow on
headed for the Mississippi but we ford
to this motel. Of course the storm

levitates. I pull the plastic drapes,
step out on the balcony.

This place we chose looks west.
The pool's rectangle glitters.
A watery sun, a babble of kids
floats in uneasy water.

By night the lights are back
and the television's large square mouth
tells the news, no mention of storm.

I wonder if it happened after all.
In the parking lot wraiths of steam
rise from the asphalt. *I have a dream:*
the water is calm as a regular heartbeat
and the little boat sails to a distant city,

the sky is uncrackably blue
it allows no disruption of travel,
no assassin's bullet.

The Chariton Review   *Steven Bauer*

THE HUNT OF THE POEM

The poet is hunter. Poem prey.

The hunter-poet discovers a scent, a sign,
a print in the dust or snow and follows the
trail of the poem-prey out of the debris of
the moment, through the chaos of personality,
into the wilderness of imagination.

The hunt is all.

At the moment of the kill, the hunter-poet and
poem-prey are one.

In the instant of ecstasy and jubilation,
emptiness resonates, reigns.

The hunter-poet approaches the poem-prey.
The thicket where it fell is empty; a thin

trail of blood leads deeper into the
wilderness.

It's always the same. The hunt is all.

The poem is hunter. Poet prey.

Wisconsin Review   *Richard Behm*

WORLD WITHIN A WORLD

Sometimes I am a young child,
Yet sometimes I am so old
That all the ages fall upon
My shoulders, and my shaking hands
Could hold the sands of every hour
That I have sifted through the timeglass
Of my life . . .
For there is a world within a world
Within a world within a world,
And like the petals of a flower
So have all events unfurled,
Uncurling toward the face of Light,
Reflecting light in colors bright
Upon a world
Within a world within a world . . .
And at times I am so young
That I feel I'm being born,
Though into what I'm not quite sure;
But I know I'm being taken
From what I thought was my security
Inside some warm and friendly womb . . .
For it is a world within
A world within a world
Within a world,
And like the universe unfolding
So have all my thoughts unfurled,
Uncurling toward the face of Light,
Reflecting light upon the sight
Of a world
Within a world
Within a world.

Unity   *Debra Woolard Bender*

VILLANELLE WITH A LINE BY YEATS

When you are old and gray and full of sleep,
My dear, I will be old and gray as you:
We'll rock together, dozing on the deep.

The clouds that glide above us will be sheep;
The tiny drops that lave us will be dew
When you are old and gray and full of sleep.

At intervals we'll watch the dolphins leap,
Then suffer ministrations of the crew.
We'll rock together, dozing on the deep.

From dawn to day to dusk minutes will creep
Melding the loved familiar with the new
When you are old and gray and full of sleep.

And if, upon occasion, you should weep,
Remembering, I will remember too:
We'll rock together, dozing on the deep.

This hand I held and hold I yet will keep;
The hearts we gave in trust will weather true.
When you are old and gray and full of sleep
We'll rock together, dozing on the deep.

Dark Horse   *Bruce Bennett*

THE THERAPEUTIST

The body will not reject plastic.
Oh, no. You may replace
all your parts—
Your lovely ribcage
like twin harps. The
charmed cave of your pelvis.

Now you are light as a bird
and your chest strums
and strums. Keep practicing.

Tired old father, how we used
to love to nestle there,
leaning our heads
against your heart.

It has flown away,
homeless. I strain my ears:
I can no longer sense
the wings' dry flutter.

Porch   *Beth Bentley*

TONGUES

I have tongues in secret places—no one
man could guess there are so many of them.
My breasts, little pink tongues when I was young—

delicate rose buds, unfolded flowers.
They moved beneath you then, love, and you leaned
kissing, spine curving down to that short sword

and another flushing flower far below.
It called you like a bee to its nectar
and was a long red throat with tongues also.

I could never name them all, with their soft
touch and harder rasp. There is a tongue for
everything—warm ones to take the frost

out of an older poet's lonely nights,
cool ones to lick away a salty fear,
others urging young boys through their first night.

My old breasts have changed in their way also.
They are no longer those young pink buds,
now bloomed into a strange coloured old rose,

petals above your face or pressed to your cheek.
Once I lost sight of them in your tousled
hair, two tongues that worked up sweaty cow-licks.

Old lover, now I press them between us,
my whole weight flattening them underneath;
against your chest their colour is like rust.

Old petal tongues drying on long white stems,
like mouths that have wrinkled in their laughter—
they stay puckered and promise to laugh again.

The Fiddlehead   *Sharon Berg*

FALSE CADENCE

I've never learned an adequate goodbye.
The naked moment when one stands to go,
Limbs frozen with parting in every eye,
Voice overaimed and shaking like an arrow
Trained on absence, risking the tossed-off word,
The easy smile, the touch unassuming yet strong
In which a final feeling stands revealed—
Afraid of the wrong goodbye, I stay too long.

Song   *Bruce Berger*

WHY I AM OFFENDED BY MIRACLES

Miracles offend because they lack proportion.
Give a picture of the Virgin a chance to cry
and right away a boy grows stigmata.
Then, before you know it,
the lame are walking,
the sick are healed,
and the hungry are fed.
What could be worse for the economy?
or more disagreeable

to the aesthete or the politician?
So, please God, no miracles,
just now and then something bizarre—
like a three-headed chicken
or a nose with a hand attached.

Kansas Quarterly   *David Bergman*

ECLOGUE

The whores are afraid to cross the street
   unattended through the swirling cars.
Still no one offers to escort them
   and so, like school-girls
wading daintily in a brook, they hold
   each other's hands and higher raise their skirts
to cool themselves in the stream of traffic.
   O Virgins, who among you is so pure
or innocent that she could run as they did
   splashing about in the blue exhaust?

The Michigan Quarterly Review   *David Bergman*

MULTIPLICITY

I cry to be broken open
and spill (sexual intercourse
is metaphor) out, dissolve in the you,
the world, the other,
to break down the walls of I.
This is an old craving, common
to all selves, atomies that feel
their separation.

Post coitum triste—we weep
for the lost, intimated unity.
From the origin, the original 'O',
the Big Bang that echoes
still, multiplication by division
brought us here. Still flying apart,
we fall continually, an endless
falling out.

The tree, were it self-
conscious, would invite the bolt
to gash it flaming
open, that still would leave it
distinct in the studded field, wound
shrinking fast, crusting over
into scar, open only to
progressive disease.

Canadian Forum   *Eleanor Berry*

THE WAY OF PAIN

1.
For parents, the only way
is hard. We who give life
give pain. There is no help.
Yet we who give pain
give love; by pain we learn
the extremity of love.

2.
I read of Abraham's sacrifice
the Voice required of him,
so that he led to the altar
and the knife his only son.
The beloved life was spared
that time, but not the pain.
It was the pain that was required.

3.
I read of Christ crucified,
the only begotten Son
sacrificed to flesh and time
and all our woe. He died
and rose, but who does not tremble
for his pain, his loneliness,
and the darkness of the sixth hour?
Unless we grieve like Mary
at His grave, giving Him up
as lost, no Easter morning comes.

4.
And then I slept, and dreamed
the life of my only son
was required of me, and I
must bring him to the edge
of pain, not knowing why.
I woke, and yet that pain
was true. It brought his life
to the full in me. I bore him
suffering, with love like the sun,
too bright, unsparing, whole.

New England Review   *Wendell Berry*

CITY

The children on the corner
play, while crowds cross streets
bolted to each other;
and the day spins around them,
spins around them in a wind
lifting the morning papers in spirals up higher.

Out of this movement a beauty comes,
fixing the shimmering day like a stage,
where actors move with the changing light,
ready to kill you for your throbbing heart.

Out of this beauty a silence comes,
a stillness where you know the truth,
where your mask falls down like a paper plate,
and you mustn't speak through your mouth anymore.

Out of this silence a willingness comes,
a way that is a way and the ending of ways;
where now you realize what you did mattered,
even had effects you can't believe are true,
even when it's told to you plainly,
how well your secrets were understood.
Now you must realize you made a difference,
that your life was a coin with the value of coins,
and the friends you had will bed down with families,
they will say, "O, he was a crazy one!"

O, City, at your death, another thing comes,
rising from the loins of your crumbled dreams,
turning like a lock in an ivory door,
opening where the people all with banners wait,
where the liars run backward to their silver cars,
and the trees are bent over hard, like dancers.

Here, at this moment, at this moment, we see
the movement of the world in the falling snow,
as shapes rush past us and we rush past them,
bundled and obscure, fearful, each with laws,
unexplored, uncharted, dangerous, and mad.

The Small Pond Magazine   *Raymond Biasotti*

MID-PLAINS TORNADO

I've seen it drive straw straight through a fence post—
sure as a needle in your arm—the straws all erect
and rooted in the wood like quills.
Think of teeth being drilled, that enamel and blood
burning circles inside your cheek. That's like the fury.
Only now it's quail and axles, the northeast bank
of the Cedar River, every third cottonwood.

It's with you all morning. Something wet in the air.
Sounds coming in at a slant, like stones
clapped under water. And pigs, slow to the trough.
One may rub against your leg, you turn with a kick
and there it is, lurching down from a storm cloud:
the shaft pulses toward you across the fields
like a magician's finger.
You say goodbye to it all then, in a flash over
your shoulder, with the weathervane so still
it seems painted on the sky.

The last time, I walked a fresh path toward the river.
Near the edge of a field I found our mare, pierced
through the side by the head of her six-week foal.
Her ribs, her great folds of shining skin
closed over the skull. I watched them forever, it seemed:
eight legs, two necks, one astonished head curved
back in a little rut of hail. And across the river
slim as a road, a handful of thrushes set down
in an oak tree, like a flurry of leaves
drawn back again.

The Seattle Review   *Linda Bierds*

AT NINE O'CLOCK IN THE SPRING

At nine o'clock in the spring
you alight with your waterlilies
and your laughter, hoping to
find a place in my life.

You believe your eyes, but I
am already coping with the first frost—
and you, in that landscape,
are as small as a snowflake.

ASFA Poetry Quarterly   *Elissa Bishop*

ALL TOO LITTLE ON PICTURES

No considerable picture
Can be remembered. Its teaching
Must be assented to fresh every time
In there-standing speech of itself.

Painting in any new order
Turns backward to Altamira,
To hornèd celebrant dancing
Always, but you must see him each time

For ever and for ever
To consider a picture
That fills silence with silence,
And the real presence is you.

Arizona Quarterly   *Charles Black*

TIDES

Here where tides come and go
and waters kiss the rocks,
the gulls also come and go
seeking worms where the tides rock.
Garbage siftings from returning fleets
and remains of battles fought under the sea

deposit their salty residue around the gulls' feet
and kiss their beaks with maternity.
The seeping limestone's chalky defense
and dissolved blood of ovaries from under the sea
subtly paint the three coral spots; and plaintive notes
whine in the birds' restless throats.
Lifting now, the gulls once more commence
their search and hang like flowers over the sea.

Here where bound tides come and go
and blood washes eroding bones,
other scavengers come and go
collecting wastes in the tubular zones.
Though bone-bound images of the mind
search for their counterparts
in seas, in gulls and in their kind,
they also reach beyond those seas and counterparts
and look to nebular seas.

And though the orbiting tides, awash
in silent tracks, are charged with a common motion,
they also move in spheres of retrogression and wash
the highest earthly bloom of matter's brief commotion.

Ball State University Forum   *Will H. Blackwell*

THE EAGLE

It is hard, alone in this room at night, to remember
the eagle. I remember how, at Anacortes, your long hair
turned to feathers, burnished, glaring like a river at noon.
And how, if you had not turned back to kiss me then,
my eyes would have been burned black forever.

So it must have been later we saw the eagle.
We had climbed the island until everything in all directions
was down. And you pointed out over the windy San Juans
toward Canada and you said *Eagle*! Did I turn too late?
Was there nothing in all that air but air?

But I remember the boat ride at twilight through the islands,
the dark cathedrals of hemlock and fir, the shadowed cliffs,
the gulls crying out against the northern cold. And I remember
your arms close as a life jacket, and the red sun spanning,
like wide wings, all that long winter, and our wake, widening.

You pointed north toward Canada, crying out. I turned.
The eagle dropped, a stone bird, down a slide of wind
to the sea. Or the eagle, like a prism of ice, melted
in a shower of feathery sparks. Or was it closer still,
so close something was living in its wrinkled feet?

Again and again your bracelets flash, a sorcerer's gesture.
The two syllables beat like wings. Again I turn, seeing all
there is to see, this disembodiment of gold or flesh, this will,

this flickering in wind and fire. Now, here, in this moment
I am never remembering, we lie always, Love, in one another.

The Seattle Review   *Richard Blessing*

THE DAYS

There are days to which God
should never have given birth.
They crawl up out of the night before
like crippled robots praying for
their death. They inject themselves
under the skin, rooting
around for the vein and
encountering only bone.
They are the days when sleep would be
the reticence of a warm ocean,
but there is only stunned fatigue
without the peace. They are
the days when the family sits
at dinner only feet apart,
each holed up tight
inside a bee cave sealed
by wax that will not melt.
They are the days from a country
back of the dark, one that we see
behind the haze of things,
making its song against the sun.

Ball State University Forum   *Paul Blocklyn*

ON THE EDGE AT SANTORINI

(Greece, September, 1978)

You understand now
what it means
to risk everything:

the body burning to a quiet speed
along the cliff-edge, the earth
inexorably sliding beneath the earth
below you like lovers making love
in their sleep, your shoulders
nestled against the black rock
(castles of lava and pumice, windows
of limestone) as you turn, flight-light
and lovingly, toward the mountain,
the hum of your engines rousing the flight-path
of butterflies behind you.

Beneath you, the volcano
humps its excavated fathoms,

God-spilled and ominous, its folds
edging the turquoise sea, churning light
like the clearest possible madness along the water
until it holds you, begs you stay tight
to the stony road and the treacherous heights,
increase your speed to just beyond danger or
lunacy, just beyond anything love or even
death can offer you.

Caution rises like a virgin's dress
over your shoulders, the sun seduces
your fingers, then your thighs, then
your past. You turn your body further
towards the edge, lean to the ageless tundra
and the expanding ceiling,

watch the rest of your life
fall like rain to the hungry sea.

The Third Eye   *Michael C. Blumenthal*

THE EDUCATIONAL ADMINISTRATION
PROFESSOR'S PRAYER

"Lord, make me the co-ordinator of Thy implementation.
Let me be the means of formulating the conceptualizations
    of Thy constructs,
    of initiating, innovating and evaluating the experiential
    data wherewith the forces of tradition may be smitten,
    the better to correlate Thy progressivist realm.

"Where there is order and stability, let me sow
    specious seeds of semanticism;
Where there is memorization, let me be aghast.
Where there is outmoded logic, and above all, O God, the
    pernicious blight of stress on scholarship, let me
    cast winds of capricious creativity.

"Help me, O Master, to combat the dark forces of books and
    examinations with vast hordes of Title II, III and IV
    gimmickry,
To spread the gossamer web of managerial theory to where
    it truly belongs, in the classroom, not the factory.

"With Thy help will youth be delivered thus, O Lord,
    from the dungeons of libraries,
    to work in the pure light of the learning resource center,
    and to dwell in a vague intermediary unit
    forever and ever."
Amen.

Educational Studies   *Gerald Bobango*

ALONE IN THE HOUSE

The doorbell rang. It was Death.
I slammed the door and ran upstairs.

The phone rang. It was Death.
I hung up.
Death peered in the window.
I closed the blinds.
Death walked out of the closet.
I ran into the bathroom.
He came out of the shower,
the water tap,
the toilet bowl.
I ran down the stairs
out the door
into his arms.

Southern Humanities Review   *George Bogin*

OLD MAN

This is a dream I needed.

I wake in my own old room
toward morning, lying next to the knees
of a girl—a young mother—born
in the milltown miles upriver.
Kneeling beside me, smiling,
she lets her long hair shelter me from
every view of myself. Except, out the dormer window,
the town's last elm.

I adore you
I tell her.
I know, she says,
with you I am quiet.

This is a sleep I am lucky to wake from.

By the time I walk down over the hill
for the *News*, she is opening her store.
She turns in the doorway, her son in arms,
and smiles. I nod and smile, trusting myself
not to say I adore her, trusting her
to dream what I have not said.

The American Poetry Review   *Philip Booth*

THINGS THAT MIGHT HAVE BEEN

I think of the things that might have been and were not.
The treatise on Saxon mythology that Bede did not write.
The unimaginable work that Dante glimpsed fleetingly
when the last verse of the Commedia was corrected.
History without the afternoon of the Cross and the afternoon of
    the hemlock.

History without the face of Helen.
Man without the eyes which have shown the moon to us.
In the three labored days of Gettysburg, the victory of the South.

The love we do not share.
The vast empire which the Vikings did not wish to found.
The world without the wheel or without the rose.
The judgment of John Donne on Shakespeare.
The other horn of the unicorn.
The fabled bird of Ireland, in two places at once.
The son I did not have.

New England Review

Jorge Luis Borges
—Translated by Alastair Reid

SEPTEMBER BUTTERFLY

On the
dashboard in my car
the September butterfly fans his orange-paneled wings.
He thumps against the wind- shield and will not see
to fly away. Please little butterfly
turn west
to court the light of day. It is
summer's end and the orange
ball slips lower in the sky. Before the night dome tightens
can't you make this one last try? So soon the night array will peer
in pinpricked splendor yawning like a cobweb
stretched across
the bay.

Poet Lore

Mollie Boring

MOUNTAIN BORN

I was born
In spittin distance
Of my back stoop.
Wouldn't have it any other way.

Oh, I left.
Once,
Went South.
'Most smothered in kudzu
And honey-dew talkin'
And it was hotter'n the fiery pit.

I like a hill
Rising 4,000 feet 'hind my privy,
And air so clear
It cuts clean to your heart,
And seven ridges
One 'hind the other
Letting in just as much world as I can stand.

Mountain Review

Marcia Inzer Bost

ANGLE OF VISION

The days, my grandfather said to me—
the days are getting shorter, summer's done.
It was high August, with an aqueous light
sluicing down the redwoods' furrowed sides,
shine of green and yellow on auburn brown.
We drove out of that luminous drowned air
to dust and colorless sky, the ridge road,
and it was only morning, only August.
His hands, knotted on the steering wheel,
lifted us out of sight of trees and river
until my eyes were full of empty light
and the days dwindled before us—
maybe he said it every year in August.
He said it like goodbye.

Buffalo Spree   *Martha Bosworth*

THE TRAVELER

Where you traveled the body couldn't go,
not for the white hair washed and combed,
the cheeks flushed with rouge,
lips wired into a smile.
No, the body couldn't go.
In all the pockets of the new gray suit
there was no ticket for the body.

I sat in the room of roses and carnations,
gray faces of distant relatives,
and watched the body stay behind
like someone seeing a traveler off on a journey,
an old man of an old world
watching his brother leave for the new.
He has lain down on a bench now
for a short rest,
no ticket for the body to travel on.

Southwest Review   *David Bottoms*

THE LITTLE SEARCHER

Day spread her lap and bade me choose—
I let go by a field-lark's whistle,
I sampled how the orchard stands,
And tried lake water in my hands.
But all my longings floated off with a single thistle.

Love spread her hair and bent on me
The splendid shadow of her eyes.
I let her pass without a sign—

For I had ever counted mine
A face I learned on a corner once from a passerby.

Death came to me: how could I choose
So royal and immense a fate?
But he gave me no chance to tell—
He laid my head against him well,
And in the twilight let me in the smallest gate.

The Lyric   *Donna Bowen*

THE EDGE

I have lived and died
on the dull edge of November,
when I stood too long
and watched the wind turn
trees as they walked straight
into the wet flanks
of a northwest gale.

In summer, I force myself
to touch the weathering
boards of old houses
as they change from spring
lumber into salt-colored
gray and pointed splinters.

And I know why butterflies go
home and worms spin wet silk.

My wells are gone dry,
and the heat of my memories
drums in my ears
like an old and wavering
pulse measuring the weak surge
of thick blood as it squirms
through the fat of dead muscle
and the cracks of broken veins.

The American Scholar   *James K. Bowen*

UNPLANNED DESIGN

Imagine my surprise when
the house I built so carefully turned
out to be a maze, and
I, standing at the end of
one long, twisting corridor,
couldn't find the door.

The plan had been to work from
outside in, like a miner or a mole, and
so the hallway twisted, subterranean, box-

like room to boxlike room, a
square diminishing, a spiral or a pit.

And now I stand in the smallest
room, the suffocating center of my own
design, the walls hung round with mirrors, my
misery multiplied into infinity—and no door.

Ball State University Forum   *Neal Bowers*

ROUTE 95 NORTH: NEW JERSEY

It shies from the Appalachians through seven states
Yet will not commit itself to ocean;
Blinded by landscapes, obsessed with its own motion,
The voyager's mind slowly gravitates

To this horizon lit by smokestacks, blow-off pipes
Tapering to troubled flames in the air,
Shaken in their torment as the ancient pair
That furnished Alighieri with the types

Of senseless search and unquenchable desire.
What drove those two, Ulysses and Diomed,
To abandon fame, Penelope in her bed,
The heroic songs of themselves, and aspire

To eternal non-commitment? What but the thought
That every man plays fool in his own house,
Bound to a fortune he cannot espouse,
Trapped in the threadless warp his deeds have wrought.

Having managed Scylla and Charybdis, how sweet
It must have been to shirk off the sublime,
Avoiding death by fame, and death by time,
To flounder where the mountain and the whirlpool meet.

Kansas Quarterly   *P. C. Bowman*

IN BED WITH A RIVER

I stood by the river where the flesh of our world
Is swept it knows not where (but I knew)
And thought how one day the bottom land
Would be fields of bedrock, how the soil by increments
Would sift into regions we only dream of farming
And be shifted in vast, lazy motions by the currents:
Steady, unseen, great winds of the oceans.
I stood by the river and tried to forget the sounds
Of the water—almost silence—heard at its edge
A musical rasp, heard the splash of ugly, edible fish
With their guts full of mud and rusted hooks, thriving,
Floating all day through the clouds of dirt.
I stood by and tried to forget I stood anywhere,
That my bones—bidding each other Godspeed—

Had not wandered gently apart to be worn beyond fitting,
To diffuse with tiny puffs into particles minutely aware,
Spinning on themselves like worlds round a star.
By the river I forgot that I was dreaming occasions
Like those built with hard blocks of the pyramids,
Spiteful and desperate, coins of an enraged kingdom
That found out too soon it would be run into the ground.
I am forgetting even you, strange archaeologist, bedfellow,
Surgeon digging in a diseased earth, that finds
A moment's interest, exhumes the token of my presence,
Withered, recalcitrant, featherweight in the palm:
A tooth, five-cusped: man.

The Paris Review   *George Bradley*

SWING ONE, SWING ALL

I suppose even molecules are driven to distraction,
Worried sick about energy, entropy and inertia,
Suffering the tensions of attraction and repulsion
And wondering how long they can maintain identity
Before losing some elemental constituent.
Even atoms and their tiny subscribers must be spun silly,
Must watch their weight, note their circles of influence.
Perhaps even Space, bearing only occasional invasions
(Speeding pinpoints of light), which exists disinterested
And cool, perhaps even this expanse, now and then,
Has to slow down and try to remember which way
It is supposed to be exploding . . .
So that none of us, whatever his talent or birthright,
Escapes his share of celebration,
Avoids his grim act of participation.

The Michigan Quarterly Review   *George Bradley*

THIRTY CHILDBIRTHS

In James Street,
as if my pneumonia had not been enough,
I started to have attacks of kidney gravel,
human penalty
for emerging from inanimate matter—pain.
The pain of one daylong attack of gravel
has been compared to the suffering
of childbirth. I must have had
thirty attacks. I thought of suicide.
One time an attack lasted three days
and in my male parturition
I screamed like a woman.
Hospitalized in Jersey City,
I had a doctor, assigned by Uncle Sam Cosgrove,
who without anaesthesia pushed a tube

up my penis, and this scalding insertion
let me be flushed with liquid and the liquid
washed out the gravel, or I peed it out.
No birth, but still
a delivery
giving me back to life.

Harper's Magazine   *Millen Brand*

SARENTINO—SOUTH TYROL

On dark days the clouds
drift through the valley's cleft,
cutting off the mountaintops.
The castle on the facing slope
from us sinks into mist.
A chill glistening is on the grass
and the thick forests are grim.
Here in the Alps, locked in
by the creeping cumuli,
we sit on our balcony
and drink Eppan wine.
Watching the *Schloss* glide in and out
of the fog, I expect at any time
to see a man-bat flap
away from a stony turret.

The American Scholar   *Philip Brantingham*

NOON GLARE

By rays sharper than the sharpest angle
Of cut glass in a jeweler's shop, noon glare
Refracts the traffic lights. No dew-drops
Moisten front lawns, no shadows cool front stoops;
Now, beams strip the neighborhood bare, and blister
Drab clapboards, arid rose beds, and asphalt drives.
You watch exhaust filter into the haze
That hangs there like sauna steam; you daydream:
You think of the dusk breeze in the park, and recall
The lust, last fall, that flushed her cheeks pink.

But autumn has its dullness, too, you remember,
For even in its dying, bleeding prism,
The sun can splash on any windshield
Sunshine, blinding as daybreak in Sahara glares.

Poet Lore   *Matthew Brennan*

NIGHT TEETH

In a plume of sky firelight
glancing across town, Juarez,

lifted from desert full
of the brown night teeth that chatter
at the moon, drunk, in tongues
of indio, mestizo mix,
of religion, of song
of roosters like conquistadores,
of pear-breasted women
who run to the yard with cleavers,
of shorn sheep,
of goats that sleep in the skeletons
of cars
& mount them by day.
Dust flecked saguaro grow arms—
the cactus shaped like an old woman.
& ocotillo, her mate, lost dreaming
arm in arm under a sliver of blazing
moon—forever night blooms.

Cimarron Review   *Peter Brett*

TO HIS LOVE IN MIDDLE-AGE

Somewhere you have been
sixteen and this is a loss
I live with. I do not
understand the way
the world goes round these
things, as though I have
got this far and must go on.

Thirty years later is not
the same. I cannot even
remember my name thirty
years ago. The world
goes round these things
like a spider's thread: soon
it will suck you out and
leave you hanging dry.

Somewhere you have been
sixteen. Letters, old
photographs and names
keep covering the tracks
between us. I have
stabbed your lovers
with a long knife, but
lacerated only you. Now
jealousy winds you tight
around me—already your
toes and fingertips
are turning blue.

Travelling, you used
the scenery as a barricade,

not knowing we would
touch and make a moon;
ten years too late
that light has reached
me here, and every whitened
bone begins to burn.

But somewhere you have been
sixteen and I do not understand
the way the world goes round
these things—as though
because I have come this far
and must go on, all the time
we've ever known still turns
between us and you have been
sixteen since it began.

    Poetry   *Edwin Brock*

PYGMALION

Those eyes still shine which promised that behind
This graceful smile, this captivating face,
This lock-framed forehead there might sleep a mind
Awaiting to be wakened, to embrace
This real world, and learn and live, and grow
An equal to that body. But I should
have known six months ago: The gods can blow
Life into marble, but not into wood.

The Lyric   *Hans Brockerhoff*

HEBREW LESSON

Three decades of my life had passed
Ere I began to learn the language of my people.
And then I felt I had been deaf for thirty years.

And now they shocked, held back so long
They split the air like lightning when set free,
They shook my ear, those ancient sounds

Which would have rung so nicely round my cradle
And have accompanied me in boyhood steps,
In my first love and deeds of manhood.

Too late now came the cradle song and was not sweet.
No, as if enraged by bitter negligence
It lashed like lightning and swift claps of thunder—

Convulsion and confusion. Yet gladly did I bow
My head to it, the way one listens to one's mother
When she is angry, and from this grumbling seemed to rise

A clatter in the desert, a headlong rush,
A lookout's signal, long-forgotten sounds of horns,
And our ancient God calling from the mountain.

Midstream   *Max Brod*
                              —Translated from the German by the
                   Literary Translation seminar of Brandeis University

SIX YEARS LATER

So long had life together been that now
The second of January fell again
On Tuesday, making her astonished brow
Lift like a windshield wiper in the rain,
    So that her misty sadness cleared, and showed
    A cloudless distance waiting up the road.

So long had life together been that once
The snow began to fall, it seemed unending;
That, lest the flakes should make her eyelids wince,
I'd shield them with my hand, and they, pretending
    Not to believe that cherishing of eyes,
    Would beat against my palm like butterflies.

So alien had all novelty become
That sleep's entanglements would put to shame
Whatever depths the analysts might plumb;
That when my lips blew out the candle flame,
    Her lips, fluttering from my shoulder, sought
    To join my own, without another thought.

So long had life together been that all
That tattered brood of papered roses went,
And a whole birch grove grew upon the wall,
And we had money, by some accident,
    And tonguelike on the sea, for thirty days,
    The sunset threatened Turkey with its blaze.

So long had life together been without
Books, chairs, utensils—only that ancient bed—
That the triangle, before it came about,
Had been a perpendicular, the head
    Of some acquaintance hovering above
    Two points which had been coalesced by love.

So long had life together been that she
And I, with our joint shadows, had composed
A double door, a door which, even if we
Were lost in work or sleep, was always closed:
    Somehow, it would appear, we drifted right
    On through it into the future, into the night.

The New Yorker   *Joseph Brodsky*
                              —Translated from the Russian by Richard Wilbur

MY FLYING MACHINE

Once again I'm integrated with machinery,
Insulated; my nerves are cables
Stretching from pulley to pulley to aileron
And elevator. My mind is a panel
Crowded with instruments and toggle switches,
A cockpit of fidgeting needles and dials.
My tremulous eyes become gyros
Functioning in vacuums like silent worlds
Turning in space; my ears are tuned
To Pitot-static tubes
That check the speed of dreams along this odyssey.

The same flesh that protects my bones
Stretches over wings and fuselage
Fluting through zones of winds aloft.
This unearthly machine burns my blood,
Exhausts unoxygenated thoughts
And exploded harmonies, accelerates rhyme
Toward selected climaxes in time.
Only my voice, of the elements absorbed,
Remains unchanged and controlled by me:
It flies inside the slipstream
Each song I write leaves in its wake.

Four Quarters   *Louis Daniel Brodsky*

WEEDING IN JANUARY

The sky is haywire alive with fire
At the wrong time; even spiders
Awaken from dazed slumbers, stumble
On weak legs to a sunned spot
On barn siding or holly leaf
From which to suspend their disbeliefs.

Curious, I stray from a heated house
Outdoors, with light coat, gloves,
And begin pulling clumped weeds
From a garden whose soggy, unturned soil
Lets them loose easily as worms
Freed from hard earth by the rain.

I am piqued to complete the immediate task
Of eradication before Winter
Remembers itself, or sees me playing
Behind its back as though no tomorrows
Stood between April planting
And January's coldest hours at hand.

A chill cast by afternoon shadows
Presses against my sweaty neck,
Stifles all inclination to continue,
Forces me inside just as the door

Between death's edge and rebirth shuts,
And snow clouds begin to form.

Four Quarters   *Louis Daniel Brodsky*

BUFFALO

Its flat, insect-blackened radiator grill
Is a buffalo's nose; twin exhaust stacks
Become the rugged creature's glistening horns.
Eighteen spinning wheels are four hoofs
Churning cement plains; its screaming trailer
Assumes the shape of a hump-back spine,
Mid-section, and writhing belly connected
By ribbed muscle and corrugated steel.

Whoever said History slaughtered wholesale
All those sons of bitches had his head
And ears fastened to the wrong rail spur.
Once again America's prairies are overrun
With snorting hordes breathing diesel fuel.
Perhaps another greed-inspired massacre
Might be an ecological blessing to protect us
From being trampled to death by stampeding beasts.

Ball State University Forum   *Louis Daniel Brodsky*

WHAT FORM THE WORLD HAS

I watch my concern for the world, how it changes: strong
sometimes, elsewhere weaker, as when the world
stands in the landscape like somebody's barn, clump
of trees. Not my land they're on. Whose,
I don't know. Or what they are. Nor
do I care. Times, though, I could think
of them as refuge, having no other and they
being offered, not then either caring what.

Or my intensest concern for the world might be
the times I find me trapped, as it were, in the trees,
boarded-up in that barn. Those times,
I hate the world, want only to break it down.

When we love the world for itself, the world we love
is one, most likely, we may have made or thought
to have made, ourselves, with love or some other power.
As if we could. Well, maybe we can
and did, but taken out of our hands when it is
as it always is, do we know was it ever ours?

I could rest content with the unseen form of the world
and never see it, believing the form were there.

Montemora   *William Bronk*

CLEANING UP, CLEARING OUT

My father's cluttered workbench stands, heaped up
With half a cellar's now purposeless junk.
How many years spent gathering all these goods—
Fuses, switches, plugs, nails, bolts and screws—
A handy man, if not a healthy one,
Repairing every break, except the last.

Old houses make requests on not old men
Old hearts in not old bodies make demands.
I clear the dust off records that he kept—
Mortgage payments, taxes, check stubs, bills—
Amused with his attempt to set at least
One ordered corner in an aimless sprawl.

Wearing old coats and gloves my father kept
For just such cleaning up and clearing out,
My brother and I haul another load
Of basement wares up to the autumn sun.
Too good a day to spend it all down there
Dragging out the past for trashmen's ridicule.

The backyard leaves almost provide excuse,
Replacing what we both drove miles to do,
To find we cannot do without him here.
My brother's sons dive on the piles we rake
And, now no longer young, we tend the fire,
Lean on our rakes and wonder at his absence.

Pulling up his pants' legs with a laugh,
He'd dance across the leaf piles we'd just made,
A father showing children how to play
Despite his knowledge and our constant fear.
Still, each trip home he'd show us the tin box
Containing all his papers, "just in case."

And this was always "home" when someone asked;
Our wives mistook us in adult disguise.
Soon one of us must try to take the cue,
Lift up our legs and dance across the leaves.
My mother knows he'd laugh to see us now,
Grown men, so sad, in coats too big too fit.

The Mississippi Valley Review   *Daniel Ross Bronson*

FOR STEPHEN

Seventeen, no great event
He says. He glides past us
With undisturbed intent.

He would photograph well
Easing into the jeep
Whose military shell

He painted red to cover
The old green wounds,
That war long over.

This boy, this innocence,
Brown, summer muscle
Flexed without pretense.

There are no mysteries
For him. The winter branch
Always leafs into light.
Supreme biology.
His days shine with chance.

I follow his car in mine.
Dust rises from our road.
Three months without rain,
Already some of the pines

I planted a year ago
Are dead. When we reach
The highway, we go
Apart. Always the wrong time

To tell my son what I mean.
He doesn't see my wave.
When I was seventeen
I didn't look back either.

Carolina Quarterly   *Christopher Brookhouse*

MY FATHER DRAGGED BY HORSES

Beyond the yard the barn is hulking
and somewhere behind my shoulder the women
are kneading and chopping their way to lunch.
Into this sun-pressed waiting
the horses come slowly, slowly
dragging the harrow where my father rides,
reins binding him over the gleaming disks.

He turns to wave
and horses, sensing the slip of mastery,
bolt for the pasture. In a jolt,
he is thrown and bound,
arms stretched and suppliant
to unleashed hooves, his body
dragged and the knives spinning,
spinning and waiting for straps to break.

Somewhere out of my sight the horses
feel his body still holding on,
and stop, mouths flecked with bloody foam,
stamping as my father rises,
wrists deepcut by thongs; and the knives hold still.

Again and again in the slowest of motions
they advance from the right
and my breath is dragged out.
This is the rhythm of every nightmare:
lovely precision of danger held in check,
rider in harmony over the animal and honed device,
and then the fall, the utter descent
to flailing hooves and a hundred sharp suns.

Cedar Rock   *T. Alan Broughton*

GIRL IN A BLACK BIKINI

Almost sexless: the white skin
of your long legs glittering
in the grey merge of lake and sky,
your body effortlessly
displayed in this morning as
you move—not girl nor woman—to
the water's edge; walking almost
in the chaste poise of marble or
self-elucidating bronze,
touchless except for the mind's faint
fine gesture of knowing, and you are
almost contained in this still air:

How that taut cord is her offing
and sea prospect; small muscles shake
and gleam wave-white in her walking,
as smoothed cloth is suspended till
the singing flower wave-caught
turns, sways to the waiting lake and
all her aching sun wave-high breaks
in the still air; and she returns,
lake sweat, sperm-wet from that first
renewal, thoughtless, paphian.

Canadian Forum   *Allan Brown*

SUNLIGHT

(for Swift Eagle)

Sunlight passes through the mountain as if the stone
were a prism. This is not a fancy of my own, not
something I imagine, even though I can close my eyes
and see the rays of sun in that shadowed land. This
is something the elders know about. Whispered to me
the other night, it was something I had known, just
as I recognized the description of the great maze of
Atlantis, the one the Aztecs copied, the design which

is that of the man in the canyons, the power of whirl-
wind in Pima baskets.

Sunlight is at the heart of it all. Sunlight is love.
Love is a sacrifice, especially when given to those
who do not understand, those who make their decisions
on the basis of surfaces. They cannot feel the sunlight
penetrating the granite of their skins.

Two days ago I was moving stones in the creek. A new
bridge had been made and boulders were pushed down
into the stream where I waded as a child. I pried
out one big stone and saw, there on the underside,
dozens of small round globules, each filled with
a tiny salamander nymph. Sightless, limbless, heads
barely defined, they squirmed within the albumen. They
had never seen the sun, yet had grown because of its
strength. I moved the stone carefully, propping it
so the eggs would not be crushed. Pale as moon they
were. Moon is the grandmother, the one who speaks
to us after we have been created by Sun's warmth.

We talked late that night, talked of Sun and Moon, of
stories the old ones told and the ways to listen. If
you listen well enough you will hear the sunlight
bubbling up through the earth all the way from the
other side.

The Virginia Quarterly Review   *Joseph Bruchac*

LOST COMPANIONS

I cannot believe them old, nor believe them dead.
I see them young and fleet, each buoyant head
lifted to dare all ills, eager to mould
an age far finer, purer than the old.
They were so blithe, so ignorant of dread.

I remember the day we climbed, the two who led
to a summit, there to see the world outspread.
I cannot believe that for them the bell has tolled.
I cannot believe them old,

nor can I accept that an unmerited
oblivion should swallow those who wed
their dream to action, who were all enrolled
in the great game, compassionate and bold.
I cannot conceive those limbs untenanted,
I cannot believe them old.

The Lyric   *Helen Bryant*

SASKATCHEWAN DUSK

Because dusk comes
swiftly to Saskatchewan,

the day is torn by night.
I have built the hours myself,
my body taking on the luminous glow
of frost that snow-birds spill.
No wasted motion, raw with scraping
rime, only an acrid fragrance
of terrible blizzards.

Whenever the noisy winds are moving
across a ruin of stubble
I will sing my dusk like the sea.
The sun and the shadows mate,
always point in one direction,
meshed tight in the red veins of winter.
No one knows how empty
night is of day, nor the true form
of the prairie gathering in the dusk.

The Fiddlehead   C. M. Buckaway

THE LETTERS OF SUMMER

The weatherman has shown us everything
stalled out, somewhere over the Pacific . . .
All afternoon there's a dead man singing
from the phonograph across the yard,
the pine trees are stopped mid-thought,
the quick-brown needles and the months—

And nothing continues to arrive.
The hour for the mail passes, and
we sit in aluminum chairs looking for a cloud,
an elbow of wind through the raked leaves,
any response, as we give in
to the torpor of our bleached lawns.

In May with all the flowers
we asked the usual reliefs, and
as though we had asked nothing of ourselves
the driven grace is at our backs;
it seems we should let it go
without so much as an arm raised or a voice,
we should simply drift on some placid, amber lake.

With dusk, we saunter toward the house like cats, as if,
treed, we had not beseeched the sanctimonious dogs.
Surely, this is the back porch of things,
a little dust, a tide of small considerations
sifting back to us veiled as the balmy August sky.
*Look to your hands in the weak light and believe
the lines will be fulfilled*—this is all they're saying.

Poetry   *Christopher Buckley*

CROCKERY

Long lilies in a blue jug
Lean like swans
From a blue pond, like the long
Sweep of the sounding of violins
From a lake of tone, like souls
All straining from an azure globe,
Each from a blue-veined pot.

Four Quarters   *Julia Budenz*

THERE'S A FEELING

There's a feeling gathering inside me
Like clouds before the rain;
A wind with a cold smell;
A wind that stirs the warm air;
Wind that raises dry leaves from the dead
To dance around me.

There will be rain—
Rain that starts as gentle drops
Disappearing into the fresh-tilled earth
Leaving no trace;
Rain that beats slow on the roof;
Rain that slides on a sooty windowpane;
Rain that whispers with the leaves
In the tops of trees,
Then bursts like tears
Onto a child's pillow,
Slashing through the air,
Slicing through my hair,
Filming my eyes,
Sluicing over my shoulders,
Running between my breasts
And down my thighs
Until I am the rain—
And the rain is me.

The Apalachee Quarterly   *Marcia Bullwinkle*

COUNTRY CEMETERY

I wrote him out a check,
One hundred for the plot,
The corner by the woods—
A quiet spot.

So now it waits for me,
I not yet old.
No spade has marred the grass,
Nor granite cold.

But where the trees are tall
Shy thrushes sing;
So is my requiem
A foregone thing.

The wind will scatter seed
Of daisies there,
Bestowing on my grave
Perpetual care.

The Lyric   *Freda Newton Bunner*

LOST WORD

I do not believe in a God
who bothers Himself in the trivia
of this planet, but
Lord, could you find me this word?
I know it as well as my name,
but it is running backwards into darkness
as I lurch after it.
It stands for the small mammal
that ate raspberry parfait
at the back door in Big Sur; the huge one
that climbed through Eric's window
and clawed at his cats;
the old one that made a shambles of his kitchen.
I say *possum, skunk,*
porcupine, knowing it is not any of these.
The word, Lord! You are supposed to be good
at words. Remember the Word? It is midnight
and I yearn for the elusive thing. I sleep
and waken. It is coming closer. It skitters by,
avoiding my eyes. I scurry from attic to cellar
of my mind. It is not there.
Weasel, squirrel, badger, rat.
I am not asking to see the dark side of the moon, God.
Only one word. Will you give it to me with Your light?
I roll to one side. The beast
turns its black triangle of a face
full on me. Ah, *raccoon.*

The Poetry Miscellany   *Jean Burden*

ASH WEDNESDAY

Brothers, celebrate with me this morning
our mortality
with hunger and the day's
dusty ritual.
And then let us praise old men
who know the ultimate of earth
but now are dazzled

with autumn leaves, snow at noon,
the slow life of plants in humid rooms;
who hobble through the villages of childhood
with no cry of wonder or lament;
who touch the last pool of memory,
water so clear and still
it is invisible,
and see the mythic coming of the night.

Old men, we praise you
who show us in a dying world
how to live the day that is
and savor it,
who rejoice
while dust turns back to dust.

Four Quarters   *Daniel Burke*

INDIAN SUMMER

October's end. A day of sunny still.
The leaves drop perpendicularly down.
The day's as hot as summer, but a chill,
Implicit in the upper-story's crown,

Dismantled of its leaves to the bare whips,
Suggests the unreality of such
A summer idyll in the year's eclipse.
A wasp, half-paralysed from the night's touch

Of frost, moves slowly as a convalescent
Across the table by the half-filled pool,
Helping the images of past and present
To merge in this day-island of renewal.

And yet how out of place it is—almost
Annoying when, our faces set for cold,
We are confronted by the summer's ghost,
Reminded of the foregone green and gold

We could not bring our prime together with,
Nor energize from grass-root to cloud-height,
Letting it pass away, becoming myth,
And memory, and finally this sleight.

Poetry Now   *Gray Burr*

THE POOLHALL

It was a room where everything was stained:
the windows turned the sunlight into fog;
old auction posters that announced the sale
of farms long lost turned brown against the wall;
the green pooltable-tops were streaked with black;
the round oak tables scarred with burns and beer.

We kids went there to breathe maturity
within that graying yellow atmosphere
so heavy with cigar smoke. For we lusted
to be beyond the itchy thirsty teen-years
and into that completeness beyond twenty-
one.

And so we watched the stained old men
bent around the scarred oak table-top,
clutching aces, jacks, deuces of spades
in leather fingers—and in our innocence,
as stainless as new fixtures, could not hear
the parable that time told in that room.

Kansas Quarterly   *Don Burt*

DEPRESSION

(for Virginia, who knows)
Take medicine! Take medicine!
—Melville

Say there were six, say there were a dozen,
say there were a thousand loaves to feed the thousands.
Who'd prefer stones? Who'd prefer to eat his anger,
his own cynicism? Many many many:
the merely sexual, the ghosts and wanderers,
the lost, the crazy. Friend, confess it,

you are one with them; and it's not so difficult
to feel how all you loved is finished, is it?
Your brilliant sex, your eyes, your brain are finished,
all that beauty. That and that and that.
All you turn toward no longer mirrors you.
The billion stars you thought so hot go out

as fast as thoughts expiring; don't blame me.
You must have always been this goddam crazy
and just never knew it. Real beasts are crowing
in terrific fires beneath us, ha ha ha,
but look at me, I don't care. I feel the ease
of whiskey and the gallows and I rest.

California Quarterly   *Rex Burwell*

RETREAT

Biafran, *sertanejo*, Pakistani—
Peculiar things, unlike me as a mollusk.
Has it been certified they really suffer?
Aren't there too many of them anyway?

In hot Honduras decent city doctors
See only *gente decente*, do not go out of town.

Officials carefully warehouse Care packages.
Americans always want to do something,
But starving should take no longer than it has to.
These people will be dying anyhow,
And there is always another one
Of the irreplaceable children.

History is my hiding.
Of all the blessed dead, not one still hurting.
No one shall now unwrite or right their time.

National Forum   *Amy Bushnell*

STOOD-UP

(a Poem for a Voice)

Twilighted reek in a blood-rugged hall—
my drumming fingers bring no one before the door.
Walled whispers. I wait,
wait for the okaying eye,
weight down left foot, right foot.
Secret as thieves, I nudge the doorknob around—
locked.
Did I board an early bus?
You woman. You witch. Bitch.
The door's swatted flat-handed. I fling down the hall.

I stretch on a bench, bored as a cat.
I put a page of my book away.
The letters are calm, so calm!
I go needle and thread through streets,
stare out of stores not to miss her.
I should go ask the neighboring gay,
I should stab at her blinds with a stick.
Why am I circling, circling her rooms like the sun?
Why am I something she'd rather wipe off her feet?
I eat a peach. I eat pizza,
I knock again, knock again

until the skylip leeches the sun away
and I wander home, home
in darkness like undeveloped film.

Prism International   *Bruce Byfield*

POEM FOR A SON

You've made yourself in clay
but it's turned out a man—
a grey man—weeping.

It is a face full of circles—
eyes, tears, a mouth.

The mouth is shaped in a cry—
some long sound wave
that could last a lifetime.

I don't know what to make of this.
You're certainly not grey,
you've a mouthful of riddles,
and mostly your cries are soundless—
internal or private
or sometimes pushed through a dream
where they don't seem to be yours.

Yet I can see you're pleased
with this grim thing
you tell me is you—
and I wonder
what have I done,
what have I made.

The Malahat Review   *Heather Cadsby*

DUE DATE

When I was young
I aimed at laurels.
I would be President,
I'd be Public Hero No. 1,
I'd personally win the World
Series in the last half of the ninth.
And later on I dreamed of being
Pulitzered, Guggenheimed, Nobeled
For being a wizard of the word,
A master builder of the mind,
A psychopompos in new worlds to know.

But soon the due date will arrive
And I shall have to cash in
All my hopes and dreams.
There is no longer time
For blowing bubbles in the air.
And I must carefully cultivate
This little plot of land
That's left to me.

What now remain are body and mind,
The wind on the cheek,
The trees bared and leaved,
The sun's upcoming and downgoing,
The helft and cut of words,
The airy solidity of thought,
And our fabled double kingdom
Of life and of death.

The Christian Century   *Seymour Cain*

CRIPPLED CHILD AT THE WINDOW

She follows their races and climbings,
eyes, through a haze of pain,
dissecting the flexed thigh's sinews,
calling each tendon by name.

Longing? Why would she envy
those games? What could they know,
who confuse beech leaf and alder
pine warbler and vireo.

At night she will visit some other
planet, her true country of birth,
reliving the light air lifting,
the fall to heavy earth.

Now her spread hand hungers
to caress green anatomies,
stretches, curving to tautness,
as they swing down from the trees—

O she dares them on hilltops and fences,
her dream wings aching for sky,
Earthlings! If you are my equals,
prove it and fly! Fly!

Song   *Melissa Cannon*

AN ISRAELI SOLDIER'S NIGHTMARE

As I look in the mirror,
an Arab stares back

frozen
with glittering teeth,
black eyes
and long fingers.

He smiles slowly
but does not cock his head to one side
when I cock mine.

The moon slips
through the barrack window
and beams of light tiptoe through my hair.

He squats in the corner
with a frayed leather book
clasped in sinuous fingers.
As he reads
my head falls onto my chest,
and I creep away, ashamed.

"There is an Arab in my mirror,"
I say to my commander.

He shrugs, and turns away from me.

Jewish Currents   *Alison B. Carb*

FLYING

Sometimes late at night dozing over a book,
the fire low and the wind high outside,
I hear above the moan in the wires
the lonely motor of a small plane,
and I wonder who's up there or if,
through the overcast, he sees our lights
and can find his way safely down the blue runway.

I have been there once or twice hunched over red
instruments, intent on some horizon
at an unfelt altitude.
How slowly the night passed beneath my wings!
Yet the air-speed indicator read one hundred and two.
One of those lights down there was home,
small, indistinguishable in the darkness, and someone
pointing: "The star that moves—that's your father."

The American Poetry Review   *Henry Carlile*

RAPTURE

Twinkle of twilight,
Stars aflame,
Soft blanket of blackness
Which shrouds thy child
With tomorrow,
Never to be the same.
Behold, the Day of days has come.
For down to the depths of the silent sea,
Across the sands of many lands,
A whisper shall touch the world,
And then a mighty cry,
For the just shall rise to meet their Lord
In the flicker of an eye.

The Pentecostal Evangel   *Randolph Carlson*

OLD MAN

Tonight we sat,
telly dead,
'till two
Just like we've always done.
Just you and I, old man.
Emptying fluid words into night's cauldron,
You dip down a spoon to find your life
relived in mine.
Old man, yours is a garden of carnations
and orchids;
mine is of wild dandelions that smile at
the sun.
So we sit,

watching the small blue-yellow flames
flee from dying turf.
The fire burns our words.
We listen
to the warm silence.

Voices International   *Alan J. Carr*

AS I GROW OLDER AND FATTEN ON MYSELF

Thank you, my children, my students,
your wiggling insistence to leave
releases me—no tears are needed

for last year's doll,
naked and not looked after,
her clothes torn and lost
from too much on and off,
too much of a child's fingering motherhood,
now able to grow older in peace

as cotton grows worn and cozy,
as a fire
steadily slows,
as a bird flies
just above a limb
to light.

I have become marbles
enclosed in cloth,
a brown suede cap I've fingered black,
a lazy second chin,
more than a third of a life
collecting its reward
for a year
until the new decade
streamers in,
afloat on cardboard horns
and drunk hurrays.

I am stuffed with myself
and ready to digest.

Poet Lore   *Joseph Carson*

THE MEASURING

You're sickly pale—a crooked root.
But one last remedy remains:
Before the dawn we'll go on foot
Through grass sleeked down by heavy rains
To the sexton's house. Already he
Takes down his spade, and goes
To walk among the whitened rows.

His wife awaits with lengths of string
Necessary for measuring.

She has no fire alight, nor words
To spare, but bolts the wooden door
And helps you out of clothes that fall
Soundlessly to the floor. Naked,
You mount the table and recline;
She comes, her eight stiff fingers
Trailing bright bits of twine. First
Crown to nose, then mouth to chin,
Pressing against each crevice, in
And down the length of your cold frame—
Whispering unintelligible names.

The feet are last to stretch: from heel
To toe each one must be times seven
The other piece. She nods, and knots
The two together, breathes her spell,
Then turns to go. I leave a pair
Of silver dollars there, and take
The string to tie where it will rot
The winter long: on hinge of gate,
Wheelbarrow shaft, or eave-trough's fall.

Behind us, where the darkness drains,
A blackbird settles on the roof
And calls back to another that rain
Is coming like an awful proof.
The two denounce the scratching sound
The sexton's spade makes on the ground—
Measuring off the careful square
Of someone else expected there.

Sou'wester   *Jared Carter*

TURN ON THE FOOTLIGHTS: THE PERILS
OF PEDAGOGY

Turn on the footlights, illuminate the stage,
Look at me the teacher, the seer, the sage!
I have my theatre, my props, my script—
Now all I need is not a descript:
Of how the actor acts, or the teacher teaches,
Nor the time-honored recipe for custard, cream 'n' peaches!

I am the teacher, I am the star,
Let's ride the performance together where we are!
We'll travel the world over without leaving this room—
And write verses of buffoonery, stanzas of gloom:
And answer the universal riddles all in good time,
Paint pretty, petite patterns and make our lives a rhyme!

Who will be my master?
Than me, who can talk faster?

Socrates, Plato, and Aristotle will be my guides;
Grammar, rhetoric and logic will be my brides.
We'll discuss feudalism, cannibalism, futurism, scientism,
Dilettanteism, materialism, Great Schism, Ism-ism!

No, I'm not Henry the Eighth,
It's more important I be Polydore Vergil the Greath!
No, I'm not Charlemagne,
I'm Einhard, here to lay it ongne!
No, I'm not Alfred, I'm Asser,
No, don't tell my mother, it'll disgracer:

She wanted me to be a physician,
Wear woolens, make money, sew heads.
Instead, I read Beowulf and Chaucer
And now sport polyester threads. . . .

Don't you know Homer, son, sit up in that seat!
Scholars live not by bread alone, they need potatoes and meat!
Don't you know Cicero or Martianus Capella?
Or Milton or Mozart or that Stratford-on-Avon fella?
Ain't isn't allowed except by the licensed, which you ain't got,
And I'm the license examiner, do it my way,

Or,

You'll sit there till you rot!

Educational Studies   *John Marshall Carter*

END OF THE AFFAIR

Darling,
why couldn't you have told me
at that motel?—
Your favorite one next to the One-Hour-Martinizing—
that we were through
after one year of coming together.
You should've broken the news
in that peeling room of ours,
near the White Star Mobil Park.
But no! You waited until
last night
and chose the wrong locale—
Your house.
Funereal for the occasion,
Windows shut,
Darkness pierced by a ragged candle,
Irises in a grey urn-vase.
And your face so doleful
among the shadows. Bad setting,
as if for a death watch.
Darling! Why not end it in style?
You, awash in perfume at our motel,
bright of cheek, fast of pulse,

all gasps until the
final joy-cry—
one last time?

Colorado Quarterly   *Curtis W. Casewit*

HOMECOMING CELEBRATION

(for Lanny)

The cicadas are dying
one by slow one again.
I lean far into their sound
and remember an Italian woman hanging
over a geranium window box in Naples.
It is time to make
a small confession to myself, and to you.
I who spend so much of my life
in the service of memory
have on occasion seen it turn over
and become something else,
something rather like the present:
your eyes a green just below sea level,
newspapers filling this house
with what the world cares,
in this age, to think;
ice cream bells nevertheless
tapping out neighborhood peace.
In the kitchen, the bougainvillea
you brought from The Valley
turns redder by the minute;
and you wear your cap from Utopia
that you never give up,
not even when you sleep.
This is the long instant that usurps memory,
this precious breath of now
when I realize that I am with you again,
that when the bright lights of faraway
places fade, this is where I come,
to this house with all its doors open,
to this ripe, soft pocket of air
we let float between us.
Like the cicadas,
inevitable as twins or seasons,
patient with whatever of this time
memory will someday choose for us,
we are both together, my love,
and one by slow one again,
moving toward the great open soaring
when we will have sung ourselves
gently free of our shells.

Cedar Rock   *Rosemary Catacalos*

CURSE OF A FISHERMAN'S WIFE

("O, flesh, flesh, how art thou fishified"
—Shakespeare, Romeo and Juliet)

May his lines lose their lures,
May his reels rust and rot,
May the fish flinch and flee,
May huge holes hex his hull.

Dark Horse   *Lila Chalpin*

LEAVE THE TOP PLUMS

Now to pick wild plums:
first you have to look for them
and believe in serendipities
or you will never find them. Many people
don't believe there are any wild plums left.

Next, wait until they have ripened
to a dull-gold-and-pink mellow sheen.
Plums, wild or no, are sour and good
only for spitting out if picked before they are ready.

Then on a sunny day—so the plums
will glisten and gleam through the green leaves
and show themselves to you—look up,
up and around, picking as you go,
pulling the branches down and stretching
to reach just one more plum.

It will not be easy.

Branches will prickle and stick,
threaten to eliminate an eye, scratch
at your jacket or skin if they can—
anything to protect their bounty.

Finally, you have a bowlful.
Do not be greedy. Pick only those
within your farthest reach. Leave the top plums,
the ones high up, for birds that will
swoop down and pluck them off.

City Miner   *Janet Carncross Chandler*

STONE

The night that lives protectively
around color, the chill we walk through
to sunlight. It's the unseen mass

below surfaces that sway
or ripple in the outer light that touches
tentatively. The thick body of stone

is definite and cool, seasonless
even after death has happened

elsewhere, been buried, flowered.
The stones we plant for death
call to that unshaken body below, below

the surface. Waiting for some response,
we visit daily, then every other week,
finally once in ten years

or never. It never happened. We never
heard. The stone set where we can see it
still speaks to us in our own words:
a year, a name—the dimensions

that meant so much; but the dark voice
of stone that supports everything
never comes. Or isn't there. I want it

to be there. I want to hear
what happens to the dead
who have broken down through
the surface.

Sou'wester   *Juliet Chayat*

WINDOW

Summer night, a woman rests
her elbow on the sill. Behind her,
a face glimmers, a curtain
streaks the dark interior.
From the street below
you see her smile, lean from
the window as if it framed
a painting. The street lamp
burns a halo in the heavy air,
and you remember
the yellow headlight
of the sun drifting down
a grey haze. Children play
hoops through fire escape rungs.
You hear the rush of an opened
hydrant; water slick as oil
collects in potholes,
and the woman in the window
strains for her reflection,
brushing her hair
in long strokes, one note
held. These nights
you would do anything
to let go: be a spark struck
in the woman's brushed hair,
a current of salsa escaping

a cafe—anything
instead of who you are,
in a sweaty street,
longing for women in windows.

The Black Warrior Review   *Anne Cherner*

FORSYTHIA IS THE COLOR I REMEMBER

To celebrate this season I must find
Some ancient poem written in my youth
When April was a constant season, blind
To such realities as winter truth.
April was all-expected; what was new
Was death and its cold logic in December.
Aprils were always here, Decembers few.
Forsythia is the color I remember.
To celebrate this April, I must turn
From all that age has taught me and put trust
In yellow blooms that fall can never burn,
Nor February hide in icy dust.
To celebrate this April, I must be
Younger than ever in my memory.

The Lyric   *Joseph Cherwinski*

ANOTHER ONE FOR THE DEVIL

Sure as Hell, the Devil
inhabited the stairway
between Dean's Drugs and Tick Tock's
clock loft
living on dust and flies,
smelling things up like sulphur,
straining the air conditioner,
eating the heat when it was cold.
That's what happened to business.
Not the malls, not the freeways,
but the Devil, goddam it, infecting
Dean with blinding hangovers, making Tick
Tock senile, unable
to remember when to eat or sleep
or how to fix clocks. The two men
sat down and hung their chins
in a sink. The deal
was closed.
And sure as Hell,
the Devil got it all: clocks, ear plugs, pills,
etc.,
the endless etcetera
on down to strings and tacks. The Devil and four
well-dressed lawyers

in the sweltering middle
of heart-attack weather
stood on the steps of the courthouse
and auctioned it off to themselves.
"Hear Ye, Hear Ye,
Be it known that on this the third of August . . ."
The Devil got it all,
and the sheriff, the doctors,
the withered bus riders
plastered on benches like bugs,
all of us passing,
we missed it. One day
there were two men in business: CLOCKS FIXED, HAM-
BURGERS, HEAT FOR SORE MUSCLES
IN A MINUTE. One day—
then, sure as Hell,
they were gone.

Southern Exposure   *David C. Childers*

MEMORIAL DAY

(for my sister, Marjorie)

Mother told me the directions
but still I'm lost
in an overgrown graveyard
while cars up on the hill
bury someone else.

The groundskeeper leads me
into the chiseled rows.
They are his souls.
He tends them now.

The lamb's head is knocked off.
A wet wind, branch, old age
or maybe kids out for kicks.
I tuck flowers into the iron bowl
and smooth the browning grass
searching for the magic word.

I come up empty.
No Alladin appears.
Just platoons of Scouts
planting flags.

The Mississippi Valley Review   *Laureen Ching*

COUPLETS FOR WCW

When I am aching with a pain or ills
that have no cure in bromides or in pills,

I take my favorite doctor to my bed:
William Carlos Williams is not dead.

Those gentle hands that healed the sick and wrote
of wagons glistening in the rain, that poet

who was the happy genius of his house
becomes my djinn, and I begin to rouse.

A little song takes form inside
my practice room; the doctor is my guide.

His stethoscope-baton directs the beat:
pentameter, not variable feet.

I'm coupling with a ghost, a shade, a god,
while worms are turning handsprings in the sod.

Dark Horse   *Martha Christina*

NO WHITE BIRD SINGS

Can white birds sing? An ornithologist
told me once there was a white bell-bird
that rang whole tones, though only as separate notes.
"Is that singing—sound without sequence?"
I said. "No, not exactly," he granted,
"but it is white." I granted him half a case.
This morning I heard a mocking bird again
and claimed my whole case back: no white bird sings.

I know some black poets who have been waiting
for just this image. So there it is, man:
an accident, but accidents are to use.
What else is a poem made of? Well, yes, ghosts.
But ghosts are only what accidents give birth to
once you have learned how to make accidents happen
purposefully enough to beget ghosts.

Bird song is itself an accident, a code
not much different from wolf-howl, warthog grunt,
porpoise twitter. It is a way of placing
the cardinal in its sconce, of calling its hen,
of warning off others. *That* code. We hear it
and *re*-code it: it sounds to us like something
we might like to try. Who cares how it sounds
to another bird? We take what we need from nature,
not what is there. We can only guess what is there.

Guess, then: why does no white bird sing
to our pleasure? Because, I will guess, songsters
nest in green-dapple. There what is white shines.
What shines is visible. What is most visible
is soonest hunted. What is soonest hunted
becomes extinct. To sing, one must hide in the world

one sings from, colored to its accidents
which are never entirely accidents. Not when one sings.

Poetry   *John Ciardi*

LAST RITES

1.
when death dances in,
tap-shoes rattling like dice
on the floor of your room,
assure him there's been no mistake;
ask if you may borrow
his faded straw hat, his grin;
ask if you may lead;
waltz him out the door.

2.
stake your claim early
to a plot of bright earth.
break ground at dawn, sowing
the seeds your father left unplanted;
reap a future in crisp green bunches.
at the close of the harvest day
lie down in the soil, head to the east,
the ancient scent rising all around.
as the sun falls from the edge of earth,
let the darkness race across your body.

The Literary Review   *David Citino*

ON THE DISADVANTAGES OF CENTRAL HEATING

cold nights on the farm, a sock-shod
stove-warmed flatiron slid under
the covers, mornings a damascene-
sealed bizarrerie of fernwork
    decades ago now

waking in northwest London, tea
brought up steaming, a Peak Frean
biscuit alongside to be nibbled
as blue gas leaps up singing
    decades ago now

damp sheets in Dorset, fog-hung
habitat of bronchitis, of long
hot soaks in the bathtub, of nothing
quite drying out till next summer:
    delicious to think of

hassocks pulled in close, toasting-
forks held to coal-glow, strong-minded

small boys and big eager sheepdogs
muscling in on bookish profundities
now quite forgotten

the farmhouse long sold, old friends
dead or lost track of, what's salvaged
is this vivid diminuendo, unfogged
by mere affect, the perishing residue
of pure sensation

The Atlantic Monthly   *Amy Clampitt*

TABLES

We've tabled it all.
We eat in silence.
I read, don't look at him.
He chews quickly, goes back to his games.

Sometimes I would lay a cloth,
blue & green, flecks of gold; almost handwoven.
Sometimes a no-iron almost-lace, in cool avocado.
Often, a pitcher of daisies for courage,
gardenias or pinks to perfume the whole kitchen.

After a year or two, I became almost blind
to that whitish mottling of the formica, the dead
yellow-green, the stylized gray flowers.
The legs' dull aluminum needs polish.
On the underside a sharp-cornered brace
waits for the tenderest part of a knee.

The surface expands—expanded—one leaf, then two.
The children sat quarreling or, like us, silent.
They've gone; we've put the leaves away.
The damn thing won't wear out. I should be pleased.
I dream of axes.

The Ontario Review   *Naomi Clark*

CHANGE OF VENUE

In the daytime
I walk in the South Bronx
Harlem
carrying my briefcase
on my shoulder
next to my thick neck
about which I am self-conscious
under my white face
about which I am also
self-conscious
but only in those parts of town

where I make a salary
on which I can live elsewhere.

In the Midwest
we have landscaped our urban decay
more effectively
in Chicago the bums are zoned
onto one street
they do not lie on every corner
in the smaller cities
you could walk the streets at night
except that nothing's open
the small towns
have no pollution
people use garbage cans
clean up their own dog shit.

I am watching the city die
I am getting paid to help kill it
it did not begin that way
too many books read
about victories
I did not realize there are no victories
without enemies to conquer
I can find no enemies
only victims whom I teach
to accept defeat
then I come home and bathe
watch my reflection in the water
see an enemy.

13th Moon   *Jill Clockadale*

LEAVING HOME

Car loaded
one sock
locked in the door.
How can he see out
with all those clothes?
Couldn't he wait and go tonight?
An owl's eyes he's got
better in dark.

I stand in morning's
skim milk light
seeing the diamonding
of latched gate
the rescued dog
street siblings
shoe-boxed pigeon.
Him, him, him—
too many snapshots!

We've said goodbye
it does not bear repeating.
The starter giggles into catch—
Wait! One more thing . . .
But he (hearing, not hearing)
drives on. Better anyway:
difficult to pick one final thing
—warning, blessing—
and make it last
a lifetime.

The Hollins Critic   *Shirley Cochrane*

THE OLD NUDISTS

Her body is pouchy,
globules of fat pocking
her thighs,
hips like immense sugar bowl handles,
breasts two smashed bags.

He is all wattles
from neck to groin,
his sternum the jutting keel
of a beached ship.

Their house
so hot in winter our minds
rock to sleep
watching them waddle
unclothed. Their familiar heads
spliced to these odious torsos.

We get used
to the faces of the old,
even theorizing the lines
and tortured gauntness
are trophies of coping;
but these bodies
seem outrageous, obscene,
decayed yellow sacks
full of wet garbage.

We hug ourselves.
Under our clothes
the loom
of our bones is weaving the flesh
of our grandparents.

The old man and old woman smile
cordially. They know
what's going on
inside us.

Portland Review   *Joan Colby*

GRANDFATHER

It says much for your life,
old man of leather, tobacco, earth and flannel,
that sixteen years after your death
I still long for the comfort
of your calloused, scarred-knuckle hands
from a hundred saws in migrant logging camps,
from a hundred picks in dog hole mines,
I remember stories of sawdust and blood, coal and bone.
I want to slip you your whiskey bottle
stashed in the pantry,
pick you the reddest banana peppers,
hear you tell the moons to plant and cut by,
old man of leather, tobacco, earth and flannel;
tell me again of your father who lost family and land
as lone Union soldier of five Southern sons;
tell me of your mother's fugitive father
who climbed the mountains to escape
the deadly march to Oklahoma;
tell me again of your marches and blacklistings,
how you never signed a yeller dog contract—
old man of leather, tobacco, earth and flannel.
Once I held up oak saplings in the sun
you skinned down to bridge a mountain stream
we are still working together;
you bared your history and held it up to the light—
now I am laying a bridge back to you.

Mountain Review   *Mary Joan Coleman*

RETREAT

I would say a band
but you would think of Sunday,
the park, the circle
of benches, children dancing
on the grass,

while I, drawn to the open space
in you by the clear notes
of a single horn,

would be thinking of cymbals,
brass, a parade, the children
pushed aside and maybe soldiers
coming behind;

I might be thinking
of war, even, and what
would you do in the battle
between my hands
when I'd nothing to play?

I might not see
the white flag you hold
like bread in your steady hands,
I might mistake you
for one of the crowd, I might
not hear the password you speak
like a whisper before the fall
of the thin baton.

The Michigan Quarterly Review   *Martha Collins*

PHOTOGRAPHING THE FACADE—
SAN MIGUEL DE ALLENDE

They are eternal as angels and demons.
Seated wrapped in clothes gladly rags,
holding for pennies their antique hats,
they wait as they always wait,
these same beggars everywhere
at every church we visit,
always the gaunt Indian mother nursing
the same gaunt baby, these archetypes
of lameness, and the diseased,
their flesh a parable of sickness.

A few miles away the freeway runs
and motels transmogrify the landscape,
and even on this square, plastics
and polyesters conquer the market,
and American Express buys us everything.
Yet, they, these changeless who waited
surely for Cortez at monuments
to other gods, are constants.

And we who would photograph the facade
aim Polaroid high, tilt viewfinder
to seek Saint Michael, putting down
a pink and wounded stony demon
and triumphing as he always must,

and to exclude from focus these wounded
lingeringly as Satan, as Christ,
in some eternal and relentless scheme
that none of us do fully cause
and cannot resolve, and, embarrassed,
we search by camera eye for Gothic things.

The Christian Century   *Betsy Colquitt*

MILTON'S WIFE ON HER TWENTY-THIRD BIRTHDAY

I have stopped scrubbing his shirts a moment
To note that I am twenty-three today.
But I cannot stop for long, the babes still cry
When their stomachs cry out to them.

My husband needs me to bring him bread, too,
So busy with his books piled high around him
And his eyes beading out like independent animals.
I must run to him soon and wring out the cloth
That cools his teeming forehead and hush the babies
So that he may grow into the greatness he already shows
Of a man who has much to tell to all the world.
Great thoughts are insinuated in the wrinkles by his mouth
And by the way he holds his pen, I can see that.
And if I am twenty-three today
Well, I will soon enough be twenty-four.

California Quarterly   *Jane Conant-Bissell*

CLINIC: EXAMINATION

Her face is a scrubbed glove,
and no wonder:
waiting is a rack of forms,
bland as macaroni,
each to be held up to
a functional ideal,
that ravishing nude model
in Gray's Anatomy.

Her antiseptic eyes drill me
as if my disease were some
subsistent flaw in soapstone
to be picked out and then burnished.
(Or a worm in a supper salad.)

Her fingers needle through
the strands of veins
(which are the fagots
of my fever's burning);
they open and close me: my folds unpleat.
Membranes part as if this were not
an odd coupling on a sterile tray
but the ordinary way
to get acquainted.

I am plasma under her cyclops eye,
a docile bivalve pried with a blunt knife;
a sheeted frog; or the rolling hills
of a treasure hunt.
Her hands must be implements
laid to my object, her face a mask.

Her fingers are tender to the swelling glands:
a two-week embryo would not elude their touch.
For also am I her baby macaque
from whom she picks and chews,
absorbed, the viral nits.

Waves   *Audrey Conard*

DRIVING THROUGH THE PIMA INDIAN RESERVATION

Out here where the summer air
is thick with the breath
of every wheat-moth that ever lived,
I take to the broken roads
that seem different versions of
the same strange story. We have

given the Pimas this arid stretch
of flood plain and ornamented
their horizons with
the busy constellations
of prosperous Mormon towns. Here

in the muddy dark, their clapboard
government mansions
burst thin, razor-edges of light
that scarcely threaten any city limit,
and everyone is safe

if we are to judge
from the pose of sleeping dogs
and the colic tilt
of an abandoned refrigerator.
This is the land
of spare parts and disregard. Cities

elbow around on three greedy sides,
and it just might be true
that these are the poorest folk
we know, hunched
over television sets, their faces
pale in the luminescent air.

And it could be just as true,
as I pass the quickest way home,
that there burns here
a greater medicine that has dappled
and feathered them with the light

of many suffering moons,
that will be returned
to the night sky when the stars
of our easy invention have
all but gone away.

Whetstone   *Paul H. Cook*

HUDSON HORNET

My father preached full, powerful;
Raised heavenly thunder as he roared,
Salvation sang,
Sang holy, phallic, masterful
Till sisters big and hallelujah
Danced out their locked-in passion.

Locked big with mastering they live,
Queens to whom small husbands cower
Drowned in vastness, female greed—
I want, I want—
Small husbands never could supply;
But heavenly and phallic deity
Drawn from my father's book and dreams—
Full-muscled, steel-loined deity
Could move them from their frigid thrones,
Could set their hips and legs to life
And holy dance them to orgasm.
How shall a mere man satisfy
What has been moved to shouting joy
By such complete priapic might?
No man for Leda after Zeus.

My father home, without the robes,
The pulpit or the book, came down
Shrunk small—to bullying the weak.
The child could never plan resistance,
Never dared defend or lodge complaint.
Despite my prayers that he would grow
And tower pulpit-like at home,
My father never rose above his times.
Behind the news he hid himself;
Beneath the used car ads he crept
And did not fix on that great Hudson Hornet—
A massy chariot fit for more than god—
But meekly in my mother's sound advice,
The humble Ford for gelded men
Androgynous and weak he chose.

God save the Sundays where he rode.

New England Review   *William W. Cook*

THE OTHER

When you come to the other side
of lust the body lays itself
down in others as itself
no longer, and the fields, till now
fallow, bloom vermilion.

When you cross to the other side
of pride the heart withers
into tinder, the wind blesses it.
Your body flares, white sticks
this side of anger.

Arriving at the other side
of terror, the voice is a dark flame
walking evenings in the garden,
your name unknown to it
if the last light calls you.

And when you have passed the other side
of hope, the shore will blaze
finally. We are all light here.
Do not look for me or ask.
You will never have known me.

The New Yorker   *Peter Cooley*

ALL UP AND DOWN THE LINES

Uncle Charlie lived alone.
He would press quarters into my palm
with his manicured fingers,
bring my mother cologne and candy;
while she bubbled thanks, he blushed.

After he had kissed me good-bye,
brushing his witch-hazeled cheeks against mine,
my father joked that Charlie was courting her.
My mother said he ought to be ashamed,
Charlie was a lonely old man
who liked to give people things.
My father answered, "Why didn't he
ever get married, and give some woman
a family?" Then they would tell me
to leave the room, while they whispered,
my mother laughing and saying "shame,"
by turns.

While I sat in another room,
holding the quarter
Uncle Charlie had given me,
hearing his soft, high voice
sputter and trail off
like a small, overworked engine,
when he spoke of World War I,
and the nights bombs whistled
over the trenches,
and beautiful young men died
all up and down the lines.

Cottonwood Review   *Robert Cooperman*

REDEMPTION

friend
Savior
woman, and all
iridescent
milk-filled
shouting
creatures

in the four
directions
of this house,
I proclaim you
stones:

be silent.

Southwest Review   *Stanley Cooperman*

I SUPPOSE HER MOTHER TOLD HER

I suppose her mother told her
That ladies cross their legs
Around one man,
And hobble after him
The rest of their lives.

On windy days
When her skirt stirred,
She wished her thighs were breathing
In another man's eyes;
That her flesh wasn't cringing
Like a bruised animal
Against breasts she wore
Like old wedding bells.

She was beautiful
In her tight thighs,
With her blue eyes murmuring
Across the floor;
But no man has entered
The conversation.

Prism International   *Francine Corcos*

ACHILLES

Did she mean that much to him that he was
Willing to brood and let his armor rot
Just to prove a point? All we know about
Briseis is that she was beautiful. But was
She a good bedmate, and did Achilles
Love her for herself, or as a trophy?

The problem is, one can't sympathize
With Agamemnon, a rotten father,
A tyrant among women, sacrificing
His daughter for a brother, even
Offending Apollo for a skirt. So,
Achilles was right to rage, dead right.

Nor did it really matter why he sulked
And stormed, why that ardent Prince of the House
Of Peleus, magnificent beyond

Metaphor, would only stir from his tent
For Patroclus; for just as his actions
Stood independently, so did his anger.

Homer knew: passion can be sightless,
Beyond reason, contrary to social
Ethics, yet heroic in its direct
Expression. Imagine where he might have
Chosen to begin his tale, at which crux,
And then think how immortal anger is.

Kansas Quarterly   *Phillip Corwin*

FRAGMENTS

15
Remembered summers are the smell of nettles,
The sun rebaking brick and the air afloat
With small flies, while spring was always cow parsley
And the nesting of birds. So we observe
The seasons while awaiting that event
Which acknowledges none. Though windows
Of a classroom which overlooked a cemetery
Made clear seasonal increases in business
And the nature of tributes.

16
Now old friends of an age keep going
And each funeral feels more like my own.
So seize the moment! Yet, what is it?
Writing before breakfast in a small garden
In Tregowis when a swish like that of water
Tells it is seven: the gentle-footed cows
On their way for milking. While somewhere
In Ampurias, Francesca quietly irons
In the cool of morning before work begins.

17
These are it then, unobtrusive, easily missed.
Eliot in the rose garden. This is not
To ignore the true giving of flesh and mind.
Yet one act of kindness, a touch of hand or breast,
Can mean more than nights of passionate gymnastics,
And as I write this, from the tree above me
The over-ripe plums fall softly to rot.
Oh come! Not so sad, love, there's good stuff still in us,
We'll play symphonies on the bed springs yet.

Poetry   *John Cotton*

BETWEEN THE TIDES

More than moon-measure
waits
at low tide;

more than beginning past ending,
full tide—
that hovering hold
when earth and ocean
ponder in pulsing quietude
the power beyond all moons,
the Stillness
beyond all measure
of time.

Arizona Quarterly   *Emily Sargent Councilman*

TWO WOMEN WITH MANGOES

One of them seems to offer her breasts
as if they were fruit, though she holds
the canoe-shaped bowl of mangoes like a gift
received. Her eyes dart off to the right,
one hand curving around the bowl's rim
as though to guard what it presents.
The other woman holds a small bouquet
of pinkish-white flowers, presses them
between her palms. In that green dress
which exposes only one breast,
she looks even more chaste than her friend.
Is it correct to call them friends?
Certainly the wash of green and yellow
in the background is not friendly, implying
turbulent weather or a growth of weeds.
If these women and their island
offer nothing we could say we need, then what
should we ask for?
                    Gaugin, at 17,
joined the navy and traveled to Brazil.
When he left his wife, five children
and impressionism for Brittany and then Tahiti,
he must have been aroused by what he found
at first—the coppery skin, the bodies uncorseted.
But these women do not look like lovers,
either for himself or for each other.
If the fruit they hold and the breasts they show
are anything to give, they're not for us:
we don't know what to ask for.
Perhaps their pose was Gaughin's own
rendition of two women, two refusals—
the head of one turned slightly toward the other,
as if she were about to speak, or had just spoken.

Cutbank   *Steven Cramer*

VISITATIONS

On the street at dusk
someone shouts out once, familiar.

Though I look behind and see no one
I'm convinced it was she
who came to me that first time, not saying anything, a teacher
or an elder sister in the fierce afternoon.

At the edge of the woods the apple tree swayed;
I touched its rough bark, looking up
through the fine green and cold limbs at the sky.
She guided my scraping knees, bare feet
sure in their hold.
Going higher, I heard my dress tear on a sharp branch
and the ground I no longer stood on was dust.
I felt only the leaves like thin muscles
against my face, and stayed there, invisible,
with the thrill of the houses below
and the clouds far away.

I knew each time she'd come would be the same,
she would speak to me in my own voice.
And now when she does I don't know her at first—
she's gone and the street lights are on
and the playground I'm passing stings
with the shouts of children.

Buffalo Spree   *Jennifer Crewe*

MOVING

The expanse of fields spreading out
filled with daisies, buttercups,
the wildest flowers, and subtle
Queen Anne's lace.
In the white frame house
the packed boxes are piled high,
time now to move on.
On the expended fields,
the deserted houses creaked
in the wind.
Chickens clawed and grovelled
in the lawn as we talked
about marriages: mine over,
hers shaking, as high
we swung our two small
daughters on the wooden swing.
"My new lover" makes me smile
at the words, makes me reel to
this wind turned day
over these expansive fields and rise.
"My husband" makes her turn
slowly leeward to the
unwanted safety of the cardboard
boxes as the shutters

of her rented house
shake violently in the wind.

Moving Out   *Barbara Crooker*

FOREIGN STREETS

I am walking as fast as I can
shifting my shoulders to slide past
men, or the knives of thieves.
And, yes, I need a man,
a man to protect me
from those hot looks on the street
which are hate or lust,
or both. Yes, yes,
I want him to go with me
into the restaurants,
into the streets.
Yes, I admit it—
living alone is dangerous
and I am weary of fear,
of clutching my dusty belongings
under my arms.
Maybe I'm weak
but I'm going to repeat it:
I want a man.
I'm sick of thinking about myself,
of closing my heart
against the day's dozen
of cripples and amputees,
the blind man with festering sores,
the filthy kids who sleep on the streets.
And my anger, that too,
yes, that especially;
and everyone tells me
that everyone is a thief.
Tonight, every corner is filled
with soldiers with their first beards
and machine guns. I want to slink past.
You won't like my saying it
but I dream of men
breaking down the glass walls
to get at me,
and the police don't come.
There is so much water,
and I wake up, crying,
"My child, my child,"
and I don't know who I mean.

The American Poetry Review   *Mary Crow*

NO FEAR

(Nantucket, 1976)

Love is a well that never runs dry
An ocean not sounded
As skies are not touched
There always, there clouded,
There stormy with sun.
There inside and outside
the outside to leeward
is easy, sometimes
the inside to starboard is oh
so, so hard.

The fear is becalming
to heart and to mind.
The fear is the drowning
in self that must hide
inside the deep bucket that
no rope can haul—to leeward
to windward, to starboard and self.

The seas cannot drown us
The skies will not fall—
Only the fog-horn
that shroud-sails our hearts.

The Massachusetts Review   *Mary Doyle Curran*

RESULTS OF A SCIENTIFIC SURVEY

About mirrors in hotel rooms: one can say

French mirrors focus on the faces; below
    the armpits lies the mystery

The British aim them so that one sees only
    with great difficulty, at an angle

Russian mirrors do not reverse the image,
    of course

And Italians spread out, with loving attention
    to the parts

The German mirror is prescriptive, marked
    and calibrated where you ought to shine

But the Swiss, ah the Swiss mirrors,
    lucidity of plate glass, perfection
    of mercury,
    fleet images frozen forever.

New Letters   *Bruce Cutler*

AGAINST GRAVITY

How things grow upright
From the earth!
A mullein stalk,
A maple tree,
A man.

No matter what the incline
Where it grows,
Each one
With earth foundation
Reaches up.

Unity   *Edith E. Cutting*

THE WAY WE LIVE NOW

The windows
look back into themselves
through the black rain

And the bells of the university
sound only a tune

You could say
this house is the ghost of one
you used to live in

where you still put on the future every morning
as shaven jaws

At breakfast
the woman you married
beats like a black hole

the edge of the edge

her flowered blouse
emptying into space like a form of algebra

and suicide is a bright bird
perching on your finger

You whistle to it
and it whistles back

a parakeet

a canary singing its throat out like a brook
the trickle of blood in a vein

You could say
you are a liar a thief and a compulsive seducer

That this is the way
we live now

The American Poetry Review   *Robert Dana*

PLOWING AT FULL MOON

The air, cold,
The hills roll up like unbroken
Swells beneath the tractor
The plow turning a wake
Wet and black.

A column of fire gusts
Up from the exhaust, the roar
Breaks through
Finally to pure silence felt
In the hands and shoulder blades.

I am with the earth and the dark,
Alone. And work is being done.
I'll go home and dream of a horse
Bowing over still water in a cedar tank,
Drinking the moon.

Commonweal   *Leo Dangel*

DAYBREAK ON A PENNSYLVANIA HIGHWAY

Clouds stretch into their
thin streak of orange.

I drive eastward, my eyes as
heavy as the semi rolling
by, lights flashing;
it joins a long
line of trucks that
reach into the dawn.

they roll,
they breathe, they
roar and sigh—
pulsating
they are alive
as surely as a
weapon, these
machines, even they

are loved.
I see the strands of clouds
moving over them like arms,
holding them
close to the earth.

Green River Review   *John Daunt*

THE WIDOW

I hear the autumn winds blow down the sky,
The year turns to its end.

I should not dread each night
That brings the strange, the nameless fears.
I know that morning comes, and with the morning—light.
But I am vulnerable now, and old,
Having so great a need—so little strength
To fight the shadowy dark,
The small, the barren hours before dawn
And a new day—that must be filled
Like an empty bowl.
I hear the autumn winds; and it is cold.

The Lyric   *Mariana B. Davenport*

WHY WRITE POETRY?

What can you do
when you burn like hot ice, like frost bite,
and you can't begin to warm
the Hindu Kush you've married.
Or when your lover tells you
that you have the intellect and sex appeal
of cold macaroni.
    You could go mad and scream in the street
    like a fire engine
    or go away and have affairs
    with wall safes and one way mirrors.
    You might melt like scented bath drops
    and float on the world like ambergris
    or decorate yourself with ulcers.
Where do you turn
when your mate
leaves you for an eight-octave bank book,
and jealousy, that self styled crown of thorns,
stomps in and pees on you.
    You could walk into the jungle
    and feed yourself piece by piece to the cannibals,
    or smilingly swallow hot coals.
    You could cry and let your thoughts flap raggedly
    in the wind, like flags hung at grand openings.
    You could go in search of the three headed dog,
    ticking like a death watch beetle
    and knowing that no one will mourn.
Or you could, like me, write this poem.

Pulp   *Pamela Oberon Davis*

THE CHANDELIER AS PROTAGONIST

The stage is set in darkness. A table, small, oval,
with a red checked tablecloth spilled unevenly over
its sides, stands in the center of the stage. The
table is spotlighted from above. Smoke rises from a

burning cigarette in an ashtray on the tablecloth on
the table. The smoke fills the light with cloudy
shapes. The shapes keep changing the way clouds do
in a calm summer sky.

Then the chandelier comes striding down the center
aisle, all flashing and wonderful. Everyone turns
to look at her. She walks slowly, knowing she is
the center of attention. She steps up on the pro-
scenium and takes a bow. There is wild applause.
She walks to the table and climbs up on it and
reaches up into the darkness and takes hold of
something unseen in the dark above the table and
lifts herself up with one arm and stations herself
exactly above the table and holds steady, just
breathing in the glow of herself.

Southern Poetry Review   *William Virgil Davis*

WHEN A BODY

(for—)

Having met as older graduate student and emigrant-prof.,
    having learned to accept, even respect,
    each other's institutional roles—
    yours having been mouthpiece for the
    administration—mine being a bad taste
    in its mouth,

Having through sheer proximity partied together
    easily and casually—consequently having
    flirted, teased and kissed, libidinously
    but always ceremoniously,

It is a wonderful (and not at all academic)
    question how it was that last night,
    after more than four years
    of comfortably complicated camaraderie,
    a casual public sharing of "chinese,"
    of Bernie's belches, of Bessie's blues,
    of B. and B. and Gin and Tonic,
    we quietly shed our social skins,
    cast off the moorings of our known,
    familiar selves, left our minds
    heaped with our clothes and
    on your sheets swam into sudden knowledge
    in a luminous sea of sense.

Kansas Quarterly   *Gene Dawson*

THE LIZARDS OF LA BREA

Little girl running in the street
carries home lizards in a jelly jar.

Her hands pressed white and waxen on the glass,
she holds them close to my face.
I watch the lizards scratch at the jar
and the sun glisten green on their eyes.
They'll be eaten by the dog
or be baked in the sun.
Lizards know these deaths in La Brea.
Only time separates them from the glass
and the dog
and the frames of their big boned brothers
buried in the clay—
their skulls bigger than men;
brittle as jelly jars.

Wascana Review   Marc De Baca

TWO GARDENS

Here in my careful garden I have nourished
Serried rows of pallid blooms
Through all the eons of my life;
Kept hedges clipped and vigilantly high,
Practiced formality,
    observed propriety, and
        for festivity have sipped discreet,
And quite occasional elderberry wine.

Then this morning, unprepared, through the
Pale filigree of my protecting wall I glimpsed
The riot in my neighbor's garden:
Alien growth in bright, uproarious abandon
Burgeoning in forms I never knew;
Exuberant universe of holy sorcery! And in the midst,
My unknown neighbor drinking from a brimming chalice.

Now in my careful garden pallid blossoms fall to ashes
Like the body in a newly-opened tomb.
As with revelation dawning,
I contemplate the possibility,
    the probability,
        the certainty
That I shall gather flowers from new and unexpected seeds,
Drink wine from quite extraordinary grapes.

Wascana Review   Arlene De Bevoise

THESIS

Death is not a period
bringing the sentence of life to a close,
like the spilling of a moment
or the dissolution of an hour.

Death is a useful comma
which punctuates, and labors to convince
of more to follow.

Unity   *William Walter De Bolt*

EUPHORIA, EUPHORIA

Despite someone starving somewhere,
and mutilating orphan girls,
and caving heads and life-long dreams;
Despite the unmitigated
horse crap of getting by intact
in defiance of self-pity
and the latest trend in ennui—
This day was typical and rare.
My kids chased grins across the lawn.
My wife sang and cleaned, at long last,
the far reaches of our basement
and kissed me, tasting of pure girl.
And I, I cracked my backhand, crisp
and low, planted corn, and hoped it
high, high in my gold summer haze.
Drunk with unevents this small day,
and me splendid with love for all.

Carleton Miscellany   *Mark DeFoe*

REFLECTIONS OF A TROUT FISHERMAN

Every man should pride himself on something
outside work, marriage, getting by;
there's a feeling I get from fishing
nothing else can satisfy,
I couldn't explain it more.

First time I seen a Brookie jump
clear out of the stream like he was
so vain he had to show himself to me,
I was hooked.
Taught myself how
to tie the best damn flies around;
other guys know of me, some ask,
"Whaddaya know, buddy?"
I love to pull the joker from my hat:
"This here's my Gaudiroyal Leaping Gnat
made by an old Passamaquoddy medicine man;
have you tried the spot a mile upstream?"

I like the democracy of a trout stream;
truck drivers, lawyers, clerks, anybody
can reel out a line. There's even a poet
comes here, though I never cared for poetry—

we get along, just fishing;
no one elbows into the other guy's spot,
everyone can have a crack
at what we're here for.

A trout is like every woman
I've felt I'd like to have:
common full-bodied Brown,
leaping speckled Brookie,
flashing streamlined Rainbow,
most still unscarred
all well-traveled
from the most challenging currents
to the deepest quiet pools,
never giving up on living
without a brilliant battle.

The Lake Superior Review   *Andrew Demon*

MOTHER

All the trees were made
of rings, their light yellow
apples like coins in the sun.
She sat in the kitchen, facing
the fall window, eyes up in the
trees, thinking them full of
planets bobbing in the blue air.
She put one of her palms over
her eyes, then laid it curved
on her belly. Inside, the birth
sac was globed with gold.

When I was born, in that same
kitchen, the sun had just come
out—mother straining to see
me and her apples at once. I
flowed through the smooth cirque of
a red river, eyes tight as fists.
The world was red. Blood was
darkness. But she held me in her
pale arms, brushing away all the
traces of birth as if they were dust.
She touched me, told me what I'd
soon be able to see, her voice as soft as water.

Apple trees are such unadvertised things.
Not many people imagine planets strung
to their branches like some brown and
gold galaxy. Not even I can keep it
up. We buried her by a river where the
water streamlines the shore like a silver
pencil. There's an orchard over the hill.
If she looks up, flicking the dirt off

her eyelashes, she can see the top branches,
the apples kindling the day—golden
babes dropping quietly to the ground.

Sou'wester   *Barry Dempster*

THE BAND

Pensioners fondle the books in the sidewalk bins
For the big bargains, two for a dollar:
Eat Yourself Slim, Secret Missions of the Civil War,
Great Train Wrecks, Photographing Your Dog.
At home on their tables the books, never finished, pile up,
Their promises not fulfilled. The pensioners pace in their
    rooms.

Sundays they're called outside by the music of the band
From the green rotunda. The musicians strain at their horns.
Their necks are pinched by the starched collars of their
    uniforms.
They appear to be playing in this heat from duty,
As if asked by friends. Others may enjoy the music
If not them, so why not play for an afternoon?

The music floats up and away over the roofs
To the window of your hilltop room, where you lie in bed,
Whispering to your one love.
All morning you've played together slowly and quietly,
Free of the need to rush to some grand finale
That drives the strivers in the town, the young attorneys,

Who crave release. Over this ample district of the present
Floats the mournful dowdy music of the band.
It mingles with your sighs as you rise to dress.
You move with its rhythms to the straight-back chair at your
    desk
Where your paper lies ready, forms for a new agreement
Between you and the town, between the town and your one
    love

As she steps outside to mingle with the pensioners
Who listen patiently to the band,
Hoping if they stay to the end
That something left behind in their rooms
Won't look the same when they return.

The Virginia Quarterly Review   *Carl Dennis*

AN IRISH WIND

Capricious wind stirs Shannon's
    gentle stream;
It shakes the clover hiding secret
    gold.

It rouses leprechauns who sit and
   dream,
Excites the young, brings memories
   to old.

It runs with emerald feet across the
   hill,
Leaves rainbow scarves to flutter in
   the glen.
It skips a stone across a dancing rill
And howls across the moors to scare
   all men.

It makes lads brave and touched a bit
   with fey;
They dare to kiss the maidens of
   Killarney.
The Irish wind on old St. Patrick's
   Day
Is magical and surely full of blarney.

Grit   *Zelma S. Dennis*

FOG 9/76

It was early
fall or late summer, I don't know
which, but the lobstering
was good. Home from the sea,
I found no one and the fog
coming in: no note, nothing save
the fog. I showered,
opened a Heineken and through
the windward panes of
our seaward house watched
the fog roll in the harbor, fog
thick as cavalry cantering across
a plain, its silence full of
unspoken deeds.
              Waiting,
the fog seemed to steepen
into waves, marshalled
in long fetches, deep troughs.
The fieldlawns before me
beneath me swelled
like Nantucket Shoals. Soon
its grayness
thickened into legend, dripping
hushed and huge off
the screens, weighing
on branches like sodden
snowfall. I
was waiting,

Slim,
        for you.

A school of angels encircled
the house. They had black
wings and choired
in the thick black
tongue of the fog.
I heard the horn of some passing . . .

I saw the fog, like beads
of sweat, on the fieldstone walls. On
the sou'west breeze I
could smell the honeysuckle, fresh
as first love.
                At last,
into the fog, I
hurled a lamp.

Poetry   *Richard Morris Dey*

I HAVE A PLACE

I lived in a very special room once—
    wide cushioned chairs, vivid drapes,
    meaningful portraits, soft bed, and
    a deep carpet.

I rarely wandered far from the luxury,
    and whatever hurt in the world was
    nursed by my room.

But the world never came to my room,
    and one day the furnishings went away.
    Even the floor was bare.

I heard my own footsteps for once
    and wasn't impressed (although
    it wasn't bad either).
    Heard myself talk, too—same thing.

I stood for a while, mindless of time,
    (no clocks anymore except the world's).

Depressed? No. If a tree falls in the
    forest and no one hears it, has it
    fallen? No then, and no now.

O I'm re-furnishing, piece by piece—
    a rocker here, a blanket there.
    But I have no heart for deep-pile anymore.

Things all have their place and I'm a thing
    like others. I have a place and always
    will, warm or cold.

Things will be things, after all,
and I sort of like them for that.

Anima   *Lily A. De Young*

WORDS TO THE WIND

The wind rifles itself up
under the cold stars;
it fills the pockets of trees,
announces itself at my arm; I have nothing to
explain to it, a man just comes this far
under the footsteps of heaven.
I explain love, I explain death, I explain
the blood charging to my hand. No use.

It wants to see how I am doing: by entering my head,
by thinning out the bones on darkest nights.
It wants to seek me out, growing
from the eyeholes like twin flowers, to enter my
mouth and snake back out, like the words I could never say.

It wants that much.
I am waiting. And what I explain
is for the one behind me, old shyness, old friend,
boy that I was. I want you to understand what keeps
your shadow growing.

The Malahat Review   *Pier Giorgio Di Cicco*

ANOTHER GIVEN: THE LAST DAY
OF THE YEAR

It is a milky morning in San Francisco.
The long-waited-for rain has arrived, and left
old cars washed clean, skiers in the Sierra
happy with four feet of snow.
In the financial district, secretaries and executives,
giddy with delight, have scattered the pages
of the year's calendar into their abyssal streets.
Down go the hours
of promotion and retirement, the terse note:
"Tell Michael the truth THIS TIME." Down goes
that fragrant moment in the one-bedroom flat,
that kiss that did or did not revise the world.

It is a time to sum up: on buff graph paper
figure the rise or fall of security:
who is freshly dead this year, who has been born,
who is recovering from his first heart attack,
how many cells the skin will have lost to weather.
It is a time to be hard-eyed and exact,
recognizing losses.

Yet, in its southern bowl, the sun has started,
over a week ago, its long return.
Lurking in the year-end loam are Dutch tulip bulbs,
the eggs of Christmas trees. Love affairs,
not even imagined, are dreaming themselves toward being.
For good or bad, shining new-model cars
idle, ease into their initial gear.

At the shadow-line on airless Mercury
one-half of the body stands in total darkness
that cannot imagine the sun, the other half
is an attitude, an experience, of light.
Somewhere on earth, whenever it is today
it is already tomorrow, forming itself
out over the absences of the non-human ocean.
It is a time to sum up, if we know how,
tell Michael the truth, if we know what the truth is.

New England Review   *William Dickey*

CONFRONTATIONS OF MARCH

In the grooved earth the old grapple
Begins again, a sweat of bursting,
Tugging, the transubstantiation of
Dead-white to green in a pennyworth
Of light thin as gruel, where March comes
Whistling down the old grid road
Like a disreputable uncle in frayed
Spats with a Gladstone bag. On the dry
Branch, a robin explores the intricacies
Of voice and place, the centuries of
Sheer hold-fast, and perplexes the air
With his asking. The wind, rising from dusty
Haunches, peers into empty sockets,
Whines to come in from the raw garden
With its knobs of dirty snow and brown
Husks of winter charity lying
Under the bird-feeder. We look long at
Each other from the indifferent polarities
Of seer and seen, until the bird wings
Suddenly into the darker reaches
Of the spruce, dislodging a single cone
Which drops away without a sound.

Wascana Review   *H. C. Dillow*

"A LIVING"

A living. Making a living
into nextness where the air
is pinched and sore with whatever

misses anything else. I want
to will rough beginnings
and even rougher ends
as I shuffle in the morning
from mattress to floor to mirror.
To begin with this flat copy
of myself, lightglared, spooked
by the vital absence.
Whose remembering lies
there behind my reflection,
inside the ordinary closet
with its ordinary goods?
The impossible fullness of image
issues from gracenotes of light,
from the sounds of day beginning—
cups knocking, a pan of milk
clicking over the gas,
drizzly leaves of an overcup oak
tufting against the window.
In the mirror I am always
and never my own self.
Believe it, believe me.
There I stand. There I be.

The Southern Review   *W. S. Di Piero*

MAINLINE

(for Gene McNamara)

Nostalgia's a rough trip.
We know that yesterday
relieves today's pain,
tomorrow's pressuring;
junkies, we shoot the stuff,
seeking the rounded vein
in the shrunken arm, filling
the pattern of hole scars.
Spoon, needle, dust
and elastic band: need
litters environment.
What matter if
the habit breaks us, if,
hallucinating, we
lose grip on now,
mortgage our then,
jeopardize genes?
Pawn the bright gadget.
When the need comes,
the monkey scratching bad,
we prowl the restless book,
the shady snapshot, murky

      movie, or the dingy song
      for source of ease. Not
      far, the pusher lurks.

Waves   *John Ditsky*

IN THE SURGERY

Its black fur is suddenly still,
the cat is dead in my hands.
I feel no heartbeat
as the long white needle withdraws
from the wet joint of its knee,
its black hair and dandruff
sticking to my fingers
as I rub across its ribs.
As black as space were its beating sides.
The pounding of my redemption began
with the Spitfires and Defiants
that crashed and thundered
in the Hitlerian war,
when I sneaked into the air
and screamed like a siren
in a safe room in Brooklyn.
Here in my hands I hold a thing
of the earth, a part
of its black night ringing
in my ears, the oldest remorse
of time. I hear it now, sounding
depths, deep, as in a sea, as I hear
the turn and moan of rocks, fall
of seeds and sleet, petal and limb.

Poet Lore   *J. M. Ditta*

COAL MINER'S GRACE

Mine is a dark and twisting place;
I walk where the serpents wait
like angels in the fallen palms.
A single eye is burning in my forehead. I
am a shout of light in these dark veins;
my long tooth is singing in the blackness
hunting for the old embrace of fire.
Tell me why the fire is hissing. In
the layered silence let me hear the choir.

The Mississippi Valley Review   *Jay Divine*

FEAR

His life frightened him. The sun in the sky,
the man next door—they all frightened him.

Fear became a brown dog that followed him home.
Instead of driving it away, he became its friend.
The brown dog named fear followed him everywhere.
When he looked in the mirror, he saw it under
his reflection. When he talked to strangers,
he heard it growl in their voices. He had a wife:
fear chased her away. He had several friends:
fear drove them from his home. The dog fear
fed upon his heart. He was too frightened
to die, too frightened to leave the house.
Fear gnawed a cave in his chest where it
shivered and whined in the night. Wherever
he went, the dog found him, until he became
no more than a bone in its mouth, until fear
fixed its collar around his throat, fixed
its leash to the collar. The dog named fear
became the only creature he could count on.
He learned to fetch the sticks it threw for him,
eat at the dish fear filled for him. See him
on the street, seemingly lost, nose pressed
against the heel of fear. See him in his backyard,
barking at the moon. It is his own face he
finds there, hopeless and afraid, and he leaps at it,
over and over, biting and rending the night air.

The Virginia Quarterly Review   *Stephen Dobyns*

NIGHT POEM

It's always afternoon somewhere
in the mind, that long slow drift
from noon
to night, scissortails slanting
across the sun like inevitable
happiness. In the giant elms
above, cicadas buzz
their seventeen-year tune-up
for now. I close my eyes.
Everything is right

where it should be: the house,
the fence, the grove of cherries snug
against the henhouse.
Inside the kitchen
my mother carries bowls of heat
back and forth, back and forth, like eternal
life. The grass, everything around me,
is filled with motion,
spreading toward perfection.

Now, in the darkening present, I hear
my own small son coming home
to supper, the evening already
beginning to form

in his mind, fireflies pulling the earth
and sky together. Stop
there.
Let it go on forever.

The Georgia Review   *Wayne Dodd*

POEM

Entombed in my heart no blood flows to you.
Shadows shine and forget, streamers of strength suck me
great as with child into the etoffe of living.
Who can say what a stone within a stone will do?
What evil possessed us to entomb and forget?
So I must tear the black tweed from out of me.
I held you only for internment. It is a sacred
miracle. The stone stirs to be free.

Have joy, my love, we live enclosed in always,
in exquisite, intangible delicacy: walk hand in hand
each long and lovely day, the rutted rue.

Poet Lore   *Margery Dodson*

INTERSECTION

There is a conflict of jurisdictions here—
city on that side of State highway, town on this—
so there's no crosswalk paved for people who meet
nature for a moment here. Grass grows, and weeds.
A dirt path frays and widens in the summer,
and leaves can be scuffled through in autumn.
Snow falls in winter, and deep prints
come single and big-stepping,
and blur with those that follow.

Spring comes, and in the moments when wheels pause
for a changed signal, there is stillness
enough to hear the voice of water in quick runnels
gathering under the snow; drip-dropping
from ice-snow heaps, and running in skidmarks,
clear and bright and noisy as if escaping from glaciers
or ice-bound country brooks.

Tomorrow this will be country mud
deep enough to suck boots from feet
in peril from the highway; but today a bird lights down
and flips a sparkling drop from its beak,
and drinks again.

The Cape Rock   *Florence Dolgorukov*

NO SIGNAL FOR A CROSSING

"Lady, you're a poet, do you think about death?"
I untangle my legs from his, listening,

knowing it's himself he wants to hear.
He tells me he dreams about trains,
"Always the same dream, the train running me down."
In moonlight he turns toward me,

but all I want is to feel those muscles
singing against my skin.
Our lives divide us. There is no signal
for a crossing, no place but here
that we can meet.

He rides me like a locomotive
chug and chug and chug and chug.
I am a field, marked in lines and grids.
I am a stuffed dummy, tied to the tracks.

Like any woman I've been shaped
by father, mother, husband, lover.
It's an old story, a long story
I've lost the need to tell.
I think about surfaces:

the angle of a hip
where lust and loneliness collide,
the grace of a smooth back,
that point on the far
horizon, the last stop.

The Beloit Poetry Journal   *Rhoda Donovan*

SYMPHONY

Horns weaving an adagio disclose
a forest in October's skin of fire
when earth at sundown, streaked with black and gold,
smolders like a tiger in repose.

Flutes blow flakes of laughter from a stream
where bathers flash like sunlight turned to flesh.
Fifes are blades of cold that carve
the year's first snow to palaces of cream.

Harps dissolve like moons of foam
breaking in whispers on a rock.
Cellos drowsily brush the mind like bees
and drop their dreams as in a honeycomb.

Violins are opulent
as Renoir's orchards humming with orange heat,
or they explode like pain,
like suns or wheat whirled from the radiant

anguish of Van Gogh.
                    The drums throb low
as Gauguin's crackling yellows, reds and greens
in a jungle night of mango leaves
where metal eyes of beasts and idols glow.

Melody builds a prism of perfumes
lured from the dyes of every instrument.
Air is woven by orchestral looms
into a robe of color, touch and scent.

Blue Unicorn   *Alfred Dorn*

FROST HEAVES

You've come into my life like frost heaves,
Buckling my autumn road into fixed waves,
Making passage roller-coaster bumpy,
Springing springs once tightly coiled
Into swaying spirals, rising steamlike.
And yet I drive, one-handed; old paths
Become unfamiliar and travel untedious:
Distances are too short, arrivals too fast.
I could ride your new road forever,
Levitating rhythmically: in ratio higher
On each bounce than the preceding depression.
Steam rollers stay home, this year.

Suntracks   *Michael Dorris*

SLEEP

I'm ready

Let others study languages
and the morphology of insects
I only want to sleep

To enter that slate palace
monument lost these thousand years
full of secret rooms

I don't care about formulas
still to be discovered
peculiar chemical marriages
yet to take place
let me mix my essential elements
my rare earths
in the marvelous alembic of sleep

There are clothes in the wardrobe
of this hotel room
that need my attention
newspapers resting on the windowsill
of oblivion ready to disapper
if I don't read them

But I have already forgiven myself
I am going to sleep

Not the sleep of quilts or pots
of water snoring on a stove

not the sleep of ancient barber shops
or town squares or women's hair
in a china jar
but my own

A sleep speckled like a sparrow's egg
weightless as a kernel of corn
with the scent of a freshly dug mine

Alembic   *M. R. Doty*

UNWELCOME

Keep your distance, Stranger Death, and call.
Halloo the house before you come inside
The yard. I'll greet you later. I'll stand tall
And strive to conquer my desire to hide.
Let me watch crimson sunsets one more year,
In autumn catch another blazing leaf;
Let me hear music on an indrawn breath,
And come to my own bitter terms with grief.
I'll fly the sky once more, see colors blend
In evening clouds, a jetstream turn to gold.
I'll listen for the footfall of a friend
On nights when air is gray and turning cold.
My mind accepts, but heart begins to spin:
The day comes soon when I must let You in.

The Mississippi Valley Review   *Irma Dovey*

CATHEDRALS

Time and again
the world heals itself
Like skin,
And we are left
With brilliant scars:
Cathedrals
And other monuments.

The Atlantic Monthly   *W. S. Doxey*

ICE

Out for a walk on the ice
the silence catches
in the net of my eyes. The ice

is green, the ice whispering
about a body
gone dreaming among its tiny acres
of light. And under the ice

the water, cupping its flat hands
around the moon, steps carelessly

out of sight. Ice in the sink
of a house gone dark, ice

in my mother's drink
spilled years ago on a rug
the color of ice. The warm ice
of igloos, the fire
of dry ice burning in the basements
of ships. And there's the ice of change

where someone's breathing
has crossed a field by itself. The trees
are there, the wind, the finger of ice
in a glove that does not care
how we are wakened.

Southern Poetry Review   *Jack Driscoll*

MORNING LIGHT

The sun, bright lemon from the blinds,
falls on the dusty books and papers
of my room.
        A thing of white skin and tissue, I
perform yoga on the floor.
        Look at my body
drifting in the sun. It dissolves
flaccid as water plates in summer
in the little Niger river.
        But the sun
is a changeless metal, the minted light of a star
inside my room.

The Capilano Review   *Louis Dudek*

CURSES

Damn blue eyes. Damn the street
boiling with girls. Damn my neighbor's
music. Damn sunshine filling the world.
Damn poem, dead on the page, accident
victim. Damn that it expects me
to read it from its blue coma. Damn
telephone, ringing good news to an empty house.
Damn my fat body, may it be buried in a seam
of coal, damned may it become its own
thumbprint, image of a leaf,
may it be released in a million years,
a little thumb of flame.

Carolina Quarterly   *Joseph Duemer*

EVENSONG

Last night when the sun went down
and the light lifted up—it was levered
off the last high land to the westward
through tier after tier of cirrus
and cumulus cloud,
all the way to the zenith—such
a finale of auroral cold fire
no one could speak here . . . We stood

like pillars of salt looking after it
a long while till it all faded
into grey-blue and dark-grey. Again
I wonder how we survive, how
we survive, when more than we had dreamt of
is given, for no reason, and for no reason
taken away.

The Atlantic Monthly   *Peter Kane Dufault*

WINTER NIGHTS

The nights hang heavy on the winter air,
Lure us to creature comfort, inner light,
Call us to shelter, hearth, and fireside chair.

We wrap our shoulders, arch them, half aware
We thus conserve the flame throughout the night;
The nights hang heavy on the winter air.

When stirrings in the blood bid us prepare
To face the long dark hours with inward flight,
Call us to shelter, hearth, and fireside chair,

Let us summon friend and kin, declare
The larder full, declare the walls are tight;
The nights hang heavy on the winter air

And beg enlivement with festive fare;
The frosts of winter spur the appetite,
Call us to shelter, hearth, and fireside chair

And feast and fellowship; call us to share
The board, for who would be an eremite?
The nights hang heavy on the winter air,
Call us to shelter, hearth, and fireside chair.

The Lyric   *Lora Dunetz*

EXPERIENTIAL RELIGION

Where to, Lady? Where do you want to go?
Harvard Divinity School, please, on Francis Avenue.
Where? Where'd you say to?

Harvard Divinity School. On Francis Avenue.
In Cambridge. Harvard Divinity School.
Hunh. What's a Divinity School?

It's a place where they study, you know, god;
it's like a seminary.
OK. Now where did you say this seminary was,
this divinity school?
At Harvard. Harvard University.

You mean Harvard University? They've got a
seminary? I mean a divinity school?
Yes, like the law school, the med school;
it's a regular part of the university,
One of the schools.

I didn't know that, that they studied god—
divinity—at Harvard. I've been driving a cab
in Boston for twenty-years, and I never knew that.
I never knew that. A Divinity School at Harvard.

Contemporary Quarterly   *Travis Du Priest*

METROLINER

Railing up New Jersey
on the jacket of industrial zones
like a zipper up the fly
of America's pants,
the train rocks. The day
all day is evening in the gray
ink of Eastern rain; the silhouettes
of electric lines are impossibly thin
for bearing any power. Poles and trestles
and meager knots of trees advance, recede,
say nothing of any purpose of conceivable world
in which they stand. The silence of country
severed by a train
is iron, mutable in time if we
believe it so. The arrangements
of commerce, the geography of steel,
all of the practical world, milks
no meaning into the bucket
of experience we are made to drink.
The liquid of time is opaque,
dumb but opalescent, shiny
like the bald pate of a pensioner
playing checkers in the park, passing
time until his end, an end inferred
from birth, as ends are figured
in the speed on any road, especially so
the straight roads, the railroads,
the tracks that show a passenger

the arbitrary skylines of the cities
they join.

Window   *Jack DuVall*

WORKING THE SKEET HOUSE

Lifting their guns easily
men call for black pigeons
stacked at our feet, each one
indistinct like a face turned away
in shadow, something flat
glimpsed blocks away in the street.
Already imagining arcs in the off-
white sky, they make themselves
steady. Even the fat are poised.

In a squat house, two of us
too young to be calm and working,
work the skeet, chilled hands
cocking the arm, a bird on its lip,
barely set before the muffled call
from outside, the quick jerk of steel,
pull, pull. Clay flecks spray
like blood, a splattering at high speed.
There is no time to think,
to joke of some other morning.
The men out there haven't the time.

When a stray piece sings in
through the only window
we flinch at its burst,
board splintering behind us
like a deep cracking in the lung.
Some moments we turn
for a split second, eyes
cold and locked, as if to say
you are the man next to me,
the one who is going to die in my place.

The Chariton Review   *Jon Eastman*

SEASCAPE WITH BOOKENDS

For some strange reason, reading the yellow novel, one
    thinks of Greece—
The blue character, blue with longing for the sea,
Steps out of the pages of the book and will not give you
    any peace.

Perhaps just this touch of sunlight on the cover
Made you slip into the blue man's skin as if you had
    swallowed mercury or seawater,

And nothing in the world would make you say: All
    voyages are over.

You feel clean, swift as a fish, yet thick and dense,
Steam like a demonic statue with roseate, redolent mist,
And all extremes of power and passion suddenly make
    sense.

When was the wishful, widening wanderlust reduced to
    lust?
Those lucid pages and the blue man mewling for the sea?
When did the thing itself, like a naked root of life, rise in
    the settling dust?

One quivers, hovers, hankers for the citron land,
Brings it all back into the less than panoramic plot,
And opens the yellow book once more, and takes the blue
    man by the hand.

What one must have, will have, to prime the cause, at any
    cost,
Is the sense of the sensation, caught and always on its
    way—
Here in the book it cannot stay forever and there on the
    sea the text is lost.

Arizona Quarterly   *Charles Edward Eaton*

KITCHEN WINDOW

How many morning suns have kissed this glass?
How many summer winds have blown the rain
Across its shining crystal? Clouds may pass
Their shadows on each square of window pane,
But nothing dims the beauty of sunrise—
I stand a moment just to view the scene:
Long fingers of old gold that gently lie
Upon the lawn's bright carpeting of green.
The warmth that steals through panes stirs in my heart
A deep response—a call to meet the day.
It is a special blessing that is part
Of sunshine I shall scatter on the way.
A kitchen window and the morning light
And I shall conquer any dread of night.

The Lyric   *Ruth N. Ebberts*

SEA BELLS

The pleasantry of the sea bells, and I talk to myself alone.
Evening calm, calm seas, peace gives me to myself alone.

Quintessential freedom, freedom to be silent as a shell,
A white scallop, once living virile in the sea, my ash tray,

A rest as in music, a slight cessation, why has brief eventide
So strong a hold on my spirit, as does the far sea bell?

The sea bell is better than speech, a universal, one sound
As against restless particularities of our tongues.

The sea bell is a secret message of the universal,
And while designed to warn mariners in the fog,

To give them comfort, set and tended by the coast guard,
The sea bell seems to me a spell and urgency of incantation,

Something far out, inexpressible loneliness,
Human-spirited. It tells the nature of the ocean,

Now silent, now restive, now roused to heavy recurrence,
An enlivening, a slumbering, a reminder, a savior.

Ships are aware of the strong, oceanic sea bells,
Aids to navigation; the soul needs them too.

If we could hear the sound of immortality,
Beyond thought, beyond reach, I should be quickened.

But to hear from the shore in rich eventide
Sea bells, they remember Homeric sailings and incertitudes,

Oceanic destructions, tempests, and safe landfalls.
Hearing them, year to year, I talk to myself alone.

National Forum   *Richard Eberhart*

"A LOON CALL"

Rowing between Pond and Western Islands
As the tide was coming in
Creating, for so long, two barren islands,
At the end of August, fall nip in the air,
I sensed something beyond me,
Everywhere I felt it in my flesh
As I beheld the sea and sky, the day,
The wordless immanence of the eternal,
And as I was rowing backward
To see directly where I was going,
Harmonious in the freedom of the oars,
A solitary loon cry locked the waters.

Barbaric, indivisible, replete with rack,
Somewhere off where seals were on half-tide rocks,
A loon's cry from beyond the human
Shook my sense to wordlessness.

Perfect cry, ununderstandable essence
Of sound from aeons ago, a shriek,
Strange, palpable, ebullient, wavering,

A cry that I cannot understand,
Praise to the cry that I cannot understand.

New England Review   *Richard Eberhart*

STONE WORDS FOR ROBERT LOWELL

Death, you are so much more powerful
Than all the weepers in all the churches,
Including Boston, that I have
To fight against you with stone words
To put you down, who will not
Be put down, despite man's imagination,
Amplitude, pained intrepidity.

He was your enemy, but couldn't you wait?
He was undefended against you.
You are the mighty one of power.
He and the weepers had to lose,
But let you know, Death,
Poems are slingshot words, Goliath.

New Statesman   *Richard Eberhart*

PRODIGAL'S RETURN

Come along, fatty-calf.
No use to butt, you haven't got no horns to hook me with
and 'tain't no good, neither, to bellow for your ma.
Folks at the big house gonna roast you for their dinner.

A rare lot, them folks there.
That whippersnapper Randy, just last spring he pranced away
dolled up fit to kill, cantering the sweetest mare
the old man had. His saddlebags
dragged at their straps—loaded deep with silver, I'll be bound.
Well, summer brought us wheat, but ne'er a note from Randy,
nor never word o' mouth for all I heard.
Old man, he turned persimmon sour,
though Buck, the older boy, didn't seem to lose no sleep.

Now this very morning, who come dragging up the icy lane
but Randy, dressed in a ragged coverall filthy enough for any tramp.
Old man, he brightened wonderful, made me fetch you up;
but Randy better watch for Buck.
Buck picked up a stone near big as your fat head;
he might just let it drop down from the silo.

Why I'll be switched! Look there, calf—
the old man standing almost young again,
one arm around each boy, repeating like it was a song,
"My sons! My sons! My sons!"

The Chaparral Poet   *Ralph D. Eberly*

HIGH FIELD—FIRST DAY OF WINTER

A snow squall comes down
from Lake Ontario leaving only outlines
behind. Trees fall asleep

and let loose their leaves, houses
turn, from hills of soil and stick,
to rocks with nothing for a heart.

Again this year, the wind rolls straight
from the Arctic—right through the field,
these perimeter trees.

I walk out from the cabin
and its fire, head spinning
with warmth through tall

cattail and red whipper weeds
toward the frame of an old Ford pickup,
muzzle dug into the earth.

I holler again
for the dog who was lost
many years ago.

This wind rustles the bones of the dead.
I feel footsteps moving under mine.

The Georgia Review   *Gary Eddy*

MUCH OF ME

The man who told the hawk
of freedom
was his jailer.
There was little need of speech,
the cage said everything.
The hawk did not sin—
he would have flown but for the cage.
The man with no eyes sinned,
the man with no dreams.

Much of me is hawk,
and sky,
and much of me
is tall blowing grass;
and my friends are
trees that stand by themselves
and summer
and birds in the high air.
And home is something
I carry within me.

Kansas Quarterly   *Chuck Eggerth*

ON LINDEN STREET

Thin filaments of
seasons bind us
together. Everyone out
with leaves to rake or snow
to shovel. Or a blight
hits the tomatoes. Edging
together, we try to talk
of how to fight something
all our ancestors fought.
But nights, each ark
seals itself, bobs
on its own strange waters.

Last night, I paddled
through a bog where dreams
shimmered like blue
damsel flies, impossible
to net. Meanwhile, to the east,
the carpenter put down
his tool chest and walked
out over the rotted
planks of his porch. West,
the woman who potted
a winter garden dove
fathoms deep to hold her
newborn daughter. Waking,
I find on my street the new
breath, the silenced hammer.

The Chowder Review   *Shelley Ehrlich*

ON READING MR. YTCHE BASHES'
STORIES IN YIDDISH

You tickle the sophisticates
with piquant translations
about grotesqueries
and picaresque exotics
in our former rabbinical enclaves—
the pitiful miasmas of King Pauper.

Oh, Ytche Bashes, what glory!
Mazel-tov to you!
I read you in English, first,
in the chic magazine *New Yorker*, no less,
with your name almost hyphenated, yet.

I envied your renown, Ytche.
As a nearby landsman
I dug in musty library stacks
and found you—

in our own sweet-and-sour Yiddish.
How much more appetizing!
How schmaltz-herringly titillating!

Only we, of the *shtetl* chosen,
can wallow in this delicacy,
This garlicked, sacramental,
raisin-winey language.

How would you translate
yaknehooze and *shatnez*,
kokilkies, lapitutniks,
skotzilkimt and *shipeh-zibbeleh?*

How would the scrubbed
and showered Amerikaner
ever relish in print
the flavor or ritual bath water—
the septic communal bilge
called *mikvehwasser?*

Or savor the erotic aromas
of illicit sourdough seductions
in the nightsoil fields
beyond the town bedlam?

How would you decipher
your antique Mishna-Talmud phrases
you constantly use in the vernacular,
like Aramaic-Targumized holiday names
like Yoma d'Pagrah?

Try to frighten in proper English
with wraiths in their shrouds
who slept overnight on synagogue altars,
with ectoplasmic homunculi
dwelling along bedraggled cemeteries.

Your kabbalah lumpen lucifers,
second-hand satans
and menopause liliths
will never startle Halloween revelers.
Only we, the ever-threatened,
can conjure ghetto-goblins
for our nightmares.

Those not of the *shtetl*
can enjoy Ytche Bashes by proxy,
but his devils and demons
and lilliput shoemakers
died with our papa-mama Yiddish
in the ovens
of sophisticated fiends.

Midstream   *Lester Ehrlichman*

THE ANNOUNCEMENT

You were at the door with the news
of a life inside and we wept
that April day, the jonquils blooming
late against the wire fence.
We turned the afternoon into a bed,
measured the moving sun with mouths.
I held your avenue of life,
that wet mystery that you and I
met in to celebrate our love.

We woke in soft rain under street light,
had a sandwich and milk, and slept
in the hood of each other's arms.

I watched your landscape change,
my worship growing
on your growing world,

and the grass stayed green that year
right through August.

Waves   *George Ellenbogen*

SONNET TO A TYRANT

When you withdraw the dagger of your grin
And sheathe the freezing saber in your eye,
When every word you speak is not a lie
That lures me to your tortures once again,
You'll haunt me like a hungry dog, and then
You'll seek my fire, my food—and when you cry
And crawl to me like one condemned to die—
You'll find that I can tyrannize. And when
My laughter stings you like the winter sleet
You will collapse upon yourself with dread;
And from that day, wherever we may meet,
In chambers where my heart has slowly bled
Or icy lamp-lit midnight of the street—
I know that I would smile to see you dead.

ASFA Poetry Quarterly   *Mary Anne Ellis*

A MOUNTAIN HERITAGE

A mountain heritage
is hard to lose.
Like a bold morning
shadow it pursues,
reaching out,
touching others
before you speak or move.
You may try to lose

it among sophisticated
trappings, suave manners,
boulevards, avenues;
like a shy noon shadow
it wanes, yet never
fully disappears.
This mountain heritage
surfaces in moot degrees,
now bold, now timid,
depending on where you stand
or whom you try to please.

Mountain Review *Joan Wyrick Ellison*

NOT BEING WISE

It was neither his hunger nor mine
which brought us to this: pickerel
are not my prey, being all bones.
As for him, he struck the spinner light,
bored with the robot wake
of my Red Devil. One hook barely
snagged the beak of his lip.

If I had remembered pliers—
but they were ashore, and his teeth were fierce.
So I left him trolling his own element
and paddled toward a safe
land operation for both of us.

He glittered free from my hands
into the shallows, and his gills gulped once.
But something, jammed into reverse
by that open-mouthed reeling,
burst inside his ruined valves
and he rolled belly up, settling
white as a slug in a bloom of blood.

Not hunger, not heart—just a matter
of my not being wise in the ways of water.

The Literary Review *Virginia Elson*

MISTAKABLE IDENTITY

Was that a crystal butterfly's wing
    shattering,
a hand-painted fine porcelain tail
    quitting its quail,
a goblet from Olympus tinkling down
    on *our* town?
No—seven young icicles taking leave
    on their eave.

The Small Pond Magazine *Elaine V. Emans*

PROMISED LAND

Tall buildings darken the sidewalks like a blight.
The ghetto coughs up garbage and dies each night.
There are no mourners.
Loose-jointed, weightless, they stand on corners,
talking, laughing, shuffling off to Buffalo—
dreaming of a future they may never know.
At night the women bloom like prairie flowers,
coy, seductive, selling love by the hour.
Face waffled with fatigue, a woman stares
at them from shuttered eyes. A radio blares.
Harlem's a jigsaw puzzle slipping into shadows.
How old is the ghetto? Ask the question, nobody knows.

Northwoods Journal   *Mary Engel*

BIOLOGY LESSON

Watch a caterpillar
eating his way
to cocooned contentment,
measuring his meaning
by foot and tooth.

Driven by hunger
and nature's timetable,
he is a force of one
against all logic.

Out of himself
he spins
his own shroud
and sews
himself inside.
Coffined
in his little death,
he sleeps
and dreams himself
into a drill,
then bores his way
to sunlight,
freedom,
wings!

Unity   *John D. Engle, Jr.*

DANCER: FOUR POEMS

(for Lan-lan King)

The dancer quarrels with solid air,
For that one foot of surface where she stood,

By the bold knife blade of her slashing arm
She carves herself as from a block of wood.

Pity the poor furred cat
Who needs four feet to do
Such leaps across the floor
As dancer does with two.

Pity the poor proud dancer who can give
Death to her ease, so that the dance may live,
Who makes, with pain to every body part,
From perfect will power her imperfect art.

Pity the poor rain that only falls
Down from the cloud-caressing sky, then crawls
Through dirt and over street. The dancer falls
Then rises like an oriole over walls.

Poetry   *Paul Engle*

ON SUCH A WINDY AFTERNOON

On such a windy afternoon
as this one
(warm. Spring winds are
often warm,
though have no reason),
I delight in little things
—the wood I carried
from the mesa—
—just enough for evening—
and the table where I sit,
also of wood.
The restless clatter
of a chime outside.
A voice or laugh
next door, and borne away
before I hear it
clearly.
Such an afternoon.
Such wind.

Chicago Review   *Theodore Enslin*

CLIMBING

When he gave up mountains he became
a window washer, hoisting himself on block and tackle
fifty stories above the street. For the love of heaven
    is an addiction like stealing
fast time from the round jail of the clock.

He loves high windows. Saves them for last,
looking down on the traffic, crawling workers

whose vision he rinses clean as fresh glass.
Pigeons swing like puppet birds under his hands.
    But does he think downward?

Does he love his fear of the lurking flaw
    in the scaffold, the crack in a faithless plank?
Does he think of the fatal journey
    between his living and his death? No.
He looks in on the nodding accountants, winks

at an astonished secretary who drops her file.
He looks out along miles of reflected rooftops,
    the sky mirrored in the invisible window.
It is like flying on the surface of our lust
    for a visible horizon.

By noon, the top windows are clear as a sudden answer,
    at dusk, pure gold,
by night, they are pure moon blue.
Sadly he rides the elevator down
and starts again at the foot of the blind wall.

The American Scholar   *Daniel Mark Epstein*

CONTENTMENT

Here I will rest beside this hill
And watch the moon and wait until
The deer come down to drink . . .

How cool the water looks tonight,
The stars are clear and strangely bright
And I need time to think.

Oh, let the others rush ahead
Where many dreams have fallen dead;
Contented in this spot, I stay.

And starlet spears of crested light
Like troubles mounting in the night
Slip with the sky into the bay!

The Lyric   *Laurence E. Estes*

WINDOW TO THE EAST

Blest is the boy who has a room
with a window to the east,
where he can watch the sun come up,
like a stallion just released
from great, dark stables of the night,
flinging its golden mane
through the morning mist, and streaming light
on a young man's heart and brain!

Blest is that son in the early dawn,
who, softly waking there,

can see Orion waiting while
Aurora combs her hair,
and watch Apollo's chariot
roll proudly up the sky.
A boy with a window to the east
is a boy with an extra eye!

The Lyric   *Virginia Moran Evans*

THE CANDIDATE

Your celebrated hand
I came to shake
lies paper dry against my skin
and almost crumples in my grasp,
it seems,
for I find no substance there
or heart.

You really never see me
with your restless,
seeking glance
slipping past my shoulder
for the next face
and skipping that one
for the next.

Moved by ambition,
you are the desert wind
building pyramids
of sand.
Not quite king—
your castle dissolving.

Voices International   *Allamae Ezell*

APOLOGY TO MY LADY

Who could hate you? Your patched-together face
plastered over your eyes like a garish mask—
all the hours spent in front of a mirror,
applying, carefully, rouge and mascara,
might just as well have been otherwise spent:
your face hangs impaled upon your eyes.

Seeing you now, who couldn't muster forgiveness,
especially knowing all you've been through?
Given the demands of thoughtless children,
and the travesty of a clutching husband,
who could be so heartless as to hate you
for trying to find freedom, and failing?

Sou'wester   *Edward Falco*

JUDAS, JOYOUS LITTLE SON

Judas, joyous little son,
roll your hoop, pop your gun,
win your race, climb your wall,
up you get when down you fall.

Here's a coin for you to spend.
Share it with your weeping friend.
Kiss his cheek, wipe his tear.
Let no sadness loiter here.

Now's your day
of love and laughter,
Who's to say
what follows after?

The Christian Century   *Norma Farber*

HOW TO OWN LAND

find a spot and sit there
until the grass begins
to push between your thighs

climb a tree and learn
the gestures of the wind

follow the stream to its source
and trade speech
for that cold sweet babble

gather sticks and spin them into fire
watch the smoke spiral into darkness
fall asleep
dream that the animals find you

they weave your hair into warm cloth
string your teeth on necklaces
wrap your skin soft around their feet

wake to the configuration
of your own scattered bones
watch them whiten in the sun

when they have fallen to powder
and blown away
the land will be yours

River Styx   *Susan Farley*

PUSHED TO THE SCROLL

We are our poems, their summation,
those written and those unwritten,
those dreamed and those lived,

the vibrant, full-fleshed word
and the stillborn word,
the said and the merely thought:
The parchment scroll unrolled
reveals to discerning eyes
careless and deliberate marks,
tentative lines, erasures,
faint, uncertain sketching
and figures boldly done;
solid characters and blurred letters,
etched language from mute mouth,
the recorded voice of the open mouth
exploding from well-filled lungs,
or sighing with slightest breath,
voice pushed to the scroll by strong heart,
and by the failing heart,
pushed to the scroll by courageous hand,
and by the hand when it falters,
pushed to the ultimate end
to leave the naked soul.

Voices International   *Winifred Hamrick Farrar*

ARCHAEOLOGISTS

they uprooted an ancient cave
and found a family of anthropoids
surviving
under the stone crust

they scraped the stone floor
and children rose up
from between the cracks

they punctured the stone walls
and found humanoid skeletons
curled up
like grotesque question marks

Canadian Forum   *Real Faucher*

SUPPOSITIONS

If I had a creature's mouth,
if I could lose this fluent speech,
if I could change the chain of being,
keep intelligence and reason without
the strain of saying, then I could read
the eyes of dogs, decipher rain and
jargon of the jays. In my mouth I'd carry
things that cannot walk, hold them gently
in the softness of my jaws.

New Orleans Review   *Margherita Faulkner*

SLEEPING ALONE

I watch the TV close its bleary eye
and drink warm milk and try a TM trance.
In bed I lie awake, following the dance
of shadows from the car-lights whipping by.
Counting by sevens fails to dupe the "I,"
who, brooding on his loneness, looks askance,
watching the clock change numbers, on the chance
the telephone must ring—I don't know why.
Your vacant place upon the pillow stares
back at me like unanswered letters thrown
in drawers; I have fogotten all the prayers
that lullaby grown children left alone
in night that stretches ocean-wide and deep.
Your absence haunts the landscape of my sleep.

Western Poetry Quarterly   *Kurt J. Fickert*

RONDEL: AUTUMN

Under the trees the leaves go down
to sink to rest in the waiting dark.
Shouting in scarlet, the maple's spark
dims to ashes without a sound;

the leaping gold of the birch is browned.
The line storm rips the bronze from the oak,
and under the trees the leaves go down.
They sink to rest in the wasting dark

where the grey November dawn has found
that the wood in its mortal torment shakes
while in lashing rain leaves bow and break
to huddle and molder on miry ground.
Under the trees, the leaves are down . . .
and sink at last to the lasting dark.

Descant   *Matt Field*

DEMONSTRATION

How thankful I am
that Jesus
did not stop at the point
of thoughtful solitude,
that Beethoven
could not keep his music
resounding in his head,
that King
was not content
merely to dream.

How grateful I am
for an infinite Presence

that moves mind
into action,
thoughts
into concreteness,
inspiration
into expression.

How beautiful I am
that I too
can sing the songs,
write the sonnets,
perform the dance
of my own being.

Unity   *Margaret Finefrock*

OCTOBER DUSK

1

On the hill above the pond
Dark seedlings of cedar
Bob in the wind above the grass
Like quail. As night comes on
Clouds come down to the hill,
And the trees climb
Into their black hands.

2

Soon the finches will be here
Again, in their winter hoods,
Saying about me:
"That is the dust from the house,
See how failure walks along
In his clothes."

3

The pond lies like a bowl
Filled with cold coffee.
I carry a mallard feather
As a candle,
Walking down under the hill
And into the ground.

Carolina Quarterly   *C. Stephen Finley*

THE DIVORCE DRESS

It curls in the closet
waiting to be lace.
It wants to be unzipped slowly,
tooth by tooth.
It wants to rustle and sway
and drop to the floor. It knows

what it is: widow's weeds.
There has been a death.

It actually is very old.
It is patchwork, a dress out of dresses,
castoff pieces that persist for years.
Nothing frays it but the moths
that live in corners of the closet
I never go to. Sometimes
I cut it up for curtains,
but it is back the next day. It has,
in fact, always been there,
underneath the borrowed and the blue,
underneath my nylon skin,
underneath the bed, visiting the special box,
turning into the other rabid vampire
that grasps my ankle every night
in its long white teeth.

During the day
it hangs suspended
like a bat. At night
it wakes women up for miles.

Moving Out   *Jeanne Finley*

APOLLO 113

(tapes found inside the recovered spacecraft)

Having come under the baleful, red influence of Mars
inside the steel rings the moon whirls out for us to dance in—
I decided the expedition be terminated.
A difficult decision. We were incised, as it were,
fractured in two, like a rare stone which then becomes
      worthless.
The choice was not wrong; it was the choosing.

The elemental powers. Their enmity is curbed by
femininity alone. . . . The ship astrophysicist
might have known the function, something like f(Fem) equals
the god's strength as it is received, responded to. But let
me rest. We ran into interference, in any case,
that seemed moisture, a deity, then the void.

No omen. Wrong from the start to hesitate! What difference
had we died on an endless series of patrols, feints
and manoeuvres in our war on the stars? Matter isn't gained
or lost, only changed: the abrasive worn down and our ghosts
spirited off. So air was reduced to water and we,
under strife, grew souls like Undines of the sky.

The Michigan Quarterly Review   *Diderik Finne*

MORE THAN

I would like to more than touch you everywhere;
More than love you
Is the way I'd like to love you.

Coming from a world locked and cold,
Arriving at the doorway of your eyes,
With more than sweet surprise, I open you.

Delight dresses me in shivers,
Dancing us together;
Love, dark red, awakens:
We drink each other's heart.

I listen: hungry for more than words when you speak;
I don't know why, I'd like to give you all my days
And hear you laugh with me,
Our laughter, more than symphonies,
The world broken open, spilling life.

Contemporary Quarterly   *Susan Fitzpatrick*

STARS SHINE SO FAITHFULLY

Nightly off Route 50
In the roller rink called Dreamland
Girls from Eden, Wango, Nanticoke
Comb their hair, pee daintily,
Lace up rented skates
And throw themselves into orbit—
Going with the music that says all
They know of what they long for

Boys skid by like fireballs
Couples clutch each other's waists
Break away and waltz in the center
Dip and spin, encircled by
Smudge-eyed little moons
Breathing peppermint
Swaying to the song called "Love
Love, love, where are you?"

And at closing time when the cars honk
And the girls spill out like candy
Old Miss Pitts across the road swears
It's Gabriel coming down the white line
But their fathers sleep on
And their mothers, sitting in the dark,
Hear Bogart saying, "Hi, baby"
Over the static, light years away

13th Moon   *Jane Flanders*

AFTER GRAVE DELIBERATION . . .

When I Go
it should be by cremation,
my ashes slipped into
an 8 x 10 manila envelope
with a second (stamped and self-addressed)
inside, posted to God
in His capacity as editor
of Everything.

I stand
a better than even chance
of being returned to myself,
along with a neat note
acknowledging my insight and my craft,
regretting that I do not,
at that time, fit
His divine needs,
wishing me luck in placing myself
elsewhere.

The Literary Review   *Elizabeth Flynn*

ARCHNE

I worked with all aurora at my loom—
The merchants at my father's house, my thralls,
Brought me gold and silken threads from Bengal,
Tyrian dyes and flax and peacock plumes.
Evenings I would dance in my rich costumes
And watch the women's eyes beneath their shawls
And hear a whispered curse at each footfall
And learn how blazing envy can consume.

When father died, the house no longer filled,
Age and solitude like friends settled in.
Yet my weaving shuttle has not been stilled;
I wave new curses; my pride was no sin:
Before the waiting wooden frame I thrill
To quicken space where nothingness has been.

Song   *Richard Foerster*

DEPARTURE

We take it with us, the cry
of a train slicing a field
leaving its stiff suture, a distant
tenderness as when rails slip
behind us and our windows
touch the field, where it seems
the dead are awake and so reach

for each other, your hand cupping
the light of a match to your mouth,
to mind, and I want to ask if the dead
hold their mouths in their hands like this
to know what is left of them.
Between us, a tissue of smoke,
a bundle of belongings, luggage
that will seem to float beside us,
the currency we will change
and change again. Here is the name
of a friend who will take you in,
the papers of a man who vanished,
the one you will become when the man
you have been disappears.
I am the woman whose photograph
you will not recognize, whose face
emptied your eyes, whose eyes
were brief, like the smallest
of cities we slipped through.

Antaeus   *Carolyn Forché*

TRIAD

I rode with my mother and father,
one autumn, in their car.
We turned down a road
where flame had caught
every tree and bush.
The incense of every leaf
filled the open windows.
There was no house in sight,
and, for an instant,
time stopped.

We came to this by different roads.
I was grown to my own colors,
but I knew myself again
to be their seedling
as when I lay comforted
between them in their bed.
I've pressed that moment
in my book of epiphanies,
now, before they grapple
with the wind
and fall.

When the holocaust comes,
we will ride away together
down this lonely, flaming road.
We will make this old Studebaker
into a pod where our hands
will meld into each other

like the incestuous points
of burning stars.

Gargoyle   *Donald Foster*

IN BLANCO COUNTY

Down here now
summer's burnt skeins
stand, old grasses abundant and
dead. The form of life's
absence, windrattled,
everywhere. The people
get old and desperate
just looking at it
and are proud
of their own stubborn
lives. To the west,
the rain runs out
and nothing else
is going to grow.
When the last dirty branch dies,
splitting in the hard winds,
old folks will
think twice about
going on,
and go on.
They have a special
way of complaining—
habitual, inward, hopeless.
More than anything,
each wants you to know
that his eyes are wide open,
that life, if nothing else,
is something he knows.

The South Carolina Review   *Russell T. Fowler*

THE TELEPHONE OPERATOR

For twenty years
she's spent her nights
trying to plug up the holes,
a headset clasping her by the ears,
holding her in place
like the secret the priest hears
in the confessional.
And, like the priest,
she stays up all night
absorbing their sins. Her
prayers are numbers and
she knows them by heart.

Even in her sleep she rolls them over in her mind:
police, fire department,
all night pizzeria.
She wonders at
how easy it is to hold
the city in her hand
like the formless soul
of a scared man.
Even the obscene caller
knows her as his wife.
She is the last one he dials
after all the others have
taken his dark voice into their beds,
persistent as insomnia.
She is the one who
cannot say no. And after
she's taken the message
and filed it in her catalogue
of numbers and emergencies,
she will put him on hold
where he'll burn before her,
a tiny light that shines all night
like the candle the priest offers
for the sinner humming
in his ear.

The Beloit Poetry Journal   *Pat-Therese Francis*

PLAY BALL!

Baseball in spring
Football in fall

Ball that we dance at
Pinball we chance at

Ball we were born on
Ball that keeps turning

Ball we will die on
When life stops burning

Then the big wrecking ball
Will knock down all

Ball in its basket
Star in his casket.

New Letters   *Robert Francis*

LOVE POEM INVESTIGATION FOR A.T.

You will probably have three children.
(Your hips are as large as a wheelbarrow's spread.)
You'll have a husband working all day, everyday,

And a home tucked away with the others, somewhere
On some borderline of suburbia, houses sprawled
And uninvestigative as similar as mushrooms
Feeding themselves and somehow becoming edible.

You'll have a kingdom out there,
White-washed but normal under the circumstance.
Your kitchen will have all the necessary pans,
Copper pots, mittens for hot things, and a family
Sitting at the table Christmas Day trying to forget,
Talking of generation gaps and the economy's discrepancies.
But a family, nevertheless, eating from that one fat turkey,
Concentrating on crouton stuffing and who will wash the dishes.

And at night you'll be alone with THAT familiar stranger,
Possibly going over current suits (He is a lawyer, after all)
And massaging his back, after, and silence flooding the room
When you stare at the ceiling listening to his regular breaths.
And maybe you'll sleep the contented sleep of security
When the night's black hole opens completely—
And I am elsewhere writing about its dark hold
Smouldering in a self-made cave, like a sold son.

Poet Lore   *Frank Frate*

THE AGE OF THE BUTCHER

That's my grandpa behind the meatcase
holding up the blood sausage; it was
the age of the butcher, a small man
dropping meat on a scale, wiping his
hands on his apron while he squinted
for the weight. My grandma beside him
with her hands full of shiny brown paper:
He's an excellent trimmer, Mrs. Dohlwitz,
excellent! I know him, my Felix, the man
to come to. Tell me, have we good wurst?

I'd already crossed the passage from
their kitchen to the shop, opened
the door, hoped they'd get the day off
to enjoy themselves. Look, grandma's
combing her hair and bending over her,
kissing her forehead, my grandpa looks
gloomy and worried. What is it, Felix;
The pains are back? Would you mind to
sit down between customers; here, take
a fig newton and a little warm coffee.
Not much of anything, just selling meat—
but it could be anything: milk, cheese . . .
They sleep from midnight till eight in
a little bed a mile behind their meat.

The Centennial Review   *Stuart Friebert*

CHARLTON HESTON

Granite—
a granite slab.
He has survived earthquakes,
doomed 747's, sunken submarines,
japanese carriers and the wrath of god.
He can stand and watch cities
filled with his children,
his wife, his mistress, his dog
crumble into greasy flame.

He is beyond irony.
His mouth doesn't twitch.

He will go on.
His numb cobalt eyes
stare at the horizon.

Better than anyone, he knows
what must be done
to save us.

The Altadena Review   *Elliot Fried*

HERE BE DRAGONS

I'm at the edge—
darkland uncharted now.
Sweet winds of home
and maps
have failed.
Alone,
with no alternative.
A tail writhes on the sunset—
redsilk sea.
What lies submerged
no sextant calibrates
and night drops
like a visor.
The spar
is in my hand.

The Apalachee Quarterly   *Ginny Friedlander*

THE HOPES

the hopes
awakened
are cradled again
in sleep

i can't help
myself:

I can't help
myself

high tension

today i survived
yesterday too:
there's tension aplenty

hoping

is a form
of forgetting

Dimension   *Dieter Fringell*
                    —Translated by A. Leslie Willson

THE LAST BITE

I think of the starved foreign children
my mother taught me to remember
whenever I felt the urge risen
to push away some of my dinner.

No Waste, the frowning legacy
served with overdone gray meat,
dry potatoes, wrinkled peas,
vinegar salad. Every bite

was duty. Fed and fed and fed,
I grew up a thin man
who daily searched for new food
and often found it. And always when

holding on my tongue the sweet juice
of what I find, I hear the call
up from a cold, famished place,
"For our sake, brother, eat it all."

The Mississippi Valley Review   *Richard Frost*

THE OLD STORIES

Renew the old stories, it is said almost every day
by poets and bartenders. The poet, as everyone knows,
is the interior decorator of the soul,
a sissy according to some—
                    yet how but through gewgaw glass,
all whirligigged, does the soul reflect itself?
These old stories, like a crab, close their fist
around the glossary of birdcalls, stench of kelp,
fingers and pineapples, around cruel articles in the closet,
to propose an extraordinary consensus.
                                The poet,
busy polishing his King Arthur chair, does not see
the traditional dark figure sneak up behind him,

and only dreams the karate blow delivered
to the back of his neck.
                    Of course, the killer is
the bartender, whose cup measures out gold or a fluid stone
that looks like gold. Somewhere in the present
the old stories get confused and there is
no other way, academically, to settle their likenesses
but by brutal dislocation.

New America   *Gene Frumkin*

SOFTLY, WHITE AND PURE

In stillness, I wait.
Within the calm lies the
expectant tension that is
prelude to a snowfall;

Then, softly, white and pure,
peace settles on my soul,
erasing imperfections,
uniting me with others
like a snow blanket blotting out
boundaries until
road and tree and house are one.

Unity   *Dorothy R. Fulton*

ARCADY REVISITED

I sense that I may someday be assailed
As one who was not master of his craft,
And sailed anachronistic ships that quaffed
The waters of a long dead art, impaled
Upon the ragged rocks that masters scaled
With a fine madness, by the muses staffed
With a sonorous gift the world has laughed
At since, and but a few of us have hailed.

I sense that, if I sail a different course,
Someone of you might sooner hear my song.
Nevertheless I know of no recourse
To new directions, for although the sea
Is full of modern vessels, I still long
To sail forgotten ships to Arcady.

Western Poetry Quarterly   *Robert Funge*

THE VERY OLD

The very old
seem to abandon life so reluctantly, like a few leftover
leaves, dried but clinging to bare branches, after watching

through the seasons all their counterparts disappear in
floating greens, golds and fading browns; their darkening
grayness seems to match the limbs that still allow them
feeble handhold, the tree to have forgotten they are there
until an exasperated wind shakes them in a fit of impatience
to the ground.

   With so little fuss and bother they seem to drift away
while no one is looking; they leave without fanfare as an
anticlimax to a story that no longer holds surprise, cutting
no swath in the air, falling almost unnoticed among their
moldering likeness, settling noiselessly to the ground,
tissues already as withered as their autumn forerunners'.

Dark Horse   *Thomas Galloway*

HEMATITE LAKE

There is another kind of sleep,
We are talking in it now.
As children we walked in it, a mile to school,
And dreamed we dreamed we dreamed.

By way of analogy, consider nightfall.
In relation to the light we have, consider it final—
Still falling from the night before
With ourselves inside it like ore in the igneous dark.

So I went for a walk around Hematite Lake
To watch the small deer they call fallow deer
Dreamed to life by sleeping fields.
Someone had taken the water,

Don't ask me who. The wild swans were
Still there, being beautiful,
And the geese lay down in the grass to sleep.
The shallows, now dry, were peopled with lilies:

Their poor, enormous heads reeled in the aquatic air.
The path was drifted in with gossamer
From the tree-spiders' nightly descent:
A monumental feather the geese flew over.

What happens is nothing happens.
What happens is we fall so far
Into a sleep so manifold,
Not even nightfall, whose gold we are, can find us.

Antaeus   *James Galvin*

SHOOTING GALLERY

I am third in a line of murderers.
I wait my turn at the Gatling gun.
Ahead of me, two snake-haired blondes
talk futures, eyes fixed on the quick clock.

Their red fingers, furled as fetuses, hang
upside down in air. Hard at work
at the machine, a one-eyed man
is shooting strings of birds who pop
absurdly back, belling surprise
with a clapped clang as the numbers mount.
I wonder at the shooter's cold efficiency,
where he trained. I wonder how a bird feels,
his neck noosed to the farmer's hands.
Right now I'm on vacation, have the time
to kill. Ahead of me, the blondes take turns
massaging fingers to practice death. My turn,
I stagger, stiff with wonder at the flood
of numbers. At the ebb, that too.
Some games I aim to lose, not win.

The Ohio Journal   *Martin Galvin*

ANOTHER CROSS

Hammer me. Let me see
What I can take, how long
Hold up my own. Oh, child, the view
From where we are is purer
Than the uncontained energy of bees
Among roses. But I want more
Than this to think back on;
Show me farther mountains frozen
In the pockets of my eyes.
So lift me up, transfix me,
High and hanging, above you,
Above this hill of clay and boulders.
And bring me shaking back
To earth, O you easiest of metaphors,
O wildest of untouched dreams.

Stone Country   *Stephen Gardner*

THE TAILOR

Ulezalka, Ulezalka,
your head laced with cancerous
tentacles like a spider's endless
web, remembers in nightmares
the Gestapo snapping commands
like castanets.

The little head
fit so snugly in the guard's
palm, baseball in a mit,
heaved against the camp wall;
the cancer shaken loose, resounding
against the bricks.

In Buchenwald
your blood line was roasted
in ovens like the Christmas
goose, served in open graves,
the hot ashes melting
the snow to black water.

Only you,
last ink spot of the line,
were left, echoing the poison
of the walls. They carried you
from camp, a mass of papier-mâché
unglued—shipped you to America.

They let you
keep your number and the threads
weaving in and out
of your brain. The numbers
counted disappearing
faces in the night.

The threads
grew until you became the thread,
they the body. After you put
the final stitches in my wedding
dress, the thread rose and floated
through the open window.

The Seattle Review   *Patricia Garfinkel*

WHITE SPIDER

Above my daughter in the tree
a white spider lowers itself on a string,
hangs like a blind eye that can establish
only light or dark. What is between
twelve and thirteen is unclear,
a quiver of thrusts and halts.
She is unsure herself
except for the way it feels to swing
her legs into space, or stretch
like the hands of a clock and balance
as if she were nothing, a negative print
of a spider, a stopped moment.

National Forum   *Marita Garin*

LIGHT MORNING SNOW, WE WAIT FOR A
WARMER SEASON

How good we imagine it would be
to see blue breaking through.

To see the snow ease up, to see
the sun blaze, eating white.

I think of you in white: your
virgin days are gone,

but I enjoyed the spring, the
quickening to fall after that

bird and bush summer. We look
into an older mirror this winter.

It's good to have this morning,
its soft descending, its mute

reminding. I stand at the window
in a room where you do not see me.

I am watching the soft falling
of the pure snowflakes, seeing
as they settle
into the earth's alterations.

Do not blame me if I stay here,
falling, delicate, merging.

Southern Humanities Review   *John Garmon*

PARIS

It's winter in Paris and women in high heels are strutting
about with their small silly dogs,
and students in black coats and long scarves are laughing
much too loudly.

It's winter in Paris and the rich stroll the Champs Elysee
in fur coats, smelling of champagne and Christian Dior,
and old men with caps on and wine-flushed faces are sharing
a joke in a smoke-filled cafe.

It's winter in Paris and skinny painted girls in pencil-
tight jeans stare hungrily from street corners,
and in the Place Pigalle a whore pouts.

It's winter in Paris and businessmen in Renaults curse
the traffic and think of their mistresses, and an old concierge,
bad tempered and fat, grumbles as she empties the rubbish.

It's winter in Paris and musicians are playing the violin
in Montmartre and lovers walk arm in arm beside the
Seine, while children dawdle home from school with pinched
white faces, munching bread and chocolate
and a sharp-faced gendarme directs the traffic with precise
impatient movements.

It's winter in Paris and an old drunk in the metro, stinking
of shit, grins toothless
and holds his hand out for a franc.

Canadian Author and Bookman   *Jane Garnett*

WELCOME TO THIS HOUSE

Welcome to this house.
We go barefoot in this place
along the passages
to the mouth of the echo. Stoop low.
Do not disturb the spiders overhead
and in the shadows along the walls.
We do not kill them. They are sacred.
They create the universe
from rock to bone, spinning, spinning.
The bones that line the way
are our fathers' bones.
They must be scraped four times a year
for offerings at festivals, and again
when times are bad
and there is little flesh to eat
from harvest wars.
Sometimes we hold the skulls and dance:
it is our way of making love.

We believe the spiders are spirits.
Everything has a purpose.
The spiders spin stars. We make bones.
We have no fire to keep away the beasts.
We are the beasts,
devouring, dancing, dreaming,
making bones to love
to warm the cold seepage of stone.

Yankee   *Faye George*

MORNING

Light breezes, drifting through the window,
flowing past curtains dancing
on scents of wild plum and apple blossoms.
Roosters crowing in alarm at a rising sun
casting its first rays on the giant elm
with a tire swing in hand.
Muffled bangs follow, from
frying pans set on the stove.
Porcelain percolators' sudden aroma
of coffee makes one hunger for
the bacon and eggs now frying.
They bury the thoughts of all else,
but the smell of the hay
to be baled today.

Valley Times   *M. A. George*

UNSEEN FLIGHT

Always I've loved the transient things that die,
After a sweet brief life, and leave no mark:

The quick, graceful flight of birds across the sky,
Stars, cigarette tips of dancers in the dark:
Blue smoke unraveled from chimneys like a thread,
Wind, rain, and roses, all things that will not last.
There is this one conviction in my head:
Beauty is worth the funeral when it's past.
I have not puzzled whether some future spring
will make me wise again the ways of youth.
Only I weep for a vanished blossoming,
Only I mourn the ashes of your mouth.
Loveliness well may pass, but all is not just
When the curse of death is upon your splendid dust.

Poet Lore   *Markos Georgeou*

THE ANGORA

I have touched her liquid fur,
Smooth as raw silk,
Sleek—white-shining—
And felt that sand-paper tongue,
Abrasive on my face.
She, wide-eyed—hypnotic—
Has stared me into dreams.

I have felt that soft purr
Singing against my chest,
As she burrowed for a spot in my heart.

And I have felt that blinkless gaze
From the rim of the couch,
As I poured her a saucer of milk.

I am sure she believes (perhaps she is right)
That the home in which we dwell is hers.

The Pub   *Jim Gerard*

PRACTICING

To sign for a single passport
is one way to begin. To take
any journey alone. To be the one
who finds the body on the beach,
eyes splintered like the agate chips
that will wrap around the neck
of every dream. These are ways of practicing.

To walk through autumn without love,
to count in spring what has winterkilled,
to rejoice in late flowers,
dried fruit. In strange countries,
to peer into the boiling pot and watch
dark hands take the turtle from the shell;
to choose the suit for the burial.

The rest are simpler ways:
to lie back as a woman lies
awash in the bedclothes with love—
to feel the last buoy of self
slip far from the hand; to trust
the blackness before the surgeon's knife,
colors fleeing like birds
in summer's wake. To step into a storm
and give freely of your breath
for every breath the wind will take.

These are the trial runs.
When the great lightness comes
like a door opening out of the body
or a core falling, swift and aglow,
you will be ready to bite down hard.
You will remember all that has left you.
And then you will go.

Cedar Rock   *Sonia Gernes*

MERIDIAN

Idly in the sun,
on one of the sunniest corners of California
we linger, looking,
pleasing the realtor's eye that reads the mind:
a house like a stage set,
shade of plane trees in earliest flower of leaf,
sun on the grass,
a gurgle of motors pausing where five roads meet;
inland those green
heights of ten thousand houses; not far, that sea.
Driveway to driveway
the neighbors, over their fences, would surely be nice,
knowing we too
must be, like them, elite, discreet, protectors
of privilege paid for:
shore, and highway, and canyons winding wide
under Temple Hills
to the Top of the World, the wren-tit's thickets, the rock
the ravens are guarding,
where deer come down, and the brush of the fox is gone;
heaven and earth,
all to be ours, ocean to wild greenbelt
greening to ripe
between the fogs and the smoglight, haze of sea
and haze of the farthest
misty ziggurat carved of the marsh hawks' slope
or still to carve,
hills beyond hills to where the invisible mountains,
in winter, rise
out of windy distance, as if the past were here

or the future born.
Home in Laguna again, looking for home,
I remember dusk,
cliffs over beaches darkening, ocean night
where now under tall
motels and towering condominiums at curfew floodlights
put out the dark.
One of the sunniest towns in the world. At the topmost
plot of earth—
on Fortune's rock, it rounds its rays like a flower.
And I think of Poseidon,
that covered the daughter of the sun when the bull in the fields
embodied the god,
the dark, denied in the palace awhile; of Knossos
fallen to fire;
of all the high walls. In the blaze of noon I turn
toward lost noonday,
not to the past but to a loftier place
than any of these,
a mountain lake too high in midwinter to be visited
by man or birds,
its beasts all hidden under ice whipt clean by stormwind,
in gloom of noon
its snow, like dust over stone, blown on. What dies.
And what does not die.

Western Humanities Review   *Brewster Ghiselin*

EXIGENCIES

When I grow up
    I want to go up
        to my loft
and make the objects
    of midday below
        into songs
        the whole world sings.

I want to take the hopscotch
    I traveled through time
        and turn it into
            a jumprope rhyme.

I want to be a rich and famous
    swingset operator
        and charge free rides
            for alligators.

I want to bark at the circus
    about my sideshow
        of freaks and familiar things
            everybody wants to know.

I want to send sack lunches
    full of metaphor and mayonnaise cuisine

to hungry eyes
in magazines.

I want to be a tinkertoy teacher
and a popsicle principal.

When I grow up
I want to be the kid
who lives next door.

The Emissary   *Michael William Gilbert*

THE PORCH

Sometimes it happens
I am having a good time
just sitting on the porch
in my big brown rocker
watching the sky sneak by.

Maybe smelling the dirt
I had turned over and raked
clean for my beans
a while ago, my body feeling
used and grateful.

Or maybe recalling a long spidery
girl I had clambered up
the sand dunes with
in Michigan once, her shoulders softly
freckled by the sun.

And maybe beyond the geranium,
perched in the wild
black raspberry patch
its mother pushed it into,
there's a young speckled robin,

fat and crabby-
looking, looking
and rocking
a little,
same as me.

Sometimes it happens
the retired gentleman
across the alley will slip
into his old
green Mercury,

tip the snappy red lid
to the back of his head,
and listen to her
purr
for a spell.

And sometimes it happens
while I'm rocking here

feeling used and lucky
and happy in my juices,
that nothing happens—

the sycamores stand,
the shade does its usual
slow business
with the leaves
over my bare toes,

and easily,
oh how easily
I fall asleep
and dream of
almost touching you.

Poetry Northwest   *Gary Gildner*

MY FATHER AFTER WORK

Putting out the candles
I think of my father asleep
on the floor beside the heat,
his work shoes side by side
on the step, his cap
capping his coat on a nail,
his socks slipping down,
and the gray hair over his ear
marked black by his pencil.

Putting out the candles
I think of winter, that quick
dark time before dinner
when he came upstairs after
shaking the furnace alive,
his cheek patched with soot,
his overalls flecked with
sawdust and snow,
and called for his pillow,
saying to wake him
when everything was ready.

Putting out the candles
I think of going away
and leaving him there,
his tanned face turning
white around the mouth,
his left hand under his head
hiding a blue nail,
the other slightly curled
at his hip, as if
the hammer had just
fallen out of it
and vanished.

New Letters   *Gary Gildner*

MOUTH OF THE AMAZON

Strumming your melodic hair
I fell in my sleep
As usual through the warm river
Of your skin,
Guiding my compatriots onward
To the mouth of the Amazon
Where we planted breadfruit trees
And played a softball game.

I was two for two with
A double and triple
And at the plate for a third time, but awoke
To receive an uplifting message from God
Sent directly through the medium of the moonlight
In your laughing eyes.

Carolina Quarterly   *R. P. Gira*

THE PURITAN HACKING AWAY AT OAK

You're sweating it out, no wonder you freeze.
You work as hard as a Puritan hacking away
At oak. Then the fine work: whittling
An Indian out of the trunk. Well, you'd say,
It takes a Puritan to argue with another one.

So we both freeze in the wind, forgetting the wind exists
To flick the leaves over and over, for the sake
Of their limberness. Any dope knows that
Who hasn't lashed himself to the lumber
And lopped all the branches, buds, eyes.

You never did like knots, pure one, as if
God who chose you to suffer in his image
Wished you to walk a straight-line plank.
You remember—that God who gambled he'd luck out
After a long run of hushed-up zeroes.

What you overlook is the revenge, the moral:
While the oak petrifies, the blade is rusting,
By nature's grace. The inexorable truth
Of the axe is: rise, swing, decline and fall.
But what do you care? You'll swing whatever Heaven sends.

But you're right, it takes a Puritan to argue.
I'm off. I heard of a mountain
Here, or there, or around, a heaving slab
Furrowed like an old fist, where my own
God hangs tapestries in a worked-out mine, way back in the woods.

Chicago Review   *Todd Gitlin*

THE PHEASANT HUNTER
AND THE ARROWHEAD

Among stray quartz pebbles turned up
by fall ploughing, it lies washed white
from November rains. Hardwood leaves
may have screened its flight,
or a hunter, running to keep
wounded game in sight, left it behind.
Finger that scalloped wedge, ponder
his methods, wonder what pointed signs
of his labors will warm in the sun
when your brass cartridge cases are gone
with the dust of thousands of game-bird bones.

Cedar Rock   *Julian Gitzen*

FIGURE AND GROUND

Ear to the earth,
I slump in the outfield grass
Like a beached body, listening
To the world confess my faults—
Twelve, clumsy from the crib,
I leaped at the clouds
As the brown baseballs
Plummeted around me, not one
In my glove the daylong afternoon.
And the coach, kicking the batting cage,
Waved me deep to left field—O gravity,
When will you love me
As a mother loves her sick child!

After the drills and the long run,
They leave the field
To me and the bullbats swooping
Low among the insects that nag
The evening air of midsummer.
I suck on a weedstem, I want
To be reborn, to come back dumb
And with fingers limber as monkey tails!

Louisiana 1957 and it's too hot to dream—
I turn on my back and watch the birds,
Their shrill melisma, flak of their black wings
Like night falling piece by piece.

Northwest Review   *Elton Glaser*

JANUARY

Here on your bed I have
a grounds-eye view

of winter; the white
falling out of nowhere.
I feel your fingers moving
like cool flurries melting
where they touch my warmth.
You bend to me and
I feel you settle
on me like a drift.
The room is silent as snow;
I call you, but you are lost
out in the blizzard of my thighs
where your kisses are
a cunning language of
their own.

Nebula   Deborah Godin

ONE MORE TIME

And next morning, at the medical center
Though the X-Ray Room swallows me whole,

Though cold crackles in the corridors
I brace myself against it and then relax.

Lying there on the polished steel table
Though I step right out of my body,

Suspended in icy silence
I look at myself from far off
Calmly, I feel free

Even though I'm not, now
Or ever:

The metal teeth of death bite
But spit me out

One more time:

When the technician says breathe
I breathe.

Three Rivers Poetry Journal   *Patricia Goedicke*

THE GREED SONG

Today, I want
everything. It's not
a lot, just that woman's hair blowing
peekaboo at her head like an angelfish
looping its plastic aquarium castle.
That dog, the one
limping . . . I want the thorn
in its paw to rise
and stitch and rise and stitch

till it's night and the moon's
bald head snaps
up from successful surgery. Let
Livia's breast grow whole again
in its bandage. There's a
raccoon praying over a smelt
in the garbage—I ordain him
patron saint of those arrested in
victimless crimes. Today, the eyes
mint gold discs of light
from the air—just pile those
coins on the bureau. Today,
I want the simple
dignity
and grace of the first
cilium that whipped me
through the dark ducts.
And I want the ducts.

Kansas Quarterly   *Albert Goldbarth*

FOR JEANETTE PICCARD ORDAINED AT 79

I

A woman grows old secretly
wrinkle by wrinkle
breast by breast
never having laid claim to herself
                                            her words
                                            her god
she sews buttons on her eyelids
zippers her bursting spirit,
her inexpressible loss.
years turn her eyes unknowable.
her anguish is buried in the comforting
earth, with the dead. you wouldn't
know if you walked on the grave she knows.

II

step forth O daughter
lay claim at last at last
on holy ground,
undefiled, unfouled,
bless before us what has been
ours, the sweet earth.
come from the dark pews where you
prayed beloved sons home from
devouring wars, the raging death.
come forward to the altar linen
embroided by those hands that
dare not defile bread you baked
but never blessed.

The Christian Century   *Renny Golden*

THE BOYS BRUSHED BY

Jesus never turned me on
Like altar boys' electric sleeves
Brushed by my waiting arm.

Angel sparks in darkness flew
To scour out the narrow arches
Where saints prayed at our sides.
The boys' black robes leaked gold
Into the aisle now burning toward the altar
Like a tongue of fire—
I rose to follow.

Burning for the boys through my ordinary clothes,
Through my love for their holy young days,
I let them take me as the bride they needed,
Knelt with open mouth to love the stranger
Jesus, though I knew—
He was not and never had been man,
Never would be man enough for me.

New Boston Review   *Catherine Gonick*

THE LONGING

At two-thirty on this bright afternoon
I am ready for a nap on your sleeping
Green rug. The fresh snow glitters outside.
My body longs to stretch and rest against
The curve of memory holding
The sheer whiteness of the dipping meadow,
The ink-blue shadow of fir and wall;
I wish to sleep in the clean lake of air
Moving through mountains to the ocean's
Reach and that darker winter swell of blue
Rolling over untenanted lengths of beach and stone;
I want to dream myself awake in silent footmarks
Stitching a line from one low house to another,
Reaching that seasoned door I can clasp and open.

Great River Review   *William Goodreau*

TO PAUL ELUARD

Farewell to the caterpillars standing in minks
in front of the Opera.
Nobody knows if they wait, if this is patience.

Farewell to the clocks fingering their wedding rings,
the murmuring moon,
farewell

to public appetite.
The seven headlengths of beauty have been cut off;
we are putting them back. In the end

the world is more like a person than not
and we are dust
only compared to what escapes us.

The professors of ethics are gathering in the meadows,
tears in their nets.
Butterflies teach us to see meanings vanish.

Not one gets away.

The Virginia Quarterly Review   *Jorie Graham*

AND THIS IS MY FATHER

up through five green
hospital floors i run the
elevator up through five
green hospital floors
to where my father walks
along the clean halls
hands in his red robe
to meet me stepping out
to meet him.
a pale hand on my shoulder,
he takes me deep-dyed in ceremony
to the nurses station
where all the work to be done
is flourished in rich flames
and slow thighs that squeeze
through the night shift.
"this is my son," he says
but i catch the stare
of the red-head with sharp brown
eyes turning her blood-dimmed face
to mine.
it is the night shift, she is the
shadow of an indignant falcon.
my father spreads his thick pale
hand with me within it
down the halls into each living
room not staked with hanging vines
of water and blood.
"this is my son," he says to
Mr. William, thickening in his heart.
"this is my son," he says to
Mr. Butler, covered to the neck.
"this is my son," he says
to whomever we pass in the hall.
the dying glide without glee
in their beds
birds fly at the windows
and turn back.
"when are you coming home?" i ask.
my father smiles and his hand opens

wide without fear floating up
to his ear, scratching.
the tall nurse catches him out of bed.
"what are you doing out of bed," she thunders.
"this is my son," he says to her
carrying off in astonishment
and fully mortal laugh of all his teeth.
and this is my father
long after his death has died
haunting the night shift hospitals
with the relish
of a gypsy.

Bachy 11   *Marcus J. Grapes*

BEYOND THE FIREHOUSE

down the flightline
to the left is a pit

of jetfuel. Touched
by a crewchief's match,

flames build a forty-foot
hell. I am covered

with asbestos and walk
in, carrying a hose

toward an old T-33
cockpit filled with

tortured dummies, their
faces staring at something

I will never see.
I rescue them again and again.

The Little Review   *Patrick Worth Gray*

THE MIKVEH

Renewal of the cycle.
Expectations and arousal.
Women leaving clean and shiny.
Young brides and pre-menopausals.

Alone, at peace, relaxed.
Soaking in a warm tub
Before the T'vila, the immersion.
Suddenly
I tighten, remembering
That the S.S. would gun their motors
Then burst into the Mikveh
And rape those "pure" women,
Those poor women.
Those poor pure women.

My lady of the lake
Checks to see
If I've cut my nails,
Removed my lipstick.
"Kosher," she says to me.
Kosher again, after the second dip.
A car motor slows down outside—
My husband coming to pick me up.

Midstream   *Blu Greenberg*

GNOSTICS ON TRIAL

Let us make the test. Say God wants you
to be unhappy. That there is no good.
That there are horrors in store for us
if we do manage to move toward Him.
Say you keep Art in its place, not too high.
And that everything, even eternity, is measurable.
Look at the photographs of the dead,
both natural (one by one) and unnatural
in masses. All tangled. You know about that.
And can put Beauty in its place. Not too high,
and passing. Make love our search for unhappiness,
which is His plan to help us.
Disregard that afternoon breeze from the Aegean
on a body almost asleep in the shuttered room.
Ignore melons, and talking with friends.
Try to keep from rejoicing. Try
To keep from happiness. Just try.

The Kenyon Review   *Linda Gregg*

TO EMILY

When I found myself faced directly,
eyes searching out mine
as if for fresh sightings or contest,
lips whose pensive stillness
changed before me to fullness
as if turned to flesh on canvas
—an old, a not forgotten land
floats close, a deeply remembered tune
from a ship out of the distance—
and then almost audibly
from the barely parted lips
the words: "Yes, yes" . . .

When I faced this in that face
I thought of you, Emily,
at the top of your stairs
all in white, a white branch

of greeting in your hand,
your impossible heart
bursting into tiny, gold-blue,
twittering, fluttering birds—

thought of you and understood
why you could not take
that first step down,
understood—when I looked into
the eyes before me, at the lips
so eloquent by now—
how you were torn,
why you would even then
have preferred to turn
and not descend to
the dark figure awaited
and pacing below.

The Michigan Quarterly Review   *Arthur Gregor*

THE SECOND VIOLINIST'S SON

You grow up with music
but what do you know about it?
The minor third my mother used
to call my name, the whole step
of the phoebe's cry—those
recognitions were in the blood.

My father, no talkative man,
shut himself in the bedroom
nights with his violin. Did he
make it speak? What did he play?
It was nothing I could hum—
a melody turned upside down.

I was concerned with the details
of growing up. Years later,
trying to sit still at a concert,
I was shaken, hard, by something
familiar—my father's part,
just under the orchestra's surface.

It was something like the plain
warp on which a complicated weft
is threaded. Or the shadowy figures
in the background of a relief
that fix the illusion of depth.
This thick layered sound

must have been what he listened for,
practicing. What I heard now
was a kind of completion he found
only outside himself.

The Georgia Review   *Debora Gregor*

WITHIN US, TOO

Strike a match,
light a candle
or a pyre—
always the same
bright pyramid of fire
leaps into being—
tongues of red and gold
reach up, whichever way you hold
taper or torch.
Within us, too, something
born to aspire,
a yearning, upward burning
spirit-fire.

Unity   R. H. Grenville

WHEN I CONSIDER

(for Emily Dickinson)

When I consider wearing white

I think of Emily.
Her midwinter eyes.
Her basket of snow.

For her, all things were statements:

The black cake
with its nineteen eggs,
beaten, beaten.
The tea trays. Their faces
scoured and blind.
The buttercups
breathing little lies
in the grasses.
And the poems.
Always the poems.

Was there one lover?
Were there two?

It matters little.
Each was put away
along with the poems,
small and perfected,
in that small locked box
of the heart
Layered like silks
or pillow slips.

Or silence.

When I consider wearing white

I think of Emily
hoarding her life like steam
from a cracked cup
until eternity opened
like a startled hand
and kindly let her through.

And I think of you.
Your face a poem
I cannot write.
The cup so precious
I fear to give.

And I, too,
am in danger, sir.

ASFA Poetry Quarterly   Margaret Griffith

RODIN TO RILKE

That sensualist Rodin, who used his mouth
and nose to sculpt, as well as hand and eye
(his models too, traced lovingly as his clay),
said to the mystified young poet Rilke,
Work! Keep working, industry's everything.
More in works than words, Rodin declared
that once he'd loved the easy, lyric line,
nymphs flowing in a wave, or wings in air;
but now he took the harder, subterranean
labor of making his way into the earth
like a totem mole, a caveman, a digger of graves.

Trying to learn the paradigms of clay,
he went for the gates of hell, not paradise:
worked up a crone, dry sticks and withered breasts.
Balzac fat as a steer, the Baptist, blind
and blackened by desert sun, mad to the world.
It's the body, the clay that matters, and secret death
like sex is the body's trophy. You have to get
down in the cave to work out the springs of man.
Black, damp clay is my master now, he said;
you see how it stiffens, fires to a beautiful red.

The Black Warrior Review   Emily Grosholz

THE DRIVERS OF BOSTON

The drivers of Boston are telepathically
connected; at Charles Circle, Neponset,
we know what
the drivers around us are doing. We must
to avoid a wreck.
On this psychic grid messages travel like electricity,
like fire in summer wheat:

I am the best
driver on this road
because I can go the fastest.
It is my divine right to
seize any opening.
I can cut in wherever
there is three feet of space.
Occasionally we are kind,
slowing down to let someone in.

There used to be a sense of humor
about this free-for-all.
Now the road-game is a battle,
feeling crowded on this planet,
scrambling for a toehold against inflation,
yearning for a patch of grass.

Dark Horse   *June Gross*

JOGGING AT DUSK

The last minutes of light. My slow shadow
moves distinct against the red dirt, muscles
and tendons easing to their new routine.

The slightest breeze feels its way through the flow
of grain and the whole Missouri landscape
is moving with me. I can hear the corn

growing, the faint crackle of feathered stalks
where the plants stand firm and green.
A mile away, the electric lights

above the football field begin to glow
like artificial stars against the dark
smudge of eastern sky while the last streaks

of light work west toward the edge of the world.
In the distance, the rough noise of a truck
winding down as it reaches the uphill

grade to Brashear. I listen to my breath
and steps forged into a single voice.
I close my eyes, glide to the blood's lonely

rhythm up a long swell of earth. The day's heat
still dances, a vague curtain above the road,
and the sad soft light of evening guides me in.

The American Scholar   *Andrew Grossbardt*

BY THE POOL

Every dwelling is a desolate hill.
Every hill is a desolate dwelling.

The trees toss their branches in the dark air,
Each tree after its kind, and each kind after
Its own way. The wind tosses the branches
Of the trees in the dark air. The swimming
Pool is troubled by the wind, and the swimmers.

Even though this is not a tower, this is
Also a tower.

> Even though you are not
A watchman, you are also a watchman.

Even though the night has not yet come,
The night has come.

The Paris Review   *Allen Grossman*

A PLACE TO LIVE

Zayde, I drove all night to get here,
My heart pounding behind the wheel,
Consumed by flame.
I am a bullet aimed at your memory,
Here to get what's coming to me, my past:
You! A man whose soul is a coin of fire.

Even in California you repeat the old rituals:
Fill your pipe with cigar clippings,
Pour your morning shot,
Wear your wrinkled suit;
A hat covers your shining skull,
Bald as a baby's ass.

Again you tell me the old stories.
They escape your tongue
As you fled Russia:
Hope and sadness in every step, in every breath.

You deserted the Czar's army at 19,
Bribed a sergeant, a fat sausage of a man,
To turn his back while
You hopped a train for the port of Vladivostok
Where you stowed away on a ship
Bound for America, *Gan Eden*.

There Jews might walk streets of gold,
Make money, movies, friends among the *goyim*;
They might write books, songs, even enter politics.
The air was alive, the people crazy with life.

Later, the air itself seemed dead.
You discovered the streets had been paved
With the bones of Indians.

Now all your friends are gone,
Playing pinnochle with the angels, I suppose,
Or else in *Gehenna* selling ice.

You tell me you will die out here,
Where the locusts are, and
If you've learned anything in all these years,
It's that there are locusts everywhere,
That a man must learn to look
Into his own face
And not turn away.

Sou'wester   *Martin Grossman*

THE RITUAL

Each day I lure the hummingbirds
into the high meadows of
light, the white fields
flowering. A thousand

Beaks seeking sweetness
in a whir of tongues.
Such a beating of
wings stinging the air!

I can fit five birds
in one tight fist and feel
the fine hearts pump.

I'm light as air
and flowing honey,
wild with
the dark bloom of the world.

Poetry   *Joy Gwillim*

NOT TO MARCH

Today my mother's letter said
that March was really showing off at home.
Yes—we've been breezy here, as well,
and it is now the twenty-third,
but not until today—
until that chance remark—
did I remember March is known
proverbially
for blowing.
Because I have been shaken
with a blowing in my soul.
The winds have had it out on me until
the very vessels of my heart have rattled
like loose shingles on a house,
loose windowpanes.

A blast! A breath—a blast! Fierce, unexpected.
Reeling within my whirlwind I have heard and known

but little other than the gale,
and still, I thought, from somewhere,
comfort.

I am disheveled now, and limp,
and I am out of breath. Not so the month,
for March has eight more days to go.

Lion,
Lamb—
hang on to my soul.

Insight   *Kris Hackleman*

WORLD OF BACTERIA

Bacteria legs, bacteria mouths,
Bacteria ears, bacteria noses,
Everywhere bacteria swim.

Some in the seedy wombs of women,
Some in the guts of clam-fish, some
Softly in the whitely dim
Hearts of onions, some in landscapes,
Everywhere bacteria swim.

Bacteria hands reach left and right
Interweaving, each strained finger
Fining down to end in slim
Root-capillaries webbing over
The fingernail's sharp raggedy rim.

Everywhere bacteria swim.

Look, in the world of these bacteria,
As through panes of leper skin,
Vermilion light, vermilion light,
Thinly shining, glimmers in;
And in that film of crimson shimmer,
Barely visible, redly dim,
Sad, sad, sad, unbearably sad,
Everywhere bacteria swim.

The Western Humanities Review   *Sakutaro Hagiwara*
                    —*Translated by Graeme McD. Wilson*

NO MADAM BUTTERFLY

Toss me a kiss, and take your leave with laughter.
Spare me your sad regrets, my heart is light.
I will remember you, but briefly after,
Perhaps a moment, or an hour, or night.
No Madam Butterfly will mourn your going,
Or wait with steadfast soul for your return.
The music plays, the wine still sweetly flowing

Will lend enchantment while the candles burn . . .
I never lacked for partners in the dance.
You called me thistledown, and we were one
In rhythm and in time and circumstance,
But you have called the end, and we are done.
Tomorrow's sun will drink you like the dew—
I know a thousand others just like you.

The Lyric   *Louise Hajek*

GRAFFITI FOR LOVERS

Fidelity belongs in the Guinness Book of Records.

Seduced by words, you'll have
Only words; if you're lucky
The word will be made flesh.

Hug your lover through misery and soon
You'll hug misery like a lover.

Change lovers as the moon changes;
Like her, never turn your back.

Absence makes the heart grow fond of others;
Out of sight means under the covers.

The older the lover, says Franklin,
The greater the gratitude;
The older the love,
The truer the platitude.

In the lines, "I could not love you dear so much
Loved I not honor more," would you
Rather be dear or honor?

Mies has no advice for lovers:
Only more is more, and still
It's never enough.

Denver Quarterly   *Joan Joffe Hall*

THE HERMIT

I live at a distance,
far enough to watch them
move in the city.
I watch the couples walk.
It's quiet here, a house
of air, soundless.
I don't let others in.
At night I can see their lights,
their woodsmoke going off into the sky.
What I do is nothing.
My wife is enclosure, my children

the windows of the house.
I don't let others in.
What a good thing this is.
What a good thing it is
to sit down alone and eat,
to enter bed empty and awake,
full of what arrives, bodiless,
in sleep. The days, the days,
I don't let others in.
How friendly they seem
in their city without sound,
without texture or smell—this distance.
They could be lifeless, or something else,
they could be in love,
they could be everything
that thrives in a life with others.

It doesn't matter, this distance I keep—
I have fires, my meals, sleep
with its net that drags their streets,
invisible, hungry.
I bring it back at daylight,
I don't let others in.
The road outside my house
leads to the city
but doesn't return—
like fish scales, like hooks.
There is no reason to take that walk.
How well I know the city.
I don't let others in.
I don't let others in.
You can't leave a wife of enclosure.
You can't leave a house of air.

The American Poetry Review   *Daniel Halpern*

ON THE DEATH OF THE EVANSVILLE UNIVERSITY
BASKETBALL TEAM IN A PLANE CRASH,
DECEMBER 13, 1977

And now we know
why coaches rage,
kick benches,
curse rivals and referees.

Here, on this corpse-strewn hill
where grief smothers hope
with an obscene fog,
finality the only prize,
the orphaned heart knows
that every contest is do or die,
that all opponents are Death
masquerading in school colors,
that each previous season is

mere preliminary for encounter
with this last, bitter cup.

Yet we would not have it so,
it must not be so:
man is not made for death.
Cry foul. Shriek protest.
Claim a violation.
Even in losing, dying,
herald the perfect play.

No scream, all-knowing coaches,
admonishing priests, scream.
Swear, chew asses, make us work.
Never quit.
What else sustains
in nights when dreams
plummet downward in darkness
to question the betraying earth?

The Cape Rock   *Robert W. Hamblin*

STONETALK

You must take the speckled stone, the dead-tired stone
out of the wind, softly wheedle him out of
the swathings, warm him, cold stone, dear
stone, whisper sweet words, rock him,
until he feels less heavy, less immobile;
you must give the silent stone your mouth
to play with,
you must take away the stone's heaviness,
you must take over the heaviness from the stone,
the stone at your breast; the stone in your lap has to
become lighter, more weightless, more floating,
luminous translucent body of redemption,
warm pulsing shell of a saint apparently dead;
you must provide the stone with last words
so that he can be freed entirely from matter,

and you must take his grayness upon yourself,
more and more, more completely all the time,
learn his lightlessness,
make silent your weak words, repent, endure
hardening until you can't feel a thing anymore,
filled with nothing but the compact meaning of your material,
cool off until you drop below zero and time,
not even aware of the wind around you,
perfectly turned into heaviness,
in order that you may, sometime,
let go from within yourself one
self-singing, solid, megalithic poem.

Dimension   *Jacques Hamelin*
—Translated by Ria Leigh-Louhuizen

THE WAKENING

Up all night
with a hundred dying chicks
in the jaundiced light
of the coop, my father steps
into the first pools of day
pausing at the door
to scrape the dung from his boots,
leaning his back to the jamb
as he thumbs small curls of tobacco
into the burnt-out bowl of his pipe.
All night his ears rang
between the echoes of his heart
with the sickly *cheep, cheep*
of small white heads agape
from twisted necks,
beaks dropped open to ask
what no one ever knows, refusing
feed and drink as they died,
twisted in the palm of his hand.
And as the sun tears itself
on the blades of new roofs where
orchards he farmed once stood,
he strikes a match and draws deep,
and the gray mare ambles into dew
from the musky shadows of the barn,
her dark tail switching
the first flies of the day.
Squinting into the light, a pain
too subtle to name settles
in his chest; and, as he begins
his chores, the morning
spreads over him like a stain.

Cutbank   *Sam Hamill*

DISPLACEMENT

Were they ever there, whether you
    noticed, forgot, looked away?

rock, tree-trunk, cliff, unmoved,
    immovable, thing in itself that

never the marvelous machine—
    muscle—could quite lever?

Or what lay buried in sand
    or shale, that nobody thought

till statesmen quarreled, bought
    arms for—worth much—oil?

Like gravity, if you've noticed,
    that simply waits for one step;

or momentum, exacting so very much
　　per milimeter at high speed; or

the waiting amanita, pristine white
　　angel of death, ruthless to the

misinformed. . . . Thing in itself
　　without self, uninvited, and always

there: you who displace the air,
　　engineer, demagogue, bombardier,

must learn to know the vacant place,
　　like a door-click after no one's there.

The Southern Review   *Horace Hamilton*

FINDING A FRIEND HOME

(for Todd)

One of these last summer nights
I sleep in your eyes,
wide awake to the lake of words
breaking at surface.
Read them, they say to me softly
like a three A.M. lover
rousing from a pool of dreams.
I read and a young boy
stands swaying in the mist of your iris.
He could be me with his shy
knot of hands and a breeze riding
his sun-shot hair.
He could be me when he dissolves
and years later returns,
the same eyes
smiling and unsure like weather.
He is you next in the clearing of seasons,
eyes shining like a promise—
and I slip from morning in your gaze,
watching your blue day and another year
whisper past unclouded.

Southern Poetry Review   *Timothy Hamm*

EXPECTANCIES: THE ELEVENTH HOUR

I lie in wait. It is the in-between
time just before the mail, minutes
of wishing, gray shadows, introspection.
I study breakfast with the care one attends
a letter. Memory is the menu's message:
words swallowed sweeten orange juice,
the aftertaste like pulp remains.

Yesterday's missives unanswered, silent
telegrams demanding immediate attention.

But nothing is immediate. Flowers drowsing
in the planter snap their dragon tails in
unison with sleep. Ink unhurries into print.
Cereal crackles with its chorus din "snap,
crackle, pop." The squeal a pen nib makes
striding over paper. Postcards, first
courses, preamble what must follow.
I savor words as "dear" & "love" until
they have an afterglow as taxing as this meal.

Subsiding is not feasting. Nothing sacred
solemn in crepe suzettes or French toast.
An exotic tongue guarantees no assuage.
I am the stranger who lives for small
unexpectancies. No Special Delivery.
You told me to expect nothing from ritual
or repast. The mail arrives late. Bills,
pleas for foreign causes, a promise of fame
& financial security, If I'll only . . . I won't.
"Never mailbox watch," was what you said.
And so I begin anew with that resolution.
The immediate is past.

Grub Street   *Karla M. Hammond*

GIRL TO WOMAN

Whose anger was it
driving me on him,
striping his red-plaid shirt,
my firing nails into his flesh
kicking and crying?

When I was twelve,
playing with cousins at Grandma Casey's house,
she made cold lemonade, and sugar cookies,
calling me to bring it.

When I leaned over setting the tray on the lawn,
this one, laughing, bowed my neck
with his heavy hand, holding me down.
   My anger sprang full grown
      to terrify the cat in all of us,
         a fury of bloody biting and yanking hair.

Grandma pulled me off of him
and laid me in a darkened room.
She gentled me, washed my tears,
then holding my hand in hers, she talked
a long careful time, my Irish-born,
wise-hearted mother's mother.

The years have used her words.
They crown my daily intent.

The Slackwater Review   *Nixeon Civille Handy*

AS ROCKS ROOTED

If we must stand alone
let it not be from dark dissent—
the arrogant "I" hating the stone
that is another's stance, sturdy, unspent.
Stand for our own truth, as rocks
rooted from the human field and piled as wall,
protecting the miracle of flocks,
and touching, and within call.

Arizona Quarterly   *Howard G. Hanson*

THE ONE SONG

It's taken many years to find
He was right that evening long ago.
When the world you live in
Suddenly turns into a minefield,
And people at every step
Vanish in quick columns of smoke,
You begin to think death is the one song.
Now I know songs about the end
Ache in the throat
Only because love is there too.

I must have been five years old.
Black clouds were rolling across fields,
And there were flicks of lightning
On the horizon
Too distant for thunder,
But near enough to crackle the voice
Of a woman singing her heart out
In the little cathedral
Of the radio.

The song made my feet squirm;
I didn't know what to do with my hands,
So I put them in my pockets.
Why do they only sing about love,
Why always love?
He laughed to my mother,
Then looked at me very tenderly,
Like I was five
And a bit helpless in the head,
And gave me an honest answer:
What else is there to sing about?

New Letters   *C. G. Hanzlicek*

FROM THE BATTER'S BOX

God is a screwball
Pitcher, I mean
That's His best pitch
With mysterious windups,
Twisting and twirling all around,
Looking everywhere,
Like Luis Tiant.

I square myself in the batter's box
Waiting for breakfast and today
To be hurled at me,
And I got this idea
It's going to be another curvy, dismal day,
Cause that's all I've been
Getting lately.

Only He throws me
An off speed change up,
A high time floating easy
At an afternoon party,
And you frowning at my awkwardness
Tell me what a dreadful bore I was,
While I beat my bat on the dinner plate,
A sorrowful strikeout victim
Of daily anticipation.

Poet Lore   *David K. Harford*

THERE

(for my daughter and son)

Somewhere, then—the bottom
Of the ocean, the middle
Of the air, the end of the earth,
Tundra, steppe, oasis—
Possibly very far away
But probably close to home,
There lies a special place mentioning my name.

Not what you call me
When we eat a meal or trim a tree,
But that which one is called
By the unending law, one's full name,

Its arrangement of ancestral phonemes designed after all
Finally to be dismantled by whatever
Whim motivates whatever veering wind—

Typhoon, simoon—

And maybe some day to be reassembled
Quite by accident, for twenty seconds
Or so,
Every totemic syllable miraculously intact

And registered prismatically in the precinct
Of a writing spider or hermit crab
Making its moral way from one meal to the next,

Until a shift of wind will lift
It and create something else
Out of it, scruple by scruple, somebody else's name
Or number: that, say,
Of a dumb animal
Seated at a hypothetical keyboard
In a proverbial laboratory
Depressing one character after another,
Until by the law of averages the imperial tissues of Lear
Are stretched out yet one more time
Upon the radioactive rack of this tough world.
A house like ours goes spinning around
Among the parti-colored science-fiction stars—

Tundra, steppe, oasis, simoon, typhoon—and
Tick, tick, tick, your names are typewritten too;

Then the voices of two special spaces
Hollowed out by the unending law
To take your neat names in a perfect fit
Will whisper, "That's it," and "That's it."

Carolina Quarterly   *William Harmon*

THE ICE CASTLE

Even now, mid-winter,
something light, alive,
is shining from the depths of it;

When I touch its perfect skin,
the light shimmers, melting
in small streams of water.

How delicate the dream
that even ice
attempts to hold.

The Atlantic Monthly   *Michael Harris*

EASIER

The tale is told of a doomed planet whose
inhabitants decided not to use
up the next few hundred million years'
supply of fish in a decade, not to pierce
holes in the upper atmosphere to keep
their armpits smelling sweet, not to leap
to unnecessarily premature conclusions
on nuclear or human proliferation.

Easier, you think, for amoebas to invent
monkeys; monkeys turn out to have learnt

Sanscrit, Greek, English, and one of their number
come up, in course of time, with the bumper
works of William Shakespeare?
                                        Probably.

The Malahat Review   *James Harrison*

LAMENT OF A LAST LETTER

(in Memory of Bernice Ames)

O, I tell you,
struggling to write the next word,
I'm of another race now.

I who
wrote creatures into the world,
O, I tell you

I cannot imagine how
I summoned them; my senses bleared,
I'm of another race now,

so weak not even feathers blow
pattern to my page, this fumbling all I feared;
O, I tell you

the jeweled hummingbird turns crow
forever, black as carrion and unscared;
I'm of another race now,

one of the dying; death will undo
all song, the flight that stirred
this symbol out of me and grew
tail, eyes . . . wings and from these letters flew.

Yankee   *Janet E. Harrison*

THE FISHERMAN

The terrible oldness
Of shoreline
Slopes to lavender light
In the trees.
The quiet there
Is a chorus of bones.
We drift past lily pads
Whose hollow bellies
Fill with dancing
Spheres of water.

In the live-well
Swims a fish that swam
A million years before
I had a place to put him.
Wet leaves kept him cool

In the long dark.
His tail waves
Like transparent feathers
In a tired wind.

A quiet rain
Dreams on the surface.
There is little difference
Now in air and lake;
The space between
A band of drunken molecules.

National Forum   *Sam G. Harrison*

WHEN YOUR PARENTS GROW OLD

(for Catherine Lupori)

When your parents grow old
your mother's stories tangle
tongue and teeth in shrunken gums
Your father hears only
fading whispers of his virtue
Bloodwhistles through his brain
sing the deafness song
Like delicate whorled shells
their subtle colors
fade and grey in the
harsh winter dusk

Carefully by lamplight
you handle them
old treaties crumbing yellow edges
at your table
Deer for their lodge
driven through tangled freeways
pursued in aisles and queues
you bring them

And the change rises and sets
moves through moons until you see
your mother staring from the mirror
and you feel her breasts
her thickened waist
her thighs under your hands
and you know at last you bear and nurture them
the old ones
as you were and as
you too will be

Dacotah Territory   *Joanne Hart*

TRADING CHICAGO

The Chicago we could have imagined for ourselves
lies on the breast of the desert on certain days, the desert

that Conan Doyle read between the lines of Mississippi and Pacific:
a city of light, yet never a Second Paris, light and singleness
being the desert's chief commodities. You and I would invest
heavily in these goods and it would all come out right—
though I have exhausted many resources trying to go it alone;
my capital would cover only half, I had to choose
the more exportable monopoly. Now I have it all on my hands,
great unmovable heaps of singleness; the hard, fine-ground
light, on those days when the weather here is dim and the distant
city glows with complementary assurance, still settles down
with a tense slowness like the blood trickling back
into a sleeping hand, not dissolved in that temperate air
but colloid, the shimmering insoluble particles
homing in on the languid streets as if there were
no other place to go.

        We walked the streets, pretending
a serious shrewdness, in our best prospective, undecided way.
The single Chicago had put up no billboards advertising
its miraculous availability, but the pigeons fluttering up
against the current of light unfurled rainbows from their feathers;
and we walked all day through the post-office and immaculate
tall banks, out again to the agreeable streets, agreeable shops
so perfectly stocked I felt sure we agreed on everything;
and at the station you examined the steel Victorian train,
gleaming like a new promise, that silently carried you away.

Carolina Quarterly   *Charles O. Hartman*

WE ARE LEANING AWAY

we are leaning away from each other.
love whimpers in the corner like an injured dog.
yesterday it refused food. today
it won't swallow anything at all.
we watch from opposite sides of the room.
this argument, burning between us like a bridge,
is no longer the reason.
something feverish is licking our fingers.
something that can't breathe scratches
at the door.

The Apalachee Quarterly   *Gayle Elen Harvey*

CONVERSATION WITH GOD

When I say my name, I am telling you
a story. I am giving you a song
singing. Singing in the crossroads,
at the intersection of planes,
in affection's impossible geometry:
reversing; angling; curling; tangential;

my own name circumscribing another's
while it is itself embraced, bound.

It is the story of a bursting suitcase,
a hole in the road, late night noises
in your neighborhood. It is the story
of good teeth, light around the corner,
seven fountains, a reserve of energy.

Inside my name, time collapses.
This too is the story. My name is
another language, not reasonable,
not hormonal, trusting. It blesses
as it moves toward your own.

New Orleans Review   *Jeanine Hathaway*

WORLD ENOUGH

In the marvelling quiet of morning
before harsh angles of logic or speech,
a woman spills over color and curve
like a dream of feathers or an antelope
frilling the arc of the earth
with leaping, body bent to the shape
of grace then gone into some deep forest
where God, surprised, blooms
like a white peacock.

Carolina Quarterly   *Jeanine Hathaway*

GETTING OLDER HERE

The moth is a shadow without a source,
an embodying solid propelled by a fast flutter,
aiming at light as if light itself
could have a shadow.

She escaped from a butterfly
who died yesterday from too much beauty.

Now she is a plain spinster, stripped
of all but blind approximate flights.
She bats at my lamp, lusting for gold,

trying to find
the way back.

Contemporary Quarterly   *Barbara Hauk*

JANUARY

Electrically, cleanly,
The news beeps its alarm,

Prints itself silently across our thoughts:
Blizzard . . . Everything is officially wrong . . .
Autos askew, related and unrelated
As by a whimsical magnet,
Snow slung low on the wires
And pop! They're down.

Cold in the walls
And up the stairs
And up your trouser leg
And over the air:
The thru-way is jammed
And on a quiet side street
An artery closes—
And he's down, too.
Sirens sound. The night's alive.

But it is not like this at all.
Out, out past the lights,
Meadows are storing this gift like cream,
Tangles of bush and twig fingers
Grow soft in its handling;
Over the cordwood and along the house
It drifts to rest,
Increases itself
Where it belongs.

Commonweal   *Richard A. Hawley*

TO THE CARP, AND THOSE WHO HUNT HER

"O, to be a dragon"
                         —*Marianne Moore*

The state set its whole official will
against you, dredges you out
or poisons the whole chain
of lakes. They break
every assumption of preservation and they can't
make you an endangered species.
You keep on,
prolific as the poor people.

You are no fit fish for those delicate
fellows at Fish & Wildlife—
rough fish, they call you. In China
old timers say you are the dragon's fry, the fish
of heaven.
            I've seen you in Wisconsin
moonlight rolling like your whales, playing
better than any other (except the otter)
on that lake and I've seen you bronze
backed in early morning, long and swift
with your big scales and whiskers, here-and-gone
through the rustled pickerel weed.

And in the evening I have seen boys mostly,
or men with tattoos and good
old fashioned hair
grease, come soft-stepping it out of the forest
to stalk with bow and arrow, keeping the wake
at their shins silent as it can be. Outcasts
of the snobs of trout and fly rods
with arrows and bows, they are by choice
non-casts.

       Oh, and I have watched you, fish
of heaven, here in Wisconsin, wrench
the bowmen your way as if, once sent, their arrows
will never stop. But, like the ancients,
a man with a tattoo bargains
for a heaven that is fierce and, once got,
hard to lose. From here, on the shore,
the captured bowmen
seem more silent and ready to fly than any
men I have ever seen. They have made
themselves, fish of the fiercest
heaven, delicate water-borne kites, breathless
at the end of your willful string.

The Mississippi Valley Review   *James Hazard*

DARK

I'll tell you why I'm afraid of the dark. It has its own idea.
It's like a bullet.
It doesn't want to know what you know.

The dark is under.
It fits a place to put a hand but I can't see.
It's like a voice behind a door.
It can be just about anything I want to hear.

Darkness comes in every size of threat:
the dark cocoon at the end of my life,
storms that turn the sky into an empty can of dark
fitting snug onto the horizon,
the dark in putting my head in my hands,
my head into the cave of a person I don't love anymore.

I'll tell you again why I'm afraid of the dark.
I can see it coming
and can't ever tell just when it has arrived.
I sense it thin and waiting between the pages of books,
but it's too fast even for a good reader.

From that place darkness
comes a phone call erratic with grief.
It fills the story called dying in your sleep
and was the only time left for voodoo to take,
for rapists to dress in.

I can't get a grip on darkness
though it wears my imagination like a shroud.
I've started hearing sunsets as cracking twigs.
I've taken to hiding a piece of flint in my shoe.

Bachy 14   *Eloise Klein Healy*

DINOSAUR

You came
nourished by
seaweed and moss
from shallow swamps,
genes frozen
against the future,
arriving too big for laps
or backyards,
at this place
of trained ponies
and humming cats,
like a mail-order gift
for the girl who has
everything,
unable to purr,
eating my roses.
Creature, you break
my china promises.
Your tongue on my face
leaves its mark.
The language you speak
died with the green,
rotting ferns
in a townless time
before flowers.
But you came,
plodding over ice
and concrete,
the light beneath
the slivers of your eyes
finding my light,
keeping it
like a hypnotist
counting backwards.
And I who have
never moved
one short step,
hang on
for dear life.

ASFA Poetry Quarterly   *Bonnie Hearn*

HARD WAY TO LEARN

A trickle of water from
a rotting snowbank tells me
the time has come to haul
one more load of manure to
the field before the frost
goes out and lets the muddy
ground suck the tractor wheels
down to the axle. The earth
will let me know when it is
ready to take the plow, as a
heifer in heat lets the bull
know when she is ready. Think of it,
forty years I farmed this place
and I still wait on it for
the time to plant. My wisdom
seems a little shaky compared
to what the land knows and makes
me suspicious of what I think
I've learned. I read signs and
add seed, ground, work, weather
and luck and hope for the best.
Strange, at my age, to be so
unsettled in my mind about crops,
weather and women—but no one gave me
a diploma when I was born.

Poetry   *James Hearst*

DRAGON LESSON

This country needs a few
live dragons, real fire-breathing,
tail-swishing, scaly, gold-defending,
maiden-snatching, nasty-tempered beasts.
Not fake scenes on a stupid TV screen,
but the real McCoy, a dragon that would
terrorize the countryside, eat a few
unbelievers, burn churches that preached
against dragons. Think how we would
huddle together, crying for another
St. George, begging for peace. Think of us
longing for, pleading for, praying for peace.
Just imagine it. And think of the lesson
our brave young men would learn, that if
they win the gold, they must keep the girl.

Yankee   *James Hearst*

KENNEDY

One late afternoon I hitched from Galway down to Kinvara on
the edge of the Burren, one of those long midsummer days when
the sun labors at last out of all-day rain and sets very late in the
evening. In dark pubs all up and down the street the townsmen
hunched to their pints silent and tentative as monks at supper.
Thinking to take my daily Guinness, I stopped, and Kennedy was
there, his picture on the mantel behind the bar.

A black-headed citizen, half in his cups, sidled over and smiled.
Ah Kennedy Kennedy, a lovely man, he said, and bought me a
Guinness. Ah yes, a lovely man, I said, and thank you very much.
Yes Kennedy, and they slaughtered him in his youth the filthy
communists, he said, and will you want another. Yes, slaughtered
him in his youth, I said, and thanked him very much.

All night, till closing time, we drank to Kennedy and cursed the
communists—all night, pint after pint of sour black lovely stout—
and when it came Time, I and my skin and the soul inside my
skin, all sour and lovely, strode where the sun still washed
the evening, and the fields lay roundabout, and Kinvara slept in
the sunlight, and Holy Ireland, all all asleep, while the grand brave
light of day held darkness back like the whole Atlantic.

The Chowder Review   *Michael Heffernan*

DAFFODILS

It wasn't the daffodils so much
as the idea of them that got
me. I was wandering by in my
own lonely manner like a cloud in the sky
feeling ugly and grim when out
of nowhere up blossomed a clutch

of yellow daffodils by the curb.
Bright things they were, good and sweet,
and I knew I liked them better than
music or money or my girl's friendly skin
the way they stood there by the street
nicer and newer and simpler

by far than anything I had seen
all morning. Oh, it was fine
to know them! I said, You daffodils
put me in mind of the clean white windowsills
of a kitchen when I was nine
one April Saturday in 19

51—my grandmother's kitchen,
her fingers dangling with dough,
the odor of pie in the oven,
the windows white as the windows of Heaven,

as if the air were bright with snow,
and someone outside them, watching.

Carolina Quarterly   *Michael Heffernan*

TWO WEEKS AFTER AN APRIL FROST

April's blossoms launch
Their smells at me
From every branch
Of every flowering tree;
There's a green
Deepening in the lawn
For the white magnolia petals to fall on—
But they blew too soon
To fall off white this year:
Bloomed white before any shoot of green,
Bloomed white where only grey black
Branches could be seen—
And then we had an April frost down here.
Only for an afternoon they lasted—
Came the freeze that night,
And they were blasted.
The pink white petals all turned brown,
And warming breezes
Haven't blown them down.
The magnolia's leaves have sprung,
But the rust brown flowers cling,
As if spring and fall
Were hung on the same small tree.
No winter's breath was ever so unkind,
Not when Orpheus turned and looked behind—
Our young spring snapped
Like a young green sapling bough;
Kore's become Persephone somehow;
The matron will not be a maiden, now.

The Hudson Review   *Steven Helmling*

COSMETIC

Speaking as a woman who has thought
        of touching up her hair,

speaking as a woman whose leg veins
        seem to grow more prominent every day,

speaking as a woman who this morning
        was hailed as "Douglas" by mistake,

speaking as a beautiful woman,

let me say:

beauty is not
in the eye of the beholder,
but in the person of
the solitary

unwatched

woman.

Northwest Review   *Gretchen Herbkersman*

THE SECOND NIGHT

This second night
Comes soft as bathroom tissue.
It lingers in pools of shadow
Where the light does not reach
Under the sofa, behind
The ruffled skirt of the overstuffed chair.

Your hands are hot; my forehead, cool.
The first night has undone me
Like a knot in a cord, and I dawdle,
Turning the pages of this book
I have read before without understanding.

Still, you have the look of longing;
Its haze descends to cloud my view.
I do not believe it would be enough
If there were two of you;
One to undo my tidy bed. The other
To hold my shrinking head
And thus encounter morning, cold and red.

We emerge from doubt and climb the stairs.
I snap my fingers to create a spark
To incinerate this mote-filled air
Halfway up, already full dark.

Webster Review   *M. L. Hester, Jr.*

WAR

Risen is the sleeper from the vaulted past,
Risen from down under and returned at last.
Huge and strange he looms there, in the twilight mist,
And he snuffs the moon out with a coal-black fist.

Cities teem with hubbub of the thickening dusk,
Frost and shadow swaddled in an alien husk;
Street-sounds of the markets halt their rounds and freeze.
Silence now. And no man knows, yet each man sees.

People in the alleys feel him on their trail.
Questions. And no answers. Faces turning pale.

Swinging in the distance, bells are whining thin.
Every beard is trembling on its pointed chin.

He's begun his *danse macabre* where the hilltops arch,
And he's screaming: "All you soldiers, forward march."
Listen to the pounding of his swart brow's pulse;
That jangling is his necklace of a thousand skulls.

Tower-tall he lumbers from the sun's last ray;
Bloody torrents follow on the heels of day.
Countless are the corpses that the swamp has spilt;
Droppings of the death-bird are their last white quilt.

*[Here three first-draft stanzas, partly in illegible handwriting
and partly repetitious in effect, have been omitted.—P.V.]*

Forest after forest feeds the flaming jaws;
Yellow bats of arson flex their zigzag claws.
Like a furnace-slavey, he hacks his poker deep,
Stoking up the embers to their wildest leap.

Hurtling without outcry into nightmare's gut,
Metropolis is choking on its own pale soot.
Over glowing rubble he gives a giant lurch;
Through frantic skies he three times waves his torch,

Mirrored in the hurricane of mangled clouds,
In the dead cold desert of the midnight shrouds.
Night itself dries up beneath his farflung fire;
Sodom has collapsed upon its funeral pyre.

The Michigan Quarterly Review   *Georg Heym*
                                        —*Translated by Peter Viereck*

ARE YOU THERE, MRS. GOOSE?

Cream sours in this weather. The black looks
we get from the sky, mutterings of doom, are bound
to have their effects. One can't laugh off
obituaries, once written.

This is the way we make our deaths
so early in the morning.

We may laugh, though, at stretches
of crisped grass, the prairie's sacrifice; we may look
across burnt blades to where heads,
ripening, bow stiffly as though acknowledging
favourable comment. No use crying off
hoppers, early frosts, men shaking their heads
at the bin doors, the spilt milk of
one summer or another.

Joe's cows are all jumping
over the moon.

Rest is still possible. Long sunlight hours
lose, untenable at best, their arguments
that appeared likely to knock our forecasts
every which way and our pessimisms with them.
We lacked faith in our opinions; years of studying
the sky should have told even the brashest
our frowns were well placed. We wanted the wit
to hold our expressions. Moments pass.

The wolf winds blow
and we shall have snow.

Wascana Review   *John V. Hicks*

FROM MISTRA: A PROSPECT

Of life the darkest part is solitude,
the realm of silent thought the soul transcends,
where waking fears in glad thanksgiving fall
like thunder from the open vaults of heaven.
The village on the hill sits poised, awaiting
capture, young champions, outriders of dawn.
But it is evening, and the trees have ceased
their dance, the echo of their leaves has died.
Upon a moonlit beach a girl appears,
who rushes to the sea to wash herself
of pleasures, fancies first conceived in love,
who turns to watch her lover rise, hawklike
into the night and vanish on the wind.
To the village she mounts and the old ones,
who sit like statues knowing they too
drew strangers under the sheets of the moon.
Toward me the girl's unblushing fingers reach,
her body moist from the spume of the waves.
In ragged caravans the spirits come
like weary serpents, a thunder of hope
as they pass southward into the evening air.
Take up your shield, my friend, the time has passed
for reverie, for freedom, and for love.

Arizona Quarterly   *Ted Higgs*

A WISH FOR WAVING GOODBYE

Later, when the scent of early leaves
from a far off grove reminds me
how we lay under their applause,
I'll miss touching the corner of your mouth
(You frowned a little even when you smiled),
but I'll keep driving north, north.
The telephone poles will recede.
Once you waved me gone,
your arm and hand drowned by hills.

I loved you. It doesn't matter.
Your heart beat against my skin,
and so entangled, we forgot
that this big world is crazed.
The gulls now cry above the wind.
Even awake, I hear them.
Life has opened its door again,
and grace, the largest space we know,
may be just across the threshold.

Suntracks   *Roberta Hill*

A CHINESE VASE

Sometimes I think that my body is a vase
With me in it, a blue-tiled Chinese vase

That I return to, sometimes, in the rain.
It's raining hard, but inside the little china vase

There is clean white water circling slowly
Through the shadows like a flock of yellow geese

Circling over a small lake, or like the lake itself
Ruffled with wind and geese in a light rain

That is not dirty, or stained, or even ruffled by
The medley of motors and oars and sometimes even sails

That are washed each summer to her knees. It's raining
In the deep poplars and in the stand of gray pines;

It's snowing in the mountains, in the Urals, in the
Wastes of Russia that have edged off into China.

The rain has turned to sleet and the sleet
Has turned to snow in the sullen black clouds

That have surfaced in the cracks of that Chinese
Vase, in the wrinkles that have widened like rivers

In that vase of china. It's snowing harder and harder
Now over the mountains, but inside the mountains

There is a sunlit cave, a small cave, perhaps,
Like a monk's cell, or like a small pond

With geese and with clear mountain water inside.
Sometimes I think that I come back to my body

The way a penitent or a pilgrim or a poet
Or a whore or a murderer or a very young girl

Comes for the first time to a holy place
To kneel down, to forget the impossible weight

Of being human, to drink clear water.

The Agni Review   *Edward Hirsch*

REMEMBERING APPLE TIMES

I came to see you in the spring,
when high were days and sun shone hot,
and often more and never not
the hand-held wine was truly mine.
Wide was ever-after time,
the apple blossoms white in wind.

I came in summer's wet and heat,
the sweat upon the lily's back;
and you a feast of wine and moss,
the ripples in the water clear.
Wide was sky, and meadow mild
the apple leaves against your face.

I brought the fall flame candle gold
when day would shine through window lace,
and neighbor boys were football kings
upon the morning backyard grass.
We laughed to see them tumble down,
and walked the apple meadow way
to shine the sound of love we made.

Now the winter breaks in cold,
and cold like splinters cracks and cuts.
Time goes tight in sidewalk steps
and clock hands snap the minutes by.
Doorknobs lock in single room sounds.
I drift across and dream the time
when ever-after time was mine.

Ball State University Forum   *John T. Hitchner*

FORTY POUNDS OF BLACKBERRIES EQUALS
THIRTEEN GALLONS OF WINE

At the end of summer
Before we exchange pine needles
For blacktop and concrete,
We have a day known as
Blackberry picking time.
It is a mark of humans
That they can forestall
Immediate pleasure
For future delight.
Thus, what could be a snack,
With a little patience
Can become a cobbler or pie.
Our children are at this level
Of gradual evolution.
They can wait, just barely,
Until the buckets are filled,
The crusts made, the oven heated,

The ice cream bought to spoon on top.
But they do not see the logic
Of waiting through winter
While yeast and sugar
Work in a frothing magic
To change berries,
That really should be eaten,
Into a hearty wine
They are not allowed to drink.

Wascana Review   *Robert D. Hoeft*

FROM GARVEY'S FARM: SENECA, WISCONSIN

i
While the sun is finishing
off the sky, wood mice
trap daylight beneath the snow,
braiding shreds of warm air into highways;
evening takes its cane to the cattle,
turns them toward the spine of earth
which leads to the open barn,
to the sound of running water
and the smell of sleeping corn.

Casually, the wind picks up its hammer
and pounds the trees into black foil:
framed by the kitchen window,
branches etch the figure of a woman
into the pliant air. Lazy dogs
crawl out of the cordwood
and go howling up the patched chimney
after the flowering smoke.
Later, nightfall takes the lady down.

ii
The greens and blues which dreams need
have gone south; sleep must be spread
over the cool, white flannel sheets
and, even then, will not come easily.
On clear nights, the moon goes
skating past the northern lights
which flicker like the sword outside Eden;
if it's cloudy, the stars drop
their pocketwatches: snow comes ticking down.

By dawn, the grey fire sounds
like an old man walking up the stairs.
The sparrows that roost in the pin oak
wind up their hearts: they tilt
against the remaining leaves
which have tucked their burned colors
inwards, like seashells. The leaves whisper
about the tide that comes and goes

around the wings of the great owls.
The sparrows listen, warm up, and wait.

iii

The day is clear and the barn is full;
there are chores to be done. A fresh sun
wakes the thunder beneath the pond,
lightening runs across the ice, kicking
at the sky. All night long the barn rocked,
the white foal galloping through the meadow
inside her: she is tired, anxious
for space; her green breath
must be turned out to the wind.

The paper is late, comes in a pickup.
Spread on the kitchen table, it says
that the boy who usually delivers
has dropped from an iceboat
into the moving water below the dam.
The weather promises to hold:
another clear night, another moon
skating into the garden, and the foal's
young eyes opening to take the cold.

The Black Warrior Review   *Ed Hoeppner*

CASTING AT NIGHT

Stripping off another yard of line,
I let it play out across my fingers,
unseen into darkness. This earth finds
its unities in night: all elements alike,
lacking definition, except that slight hint
of something civilized ridging light
around a distant stand of cedar.

I can feel the trout: thin bodies
lingering behind that frieze of rapids
audible below, exploring every cul-de-sac
of sediment and weeds in the hollow
pool beyond. I can feel their hunger
as something palpable, place
their feeding forms in blackness.
Still, I'd just as soon ignore them,
exercise the dumb machinery of bones.
Tonight, I find my own unities
in darkness: feel all sky and water
through my fingers; this weighted line
buzzing back and forth, threading
night behind me with the dim
vocabulary of rocks and stream ahead.

Sou'wester   *Allen Hoey*

HIMSELF

The one most like himself is not this mirror's
Dishonest representation
Of a familiarly strange person

Growing more crinkled around the eyes,
But one on whom he has not set his eyes,
One he knows is in this house with him.

In this very room there is
A youth he has outgrown, whose ease
With the world is greater than his own,

Whose gifts are greater than his gifts,
Whose joys are deeper joys
Than any he has known.

By the time that he began
To grow apart from that potential grace
He had never worn its face,

His callow years were all a waste
Of foolish choices and false satisfactions.
The blessing given him at last

Across the alien years
Is that he now may judge his actions
By what that one most like himself would do

Whose ease with the world shames his unease,
Whose delight exceeds the joys he's known,
Whose gifts are greater than his own.

The Hudson Review   *Daniel Hoffman*

INDULGENCES

Peaches so sweet this summer
I can smell the blossom shining through them.
Tomatoes so big the vines can't hold.
I sit under crab apple trees beside my son
and the day has a meaning so clear, so comfortable
I could carry it under my arm.

We are all dancers out under the moon
but not the reason the sun wakes.
This evening in Colorado there will be a man
walking his shepherd along a quiet street.
A lady in Japan will press flowers
in a book of Rilke and cry softly.
And it will rain on the warm earth.

National Forum   *Michael Hogan*

THE FISHERMAN CASTS HIS LINE INTO THE SEA

The fisherman casts his line into the sea.
The woman waits in the house upon the hill.
The fish swim in the dark, and cannot see.

Far to the east, beyond where he can see,
The buoy rises, falls, and clangs its bell.
The fisherman casts his line into the sea.

And on the high hill, the empty tree
Stands by the house, the woman at the sill.
The fish swim in the dark, and cannot see.

Jesus, fishing the dark Galilee,
Thought he heard a cry from a far hill.
The fisherman casts his line into the sea.

The woman sees the starlings fill the tree,
Emptying the sky above the hill.
The fish swim in the dark, and cannot see.

The house stares blankly out to sea.
The woman hears the silence in the bell.
The fisherman casts his line into the sea.
The fish swim in the dark, and cannot see.

The Midwest Quarterly   *Robert Holland*

ICE CREAM IN PARADISE

(for J.A.M.)

What the child wants longs the man for:
"Will there be ice cream in heaven?"
O no child, for when you ripen
you will not want that,
at least not there. Ice cream
or pears or apples, these are
but trifles. How your heart grows
is learning better. And from these simples
you'll turn to cures, you'll want
just what you must want, to be just,
to be loving, to be graceful. Do you follow?
It is a harmony of all your soul.
"And will there be harmony in heaven?"

The Southern Review   *Robert Hollander*

YOUR WOODS

I can't do it often.
My wild cat sleeps
splayed on the sofa,
underchin up like a fishbelly,
a floating wreckage

on the airy currents
of his birdstorming dreams.

Gently, I lower my face
into the downy fur
and its scent of clean oils,
woodsmoke and rosemary,
and this fragrant memory
so subtly awakening
and so tentatively kneading
its claws into my temples.

Primavera   *Margaret Holley*

THE MEETING

I turned upon the world an inward eye,
shut all my doors so that I might not see;
drew back my skirts to let the world pass by
and would not stoop to feel its touch on me;
shut up my hopes with all their fragile fare;
fed my own angers; felt their fierce reply,
and, dead myself, let long-dead specters tear
this beauty that should live in those who die,
and in my fury felt my deep soul burn
that flamed itself, and knew itself as flame.
No greater fool had heaven ever known
than I was, till I heard you speak my name . . .
when the wide world had changed my day to night
then you came forth, and all the earth was light!

The Lyric   *Jocelyn Hollis*

FAMILY PORTRAIT

Features frozen in time,
We sit stiff,
Staring into the future,
Mindless of the day
Dust would frame our dreams.

All dead now,
Our names lost
To new generations;
We hold the pose,
Captives of the camera.

Delta Scene   *Rebecca Hood-Adams*

IN THE CANADIAN ROCKIES

Here majestic mountains tower—
Ball, Columbia, Eisenhower—
Beckon, threaten, smile, or lower.

Glaciers in the sunlight glisten,
Emerald streams down gorges hasten,
Roots to cliffs bold pine trees fasten.

Underfoot, blue gentian, yellow
Dryas, rose and purple mallow,
Smooth and shining-green wolf-willow.

Mountain goat and horned sheep scramble
Over rocks where waters tumble.
Bold and fearless the ensemble

Where majestic mountains tower,
Beckon, threaten, smile, or lower—
Ball, Columbia, Eisenhower.

The Lyric   *Virginia Shearer Hopper*

CHILDREN'S LENTEN WISDOM

Ashes, ashes, all fall down
Upon their knees before their God;
Ashes, ashes, all fall down
And bare their backs for chast'ning rod.

Ashes, ashes, all fall down
Christ's forty days to emulate;
Ashes, ashes, all fall down
Upon their sins to meditate.

Ashes, ashes, all fall down
Anticipate the Christ's return;
Ashes, ashes, all fall down
The discipline of sorrow learn.

Soon the pocketful of posey,
Soon the Crucified will rise;
Soon the ring around the rosey,
Soon Easter anthem swell the skies.

But now we learn from children's game
The time to smile, the time to frown;
Recurring Lent is still the same:
Ashes, ashes, all fall down.

Christianity Today   *James A. Houck*

I SHALL NEVER GO

I shall never go to the Caribees; the sand beaches,
The luxuriant tropical growth, these I shall leave
To the natives with tawny skins, to women with black hair,
To bold adventurers who spit salt spray and sing
While skippering their craft among the reefs and shoals.
What devil drives that we must glorify all foreign climes?
Our lives are brief enough. I hear no final answers

From those tropic shores, no more of love or hate
Than I receive from my own consciousness of humankind.
Thus long ago I cast my hero's role in contexts
Nearer home. A few short miles away the cliffs
Drop just as sharply to the sea, the kelp beds
Rise and fall in tides and currents fierce enough
To make the best turn pale. Blue water sailors know
That death comes close to shore no matter where
And that, despite our dreams, the gods prevail.

Kansas Quarterly   *A. J. Hovde*

FOUR FAWNS

This morning came down
Through pinewoods
To eye our pond;
    Moving about, they startled . . .
    Then blended away.
But I think I caught one picture—
At least in the heart's camera—
    Their disclosure, in nature,
    Reminds me of you, of blending.

The New England Galaxy   *Barbara Howes*

THE HOUR OF PRAYER

How glorious is the hour of secret prayer,
When one withdraws to some familiar place,
Perhaps a quiet room with desk and chair,
Where supplication meets refreshing grace!
As Aaron moved the sacred veil aside,
And gazed with wonder on Shekinah fire,
The praying soul with vision clarified
May also to the holy flame aspire
With gifted utterance as the Spirit wills,
And glowing unction in a mind renewed.
O rapturous moment when the Lord fulfills
His promised word in blissful solitude!
Though one may simply kneel at desk or chair,
How glorious is the hour of secret prayer!

The Pentecostal Evangel   *Albert L. Hoy*

VOICE OF THE CROCUS

Bedded in tranquility,
Blanketed with silence,
I slept.
But now, while winter lingers,
Slowly, slowly,

There comes the nudge of life
That will not be denied,
    The urge to seek the light.
    Slowly, slowly, I find my way
    Through darkness of the soil,
    Upward, ever upward
        Until the final thrust
        That penetrates the dark
        To let the doubting see
        Resurrected life in me.

Unity   *Mildred N. Hoyer*

MODERN AMERICAN NURSING

I think you have to be Catholic to be a nurse, stretching
    yourself taut upon a cross of mea culpa, mea culpa—
    I'm not doing enough.
I will take on twenty patients—no, make it thirty—and
    all with the most catastrophic of diseases and treading
    on the borders of death.
Running down long, neon hallways, lifting bottoms onto
    bedpans and poking little glass tubes into all manner
    of human openings in search for various meter readings.
The telephone will ring incessantly in a harsh contest with
    the old lady down the hall who cries all the time, all
    the time, and supervisor will tell me my white shoes are
    unpolished; she's pulling one of my aides to work in the
    ICU and was I really sick that day I called in?

I think you have to be a third-world person to be a nurse,
    to suffer centuries in poverty and shadow until rage
    is a simmering and brooding creature.
Knowing both the subtle and outrageous forms of punishment
    that take centimeters of dignity slowly, slowly, until you
    are a perfect human form curled around a charred and
    rotted tube all beneath a white cap. Functioning.

I think you have to be a woman to be a nurse. Smiling sweetly,
    nodding, acquiescing, accommodating and turning around
    again to save a life more important than that of its
    savior, who indeed would never think of saving herself.

Anima   *Lucy Hricz*

NEWTON'S THIRD

To every action, they say,
There is an equal opposite.
Such balances entwine
To check all motion.
The leaning mast shows with infinite
Precision how the ship's keel

Counterpoises each catspaw puff.
And thus in war, when titans grapple,
All thrusts dissolve to the force-free
Quietude of No Man's Land.

And so it is in poker, when the
Tight circle of computed chips
For one instant exactly measures
Each man's estimate of cards
                            he cannot see.
In those seconds his calculation sits
Sound, even though the downfaced cards
Shall repudiate his shrewdest bid.

With us, my dear, all cards
Now stand upfaced bold.
                    There's your horny
Seven, my knave, your wild deuce,
Your loving five, my bitter ten.
Now, you must agree, no sane player
Would put down chips of reckoning
Against upfaced cards
Where the player's fate is known
Before the bidding starts
Except, perhaps, in Stud;
Would you then, milady,
                     take a turn at Stud?
We've played before.
Four cards up, and one card down
Upon its face. No? Not today?

And so we hang, by Newton's Third,
In perfect counterpoise
                    on undialled phones.
Though subtle balances entwine,
The web is cut
Leaving just the bones,
And five cards up.

Canadian Forum   *Jake T. W. Hubbard*

MINE

Work in a mine and become a mine.
Let coal grind into knees
until the skin is tattooed gray.
Let coal dust work into eyelids
until it can't be scrubbed out
and farmboys sniggering eyeshadow
hustle fights in bars. Work long enough
in the earth, breathing earth,
and coal blacks over the lungs,
sparkling dark in the dark of the body.

Work in a mine and become a mine.

From age, from grief, from chance expression,
each line in a miner's face
is there forever—drawn in soot—
until the men become ink drawings
smudged into someone like themselves.
On Florida's pink beaches, surfacing,
they embarrass their brown children
and cannot relax. With each deep
probing cough, they are mining.

Southwest Review   *Andrew Hudgins*

MY RELATIVES FOR THE MOST

My relatives for the most
part
were not pillars holding up stone roofs
but rather planks stepped on
taken for granted
until the splinters lifted up
inclined and pricked an intruding toe
My relatives for the most part
were not words tossed
through the corn and strawberries
under the mules' feet
making ink out of water and wait
when they grew something that had no claim to share
My relatives for the most part
knew nothing of taking life
away with a pointed scorn stick
they just knew whittling ways
of making wood
fly away in the night
from logs that became generals and boats
that held their tongues and hulls tight
about the rich human waste
that kept itself under outhouses
rather than make the corn and strawberries
stop the white man's mule stop
in his traces.

The Massachusetts Review   *Frederick B. Hudson*

MILL AT ROMESDAL

(for Dr. Calum MacRae)

One look at this mill and the adjacent croft,
the local intimate way grass slants to the mill,
the sea beyond the broken waterwheel, and we know
here we could keep some private promise to improve.
We could reinforce the floor

where grain was milled, repair the tracks
for the grain cart, redivert the small stream
back into the flume and start the mill again.
Send the word out now: your miller
is open to all who bring raw grain.

If we could turn our lives that way, the way
the mill stones turned, slow and even,
the milled grain falling dreamy all day
every day but Sunday into carts, we'd find
some recent peace, a composure we never quite trust
in family portraits. We'd be wise to allow
for the loch that hammers inside
and that man not on record who broke one day
in the byre and demanded the cattle say thanks.
With this loch pale in our faces and money
collected last year for milling turning
to dust at the touch, we really are happy, are happy—
our voices run down late summer,
the stream without pressure and the waterwheel limp.

If we count bones found on Skye, we get
Celtic, a lot, Viking, very few, despite
three centuries of occupation and Nordic names
that hang on: Hinnisdal, Monkstadt, Eyre.
The Viking bones found here

don't care what we or the man they belonged to did.
They don't blush for their part in oppression,
innocent women in shock.
There's a way of saying, "Yes! We were rotten, so what?"
Of saying it anytime we want to the sea
that answers softly in Gaelic and doesn't indict.

We won't restore the mill. The waterwheel's
broken beyond repair and, if we got the two stones
back in gear and grinding, no one raises grain
today on this island. The modern Norwegian ship
needs papers to sail these waters. The Viking bones
are in Glasgow for date and classification.
We own the mill in the warmest sense of own.
Let's keep it run down. Let's keep the crofter's cottage
empty and cold. If anyone asks for a miller
we'll say, that's what we were once, and worse.
This is what we are now.

Poetry   *Richard Hugo*

THE ROAD OF BIRDS

The fields close in on all sides,
Slide across late summer air.
Mengel's farm settles with age.
I kneel
And the ground rises with grackles,

Yellow-shafted flickers, larks.
They vanish around cornfields
Or into the locust trees.

The road rises, too,
Toward the old lime kiln
And the meadows of alfalfa.
I walk there past the stream,
Past the rock fence
To the woods,
And sit there,
Watching as one by one the birds
Appear, disappear,
Grow silent in the light
That folds itself against the coming dusk.

I can feel a turning over in the air.
Yesterday I saw the phoebe's nest
Brimming with a second brood.
North of me wings fill with migration
Near ridge or river bluff.

When I stand,
A moth tilts against the flat light;
A female killdeer
Flutters the air with her cries.
I follow her to the dirt road.

It's late now.
Suddenly the killdeer
Flies over my head back to her field.

Watching her,
I think of all the distances
Of coming night,
My own motions into love or dreams
And the earth spinning,
The universe endless as blood,
And nothing ever really at dead rest.

Sou'wester   *Harry Humes*

LIFELINES

This rain that has come from far away, like breath:
The veins of my eyes are empty and it fills them.
I cannot remember where it has beaten so long.

I have written to the water of my trials:
Of the parts of my hands that are vanishing, of the lines
That are already gone. I have told the rivers all
My doubts, and the sea
Has somehow uncovered the things
I could never confess. Now, suddenly at the end
Of a lifetime's correspondence, a cloud has risen
Out of my sins, and water comes
Falling into all my empty beds.

Now like a bridge lifted out of the sun,
Like the arc of a shadow over rivers, my vision grows
In colors of that water, and spreads itself
Before me, wide as a heart.

So many things I know can never be
Forgiven. Things that have disappeared
And cannot be washed away.
But the rain is tumbling now, blind as a pulse
Down through the streams of my palms,
The deep lifelines.

The Chariton Review   *T. R. Hummer*

ANTS

It is springtime and the ants come into the house.
They are searching for something, not in lines yet
but scattered all over as if a great wealth had been
changed into pennies and thrown about the room.
This is how it feels to be lost in a long depression.
They stick to what's what. They feel every surface
with feelers, like hands searching dressers in the dark.
Small and full of legs they crawl below the oceans of air
that smell of lilacs and roses, and do not get involved.

New Letters   *Lewis Hyde*

THE LAST FLIGHT OF THE GREAT WALLENDA

A hazy day in Puerto Rico
And the crowd takes its heat from you,
Old Master, Great Ropewalker, raven.
Up to the rooftop with lithe gait you climb—
A quick trick, you pick up the pole, pause
While you and the air weigh the wires,
Your labyrinth across the street.

Below, we rage and build our pyramids
On our own shoulders, tight or slack.
Some of us hang on with circus-act finesse,
Some vaudeville in the ring,
But you leap to our pounding hearts
And tease us with your stunt.
We love it when you make it one more time,
Melting along the rope, drop by waxen drop.

Go ahead, Wallenda, fly.
Clutch your pole to seek a balance,
Curl your toes to a grimace
And mock the windburst from the west.
Dazzle us and strut your life
above our heads, inch by defiant inch.
Shout an answer to our gaping mouths
In your own "oh's": life is a dare.

And when you fall and crush your bones
And drown your carcass in cement
We flee, wing-clipped sparrows,
From the thud.

The Altadena Review   *Barbara Helfgott Hyett*

MY OWN HOUSE

As I view the leaf, my theme is not the shades of meaning
that mind conveys of it but my desire to make the leaf
speak to tell me, Chlorophyll, chlorophyll, breathlessly,
and I would rejoice with it and in turn would say, Blood,
and the leaf nod. Having spoken to each other, the topics
would become inexhaustible and think, as I grow old and
the leaf begins to fade and turn brown, the thought of
being buried in the ground would be so familiar to me then,
so thoroughly known to me through conversation with the
leaf that my walk among the trees, after completing this
poem, would be like entering my own house.

Chicago Review   *David Ignatow*

WHAT I DID LAST SUMMER

I listened to the foliage grow at night,
the lilacs glowing purple underneath a moon I set
my sights on early, rhubarb rustling underneath
the bedroom window in a wind that filled the air with pollen flecks
of imitation snow and gave a ghostly texture
to the world of darkness. In the morning
I'd arise and send a message through a can strung taut
between my bedroom window and a tree, consume
a soldier's breakfast from a bowl and go out riding
on my Hawthorne like a scout the cavalry
was so dependent on in Wagons West.
At noon we ate our jelly sandwiches and listened
as the radio reported grave statistics from the war.
To give the day perspective I'd go out again,
a playing card attached between my spokes
to let the forces know that I was still a child,
to warn the Crow who rode with Custer I had taken sides.

Neworld   *Ron Ikan*

INVOCATION FROM A LAWN CHAIR

A wildness in the grass has closed
beneath the mower's roar. Composed,
the weeds; the sidewalks hosed.

Here no clover vagrancies

are fumble-buzzed by fuzzy bees.
How neat, complete, the tailored trees.

In pink and ivory double row
along the concrete patio,
two dozen powdered roses grow.

Christ! for the smell of some liondark jungle,
regal and riding on beat of drums!
Pound, you June, and swell with blood
and heavy stalking secret
come:
trophic ambush of the moon.

The Christian Century   *Mary Jean Irion*

HOLDING ON

(for his father, prematurely old)

1

This morning he studied the dead wasps
caught between the pane and screen of
a window some winter warped shut
        when he could still remember
        the old words for knowing.
        For weeks now the deer have
        shed their antler moss.
Men in the field behind him are steering
the billowing pea sacks like sails.
        He tells me quietly there are
things that always remember, as—
this morning we stood beneath the pine
plucking kernels loose from cones,
        fingers webbed with sap,
becoming, almost, the trees themselves,
until a crow's first scream called us back.

2

My daughter has been tugging worms
        out of small spike holes
        robins have left in the sod.
They stretch—elastics, she laughs—
        snapped loose like dead
        skin around her fingernails.
But we have avoided a dead owl in
        the grass just beyond:
and I have read where Swift describes
the brain as carrion corrupted into worms
        still holding the loose
        shape of the mother animal.
My daughter has been tugging worms
Beyond, a windfall light is falling

into yellow grass beneath the trees.
It's her way, she says, of imitating birds,
a way of learning how to fly.

3

      He sits at the top of a hill,
his face sagged like those on pumpkins
we used to keep till they rotted,
      counting branches that are filled
with the gauze nests of gypsy moths,
his thoughts rising not from himself but
      from the rock-filled field
      where they have been woven,
      and he lifts a voice up
into the sun for just a moment,
a thread passing between his teeth,
loud kite in a remembered sky.

Prairie Schooner   *Richard Jackson*

MAKING AN IMPRESSION

I am here again
in this sleek, yellow, plastic place,
crowded in by chrome and gray metal
apparatus, which makes me think
of the unblinking eyes of German
technicians, scientific craftsmen—how they
carry on the marvelous tradition, precision;
and it is true, there are "racial traits,"
springing from what impulse, I wonder—
the imitation of the past? a chauvinistic wish
to fulfill, make real the national type?
place handholds on identity? I am lying
back on the reclined yellow chair, my head
caught within the padded V beneath it, and
a blonde girl in a white dress has her fingers
inserted in my mouth, pressing
against my lips, holding me open, waiting out
the sixty seconds for the impression
to harden, and I think:

why should I not eat up her fingers,
suck them down into me, be-
come a dragon suddenly, with fire
in my throat
and no need of teeth.

Cedar Rock   *William (Haywood) Jackson*

AUTUMN ORCHARD

Here was the autumn orchard where now stand,
Identical, the new, the gleaming houses.

Would I might hold an apple in my hand
As easily as memory arouses
What once was here, for I am seeing now
The western sun behind the burdened trees.
Would I might pluck one apple from the bough
As easily as I remember these.

How can I learn to walk serenely here
Beside conventional roadway, step, and door,
Who cannot free the wish, nor hide the tear
For what is lost, for what has gone before?
I should be told that there is, after all,
An essence and an irony in fall.

The Lyric   *Catherine Haydon Jacobs*

EMBROIDERY

Every time we meet,
it's so surprising,
you are always other
than I had remembered.

Why does my mind
keep playing that trick
of editing impressions?

Your kisses are not soft,
your voice not gentle,
you do not look at me
in any special way, just
in that certain way.

Rounding the jagged edges,
polishing highlights,
cutting and splicing,
dubbing in music,
the whole homogenizing
process begins
the minute our backs
are turned.

Two separate points only
—kick and wrench, that is
meeting and parting—
give no scope for enlargement
or diminution.
They are real.
They have no dimensions.

In between lies
embroidery.

The Malahat Review   *Maria Jacobs*

THERE IS GOOD NEWS

a law
removing from use the monosyllable *love*
for a period of three years; pro-
mulgated by a poet, and un-
enforceable. But a law.

The monosyllable
(which I may no longer name)
will be unavailable to:
carbonated drinks; pimps; all ad-
vertising agencies; candidates;
graduation addresses;
haute couture; hill-billy
bands; and, under the worst penalties, all
Interested Parties.

This will deprive
children; those dying; lovers; and those
other needy. But it is hoped
that in the fourth year
someone as yet unknown
will enunciate a syllable
of force
so tall as to unite
roots and
heavenly bodies.

Yankee   *Josephine Jacobsen*

POEM FOR MY MOTHER

What do you say to your mother on
Valentine's Day? I am usually saying good-
bye and there I am in the driveway
leaving, waving to you in the window;

you with your apron your warm smile but nervous
hands, your dance of weak knees
and the broken look in your eye. But I wave
you wave, maybe I honk and around the

corner I curse, slam my fist on the
dash, hating the way I hurt you but
then I sometimes remember in spring from our house
how we used to watch the robin family how

even then I felt like a little bird with
wings and you always you being the one
who builds the nest and keeps it there and
that's the price you pay raising the kind of bird

that flies.

Nitty Gritty   *Lowell Jaeger*

SONG OF THE FARMWORKER

I work like a pump in my own sweat
till one of us drops, the sun
or me. I work with a pulse
splitting my skin for that one slice
of white bread you hang on a hot limb
so it dries. Boss man,
you're the only thing dark
in a long field of fever and light.
You're the shade at a distance, that hurts.
At night, all my fluids
are gone, and my sore blood won't budge.
With no spit to oil my mouth,
the bread which is all crust, the one
piece, won't go down,
it won't go down.

Confrontation   *T. R. Jahns*

AFTER YOUR DEATH

it happens
even in my own house
I get lost
half way up the stairs
or opening a door
I forget where I am
what I'm doing
& so I panic
grabbing hold of a bedpost
or burrowing in the stairwell
listening to everything:
old wood boards
squeaking like muffled crickets
footsteps moving around in the kitchen
the voice
from a radio or TV
a clock ticking away in the next room
I stay frozen
perfectly still
& glance
at the walls
pictures
furniture
my own hands
trying to remember
but it's only your face
held up in mid-air
floating toward me
that I recognize
that places me

again
inside
this small body.

Sou'wester   *David James*

WOMEN CALLED BOSSY COWBOYS

The journal Literary Gazette says dozens of irate
men have written to complain that liberated Soviet
women are losing their femininity and acting like
men in their smoking/drinking/cursing and having
free sex

The Soviet Union's new breed of working women have
forgotten how to be women

Every man dreams of a woman who's soft/loving/
expressive/affectionate/modest and shy

They're getting harder and harder to find

Men are getting fed up with crude women who have
the manners of cowboys/their bossy shouts around
the house/their shabby ways of dressing/their
swaggering way of drinking bottoms-up like a man/
turns the home into a crude barracks

Every man would like to see in his house an
atmosphere of softness/warmth and purity

Even at the front in the Second World War girls
wearing boots and greatcoats managed to keep their
femininity

Now it's hard to distinguish the girls from the guys/
their vulgar laugh/swaggering walk/cigarettes/and
their language makes even strong men blush

Women assume a great share of the Soviet workload.
They make up 52% of the collective farm workers and
48% of the factory workers

Canadian Forum   *Beth Jankola*

THE WAIT

No use trying to hurry it. It

will arrive when it's ready. Nine months

you say? Then you cannot delay it.

It has already decided what
you will name it. It will push you off

your chair, take your place at the table.
It is planning to sleep in your bed,

wear your pajamas. In due time it
will feed you rat poison, or run an

exhaust pipe into your room. Oh do
not weep. All is planned and natural.

Even now it is curled in a fist.

Thumb in mouth it is laughing at you.

The Atlantic Monthly   *Phyllis Janowitz*

DEATH

Listen,
she spent her days.
Her coins ran out,
the machine shut down.
That's all.

No cry, no call,
no rage can turn the current on again.
Only the coin of a day
and all her coins were spent.

Into the slot
one
by one
until the last.
And then the current off.
That's all.

Look, there was a locked box that leaked coins—
some gala in the hand,
some acid-bit,
that bent, this nicked.

Coins Spent.
Current cut.
That's all.

Xanadu   *Mildred Jeffrey*

DIVORCE

I picture it as coming
home alone on a frigid
dark night in shall we

say January to an empty
house: no heat on, no
lights on, no one there,
every last one of them
elsewhere, and nothing on

the stove, the stove cold,

the ice box and cupboards
bare, the mail all ads,
the phone dead, the TV
unplugged, on the stairs
a singular ringing silence,

and on each floor and in
each room no
one.

Carolina Quarterly   *Kate Jennings*

WESTERN MOVIES

The Black Hills are threatening to run dry
On Deadwood at daybreak and distraught Indians
Are reflecting on who should lay the girl
With the mica eyes, who should die a noble death
At the hands of a self-appointed hangman—
Constant rewrites in the script.
A school marm brushes up on her Chaucer,
Traces English lore in the dirt
Of a western town for the benefit
Of the miners' sons who are dying to leave
Their marks on the expanding West,
Become bigger than life in a director's dream.
Smoke leads a drunken husband home
And a hunting party points itself toward Hollywood
Just as the screening room door slams shut.

Contemporary Quarterly   *Jeffry Jensen*

FLEETING RETURN

What was he like, my God, what was he like?
—Heart to be heartless so, mind to be shallow!—
The passing by of breezes, was he lithe
As that, or as the fleeing of the Spring?
As light, as fragile quick, as airy as
A summer dandelion; irresolute
As a slight smile which might yet lapse or laugh;
Vain as a banner snapping in the wind!
Banner, dandelion, smile, fugitive
Spring in June, the breeze's purity:
How crazy was your circus, and how sad!
All your change was for nothing—memory,
The blind bee of bitterness. I do not know
What you were like, but only that you were.

Contemporary Quarterly   *Juan Ramon Jimenez*
              —Adapted from the Spanish by William Moritz

THE BOARDING

One of these days under the white
clouds onto the white
lines of the goddamn PED
XING I shall be flattened,
and I shall spill my bag of discount
medicines upon the avenue,
and an abruptly materializing bouquet
of bums, retirees, and Mexican
street-gangers will see all what
kinds of diseases are enjoying me
and what kind of underwear and my little
old lady's legs spidery with veins.
So Mr. Young and Lovely Negro Bus
Driver I care exactly this: zero,
that you see these things
now as I fling my shopping
up by your seat, putting
this left-hand foot way up
on the step so this dress rides up,
grabbing this metal pole like
a beam of silver falling down
from Heaven to my aid, thank-you,
hollering, "Watch det my medicine
one second for me will you dolling,
I'm four feet and det's a tall bus
you got and it's hot and I got
every disease they are making
these days, my God, Jesus Christ,
I'm telling you out of my soul."

Poetry   *Denis Johnson*

INDIAN SUMMER HERE, YOU IN HONOLULU

(for Elizabeth Shinoda)

It is the Gulf Stream wind's illusion,
This summer weather when it should be fall:
Cordial vapours buoy the tricked out leaves
And lure the bees once more into the cider dew
Of orchards. In the bogs, the migrants
Pause knee-deep in the wash of burgundy
Fruit, drawn by the tilt of blue-winged teal
Into the tamaracks. For them,
The south is here, now.

And you,
Inured to summer on an island of slow time,
Sift thought-out leaves of other poets' minds.
Immune to sudden warmth's intrusion,

You could not know the hope false seasons bring,
Or how a tropic wind's delusion
Argues truth far into winter toward the spring.

So I am drunk on mellowed air
And, like the aging year, this summer spirit's
Willing fool. She winks and her laughter blooms
Along her path. But the wind
In the wake of her skirts is cold.

National Forum   *Donald Johnson*

STUFF

Pretty white lady
In the glassine bag.
Disguising reality
Under the name of scag.

Many a night
We made love to the moon.
I'd be so high
In the dopefiend's swoon.

So peaceful the words
You spoke to me.
This world ain't nothing,
So let it be.

Many times I had
A problem or two
But they all went away
When in came you.

Some take you in toots,
Called a one and one.
When we got together,
I'd like to gun.

I'd do anything
For your glorious high.
From robbing and stealing,
To telling a lie.

You were well quiet kept,
We know this by far.
It was the money-making nigger
Who made you a star.

You was always cool
For niggers like me.
When you choked alabaster kids,
It just could not be.

Then they showed up
With that methadone thang.
Hitler's tonic,
With a mixture of tang.

Since dual wrongs
Could not make right.
I put you down
And began to fight.

A question to the public,
So fitting you see.
Dare to answer,
If honest you be.

'Tis a funny thing
Here in the pen.
We can't get out,
But the lady gets in.

Southern Exposure   *H. B. Johnson*

ON THE DATES OF POETS

I open an anthology
and thumb through the pages. Starting somewhere
around the turn
of the twentieth century,
maybe with Graves,
most of the dates are incomplete,
as if the ledgers were only half carved.

Parentheses enclose
each poet's year of birth, a dash, and then
an empty space,
as though, if I would hold my praise
and wait, more numbers might appear
and he enjoy
the consummate symmetry of the dead.

Kansas Quarterly   *Michael L. Johnson*

THE CORNER

One house in my walk holds a corner
where hollyhocks fade in the too much sun.
The flowers are a stoppage of being,
stringing back this time to the lost ones:
all the old Finnish grandmothers
and their brown cotton stockings,
the smell of kerosene stoves
and the lack of singleness.

If I do not think too long
I can understand the aging words,
the laughter which comes from the very sound
of the rich words, the stories and tears
over outraged foolishness.
The adolescent survived the fighting

now/then/when
with children whose parents
heard other words
and took the royal chance that hollyhocks
and the sound of Finland in your blood
could outlast the many suns of future days.

The Georgia Review   *Rita Johnson*

SOME SCRIBBLES FOR A LUMPFISH

I've tried pitying you
For each way
Grace has spent itself
Far inland
On the slightest
Weed, left you treading bottom,
The shape of the ache of a slapped cheek.

But as the air admits
Bums easily as debutantes, I'm learning
What's ugly in you
Is my own
Failure to hear in the heart's frumpy
Drudging

That closet fugue each lifetime brews,
As if what persists awhile, no
Matter how slurred
Or humdrum, cannot help but gather to it

A little swank
And glide.

Northwest Review   *Thomas Johnson*

NATIVE AFRICAN REVOLUTIONARIES

As I watch the moon
casually rising tonight,
I am reminded of the hippos of Botswana.
Every night they rise out of still pools
to feed.

Walls surround mango orchards.
The hippos of Botswana travel like darkness,
darkness that penetrates any barrier.

The hippos of Botswana stand
in mango orchards reflecting
the moonlight like grey planets.
At dawn there are no ripe mangoes
for miles.

Carolina Quarterly   *Paul Jones*

TANGO

I am that binge you need
in the middle of the year
when your Christmas bonus
your vacation
your raise
are still months away
I am the dissonant note
that helps you through the monotonous harmony
that you say is your life
I am that instant of madness
that lets you endure the rest of the hour
the praise so convincing it dispels your doubts
the urn into which you cast your pathetic "you-don't-understand" 's
your little daily frustrations
your:
the-coffee-is-cold
who-opened-my-letter
another-gas-bill

I am the one who awakens the unknown recesses of your skin
the one who makes you say
when I'm with you I feel like a schoolboy again

I am
in other words
that woman you take to a hotel
the night you're out drinking
the one whose name you forget to ask
or ask if you could see again.

Review   *Elena Jordana*
                                —Translated by Kathrine Jason

SONNET FOR A LOVED ONE

There is a world of pain beyond the heart
Where sunlight shines unseen, birds sing unheard.
Lord, if you have no compass or no chart
To lead me there, give me one guiding word.
It is a world where values are compressed,
Where hand on hand is eloquence profound,
Where sleep is a gift held dear and blessed,
Where whispers are cacophonies of sound.

My loved one lives there, Lord, and I would go
There, too, just long enough to memorize
Its boundaries, just long enough to know
Its hills and vales, and how the landscape lies.
I find this world of mine no longer fair
With a world of pain so near I cannot share.

The Lyric   *Dorothy Joslin*

WAITING CAREFULLY

At the edge of this pale
Shredded lawn, July
Simmers in the street:

Long-boned girls
Walk their hips around,
Sweat on the lips,
Those fine-haired thighs;
They are brown,
Utterly possessed.

Young men on leave
From their stiff universities
Swing cameras and rackets,
Squint into conversation
And smack hot pavement
At jogging speed;
I do not know them.

My chair is cracked,
Split at the canvas seam.
It is a familiar risk.

I would not dare the trip
To town, where cars shimmer
In narrow one-ways,
Where tawdry hotels spill
Stale perfume, and sleeveless women
Stop all traffic;

Better to take my chances
With a broken chair,
Forge a book of dreams,
And await some subtle invitation.

Poet Lore   *Nancy P. Kamm*

COMPENSATION

I cannot rival Helen's face—
For me no thousand ships set sail.
Nor have I Cleopatra's grace,
Or Mona Lisa's, fair and pale.

No lover ever wore my glove
In joust, or carved my name in jade.
No secret tryst, no tragic love—
But, oh, the loaves of bread I've made.

Our Family   *Virginia Maughan Kammeyer*

YOU ARE MORE THAN I NEED

(White Mountain, July, 1977)

Let the still yellow goldenrod, hot with sun, come back.
Let subtly inked ferns, wind-fanned green, come back.
Let the haze over earliest roofs, blue as cold feet, come back.
Let the mauve-eyed, shawled spinner moth come back.
These I have said morning and night to.
With these I have accepted silences.

Let the starched, dark mantilla of pine, floating, come back.
Let the rain-fretted dust, slick on the window, come back.
Let the slow pointillism of the screen door come back . . .
In these I have bought games with time,
In the points of bird feet marked my knowledge,
Set my scores and messages,
Left my love and returned to it,
Loose-gaited and light.
And you, like an old Canadian trader, come whistling warning.

Poet Lore   *Rebbekka Kaplan*

FIDELITY

During the dream
in which my wife died
and Felicia draped her thighs
over my quivering hips
while our tongues wrestled
and matted hair spread a reeking paste
across our bellies,
The baby whimpered
in the next room,
a tiny cry pinched from fitful sleep:
When my wife stirred, sat up, listened,
waited,
then lay back gently, searching out the darkness,
I pressed into her warm curve,
trembling a little
with love,
forgiving us both for the bitter spite
that wracked our days,
and sank helplessly toward the old dream,
in which Felicia died.

Kansas Quarterly   *Jerry Kass*

THE CYCLISTS

On the cover of the book of 19th-century
etchings, three lady bicyclists,

their black eyes fixed on the front wheels,
race toward an unseen goal.

Billowing behind them, their hair & skirts & scarves
thrust them continually out of themselves—
till there is only wind & the spokes shivering
to a thin chrome light. And though

at any moment their mushrooming skirts
could catch in the treacherous rear wheels
& drag them down,
                    the skirts
do not catch, & the cyclists race on,

locked in the story the wheels tell
each of them—a story of covering ground;
of a woman who went & never came back;
of nothing at all,

the spokes whirring till they vanish,
the feet & the pedals a single blur.

The Paris Review   *Lawrence Kearney*

IN THE DREAM OF THE BODY

The cedar took over an hour of digging,
and cursing when the shovel stuck on a root
or a rock, pitifully small when it came out.
There was sweat in my eyes and hair
as I pulled and rocked the trunk;
the ground heaved, a last root snapped
and I hauled up the tangled shape.
It was damp; clay covered both of us
like lovers come back out of the earth.

Sometimes I could just sit in the front yard,
not even reading, only the landscape,
the park across the street in mind.
If I spend enough time here
I'll become calm as an old farmer
watching the branches on a hillside.
Later, when no one's around for blocks,
I'll try to think what the trees were like
and remember trucks passing in the background.

If I had a woman's body, I think
the shadows and the roundness would excite me.
I'd wrap my breasts in thinnest satins,
for the outline, the sheen of myself.
The air would be full of motion.
In cotton I'd walk back and forth past the mirror,
the smooth cloth touching my body,
and know my breasts were perfect.

The dream has only inertia and loneliness.
Sitting here, some days there's nothing I want.
That's a lie. I wish the morning would lead me
into the shade by the porch. I want something
substantial as fatigue to lift my arms toward,
the sunlight present in some other life
beyond the woodpile, the air I could almost hold.

Cut Bank   *David Keller*

HEIR TO SEVERAL YESTERDAYS

I should have been a gypsy child
Whose days were patterned by a wild
      Magyar waltz;
Instead, I fed on apple pie,
Watching corn grow, taking my
      Epsom Salts.

My mind was miles and years away
Where jungle-crusted cities lay
      Half-forgotten;
But my dusty days were bound
By chores that had a common sound:
      Chopping cotton.

I dreamt of caravans to Tyre
And treasures hedged by dragon-fire;
      Xanadu!
My dreams grew dim as days sped by
While I matured and married my
      Betty-Lou.

I hide my secret vanities
And daily pace on sanity's
      Very edge;
I lie beside my wife each night
And mourn my wasted, would-be, bright
      Heritage.

The Lyric   *Parham J. Kelley*

THAT MAN IN MANHATTAN

He thought if he could surround himself with quotations
they would form a chain mail virtually impenetrable.
He collected books of all sorts to this end, even geographies.
One never knows when one may confront a territorial adversary.
He knew personalities that functioned on the principle of
Manifest Destiny.

Manhattan harbored, besides steel, concrete, and glass,
human accoutrements. Man as signpost, man as gutter,

as pristine steeple, as lethal weapon. He had seen these.
He lived in Manhattan. He wanted to be prepared.

He was not physical, metaphysical, or passive, only himself.
He figured if he could collect quotations like butterflies
skewered permanently to the bland wall of his mind, he would
at the least add color and the surety of captured beauty
from a world not his.

Kansas Quarterly   *Shannon Keith Kelley*

NOCTURNE: LAKE HURON

(Mackinac Island, Michigan)

"Dull sublunary lovers . . ."

Tonight the fireflies flicker on, then off;
almost invisible, the small-winged bats
dart from the awnings of our rented house
on Lake View Drive. We swelter in the heat
of circumstance. What was and what must be
yield to a fragile reciprocity.

Beside me now, you slumber on at peace
among the pillows where at last you smile
through random dreams I cannot hope to share.
We're strangers still, although I call your name
across the calm interstices of sleep.
Your breathing answers, regular and deep.

I watch the city lights across the straits
commingle with the ageless glint of stars.
What brought us here, two transients in touch?
What lit this colloquy of love and pain,
this congruence of bodies dimly creased
by what the night's frail energy released?

Out on the lake the midnight ferry sounds
its fog-horn once before it turns to dock.
You wake: your eyes like distant satellites
orbit the wanton stars of our brief tryst,
knowing it is the tentative we spawn
as we move slowly round to greet the dawn.

The Southern Review   *Conor Kelly*

EIGHT MILES SOUTH OF GRAND HAVEN

You can see the beach and the waves, you can see the sky
and its few clouds, but you can't see the land on the other
side: so then, this must be the ocean!

And then, there is an Indian north of here who would still
be alive if he'd slept in the bottom bunk, and an old man

who walks through the pines, looking for a boy with the back
missing from the top of his head.

So then, there is the fish gasping for life on the flat sand,
its eyes open forever and the dog, its eyes closed, looking
for air in the arms of a large raccoon at the bottom.

So then, there is the creek, with the warm urine of towns,
there are the turtles, dying between roadsides, and there
is the note behind the final piano, "This is terrible. The
steamer is breaking up fast. I am aboard from Grand Haven
to Chicago."

You can see that here, of course. But first you must feel
her wood, the moss-grown hull of the steamer, Alpena, under
your feet as you swim.

And then, there is the grip of the sailor's hand, part of
the water since 1880, around your modern ankle as it poises
above the wreck.

So then you can walk in the storms at night and damn god, you
can live with the flashes of sulphur and the way the roof
lifts in the wind from its calm place over the horse's head,
over the diners who pray before breaking bread.

And so then, you can look at the brown sand and the waves,
like an Indian in an upper bunk or a boy who has blown off
his head, and see that and the sky, with its few clouds, and
that this is an ocean because there isn't any land on any
other side.

The American Poetry Review   *Dave Kelly*

AN EASY POEM

(for Elizabeth)

This is an easy poem to make
because it is entirely true and therefore has no need
for barb wire around it. It could no more break free
and tell a lie than the ocean could.

This is an easy happening
initially taking place outside of a psychiatrist's office.

A man and a woman meet.
They exchange glances.
They exchange tales of woe.
They notice the psychiatrist's bicycle
chained to the radiator of his waiting room.
They laugh
to think that a psychiatrist is paranoid too!

How simple the poem was that day,
urging the man to ask the woman out—
first for coffee, then for something darker,

and hotter. The woman invites
the man to her home. She cooks him
lambchops and potatoes as white as milk.

Suddenly, as in all easy happenings,
Fate steps in and cracks the woman's front tooth.
Oh no! Why did it come at this easy moment
when love was about to flow
like a faucet? Oh no! She is now the crone,
snaggle-toothed and quite a different story

than the laughing, golden haired woman
waiting in the room
outside of the psychiatrist's office
for a sign, something
that would change her life. The man

runs out of her apartment. Nothing
is easy he says. Call me when you get another
tooth. This was an easy poem to make
the whole truth,
and nothing but the truth,
so help me God!

The Hollins Critic   *Terry Kennedy*

THE STAMMERERS

They are there on the other side of the hill
armed with voices; someone calls out to them: Repeat—
and a thin staccato fire is returned
like a retreating echo.

They may not, like others, always say
precisely what it is they mean; lips meddle instead,
the tongue's disobedient, and the heart
must pause for alternatives.

In timing their utterances, they may make
metronomes of their feet or sing at inappropriate
moments; they need not bite down on metal for control,
however, nor should their tongues be trimmed.

They are not contagious. Given pens they often write,
given spoons they tap out messages, before
mirrors they are often eloquent without revision:
it is the tongue's easy wag that is deceptive.

Poetry   *Margaret Kent*

SUMMER STORM

When, for days, heavy air
Hangs in the Western
Mountains of Maine,

Life slows.
The waters are scarcely
Rippled and birds
Settle deep in the evergreens.
Folks say the weather
Is building.
Hazy skies soak shallow streams
Dry. Lawns dull, flowers fold
And dust rises from dirt roads
Which resemble
Arid tracts of desert.
Without warning, but as expected,
Great rumblings are heard in
The distant hills.
Black clouds fill the horizon
And jagged bolts stab at
The earth.
Legend has it, Thor is
Wielding a mighty hammer
Today.

Indiana Writes   *Richard B. Kent*

LITTLE SIS

Whoever you are,
7 or 8 years old like me,
and like me, no doubt,
a little dangerous,
and fearless too—at the
time—maybe you'll find
this little book someday
and remember that while
we were exploring
the wilderness
between Liberty St. & Root River
(between the Marquette St. Bridge
& the factories)
we stumbled upon
the hut of some teen-age boys,
who held us captive
for an hour, and made
us take off all our
clothes.
Then they let us go
without any further harm,
and walking, shaking
in my baby boots
up that hill, I felt,
not ashamed, but suddenly
as if you were my sister,
and that we had

had the same dark hand
brush against our one innocent
life.

New Letters   *David Kherdian*

EASTER EGG

If you must crack it
Let it not be

Hard-boiled,
Soft-boiled,
Coddled,
Scrambled,
Once-over-lightly,
Fried in grease.

Let it be fresh!

Or better yet, wait.

Quietly at dawn
Or armed with fragrance,
Expectantly, in fear
As they that approached
That round, hard, lifeless wall

And found it burst!
The empty shell alone
And silken inner shrouds.

For that, God-planted
In a mother's womb,
Endured in silence
The suffocating,
Prescribed imprisonment,

Then hatched
And lives!

The Christian Century   *Alan Kieffaber*

IN THE SMALL BOATS OF THEIR HANDS

In Mexico women have hands strong enough
they can still go down to the river
and pound their black skirts clean.
Their hands lie open on the rocks
the way they offer tortillas in the streets
or unfold to a husband's touch.
A woman can carry everything in the small boats of her hands:
the same shell for so many years
it presses to whorls on her fingers,
small fish,
coins left overnight on the dresser.

But the bones in a woman's hands are lighter,
harder to bring home
when given up to the world.
There is nothing a mother can tell her daughter
when she places a piece of bread in her small hands,
folds her fingers around it.

The Georgia Review   *Pamela Kircher*

I LOVE OLD WOMEN

I love old women
who walk slowly
when everyone beside them
is scurrying,
who remain silent
when everyone behind them
is shrill,
who smile when the clock
sounds the hour.

I love old women
who pick up the pace
when everyone beside them
is lagging,
who speak out
when everyone before them
is mute,
who scream when the clock
winds down.

I love old women
who do not seem to notice
that you are noticing,
who when they say *Good morning*
perhaps are serious,

strands of fine blue hair in place,
but moving,
always and forever and forever moving,
in the wind.

Wisconsin Review   *William Kloefkorn*

CIRCLES

The light at this hour
benign, clear.
Swirls in the carpet—
motes in the air
of childhood.

The table you wheeled in the door
in sunlight that day
now here in this room.

Years of light
between us, light years.
I reach out my hand
to that hollow
place. I feel it
as one explores
an old wound, the flesh
bunched and scarred.
The light describes circles
along the wall. I see
things differently now:
each day
transforms
into another day.

The Hudson Review   *Elizabeth Knies*

OCTOBER

i
Autumn comes to its senses
like Beethoven walking into a dark room
and suddenly recovering his hearing,
and what he hears is moss withering
on the gray stone sill
and sunlight dragging its pulse
through lichen and lost bird feathers.

A leaf breaks its hinge at the bark
and leaf by leaf they fall
and flurry in the wind
till drains are skinned with sheets of damp yellow
and the roof drips where gutters overflow.

In forests, the momentum of sleep becomes
more powerful than a fall from a great height.
Locks tarnish. Ice armors the pigeon's foot.

A dog barks on and on, distraught in rain.

ii
Why are we so sleepy, think the wasps,
and the next day they aren't there.
Tonight the humus is warm as a bed,
but a cold wind with a wet edge
blows an inch above the ground
and the air is filled with autumn grist.
Under the moon: a drift of crystal.
Tomorrow the front steps will gleam,
darkened to slate by melting frost.

Southern Humanities Review   *Fredric Koeppel*

THE WEDDING

This morning on the beach where the last wash of spray
Had frozen on the sand
I found a wild duck crevassed between the rocks.
The hard sun lit it like an emblem:
Death's finality.

My body claims me
The way the duck
Is the white, black, gray of its feathers,
The way the last frozen wave owns winter.
Dead, it will be all I am.

I don't understand about death.
My dead aren't stiff and absolute,
They drift back,
Snow humped on the earth, the gray fur lining of a glove,
Fragments stubborn as fossils
That flutter and stir,
Voices in my cells.

Those cells are my body,
Those images alive in a brain
Dying cell by cell.
I try to imagine this life, this death,
A light that loves them both.

The Massachusetts Review   *Sandra Kohler*

KENNEDY AIRPORT

Those greetings! those goodbyes!
I am passing Kennedy Airport—would know it blindfold
by the glad snarl of jets.

Many times, living near, we told each other:
Let's take off and arrive
with those great dragon things one night,
and from a side let's watch some families
go through their griefs, their joys!

Now the terminals are blended in my head,
and our passengers—going, coming—and the years;
arrivals too late, departures too early,
meeting places botched,
fragile names blared like hospital personnel . . .
only the pattern is clear:
children wrenched away, and again, again,
wrenched away, after each crumb of a visit,
to Chicago, Ann Arbor, finally Kermanshah,
our noses rubbed in the fact, again and again,
that they were not part of the unit any more,

that the nest was down to two . . .
and other arrivals, other departures,
always with huggings, tears;
always a clutching, not a clasping of hands.

I cannot pass Kennedy Airport without aching,
though for us it means London as well, Amsterdam, Firenze;
though for us it means greetings as well as goodbyes
(unlike my grandmother, she who coughed forth her soul
in the back of a wagon alone
on her way to a doctor too late
on a snow-cursed Polish road
without a goodbye from her husband
but greeted by God at least, I would like to believe;
unlike my grandmother, who never did make it to America
where I hoped all my young years to greet her;
and who never even came to the depot
on those five nightmare mornings
as her children were wrenched away,
goodbye after goodbye,
depot with no greetings, only goodbyes,
till her nest was down to two;
without ever one telephone syllable to breathe or recieve,
one word to decipher or place on a postcard;
waiting, waiting for the steerage tickets
her five American children and their mates
never did grow quite prosperous enough to send).

Midstream   *Aaron Kramer*

OVERCOATS

There is a dream of eternal warmth,
a strangle scarf, buttons that must
hold taut; there is an overcoat I wear
beyond my final prairie storm,
because taking it off I would only discover
another coat inside, and inside that another,
older, with frayed elastic cuffs,
then buried under it the Mackinaw of
eleven pockets worn on my first date,
trying to win Elizabeth Holsinger, golden,
composed, the desire of every boy
at Sacred Heart School; there, in the recess
of some pocket as yet unexplored, I misplaced
the most important movie tickets.
But this time the endless, anxious crowd
at the Victory's matinee could at last
surge forward because we,
Liz taking my arm hard as I prove worthy,
could finally enter, though even
in the darkness she would see
I wore underneath my soft
rabbit fur collar of childhood;

she would laugh as I stuffed
it under the seat, but
there would be another and another:
they would become unbearably tighter as I
hurried, explaining there is no
end to the overcoats of childhood,
and if, but this could never happen,
I removed them all, she would only laugh
with all shrillness at the palest small body.
By then, everyone would be looking.

California Quarterly   *Larry Kramer*

SENSATIONAL RELATIVES

(for my brother, Peter)

Last time I left
Bill's Twilight Lounge
with a young black poet
whose words hit home
like the shiny gun
that got him on probation
and my sixteen-year-old brother
who passed for eighteen
and was fascinated by sensationalism,

we were driving up
to the Lorraine motel
to catch the tail end
of King's commemoration
when the police
shone a flashlight
in our faces.
The poet had left.
My brother, I taught
not to talk back
the way I'm talking now
because there's a time and place
for blah blah blah—
the police said I had thirty days
to get my registration changed
to Tennessee.
I thought about mobility.

My brother thought it was a joke,
something he'd seen on TV—
Beale Street's most celebrated gambler's
reply to the police
when told he had 24 hours
to leave town,
"That's OK—
here's eighteen of them back."

He got in his car,
bags already packed,
and drove straight up Highway 51
into Chicago.

We left for New York the next day.
Tennessee was ablaze
with red-bud trees.
Calves roamed the Virginia fields.
My brother pointed out
farmhouse hex signs,
and my cat watched
New Jersey birds
through the windshield.

We knew we were getting home
when we picked up WLIB
"where the Third World comes
    together,"
and could finally joke
about the Ku Klux Klan
back on prime-time radio
in Memphis.

And then all I remember
is throwing my arms around my mother
and wearing fancy clothes again
and wanting to get married
and pouring white sugar into tea
and promising my grandmother
I'd never change.

The look in my grandmother's eyes,
dying, but sure
she was keeping on through me,
was the same look I saw
the very next day
on emerging from the subway
into the bright lights of Times Square,
when three white cops
threw a black man
down to the cement,
crowds forming fast
as spittle in their mouths.
One of them
pushed a gun into his back
and he looked at me
and surrendered.

My own sister
must have looked that way
at knifepoint,
demanding forgiveness
while some dude
demanded back
ten dollars

for a blow job
in an alleyway on 42nd Street.
I woke up early this morning
trembling the way she trembled
on the cold Hudson River pier.
I got up and drove towards the Mississippi,
flooded with the same tears.

I reached Fayette County,
third poorest county in our country,
and stopped a kid bicycling along the
    fields.
I asked if he'd heard of John McFerren.
Or the Fayette County Civic & Welfare
    League?
He looked at this white lady
in a car with California plates
and said Ma'am, he didn't know.
He said Ma'am a hundred times.
I said John McFerren was a hero
I'd read about in a book.
I looked at his face
and hurried home.

Now I'm back,
diary and diaphragm in place,
"I Am a Man" sign
hanging on a door,
left over from the sixties.
I'm dealing with the same shit,
like watching Greta Garbo on TV
and thinking I have TB.

It's possible God
kicked his foot into my lungs
the way the white man
beat up John McFerren
for registering to vote
in Fayette County.

But nowhere in Fayette County
did I see the pain.
Only spring
crying out in beauty,
roots pushing through hard soil,
people talking through the sunset
about catfish struggling on a line.
Catfish didn't register
to swim this brook.

Southern Exposure   *Alexis Krasilovsky*

THE TRANSANDEAN RAILWAY

Two winding rails
have split the pressure,

tamped their platform through
frequent drifts, gutted mountains,
spliced frontiers, and remained
long steel parallels.

Darkness swallows the train.
Passengers sip maté
in a rumble of politics;
Rosas returns to haunt
Allende. El Che applauds.
An avalanche of words smothers
the rails. The whistle
screams for relief, scalded
by its own steam.

The tunnel withdraws.
A brilliance of snow walls
and craggy fingers calms
the spine, freezes rage. Tracks
smile up ahead—for they
have been here before.

Wascana Review   *Thomas Kretz*

MOCKINGBIRD IN WINTER

In the dead of winter, when
The wind was whipping rude
To some street workingmen,
Huddled for fortitude
Around a pot of fire,
A bird upon a wire
Looked down, remembering
The time that it was summery
And not Decembering,
And sang a winter song,
A few notes unrehearsed
In one inventive burst,
Upwelling from that memory.
But, struggling with a feather,
It did not sing for long,
And sailed off on the weather
That whipped the huddled men,
Because the time was wrong.

Poet Lore   *Ernest Kroll*

PENNSYLVANIA ACADEMY OF FINE ARTS

(Summer Branch)

Visiting you, we slept in the arms of
Great trees cradling the dark around

Our rooms, where legend had the
Steel-willed, terse, much-slept-about
Virginian stretched out for the night
Before us. But that's not the point.
You said the land was made for paint;
We looked to the morning for the proof.
Morning supplied it truly when
The head academician, chief
Technician, wizard and master,
Rose in the east and with a flash
Filled in the fine detail complete
To the least flower, to the last leaf.

The Hollins Critic   *Ernest Kroll*

WORDS WORDS WORDS

I love you! You say, "I don't believe you."
My word it seems is not as good as gold
and the old *roses are red violets are blue*

is old and I am thirty-six with or without you
and action speaks. Your back to me is cold.
"I love you," I say. "I don't believe you

for a minute!" You say it like you mean it. At forty-two,
you'll buy no noisy bill of goods. You've been sold
old roses, red violets, you're black and blue

with compliments! Darling, I don't know what to do
to stop my mouth. I feel, therefore I am bold:
I love you. But you say, "I don't believe you

mean that." O.K. All right. The air turns blue
at twilight, I close my empty mouth and go—
I'm old. Roses aren't red, violets aren't blue

anymore and singing hurts, breath hurts. Two
days later you reconsider, come in from the cold,
older. "Roses are red again, and violets blue
and I love you!" You don't say. Well, I don't believe you.

Aspen Anthology   *Marilyn Krysl*

THE LAYERS

I have walked through many lives,
some of them my own,
and I am not who I was,
though some principle of being
abides, from which I struggle
not to stray.
When I look behind,
as I am compelled to look
before I can gather strength

to proceed on my journey,
I see the milestones dwindling
toward the horizon
and the slow fires trailing
from the abandoned camp-sites
over which scavenger angels
wheel on heavy wings.
Oh, I have made myself a tribe
out of my true affections,
and my tribe is scattered!
How shall the heart be reconciled
to its feast of losses?
In a rising wind
the manic dust of my friends,
those who fell along the way,
bitterly stings my face.
Yet I turn, I turn,
exulting somewhat,
with my will intact to go
wherever I need to go,
and every stone on the road
precious to me.
In my darkest night,
when the moon was covered
and I roamed through wreckage,
a nimbus-clouded voice
directed me:
"Live in the layers,
not on the litter."
Though I lack the art
to decipher it,
no doubt the next chapter
in my book of transformations
is already written.
I am not done with my changes.

The American Poetry Review   *Stanley Kunitz*

ROUTE SIX

The city squats on my back.
I am heart-sore, stiff-necked,
exasperated. That's why
I slammed the door,
that's why I tell you now,
in every house of marriage
there's room for an interpreter.
Let's jump into the car, honey,
and head straight for the Cape,
where the cock on our rooftree crows
that the weather's fair,
and my garden waits for me
to coax it into bloom.

As for those passions left
that flare past understanding,
like bundles of dead letters
out of our previous lives
that amaze us with their fevers,
we can stow them in the rear
along with ziggurats of luggage
and Celia, our transcendental cat,
past-mistress of all languages,
including Hottentot and silence.
We'll drive non-stop till dawn,
and if I grow sleepy at the wheel,
you'll keep me awake by singing
in your bravura Chicago style
Ruth Etting's smoky song,
"Love Me or Leave Me,"
belting out the choices.

Light glazes the eastern sky
over Buzzards Bay.
Celia gyrates upward
like a performing seal,
her glistening nostrils aquiver
to sniff the brine-spiked air.
The last stretch toward home!
Twenty summers roll by.

New England Review   *Stanley Kunitz*

AMONG FRIENDS

Now that I live no longer among mountains
of any sort,
people have asked me what I do now for sport,
what I have taken up as perhaps a hobby
or what I have forced myself to endure
or make the most of.

And I say I have married and settled down,
and that is the all of it—
except that a dog lives with us and makes vast
demands, which we take delight
in indulging,
and that the weather here is durable and bright.
That I grow a garden,
weed it all day,
and by night
water it.

And they shrug and are glad.
And spill out their own sad stories,
For they, too, have been on the heights,
and have come down.

The Southern Review   *Greg Kuzma*

TALKING ACROSS KANSAS

All afternoon we lie, stretched out
on your lounge chairs. Our eyes
don't meet. Whatever we talk about
seems to repeat itself, in sighs,

like driving through Kansas, the red
barns, the occasional farmhouse fringed in green.
I keep waiting for something we haven't said
to disturb the flat horizon like the scene

of a summer storm, with jagged streaks,
crashes, and sheets of rain.
No, not this visit. Nobody speaks
of anything as vertical as pain.

Words pass like salesmen on road trips.
We get up when our talk has outlived the heat,
and notice our backs are crossed with strips,
like lash marks, or rows of uncut wheat.

Dark Horse   *Paula Kwon*

WESTERN WAYS

The simple-minded interstates have it now, and the motel-
and-filling-station towns: Holiday Inn, Best Western,
Quality, with Gulf and Texaco: the clean featureless

caravanserais: gas pools good beds sanitary
indifferent food. Oh yes, but beyond and outside lie
not only reservations and actual ranches but also

that special little town of the plains, at intervals strung on
the gleaming straightaway of the tracks. First seen miles
   off,
green smudge, white silos at the southern edge, and the
   northern

marker of the water tower: Hays Russell Kit Carson:
oasis groves in the grasslands dropped there out of the
   nineties.
Yes but sometimes the cruel flow-ways have passed them,
   leaving

a once proud road now secondary; coarse grass and
   broken
windows and festering boards, decay without circulation,
stare at us in squalid reproach, at us, the suburban

passers-through on our way from urban to coastal urban.
We might have lived another life by the silo and water
   tower.

Sometimes in the great desert the Greeks imagined
   Atlantis.

Poetry   *Richard Lattimore*

CHRISTMAS MORNING

snow fell
        on the smiling of the sheep
            and the chewing of the cows
till all the world gave flame
        in the squeals of the pigs
            and the skitter of the foals.
I woke and knew the cold
        from the quiver of the dogs
            and the huddling of the birds
watched the fields fall away
        to the trudging of the farmer
            and the bending of the lane.

Above the tree rose the day
        with the driving of the tractor
            and the sticking of the gate
and each barn door framed gold
        round the bundling of the children
            and the rhythm of the ladder.
So it was that I came
        by the multitudes of the bales
            and the beaming of the rafters
to dream and know and tell
        of the overflowing of the loft
            and the sharpness of the straw.

The Centennial Review   *Steven Lautermilch*

FOR MY WIFE

We are being born again,
getting second breath in skin and bone, vein
and artery, that once in grunion milt by sea and riverbed
died to take to air.

Through you I find new sight, see the egg
face to face, know the fish, grasp the tree and vine and
blossoming play the ape, to pay out more, still
more this cord, our life-line, into time, into space.

With such grace you grow awkward, pantomime and trance
the moon and tides in their slow dance around the earth.
And then, delivered and light, how you shine,
how you shine.

The Centennial Review   *Steven Lautermilch*

GRAY DAYS

On the gray days, when the sky
        withdraws,
Days without color, current,

character,
When everything draws back into
   itself
Its passionate assertions, when
   even grass
Cannot be called green, brown,
liv-
   ing, dead—
On such days, old-timers used to
   say,
Dutchmen hanged themselves;
   you could not buy
Clothesline on the Northside.
   What irony:
These are no days for binding,
   knotted things,
For painful definitions. For a time
On these gray days, tiresome
   mutability
Itself is halted. There can be
Surcease from brightness that
   slashes,
Glory that stuns, decisiveness.
   Look steadily
On the gray days, rest in the
calm,
   the slow
Remote serenity of something
   gray.

Newsart   *Joanne Lawlor*

THE HARVESTER

I go inland each afternoon.
I pick green grapes in fields shadowed with leaves.
I pluck them out of their grove to be taken into town.
   birds whistle.
in afternoon the sun ripens the grapes by touch.
heat waves rise between the vines
like channels of the sun's tide deepening.

Taking a bunch, I fill my hand,
my fingertips are wet from their skin.
beneath red trees I lean against the shade.
bees bounce over the grapes,
I follow them till I sight the comb.

I never think of being alone.
my heart beats as the sun beats.
I breathe when the leaves rustle.
I feel the stubble of dry grass scratching my feet.
my ears buzz. and when,
with my tongue, I squeeze a grape

whose skin is smooth with afternoon dew,
I taste honey and wine.

The Centennial Review   *Terry Lawrence*

AUBADE

*(In reply to a poem on the dread of death,
by Philip Larkin, of the same title)*

Long ago when I shouted in red letters
to my friends in the street after
our team won on the grade-school playground,
I felt Something brush lightly against
my resting sore ankles.

When later my voice went over
long vibrant wires to talk with
a crippled sister, Something
touched my own body, less lightly.

I know now that Something
may take my acrylic painting of
redwoods fog-crowned, unfinished, or from my piano
lift the next-to-last chord of a Chopin prelude,
or erase the not-quite-right phrase
my hand gave to a poem incomplete . . .

After a short while, who will care?

Or maybe tomorrow Something will lean on
my shoulder to watch these California toyons
raising their red berries to
hundreds of hungry robins;
or, matching my limp, walk with me a last time
under trees that the darker night sky
talks to in special wind patterns . . .

After a short while, who will care?

Or it may be that someone, somewhere,
will care as much as I did,
—and paint or compose or write
with that exquisite talent
I tried for, but lacked.

But Something, perhaps, will stay with me
under closed eyelids, even while
my rigid body lies whiter
than written-off silence, as on
that long ago midwest morning, March born,
I was far too young to know
the white flame, or the cold whisper of snow.

Buffalo Spree   *Ruth Lechlitner*

SONG IN WHITE

Clouds fell
sometime in the night:
come morning,
everything was white
and you could see the cold breath
of the sky
touching every still object
with white crisp froth.
There was a world
white on white,
and the cold steam of the clouds
washing over and up
and opening around stark trees
and white round hills.
And a silence
moving like the clouds
across the face of the sun.
That, too,
was white.

Prism International   *Anne Le Dressay*

YOUR LIGHT

You brought me bdellium and onyx, stones
you found in Genesis. I gave you plums,
fresh raw oysters, aged Jamaican rum
and Camembert. I loved your muscles, bones'
renitence. Later I watched your light
glimmer through darkness.

                    Now, a world away,
you send no word. I wonder, wait the day
of your return, wrestling with heavy night.

Poet Lore   *Ann Lee*

THE MIRRORS OF JERUSALEM

1. This is no country for hedonists

  In the Jaffa Street cafes they serve
pious carrot juice. At breakfast
the shredded beets have no blood
& the yogurt in stiff white cups
has a scrubbed & meagre taste
unrelieved by the honeypot.

On the busses men brawl
about politics, politics. Tautly-
tongued sabras strut in Zion Square

& everywhere the soldiers bear their rifles
deceptively casual.

There is no dancing in Jerusalem.
Only the taxi-drivers & old men
are singing their rumpled songs.
Newsmen are grim: no Brinkley pomade
or crazy widows who stash
their money in mattress ticking.
Here there is no madness
except a paranoia common as the sun,
rung by Russian tanks that hulk
between the olive trees.

But once in these Judean hills
holy craftsmen hewed pomegranates
from the stone; roses, grapes
& seashells whose lyre-shaped grooves
not Persian, Greek, or Roman,
Crusader, Turk, or tourist
have dared to rub silent.

2. *This is no country for puritans*

The Shrine of the Book hovers
above Jerusalem like an upturned breast.
In the old Jewish market off Jaffa Street
women with embroidered shawls
press the plump chicken feet
dangling from open-air stalls. Velvet-
brimmed Hassidim wipe the herring juice
from their beards, spit, & dip their fingers
into vats of olives in the shout-
&-spice-riddled air.

On the busses there is always music.
A sabra with six gold chains around her neck
hugs a soldier whose collar hangs loosely open
in a garden of flesh-colored roses.
When the drone of a jet
upsets his siesta, the rabbi shrugs; resumes
his dream about darkly-haired women
who serve him grapes & fat pomegranates
in bowls of shimmer.

Yet once in these sands
the protocols of guilt
germinated like the gray
& purple thistles
that everywhere poke from the roadside.

Webster Review   *Barbara F. Lefcowitz*

THE MIND IS STILL

The mind is still. The gallant books of lies
are never quite enough.

Ideas are a whirl of mazy flies
over the pigs' trough.

Words are my matter. I have chipped one stone
for thirty years and still it is not done,
that image of the thing I cannot see.
I cannot finish it and set it free,
            transformed to energy.

I chip and stutter but I do not sing
the truth, like any bird.
Daily I come to Judgment stammering
the same half-word.

So what's the matter? I can understand
that stone is heavy in the hand.
Ideas flit like flies above the swill;
I crowd with other pigs to get my fill;
            the mind is still.

The Kenyon Review   *Ursula K. Le Guin*

THE MIGRATIONS OF PEOPLE

The story was always the same—
sooner or later, the strangers arrived, moving
from flood or drought, down to the peaceful long
    held land,
where rain fell in season
and the sun came as usual to lie gently on wild
    sweet oats . . .

So the barbarians took the black land by the river,
built their houses under the trees, known and named
from time beyond time.

The people fled like deer in the woods,
leaving their houses, mud plastered by their fathers'
    hands,
leaving the bones of their ancestors, and the holy
    niche by the fire.

In the new land, the old gods looked bleakly down
    on the strange hearths.

Now there were no more forests,
only rocks and sand, and a bush here and there.

Still, while the people remembered rivers,
the blackberry grew out of rocky soil,
and the sweet red fruit astounded, sharp and
    surprising
as the probe of the thorn.

The sun seemed more powerful here,
spreading its setting brilliance of rose and amber
    and orange

over a wider sky,
splashing its color onto the household god,
making him seem again transcendent.

And sometimes the exiles, from their bones' centers,
yearned outward toward the rocky land.

The Christian Century   *Dorothy Leiser*

HENRY MILLER: A WRITER

when the photographer comes in
the old man wraps his bathrobe
at the neck
winces at the light
his bony hands, purplish and big veined
tugging at the walker
that pushes age into a prankish smile

"i've so many ailments
but i'm alive to the fingertips
it's amazing the tricks you learn
when you're crippled"

where is paris, big sur
the boys from brooklyn?
in the small house of frail posters
chagall-like watercolors
he gestures to the wall
and bounces a ping-pong ball
across the floor
till it comes to rest
with his one good eye
in the corner

i see the still wet lips
that once opened the loins
of pampered graduates
that moved across waters like a fog
warning the dry grass of suburbia

but the children are gone
into their own neon rhapsodies
forget the words
"the whorehouse is the slaughterhouse
of love"

he is rabelais and li po
and seraphita and cendrars
driving a bugatti through the amazon
with one arm

he laughs at presidents
shuns chatter in his home
"age deserves some rights"
loves sex, hates pornography

the feminists with their movements
are chauvinists, mailer's long-winded
"can't he write a simple sentence?"
the japanese woman is a soft hand

he stares at the oranges
of hieronymus bosch in the toilet
where "meditation is best"
and picks his teeth with a silver pin

the rooms flash the ancient thirst
forty years too late
the wicked tongue is still there
but not the long streets
or the shack overlooking the pacific

"am i all right" he asks

is my eye open?

Bachy 12   *Carol Lem*

WAKING UP

One summer morning the sun fell gold
on the dark green loops and swirls
of the living-room carpet.
Shadows slipped through solid light
like echoes of a bell, dust swirled thick
in the bars of light. I lay on the floor
curled into a ball in the broken light,
listened
to the high thin ringing in my ears,
the dull thumps and talk of the family getting up,
cars, a plane, the wind.
The furniture glowed scratched red;
in its shadows the carpet
shifted into intricate patterns
all around me, a swamp, a jungle of curves
where I was lost, pressed down by the weight
of the light. In the silence
I could feel through the floor the low rumbling blasts
of factory whistles, just hear
bells, far off, very faint.

Combinations   *Edward Lense*

NORTHWARD

Northward at night
In wonder I spied the world:
A bewilderment of stars and seasons
Glittering, wheeling on and on

When time was always within
The purview of my telescopic eye.

Arizona Quarterly   *Dominick J. Lepore*

ANY NIGHT

Look, the eucalyptus, the atlas pine,
the yellowing ash, all the trees
are gone, and I was older than
all of them. I am older than the moon,
than the stars that fill my plate,
than the unseen planets that huddle
together here at the end of a year
no one wanted. A year more than a year,
in which the sparrows learned
to fly backwards into eternity.
Their brothers and sisters saw this
and refuse to build nests. Before
the week is over they will all
have gone, and the chorus of love
that filled my yard and spilled
into my kitchen each evening
will be gone. I will have to learn
to sing in the voices of pure joy
and pure pain. I will have to forget
my name, my childhood, the years
under the cold dominion of the clock
so that this voice, torn and cracked,
can reach the low hills that shielded
the orange trees once. I will stand
on the back porch as the cold
drifts in, and sing, not for joy,
not for love, not even to be heard.
I will sing so that the darkness
can take hold and whatever
is left, the fallen fruit, the last
leaf, the puzzled squirrel, the child
far from home, lost, will believe
this could be any night. That boy,
walking alone, thinking of nothing
or reciting his favorite names
to the moon and stars, let him
find the home he left this morning,
let him hear a prayer out
of the raging mouth of the wind.
Let him repeat that prayer,
the prayer that night follows day,
that life follows death, that in time
we find our lives. Don't let him see
all that has gone. Let him love

the darkness. Look, he's running
and singing too. He could be happy.

The Georgia Review   *Philip Levine*

EVERYTHING

Lately the wind burns
the last leaves and evening
comes too late to be
of use, lately I learned
that the year has turned
its face to winter
and nothing I say or do
can change anything.
So I sleep late and waken
long after the sun has risen
in an empty house and walk
the dusty halls or sit
and listen to the wind
creak in the eaves and struts
of this old house. I say
tomorrow will be different
but I know it won't.
I know the days are shortening
and when the sun pools
at my feet I can reach
into that magic circle
and not be burned. So
I take the few things
that matter, my book,
my glasses, my father's ring,
my brush, and put them aside
in a brown sack and wait—
someone is coming for me.
A voice I've never heard
will speak my name
or a face press to the window
as mine once pressed
when the world held me out.
I had to see what it was
it loved so much. Nothing
had time to show me
how a leaf spun itself
from water or water cried
itself to sleep for
every human thirst. Now
I must wait and be still
and say nothing I don't know,
nothing I haven't lived
over and over,
and that's everything.

The Georgia Review   *Philip Levine*

ASHES

Far off, from the burned fields
of cotton, smoke rises and scatters
on the last winds of afternoon.
The workers have come in hours ago,
and nothing stirs. The old bus creaked
by full of faces wide-eyed with hunger.
I sat wondering how long the earth
would let the same children die day
after day, let the same women curse
their precious hours, the same men bow
to earn our scraps. I only asked.
And now the answer batters the sky:
with fire there is smoke, and after, ashes.
You can howl your name into the wind
and it will blow it into dust, you
can pledge your single life, the earth
will eat it all, the way you eat
an apple, meat, skin, core, seeds.
Soon the darkness will fall on all
the tired bodies of those who have
torn our living from the silent earth,
and they can sleep and dream of sleep
without end, but before first light
bloodies the sky opening in the east
they will have risen one by one
and dressed in clothes still hot
and damp. Before I waken they are
already bruised by the first hours
of the new sun. The same men
who were never boys, the same women
their faces gone gray with anger,
and the children who will say nothing.
Do you want the earth to be heaven?
Then pray, go down on your knees
as though a king stood before you,
and pray to become all you'll
never be, a drop of sea water,
a small hurtling flame across the sky,
a fine flake of dust that moves
at evening like smoke at great height
above the earth and sees it all.

The Iowa Review   *Philip Levine*

EXCEPTIONAL

You know, I see, that four score years and ten
Are rather more than the allotted span;
And each familiar face that drops from view
Reminds you of the limit placed on man.
"My time will come," you say. One bit of earth

Has been reserved for you, because that plan—
Your sons will know it as your fathers knew—
that plan of death began as life began.

Ah, yes, you know, and yet within your eyes—
Still young, still eager, pleased, still bright—
Within your old eyes, young beyond their prime,
There flits a strange invincible surmise,
As if you hoped, of all mankind, you might
Escape the infallibility of time.

Western Poetry Quarterly   *Thelma Lewis*

THE FOUNTAIN

Poor fountain, dusty, clogged with pebbles,
old heart that used to race: I know that ache
of absence, that hubbub of life
you loved so much. I know what it's like.

Maybe things will change. Maybe the mountains,
feeling the weight of all that snow and ice,
will send the waters bursting into your pores
and get you going again. It would be nice

to feel the old pulse throbbing, that face
of fresh waters fountaining young again,
and the lovely girls bustling around you,
come for cool waters and thirsty men.

Poet Lore   *Pavlos Liasides*
                          —Translated by Edmund Pennant

AFTER THE DEFORMED WOMAN IS MADE CORRECT

Their pink mouths opened wide,
the neighbors' children
wondered at the bone
where my eyes should be,
my sight like a bird's at my temples.
They marveled at the out-sized
arc of my nose, and none
misunderstood me.

Years ago I grew used to whispers.
The mirror, the deep water,
their surfaces broken—
how will I know myself
among them?

The surgeons applaud their grand performance.
How long will I dream
about their touch, that pressure
like hooves, as they lifted my brain

from me in a trance so my skull
could be altered?

I fear they will shrink my mind forever.

Now days must pass before I can see this face,
know these constructions outside,
and for all this confusion
they must carve again, measure duty
by repair, so nobody startles.

I will pardon them their stare,
my scars like paper cuts
making maps of my flawed beauty,
forgive the dependable their appearance,
and the men at the bus-stops
with their averted glare.
I will pardon them
my mars.

Sou'wester   *Robert Lietz*

QUIET BY HILLSIDES IN THE AFTERNOON

quiet by hillsides in the afternoon
out of my window I have walked to a place to lie down in
and the lavender grey holds me
I am framed by the window I have walked through
it shapes me
as the shape of longing I stride on the hillside
looking for patches of lavender grey
that mount themselves there
when the sun shifts they are gone
uncovered in the shifting light of late afternoon
it is then that I find them
when nothing is high or bright
but slanting light seen from the window
slants its grey across hillsides
and shapes of longing catch their clothes
on all the thistles and foxtails there are
the hill is full of them
slanting sideways in the air
when we all lie down together
pushing our shapes together
finding shadows to lie down in
and the quiet that finally touches my palms

Bachy 11   *Martha Lifson*

THE OBSESSION

There must be something that links them all,
Some statistic I could spot:

The way that each walks down the hall

And leaves, saying, "Yeah, I'll call."
He was different? No. I forgot
There must be something that links them. All

The time I see the pitfall
Of their similarities; more often than not
The way that each walks down the hall

Stings me, their echoes like the last steps in a stall
Before a horse runs out, the long-shot.
There must be something that links them all.

I compare their ages, pasts: the small
Things we tell each other. I plot
The way that each walks down the hall

And wonder what causes men to have the gall
To leave: my father did what
He could, linking his children all
Together when he walked to the end of our hall.

Aspen Anthology   *Rosy Liggett*

CALAMITY JANE GREETS HER DREAMS

She dreams of swimming the Platte
with Custer and his army.
The current takes her on
to tubs and washboards
scrubbing her intricate lies,
tracking the past
to the wild man she could trail;
she leaves him with an empty
gun in the barroom.

Surfacing, always surfacing.

Notorious years,
       hello, again.
The two of them, swaggering
in brand-new buckskins,
always a good show . . .
whooping, chaotic, done.
She pictures her face and breasts
lit by that tin badge
flashing in the sun.

Carolina Quarterly   *Kathleen Lignell*

MISMATCH

The courts wait, wide open.
Children fool, dreaming airily of shots.

Heavy men puff, out of step,
laboring to regain
what dribbles out of bounds.

Today I overslept and found
the sides chosen with a place
for me. Match-ups disclosed
how far short my team must fall.
Play or decline?
I played.
        I lunged for something gone,
a ball that spun away, bodies
slipping through my arms like smoke,
before I'd thought to move.
They wove a net that tangled us
where we stood, as they danced
and floated up to the rim.
Yet, once before, it happened:
secure in their heightened grace,
unaware, they sparked and fanned a flame
that burned clear down to my sneakered soles—
and we got ahead, somehow, and stayed
there, hanging on until the end.

Southwest Review   *Carl Lindner*

LIGHT SHOWERS OF LIGHT

All this time we have been drinking
deep from Cartesian wells
and, no matter how sequential,
they cannot quench unfocused thirst.

Small rains will serve us wholly.

Calling on clouds may be a valid calling,
and receiving is a beggar's art.
It is the only art.

The Christian Century   *Kathryn Lindskoog*

APRIL

Clouds are giving way: bushes
along terraces shiver and glow.
Spring has waited as long to be touched
as a girl who hates her modest dress.
It is brown, thick as winter, and the few
bright days hardly make a dent in it.

She smiles—white flowers of the cherry
tremble into blossom—but he cannot believe
she will allow bright fingers to burn a trail

up her smooth thighs, and cause the forest
he has imagined—huddled in darkness—
to sizzle into being with his touch . . .

With a nervous glance he pulls back
and perversely she summons the rain,
the shock of it drumming
on the crowns of petals
like a dentist's tiny hammers
to localize her pain with pain.

Descant   *John Linthicum*

THE RADICAL IN THE ALLIGATOR SHIRT

(with acknowledgements to Kenneth Koch)

I used to be a radical
but now I wear an alligator shirt

I used to lead peace marches
but now I'm an assistant dean

I used to address the crowds
from the steps of South Building
but now I fall asleep after lunch

I used to debate the Dow Chemical recruiter
but now I invest in the market

I used to sit-in against the marines
but now I get lost on the beach

I used to tell my students the truth
but now I think that youth is a stage

I used to distrust anyone over thirty
but now I know why: they knew better.

Carolina Quarterly   *Lou Lipsitz*

THE SIXTIES

Negroes turned black overnight.
The cars grew flat.
Mickey Mantle broke a window
and we've been paying ever since.
Anarchists lept from classrooms,
fully armed, and cured
our incurable disease—
parts of ourselves hardly
mentionable opened up
to strangers. The purpose of poetry
was to scare priests.
We made love like a train,

full speed, and never looked back.
Someone tied our dreams in a sack,
saying: "you can't fly
if you don't drown," and tossed
us out with the cats.
That was life in the sixties:
crawling out of the water
and onto the tracks.

California Quarterly   *Thomas Listmann*

TOURS

Consider our Disneyland tour by the Yangtze:
water snakes glistened like steel lances,
toads on rocks stared like witch watchers,
hunters shouted in the woods, "The wolf!"
Morning long we crept through thick bushes
after a fox, answered Pu Ku birds and sent
the spring away; we saw maple trees shed
blood into the pond, the November snowfall
transform hilltops into silver pyramids.

More thunderbolts cracked, more outbursts
from the Siberian prairies; the sea-going
ship at Huang Poo harbor was ice-cold,
the farewells grieved me then grieve me now:
over the gleaming roofs of the Small World
looms the Haunted Mansion above the banks,
graveyard owls hoot over traffic sirens;
bright as flowing car lights, fireflies
surprise livid skulls, and in the smog a
pair of woman's legs swings, dust-hued.

"Great changes have come with the Revolution.
Mother fell in the field, too old to work."
That's all you know, my sister; that's all
you have to say in the letter, three decades
after our first tour by the Yangtze River.

New Boston Review   *Stephen Shu Ning Liu*

GUNFIGHTER

everyone writes of him, myself included,
in spite of his own notorious illiteracy,
which spared him literature;
high, middle-brow, and low,
he preferred poker: high-ball and low.

he didn't live quite long enough to be played
by anyone who has played him.
he didn't stamp and paw like a centaur,

like edward villela or the chorus of *equus*.
there weren't no neiman-marcuses
selling cowboy boots by bill blass.
he missed a lot of meals,
but never mythed his morgue.
he'd a-shot a man mighty dead for *that* pun.

a greatly overlooked consideration:
heat makes men miserable,
also mad in every sense,
nor does tequila cool like gin-and-tonic.
no memsahibs in gila bend.

he had a lot of names,
but none was finn maccool.
christ was a swear word
and sanjuro too much of a mouthful.
he would've preferred *the magnificent seven*
to *the seven samurai*
because it was shorter.

people assume they've seen the last of him,
but history's not necessarily linear.
we poets all would like to be him,
though he wouldn't have wasted precious
ammunition on us.
i'd just as soon he'd shoot his way
out of all poems, mine included,
but especially those that can't tell
murder from phenomenology.

The Literary Review   Gerald Locklin

THE LIBRARY

This massive, carved medieval harp of Irish oak
no longer sounds in the winds from ancient times gone
    out
of Celtic towns. It rests in the long, high vaulted room
filled up with one million books whose pages chronicle
the works and ages both in *our* land and in Ireland.
For a hundred years no student has bent here above
those huge, leather volumes that burgeon on the balconies
like matched and stacked rows of great pipes
for the unplayed organ of this magnificent place.
But both pipes and harp seem still to come alive and turn
Trinity College Library
into a fantastic temple when we stand over
the twelfth century Book of Kells,
which James Joyce so loved he carried a facsimile
to Zurich, Rome, Trieste. "It is,"
he said to friends, "the most purely Irish thing we have.
You can compare much of my work
to the intricate illuminations of this book."
Its goat skin pages open up for us under glass

in a wooden case. At this place:
a dog nips its tail in its mouth,
but this dog is of ultramarine, most expensive
pigment after gold, for it was ground out of lapis,
and the tail is of the lemon yellow orpiment.
Other figures are verdigris, folium or woad—
the verdigris, made with copper,
was mixed with vinegar, which ate into the vellum
and showed through on the reverse page.
Through the text's pages run constant, colored arabesques
of animated initial
letters—made of the bent bodies
of fabulous, elongate beasts

Poetry   *John Logan*

BATCHES OF NEW LEAVES

(for Maureen)

batches of new leaves
spurting green out the window
backyards filling up
with bird song
as i sit gazing
seeking snatches
of poetry
and then you come
swinging braids
running cold fingers
down my back
beneath my shirt
pressing crotch to my shoulder
dipping and encircling my nose
with lush warm lips
as the heat comes on and rises
from between the legs
of this desk straddling me
but
it's just a tender moment
and you say goodbye
kid
as you swing away
leaving me
to fill my hands with
this poem for you

Wind   *Jonathan London*

112 AT PRESIDIO

The sky, a dome of glaring brass,
presses close upon a dust-dry prairie,

where sand, stone, brittle tumbleweed,
and even the scuttling diamondback all seem
ready to burst upward into sizzling smoke.

The horizon swims in distance, its rim
of dark mountains a nebulous promise.
Here, in mid-afternoon, the sun flames
in white fury—burning—burning—
Stark in the midst of this hellish vista,
as if propped by the thin, dark bracket
of its shadow, leans an ancient windmill.

Teeth rusted and snaggled, creaking blades
broken and askew, this tottering hulk
rises defiantly, an insane ink-blot
upon a blaze of sky, gaunt survivor
of an age we had long believed
outgrown.

Cedar Rock   *Virginia Long*

ELEGY FOR MY FATHER

(Doniphan Louthan, 1920-1952)

I do not remember the day you disappeared.
I was too young to understand,
still small enough to curl up in your hat.
When I questioned mother
years later, she told me you had gone
to heaven, but I knew better.
You were in her heart, and kept it beating
by pacing back and forth.

Ploughshares   *Robert Louthan*

THE BEASTS OF BOSTON

On the ledges of Newbury Street
the birds cling to their cages;
lap dogs take cocaine from jeweled
spoons; only the declawed cats
dream without poppies.
Perhaps, as they say, there
are still bears on Beacon Hill
brave enough to meet the lions
in Copley Square. At night growls
spin through the air like hoopoes;
they hollow the Commonwealth
canyons.

First, believe in bears.
    Then believe

the Phoenix, rising, broke
the windows of the John
Hancock. Or was it the Great
Auk lost on its way
to the State House, sucked
in a downdraft, caught
by its own reflection?

The lambs, they say, are bearing
sharpened witness underneath
their wool. The better to cut
you with, grandfather.

     Know this: ever
since the tigers ate the swan
boats and the Pru was taken
by foxes, it hasn't been shadows
they stalk on Newbury Street.

Yankee   *Betty Lowry*

ANOTHER MEETING

Thirteen will attend,
Intellects fat and thin.
Egos playing pretend
In the vacuous din
Of vying moods,
Tissue paper skin
While one broods
And shrinks within—
As another meeting
Is about to begin.

Ball State University Forum   *Lawrence A. Lucas*

RAIN

Exclamation points surprise
the trees
whose tongues have been hanging
a month.
Barefeet
in little rivers
along curbs
run to sea.
Cars make clean sounds
over shiny roads.
Outside the garage
I pick up a stone
smooth as the palm of God.

The roof beats poems down.

I fall asleep, lamp on,
awaken by a cloudburst
of thoughts:
all over the city
thousands of windows
and rain passing
through uneven light.

The Christian Century   *Sister Mary Lucina*

THE CHILD'S DREAM

If I could start my life again,
I'd keep the notebook
I promised myself at nine—
a record of all the injustice
done by adults: that accusing tone
when they speak, the embarrassments
before relatives, like the time
I had to put on my swimsuit
in the car, while Mother chatted
with an uncle who peered in, teasing.
And *wouldn't* they be sorry
later, when they read it,
after I'd been run over by a truck,
their faces darkening
like winter afternoons.
And I, of course (if I survived),
would have a reminder,
in my own hand,
so I'd be the perfect parent,
my children radiant as the northern lights.
It's like poems you hope
will be read by someone who knows
they're for him, and cry
at what he did or didn't do,
wishing to touch your face once more,
to cradle your body.
You can almost hear what he'd tell you
with his voice that sounds
like the sea rolling in
over and over, like a song.

The Georgia Review   *Susan Ludvigson*

THE PALACE FOR TEETH

tired of lips and gums,
tired of cooperating,
my teeth shift
getting ready to make

their move.
they want a view;
they want turrets and banners;
they want goldfish and moats
and ladies-in-waiting;
they want a place to live in.
teeth!
you have chattered all night.
give up this idle dream.
look around.
your roots are here.
think of your roots.

The Chowder Review   *Abigail Luttinger*

CAT OF MANY YEARS

On soft puff of satin he now lies,
sleeping hours away—
Cat, how hunted tirelessly through long seasons,
who leapt with butterfly-desire,
who batted crisp brown leaf, who stalked elusive bird.
    I remember gray silken stripes—
kitten who probed ledges; sideboard, tables—
padded feet delicate as velvet
in their diagonal search, not a glass tinkling . . .
remember how draperies were pathways
to heavens; then always the fall
on four spread paws.

                    From darkness, cricket-sound
flutes—he opens slumberous, sulphur eyes,
languourously stretches, smoothes ruffled fur
with rough, wet tongue.

                    Insistent sound flutes—
he tenses, leaps to floor, to door,
mews loud demand . . . *Go with care, Old One!*
    Like quicksilver, he flows into night.
Cat, under myriad stars, do you forget years?

The Educational Forum   *Gertrude May Lutz*

SONG FOR A NEW GENERATION

When I was a child I liked being with people,
but even better, I liked being alone . . .
feeling cleanness of a day washed clear with wind;
watching shine on leaves moving with soundless music,
tuned to bell sounds in my heart that no one heard
except myself; knowing pathways by their crushed
pungence, the stain of green a brand upon my toes;

and I recall how wind-shaken pear blossoms fell,
a smoothness to my touseled hair, each white petal
a flake of purity.

        Yesterdays tilt toward tomorrows.
Time has a way of becoming vague—pathways
grown over with hours and days; years like a hedge
between memories. Yet in the eye's mirror there is,
standing small upon a sun-drenched universe, a child
listening to shape of song rising into immeasurable
blue, and the child is the rapt child that I was,
wearing my name and face.

The Educational Forum   *Gertrude May Lutz*

SURFACES

I always thought that
there is something
beneath every surface,
waiting to be
revealed. I watch
the bluejay pick
among the brick rubble, wonder
what is beneath
the bluejay's surface.
I cut open the bluejay.
I find a beetle. I do not
wonder what is beneath
the beetle's surface.
I have looked
beneath the surface
and there is nothing,
except, perhaps,
another surface.
Mystery is simply
a manipulation
of surfaces.

Kansas Quarterly   *David Madden*

SHELLS

I

In the long summer days when I was four
We'd drive the throbbing black sedan to the beach
Where Grandma lived. Upon that hot, bright shore
Lay glittering shells of amber, pink and peach.
The sun flamed; green waves tilted bells
On buoys far away. Beyond my reach
Beneath the waves and weeds were countless shells,

Clustering cool and distantly alluring.
"The homes," my mother said, "of animals."
I pictured tiny ones, inaudibly whirring
Through lavender and lapis trumpets masked
With filigree, blue sea grass darkly stirring.
I plucked a shell from hot sand as I basked,
Peered where the spiral center was sun-dried.
"What happened to the animal?" I asked.

II

Later, my Grandma sold the summer place
Grown bare and eerie after Grandpa died.
Now she arranges shells in a wooden case
On long smooth glassy shelves, intensified
By soft lighting: cowries, luminous
As memories. They glow with pink inside.
My Grandma dwindles flamelike before us.
Somehow she's frailer every time we come.
Her shells grow fluted, clear and nacreous;
Her tall clock ticks a deeper, sharper drum.
Where tiers of photos mirror past events,
She flickers out to bone and calcium.

The Lyric   *Medb Mahony*

HARVEST

In spring we tried with sharpened spade to dig
Bermuda roots and shoots of ribbon-grass,
Tender before they toughened. The flaxen flag,
Fastidious, remote, stood in a weeded place
And seedlings meant to bloom in drowsy hours
When spring was past, were set in promised rows
To open into tawny harvest flowers
And compensate for withered lilac sprays.

Now in autumn, weeds we missed in spring
Go furtively to seed; the crab and rye
Send their futures forth, inexorable and strong
As zinnias and asters. Oh, bitter meadow rue!
What spreads into our garden, gold with leaves
That drop into the slanted suns of love?

Poet Lore   *Jeannette Maino*

SKY PATTERNS

Against a sharp spring sky
a cloud of silhouetted birds
is a scarf blowing,
sand swirling,
surf curling,

whip lashing.
Black birds banking,
beating around the single dark crow that floats,
a rotted log becalmed in sea,
beset by waves, motionless.
Flowing birds with one identity,
one skeleton emotion, supple as a snake
coiling in sky,
swooping against the kernel of evil,
the cutting edge so thin on blue
it disappears, then curves again into the eye;
turning, swaying, sweeping birds
intent on the dark point of their predator.

Poet Lore   *Jeannette Maino*

NEIGHBORS

The green snakes in the mulch pile note
Not all people are all throat.

The grey toad in the bean patch finds
Not all folk have lumpy minds.

The martin in his chalet house
Sneers at neither dog nor mouse,

Observing they are not like cat.
The martin is above all that.

So one must marvel as one goes
How each illiterate barn owl knows

One must weave webs, one watch wheat
    sown,
Each minding business born his own,

Content that he acquire no labors
Characteristic of his neighbors.

Yankee   *Charles Malam*

ABOVE THE WALL

Suppose—
Ah well, suppose
That there could be no avenue between us,
That these ample rows
Of ancient child-remembered trees—
Suppose that these should go,
Their simple need outgrown,
And there, instead, a thoroughfare,
A rising flood, a wall of stone.

Then still my dear and still,
Though nothing should remain

Of our so long inviolate,
Our quiet lane,
Though neither you nor I were there
To meet again—
Still suddenly upon the air,
Across the flood,
Above the wall—
Still should I surely
Hear you call.

The American Scholar   *Susannah P. Malarkey*

CONVERSATION

You making small talk to hide reality;
Me staring through my hands,
        braided into knots in my lap.
We compete with gestures, and play games with our eyes.
The winner gets knives,
The loser gets to cut the silence.
Now we talk.
There isn't any sense of release,
        no easing of tension,
        no lifting of spirit.
Every word just cuts deeper into an old familiar track—
        the sound of a worn-out needle hurting a song you love.
I think we've played this one before.

Voices International   *K. Malley*

COLD SNAP

All the new flowers flat
on their faces in the garden.

Already our day is broken, snapped
like the daffodils
now sunk in mud.
I sit on the ruined bed.
Why should I try
to tell you why I turned
from you in sleep, even
as the lawn sprouted
its grey hair overnight?

The sun coming up is enough
for you, and you will say
spring permits this sorrow, but
it is more than a change
in the weather, more
than the spiked grass angry
outside the door, the litter

of leaves, the blossoms'
collapse, and please:

I don't want that fistful
of glazed tulips you will bring.

The Georgia Review   *Kathy Mangan*

CANTICLES TO MEN

(A Sonnet Sequence)

THE FIRST

How can a long-used body reconstrue
the time of innocence? The mind must strain
backward across old knowledge to the new,
unstroked, unpenetrated flesh; the pain
of nipples hardening to the boyish touch,
the pulse of sudden heat . . . and yes, the round
smooth neck of youth, the sudden alarm of such
hard arms, hard lips, the insistent tongue, the sound
of breathing. But then, they were each somehow afraid,
so young they were, so troubled in ignorance
they did not dare go further. And so they stayed
kissing and clinging in a murmurous trance,
over and over whispering other's name—
until, one day, he hurt her as he came.

MAN OBSERVED

You must know everything about a man
to savor his difference: the way his hair
grows on the nape of his neck, the line of the span
from hinge of jaw to chin; the solid or spare
disposition of flesh, and how his wrists
join to his hands, his ankles to feet, his feet
move as he walks; the way his body twists
and whether his arc of movement is complete
or spasmodic. Notice the texture of his skin,
furrowed or taut; the way his lashes grow,
his eyes are opaque or clear; how thick or thin
the bones of his fingers are. These you must know
to know what a man is like. And how he drinks,
and whether he lies to cover what he thinks.

New Letters   *Marya Mannes*

NOW I AM A MAN

As a boy,
I balanced
cockily on neighbors' fences,

romped dusty hills,
splashed knee-deep through mountain brooks,
hated my father and loved my mother.

As a youth,
I blushed,
bragged,
stormed young girls
on sun-kissed banks in dreams,
hated my father and loved my mother.

As a young man,
I married,
stiffened,
half-contained,
grimming away
to pay for love.
And I hated my mother and loved my father.

Now I am a man
trying to cry—
but with no one to blame.

Inlet   *Russell Marano*

A BOOK OF VERSES

The book slides from the shelf, pops open
to my fingers' touch. Not, love, as I would
now have you come to me. It has taken me
long to see the lifting force not
of reluctance but of independent pressure
that carrying you both towards and away
makes us closer than when your being soft
honeycombed our mutual yieldings with delusion.
Inside the front cover, your maiden name,
finely scripted, stares out at me, and in
the bottom corner an old sticker clings
and whispers: "The Book Nook, Lawrence, Kansas."
It is a book of poems bought with hard-
spared dollars. The poems also are spare, hard,
but some elaborately formal over a river of wit;
and I think of how you still read
with a steadily sharp and sensuous possession
and rarely with my own intermittent
carefulness of attention. Just as firmly
you put books aside and let them wait out
their years for the chance of your returning.

But you have always come back to your
commitments no matter how hard your thoughts
of putting them down. I, too, have been
like a book in your hands to be lifted up,
put down, laid aside, but only for instants,

and all the grace of your strength has
seemed to stem from your resistance
to the brutal or playful nothingness
to which everything at some time
seems to reduce itself. I used to think
of finding in the caves of my imagination
a breath to blow the world into shapes
that would open for your needs, barely
knowing that I was inflating a secret
wish of shaping you for my own dreams.

Do we converge towards love
only as the eyes trace through a book
for quick minutes? Or have we come
to give each other a long easier breathing
that widens to meet an opening world?

The Mississippi Valley Review   *Mordecai Marcus*

WINTER WATCH

So it comes to this, then:
backward toward a time when
memory is a scar cross-
stitching pain to joy, grief to loss
across a darkening valley where
already the horned owl waits,
perched in the larch for nightwatch,
his lantern eyes scanning the stillness
of abandoned home, woven tuft of weed
& matted hair nestling in the sycamore's crotch.
So begins the trilling of first cold,
crisp October whose blue clarity is
a lullaby to settle the cornshocked field
before winter locks in, setting its
teeth on edge & every eave:
wherever water seeks to run,
the hard cold fact glistens:
here winter nails us in
between hearth & dark
corners where already
our stories grow too dark to tell.

Carolina Quarterly   *Jeff Daniel Marion*

GOLDEN GATE: THE TEACHER

I am a bridge.
I lead them across the river
    of ignorance
To the isthmus of knowledge
    wherein lie

The berries of wisdom
  ripe and sweet
For just the taking.
Lovely berries
  sweet and drippy,
Juicy, heady, evergreen.

And they come. Singly
  and in droves.
Sauntering, running, galloping.
Some camp on the edge
  and go no further.
Others romp and play
  while some few discover
Juicy, drippy, tasty berries.
Sweet to look at; sweet to taste,
Luscious to lick on the lips.

Educational Studies   *Lilyan S. Mastrolia*

RUSTON, LOUISIANA: 1952

The man plays harmonica at midnight,
stomping around the kitchen,
and the sound of Oh Susanna wakes the child.
Here is the woman walking her children
before dawn, the clacking of the stroller
down the empty streets of the town.

Years leave us but the real snow
is still in the picture, the small girl
with socks on her hands
smiling thigh-deep in snow. You leave us for good
but I face the blackboard easel,
my chalk letters.
This is the picture of the girl turning her back
when the father says goodbye.

Every year a small child in me
grows larger, surrounded by the ribs of the past.
She rearranges the chronicle of pictures.
The years behind us become smaller,
clearer, as in an engraving
or the trees on a familiar street, repeating
and repeating.

Denver Quarterly   *Cleopatra Mathis*

AN AIRLINE BREAKFAST

An egg won't roll well
nor a chicken fly far:
they're supposed to be local.

Like regional writing or thin
wines, they don't travel well.
I do. I can pack in ten minutes.
I remember what I love when I'm gone
and I do not and do not forget it.
The older I grow, the better
I love what I can't see:
the stars in the daytime,
the idea of an omelet,
the reasons I love what I love.
It's what I can see I have to nudge
myself to love, so wonderful
is the imagination. Even this wretched
and exhausted breakfast is OK:
an omelet folded in thirds
like a letter, a doughy roll
and some "champagne": sluggard
bubbles half the size of peas.
But the butter's unsalted
and from the air the earth
is always beautiful, what little
I can see of its pocked skin.
Somewhere down there a family
farm is dying: long live
the family farm, the thinning
topsoil, the wheat in full head,
the sow in her ample flesh.
We're better organized than hunger
and almost as profligate.
Across the farmlands a few
of us in a plane are dragging
a shadow-plane, an anchor
that will not grab.

Antaeus   *William Matthews*

IN COLUMBUS, OHIO

Cautiously, hoping that nobody sees,
    I stop my hired car outside your house.
You are not there, but far away
    in California putting your children to bed—
Nor have I seen you once in fifteen years.
    It's past eleven: your mother's floating by
A window in a purple robe, your father's
    reading a book. They have both been sick.
Like all their friends, they've had their
    operations, retired from their jobs, and begun,
To their annoyance, talking—like any poet—
    of the past.

What if we had married? The notion seems
    outrageously absurd, and yet, before our lives

Began in earnest, that, as I recall, was once
    indeed the plan. For years, I preferred your
House to mine, your parents to my own. . . .
    And then I loathed them, thought these shadows
At the window pane were guilty of offenses
    intellectual and moral, that they drove you
Crazy to extremes of anarchy and lust through
    their chaste example and their discipline when
All the virginal austerity was mine.

What I want to do, you see, is to leap from
    the car, pound on the door, and say:
Forgive me! as they stand there staring in the
    autumn night. . . . (Perhaps we'd spend
An hour drinking brandy then, and tell long tales,
    and show each other photographs,
And shake hands solemnly at twelve. . . .) But
    of course I don't do anything like
That at all. I start the car and drive on East
    as far as Philadelphia.

Salmagundi   *John Matthias*

EUREKA

She spoke no English,
I, no Vietnamese. Yet
she lapped up words
like a matter-of-fact mimic,
her face expressionless.
Good morning
good morning.
How are you today
how are you today.
Fine thank you
fine thank you.
  . . .

  . . . .
And then one day a thunderstorm—
Good morning
—a no good morning. Yes teecha.
This day, the words, they came
not from her tongue
but from her mind.

Educational Studies   *Ruth O. Maunders*

A SHORT HISTORY OF THE TEACHING PROFESSION

Fifty-two years ago
when the first grade tumbled
like a gaggle of geese
into her classroom, they looked up—

startled—at the tall tree
the teacher was to shelter them.

Slowly they quieted to her
gentle intimacies of phonics,
bittersweet learning to read.

Today, one of those children
stands beside her
looking down at the face
weathered with hope,
touching the hand.
Bone and flesh hardly intervene.

All those words that fountained
from her have gathered into streams
that fountain other streams
forever.

The Christian Century   *Sister Maura*

WHEN IT RAINS

(for Sara and Bob)

Across the street, apples fill the gutter.
They float when runoff rises out of the dammed
drains, and half of them drift away when the storm
lifts over our mountain for the east.
I call them Seek-No-Furthers, but they're not.
They are Jonathans or Gravensteins,
almost bitter and from the wrong season.
Sometimes when the house begins to smell
of bruised apples, I make a pain of them:
not the world starved for wormy fruit, or old
women reduced to rotting plums: but a game
I imagine of gathering only
the ones that have fallen in an hour
of rain. I watched them drop and roll
and lift in the sluice. Now, I want to fix
their broken stems to the right branches,
turn, and watch the accidents that happened,
certainly as apples, around me.

Kansas Quarterly   *H. A. Maxson*

DRIVING; DRIVEN

a loose knot of geese crossed the road, vain & squabbling.
traffic resumed until the sheep came, anxious to please
shepherds who did not wish to cross but use the road. we
furious motorists honked, honked & nosed through. again,

traffic resumed, & swelled into a superhighway; but
hitchhikers encroached for miles, finally clotting flow

into one slow hot line. the police were not around, & all
the hitchers got rides, murmuring, "wherever you're
    going."

then, no further problems. everyone arrived on time
in the capitol & went to motels or houses;
by dusk, curfew had manufactured silence. all night
we travelers dreamt our vacations, considered how,

were we in charge, we'd dispose of the asphalt & oil
of the world, where we'd drive, how we'd survive.

Poetry   *David McAleavey*

OUR MOTHER'S BODY IS THE EARTH

    Our mother's body is the earth,
    her aura is the air, her spirit
    is in the middle, round like an egg,
    and she contains all good things in herself,
    like a honeycomb.
    She squats and the rivers flow;
    her breasts are the hills,
    her nipples the trees.
    Her breath scatters leaves
    on the shifting sands of her belly,
    and her knees roll out caverns and canyons below.
    Her menses makes the ocean floor shift,
    and tidal waves proclaim her pain.
    When we, her children, return to her,
    in ash or in dust,
    her flesh is scarred with accepting us back,
    and her intestines growl at our death.
    Mountains erupt with her agony
    and pour us back into the sea
    to hiss and spume her orgasm.

Anima   *Mary McAnally*

LATE AUTUMN WALK

    From inside nothing is plausible
    But the need for a change. Leafing
    Through the backcountry's paisley
    Ups and downs sways anyone out
    For a spin, flamboyants thrilling
    The air, a breath of which leaves
    One lightheaded with their conceits
    Whose bare, forked facts of life
    Will be raked against a winter sky.
    Or, steaming behind the kitchen window,
    To watch a solid week of drizzle
    Targeting the pond, tapping out
    On oak-leaf clusters monotonous

Ultimatums some have challenged,
Some accept. The wildings drop.
Sumacs flare in spiky disarray.

By November, it all comes clear,
And yesterday's mild invitation
Drew me outdoors—past the pond,
The pasture, into the gulley and brake
Whose angry dyes a frost had left
As nutskin, tobacco, cider, plum.

The Yale Review   *J. D. McClatchy*

THE LIGHTS GO ON

The bar my girlfriend works in is a dive.
Nothing left unwatched is safe there.
Even the shambles who runs the place
lost his battery to punk commandos.

My girlfriend has to pay her way, though,
and I can't give her much to go on.
At least it's something; the tips she gets
wouldn't keep an orphan in hand-me-downs.

For this she's Miss Red Cross to the troops.
Sometimes bonzai throws its arms around her
before relief can haul it to the gutter.
My girlfriend clings to whiskey in her station,

trades ironies with the handsome bouncer
and tells me nothing. I was the same:
glued to adultery by last call I'd move
anywhere but back. So the lights go on,

my girlfriend begins lugging the empties in,
wipes up after the dead and wounded,
then counts her take. All clear at last;
I follow her outside like a white flag.

Contemporary Quarterly   *Mark McCloskey*

VIEW FROM THE WINDOW

Awake now,
Fully sensible of my own chains.
I do not own this day,
This day owns me.

Outside the window of my cage
I see a chained monkey, there in the
Wheeling shadows where
Day casts its omens. Already
He fights *his* chains, shrieks obscenities,
Swooping from tree to tree like
The bird he is not.

He shrews, sunders in brazen defiance
His dark coagulation of leaves,
Arteries of branches.
I admire his spirit.
But soon someone will come, give
Him breakfast and
His hunger will accept his chains.

Now I hear *my* chains rattle in
The coiled silence of my own madness.
I writhe for space, for one wing-free sweep.
But there are milligrams to go,
Electrodes to accept. And after
The currents have split the atoms of
My own madness, I will hear
All the day long
The fall-out of our clinking
Brattling chains . . .

The Smith/20   *Jane McCoy*

I HAVE SEEN

I have seen
wind wring blood
from snow

I have known
ice to the bone
and deeper

I have watched
seven sure lovers
ride the road out

Still I flinch
at your easy touch
light
against my skin.

Prism International   *Kathleen McCracken*

AUGUST, AT AN UPSTAIRS WINDOW

A haze is on the lake; the dipping grasses
Seem blurrier in the distance than they were,
And stiller. A swallow swoops, a duck passes.
Nothing exotic happens. There's little astir.

I hear with keener hearing a piano playing,
Varying, repeating itself. Someone I love
Is down below at the keyboard, slightly swaying
To an exercise of Czerny's. It is enough.

The Lyric   *Harold McCurdy*

ON TEACHING DAVID TO SHOOT

Bullets splat downrange,
dimpling the target with holes.
Even from here I know his group
is tight. Tatters of cardboard
flutter, dead before
they reach the ground.

Twelve, head down with pride,
he works the bolt with stubby fingers,
each motion intentional, impressing me how safe,
how competent he is. Flies buzz
on his face like after battles.
I watch his living hand wave them away.

Here, between two banks of dirt,
I have taught him the secrets of balance,
of double sighting the target, eyes
not squinting, focused on the dark circle
and thinking the bullet there.
I have not told him everything.

When the paper appears splattered
with buckshot, together we crunch
over shells and deep ruts to the board,
put up a fresh target.
Cockleburs yellowed by sun
stab my legs like old regrets.

This son I would with choice
raise in another country
where the only trajectories
are flights of bees to the moist
dilating cups of tulips
yellowed with pollen.

Clipped in place, the target
waits like a child.
Together we crunch back
to our positions, and reload.
I tell him ready, aim
And he takes aim. And fires.

Southwest Review   *Walter McDonald*

EASTER MONDAY

Gray as a government holiday,
until across the road a cross
blossoms in the cloister, surprising
as Jesus himself must have been
at first. It is too brilliant
for belief: I must touch it,
I must see its wooden feet, I must

remark its missing nails, I must
observe the chicken wire where
the children twisted the thin stems
until they bled and hung dead.

But it still flowers today,
and I bless this body of light,
saying, *forsythia, jonquil, rose,
carnation: my Lord and my God.*

The Christian Century   *Michael McFee*

ARE THE SICK IN THEIR BEDS
AS THEY SHOULD BE?

Are the sick in their beds
as they should be—
healing, dying,
groaning,
bleeding, urinating,
defecating, vomiting,
running their sores
all in their appointed places?
Are the nurses and doctors at their stations?

Are the children at their play
as they should be—
laughing, pushing,
dirtying, tormenting,
sneaking, eating,
peeing, peeking,
joyfully singing
all in their appointed places?
Are the loving parents at their stations?

Are the dead in their graves
as they should be—
moldering, food-giving,
ghosting?
Are they in their appointed places?
Are the caretakers at their stations?

Quick! All of you
who are predator, prey,
hooker, pusher,
mind enricher,
fear monger,
and all the others—
find your appointed places.

Ah, we are each at our station.
Nothing is amiss.

Cedar Rock   *Joan McIntosh*

EARLY MORNING OF ANOTHER WORLD

After squid and cool white wine there is
no sleep. The long tentacles uncurl
out of the dark with all that was left behind.
Promises expand promises. A frayed mouth
loses its color in the dawn.

How easily the wine pours, the sand pours.
The hours mount with the waves until nothing
can be turned back. Wine glistens on lips,
a thin transparency of rose like everything
in this world.

Eyes appear out of clear water, blue shining
in the silvered surface which is itself clear.
Hands are asleep as two small squid out of water,
drying, miles now from the sea.

The avenues outside are banked with snow. The snow
is falling, filling empty vases, flowerpots that
have forgotten flowers, all memory of color.

A woman's face composes, beautiful, lean,
in the icy window, a face returning after many years.
Her mouth pulls at a smile, a final, frail act.

Perhaps she will laugh at this harvest of snow,
at the wind's stinging music, at the long nakedness
of the sky which holds nothing, which holds
the answers to all the questions she will not ask,
she will not know.

The Yale Review   *Tom McKeown*

TROUT FISHING IN VIRGINIA

The Exxon man tugs his CATerpillar cap,
rams a nozzle in my tank
and talks of fishing—
says he waded creeks all day
til heading for Baltimore at seventeen:
    "Never needed hook 'n line."
I picture a farm kid with fast hands,
ask about technique:
    "Simple.
    Ya heft a boulder high's yer head,
    womp all the rocks in the water—
    fish down under float to the top
    goofy as hell."
Overflow gas gags the tank,
stains my VA plate.
    "Cash er charge?"

Southern Exposure   *Michael Beirne McMahon*

LONELINESS

The psychiatrist works below the cliff.
And it is sad to see the patients climbing,
the leaves falling, the fogs leaning,
all against that rakish face, that lush leap.

From the top you see the sunny cat on a roof,
you feel blinding as a mountain goat.
You have to get ready
for a more complicated life.
You have to tell him the simple things
don't know how to put their round heads together.

You come from a country with high sides.
Building a stairway is like laying a fire.
People have thick legs for all the verticals.
There is no ambition, just fitness
and the cantering of bells.

You don't know why you go up and down.
He says just talk, but you can't describe it.
You come from a land of music.
You could never refuse a scale. You begin,
"This week I suffered these words and tune.
Maybe just listen to my voice."

The Agnie Review   *Sandra McPherson*

NEW ENGLAND GREENHOUSE

Nothing doing here,
no goings on.
Not a soft-lipped orchid
or lily is loose.
Whatever is, is.
The sky is the sky:
what served for heaven
has fallen, is glass
the rats translate
to sand.
What was a greenhouse
is a whistle for wind,
a scurry.
Where once the sun
kept house
and smooth gears moved
the heavens
with a sort of hum
is nothing now, nothing
but snow
curled in corners,
rust half through
with a boiler and coils,

and a sapling
up from the cellar
heading strictly
for the clear cut sky.

Yankee   *Rennie McQuilkin*

THE COAL MINE DISASTER'S LAST TRAPPED
MAN CONTEMPLATES SALVATION

Over and over again he remembers that huge black sound.
Some of the men were caught,
their mouths wide as caves, others
stopped in the act of running.

When he woke alone, in a 6-by-6-foot tomb,
he faced upward
where the sky should be.

For a few hours, or days, he dug with his nails
while the lamp on his forehead burned,
one weak yellow eye. Once he thought
he heard their shovels hushing in the coal,
their white prayers far above him.

Now nothing but the constant wheeze
of darkness.
Even while he lies down and sleeps,
his hands dream of digging, eyeballs
still flicker under their lids,
trying hard to remember
the color of light.

Midwest Quarterly   *William Meissner*

FALL

The prophets have died in the desert.
The angels with drooping wings
are marched off in threes
and assembled in the square.
They'll soon be judged,
asked what sin
drove them from heaven.
What mistake, fault, betrayal?
And they, with a final act of love,
Will gaze at us, misty with sleep,
and not find the devil's own daring
to relate that they fell
not from sin, not from sin,
but from weariness.

Webster Review   *Gabriela Melinescu*
                    —Translated from the Romanian by
                    Michael Impey and Brian Swann

IN THE HALF-POINT TIME OF NIGHT

In the half-point time of night
I wake.
The moon is full. It is mid-June.
I am awake often in the night.
Sometimes I get up and pace through
the house, watching
the clock move.

If there is any wind, I can hear it.
If the sirens from the fire house
at the end of this street go off,
I listen and wonder.

Once I went outside and saw
a falling star.
It made no sound from where I stood.

Falling is the sound I make
when I dream.

Once I woke with a cricket on
my pillow, turning the bed
into a field with its rubbing noises.

I like best waking at some
strange hour
with your hands moving over
my body with want, you pushing
closer to me—

and I, bursting with flowers.

Vagabond   *Ann Menebroker*

STEADY RAIN

All morning the mist
has rendered
the foothills elusive
and green. Here, close by
their base, I must share
in the mountainous gray
weather. When I look
east from within
this swath of rain, out
to the open prairies,
I can see that the
sky does brighten.
But it hurts
my eyes to look out
so far, to that long
luminous horizon
where you are.

Southern Poetry Review   *Lynn Merrill*

WHEN I CAME TO ISRAEL

I saw my daughter
when I came to Israel.
She sat between its wars
by a soldier on a hill.

Stones and olive trees
and the bright air all around . . .
So many stones! like stars
painted yellow and brown.

Suddenly, my son appeared,
carrying on his back
the soft horizon
like a huge, blue knapsack.

He strode from a field
and lifted me,
the way a young cliff
lifts the grey-haired sea.

My little father, he said,
at last you're here.
The fields, the orchards,
everything seemed so clear.

Then my daughter ran
down down the hillside,
excited like a stream.
She called me; and I cried.

But my wife was a dove
in the wailing wall.
She lit the moon.
Snow began to fall.

And she laid the snow,
as if at home again,
proudly, under the lights
of Jerusalem.

Jewish Currents   *Bert Meyers*

COPS AND ROBBERS

Oh, neighbors! I'll have such a quest shortly.
He's one you all know by heart, by the ties
That keep you short of the death he bids morning.

He'll come, attracting attention to his last footfall—
My door. With black, with badge, with lugging stick,
The unobtrusive way he pulls bodies out of the wreck.

Except, he makes his own weather conditions.
Every hair beneath his short-sleeves fills me with
Lust for the speeding violation; yes, it is best

To make masochism as socially acceptable as I can.
It is clear, from the way his one-sided glasses peer
Down at me, that I am to fill what the public's lust

Denied him up to now, and I reel with expectations.
The car saddles nonchalantly at the curb, curtains
Part, questions seep through in highly distilled murmurs.

He stands gaunt in the doorway, my hands go out—
I surrender! Oh, but he is here, damn the neighbors!
Criminal, he wants to be my toy, my crazy plaything.

Kansas Quarterly   *Bill Middleton*

AS IN THE LAND OF DARKNESS

Here, on this earth soft
as ash, even your serpent-
handled cane is worthless.
You struggle through the deep
field, sun warm on your face,
your free hand running over
the prickly crowns of pokeweed
and goldenrod. I point out
the swallowtail butterfly
fanning its wings on a harebell
blossom, the hawk floating
high above the wooded horizon,
but nothing penetrates
the pupils thick with mist.
Turning to take your weed-
scratched hand, your face
is radiant and wordless.
I stop to wonder at our
stubborn appetite for joy.

Buffalo Spree   *Robert Miklitsch*

BURY OUR FACES

Adultness is thrust upon us
when the last old man
of our childhood dies.
We attach to each other
like coral polyps,
abandoning our parents
to their fears of death;
we marry of primal necessity
and are reborn with our offspring.
Riding life like a train,
progeny are the newspapers
we bury our faces in.
Only when they're thoroughly read

and folded away beneath the coach seat
do we glance out the window
to see how many counties are behind
and how closely looms our destination.

Kansas Quarterly   *Bob Millard*

NOCTURNAL VISITOR

My lover is ridiculous.
He stumbles in my door
without any warning.
It's three o'clock in the morning.
He turns up at all hours
soaked with rain.
He has lost his jacket.
He's strung out on cocaine.
When he is here
I have a string of tiny explosions
in my brain.
Did he really say that?
If the police came by
they would say
Lady, lady, you mean you let him in?
Oh, officer, he is a fine
example of the truly criminal mind
and he has strong white teeth
to bite me with.
Come in, wolf.
Rip-off artist,
junky.
Every mother's nightmare,
love.
He spears me like a fish,
he rocks me like a wave.
He catches me up
and lets me fall.
There is no surety in love,
there's no safe place
except in living alone.
Asleep, this stupid boy is beautiful.

Centering   *Carolyn Miller*

THE TOUGH ONES

O beautiful bones,
your hungry father devours you,
middle class goods, no more dreams
of winter wheat, no more seed
to plant.

Drying out my skills,
o little jail in Louisiana with yellow shades,

dead fish, big back rooms in January,
bailiffs with their engines warm
cleaning house.

Cold winds blow
through the soiled sheets,
old brown men bringing their lives out into the light,
a maiden with small breasts nursing
a dying candle.

It is like that on a lost morning,
all blue and swollen, the sea on the rocks
and the gulls of the universe
feeling their bodies
for bruises.

The Hollins Critic   *Errol Miller*

MAY YOU ALWAYS BE THE DARLING OF FORTUNE

March 10th and the snow flees like eloping brides
into rain. The imperceptible change begins
out of an old rage and glistens, chaste, with its new
craving, spring. May your desire always overcome

your need; your story that you have to tell,
enchanting, mutable, may it fill the world
you believe: a sunny view, flowers lunging
from the sill, the quilt, the chair, all things

fill with you and empty and fill. And hurry, because
now as I tire of my studied abandon, counting
the days, I'm sad. Yet I trust your absence, in everything
wholly evident: the rain in the white basin, and I

vigilant.

The Agni Review   *Jane Miller*

ON THE WINGS OF A DOVE

Once after he'd come back from Ohio
he worked at road construction for a summer
back up on the Laurel and Ivy Rivers
in Madison. After work, instead of going
all the way to Asheville, he'd stop by
a bootlegger's in Marshall, buy some white,
and drive to a place down on the French Broad River
below Redmon Dam. Pulling his car
down a sandy road, nosing it back
into the willows and sycamores so far
they closed around it, he'd sit there after sundown,
the smell of tar and sweat and asphalt in his clothes,
smoking and drinking white, listening to bluegrass
on the radio, watching the river, mountains and sky
run together in the coming dark.

Catfishermen built fires along the bank
and over on the island, and hung their lanterns
out over the water. His troubles sat
right under his breastbone, black
as a treeful of starlings, all talking at once.
But when Bill Monroe and the Bluegrass Boys
played Wait a Little Longer, Jesus, or Blue Moon
of Kentucky, and his mind throbbed and hummed
like pistons under the hood of a good truck
hauling his thoughts over an open highway,
and the lights on the riverbank, and out
on the island got in tune with the bluegrass and throbbing
pistons, and his mind turned into a whining sawblade
spinning so fast it grew invisible and quiet

the starlings under his breastbone stopped talking.

Then, white doves rose out of his ribcage
and flew out over the river toward the island.

Carolina Quarterly   *Jim Wayne Miller*

A CLASH WITH CLICHES

The peace in the valley will sing to me like a choir
when the end of a perfect day laughs at me wryly.
I shall lie in the grass of green pastures as in the
    trough of a wave
that has washed me clean of the day
as I lean back to finger the scars of a good fight
like a lonesome child who plays with himself.
Oh, it will be good to get out of the wind
after a high on the raindrops,
for sleep is smoother than wine, swifter than prayer,
    sweeter than love
in that time when all the cliches standing tiptoe
take flesh of my tired bones.

New Letters   *Vassar Miller*

ONE MORNING

I wakened to love and music, coaxed from the shelter
of sleep's green grove to a bustling kitchen
where affection is spoken in golden vowels of eggs
and crisp consonants of bacon, in airy whispers of biscuits,
in the sibilants of milk and butter;
where a blind boy plays on his squeeze box, but the melody comes
out of this rancid land, pinched by the sun,
pocked by the wind, chewed and spat out by locusts,
suckled on drouth, singing with cracked lips
that nevertheless life's sharp edges
are tucked away if only for moments

of a remembered morning
wakened to love and music.

Kansas Quarterly   *Vassar Miller*

FOR YEARS

At midday
sparrows gossip on
the window ledge,
wisps of cirrus
drifting overhead, passing
beneath a shredded
collar of moon.

October declines—
a scrawl of blackened pods
hangs from the locust;
grasses arch, stiff
with frost; sleet,
crossing the plains,
beats its tatoo.

My father used to nap
in his chair after work
and a long drive: sunlight
paled in the west
windows, threw fading patches
on the rug.

For years I knew
why he did this,
and have done the same,
slipping down
wave after wave
where the trough opens
wide below,

not anxious ever
to rise again, emptied,
breathless,
and find only the room—
single window, door,
a tree outside heavy with snow.

Descant   *Ralph J. Mills, Jr.*

A MUSICIAN RETURNING FROM A CAFE AUDITION

(of the Owner)

Now that guy was a real fruit. A peach,
To be exact: smooth, sweet-smelling, kind
To the eye, fuzzily attractive. Oh, but to the reach,

To the closer look, damned if you don't find
Him a rotten dripper, bruised on the back side,
Brown from sitting on his soft butt;
Past ripe, but unaware that the tide
Of his past-ripeness is flowing, hungry to glut
On his easy pink pulp: O God! drop
A blight on cafe owners, the entire crop.

Kansas Quarterly   *Michael D. Minard*

OLD EGO SONG

Old ego climbing out of the trap door on the top of my head.
Wearing his bald ego feathers, strutting around the
house, turning lights off and on. Bald ego stepping
out to pick up another pack of cigarettes—flying high—
ego-eyed.

Old ego coming back from the grocery store, climbing back
in through the trap-door. Thinks he's 30 years old, thinks
he really knows how to tune up a Volkswagen. He even thinks
he can dance all right, though we all know better.

Old ego sitting down in his chair thinking back on what
happened this morning. Thankful he turned down the newspaper job.

He should be out grilling steaks in the backyard.
He should be eating meat.
But he's just chuckling to himself
and he's not saying what it is.

I suppose we should leave him there,
alone, nodding off to sleep, dreaming.

Kansas Quarterly   *John Minczeski*

CHANNEL WATER

(Song for the 16th Century)

Narrow water, channel water,
mainland now but once the daughter
of North Sea and Ocean wide—
stormy Circe, changeling bride—
be you gentle, smile you fair
as the rose-sweet summer air.

He who is my heart's delight
sails for France this very night.
Keep him well, that I may say,
"He is safe now in Calais."
Narrow water, smile you fair—
guard him well whose child I bear!

The Lyric   *Virginia Scott Miner*

SPRING SEQUENCE

5
I hear it in the river first
and step outside. This rain
has not climbed my hill yet.
Then, tiny pricks
on the roof. It begins.
Water over water: a perfect time
for love, all the creatures
hiding under leaves.
Alone on the porch, I
whisper familiar names to the wind.

25
Sometimes I think it is
the waterfall, but I know
it is the wind I hear
long before it arrives
at my clearing. West,
the beech trees are calm
as squaws in their blankets,
then after the sound of it
they begin to sway in quiet
pleasure. At last it is here,
the smell of rain on the way,
the burning left for another season.

The Black Warrior Journal   *Judith Minty*

FOR MICHAEL

When the storm
gave me its dark clouds
for hair,
I became this black baby
lying in my mother's arms.
And when the squirrels
gave me chestnuts for eyes,
I watched my body
grow nipples,
watched them grow slowly
throughout covered nights.
And when I grew older,
I spoke words
that hid
behind venetian blinds.
And when I came to you, husband,
I came as a black feather
that had moved
against wind.

Open Places   *Karen L. Mitchell*

THE FISHERMAN'S WIFE

In December predawn
I ferry him to Stonington.
Rustling inside his oilskins,
he holds his knees to his chin
and dozes; already at sea,
he rocks in the seat beside me.

Three times I rolled the vows
over my tongue for luck.
Before we used to lie tangled
amid fishnets and tackle.

We cross the causeway.
The smells of salt and mud stir in him;
he rejoins the crew.
The tides rise and fall:
a great sponge somewhere
squeezes and lets go.
The bay moves,
the seaweed hissing.

Going home, other cars seldom pass,
but each set of lights draws me.
I slide slightly toward the twins,
the double arms,
the tendril company,
wrapping me, gathering me.

I learned
the first wish brings you wealth,
the second,
wisdom; the third
undoes all three.

The granite blocks
that line the causeway
flash by like fish.

Dark Horse   *Nora Mitchell*

GOING TO PRESS

Those Denver evenings I'd drag myself
down to the green but treeless "park" hemmed
by light traffic, construction sites, a hospital,
whose reedy seepage deepened, widened, did
all it could to assert pondhood. Sprinklers
would be hurling ack-ack. Down I'd flop
into a start of coolness, watch little fish
dimple the surface, lip flies and flip out
flightily, plop-plop-plop like a skipped stone.
They soothed me, some. I'd think about the moors.

An hour's drive and a whole day's exhaust fumes
divided park and pond from the Front Range
smudged by dusk, posing a low profile
cut out of soft black construction paper
with kindergarten scissors, a set
for the melodrama Sunset. Wrenchingly desirable.
Impossibly remote. Flung there instead
I'd feel my unplugged brain click
like a cooling iron, its root system of fine
wires threaded through abdomen and back
be easier, tic by tic.

Those hag-ridden evenings I sensed, dully,
how *extremis* in some forms can only be
relieved by increase, ever. *Press* the Swedes say
naming that state of strain, that desperate state,
and humble me again
to hear Giles Corey, aged family man
killed for a witch in Salem, flat on his back
in a green field the final days of his dying,
crushingly burdened, breathless, swollen, protruding,
croak his two words: More weight.

Poetry   *Judith Moffett*

FEBRUARY

Here, it is never enough
to say things will get better
or a man's a man. Nothing
is that simple, we admit,
but we try—we have that
to say for ourselves. Here,
we remember nothing
but the time we knew nothing
of this town we have named
February, after the month.
If there were more to say
we would mention only
that for each person
in February there is either
one ill or one blessing
and no one knows which.
Thus, the child
beaten by his parents whispers,
"I understand, I understand,"
just as his father believes
he knows. And the woman
whose beauty makes her
desirable is vain enough
to think it can't last.
In a town as small as the month

is short, we have come
to live with more than enough
and everything.

The Black Warrior Review   *Larry Moffi*

THE WORD MAN

He collects used words
on our block where once
we were proud spokesmen

of the neighborhood. Ice-man,
rag-man, peddler of wooden
nutmegs—we have haggled

them all obsolete. Now
we can deny no man. We sell
him words for a song,

and dance to his bell's toll
like idiots. We sold him
ugly and *sinful,*

and felt better for it.
Later we gave up derivatives
and possessives; soon after,

old favorites—*tessellate*
and *flinch.* Tomorrow
I will sell him my name.

California Quarterly   *Larry Moffi*

CHRISTMAS AT VAIL:
ON STAYING INDOORS

I knew the town from nightmares,
recognized at once this white pavement:
do not tell me it is only snow.
Underneath the frost the streets are just as white,
immaculate as condominium walls,
clean and pure. In the bistros we dine
endlessly for recreation: steak and fish.
(No hunting is allowed.) We can eat fruit here
and not expect retaliation. (Not a single tree
died for these chalets; they are built of inconceivable
alloys of indigestible material.) There is no killing here.

Even when we walk outside, we stay indoors.
Automatic sentries guard us, blindly approve
each time we pass from LionsHead to The Village.
All the buildings are provided with glass eyes.
I have become convinced that huge machines

inside the mountains manufacture breezes
to slap our cheeks from white to red.

There is reason for the loudness of the wind.
It covers the gnawing of trapped rodents,
the steady drum of taproots seeking water.
Every wall in Vail is hollow. Inside,
the ghosts of laborers clamor
like steam-pipes in the night.

Underneath a fireplace stacked with spruce logs
there is a hill of gifts. Nearby, a newspaper
carols inaudibly of rape and of starvation.
We burn it after dinner. Its ashes
drift like blackbirds over Vail,
detonate on tame hills like grenades,
liberating the ground. The mountains,
rising up like fists, surround the town.

The North American Review   *Pat Monaghan*

THE TRIANGLE LADIES

The Triangle Ladies
want you tonight
on the chalk brick streets
spending the hot away.
They want your blue curls,
your long strides,
the David dip in your hip.
You
walk with them
wearing new shoulders
wide as your blue car
gliding cool and thick
over lighted bricks.
        Silver chain purses flash
on rubied wrists
draped over your silk tweed sleeves.
They rub the roseblades on your cheeks
and hush
at the gold flesh of your throat.

I want to go with you and the ladies
into the Oyster Bar, to sit
beside you on the red seat,
to eat the clams you call for,
to drink the beer you pour from the glass pitcher.
I want to straighten your collar wide
and touch with the tip of my finger
each spark
in your row of moonpearls,
each movement

in the white swell of silk night ocean
        spilling around us triangle ladies
—the sweetest sea.

The Mississippi Valley Review   *Carol Artman Montgomery*

EXISTENCE

There is a careful look
to cows
brindled and unmoving
on brassy humped hills.
Some child has
mused on morning,
wondered about night,
then placed cows there
to remember what
existence is
before it gets wiped off.

The Christian Century   *Sheila Moon*

BELOW BALD MOUNTAIN

Having never read or wanted to,
the farmer squints for a message
on the mountain,
some explanation for arthritic legs
and the eyes that mistake
apples for pears.
This season for the first time
he listens to the wings of birds.
The somber migration rustles
like corn stalks.
In it he finds his own words.

Mountain Review   *Janice Townley Moore*

THE ARGUMENT

The argument begins the week we marry.
He asks me to have him cremated
at death, to have his ashes scattered
over deep woods humus, feeding spiderwort and ferns,
wild strawberries, his remains living again in that way.

I tell him no. It is tradition in my family to fill
stone-marked graves of a certain brick-walled tract;
our places wait. Death will not remove
you from this family. Like those there now,
you will be visited, brought flowers: a lily
at Easter, mums on your birthday.

You will be addressed. That you do not answer
will make you no less in family eyes than sullen
Uncle John or Sharon of the vodka.

But now, he says, it is a documented fact
that the soul leaves the body at the millisecond
of the last inhalation, long before burial. A Swedish doctor
has rolled beds of the gravely ill onto scales,
has measured the loss of the soul's weight
at that precise instant. Do you need to sit
beside the buried rotting peel of a banana
to recall its fruit?

Poetry   *Jane P. Moreland*

ORPHEUS TO EURYDICE

(for Laurence Lieberman)

1
As you know, I have not lost you.

It would be presumptuous
in the violet evening
to imagine a freedom
apart from the terrors you have designated,

apart from the body's decay,
the cancer hiving within
and the sullen taste of puke
with which the story ends.

2
Less trade now in this city
which I've loved ever since my childhood's
wintry nights—

but an immense bustle of
decay, as peddlers, jugglers
throng the avenues

and I seek to follow the one
of all these millions
who will hand me your gift—

as it were a flower.

3
Many years have passed since Europe,
dying then as always,
sent me the message shielded
by your green-grey eyes.

I drove you out the back roads—do you remember?
and put my arm across your shoulders
tensed slightly under
the white angora.

4

Men are killing men,
they're killing women and children:
whites and yellows are good at it,
blacks and browns catching up fast.
Do you like the touch of blood in your tapestry?

Yes, adored, you do—
and all the more, I expect,
since you can read in their swine-snouts
how ready they are to grovel.

5

Three times I came into you:

in the garden one night of mid-August
when a wind was stirring the shrubs—
on the river's bank while crows were cawing
down a long September afternoon—
and again after the first frost
when the fields had lost their color.

Then you died and rotted.

6

When I went looking for you
the lands were grey and locked:
the straight had been made crooked,
the messages put into code.

It seemed to me, though, that one old crow I saw
in his uneven passage
from bare tree to bald ground
could riddle me out the answer.

7

And the city was a screen of images
that closed you off
in their virtual past:

The childhood park of games
where we played in my made-up country
falling and scraping our knees—
the soiled room where I encountered women
tangy in the sweat of summer
(you were there, in all those women)
and the first songs came.

8

The smoke of the city at night
rising from obscure chimneys
smirches the moon.

A month after you died
I saw a bat skimming
from the cornice of a public building
and followed his lurching flight above the warehouses . . .

He had no message from you.

9

How to make the descent, then,
to your silent mirror?
The old paths are blocked by
history's debris
and we find we dislike the new ones,

their way ever downward
empty of mythologies
with at the end a few bland ghosts
starved to wisps of gesture!

10

And the mystic inner sea
is itself problematic.
I shall find a raft for the crossing, no doubt,
and abandon it on the far side

and making my way through the grey lands
in birdless quiet
attain at the last but a city full
of the shadows of jugglers and peddlers.

11

To find you, to lead you back by the hand,
adored one terrible with claws!
I lust for your haunches
as the old ones lusted for the Sphinx

and am not reconciled
that you be stuffless now
serene in your shadow-pasture
in the last reflex of the mirror—

not reconciled, nor shall be,

12

even though the harsh deaths,
the murders, are continuous
and I do not wish to see the blood
mirrored in your eyes—

even though I well know
you love what is and will be
and may not deflect by an eyelash
the hand that strikes to kill.

13

But see, now,
your eyes are passageways,
your breasts the memories of fullness,

and those strong legs that clasped me thrice
have walked you into the shadows

from which I say I shall reclaim you
lucidly as though
you bore a second history of my ancient self.

14
What remains—my song?
To be bandied among the jugglers
and parceled out by the peddlers, to be sure.

It is something given
as all else is given here—
once in the tangled steaming heap
and once in the mirror.

15
I greet each day as it comes.
May the sun rise and set
with my blessing always
of man and song.
How endless it all is,
how without compunction!

Already I have turned and looked—
and you, already, have been lost again.

New England Review   *Frederick Morgan*

FEBRUARY 11, 1977

(to my son John)

You died nine years ago today.
I see you still sometimes in dreams
in white track-shirt and shorts, running,
against a drop of tropic green.

It seems to be a meadow, lying
open to early morning sun:
no other person is in view,
a quiet forest waits beyond.

Why do you hurry? What's the need?
Poor eager boy, why can't you see
once and for all you've lost this race
though you run for all eternity?

Your youngest brother's passed you by
at last: he's older now than you—
and all our lives have ramified
in meanings which you never knew.

And yet, your eyes still burn with joy,
your body's splendor never fades—
sometimes I seek to follow you
across the greenness, into the shade

of that great forest in whose depths
houses await and lives are lived,
where you haste in gleeful search of me
bearing a message I must have—

but I, before I change, must bide
the "days of my appointed time,"
and so I age from self to self
while you await me, always young.

The American Scholar   *Frederick Morgan*

MY CHILDREN'S BOOK

This story goes on a long time,
Children, and how shall I appear
For years in your translations?
As the kind bear I am
In our polite family mythology?
Or Mr. Fear-in-the-Forest, the Man
Who Made the Mountains?
       No.
All Sunday in your recollection
I grouse in my chair in our story
Reading my dull thriller,
The Case of the Ordinary Man,
Quickly through to the predicted end.

And do not wish to be interrupted.
Not much is true, we know, in our story.
Still, in it each of us gets something
He wishes. And what that comes to.
We are writing it now. You
Are taking it down
In part from my dictation. This
Is one book I shall not finish. I
Leave it to you. I
Wish I could see how it will end, I
Wish you could tell me. This
Is the exciting part, do not interrupt me.

The Georgia Review   *John N. Morris*

THE RIGHT TO LIFE

In the novels I shall never write
The characters wait
For me to allow them to happen.
They have been patient there
In that nowhere for years
As in their causes.
But now they are stirring.

They say, *Instar the sky.*
Give us our children.
They believe in their lives,
The paper wind, the ink houses.

Optimists, theologians,
They suppose they
Would be made to suffer
To some purpose. They argue
As from a design.

They believe in their lives.
Because they are mine
I cannot bear to tell them
How in my words
I would find them wanting,
How suddenly some morning
I would tear them to pieces
Because they are mine
According to their deserving.

New England Review   *John N. Morris*

THE HANDS

Yes, our faces are ten blanks
but bearded with the ghosts of
quarter moons. So we are wise, wiser
than you who go clothed in fur,
than you who have eyes.

Prism International   *Daniel David Moses*

VOICE

My voice has been imprisoned
in the voice of a crowd in a stadium,
before the grandstands empty
leaving behind my voice among the stragglers,
in idle conversation, in the odd shout.

I wanted to have a river to work with,
a voice that thirsts and drinks,
swimming and diving among the nude bathers,
surrounding the body it chooses.

I did not want my voice to be only a difference
of shadow as a black pine is in the night.
I wanted my voice to be a different, moon-like thing
that those on foot can see by.
I wanted my voice to reappear
suddenly in the night,
to last after touch, taste, sight, hearing.

The Michigan Quarterly Review   *Stanley Moss*

MEADOW GRASS

(for Marie Mellinger)

There is more to this meadow under the mountains than
    mere names
of fescue, blue Timothy, panic grass, Fox sedge, hop
    sedge—but my eyes
keep coming back to the dark strokes of plaintain, each
    head as if surrounded
by a ring of pale insects, a curious, almost ugly crown

The Cherokee called these weeds "Footprints of
    Englishmen"
Wherever the settlers went the plaintain grew, broad leaves
escaping under their heels, the wayward wagon tracks
grew like dark stars on the banks of a Devon lane
seen here against clay of the same colors: oxblood to
    orange,
foxbrush, fernseed, the outrageous rust of men
washed into creeks in the runoff of heavy rains
mingling Greek blood and Trojan
like Scamander in the old tale
some settlers had by heart, and more never heard of

The roots of red flowers went to the chiefs and warriors
Yellow and white were squaw flowers, went to the
    mending of women
Children sucked on the creeping stems of the pea plant
    and grew eloquent
in a language that no longer mattered. It was the
    settlers' names
that caught up with the changing meadows—wort, balm,
    and bane
Gerard and Culpepper claimed them

Not the Seven Bark, nor the lovecharm Pipsissewa profited
in the eclipse of the Sun Spirit and the Star Maiden
only the transplanted plaintain—spear, vinegar sponge,
    corona of insects
only the Deptford Pink, Venus's Looking Glass,
    Mouse-Ear . . .
The weed-strong invaders clung like pea plant to the alien
    clay

I would escape a moral if I knew how
or remake one if I could stop my wandering
The grass changes under my feet. Words, names, change
    in my mouth
under a shifting, mostly indifferent sky

Poetry   *Michael Mott*

PLAYING CATCH

(for my Father)

The instant released, it spins
and you relax from your stance,
an old man, without a hold.
What survives is the bright sun,
a bird's song, the breeze, rolled out
of concentration:
                              being:
a dull shout peripheral
to the smooth ball.
                                        You
wait alone, your man's body
weakened leaning at your pitch,
thinking; thinking part of it
gone
        to me at the far side
of your lawn, some continent,
another world.
                        And I slip
with the dizzying thing, claim
the grass is damp, and each blade
bent on getting back at us.

Our play spreads too wide around;
in the shade my daughter stirs,
moodily wakes, wants to cry:

we have broken into dreams.

Pig Iron   *Keith Moul*

NIGHT SONG

Among rocks, I am the loose one,
among arrows, I am the heart,
among daughters, I am the recluse,
among sons, the one who dies young.

Among solutions, I am the problem,
between lovers, I am the sword,
among scars, I am the fresh wound,
among confetti, the black flag.

Among shoes, I am the one with the pebble,
among days, the one that never comes,
among the bones you find on the beach,
the one that sings was mine.

The Ohio Review   *Lisel Mueller*

QUESTIONS AND ANSWERS

Have you cast your net out over the world?
I have cast my net.
Of what did you make it?
Of yarn.
What did you take for yarn?
Silk, nettle, cobweb, and steel.
Where did you get it?
Silk from my mother's white hair.
Nettle from my husband's eyes in bed.
Cobweb from my sister's bridal ring.
Steel from my nursemaid's wooden rosary.
How long did you work on the net?
A hundred years.
Where did you cast the net?
Over mountain and valley.
What did you catch?
Feathers. Little feathers.
Is that enough?
That's the world.

Paintbrush   *Doris Muhringer*
                          —Translated from the German by Beth Bjorklund

DEJA VU

Memory comes, like the shadow of fog,
quietly. Wings flutter, invisible;
recognition trembles in silence,
wind chimes in the slightest
of summer breezes.
Why does this scene, this object,
echo in the hollow of the spine?

What dormant knowledge rises
like moon-pulled water, to tell us
what has come has come again?
Do vanished lives
cry out from secret caverns?
Is it all
illusion? What
tugs at the sleeve of the soul?

The moment
passes. We scrutinize it later,
turn it over in the mind
like a pearl. Like a pearl
it hides its core, its cause.
The feeling, lingering,
like the ghost of the mist,
disturbs us.

The key fumbling for the hand.
The echo groping for the sound.

Northwoods Journal   *J. B. Mulligan*

ENEMY, ENEMY

My enemy is dead. The news arrived
This morning in a rush, and all that I
Could find in my emotions was a dry
Grin, and yet . . . The man is gone, unshrived,
And justly unremembered here. A few
Of us, who still remain and knew him well
Enough to know the market drop in Hell
On his arrival there, complain. His due
Was even less than this, and yet . . . I ponder
On this beast and once again the fog
Collects upon my window, and the dog
Howls on paths too old and cold to wander
On. Hate cries hot, and I regret
The civil words I have to say. And yet . . .

Western Poetry Quarterly   *Cecil J. Mullins*

RECOLLECTION

When first our eyes engaged the startled Bird
Of love, and followed the shadow of her wing,
We recognized her Form without a word,
And left her nameless at the virgin spring.
I waited seven years to hear her sing
A name I knew, and when at last I heard,
It seemed a water thrush sang three sweet notes—
And turned her head, thinking some danger near,
And flew away to hide in deeper shade.
I hear the echo of those broken notes
In every accidental sign you've made,
In every chance remission of your fear.
Give me your hand! She can't be far away—
This time we'll see her tip her head and sing.

The Lyric   *Marilyn R. Mumford*

THE SILVER RACER

Before the days of duty
when beauty was waiting
behind every bush and moonrise

I kept my special toys
under the window with
the secret hole in the wallpaper

And as the moon crisscrossed
itself with winter limbs
and night wings flying

I rolled a little silver car
with red wheels on the sill
till I fell asleep against the glass

And no one believed me
when I told them at breakfast
that I rode in my car where God

was as small as a june bug
and sat beside me as we drove
across the rug to the mouse hole

Southwest Review   *Joseph Colin Murphey*

CROCUS

You are wrong about the crocus,
the bulbs closed tight beneath the still
unbreathing snow. You can't rouse them
to bring back that Easter garden
of violet deaths and golden resurrections
slipped from our childhood eyes.
Even if your yearning could find
that Sunday morning faith, long ago uprooted
with our cellophane grass and paper flowers,
how could its faded heat sink down
through frozen earth to stir the crocus
and raise it back to life?
Yet you say the crocus will be first.

But this morning I passed the East Gate
near Delevan and Main where early sun
dredges snow in Forest Lawn,
and I saw that the first to rise
are as low and gray as weathered bone:
the rows of stone. Slowly they melt back
to sight, not blooming, not singing,
but tuned to the reappearing sun
like impassive faces on Easter Island,
patient for some promised resurrection.
Flowers they are of rare old names.
Call them simply forget-me-nots
and see they are flowers of revelation.
Each year they are the first to rise.

Harper's Magazine   *Joan Murray*

LIED IN CRETE

I gaze out a hundred windows:
a silent air

rolls over the fields.
Your name along a hundred roads,
night coming out to meet it,
a blind statue.
And yet,
in the stillness
of Mycenean dust,
I could already
sense your face,
your promised shape,
rising to haunt
the grave substance of my dreams.
Only there do you answer my call,
every night,
your sleepless memory,
your wakeful absence
distilling a vague alcohol
through the slow shipwreck
of the years.
I gaze out a hundred windows:
a silent air rolls by.
In the fields,
an acrid Mycenean dust
announces a blind night
bearing the salt of your skin,
the ancient coin of your face.
In that certitude I rest.
In happiness.

Review—21/22   *Alvaro Mutis*

TOO MANY MILES OF SUNLIGHT BETWEEN US

Sitting upright in the 2 a.m. blackness, off-balance,
blank, I make the image of your body flower in the darkness.
Like the sun, I keep it alive by staring at you tending
the colorful faces and wild plumage of what seems impossible
for me to grow. I've grown silent twisting with the houseplants
I keep dying of neglect.

Your garden rises in a slow commingling of sunlight
and laughter until I'm over my head, under the covers,
throbbing, thinking I can't do this any longer.

I want to be buried in something totally unimportant
and not find your neck-twisting body at the bottom of it.
I want to find myself at the end of the day in love
with the simple curve of a comma, which I now see as a scythe.
I want a pause in which everything sighs and goes back
to normal: the miles of sunlight between us as simple
yellow space. The blackness, blank.

Cedar Rock   *Jack Myers*

TO SUMMER

You can only have a lot of power,
never enough:
the strength to lift
rivers from their beds
one drop after another up,
millions spirited heavenward
lifted in the giddiness of sunstroked days
above the drought and dead cattle,
the mud and fester made
not from their leaving
but their failure
to return.
And in your long absence too
you can paralyze the flow,
ice the brooks,
freeze stone
banks.
You can also return late,
stay too long,
appear surprised,
come to tempt
or disappoint.
This we know,
we who eat what will grow,
rise and sleep, and leave
just once.

The Paris Review   *Alan Nadel*

THE FISHERMEN'S WIVES

The fishermen's wives
Smelling of seablood and foam
Have exchanged their pink cheeks
And feather hair
For the heads of fish
Their breasts
Once circles of soft and shimmer
Have turned into fins
Scaly and wet with salt-milk

The women
Whose husbands are fishermen
Grow green and cold in nets
All they know of moonlight
Is that it moves the tides
And causes their deep fish parts
To drip bright red brine

The wives of magicians
Make love inside of top hats

And turn into rabbits
Before the third act
While executives' wives
Attach leather handles
To their shoulders
And give birth to paper children

Praise to the doctor's wife
Who heals herself

God bless
The mortician's wife
Who lives forever

Black Maria   *Elaine Namanworth*

YOURS TRULY

Sometimes a wild thing
will walk right out of the woods
into your hands
and you, thinking of something else,
kneel and recieve it
as though it were yours to stroke
from the very first—
and then it's gone,
the after-color of fox fading
into the woods and the woods
darkening shut behind it—
while you stare down at spread hands
measuring an emptiness
nothing else can fill . . .

and this is love
and this is a judgment.

Poetry Now   *Leonard Nathan*

VOTING MACHINE

nowhere can flesh feel more limp
body more spilled
than casting among millions
one vote
to kill the censor
dismember the thief
smash the pretender

with all my weakness i
pull the lever
against all tyranny at least
i scratch my mark
wiggle a negative

never a force of
nothing

however miniatured
i will speak
me

Poet Lore   *Norman Nathan*

I CAUGHT THIS MORNING
AT DAWNING

I caught this morning at dawning,
And the sun on the last night's snow
Revealed that there was no footfall—
Only the soft silent flow
Of Earth and Earth's undulations,
And the white unbroken snow.

This is our soul at each dawning,
Silent and perfectly white,
Unblemished it follows our contours
As if somehow God's delight
Is to cover us softly with mercy,
And renew us over the night.

Unity   *Dennis Neagle*

THE PRINT-OUT

at first light
this very day
a pick-up flight,
starling and grackle,
blackbird and may-
be the odd jay,
a motley lot
that'd heard the word
though not of mouth,
was heading south—

transmitting it
by bit and bit
of one design:
wings shut/minus
wings spread/plus,
the no, the yes,
saying what they
were meant to say,

that out of those
implicit clues
we might suppose

that there are some
for whom
what everyone knows
is noise
is news

The Mississippi Valley Review   Howard Nemerov

CEREMONY

At five of this winter morn the hound and I
Go out the kitchen door to piss in the snow,
As we have done in all solemnity
Since he was a pup and would wake me up to go.

We mingle our yellow waters with the white
In a spatter of silence under the wheeling skies
Wherein the failing moon lets fall her light
Between Orion and the Pleiades.

The Mississippi Valley Review   Howard Nemerov

PRAYER

(for D)

Your golden loins slake my lust for treasures.
Unnameable gifts, scarcely imagined
in dreams haunting the crazed poets, bless me
like the rapture of field mice missed by owls.

When the troll slivers from my breast, do not
miscue ugly mischief from the dark past
which rants slavering, in the Town of Tongue,
like the rabid fox that spreads its disease

Unknowingly. I gaze from my study
at the solstice trees, savoring designs
shadows throw on the impervious snow—
think of you, who's made do with barely more.

Both are beacons: the faith of maple trees
in midwinter, my love for you always.

                                        February 14
                                        Mike

Buffalo Spree   Mike Newell

UNTITLED

Meyer and I, we drove
that old Nash across midnight,
Iowa, Illinois, lurching as far

as possible out of high school
and Dakota's dust. We coasted

into Chicago off old Highway
Twenty, first time in our life, me singing
country, the seats down, twanging
a five-dollar guitar at the kind of
smoke we never breathed before. We
stayed awake for days, almost caught
a homerun ball in Comiskey Park, found
a whorehouse by accident, rolled

on by, around the big lake to
Michigan, college, no
insurance, no brakes
the whole way!

Great River Review   *Herman Nibbelink*

SOUTH OF THE BORDER

Come dance with me—
My eyes flash
dark under my sombrero,
my white smile zings
like a light whip-lash.

Come dance with me—
My feet dart
swiftly as blackbirds,
My broad red sash
makes happy breeze
as we sway and part.

Come whirl and twirl
to the tambourines
that quiver and laugh
like little spanked girls,
to the clackety-click of castanets.
In the glide and the spin
your heart forgets
to cry, to cry with the violin.

The Lyric   *Virginia Real Nicholas*

SINGS A BIRD

—Pretty, pretty, pretty!
sings a bird up in a tree.
—Winter's gone with winter's grief,
and spring comes greening in the leaf,
and joy will drink the sun with me.

—So sweet, so sweet, so sweet!
sings a bird upon a fence.

—Now April ripples like a brook,
and love's the music in her look—
who will walk when he can dance?

Writing   *John Nist*

MADE TO SEE

The day dies beautiful.
And so the year.
The light slants long and fades.
Then the first stars appear.
Thus the night comes on.
Always.
And it's for this
our eyes were made to see.

Arizona Quarterly   *John Nist*

SHOPPING

Frozen lemonade, frozen limas.
Now we fill our hearts like baskets, silently.
Strangers slide by like voyeurs,
their eyes sullying the sallow chicken,
nude parts severed from the whole.
I pass a sunglassed neighbor
as mysterious in her mission
as a wrapped cauliflower.

At the counter,
eyes bristle in mascara.
Cold hands cover my parts,
get to know my needs and desires and
how much they cost.
Guilty of knowing,
I pay and pay.
Remorse covers me in brown paper.

Buying and selling myself over and over,
like an old whore
I gather my sacks and
adjust my change, sinning in
tin and silver,
naked as that
yellow chicken lying broken but
efficient on its shelf.

Primavera   *Jane Chance Nitzche*

NIGHT DRIVING

The tires revolve, blurring
Houses into a streaked darkness.

Speed mesmerizes,
Drugs away my caution:
I am invulnerable, encased in this car.
Its acceleration triggers scenes
From our accident:
Four almost dead; the totalled car,
Nose reversed in its metal face.
My mother still wears its scars
On her face,
Brands of five operations.
I was left whole
But addicted, needing to hear
Tires whisper speed,
The thrusting through sidelit blackness,
Hurtling towards impact:
The wanted collision.

The Agni Review   *Sharyn November*

IN FRONT OF THE SEINE, RECALLING
THE RIO DE LA PLATA

(for Octavio Paz)

No landscape ever fancies or delights me,
Octavio, if it does not offer there
in the mystery of its hills and of its plains
a lustrous gift of water which endures
only as long as the fluent eyes we adore
within the passionate oval of a face
or in the love that just a mirror holds.
No landscape has such clearness in the mind
nor plants itself with such pure resonance
as that which in our musing yields to us
a starry sky draped across the water,
with cities and with people who would cross it
and bridges studded with doves, beneath full moons.
Rivers seem to find their way like veins
which, springing from the heart, return again!
They're like blue ribbons that join one golden heart
with another, as in romances or necklaces.
I wanted to show you an enormous river:
at times it is mistaken for the sea,
we call it, though, the Rió de la Plata,
(the rivers of America are so large!).
That it have the cast of silver hardly matters,
only that I always witness it,
yellow or iridescently rose-colored,
without houses and without people, over the clay;
a river in which the vacuous clouds are reflected
with all their steps of stone and looming towers,
with their iron summits, with their angels,
that arises from the light among the shadows

like the raven's wing within the branches;
and that river I have seen in other rivers—
in the Tiber, and the Arno, and in the Thames,
in the verdant Rhone, among the foliage
and here within the abundant waves of the Seine,
like when we recognize amid a crowd
some just discovered face that once was ours.

New England Review   *Silvina Ocampo*
                              —Translated by Jason Weiss

REQUIEM

Farewell my friend,
Peace and rest,
You yield a smile
To death's caress.

Flowers expire
Too close to June
And kind hearts tire
Too soon, too soon.

The Lyric   *Martin T. O'Connor*

LOST OBJECTS

Night after night I dream about my losses.
First, a topaz ring,
Second, the words of a promise,
Third, a revolution, fourth, a dollar in change, fifth, a
    canary
Dead stiff on the floor of his cage, his bird-fingers tensed
    into string.
Once, a house with a shingled roof,
A cat that lived in back of the house,
Two lemon trees where the cat is buried.
A view of the bay, a lover, a country,
Ten years of my life.

All of it pouring like water down the drain of some
    monstrous spillway,
Making a whirlpool, tugging at my chest, pulling my
Closed eyes oblong, my closed brain sullen.
The flood makes a pressure, it thumps in my forehead,
Pulls my hair, my bed, into its vortex
Over the rim of the funnel
Round and round like a cartwheel.

I'll struggle, I say. I'll grow extra fingers, reach out, grab,
                hold, salvage
Some of it, any of it:
My father's eyesight, my oldest child's talent, the key to
    my house, the short way home.

Poetry   *Diana Ó Hehir*

TIME-TRAVEL

I have learned to go back and walk around
and find the windows and doors. Outside
it is hot, the pines are black, the lake
laps. It is 1955 and I am
looking for my father.
I walk from a small room to a big one
through a doorway. The walls and floors are pine,
full of splinters.
I come upon him.

I can possess him like this, the funnies
rising and falling on his big stomach,
his big solid secret body
where he puts the bourbon.
He belongs to me forever like this,
the red plaid shirt, the baggy pants,
the long perfectly turned legs,
the soft padded hands folded across his body,
the hair dark as a burnt match,
the domed, round eyes closed,
the firm mouth. Sleeping it off
in the last summer the family was together.
I have learned to walk

so quietly into that summer
no one knows I am there. He rests
easy as a baby. Upstairs,
Mother weeps. Out in the tent
my brother reads my diary. My sister
is changing boyfriends somewhere in a car
and down by the shore of the lake there is a girl
twelve years old, watching the water
fold and disappear. I walk up behind her,
touch her shoulder, she turns her head—

I see my face. She looks through me
up at the house. This is the one I have
come for. I gaze in her eyes, the waves,
dark as the air in hell, curling in
over and over. She does not know
any of this will ever stop.
She does not know she is the one
survivor.

Mississippi Review   *Sharon Olds*

TRAIN TO REFLECTION

through the black pockets
of the underground city
the screaming subway
sounds like an animal in a trap
I watch the twisted faces

walking like shadows
balking near the exit.
I see myself for the first time
in the tunnel glass
lost in an ocean of stone
the human echo
howling in pantomime
just another face
on this train of clack clack
clack clack, clack clack
the 7th avenue train moves like a sewer
by steel the parody by silence
I sit bouncing in a plastic seat
the chug-a-lug rhythm
while the train flashes
and roars through the storm
heatwave these thoughts
in the heads of passengers
at midnight
somewhere under New York.

Nitty Gritty   *Lawrence T. O'Neill*

SPEAK

Again I keep watch.
I bring you water, brush your hair.
I call the doctor, knowing
nothing will make you better.

You've taken to bed
forgetting the house:
the green chair, the children,
the dress hanging limp from the curtain rod.
And Father home early, impatient for supper.

As I rise to leave, you call
until your voice fits me,
your head rooted to the pillow,
legs lost among the sheets

that twist to kiss you, discovering your face
as I've never seen it—
the high, sharp bones—

and here across your forehead
the blue vein that holds your life,
of which you will not speak.

Carolina Quarterly   *Bea Opengart*

THO WE ALL SPEAK

Tho we all speak
the same tongue,

there are places
in America that
are not home.

I've moved thru
the shutter of towns
on my way home
so I know what
I'm talking about.

If I'm to die
along the way,
let it be
where mountains
never speak

unless spoken to,
where waters show
as much courtesy
to me as to
a speechless sky.

Mountain Review   *Daniel Ort*

ANXIETY ABOUT DYING

It isn't any worse than what
I discover in the dentist's chair
under the nitrous oxide.

The whole jaw is going, I complain, the gums, the bone,
two enormous fillings lost. What do I need?
Maybe a guillotine? says my dentist, the joker.

The only thing I have to fear is fear itself, I tell him.
You believe in that bullshit? he says,
setting to work on my rotting bicuspid.

Now comes the good part. Breathing the happy gas,
I get answers to all the questions I had
about death but was afraid to ask.

Will there be pain? Yes.
Will my desires still be unsatisfied? Yes.
My human potential remain unrealized? Yes.

Can a person stop minding about that? Certainly.
Can I commend my spirit to the seventeen
angels whistling outside the dentist's window?

Of course. How nice the happy gas.
What a good friend.
I unclench my sweaty little hand.

I wave goodbye to my teeth.
It seems they are leaving by train for a vacation.
I'll meet them in the country when I can.

Poetry   *Alicia Ostriker*

LULLABY

(to Robert Louthan)

This is where
the light sleeps.
This is where
the light goes down

on its knees.
These are the prayers
it says.
These are the blind

and frightened
who come to listen.
When the voice stops,
they all go to sleep.

Memory goes to sleep.
Memory is always
the last to go.
Usually, it turns

to sleep
on its other side.
Then the coffin sleeps.
And the hammer

that built the coffin
goes to sleep.
And the lumber.
And a few of the nails.

The Iowa Review   Sue Owen

THE GINGERBREAD HOUSE

We made our little girl
A gingerbread house.
Despite sweet cement
It leaned as if it yielded
To a hurricane wind.
Our baby took one look at it,
Said it was a witch's house,
And burst into tears.
She was a prophet in her way.
During our estrangement
The witch flew out the window
Riding on the storm.
She cast a wicked spell
That made us hate each other.
And now between the two of us
In the finest fashion

Of the old fairy-tales
We gobble up our child.

Kansas Quarterly   *John Ower*

MISSOURI TOWN

In windy June, the prairie grasses bow.
Built on the section lines, the roads decide
the lay of farms, where barns and houses go.
Now outskirt clusters start to override

the farmers' patterns: Elevators rise
white by the tracks, and gas-pump taverns keep
their liquids dark and cool. Cemeteries
bed lovers in a brief or final sleep.

Respectabilities begin once more
with numbered houses, where domestic grass
is trimmed as close as military hair.
What happens happens back of curtained glass.

At the town's heart, storefronts around a square
look to the shabby courthouse, red and tall.
Gossip and document converging there,
a dry old clerk in sleeves gathers it all.

Poetry Northwest   *John Palen*

SUNDAY IN SOUTH CAROLINA

Why, when Sunday closes the lid on this world
and all that leaks out are the Baptists
and the sounds of various tinkling hymns
and tinnish chimes,
        do we stand, awful and amazed
at the uninspirational silence that lacks.

Weeks of this leveled at us in sevenths
should eventually calm or inure us,
but we fail to meet it. We cannot buy
a coathanger, only *Playboy*; no beer, but cigarettes;
    we buy what we do not need
    and by doing so
        celebrate the empty masses.
pitifully beaten at our game,
        we are like Bach
in the hands of an amazed Einstein
beseeching a bored friend:
        the music is the method, my friend,
        and this simple universe but a jewel
        set in a cheap but perfect ring.

Southwest Review   *Robert Parham*

TANYA

One day after school
I was running the tracks
back into the country
in early spring, sunlight
glazing the chips of coal,
old bottles and beer cans
shoaling the sides. I ran
for miles, stripped
to the belly, dogwood
odors in the air like song.

When I stopped for breath
I saw there were women
bending in the ferns.
They spoke in Polish,
their scarlet dresses
scraping the ground
as they combed for mushrooms,
plucking from the grass
blond spongey heads
and filling their pouches.

But the youngest one
danced to herself in silence.
She was blond as sunlight
blowing in the pines.
I whispered to her . . . *Tanya.*
She came when the others
moved away, and she gave me
mushrooms, touching my cheek.
I kissed her forehead:
it was damp and burning.

I found myself sprinting
the whole way home
with her bag of mushrooms.
The blue sky rang
like an anvil stung
with birds, as I ran
for a thousand miles to Poland
and further east, to see her
dancing, her red skirt
wheeled in the Slavic sun.

The Hudson Review   *Jay Parini*

SECRETS

The secrets I keep
from myself
are the same secrets
the leaves keep

from the old trunk
of the tree
even as they turn
color.

They are the garbled
secrets
of the waterfall
about to be stunned
on rock;
the sound of the stream's
dry mouth
after weeks of drought.

Hush, says the nurse
to the new child howling
its one secret
into the world,
hush
as she buries
its mouth
in milk.

On the hearth
the fire consumes
its own burning tongue,
I cannot read the ash.
By the gate
the trumpet flower sings
only silence
from its shapely throat.

At night
I fall asleep
to the whippoorwill's
raucous lullabye,
old as the first garden:
never tell
never tell
never tell.

The Atlantic Monthly   *Linda Pastan*

PARTING FROM MY SON

The plane wheels lurch, leave
the tarmac, tightening
the inescapable cord.

               The tug
brings sudden tears. No use to call myself
a fool. Time has no help for
what ails me.

Son, grown to a colossus, striding
the streets in your high boots, spinning

your gaudy fantasies,
your desperado moustache is
no disguise to me.

I leave you where the wind
blows cold off the river   and

your dreams are not enough
to keep me warm.

New England Review   *Evangeline Paterson*

BIRTHDAY PARTY

Eighty-four years ago,
the changing candlelight
created shadows of her
birth. Today, the same
illumination foreshadows her
death. Delicately.

Her daughter begs her to make
a wish. She would like
secrets again. Her own life.
Privacy. But her
daughter has her own ideas
and does not understand.

The candles are hard to blow,
but daughter insists.
She might as well cut down trees.
Her eyes fill with tears.
They applaud. She looks away;
the lights are cruel.

Cedar Rock   *Patti Patton*

INDIAN MOUNDS

Eight and already bored,
I dug holes because the dog
Did, splashed myself
In cool red clay certain
That something was hiding
There beneath sleeping grass.

Small persistent hands
Scooped up mountains,
Smothered black ants
Until my fingers throbbed
From dirt securely wedged
Beneath my nails,
Hard pink moons rising
Through clouds of dirt.

There, shining in summer's
Wavering light, teeth,
Age-smooth and yellow,
Stirred the dust
And my own small heart.

I brushed them free,
Let them rattle in my fist
With the first rays of light.
Through decayed jaws
The voices of a thousand
Dead spoke to me
In my youth, do not forget
Us, child, we fathered you
In the dark ignorance
Of our time, then chanted
Out our death and yours.

Voices International   *Angela Peace*

NIGHT HARVEST

O gentle, restless earth
Where the green ears shall grow,
Now you are edged with light:
The moon has traced the fallow,
The furrows gleam with night.

This is the poet's hour:
While others lie abed,
I sow the dark hills late,
Scatter like sparks the seed
And watch the dark ignite.

O gentle land, I sow
With my heart's living grain.
Stars draw their harrows over,
Winds send their melting rain:
I meet you as a lover.

The Lyric   *Susan Pence*

WHEN AT NIGHT

My father sleeps in the sun porch
on a strange white bed.
I know what *gestorben* means.
Nobody said.

One day my father picked me up.
Ach du lieber Augustin, he sang, he sang.
Around, around the living room,
The big house rang.

He loves my sister more.
Sister's small and fat.
When I grow up I'll be like him—
gold mustache and a straw hat.

What does dying mean?
Is it living like a stone?
Being everywhere at once,
like river mist or rain?

Mama cries and cries.
She's wearing out her eyes.
Be a big boy, a good boy.
I don't cry.

In Mr. Gumbie's yard
the trees are clipped and strange;
the branches wrapped in gunny sacks
like bandaged hands.

Gumbie's in a box.
I saw, across the way.
They put the lid on.
They took him in the rain.

His face was brown as leaves.
He was bent and sick,
inching past my window,
loose coat, tapping stick.

I dream about my father.
Wind and cold rain.
He doesn't have a face.
The wind blew away his name.

Poetry   *Mark Perlberg*

THE CLARITY OF APPLES

(for Nicanor Parra)

The ancient tutor, awaiting failure,
spoke slowly of diverse things which
cannot be taught:

The clarity of apples
The architecture of sand
The fear of grey eyes
Memories of corridors.

The animosity of owls
The gentleness of knees
The deafness of marriage
Resurfacing pride.

The fragility of ice
The lumbar structure of giants
The lucidity of rain

Understanding a fanatic.

The reasons for civil war
The confidence of bears
The repentance of laughter
Haste and chance.

Colorado Quarterly   *Terry M. Perlin*

WINTERSCAPE

Sad to see the leaves abandoning
the twigs and branches that had long adorned.
I watched them wafting, lifeless, and I mourned
that there would be no leaves again till Spring.

Yet solace, in the evening hours, was mine,
when I, my vision fixed on leafless trees,
beheld the loveliest intricacies.
Complex design on exquisite design.

All summer long my casement window view
was blocked by trees grown fat with leaves, and tall.
I saw no moon late Spring or early Fall;
but now . . . oh now the moon comes shining through!

The Lyric   *Jess Perlman*

RECOGNITION

On the boulder a lizard
bobs on his forelegs, quick push-ups that
flash his blue throat-patch in jaunty warning.
Dark eye cocked warily,
he lets me creep closer, sit near him.
We slow to witnessing.

Wistful brother, I know you could flick
like the tip of a whip across the rocks.
The sun has ignited your speed,
the puff of your rapid heart.
Your reined swiftness holds a deep quiet.
Around your rapt eye, fixed on me,
the season billows, clouds swirl up.
You are more still than the limestone
bones of the mountain.
I feel two hundred million years
circle the galaxy. Blossoming
rises on the foothills.
Swift and slow mingle.
The world of our wildness
hangs in a balance of breath and watching,
a tiny trembling. Day tatters in the wind.

ASFA Poetry Quarterly   *Georgette Perry*

THE LESSON

One thing you taught me I'm grateful for—
to judge a man by the place he's most at home.

You, in spite of the B.A. & the M.A. & the LL.B. & the Ph.D.
& even in spite of Yale,
are still at home with
scorpions & dust storms,
dry riverbeds, flash floods,
95 on the highway, 110 in the shade,
& 5 deserted acres to feed 1 cow.

Your daddy keeps a gun in his glove compartment
for rattlers,
for the Indian who messed up your sister,
for goodtime Saturday nights in the Legion Hall.

There are 2 prisons & 1 jail in your town,
there's death for those who run,
& yet you are at home there.

"Never anything happens you can't wear jeans."

Kansas Quarterly   *Elizabeth Peterson*

FROM THE POINT

Far under the waves glide in, in rippling lines
that break creamily, slow motion, white foam spreading
along each crest as they crumble, falling like nine-pins—

The vast, blue bulk of the sea, fanned out and edged
with a bank of snow-puffed clouds—
                          Bird chirrups, whistlings,
the cries of children playing across the valley
(The one in pink is mine), and the town of Lynton
perched in the lap of Hollerday Hill, its houses
ranked in Victorian rows, slate-grey, red-brown,
shining in the sun.

                    To the left and down the road
I can see the house where the Buddhists sit and breathe,
taking it all in, and letting it go,
half-hidden by the yellow-brown bouquet
of trees, and further up the valley hemlocks marching
the steep hillside, the Inn, the small grey bridge
and the end of the cottage block where for one year
we've lived so happily.

                    May flies round my head
in a sudden swarm—moving up, down, sidewards,
trailing their long thin bodies like helicopters,
speckling ocean, town and valley, moving up, down,
sidewards—moving—always moving—never resting.

Kansas Quarterly   *Paul Petrie*

REMEMBERING HOME

The sea called;
Her siren song came to me in
     winter's night,
Murmuring old lullabies,
A whisper of grey-blue waves
Gently lapping at an empty shore.
And, in a memory,
I again looked out over the stone
     breakwater
Into eternal distances.
I saw the setting sun hung on the
     edge of day,
Its glowing crescent shimmering
     through the dusk,
To caress the sea with last warmth.
The town dozed in the shadow of night,
Rocked in the arms of the soft sea
     breeze,
Kissed by the twilight breath
Of the zephyrous west wind.
And, in sleep's enveloping haze,
I saw my home
So far away in time and reality,
So close in heart and soul.

The Atlantic Advocate   *Susan Petrykewycz*

POKER POEM

If I told you a rookie
drew the case lady
on the last card,
sandbagged me out of
better than six bits,
you wouldn't understand
the game, not at all.

Lower your eyes. Nickels,
quarters, dimes sting across
the table-grain, sorry wine
or old uncollected IOU's
shuttle between hands
always holding something—
cards, smokes, wine.

Like sprung rhythms
the cards hit their spots,
as natural as fate
or the storytelling
of pokerplayers,
sitting over low stakes,
drawing to inside straights.

Window   *Michael Pettit*

HOME IN INDIANAPOLIS

Pine cones on the ground of the park,
a long hill good for sledding in winter,
and on autumn afternoons
air that was rare with burning leaves.
All this before my gradual turning—
the subtle parting of our lives.
Now living fifty miles south seems
like being in the real South.
The accent is different, insects larger,
foliage somehow almost tropical.
It's twenty years since I've left,
and lost the key to my parents' house.

Driving north in dreams
the year is always yellow and red.
I steer toward a yellow window
on a dark street.
My childhood is behind the curtains:
my parents still new, the smell of
fresh paint brightening the kitchen,
apple pie and milk, or cold pears
set aside before bed. And after sleeping,
waking to the coolness of a blue morning,
a fine day of sidewalks and leaves ahead,
the light so clear—and knowing
it can never be so clear again.

Centering   *Richard Pflum*

LUMP

(for Dr. John Prutting)

You are a hard-boiled egg. Me?
no hard-boiled detective. But,

you are what I detect one day,
what propells me to see Dr. P.

You are a death-baby, I cry.
You'll grow inside me till I die.

You are a death-toad squatting,
spitting poison into my blood.

You are a lump in the breast,
cleverly disguised as one in my arm.

You are the Big C that killed Granny,
Uncle, and now wants to kill me.

You are an inelegant swell. You,
Lump, are the creep who crept up

till they cut, leaving a stump,
my arm hacked off, a leg of lamb.

But, Lump: you are "perfectly benign,"
says Doctor P., rolling you, curiously,

between two fingers. Lump, you are
only a torn muscle, a thing fallen

below the biceps. Lump, you are
a reminder of all fallen things: Troy,

Rome, boys who built up their bodies.
Mine is a cake fallen in the oven.

Lump, Lump, you are a hard lesson:
Learn to take one's lumps.

The Ontario Review   *Robert Phillips*

REFLECTIONS

Old homes and human lives—both
So apparently sound, so deceptively vulnerable.
Commanding the north shore, atop a hill
The abandoned home hunkers—walls disintegrating,
Naked ribs exposed, foundation crumbling,
Chimney stones in a heap below the kitchen.
"Caution" reads one sign, "condemned" the other.
And one knows it's best to keep away.

Sure, once when this was but a dirt road
And these hills deaf to the diesel's call,
Before the Chicago junior execs
Paved the lawns in front of their split levels,
Winter fires roared in this stone chimney,
A horse or two stamped in the stable behind,
And children peeked from behind lace curtains
At ice on the lake, at winter's first snow.

Even then, I reflect looking at
The fir studs and exposed lathing,
The place was a firetrap.

Today I have called twice and received no answer.
It is cold, and there is no mail service.

Ball State University Forum   *David R. Pichaske*

THE VOYEUR

Undressing her hair,
she drops the tortoise shell combs
on the dresser.

Beneath the open window,
the privacy hedge snaps and cracks
like bones of old men.

She wiggles out of her slip,
checking the door chain,

locking the light out.

The familiar stranger stands there
watching the ritual of undoing;
reaching out, quivering, licking up
something like spoiled sweets.

Cedar Rock   *Deanna Louise Pickard*

TECHNIQUE

The roofers roof from the bottom up,
new tarpaper & new shingles to make it tight.
And when they finish one side (provided
they travel on schedule), they straddle the beam like monkeys
& eat their noon meal in the sun.
They all bring sandwiches, they all make smalltalk.
One clawhammer & one ballcap per man.

Just as easy—easier, I would think—to descend the other side
& chew at leisure, safer, on the grass below.
That's not a bad view & there's room to stretch.
One way or the other, I'd say,
they'll have to make that long climb down.
My way they could finish up (I mean
on their own time) their coffee & sandwiches &
look up satisfied, fed to the teeth, to see what's left to go.
My way they could cut by one
their descents on a full stomach, & keep their work
all ahead of them.

The roofers, though, are not paid for technique
but for beating the clock to that blue weathervane there.
They have their habits to a nicety
& won't hear more about it. They like best of all
to ride a roof that's going nowhere fast
in full noon sun: the damnedest hottest spot imaginable:
& eat & drink & wave their hands, clear at the top.

The Chowder Review   *Philip Pierson*

AKRIEL'S CONSOLATION

This morning I wrote a poem
on the sadness of this street:
loud new youths, rude new neighbors,
rot in the walls, ruts in the pavement.

Said my angel Akriel,
invisible, soft-tongued:
"Stop your griping, Bill Pillin!
All things grow old and rotten.

At least your derelict street possesses
a bracing authenticity

unlike the illuminated stage-sets
of the bourgeois boulevards.

You may even grow fond
of rotted planks and decaying plaster
and include them in one
of your mist-ridden night poems

which do, after all, make some sense;
whereas reality is random and misleading
unless changed in the eye: golden
flickers of dust in a lighted window."

Bachy 12   *William Pillin*

FOR ALLEN GINSBERG, WHO CUT OFF HIS BEARD

Now your cheeks are as old and bald
As that withered plate you call your head,
And still you bang your wheel and chant
The sad songs we thought were manifestoes.
You made us poets long before we learned to scan
The best that critics have thought and said.
We, too, howled for the dead we did not know.
Now, even your beard has gone bad in the teeth
And anthologies make you fit for study.
Buddy, can you spare a rhyme?
Anything to get me over the shock
Of finally meeting you face to face.

The Cape Rock   *Sanford Pinsker*

THE HOMES

It billows in a gust of wind
but doesn't tear. You're telling me
it must be rebuilt every day. Does the spider
have nothing better to do?

Here is another one, two of them
rolling down a wire from the top of one fir
to a branch of the next.
This one by the door has caught
the first hard beam of sunlight falling off
the roof and set it spinning in midair.

In wheels, the spokes only seem to mesh
when the children's bicycles speed out of sight.

These that seem to turn unravel, thread
by shining thread, and fly like disheveled hair
from the eves, the hectic trees. At the end
of a season, you declare, say love or ruin,

the delusions are a skyline
crumbling faster than the heart

can reconstruct it. You are telling me
we do not grow but are reduced to some

faith, frail and repeated as this filament
that seems to lengthen from no branch at all—
can I believe you—that it swings the creature
clinging to it through enormous absences, sufficient
room to start again.

Prairie Schooner   *Anne Pitkin*

FEAR

In the echo of my deaths
there is still fear.
Do you know about fear?
I know about fear when I say my name.
It is fear,
fear with a black hat
hiding rats in my blood
or fear with dead lips
drinking my desires.
Yes. In the echo of my deaths
there is still fear.

Review   *Alejandra Pizarnik*
                                        —Translated by Lynn Alvarez

FIRE. 10/78

my father used to show off by putting his forefinger
into the orange flame of his steel cigarette lighter.
now all lighters smell like him.

or he'd pass 8 cars, waiting for the passing gear to
kick in. in a game too real for me, not enuf for him.

he used to stand outside, hands grinning in his pockets
, w/ my mother pleading from inside the Rambler, as the
lightning charged the thin air. he used to chew grape
seeds & never spit them out.

or in the campfire he would suddenly grab a burning log
& shift it around.

or i'd be on the back of his bike & we'd ride on the stiff
sand of the North Sea. The white brows of the sea touch-
ing my screams & disappearing in his laff in the white
brows of the sea.

or he'd stand near the edge of a cliff in new hampshire
w/ 4 or 5 toes hanging over; a swift kick from a gentle
gust & our fears would all be gone.

Carolina Quarterly   *Bart Plantenga*

WHISPERING CLOUDS

By nature shy, by nature
used to snowing, spreading winter's pall,
they had to ponder meanings,
to weight with gravities of blood
sky's verity.

They're shy. They're soft, small clouds
drifting and uncertain,
monotonies of form
within massive greys.
Floating in from the eternal sphere
in nature's mold,
they shrink from the irrevocable press;
you can't tell one from one.

But make ready—
see them venture forward, put on color,
see them wear firm lines amid the crowds.
Hear them: they come,
come with a rattle, a jingle, a tone and a word.

Northwoods Journal   *Mariquita Platov*

SEA TURTLE

Long after his great carapace was wrenched
And torn with grapnels, slung on hooks and hung
Endwise above the pier; and sailors drenched
In slime and blood had carved and hacked among
His giant parts, had ripped his sea-green limbs
And cut his ancient head away; when all
His form was bleeding film, a crimson lens
Of gelatin upon the dock: withal
The great sea turtle's massive heart beat full
Against the plastron, throbbing audibly
Its plea: this was no easy thing, to still
A century of roaming through the sea;
And beat long after sunset had dispersed
The blood wrung from the cursing sailors' shirts.

Poet Lore   *Liston Pope*

WANDERER

(from the 'Scivias' of St. Hildegarde)

Where did I dwell? I dwelt in the shadow of death,
as did a mystic anciently aver.
Where did I walk? I walked on the primitive
pathway of error, was a child of earth
(and down the years my speech betrayed my birth).

What did I hold for ease against my breast?
The flimsy comfort of a wanderer
for whom there is no rest.

Two children vied for life in me: I fed
the greedy one whose talent was to beg
(no one had warned me of the cowbird's egg).
I let the little one grow thin and pale
and put a blame on life that she was frail.

How did I ever come then to the light?
How did I ever, blind with self, discover
the small strict pathway to this shining place,
I who betrayed the truth over and over
and let a tangle of dark woods surround me?
Simple the answer lies: down cliffs of pain,
through swamp and desert, thicket and terrain,
oh, someone came and found me.

Commonweal   *Jessica Powers*

WINDMILL IN MARCH

Ragged and gray as the salt-cedars
on the prairie's weathered edges,
I've stood all winter long
waiting to lift my bony arms
in praise for any alms,
to whisper blessings at each crumb
of wind or bright-cupped coin.

A patient mendicant, my hope's
been like an insect's bulging eye
that gathers from all sides
the splintered light.

And now, although the fields
are dun and not one green thing
pokes its head above the ground,
March sets me creaking, humming,
wheeling as if I had the gift
to spin fine summer back,
the power to bring birds and wheat
and gentle rain again.

New America   *Katharine Privett*

THE WAKE

In Newbern Tennessee he lies awake
Listening to the rocker's creaking rungs;
Downstairs the old man nodding in the dark,
His head bobbing eccentric pendulums,
Disturbs the quiet of one sleep.

The winter night is clear and cold,
Carrying noises farther than ever,
Beyond the house, the northwest field,
The lane that borders, rutted and washed.

Hardwoods, audible in a sharpened wind,
Blend with long whistles from the freight
Whose engines rumble through the center of town
And fade again with echoes like a chill.
Downstairs the old man is rocking in the dark
Or should be, as the chair is creaking still;
The house is creaking in the winter wind,
Filled like a family's hard-breathing sleep
That, cooling, moves from room to room.

The Southern Review   *Wyatt Prunty*

ROW OF HOUSES

No heralding daffodils
Gladden these bare
Dooryards in spring; no scent
of spice bush or pear.

In summer, no marigolds lift
The spirit; no tall
Čannas. No scarlet hip
Signals fall.

What human blight has spread
To this dismal row
Of houses where only starved
Antennas grow?

The Lyric   *John Robert Quinn*

NINE YEARS AFTER VIET NAM

Nine years after Viet Nam
where friendly woodchoppers by day
would be Viet Cong by night
I'm still on Recon Patrol.
Everybody has slant eyes.
It's an M-16 world.

Teacher by day, tonight
I'm at the trigger
of an electric typewriter.
This paper has yellow skin.
This poem has slant eyes.

Descant   *Leroy V. Quintana*

TWO CLOUDS

(for Jennifer, March 20, 1977)

Smallest breath
on the pillow, we counted
all the months,
first day of spring, first day
of summer, and each night now
as your silence
draws us back to you, here
where these soft leaves are leaning
over a little water
inside this circle
painted on your bed, and that cloud,
that aimless puff, goes on
floating through the same perfect sky.
If there's a secret,
I won't ask.
If there's one good explanation,
I don't want to know.
Your blue eyes
catch hold of everything
that pleases you,
and you know
what I mean when I say, *Look at that!*
That I mean, Look at me.
I'm just asking
for another reckless smile,
as if one more would rescue
the morning's gray
indifferent weather, and nothing
would be left to speak of
but this
feathery branch of the willow,
or the shadow of the next
lodged above it,
or the shadow of the cloud
that sweeps the grass and is gone.

The Michigan Quarterly Review   *Lawrence Raab*

THE RAGGED ROBIN OPENS

The ragged robin opens,
and the sunflower pleads
with the heavy-eyed horizon;
the crickets are rasping now,
in his hollow the hornet horns,
and in the velvety evening
a fluttering woodlark has written
his sleepy mood on the sky;
farther on, out on the meadow,

within the drizzling darkness,
on the tracks of sidestepping
hares the grassblade shudders;
the birch, in its silver shirt,
strolls in its leafy litter,
and tomorrow, in these regions,
we see yellow autumn, a visitor.

The Michigan Quarterly Review   *Miklos Radnoti*
                    —Translated from the Hungarian by Emery George

CREATION MYTHS

The cosmologists are wrong:
Worlds are not created with a bang, light
Exploding, heat too intense to measure, primaeval
Gases swirling into violent new chemistries.
Worlds accrete, drop by drop, as slowly
As time flowing—slower:
Worlds fit like microscopic bricks, puzzled
Into shape one color at a time; worlds are fabricated
Like the worn, hand-rubbed creations
They always are. Like this morning:
Taking the children's wash from the dryer
I saw that the pieces had come together, at last, without my
        knowing,
Had made this world around me, roofed me warm
And well, held the healthful and let the noxious
Go. Good riddance, good morrow: I greet
My finished cosmology, I smile as a theory vanishes.

The Michigan Quarterly Review   *Burton Raffel*

UNTITLED

See all the people gettin' off the bus—
All the bastards come just to look at us;
I can't help but think it's a crime—
They've better things to do with their time.

A sixteen-year-old girl says what did you do?
I was caught raping a little moron like you;
And when the preacher asks how'd you break the law—
I was robbing Peter to take care of Paul.

There's not much of a lesson here to be taught—
We are just like you, except we got caught.

Southern Exposure   *Mark Rahschulte*

MEDITATION

Lord, what is man?
            He looks into a glass

and sees a physical figure
      looking back at him,
the two waiting immobile
      for him to reappear
as the world knows him,
      by name, by work, by habits,
in what particulars
      he is significant,
and . . . why should it be embarrassing
      to speak of this?
. . . in what endearing;
      is he honest?
and how he looks
      when meditating;
all in a semblance characteristic
      as his bones,
including that shade
      in the inwit of presence,
his secondary at the subliminal portal
that stands for more
      potentiality than appears,
the quiet continent
      behind it feeling boundless
(the worse for him).
The final scene, the only scene,
      inherent in glass,
is that looker
      waiting for it to happen
and caught in the act.

Chicago Review   *Carl Rakosi*

LOVE IN MAGNOLIA CEMETERY

No one knows us here.
I could be Lelia Hartlett, b. 1896,
my crinoline rustling through grass
on an errand of grief. Or we can be
the initials carved into the crepe myrtle bark
where Robert goes on loving Janice
despite sapsuckers, borers into heartwood,
the changing directions of wind.

Everything here
except granite
seems made for love, I say,
as you bite my shoulder
and Easter explodes with resurrections
of azalea, forsythia, dogwood.
There is even a pond
for lovers to comb water across their faces
like tears. And the wind here
never ceases its shuffling of leaves,
redispersing stories

from the four corners of earth,
the only denouement worth keeping track of.

Should we—here? In your eyes
I see the headlights of cars
driving home to soft beds.
If I were Lelia Hartlett, my time
would have been up three years ago.

Love, I forgot to mention
someone we know is buried here.
I always save my best lies
for love. Look: magnolia buds knot
and swell towards July
and the space on our stones
still glares with uncut granite,
open-ended, waiting for legends.

Kansas Quarterly   *Paula Rankin*

THE FOURTH OPTION

There is one sure way
To change one's evil ways
There is one way
To grow new hair and make new friends
There is a way
To beauty, love, and easy money
There must be a way
To win the hearts of small dark girls
There should be a way
To vanish when friends aren't enough
When cooking doesn't help and burglars are everywhere
There should be some way

There could be a way
I sometimes think
To tell the people everywhere to go away
To say bye-bye I'm off to Florida
Won't be back for years and still come back in years
And find it all the same
There might be a way

There may be the way of the goat
Who eats what he can and eats the cans as well
There very well could be a way
There is only one way, to be sure
There is a way

Kansas Quarterly   *Henry Rasof*

POSTSCRIPT, ON A NAME

Ezra Pound (his fingers, bones)
lies beneath Venetian stones,

ivy laced, in lupine bound,
lilac, laurel all around:

Here you read me, here my name—
Pound inscribed in marble fame,
Almost breathing, almost brave—
Concentrates what Time forgave!

Poetry   *Stephen Ratcliffe*

INSIDE, OUTSIDE, AND BEYOND

(Cambridge, Holy Week)

Inside
the voices of the boys
wash through the shallow runnels
cut in the dark, male fabric of the chant
swiftly and mindlessly
as clear, cold water,
alleluia.

Outside
the gardener in rubber boots
piles fresh cut grass
under an ancient tree;
the blunt gray tines of his haying fork
move inexorably
through the matted green,
miserere.

Beyond
the mutilated willows by the river,
savaged to keep the channel free,
wait with the certainty of mud and roots
to be reborn,
gaudeamus.

Salmagundi   *John Ratti*

SONNET TO SEABROOK

In New Hampshire's green paradise this June
one sees the slowly radiating scars
of what may become an Inferno soon,
and even demonstrators bring their cars.

An ugly crater's opened in the earth,
by those devil's toys, earth-scraper, -mover.
Men strangely take an insane pride, giving birth
to disaster, like a twisted lover.

Where are our Thoreaus and Emersons?
Lying in their graves, not so deep as this!
The earth is hollowed, spooned in helpless tons.
Death is promised in slow doses, like bliss.

Technicians tell us Armageddon's fine.
Cranes hover over shale. Slow rivers shine.

The Massachusetts Review   *David Ray*

BOOM

Oyster boats are moored
    under the boom on the dock
    and the boom swings
    creaking on its line

As long as the wind touches it
    the boom swings
    back and forth
    gently creaking

I am like that boom
    moving when you touch me
    speaking when you touch me

New Letters   *Julian Lee Rayford*

LOVE POEM

Warned, warned for years
what too much love would do,
I settled for never enough.
I did not have a body,
sleeping in the attic,
spare and still, suns falling
past the tiny window, blooded,
always the maples
whispering below, rattling
with leaves, rattling with emptiness.

Too much sleeping woke me.
My arms opened first, so tired
of carrying their loneliness.
Now my body belongs to you;
it cannot help itself.
The fears that come to me,
night and day, are not of love.
There is no darkness
in this. The sun paints
our bodies simple and shining.

Ploughshares   *Susan Irene Rea*

RETURN TO THE VALLEY

Running the earth in those years of meadows,
A smile brought the world tumbling in apples;
The valley billowed green and the days were forever
And God sang in the slim rain.

Cattle shadowed, warm, broken in water, horns tipsy;
And there were strawberries.

Meadow years,
Strawberry years, barefoot in the glad mud,
Forever years.

So I return now
Knowing a new forever,
Afraid.
I have been to a meeting of seas and suns
Devouring horizons.
I have forgotten how to touch strawberries.

But in my sleep they creep into my hand,
Their rough cones nose my palm,
I awake to weightless hours
And marvel at the simple amnesty of soil.

Event   *Elfreida Read*

REMEMBERING HIM

He was so compounded
of peach juice and smiles
that not to love him
would be
to refuse nourishment

His eyes had
the sudden sweetness
of rabbits
startled at the lettuce

His stubby hands
left the tools of work
waning at dusk
to take his violin
and so caress its purring throat
that clear Italian voices
sang the twilight stars out
for his figtree audience

So total
was the ambience of this man
I would give
all my blood tonight
to see him
for just one word again

I loved him so

Kansas Quarterly   *Joe Reccardi*

MY GRANDFATHER ALWAYS PROMISED US

The streets outside have ice on them.
On the 19th century farm where I grew up,

where my grandfather was a tenant farmer
for the old lady, her two mean dogs,
her large stone house & her constant small investments,
a cow slipped on the ice in those fields
& lost it, her life, though the cow inside her
was saved. My uncle & I fed the calf throughout
the entire winter, first with a bottle & then
from a gray pail, the milk of some other cow.
Where I live now
the old in the neighborhood are having their hard time,
the ice outside is hard for them.

Dogs blast at their heels, the wind chill
doesn't quite excite the blood that is already
slowing down & tired of running to catch them,
the ice seems to go on forever & the weather
stays where it is, everywhere. The old
have the absurdity of cows on these streets,
the grazing absurdity of cows. The young look
like dogs, the home-owners like wolves,
the sky itself so many nomadic animals,
clouded & quiet. Whether it's the field or the street
that gets us, I couldn't
say—but I can see my grandfather
moving towards the barn through perfect ice,
while the fields of his century move far,
& then farther away.

New Boston Review   *Liam Rector*

MELISSA

She is named Melissa.
Her other name has changed so often,
it is easier, just Melissa.
No longer do the men silence their joking
and look as she passes their tables.
For years she flung cocktails here
until closing time and then

the manager fired her in December
when she had pneumonia
and business was brisk.

Out of habit, she returns,
her eyelids dark,
sunken.

Sometimes the bartender
after close up
buys her a drink
and into the northeast of the morning
unshoulders the weight
his evening has carried.

She has no other name.
It is a soothing name.

A bird's song after rain.
Melissa.

Canadian Forum   *Carolyn D. Redl-Hlus*

ABELARD AT CLUNY

Now you've been an Abbess for years:
Your thighs have likely grown fatty,
Silver drops of grey pervade your letters
And all your ermine metaphors have died.

And I tiptoe in marble halls,
Wander through orchards at will,
Cool my crystal feet in holy fountains.
Documents are fuzzy now, and futile
Rhetoric amuses me.

But visions of childhood still sing in the trees.
Orchard vision catches us dancing,
And I curse Jerome and history,
Quicken my step,
Retire to my penitential madness.

Colorado Quarterly   *Grover Rees III*

BOTANY LESSON

How can a flower stand out
     in a garden of mediocrity?
The genes that made its genes
     bore the vast, white-petalled sea.

Spontaneous mushrooms? They rot
     in forty-eight hours by the foot of the ash
into a brown stain. A dot
     on the sky in lower case won't last.

I can't tell which way
     a thing will go. Men, too, pervert
themselves, end locked in jail
     or licking self-inflicted hurt.

Hold high a wet finger: Does wind—
     quick—kiss it? When the sea is calm,
all boats ride evenly;
     a grain of sand blinks in my palm.

Then, as a storm, the beast
     bursts. Its hands terrorize the waves.
One man rises—the priest;
     the rest bend low in the wind—the slaves.

The American Poetry Review   *F. D. Reeve*

WALTZ

We dance without passion but the movement
is reminiscent and I could follow you,
if I chose, with my eyes closed. I lay one finger
on your cheek like a scar. Your skin is white, cool.
I have never wounded you, although once
I wanted to. Tonight I enjoy the fine,
unmarred texture of your skin and the ease
with which you embrace me. How delicately
we touch the ones we do not love.
I can feel the convulsion begin, the raw edges
of a wound moving like a mouth in speech.
I turn away and my gesture is formless,
awkward, the movement of a prehistoric fish
dredged up and exposed to light for the first time.

Southern Poetry Review   *Heather Tosteson Reich*

FATHER

Father is, dedicatedly,
father. The ship's captain
seeking one white whale in waters
not yet scented.
He knows innocence and
comes a long way from it,
stretching the horizons like a Queeg,
but liberal.
Quartered by respect for unskilled
help, alert to undertows the
seasoned know alone, he holds the helm.
Salted by experience,
faith sprayed, wise, buying time
in spite of mutinies
a green crew wages.

The great whale looms, building foam
in wakes as steep as mountain ranges.
Masterfully, he veers, unsleeping,

while below deck, unwittingly,
the crew plans its escape.

The Christian Century   *Lois Reiner*

THE OTHER SIDE

Soo Line, Reading, Pacific Fruit,
Nickel Plate & Wabash, Lehigh
spell out their routes and go by,
but now I am looking through
empty cars, each door slid open.

Held in those passing frames
on the road going past the switchyards,
I am a small boy standing
beside his grandfather, who wears
a Railway Express guard's
pistol and nightstick,
who was thirty years a carpenter
for the Chicago, Burlington & Quincy
till the day he brought me to the yards
to watch his old apprentices
crowbar inlays and veneers, salvaging
the sleepers White Wing and Pere Marquette
to carry freight. After that,
the hammer and screwdriver loops
on his leather apron
gaped from a cellar hook.

To this day I can press
my thumbs into my eyes and see
lines of light in the shape of
nails, auger threads, files
as finely scored as fingerprints,
wood shavings and the grain
in the handle of my grandfather's plane.

Through the open doors clicking past
like a slide show, I can see him
drawing his nightstick along
the sides of boxcars,
bumping it over rivet heads
to drum the riders out of
their sour corners—three or four
routed on each patrol,
though he told me he never saw
the same one twice.

The Ohio Review   *Thomas Reiter*

THE VISIT

An owl swoops
over the dry field.
The ancient fear whirls
beside my ear.

Socrates accepted
with unbelieving grace
the unphilosophical opinion
that hemlock would save the state.

Thomas More, at first secure
within the leaves of law,
blinked mightily, and for the last,
as a petticoat uttered judgment.

And the black-robed patriot
(you, Campion, are closer to my heart)
affronted the imperial theme
before he kissed the daughter's axe.

Wings beat
on my anonymous door;
little men lack
the consolation of history.

Sou'wester   *William J. Rewak*

DIVIDING THE HOUSE

Eloquent as stuck drawers, we come out
with everything, too late, too hard.
Today no tears—we're praising
self-sufficiency, the adaptation
of higher animals to early loss.

What you wear shears off
from what wore you.
For your endurance, take the house.
I take, for wandering, the car.

They're all so odd, the props
of intimacy stranded in the yard
with the perfection of toys.
Though there were no children of this marriage
but you and me, I wonder
how they will do without us.

The Ohio Journal   *James Richardson*

BRIDGE OF THE CAROUSEL

The blind man, standing on the bridge, as grey
as boundary markers of a nameless realm—
he is perhaps the one thing, ever constant,
by which the sweep of galaxies is set,
the silent middle point of all the heavens.
For all around him wanders, flows and gleams.

He is the unmoved righteous one,
set down among the many tangled routes,
the somber entrance to the underworld
amid a blindly passing breed of men.

Denver Quarterly   *Rainer Maria Rilke*
                    —Translated by John Drury

HOW NIGHT FALLS IN THE COURTYARD

On coming to this sprawled and lazy city,
I vowed to live in courtyards and eat papayas

on and on into infinity . . .
to lie on the beach and feel the sun
suck hotly on my naked skin.
This I have done.

Such a short space of time to root a coleus in water,
soon plant it in the dirt
terra cotta-pot red,
and see it spread to claim the sun.
Such a long day, in little time again
it passes on.

The neighbors call their cats inside
with strange little baby-talks of cat-love.
Of course, we're forbidden to pick the roses,
all pink and red at the front of the walk,
so we bury our noses in them for a moment
and pass on.

Perhaps we'll sprout some sinsimian
or write a screen-play
or go to a fire at twilight . . .
This is a place of limitless possibility.
Nervous but content, we bask in the light
and pass the pipe around.

Neworld   *Christine Rimmer*

BLACK

The way in which blackness appeals: it beckons, calls.
Blackness of caves, deep mines, dark cellars.
Black of coal,
black of the fur of panthers.
Black funerals, black moods, black tea, black thorn.
Black vultures.
Black walnut.
Black magic, black skin.
We are black and black:
    we come from blackness and we return,
       a long, dark, improbable journey.
Black grouse, black bryony, Black Hand, Black Death.
Black bile, black birch.
Black box.
Black horehound.
Black oak. Black rot.
Black humor.
Black sheep.
Black out.

Poet Lore   *Nicholas Rinaldi*

YIELDING

It is the quality that most resembles
the breathing of stars

or the way my cat's long hair
ripples as the wind passes over her back.

In the garden the flowers
are yielding always to the desire
for color: deep pink of petunia yields
to indigo tufts of ageratum
and purple bouquets of alyssum.

At night, when I feel you naked
against my hips, nudging
me like a boat bouncing
against a dock, I turn
my drowsy body over
and yield to your sleep-warmed skin,
pleasure of chest-hair
and insistent, firm thighs.

It is to yearn for release
and then—
    to give way.

The Spoon River Quarterly   *Shellie Keir Robbins*

I NEVER SAW THE TRAIN

that came through our town
at ten every morning

you could set your watch

the whistle
starting way off

coming fast
until it was
a scream
louder than a woman
in first labor.

We stopped
rakes idle
ironing boards cooling

while the windows shook
and the crockery fell
from the kitchen shelves.

The whistle
was in the next town
long before someone said
the words

let out
like a breath exhaled
so it was the last car
following down the track.

"There goes the Riley."

Indiana Writes   *Jean Roberts*

POEM FOR MY DEAD HUSBAND

In the steadying breadth of day
I can recall you
with a lit clarity
from my still burning wick of love
(which neither time nor others' hands
could pinch).
But when blindfold in dreams,
your remembered breath on mine,
I, muddling,
fumble to rebuild your face
which, half-forming,
fans
lost mental conversations
repeated and repeated and remade.
Till fighting that wet stranglehold of sheet,
I, sickening,
sweat remorse and wake.
If only I had lept and run
when you were still in sight
to say
and say again
the words you walked towards.
But in my stunted heart
I dawdled, looked away
and hobbled off
on mean and crooked feet.

Centering   *Sheila Roberts*

THE PARTY AT THE CONTESSA'S HOUSE

There is a party tonight
at the Contessa's home.
Years ago, she owned the house
and lived there, fading
from a turn of the century
opera career. Hidden in the country,
the house rises up with white bell tower
and narrow double doors. Inside,
the sunken living room where her guests
gazed up the wall and watched
as Madame sang from the balcony.
Her pet black snake coiled
around every wavering note.
The secret behind the bookcase:
shelves for hidden memories
of records, yellowed programs,
photographs, the ring she wore
on opening night performances.
The stairs to the roof to the night

to the stars to the past. Tonight,
the winter wind is blowing through
a clear sky. In the distance,
maybe twenty miles away,
city lights mark the horizon.

Descant   *Brian Robertson*

THE COWETA COUNTY COURTHOUSE

What jailhouse bars are more black
or more cold and hard than the pavement
of this, the open highway? I feel my
body sway east back and forth almost
as though I loved the gusty air of
passing trucks. Don't they too know
the cold shoulder of a new horizon
every afternoon? It's so much more
stale and changed from the sunup
of the morning. I know freedom
like the sign of a city by a freeway
out in nowhere. I know how freely the
cold sinks in through this old leather
coat. But why do I sometimes find my
collar turned away from the road and
walking at my feet when a car slows
to draw near and I see what for a second
seems it could almost be a familiar face,
before the collar lifts around the corners
of my eyes. It's like I almost didn't
need a ride at all. My memories of
nights beneath the February stars and
those in truckstop bunks or with
some dude who picked me up outside of
Washington: all those glorious nights
find themselves rolled up and intertwined
with one in the upper floors of
the Coweta County Courthouse, where
I knelt and cried and almost prayed.

Newsart   *James Miller Robinson*

THIS EVENING, WITHOUT BLINKING

If you watch
Between this ten minutes and the next, across that field
Of half-mown stalks and fallen weeds, the scatter
Of blackbirds rising from the stubble, settling
In the locust tree, rising again; if you stare
Intently at the broken shadows of the poplar
On the hillside, at every point and particle
Of their blossoms and burrs, at the hard surfaces

Of the acorns in bulbs and clusters of wooden balls
Among the oaks; if you notice the fur and fuzz
Of every stem and seed, the twist of the wheat tassles
At the neck, buttons of sound, hush of lashes;
If you watch without motion, as still yourself as
Some lax shell overturned in a creekbed, you will
See the hair of each feather, all the stones and ferns,
Every thread and needle of the landscape flash once
In brilliant gold, sparkle like cut-glass figures,
A moment of candles in one bright light of everything
Before the dark.

The Seattle Review   Pattiann Rogers

HUMAN DILEMMA

Climbing mountains
Sailing oceans
Fording rivers
Going nowhere
Holding what cannot be held.

Turning skyward
Finally inward
Holding what can be held.
Changing until we find that which
    cannot be changed.

Unity   *Jim Rosemergy*

POETS OBSERVED

Young poets swim in schools like minnows
As time or tide their number winnows
A few survive in deeps, very
Wily, large, and solitary.

Arizona Quarterly   *F. C. Rosenberger*

DAVID HOMINDAE

(after Michelangelo)

For stone that breaks the giant hold, for strength
I love you not, but love the languid length
Where right the slack and narrow arm now takes
A certain fortitude that weakness makes.
Then, after turbulence, I love your grace
At end, when grace is grace in rest. Of rock
Your softness; yet no hardihood let mock
Your maleness, closed and petaled in its place.
I love for life, for so short days, for bud

Laid out on block, for chiseled pallor, blood—
More than the upward rising of the lines,
The deep dependence downward that defines
A homily to God by mortal strain,
The manly droop of marble.
                                        And its vein.

Southwest Review   *Marjorie Stamm Rosenfeld*

NATIONALISM

I'm so tired of being a Jew, an Arab,
Even an American . . . and all the flags
That spill our blood. Those Germans—Lord!
What was it they did 32 years ago?
What did Russia do when Stalin lived?
And France, England, Spain—name their crimes,
Name their colonies, name the years?

I'm so tired in the heart of all the parts,
All those orthodoxies that go with bullets—
Fired by boys, by men, by women—and bombs
Among the Irish when whiskey is so much better.
So tired of the latitudes of platitudes,
Sums of sentiment and the G.N.P.'s ghosts—
The First World, the Second, and the Third World.

Better not to develop; be like Iceland
Or some islands still lost in the South Pacific;
Be anything but a nation with a flag.
Burn them all! with the German going first,
Then the Russian—then our own bursting through air;
And we'll dance internationally. Dance! Dance! Dance!

New Letters   *Harry Roskolenko*

LISTENING-POST

Sometimes, in the palpitating chrysalis of night,
Locked and sealed within my citadel of flesh and bone,
I strain to bend and focus every thought,
Every drifting microvolt that rises evanescent
From the ceaseless resonating circuits of my brain;
In my winding-sheet I strive
To forge a field of force,
A personal polarity, a telescope
To scan the numbing vastness stretching
From the borders of my bed.
Like those huge and humming shells
That stand on barren heaths
And sift the sounds of space,
Back and forth I range, searching,

From the pathways of the evening star
To the pastel gladness of a child's
Lost world, searching for the gem-like
Source, the ruby beam to lase the lock.
And always, the signals are the same:
The measured movements of my mortal heart,
The startled slitherings of my mortal guts;
And over these
I have
No dominion.

Voices International   *Martin C. Rosner*

SALESMAN

He sells door to door,
Rings the bell and waits.
Madam, would you like to live forever?
Home Office tells him
take it easy with the product.
He holds the thick thumbed book behind him
like a child's surprise.
Madam, would you like to live in Paradise forever?
Jesus, clean and courteous, invites me.

O Lamb, forgive them their computers.
In this ghetto of green lawns
your prospect's zero.
I, the least religious Jew, must die
six million times. You're late—
four thousand years. Competitors
have worked this street—both sides.
I nail their message
to the doorposts of my house,
upon my gates
O Lamb, I praise
the perfect whiteness of your shirt.

Great River Review   *Ruth Roston*

HIGH SUMMER

High summer
and every thing relents,
bird song goes slack,
the grass is less intense,
even the weeds relax.
But in the meadow,
thistle blows
and flutters to the ground
where finches chirp
chicoree of dissent.
Their summer song

still sounds anticipation
as they slit seeds
and take the thistle down to nest.
Such is ever the evidence
against our consternation—
that always there is something
that will not repent,
some counter, some event
that seems for all the world
as though in celebration.

Sou'wester   *Guy Rotella*

TEMPORARY PROBLEMS

*("The burial place of an Indian who lived more than
five hundred years ago again delayed construction on I-75
near Fort Lauderdale. State road engineers have
several alternatives, all costly."—News Item)*

Why we should hesitate is not quite clear.
Your bones will feel no pain; all due respect
Will naturally be shown. Perhaps a quiet
Ceremony, with a Seminole
In total tribal garb to give the chief
Address. In token of our gratitude
For the richness of your heritage, we'll move
Your grave with care, out of the way of cars.
The sun you loved is still our number one
Commodity. You'd understand, we're sure.
What's that your dust is spelling now?
Swamp and fire feed the Spirit's eyes?
That's very nice. He'll bless our enterprise.

National Forum   *Larry Rubin*

IN THE SEASON OF WOLVES AND NAMES

I've reached the end of my names.
My children slip through my skin,
luminous fish of my flesh, in pursuit
of their restless sea, the way of children.
The girls have woven white blossoms into their hair.
As they dance, bare-legged in long grass, petals
spin down them. The boy was born with leaves
for fingers, feet deep into the lap of Earth.
They share a secret. They know the meaning
of names, believe in the paths
they are digging through water.

With no wolves at their back, they do not guess
how I howl all night at my wolves, how I see
through the disguise of their ember eyes, wet fangs.
Tiresias fondling the points of my new breasts

in the park. "I like this. I like this," he whispers.
Mismated Narcissus hunting me down through smaller
and smaller circles, hissing "Not you. Never you."
And Penelope, who forgot. In the whirlpool eye of the giant,
I drown endlessly without forgiveness.

How they crouch at my door, pelts glinting
in the shadow. How tall their tongues,
flaring out of the darkness. They know me well.
I always submit, let them chase me
across the margins between my seasons
into this soundless cavern, stripped
of all names but the one they are hunting.
They have me where they want me—hamstrung, belly-up.
They ransack my body to find that last,
merciless name, the one I can never say
for fear the children might hear me.

Prairie Schooner   *Mariève Rugo*

SUNDAY

Sundays when the wind blows
are the corners of clean-washed sheets
as they flap dry in a summer sun,
or the white silent spaces that hang
between the black hands of a clock.
Winter Sundays strike the ear
like new bronze bells
and when the day is bright
ring in the sudden sunlit spots
beneath the needles of a pine.

A gray Sunday is a cat
that paws among ashes on a moonless night,
it is the dust on a shelf of old books
or the dust of a moth crumpled in a hand.
A spring Sunday turns languorously
as a sinking bottle,
it is like a blue lake above which
the gulls circle and glide,
drifting all day—
casting shadows without a sound.

Poet Lore   *Lawrence R. Rungren*

from THE WEDDING POEM

The night before you left, as you lay
asleep on your stomach, I touched
the smooth, sad curve of your waist and hip,
not knowing if you would come back.

You were gone for a year.
It would rain, staining beech trunks, pinning

leaves to the ground; that dank smell of pavement
rose from the streets.

I rapped the copper pan on the range
just to hear it ring. My days
were winds that blow against an alley wall,
or steam from a simmering kettle

forgotten on the stove.
When the sun sank down near the hills
flocks of birds would hurry toward the woods,
toward fir trees like narrow tents against the sky—

sparrows, chickadees, swallows and crows,
in broken, swooping lines, as if pursued.
And I longed to take shelter
in the forest of your hair.

The Beloit Poetry Journal   *Lawrence Russ*

GUYANA

Tall candles' tapered waxes scent the air.
The organ pulses low. The loaves and wine
Are spread where golden Sunday sunshine glows
Through leaded panes. The invitation calls,
"Come, take and eat." We share the mystery
Of sacrifice and strength. Our hearts are bound
Each to the other by a common thought
And purpose, tapping hidden wells of joy;
But still we hear primeval throbbing drums
That stultify all reasonable thought
And call to dark communion's pseudo-grape.
Obediently we file, partake of death
Of self, and cede to others power of life.
Or death.

The Christian Century   *Fern Pankratz Ruth*

LESS IS MORE . . .

Each day we settle for a little less.
Sleep, food, the deep
dreams that once sustained
us. Now we doze, victims
of blankets, and remember nothing
on waking. Nothing, that is,
but the cold sweat curling our thin
hair grotesque, like a baby's.
Something withdraws flavor,
something leaves out the key
ingredient. Now we favor icecubes
and ale, but there is never
enough. We freeze or get drunk
too soon and always forget

the piper until morning
when we pay the usual fee
with aspirin. All day the dullness
settles. We taste dust in
our tea. Our coin collections
are dull, no excitement in those
blunt boxer's faces, those eagles
rubbed featherless by the pecking order
of gathered coins. And we read less
of the paper every day—headlines
and leads, enough of course
to make us want to cry, enough
to make us ravage the TV Guide
for 'thirties movies when
no one settled for less, where
the legend of our childhood lives
basking in the huge limelight
of the Great Depression.

Poetry   *Vern Rutsala*

EAGLE SQUADRON

Haze, and out of it we appear,
my mother and I walking
from the matinee. It is cold.
We walk fast. I feel the ice
in my chest. We have seen
Eagle Squadron at the Laurelhurst
and Spitfires buzz
above our haze, Heinkels fall
hard behind the watertower.
It was a good show and like
good ones follows us a while.
But now the haze goes colder.
Snow begins to fall
and the streets all lose their names—
but slowly, so slowly we
don't know we're lost until
we are. Then we wander
the strange city for hours until
my father appears, driving
the roadster slowly, head
out the window, and calls us
to the warm dashlight of home.

The Iowa Review   *Vern Rutsala*

THE DEATH WATCHERS

This is a room with a death
happening in it
thin and patient.

Women who have kept vigils
in other countries
would recognize it . . .
the smell of fever and fear
and the curtains blowing fitfully.
Everything here has an old pattern.

He pushes covers slowly back
to cool his legs.
Crossing them is slow hard work,
like walking in deep sand.
He's folded away most of his life
sorted and clean in drawers,
but the shreds he's kept
will be enough to die with.
It only takes the energy of one last breath
to finish the job.
He makes each necessary effort
conscientiously,
dying his death himself.

Sounds from the wet street
interrupt all night,
but past watchers sit in our minds
and comfort us like the fingers of rain.

Primavera   *Alice Ryerson*

THE AVENUES

Some nights when you're off
Painting in your studio above the laundromat,
I get bored about two or three A.M.
And go out walking down one of the avenues
Until I can see along some desolate sidestreet
The glare of an all-night cafeteria.
I sit at the counter,
In front of those glass racks with the long,
Narrow mirrors tilted above them like every
French bedroom you've ever read
About. I stare at all those lonely pies,
Homely wedges lifted
From their moons. The charred crusts and limp
Meringues reflected so shamelessly—
Their shapely fruits and creams all spilling
From the flat pyramids, the isosceles spokes
Of dough. This late at night,
So few souls left
In the place, even the cheesecake
Looks a little blue. With my sour coffee
I wander back out, past a sullen boy
In leather beneath the whining neon,
Along those streets we used to walk at night,
Those endless shops of spells: the love philtres
Or lotions, 20th Century voodoo. Once,

Over your bath, I poured
One called *Mystery of the Spies,*
Orange powders sizzling all around your hips.
Tonight, I'll drink alone as these streets haze
To a pale gray. I know you're out somewhere—
Walking the avenues, shadowboxing the rising
Smoke as the trucks leave their alleys and loading
Chutes—looking for breakfast or a little peace.

Poetry   *David St. John*

MORNING

I get into my blue wolf-car.
I slam the door like a pat on the neck.
I shove a Neil Diamond tape
into the slot. Just before I
tear off the knob
I turn the volume so far beyond high
that the dash shakes and the red needle
goes from full
to damn near bursting.

I say go ahead Neil.
Sing that sad song.
It don't matter Neil.
Everything sounds good today.

I know this car:
it can run all day
topping hill
after hill
over any creek
the wind whirling around us
running anywhere.

Show me a road.

I tell the man mowing weeds
at 70th and Vine
to have a seam-splitting hell of a fine day.

I press the pedal,
the bottom of my foot
loving the give of it,

and I am gone.

Prairie Schooner   *Marjorie Saiser*

OPEN HEART

He withdrew his hand slowly
Just as my own slid over its back
Index finger plunged between

the sucking, mulching cusps
Squeezing the swirling current
Of blood between our flesh;
How close to the center I had come—
A hard knot of muscle
Fighting for breath,
Awaiting a small steel cage
And its white plastic ball
Swimming in place
Sending our hearts racing to shore.

Bitterroot   *Michael Salcman*

STAYING UP ON JACK'S FORK NEAR EMINENCE, MISSOURI

Our low cabin above the river is lost
in its own wood.
Everything breathes clearly up here.
This is the place where life can stop
being planned by day. By night
the world will have moved from under our eyes.

for we can't tell
if the valley floor will rise up again
in evening mist, the close hills leaving us
a sheer edge of quiet,

or if the dark will release shy things in our minds,
gnawers and scratchers,
those strange shapes that close up under lights,

or if we will sleep at all
in our damp beds, and not watch for the earth
turning through a dream towards dawn
to reveal in the still flash of morning
the old magical forms: leaves and far-off trees
now gone black in the high country of the moon.

Encapsuled in space like pilots,
we could sit on this screened porch for years
with gin and stories
while the river works its slow way into stone and mist
obscures our past
like sleep, like the valley's continuous sleep.

Bitterroot   *Albert Salsich*

ENGLAND

At times I thought the country itself was a cloud
High up on the map, a sheepwool shape in the sea
That might as easily rise to break blue sky.
But meadows dipped beneath rough cows and horses;
Rippled with short-fur grass, the scruff of earth.

As if, like me, they longed to come in early,
The cold days shrank from darkness. False as ice,
Thick mist released itself by vanishing.
I pedalled home uphill and saw the light
Foreshorten, felt my bearded breath fall back.

Those mornings I would wake to watch the leaves rain.
Too damp to burn, their colors ran and blurred,
Turning a mottled surface underneath.
Seeped in a world as soft as my intentions,
Through miles of glass and cloud, I thought of you.

The Atlantic Monthly   *Mary Jo Salter*

ON THE PAVEMENT

The only monument
to the careening weep of car
was bled in black on pavement.
It washes in the warm rainshower,
glistening streetgrease;
it will leave no pain, no
remembering in the street.

Streets forget no more than remember.
Streets simply never sense
the images they might forget, recall,
or distort. The faces of streets
soon take their character
from the things they wear,
in black tar, in rubber remnants,
in the sprinkle of glass
flickering in mobile streetlight.

So the consuming crunch of car
body in red paint against the wall
is rouge for a dark face.
Streets wear the makeup mute,
and protest only to the jackhammer.

Great River Review   *David A. Sam*

OLD HOUSE PLACE

Although the house is gone, how well I know
This place has held a house the way a hand
Can hold a bird, the sky an afterglow
Of sun that has receded from the land
Except for diamonds in a windowpane.
No need to prove that there were people here
By broken china, rusted weathervane—
A ghost of habitation hovers near.
A house has some enduring quality

That marks its site after the walls are downed.
It seems that each domesticated tree
Protects this acre of deserted ground
Against encroachment from the spreading grove,
Remembering that once it sheltered love.

The Lyric   *Velma Sanders*

ORCHESTRA

The conductor's cocked twig turns out
to be a mountain hike through the kettledrum's buttered thunder
and a flute birdwatching our daydreams. Then tremolo
slurs the violin-section's left fingers in unison,
like sand-lilies curled against wind.

Lull of bassoons, solo trumpet. And back to the bones
of this music we came for; we came to hear structure
but find the female bassist pretty; or pretty, considering.
And a strain colonizing us earlier as oboes
claims us again as trombones
swimming underground, past ore lying in the veins
of solar gold like smashed cars, delving geodes of mineral skies,
white tie and tails, durable evening gowns
giving lessons by day, not making much money.

But we've come to follow album notes. Except for this sadness
hearing dull uncles, aunts, neighbors, second-hand cousins
tell us all they had meant to say,
this sadness at finding we love them
in the faces of strangers, the fog wrists of cellos
turning us into little wells of deep space,
pouring us into and out of our lives—
like all we had meant them to be
if only we had remembered.

The Georgia Review   *Reg Saner*

COUNTRY LANDSCAPE

This involves more than just the water standing
in the open field like an extended gasp,
or the one cloud drifting
toward a horizon I would never have imagined

so black,—did I say *red* cloud?—or the newly-felled
tree's split membrane pulsing in the summerlight.
And it's not just the crops in a row like reasons,
either, that are responsible for this attitude,

although, paradoxically, that's what I've put down.
Sometimes I think it's the difficult matter of the heart.
Sometimes it could be almost anything except
what I've mentioned. All those things I decided against.

Perennial beauty. The dream of moss. So much silence
wasted on us. This is the best place for it.
At least one mile is the distance between
the waiting weather and where you stand, at any moment.

And the question you'd be asking yourself here
is of the possibility for a better life, for greater desire,
though that is obscure, and the feeling of taking part.
The sad gulf that opens in the blood, like a window.

Later, the moon and stars would rise
like boats diverging on a bay—
even then you wouldn't know what it means.
Unlike the stars, you would lose your breath,

you could hear your heart skipping stones,
and the memory of someone who once said:
"your affections are seditious."
There are always sounds here. And small birds

that are learning to become chords—
as if the immense wind were not enough relief,
extolling in the leaves which so often surround us.
Between you and me is an empty gesture,

I only recently understood that. And that gesture
has me sitting here sorry about this piece of paper
which doesn't take into account the difficulty
of a street, a street repeatedly unconcerned with questions

of faith, or men on the move. I don't know what to say—
there are so many personal moments effaced in this light.
It's like this: dead insects blow across the floor.
They have never forgotten.

Poetry   *Sherod Santos*

THE EPISTEMOLOGIST, OVER A BRANDY, OPINING

Relaxing here with brandy and certitude,
Consider our imprecise grasp of things, fuzzy,
Nothing what it seems,

And not even the equations of the scientists—arcane,
Useful in prediction—can convey the confusion, the *buzz*,
Of the hidden complexities,

Simplicity merely being the mind's abstraction
To be able to deal with something. Remember,
Simplicity is parochial.

Think of our isolation! Our blinkered view
Of what's going on around us! It's been set
By millions of years,

So it works well, bringing us food and progeny.
Only sometimes a whiff, something out there,
The message unclear.

Sou'wester   *Robert Sargent*

THREE THINGS

I carried two things around in my mind
Walking the woods and thinking how to say
Shiver of poplar leaves in a light wind,
Threshing of water over shining stones
A brook rippling its interrupted way—
Two things that bring a tremor to the bones.

And now I carry around in my head a third.
The force of it stops me as I walk the wood,
Three things for which no one has found a word—
Leaf ripple, that shining tremor under the skin
Deep in the flesh, a shiver of more than blood
When lovers, water, and leaves are wholly one.

Yankee   *May Sarton*

BY WINTER SEAS

The long tides shudder over hidden rock
    As shudders now the bird in winter fear,
And shudders too the ghost whose omens flock
        Like vultures to unsphere
        Its tired centricity
        And shred its will to be.

What matter now that joy was in the waves
    And birds were venturesome as morning light,
When ghost resigns its urge to fresh enclaves
        Of dream, admitting blight.
        Of that mortality
        Which is its mystery?

Arizona Quarterly   *George Brandon Saul*

THE FAR NORTH

        Ah well, the night,
        the sky, the blue
        morning again
        braided and impossible
        in disentangle.

        It is 38
        Below Zero. Here you come
        like ice out of the far north
        dragging those wizened genitals

        behind you. Grease, skins,
        seal flesh and dogs. Times
        like these you forget
        whether you are really
        there. Admit it,
        you haven't spoken a word

in days. Wrap yourself in rabbit
fur and whistle the dogs
to your side. There are women
out there on ice: muscular calves,
breasts lifted high, palms held
out. They are the chorus
line from a Juneau saloon.
You are home. Now they dance
toward you, legs up, kicking
the moon, dancing clear through you
and back out on the ice.
You've finally discovered
it's dreams like these
that burn holes in the sky.

Four Quarters   *Terry Savoie*

HELLO, SISTER

(78419)

Hello, sister. I saw you today from my distance.
Even then the good woman smell reached me.
Perfume and magic.
Your face was smiling/frowning/worried/happy.
I saw all this from this window of mine.
It's all they let me see of you.
They think.
Do they forget, or just not know,
That I can taste yesterday more
Sharply than any of the todays I've seen yet?
Or that I can reach out and touch
You in my mind? A solid ghost of what used to be.
The softness of just your passing can't
Be erased from my memory.
Until I see you again, if ever, I think of you.
One favor before you go? Smile for me.

The Pikestaff Forum   *Mark Saylor*

REFORMED DRUNKARD

He wakes in a new world and wears new eyes;
His tongue is sweet, as if all night
Summer rain has been his drink
And has rinsed his gaze. His razor moves
With confidence around a temperate smile.
He puts on laundered clothing, knows that vigor
Is stored like legal tender in his purse;
His motion is exemplary, moreover
His wife now wears a different face.
That stare of apprehension and reproach

Has disappeared; she looks on him with pride,
Especially when at dinner he declines
Without perceptible distress or effort
His host's warm invitation to take wine.
She smiles, approving, with the smallest nod;
He is her favorite child. The vicar, too,
Approves, has even stated publicly
That he admires the man, regards
His abstinence as evidence of courage.
The vicar is wrong. Courage or its absence
Is irrelevant.
               Sometimes, not only in his sleep,
He dreams about that other world, returns
To shiver in a gray chemise of sweat.
What he feels is mainly fear, but something more—
Mixed in that pathogenic stew
Are flavorings of desire, relief, regret.
Something warns him not to analyze
The potency and quantity of each.
He walks a straight line very carefully,
Step by step, day by day. It will lead,
He believes, where all lines lead,
But that is not
For him to think about, far less to say.

The American Scholar   *Vernon Scannell*

A SPRING DAY ON CAMPUS

Small birds play in the ivy
As I walk back from the library
Forlorn
With *The Death Notebooks* in my hand.

She died in the garage
In her car
After a light luncheon
And tea,

My sister in the faith
Rowing toward God
The laughing God
Who helped her ashore.

I cannot think of death:
The birds in the ivy
The love in my life.

The Christian Century   *Gilbert Schedler*

SOUTH SHORE LINE

The train has stopped running
all the way

but the cars lie like dusty
stones in the pale eye
of morning.
Morning smells of burnt cigars
and urine drift across the
horsehair seats.

You angle your head against
the glass and look through
glazed soot at the flat
green farms.
They blur but you look on.
There is little choice.
Who can read while iron wheels
shake your spine to jelly?

But you learn to sway with
the train.
You learn to recognize things
before they happen.
Like the crushed gray sulfide
sky that is Gary,
or the squeal of the rails
coming out of East Chicago.

The ride back at night is
worse because the world
is blind and every inch
is the same.
It is better to be drunk or
asleep than to watch
the dark glass for hours,
waiting for the pins
of light that burn against
the sky.

With a sudden burst of
pure noise
we rattle over a curve
dragging the night behind
us on a web of steel.

Indiana Writes   *John Schlesinger*

NO

The world says No.
It has a genius for No.
Everything is No.
In the beginning was Yes
But the world says No.
By the world I mean the people.
The people No.
The people say No.

Authority says No.
Power says Yes to itself
But No to everyone else: it says No.
The police say No.
Sometimes, assuredly,
It is necessary to say No.
But I say No,
It is not always necessary to say No.
When the new child wishes,
Someone always says No.
When the dog barks
At his own wagging tail,
Someone says No.
When the cat runs sideways,
His back up, playing,
Someone says No,
You'll break the lamp.
The world says No.
When someone has a new idea,
The world says No.
The world likes to say No.
No means I know better.
No means I am stronger.
No means I am Yes and No.
The world says No.
The people say No.
Authority says No.
Power says No.
The police say No.
The teacher says No.
Love might even say No.
No is the genius of the world.

New Letters   *E. M. Schorb*

A DELICATE BALANCE

I've never felt it true
the heart observes the score,
that loving less insures
one will be loved the more.

And when I was inclined
to be a bit apart,
I didn't think the distance
was in itself the start

of love, just that you wished
to make your feelings clearer.
Now, withdrawn in turn,
you are, I sense, the dearer.

The Southern Review   *Laura Schreiber*

TO A BUTTERFLY

Sun is a rose window
through your silken wings.

Motionless, you cling to my palm,
remembering a womb that tore,
and spilled you out to crawl.

My heart is still too,
my breath gauze in my throat.
When you fly, I will follow.

Canadian Author and Bookman　　　　　*L. Pearl Schuck*

FRAGMENT OF A PASTORAL

Here might we live in . . . not quite peace, but relative
obscurity. Trees and mountains: this is metonomy.
　　　　　　　　　　　　　　　　　　　　I loved
　　Brooklyn
On your behalf, but was it what we dreamed of under the
　　air-vents
of August nights, in summer's tired plunge toward a red
　　dawn?
It was all we could do to take "taking seriously"
seriously: eyeglasses, eggs, the *Times*, rhubarb, rhubarb,
peas and carrots, hail Caesar, ciphers for the endless
adulthood of Sunday breakfast, products of who knows
　　whose fancy?
To understand those moments, to sort them justly, I
　　can't believe
we thought it possible. Like trying to live
on Benzedrene and Life Savers, you just can't,
eventually.
　　　　　　　　So this: a partial remedy for the quandary we
　　argued
over cups and cups of coffee, perhaps worse than no
　　remedy,
but who will be the wiser? Only we must become small
　　enough
to live in this broken world . . .

Poetry　　　　　　　　　　　　　　　　*Barry Schwabsky*

RAIN

There is more than one rain. There
is the rain that drones, how far
how deep I don't know, and the one
that rattles leaves and gutters
chattering windows. Yes, and another,
wind rain, think of wind rain, how

it flattens and angles. See, there
are three rains. And what of the
one we don't hear or see, the one
the brain doesn't know, do you know
this rain? Yes, and I know another.
I smell this rain flowing the sky
and I look to birds and flowers
tuning, and the air, how it slows
down. There are more, listen,
listen! Do you hear the deep rain,
how far how deep I don't know.

Portland Review   *Peter Sears*

THE FATE OF BIRDS

The fate of birds disturbs me,
How they fall prey to fang and claw,
Fry on the high hot wires or
Whirl in disconsolate winds
Like dead leaves, smashing
Their matchstick bones on transparent
Panes that harbor the mirage
Of comfortable safe nestings.

Swimmers of the sky need more
Than just a modicum of luck
And the long day's blessing:
When the carnivorous shadows cross
The floating moon and the furred
Assassins purr among the trees,
There should be reassuring voices,
Silent, in the flutters of the heart.

Western Poetry Quarterly   *Kenneth Seib*

HICKORY STICK HIERARCHY

When I was young my adult peers
Insisted some day I'd recall,
While pondering over vanished years,
Those spent at school were best of all.

Indeed, this statement might have earned
From me an acquiescent nod—
If all my pedagogues had learned
To spare the child and spoil the rod!

Educational Studies   *Len G. Selle*

THE MORNING OF THE RED-TAILED HAWK

In holy books, in church, I hear curses,
see stones hurled at bodies caught in acts

that spurn the law of Moses and of God. I,

like Saul, have judged, held coats in hands
washed clean in the blood of a Bible-belt Lamb.

But, from my window now, I follow the red-tailed
hawk, gliding, imperceptibly adjusting
to turbulence, scanning his territory
for unwary rodents in the tall marsh grass.

I too cruise, needing emotion, words to write.
Today, I intercepted a man's glance, saw his eyes
smoothing the light hairs on another man's arm
as they walked the beach.

These two are lovers in some sheltered cove,
where my claws could intrude, sharp
as the red-tailed hawk, his talons sunk in flesh.

I will not write their names. Deeper than books,
than church, I have caught some ancient pain,
accepting it to cup, as in a chalice,
between my trembling hands.

The Beloit Poetry Journal   *Bettie M. Sellers*

BENT TREE

I go a long way back to find that bent tree.
Alone in the middle of the garden, it had a knot
at its center, a small space where as a child
I imagined animals once lived.

How the time has passed since I tagged that tree,
lobbed rope over the branches and swung below
all summer long. Afternoons I'd fall off into deep dreams
and open my eyes to see the world, the thick leaves
twitching above me in the wind like birds.

I remember years later looking for you in summer,
wondering where you might be on such a warm night.
Everything we hoped had disappeared so fast.
And for nothing more than a fond thought I imagined you
beside that bent tree, your hair again long and
your skin wild, chanting my name at the fat moon.

The Hudson Review   *Peter Serchuk*

A MIRAGE

If spring should rise like a heron
From misty corners of her joyless eyes
And fly across a sorrowing length of blue
Staked with black to the freshness of round white worlds,
Would the flight transform the glaze of grief,
Free vision, and fill the eyes with stars of light?

Would the round white plains really shine again
And winter's half-closed lids heavy with memories
Of change and loss, cold as any frozen marsh,
Open wide and look with joy on sun-filled daffodils
And splendors of a heron rising from a misty marsh?
Dew falls from frosty reed, and flowers bend in the wind.

Poet Lore   *Ruth Setterberg*

WHAT IS LEFT?

After the bars and the gates and the degradation
What is left?
After the lock-ins and the lock-outs and the lock ups
What is left?
I mean, after the chains that get entangled in the grey
    of one's matter
After the bars that get stuck in the hearts of men and
    women
What is left?
After the tears and disappointments
After the lonely isolation
After the cut wrist and the heavy noose
What is left?
I mean, after the commissary kisses
And the get-your-shit-off blues
After the hustler has been hustled
What is left?
After the murderburgers and the goon squads and
    the tear gas
What is left?
I mean, after you know that God can't be trusted
After you know that the shrink is a pusher
That the word is a whip, and the badge is a bullet
What is left?
After you know that the dead are still walking
After you realize that the silence is talking
That outside and inside are just an illusion
What is left?

I mean, like where is the sun?
Where are her arms and where are her kisses?
There are lip prints on my pillow
I am searching

What is left?

I mean, like nothing is standstill and nothing is
    abstract
The wing of a butterfly can't take flight
The foot on my back is part of a body
The song that I sing is part of an echo

What is left?

I mean like, love is specific
Is my mind a machine gun?
Is my heart a hack saw?
Can I make freedom real. Yeah

What is left?

I am at the top and bottom of a lower-archy
I am in love with losers and laughter
I am in love with freedom and children
Love is my sword and truth is my compass

What is left?

North Country Anvil   *Assata Shakur*

COLD FRONT

Old women in this town never sleep
on nights like this.
I hear them blinking across rooms
from house to house, wool blankets
pulled to their chins,
blinking back fathers, husbands, sons—
the blood trembling with the rattle
of precious china.
The wind rides through windows
tossing black rose boughs,
worrying a shutter all night.
In the deep cellar the furnace
clicking on, clicking off,
the floor boards sighing
against bent nails;
the ticking in the walls,
the night scratching to come in,
the blackness flowing like a river of lost bodies—
the house finally swept up with the circling
leaves, the old ladies
of the town
swirling on galactic beds,
the street lights winking out
one by one,
the air full of bones.

Tendril   *Peter Sharpe*

PREFACE

Mother, don't read
my poems.
You'll feel like you did
the day my brother took us
aboard the KC-135 he flies.
In the cockpit

admiring all those terrible
gadgets, a hundred
clocks with their numbers
and later
on that tin roof of a barn
he said was the wing
you were afraid for yourself,
for him: as if
the child you knew
had quietly changed
into a strange
incomprehensible man.

Moving Out   *Carol Shauger*

JUDAS, PETER

because we are all
betrayers, taking
silver and eating
body and blood and asking
(guilty) is it I and hearing
him say yes
it would be natural for us all
to rush out
and hang ourselves

but if we find grace
to cry and wait
after the voice of morning
has crowded in our ears
clearly enough
to break our hearts
he will be there
to ask us each again
do you love me

Christianity Today   *Luci Shaw*

A FRIEND'S PASSING

(Homage to F. D. "Dick" Cossitt)

Oh you tall traveler,
driver of red convertible,
toucher of people,
welder of shapes,
maker of bronze flowers,
aesthetic wanderer,
father,
lover,
writer of words,

talented one,
friend . . .

Drive now in the votive chariot
    of your own design
fashioned of bright metal.
Your passing marks us with wounds
    of melancholy
        that will not heal.
The memory of your gentleness
    remains
with promise.

Inlet   *Barclay Sheaks*

THE DEER

The deer is patience,
the deer is what we see standing
in the woods, half its jaw shot off,
just staring.
You ought to kill it now
but you lift it into the back of the pickup.
At home you pack the broken bone with mud.

Healing, she moves toward you.
Shy, she rubs her head against your leg.
What I've loved in myself and others

is in the dream I have of this deer
though she was real: she came out of the woods
bleeding, she knew how to die
but healed. The deer that walked
one day back into the woods

is standing by a pond now, alert,
in a wash of sunlight.
How quietly she stands there
as if there were no way
to not belong in the world,
as if it were this easy.

Poetry   *Laurie Sheck*

BREAKFAST

These are the stone paths
of an early morning.
I walk up steps through courtyards
and camellias; all are wet
and have a cool smell.
On their other side,
I will open a door,
climb the stairs,

open another door.
You sleep behind it.
When I turn the lock,
or when I settle
on that narrow bed,
the first vibration of your voice
will cleave me like a split pear.
The taste of you will be
the first thing
to pass my lips.

Yankee   *Robin Shectman*

HOW TO AMUSE A STONE

command the stones in a loud voice
or speak to them
just to the left of silence
or sing them a love song in Spanish—
they will not respond

write a letter
in it confess all your sins
place it under a stone
leave it there for months
and when you return you will find
your letter unopened and unread

stones have a sense of dignity
greater than that of kings
a sense of honor
stronger than that of friends

stones are fulfilled like prophecy
tendentious as rain
and have a sense of humor
more subtle than we can comprehend

it takes a long time to amuse a stone
first you must capture one
carry it away
imprison it with mortar in a wall
the stone will not complain

then you must wait
and years after you are gone
under another stone on which
some stranger carved your name

the mortar in your wall will crumble
and the stone you captured
will fall to the ground
amused and free and going home

Poetry   *Richard Shelton*

LENT TENDING

These February days, though few,
lie long upon us. They cling
like last month's worn and weathered snow,
the soiled and broken crust askew,
but deep below the frosty claw holds firm.
And will it never end . . . we sigh year
after year. While all the time we know
that, far or near, the trend is warm.
Surprising life prepares. The One
approaches now who all our winter bears
toward its final overthrow.

The Christian Century   *J. Barrie Shepherd*

THE GROUNDHOG FORESHADOWED

Someone stole a winter from my life,
its wet kiss wiped clean
in the windows open overnight,
a bedroom quickly summered,
cold bled from every pore.

There is nobody to stuff hands
inside my pockets, to huddle with
in the doorway blocking December.
My blankets have dwindled
to a topsheet I don't share.

The moon is empty and still
swollen, heated from its long run
like a dog's tongue, by words it holds
declarations attached to hot
nights and longing spring winds.

I shall go out and steal back winter;
having gone too long without it,
I am no father to this spring.

Kansas Quarterly   *Steven Sher*

EARTH CHANGES

When Mama lay dying
Papa came in from the fields;
he said he heard her soul cry out,
he said the earth was changing.

He said he felt the sun setting
in broad day, out there plowing,
and his name come to him
from the inside of his head.

He came, talking, through the screen door,
with clay stuck heavy to his boots;

he didn't stop, he didn't pause,
he came right through.

He walked straight in to Mama
and put his hands around her head.
They were so large, those hands;
they both reached to cradle Mama's head.

Her eyes closed at that,
his lips smiled a bit,
and then her body shuddered,
lightened, and went limp.

When he sat on the bed, silent,
I took his face in my hands.

Great Lakes Review   *Kent Shire*

URGENCY

I'm not ready, I shout.
You smile, eyes trailing off behind me.
See, you're detaching yourself already.

I drive across the city on errands.
Weakening now, you stay behind to rest,
to write notes that will encourage me.
The bed is covered with small packages
you are wrapping to leave for the children.

On the beltway I realize I will never see you again—
I'll be widowed like my mother, staring out the window
at dusk, my children searching each car.

It's spring. I'm cluttered with details.
I am missing your last hours, the final calm
when the house falls silent and your face
turns ethereal.

I push the accelerator to the floor.
A scent of flowers enters the car. It's dark.
The children croon soft, repetitious songs
in the back seat.

The car slows. The headlights go out.
Trees hang like shadows across the road
scratching the doors as we pass. I see your face
on all the mirrors.

Like a boat moving through weeds, the car glides
silently to a stop. Thick flowers and leaves
cover the hood. *O my husband, what is this
strange land I have no desire to explore?*

New Orleans Review   *Betsy Sholl*

THE SPIRIT OF 34TH STREET

Doors opened with a silent scream,
    like photographs of anguish;

the subway paused, shed cargo
and raged on.

She lurched aboard,
sagged into a vacant seat,
frail weight of her gray years
hunched with cold.
Numb fingers plucked at rags,
drawn close against raw misery.
Knuckles, cracked and swollen white,
clutched into a plea for warmth.

He, dark and lithe,
swung down the aisle,
taut jeans dancing
rhythmically.
With Latin grace
he, sidling past
her patient form,
in one smooth gesture
disappeared through subway doors,
leaving in her lap,
like folded dove wings,
his black leather gloves.

The Christian Century   *Peggy Shriver*

TORNADO WATCH

Lightning slices above Texas City,
the refineries and Dairy Queens.
Our dining room table is a table cloth
spread over a dozen cases of Lone Star.
A piano is rolled into a field.
The land has been unzipped.
Two men stand on the piano
& count oil wells.
We send out invitations,
but only piano keys arrive.
We send out appeals,
but we can only smell
an overheated radiator.
What muscles the land has,
a violence of separation.
A window flies across a pasture.

Southwest Review   *Paul Shuttleworth*

WHITE PINES

Their boughs curve upward in praise;
regal feathers painting the air,
the houses and farms;

soft cry on winter nights,
ghosting under the door;
they haunt the fields with their absence,
in search of stolen brothers, groaning
down wind, down highway and river
to the deaf and hungry cities.

North Country Anvil   *Barry Silesky*

THERE ARE IN SUCH MOMENTS

the frequency of bumping
a passerby on a crowded
northern street, the tidal
times of an elevator, the
heft of a trashman's joist—
there are in such moments
of mundane distillation
more than meets the eye.
for example, in screwing
the gasoline cap onto my
car that so resists the
groove, i have the very
chance for sensitivity in
my touch, and so i grasp,
taking the deepest of
inward breaths, a rivulet
recalling the river, and
as the air passes ever so
slowly outward—as the
hopeless sigh of a balloon
pursuing friendship—i feel
eyes closed the invisible
but perfect engagement of
the cap and the metal torso
as if a silky thief at the
moment the vault's combination
submits like labiae to reveal
untold gems and endless nights
of thrashing.

Colorado-North Review   *David I. Silverstein*

MY FAMILY'S UNDER CONTRACT TO CANCER

every few years,
renewing its option,
it claims another aunt, uncle, cousin,
relegating our infrequent gatherings
to the level of witch hunts;
eyes probing chests

374 / Anthology of Magazine Verse

for evidence of disguised mastectomies,
the hoarse throat of a lingering cold—
solid proof
of its black progress through vocal chords
and God pity the poor fool who,
inhaling carelessly,
breaks into a coughing fit . . .
condemned for the rest of the evening
to know that
behind every affectionate smile,
every tender hand clasp,
he's watching another name
scratched for the Christmas list,
another reunion table
minus one more chair.

Canadian Forum   *Greg Simison*

WATER ON THE HIGHWAY

Water on the pavement moves before me.
Witch water, I say, as though some sorceress waits,
snapping her crooked fingers to make it disappear.
It is real, I tell you. It evaporates,
or seems to, and it is always there.

Last night a friend talked about going home,
the roadmap she followed, the bridge she had to cross.
As I listened, I studied her words on paper
describing a house with stained glass windows,
a wicker chair, her father's face. I want to believe
poets who say this is the way home, who go and come,
traveling lines as concrete and safe as any interstate.

The sun is hot today and my map is marked, open.
I drive home knowing, as I go,
I will have to cross water to get there.

The Georgia Review   *Nancy Simpson*

FOR MARIELLA, IN ANTRONA

We are women of different origins,
you with your handmade sandals
and I with my knapsack and boots.
But when we met by the lake
near your mountain village,
we spoke as easily as sisters.
I told you of the men I loved,
how they formed patterns in my thoughts
like the patches of moonlight on the water.
You said you did not need men.

As the moon teased and tugged
at our shadows, you recalled

how the villagers fear the lake;
even your mother believes it's bottomless.
But not you. I watched you undress,
climb to a slippery ledge and leap
headfirst from that height.
I thought of your mother asleep
as your body, a brilliant
naked crescent, pierced the surface.

In mock modesty the moon slipped
behind the mountains while you
shivered into your dress again.
We said goodbye and returned,
you to your home, I to my country.
But whenever a lover's hands
slide under my clothes and reach
downward to an opening in the skin,
I see you diving, diving into the
darkest waters of your birthplace.

New England Review   *Tobey A. Simpson*

POEM OF THE MOTHER

The heart goes out ahead
scouting for him
while I stay at home
keeping the fire,
holding the house down
around myself
like a skirt from the high wind.

The boy does not know
how my eye strains to make out
his small animal shape
swimming hard across the future,
nor that I have strengthened myself
like the wood side of this house
for his benefit.

I stay still
so he can rail against me.
I stay at the fixed center of things
like a jar on its shelf
or the clock on the mantel,
so when his time comes
he can leave me.

Quest   *Myra Sklarew*

THE ACCOMPLICE

It's the way she moves
So the store detective won't notice
The direction she moves in.

The color of her hair makes too much sense
To him, a shade of brown
That means stirring maple syrup
Into oatmeal at the age of four.
She's no longer a woman in a blue dress
Pausing at housewares,
She's Sis looking for something
In the pantry.

As he follows her down the racks
Of party dresses and little overcoats
She's Reverend Banks' youngest daughter,
The one who carried a matron's pocketbook
Through fifth grade. He's chasing
Her home from school, he's late for piano lessons.
Among the bras and girdles
She's Mother, getting a bit stout
From nibbling while making dinners and living
All day among leftovers,
Who says "Son, don't go very far."

But it's her arrival in bedding
That's my signal to act.
Now he's imagining passion, adoring
And being adored. When she takes off
Her shoes and tests the firmness of the mattress,
We have him where we want him.

Walking with aplomb
Through the electric front doors
With a television set under each arm,
I think affectionately about how I depend
On her, how when she holds you
She holds you up.

Antaeus   *Ron Slate*

SANDPAPER, SANDPIPER, SANDPIT

sandpaper (sand pa•per) *n.-s* I. Paper that
is covered with sand or some other rough,
abrasive substance used for smoothing or
polishing a surface.—*v.* sandpapered,
sandpapering, sandpapers. To work with it
or as if with it: *My mother* sandpapered
*the edges of my father's moods until she
made their marriage smooth.* See *true grit.*

sandpiper (sand pi•per) *n. -s* I. An Eastern
shorebird that walks at the water's edge
quite rapidly; it frequents the flats of
the tidal estuaries whenever the beaches
of the region are enveloped in a chilly
fog; it is streaked with a brownish gray
or a buff, but it is completely white at
the breast. 2. A woman with the impulsive

movements of a sandpiper: *She hurried on*
ahead of me just like a little sandpiper,
peeping with pride.

sandpit (sand pit) *n. -s* I. A deep hole
in the sand. 2. A point of depression.
3. A hollow of loneliness that is left,
if a loved one is lost. See *true grief.*

The Georgia Review   *Warren Slesinger*

IT'S TRUE I'M NO MISS AMERICA

But if I were a dandelion weed
Sprung up in seedling symmetry of green,
With sun and mud the summit of my need,
A little bland anathema, serene
Amidst the sleep and silky summer grass,
You would not grudge my ugliness; you'd pluck
My ragged yellow blossom as you pass
And stick it through your buttonhole for luck.
You'd say that there was beauty in the beast.
And when the luscious velvet of the rose
Was limp with age, and its plush petals creased
And dropping slack in stuporous repose,
You'd sow your wishful love upon the air
While blowing kisses through my hoary hair.

Poet Lore   *Stephanie Slowinsky*

PHYSICAL FOR MY SON

I took you to the clinic today,
Somewhere between school and suppertime,
With my jaws tight, my fists clenching
Over committee minutes and burning potatoes
Until the lab tests came in lintless white coats
And punctured a finger on your grubby left hand
And invited me into your inner ear,
The otoscope bringing me breathless
Into a chamber I had not known before,
Aware that you, having lived inside me,
Know somewhere more than I'll ever know about you,
Reaching—
Like when the technician with sterile fingers
Finally washed slides in the stainless steel sink,
And I wanted somewhere to save your blood.

Kansas Quarterly   *Barbara Smith*

PELVIC MEDITATION

The August night thick and black on us.
We lie under Emma Goldman's ulster,

holes of white-hot stars, suspicions of wind,
whatever will come through the pin pricks—
delight, fault, our own dubious lives.
And hot, hot things rising through the fabric
of air with the fervor of one childhood summer,
before they fall, morning's heavy water, and bend
the stems of iris. The gravity
of buttock and back flattens the springs,
their stifled metallic noise—reticent crickets.
We're restless; scapulas cut up the sheets
and it's then I take my hand to the place
between your thighs, to the fine coarse hair,
and the thin ridge of bone I feel there
with wonder. I had come to think of you
there as opening, soft cleft, let's say it, *hole*,
And I know the figure of the pelvis: the twin wings
between the spine, the two eyes below in the anterior. . . .
Yet I thought *soft, wet,* and *opening* like the scalloped space
between the curtain and the sill when we have wind,
like the gap in the hedge in front of Emily Dickinson's
we walked through. There's my ignorance. Big,
before the lips, beneath the hand, gaping
in dialogue of solids and voids. And holes in the night
like aureoles, like history palpable and female
and the night rising and the wonder
in spite of what you have to call *dumb,*
dumb, and the bones soothed in atonement,
the woman as witness, the clamor of crickets.

West Branch   *Bruce Smith*

THE ROUNDHOUSE VOICES

In full glare of sunlight I came here, man-tall but thin
as a pinstripe, and stood outside the rusted fence
with its crown of iron thorns while
the soot cut into their lungs with tiny diamonds.
I walked through houses with my grain-lovely slugger
from Louisville that my uncle bought, and stood
in the sun which made its glove soft on my hand
until I saw my chance to crawl under and get past
anyone who would demand a badge and a name.

The guard hollered that I could get the hell from
     there quick
when I popped in his face like a thief. All I ever wanted
to steal was life and you can't get that easy
in the grind of a railyard. *You can't catch me,*
lard-ass, I can go left or right good as the Mick
I hummed to him, holding my slugger by the neck
for a bunt laid smooth where the coal cars
jerked and let me pass between tracks
until, in a slide on ash, I fell safe and heard
the wheeze of his words: *Who the hell are you, kid?*

I hear them again tonight, Uncle, hard as big brakeshoes,
when I lean over your face in the box of silk. The years
you spent hobbling from room to room alone crawl
up my legs and turn this house to another
house, round and black as defeat, where slugging
comes easy when you whip the gray softball over
the glass diesel globe. Footsteps thump on the stairs
like that fat ball against bricks and, when I miss,
I hear you warn me to watch the timing, to keep
my eyes on your hand and forget the fence,

hearing also that other voice that keeps me out and away
from you on a day worth playing good ball. Hearing
Who the hell . . . I see myself, like a burning speck
of cinder, come down the hill and through a tunnel
of porches like stands, running on deep ash,
and I give him the finger, whose face still gleams
clear as a B & O headlight, just to make him get up
and chase me into a dream of scoring at your feet.
At Christmas that guard staggered home sobbing,
the thing in his chest tight as a torque-wrench.
In the summer I did not have to run and now

who is the one who dreams of a drink as he leans over
tools you kept bright as a first girl's promise? I
have no one to run from or to, nobody to give
my finger to as I steal his peace. Uncle, the light
bleeds on your gray face like the high barbed-wire
shadows I had to get through and maybe you don't
      remember
you said to come back, to wait and you'd show me
the right way to take a hard pitch
in the sun that shudders on the ready man. I'm here

though this is a day I did not want to see. In the
      roundhouse
the rasp and heel-click of compressors is still,
soot lies deep in every greasy fingerprint.
I called you from the pits and you did not come up
and I felt the fear when I stood on the tracks
that are like a star which never makes it
into any kind of light and I don't know who'll
tell me now when the guard sticks his blind snoot
between us to take off and beat the bastard out.
Can you hear him over the yard, grabbing his chest,
cry out *Who the goddam hell are you, kid?*

I gave him every name in the book, Uncle, but he
      caught us,
and what good did all those hours of coaching do?
You lie on your back, eyeless forever, and I think
how once I climbed to the top of a diesel and stared
into that gray roundhouse glass where, in anger,
you threw up the ball and made a star
to swear at greater than the Mick ever dreamed.
It has been years but now I know what flowed there

every morning the sun came up, not light
but the puffing bad-bellied light of words.

All day I have held your hand, trying to say back
    that life,
to get under that fence with words I lined
and linked up and steamed into a cold room
where the illusion of hope means skin torn in boxes
of tools. The footsteps come pounding into words
and even the finger I give death is words
that won't let us be what we wanted, each one
chasing and being chased by dreams in a dark place.
Words are all we ever were and they did us
no damn good. Do you hear that?

Do you hear the words that, in oiled gravel, you
    gave me
when you set my feet in the right stance to swing?
They are coal-hard and they come in wings
and loops like despair not even the Mick
could knock out of this room, words softer
than the centers of hearts in guards or uncles,
words skinned and numbed by too many bricks.
I have had enough of them and bring them back here
where the tick and creak of everything dies
in your tiny starlight and I stand down
on my knees to cry *Who the hell are you, kid?*

The New Yorker   *Dave Smith*

PINE CONES

Any way you hold them, they hurt.
What's the use, then?

Once in our backyard, by a sparrow's hidden
tremor there in the green wish of spruce,
a full but unfolded body

hung. It bore every color of the world and was sweet
beyond measure. The canyon wind banged
at this then went elsewhere.

Something happened that night.
The sparrow seems to have seen what it was.

Look at him huddled there, mistakably some other shadow,
the sly outlines of his body almost blue as spruce,
the sun like a big wall nearby

and you stepping through it, big, that big
he would almost give up his only wish.

Almost. Almost. Almost.

Isn't this the way hearts beat in the world,
the way pine cones fall in the night
until they don't?

When you pick them up, as children do,
the tiny spot appears in your palm,
red as the sun's first blink
of love.

And that sticking unabidable tar.

The Georgia Review   *Dave Smith*

ALLEY-WALKER

walking down the alley
looking for you the black man
standing in a back doorway
eyeballed me
I could tell he wondered why the hell
I walked down the pitch black alley
like I owned it kicking at a beer can
like some hooker who walks the streets
around the corner on Western Avenue
a Hooker Row where L.A. ladies-of-the-eve
wearing sequined T-shirts
lame open-toed wedgies walk slow and easy
as if the wind blows their asses side to side
the way it does palm trees
he probably thought I was on my way to roll
some poor John behind the garbage cans
and stuff his empty wallet into a
Dempsey Dumpster
but I was looking for you
thinking you'd run out on me
took off in your green Mustang
leaving me there to pay for all that champagne
not a dime in my bag
to call a cab or a friend
you bastard I walked through the back door
of the Troubador the bouncer afraid
to ask me if I had a ticket
walked past the booths and stools
the men's rest room
to the bar
where you sat drinking our champagne—
"Jesus Christ, baby, I've been looking all over
for you
Where the hell have you been!"

Nitty Gritty   *Joan Smith*

CHECKING THE FIRING

I could lose an eyelid and see forever
or go blind with this desire
to see inside the kiln
where small apocalypse surrounds

the vessels our fingers shaped.
Base and rim glow to bisque
as vases remember the turning wheel,
the slip, the palm, the spinning center.

We wait nervously for the perfect
moment to cut the fire
so a careful cooling can begin.
I look into your unblinking eye
where a bronzen and gold-wreathed glow
says this is the exquisite instant
of highest heat, the crux
we must weather to survive.

From soil and water we have rounded
the forms to hold a life.
The moment of our making, love, is now.
I see it etched in fire.

Buffalo Spree   *R. T. Smith*

GETTING BY ON HONESTY

at the edge of the macadam parking lot
behind the employment security commission
where I go to pick up my check
there is an oak tree & on rainy wednesdays
when I arrive for my appointment its
leaves drip deep green & the sky seems a
great grey hand stretching to the sea
I never want to go inside & this oak tree
is my only excuse
the sky a constant reminder

there's something sinister in the game
we play
my friend the clerk wants to smile but
by law cannot
occupation? she asks
poet I answer
present employment if any?
paid poet.
got something for me? she whispers
palm down I slip her a sonnet
on the sly
sign here she snaps
handing me the check
she lifts her pale freckled face
close to mine & for just a moment
I believe she might smile
but america is all business
next week, she says
I'd like a rondeau

Green River Review   *Stephen E. Smith*

STILL LIFE

This still life is still life after all.
These massed hydrangeas standing near the wall
as big as cushions puffed up on a chair
loll their heads like pink clowns in the air
who just perform and do not need to know.
They bloom with blue like heaped up mountain snow.

These flowers bring such fullness to the room,
they stand like resurrections from the tomb.
Now at season's end with tarnished golds
the year rots like a mirror which still holds
blue and silver merging with the frame.
These are colors with a flower's name.

We sit and watch their clouds of pink, their sheen,
the way they look both savage and serene
drawing the light and holding it at bay:
a storm inside a storm that has been stilled
with something finished, something unfulfilled.

Waves   *Vivian Smith*

THE PIANO TUNER

(for David, who has the good sense to play the piano)

No telling his age
or how long he had been blind;
no telling about his sense of time
or his family or his loves.

With cane and magic bag, along
came Mr. Green in the afternoon,
quiet and punctual as dusk.
He knew somehow where the piano would be
and began by taking a history,
speaking with it, his puissant hands
floating above the nervous system . . .
saying it was old,
perhaps older than the house,
and required gentleness.

His eyes were fixed
in a lifted, photographed gaze
as if he peered out from under a cap
at every star
(whose names he knew).

All of us felt
the vivid sense of being honored
beyond our worth
by his gift of presence.
He spent hours coaxing,
showing where it went wrong:

standing over the aged heart,
sighted fingers skillfully lost
among loose wires and felt-capped hammers,
reuniting the larynx and its truthful voice.
Together they spoke as if at prayer.

So nothing really to tell;
you should have been there.
These are words
written around a poem
who entered our house
and after hours of being who he was
drew his hands and ears away
from the old piano
and said softly
"thank you."

Poet Lore   *W. Atmar Smith II*

EPITAPH OF A STRIPPER

Here lies the stripper stripped, disrobed for good;
Death wholly bares what life but partly could.
The house lights dim: each pointed, star-tipped breast
Invites complete approval east and west.

Bits 10   *William Jay Smith*

DENIALS 1

She was a gently shaking chandelier,
shivering, shivering. You touched her and
she trembled; you touched one brittle crystal
and the flick of it went shivering, shivering,
shaking across her frail transparencies,
flashing from facet to fragile facet;
each slender leaf sent trembling to the next
its slim vibration.

She was a bright and icy chandelier,
a click and quiver of clear, unvowelled sound.
You passed across her like a wind through leaves;
you rippled away in the shrill, white air;
you shook her through and left the way you came,
changing nothing.
She was a ringing tree of fragile glass,
shivering in a leaf storm.

The Mississippi Valley Review   *Jane Somerville*

INITIAL RESPONSE

That was a year of suddenness,
even behind the walls of a girls' school.

Our bodies began to bend, turn serpentine;
it was remarkable how we digressed.
Our lives lifted from history books
to wonder at trappers caught
with their women in deep Montana snow.

Past windows circling classrooms,
we found our bodies corresponding
with the limbs of windy trees,
and our hearts flew forward
to aviators chanting battle hymns
tilted at the sun.

We were swept along the curve
our lives took on. Little else
was real. We blew
like a three-cornered sail,
lightning striking all the way.

The American Scholar *Katherine Soniat*

ANGEL

Tonight I find the
Calendar with its days
Marked like targets.
It has to do with
The rationed water
Falling from the North
And my woman asleep,
Legs pushed up to her
Veined breasts, heavy
And tilting with child.
She turns to expose
The belly rising
—not pure and rubbed white—
But tangled in TV
And telephone poles
Howling through boredom.
My hands patrolling
From throat to her dark
Spade of kinks, I
Think of that good day
When this child will kick
His joints into place
And the eyes circle
Points of clarity.
Already the fingers bloom
Like candles, the hair
Parts in a warm flow,
And the pocked buttocks
Are globed with fat.
I know this, somehow,
Though it is July,

Weeks before our dark
One slides like water
Into light, his hands
Tightening on air,
Or the cord that links
One life so he should
Turn, beyond knowing,
To what is also his.

The North American Review   *Gary Soto*

OWNING A DEAD MAN

The geese fly off, but sometimes they don't take
their voices with them. Stretched out like this,
I think my future is simple, like a cornfield
filling with light. I'm happy,
because of the way the geese have left their shadows
drying on the lawn around me, and the way
the long docks lean out into the water,
letting the unpainted boats knock against them.
Once, my mother told me, a woman came to this place
with an urn that held her dead husband's ashes.
The woman's pale hands tossed bits of gray-white
bone and soot onto the marsh, where the quail hid.
My mother was angry that the bones had trespassed
her land. *In a way*, she said, *I own a dead man*.

Now as I lie here, I think of the coming winter,
of his bones, mixed with the bones of the mouse
and the gull, cleansed and shining in the new snow;
but if I try to think too deeply, it's as if a bird
were pulling straws from a dried out nest!
So I wonder if I have ever witnessed the middle
of winter: the birch trees' inability to lose
anything more, or if I have ever seen myself
as more irrelevant than in December—
In that cold and stillness, my blood
and my muscles contracting as I tramp through the snow
couldn't possibly mean anything. And there *are* days
when a landscape feels nothing for its real trees,
only for what lies still in the snow,
or only for what has been.

Poetry   *Marcia Southwick*

THE LAST FISH

Early to meet you, watching a man
At dinner all alone up front
In our restaurant, I caught his gaze;
He looked at me not seeing me,
Working the mangle of his jaw
In a trance of such rapacity

He seemed then like a monstrous fish
Who sieves the seas for life until
He's taken all, and starves, adrift
In Emptiness. We have our fill
Who die of our consuming need,
Cursing the hunger as we feed.

Kansas Quarterly   *Barry Spacks*

MIRROR IMAGES

I never look at myself
In the mirror anymore,
But sometimes the image
Sneaks up on me
In places like the ladies room
Of the Sheraton-West Hotel
When I'm washing my hands
Over a gold-flecked sink
Under a pink light.
Then my eyes lock in
And accidentally focus.
What I see
Is not at all me,
But some other lady
With wrinkles around the eyes,
Porous cheeks
Downed with fuzz
And just the beginning of liver spots.
Oh God.

Neworld   *Laurel Speer*

THE ORCHARD

The cherry trees, mindless of the field
Flaming into spring, mimick winter:
Petals falling make wind a blizzard.

Over the grass, tips of branches bleed.
As from an offered beast, fruit
Darker than sunset drops to the ground.

The sun that spreads green moss over rocks
Splits and shrivels cherries, bleaching
    their stones
White as bones, white as petals in the grass.

Jam To-day   *Michael Spence*

WAKE

Ash in the air. Ash in everyone's mouth.
You wake to a room without doors or windows.

You should have known.
Last night the oil lamp hissed, wick
twisting into a death you didn't recognize.
And now the body's wet wood will not rise.
Listen. They call you, black-shawled women,
crows glittering in their palaces of straw.
Forget them. Go to the dead place
the dead know losing your past
as snow loses itself on water. Go now
or the trees will touch their fingertips
to yours. I am your soul.
I am who you turn to when the world stops.

The Yale Review   *Elizabeth Spires*

FUGUE

Entering the darkened room
where you are plying your flute
imperfectly, the children playing
while a fugue spills from the record
player, I repeat the cadences of hurting:
the phrase, predictable,
is mounting more intense
successive times.

Beyond the rectangle of window,
the sea flashes toward me, framed and blue:
it is such perfect happiness, suggested,
I shall never reach.
The notes of the music slip by, silvery
and gasping: your wrong notes
and my uncertainties.

This would make a perfect ending,
I think, breathless: children murmuring,
oblivious, the music
sonorous, baroque, repetitive.
You drive your flute, stumbling, by
ear, or by will,
unable to sight-read the phrasing,
and I stare outward at the ocean
making no wrong moves;
no right ones either.

The American Poetry Review   *Kathleen Spivack*

TROUBLE-SHOOTING

On still days when country telephone
wires go south, go home, go quietly away into
the woods, a certain little brown bird appears,
hopping and flying by starts, following the line,
trying out each pole.

My father and I, trouble-shooting for the telephone
company back then, used to see that same bird
along old roads, and it led us to farms
we always thought about owning some day.

When I see that bird now I see my father
tilt his hat and flip the pliers confidently
into the toolbox; the noise of my life, and all
the buffeting from those who judge and pass by,
dwindle off and sink into the silence,
and the little brown bird steadfastly wanders on
pulling what counts wherever it goes.

The Black Warrior Review   *William Stafford*

IN ITS PLACE

At your burial
I thought I died a standing death.
I was pitched in soil, as solid as a tent stake
and heavier than the earth.
We were both lowered.
For months
my rooms sang your terrible music.
Your smile trailed me like a fury.
Space crowded my bed.
I thought love had gone underground.
But today
your eyes, the blue,
after circling the eucalyptus like a vulture,
watched me pour the morning milk
and, seeing my rumored carcass was a lie,
the blue settled, finally,
in the sky.

Contemporary Quarterly   *Carol Stager*

THE CENTER OF THE GARDEN

(It is so . . . comfortable. You need not put on your
best toga.—Pliny the Younger)

The garden is only for you. It is a shell
in which you live. It is a wall
to keep you from the world. You are the center.
Not the pool where dryads
pour water forever in meaningless gestures,
nor the stairs with stone balustrades
where eagles spread their useless wings of stone,
nor the clipped alley between cypress hedges.
You are the garden. Let it circle round you.
You are the heart of the maze, where the laurel
draws its own pyramid, shakes out its limbs,
overhangs the path and takes the form of trees.

Leave Daphne there,
her freed limbs shaking in the autumn wind.
See the colors of autumn—chrysanthemums, asters,
the lawn covered with leaves where yellow and red
rain from the trees, and for your pleasure
the black-crested quail wander over the lawns.

The boat drifts farther away; it is leaving,
and flocks of traveling common birds feast on the red berries.
The orange trees
set here and there forget the terraces
and the path curves away between the pine trees.
You are inside the garden, and it takes your form.
It is real now, not a plan, not even a vista,
but a warm wall in winter, an old coat thrown around you.

The Atlantic Monthly   *Ann Stanford*

POEM ON THE END OF SENSATION

Winter begins
always
with a fixed angle
of vision,
an acute or obtuse
perception.

Afterwards
doesn't matter
when snow drifts
like nuns slow
over the gray nights
and the moon is ringed.

Only a few of us
can endure
this cold hardship
of vision,
only a few of us
even want to.

Life in summer
is short
and to the point—
like a slash
like a youth
at love.

All its
pleasures are made
like this:
short lines
quick rhythms
abrupt conclusions.

Canadian Forum   Ken Stange

AT EIGHTY

At eighty they took the scales
from his eyes, and he saw
trees like men standing; the stability
of the permanent dark
conditioned him to stillness
till light flooded the cells.
Concept became percept; in the wake
of summer the sycamore
changed, was deciduous.
He looked in the glass
at the bare boughs of his face.

Webster Review   *Rosamund Stanhope*

TEN SONNETS FOR TODAY

Ten sonnets for today should be enough
    to lead me from the heavy conversation
about ex-lovers which asserts its stiff
    despair against me now. My inclination

is rather to produce more luscious lines
    like leaves around the Creuse than think of
        girls
I'm glad to see no more. The vital signs
    of memories reveal that flowing curls

or Marxist dispositions don't suffice
to hold my interest. Faithfulness is nice
    but I am disinclined to lay my limbs

to rest in a cold fen. I'd rather hear
more Mozart or see pictures by Vermeer
    than still pursue a star as its light dims.

Canadian Author and Bookman   *Phil Stanway*

CIRCA 1814

In the old part of the cemetery,
the stones,
the white bone-ivory, lean.
Not like crisp-lettered fortresses
stand the stones
in the old part of the cemetery.
The rain has lacquered words
into thin enamel
nicks. Hand-cut
marble leans away from the wind
like wafers,
brittle as the green bones
beneath.

Yankee   *David Staudt*

THE WING FACTORY

It is here the bones
are assembled
with their incredible spaces,
their interlocking moves.

It is here where you learn
how to use them,
how to get accustomed
to their giant sound
behind the neck.

Here, behind the eyes
in a building like a greenhouse
and an aircraft hangar,
you practice where the wind

lifts you out over the tiny surf.
Here you need no reflection;
above glass, you could
give lessons

as you ride above
memory,
how to steer
this shadow
over the wrinkled air.

Here in the wing factory
you are the only worker,
and without sweating
in the dark

things come out
smooth, brilliant,
all feather and fire.

Denver Quarterly   *Dona Stein*

MODERN LOVE

In a month all these frozen waterfalls
will be replaced by Dutchman's breeches
and I will drive down the road
trying to remember what it was like
in late February and early March.
It will be 72 degrees on March 24th
and I will see my first robin
on the roof of the Indian Rock Inn.
My wife and I will go in to stare at the chandelier
and eat, like starved birds, in front of the fireplace.
I know now that what I'll do
all through supper is plan my walk
from Bristol, PA, to the canal museum.
I will exhaust her with questions about old hotels

and how much water I should carry
and what shoes I should wear,
and she will meet me with sweetness and logic
before we break up over money and grammar and lost love.
Later, the full moon will shine through our windshield
as we zig-zag up the river
dragging our tired brains, and our hearts, after us.
I will go to bed thinking of George Meredith
lying beside a red sword
and I will try to remember how his brain smoked
as he talked to his wife in her sleep and twisted her words.
Where I will go in the six hours before I wake up freezing
I don't know, but I do know
I will finally lie there with my twelve organs in place
wishing I were in a tea palace, wishing
I were in a museum in France, wishing
I were in a Moorish movie house in Los Angeles.
I will walk downstairs singing because it is March 25th,
and I will walk outside to drink my coffee on the stone wall.
There will still be drops of snow on the side of the hill
as we plant our peas and sweep away the bird seed.
Watch me dig and you will see me
dream about justice, and you will see me
dream about small animals, and you will see me
dream about warm strawberries.
From time to time I will look over
and watch her dragging sticks and broken branches
across the road. We are getting ready
for summer. We are working in the cold
getting ready. Only thirty more days and the moon
will shine on us again as we drive to Hellertown
to see Jane Fonda grimace and drive back
after midnight through the white fields
looking for foxes in the stubble,
looking for their wild eyes, burning with fear and shyness
in the stunted remains of last summer's silk forest.

The American Poetry Review   *Gerald Stern*

IMMENSITY

Nothing is too small for my sarcasm. I
know a tiny moth that crawls over the rug
like an English spy sneaking through the Blue Forest,
and I know a Frenchman that hangs on the closet door
singing chanson after chanson with his smashed thighs.
I will examine my life through curled threads
and short straws and little drops of food.
I will crawl around with my tongue out, growing
more and more used to the dirty webs hanging
between the ridges of my radiator and the huge
smudges in that distant sky up there, beginning

more and more to take on the shape of some great design.
    This is the way to achieve immensity, and this is the
only way to get ready for death, no matter what Immanuel
    Kant
and the English philosophers say about the mind,
no matter what the gnostics say, crawling
through their vile blue, sneezing madly in the midst of that
life of theirs, weighed down by madness and sorrow.

The Paris Review   *Gerald Stern*

ACADEMIC AFFAIR

Everyday between classes intently over coffee in the Union,
Conscious of our new-minted Ph.D.'s,
We talked.
Your hands, thin, angular,
Defended your fragmented modern world
Against my well-ordered medieval cosmography.
In dreadful innocence, we quoted Donne:
"Difference of sex no more we knew. . . ."

Now, sitting across the table in the Union
Over cold coffee, smoking in tenured comfort,
The image is always there before me—
Your body, thin, pale-gleaming in the moonlight,
Blurring into my well-ordered medieval cosmography.
I think you see it too—
A dream, perhaps simultaneously dreamed,
That hangs between us,
Palpable as the smoke from your cigar.

Sam Houston Literary Review   *Brenda S. Stockwell*

MORNING SONG

Flush and burn, your fever rose all night.
Your sleep was troubled; and even though I knew
This had to run its course, throughout the night
I tried but could not think of anything to do.
Often you cried out in that sleep, far away;
And wherever you were, I thought I could see
That whatever it was you kept wanting to say
It did not seem to have to do with me.

The tired eyes open. You see now that I see,
Swirling and tangled, inverted, how
In this firmament the blood streams and races.
Your smile and damp hair rush up to meet me,
Or is it I to them? This skin's blaze and glow—
The beads of dew on these most secret places.

Quarterly West   *Leon Stokesbury*

WORDS TO MY MOTHER

I don't ask you to tell me the great truths,
Because you wouldn't tell me; I only ask
If, when you carried me in your belly, strolling through
Dark patios in bloom, the moon was a witness.

And if, when I slept listening
In your breast with its Latin passions,
A hoarse and singing sea lulled you to sleep nights
And if you watched in the gold dusk, the sea birds plunge.

For my soul is all fantasy, a voyager,
And it is wrapped in a cloud of dancing folly
When the new moon ascends the dark blue sky.

And, lulled by a clear song of sailors, it likes—
If the sea unlocks its strong perfumes—
To watch the great birds that pass without destination.

Webster Review   *Alfonsina Storni*
                                          —Translated from the Spanish by
                                          Marion Hodapp and Mary Crow

FLY, LADYBUG

Ladybug, ladybug, fly away home,
Your house is neglected, your husband has gone,
Your children have married and left you alone:
    Ladybug, ladybug, fly away home.

I came to hear music, guitar and trombone;
A sad singer clings to a frail microphone.
My father has taught me in summers long gone:
    Ladybug, ladybug, fly away home.

Young folk are swaying in murk and in gloom;
The world is so weary it leans to its doom;
My father is calling in soft teasing drone:
    Ladybug, ladybug, fly away home.

The bar stools are empty, the barflies have flown;
My flesh is so heavy, it pulls on the bone;
My father is asking, and sad is his tone:
    Ladybug, ladybug, where is your home?

Alarm bells are ringing, and sirens make moan.
I thought I heard Ladybug give a great groan.
My father's sweet nickname for just me alone:
    Ladybug, ladybug, I'll see you home.

The Lyric   *Annette Burr Stowman*

HOOT OWL SHIFT

From darkness into darkness
they plunge, through the sockets

of earth's cryptic skull,
flesh and soul blackened in descent,
the shaft a catacomb
of vast, impenetrable silences,
short-winded and leadened
with doses of slow dying,
these tombs of spectral visage,
these miles of bituminous stone.
While coaltown sleeps,
the digging continues,
the mountain a provider,
a sarcophagus, a crown.

Mountain Review   *Robert Stricklin*

LULLABYE

Snow is lying on my roof.
I cannot breathe.
Two tons of snow lie on my roof

heavy as the sea,
the loft of grain,
the desert as it gathers sand,
and I have only two small flames
beside my bed. I hear the sea

when I lie down, the sea
inside my head.
The candles sputter when the wind blows.
Snow falls from the trees

like sacks of grain.
No seed can root in snow.
It cannot breathe.
My roof is like an unplowed field.

Who walks upon it?
Rafters creak
as if a wish-bone cracked
and I had wished the sky to fall.

Carolina Quarterly   *Kathryn Stripling*

CIRCUMSTANCE

(for David Ignatow)

In the shabby cafeteria on the lower east side,
the members of the group gathered,
forming like crystals on cracked,
thick-lipped plates. They were regulars,
writers who frequented the place after work.
With their nickels and dimes, their heads
turned toward art even as they turned the knobs

of the food windows.
It must have been a time
when there was still enough time to grasp after
the same future, everyone equally poor.
When snow felt good and filling on the tongue,
when everyone was promising.
A time when to struggle with art meant
filling yourself with things you couldn't eat,
when circumstance swallowed you whole
and offered you up again
and again until you gave in
and thought the bloody well hell with it,
only to return to the cafeteria the following evening,
as everyone knew you would,
your shoulders lightly covered
from the softly falling snow.

Pulp   *Laurie Stroblas*

TEA

Spirit Lake, Iowa, this January morning is ten below
and drifts. I shovel steps, driveway, mail box;
come in, brew a pot of hot tea and think of Ceylon,
its hills covered with dark green shrubs as tall
as the women who pick the uppermost leaves.
They chatter like finches, weave in and out with flat,
round baskets. I see their blue and orange dresses,
the hot yellow sun, the broken umber carvings
of dancers in bas relief, holding their positions
for centuries where delicate hands spread leaves
to dry on the stone porches of ruined temples.
I sit in my kitchen, the scent of Ceylon,
the sun of ancient dancers in my mouth.

The Seattle Review   *Ann Struthers*

GRAVESTONES

Some of the grandest have chosen marble,
ignoring how it sugars off,
how years of rain and frost erase
name and span and pious verse
until they seem faint shadows
a deep snow casts
over holes in earth.
We walk around these monuments
that look like melting wedding cakes,
angling our shadows and the sun
to coax out sense
sunk irretrievably back to stone.

Slate is the native rock.
It accepts only the strict, the shallow line,

the intelligent tap of the chisel.
But what is etched on those tall,
thin sheets is crisp for centuries.
The designs are primitive, the spelling
erratic. It's the simplest stone,
and supports this mountain burying ground.
In touch, it is the nearest thing to bone.

Ball State University Forum   *Floyd C. Stuart*

FEAR

Imagine the lake behind your house
imagine him taking you back there
at dusk back through the woods
where the path was laced with darkness
imagine the lake beyond the trees
where you went to swim with his friends
to strip down your pale skin
and float like the moon on the water
imagine the lake behind your house
admit that the image is dim
admit that he takes you there no more
you have become too frail for him
your bones are showing through
and he hates it the sight of your bones

You should have kept it a secret
the dream of you watching yourself
in the mirror your left arm trying
to open your ribs and free the thing
that flaps in the darkness within you
your right arm pulling the bones closed
afraid of what you could find inside
and of what it could do once loose
you should have kept it a secret
you should have known what he would do
that he would call it guilt and shame
and now as you feel the flutter within
you must decide whether to live
encased in his fear or facing your own

Kansas Quarterly   *Roger Stump*

100 YEAR OLD WOMAN AT CHRISTMAS DINNER

Propped in a cave of pillows
She is poised and frail—
As the whorl of an antlion's hole
Breaks at the point of a shadow.
She grows around the tree.
Her cheeks and nose are rough as a peak.
The lights hang like rings from her ears,

Splintering on her muddied eyes like coal.
Hairs grow from the corners of her lip,
Blowing and seasoning
As the winds promote the wiry
                          grasses in the fields.
And her hands are the crabs
That sleep with crisp white
                          shells of the sea.

Outside, the young white gums bend
                          and blow,
And the birds whistle in their juicy ears.
Around the land are the stoical humps
                          of eternity,
The crusts of myth and stones
And lumps of spiders in the trees.
She is misplaced in the cubes
                  and spaces of our world
And groans to be with yesterday's
                          immolate toys
Bending in the green rain.

Canadian Forum   *Colin Style*

VIEWS

You shout to me
during your fast sprint
into the night.
Snow spills a glut on the dark side
of the lawn, throwing a shadow
across the gulley,
a great shiftless fog.

Your words are a pointed rib
thrown into the air, lashing my eye,
but it is the wind that brings
me to tears, I am broken
by silence—
a ghost moving inside
my boney quarters
that has moved in with me
taking all the hot water,
tasting all the sweet meat,
drinking everything in one long gulp.

It is as if I see myself
for the first time
out on an ice floe, a young Lillian Gish
with a petal, angel face
in the streams of the White River
the sun has flaked to ice
and I think of the river again
in the August morning

when the only cool things
were chunks of odd white marble
found at the river's edge like teeth.
Then I think of the lost sweetness;
the body outside the shadow moving
down once more.

Beyond Baroque   *Harriet Susskind*

POET'S PRAYER

To justify the quiver in my quill
Before the mood of inspiration fails,
Let words that keep the soul from going blind
Build views beyond the vacant windowsill,
Then nullify the night and tip the scales
With sun. Show me truth and ways to find
The element of beauty intertwined,
And I will coincide with mountain trails
That aim for heaven from the highest peak;
Or sail with Neptune in the wake of whales,
Thus culling pearls and coral to distill
The sea. And lest my ways become oblique,
I pray that wisdom be the first to speak
With music chanting like a whippoorwill.

Western Poetry Quarterly   *M. L. Sussman*

CHILLED BY DIFFERENT WINDS

We walk together, breathing different air,
Heart-chilled by different winds, consumed by fires,
Unruly flames that soar or veer or glare,
Igniting embers of unvoiced desires.
But each of us walks with demanding ghosts
That interfere to complicate the hour,
Or leave us stranded at bleak starting posts
Without a race to run, with wine turned sour.
We lean precariously out to reach
A hand, a smile across the widening space,
But have not learned the subtleties of speech
Or touch to give our faltering spirits grace.
We walk together but advance alone,
The winds of difference freezing us to stone.

Voices International   *Alice Mackenzie Swaim*

ALONE WITH THE DAWN

Alone with the dawn light unfurling
and a plane's drone cracking the lone acres of sky,
then the birds' silence seeping.

You are asleep beside me,
still & strong, your breast's muffled mound
heaving. And as the dance of sunrise goes on
I watch you, my eyes tunnelling through
the twisted years to those morning days
when fires were stoked in our blood
and even our locked sleep kindled their flickers.

And if we are quieter now, like worn storms,
in this calm place inside, your touch is treasure
—an anchor in treacherous tides.
The night's stars float hidden
in the day's blue glow.
We have come with our longings like pilgrims
longtimeago, and we have stayed.

Alone with the dawn & your secret dreaming.
Already the birds have woken,
rubbed their little eyes with song.
But it's winter, I will not wake you yet.
And tonight I had no need of sleep
beside you.

Green River Review   *Matthew Sweeney*

GRAVE CLOTHES

The undertaker asks for clothes,
and confused by this last dressing
I call up and inquire delicately,
"Just outer clothes or everything?"

So I pick out the best bra and girdle
still stiff and white in their labels—
it seems unfair, if appropriate, to bind her
at last in the panels and slides of her ladyhood—

next a suit and blouse—
an ersatz of satin curdled by too much ironing—
rejecting her last cocktail dress
and the memory of a final tourney with youth,

the turkey neck and creased bosom
heaved through a gilded tissue of silk—
finally a pair of shoes without worn heels,
stockings a ladderless nicotine veil.

But I forget these are not for her,
but for us, the gauze of stockings,
the compress of clothes
to bandage the wound of mourning.

Staid in maroon double knit and pearl buttons,
peeling their imitation,
she is shut into public display
the lily of her age gilded by the undertaker

who afterwards offers me the shoe trees,
the shoe box, so small a replica.
I refuse, wanting nothing back,
and go home to throw out the adjuncts of the body—

the bridgework soaking in a glass,
the hearing aid coiled in its plastic box—
yet wear her coat's imitation fur to the funeral—
a last dressing.

Denver Quarterly   *Karen Swenson*

MAXIMS OF A PARK VAGRANT

A young man is spaced out on the lawn.
He waves his hand and talks with no one I can see.
There are idiots, and idiots. That leaves room for one.
One is too tired to be angry at the barber in front of his shop
who gave one wrong directions. Or with the blonde
chattery slavic girl who turns out
to have wasted one's time so exquisitely.
One is a magnet of derision with one's oddly shaped load.
Telephone voices are brown and corrupt. Harmony resists.
Cars become the armour people need
from within which to exhibit their savagery.
They are always forecasting thunderstorms.
One thinks they forecast too much
that may or may not happen.
I think they forecast too much that pleases them,
even by making them afraid.
One returns the same way, where one, another one,
has gathered to a corpse on the wide grass,
face down. Listening for listeners.

Canadian Forum   *Nicholas Swift*

ANIMATION AND EGO

A man walks through a district
of perfume and dress shops,

and wherever he turns,
whatever his eye might spot

through the sunlight, shadow,
and damp odor of traffic,

he sees only the cold beauty
of women in windows.

If a mannequin leans
offering her perfect hand,

or the woman sitting in bed
whispers a few words,

he knows, as the body absorbs
sight and sound, they're calling him.

And if they stand as stiff
as stone, not even a subtle wink,

he thinks each inviting gesture
is saved until the streets

empty, until his fingers
touch glass, freely,

leaving a handful of kisses
on their billboard smiles.

The Georgia Review   *Jody Swilky*

A VIRTUE OF SHAPE

The woman let her hand trail
In the water. With her fingers
She drew lines, representing waves.
Other waves the boat made, passing
Close to shore through the water
That was cold and clear. The evening
Coming on was a part of what she saw,
And the man across from her, rowing.

What could spoil such a lovely ride?
She let her hand trail in the water.
The boat continued, and the fish
Below. The wind picked up a little.
Had she noticed them before:
The wind at odd intervals,
The colored fish heading into shore?
It didn't matter—the ride would continue
And night arrive; eventually,
Against the border of sky,
One element would stand out to speak
The weight of these things: meaning
Being a virtue of shape and order.

The Agni Review   *Thom Swiss*

ASSUMING THE NAME OF ANY NEXT CHILD

He came into the world with showers
He came into the world with rainbows
He came into the world with more poems than you
    can count in thirty years
He came into the world with all the philosophies
    disguised as moods and dancers
He came into the world with problems, people, moving
    molecules, disturbed acrobats,
all the alphabets, all the languages, all the

Olympic games, all the architects,
all the boat builders, all the artists and craftsmen,
He came into the world with all the technicians of the
    sacred as propagandists,
yogi teachers, instructors for Nijinsky and Einstein,
He came into the world with all the seeds and suns and
    galaxies ever to come,
He came into the world with all the instincts and
animals, sands, and sounds,
He came into the world with Absolute Continuity.

Great River Review   *John Tagliabue*

THE INSECT SHUFFLE METHOD

book mites are eating the bindings
of my science fiction books
causing pages to slip out, intermingle
as I pick them up
forming fantastic new worlds
more logical, more incredible
than their previous incarnations

new texts, new myths
flying, bound outward, for Alpha Centauri
fresh as the *Tao Te Ching*
heroes find themselves
in new, even *more* incredible situations
villains pop up at even *more* unexpected times
space warps and black holes
run rampant through the new universe

it is all too wonderful. I feel
like Balboa or Timothy Leary
or at least Ezra Pound, cackling softly,
at this new expansion of the mind
facilitated by The Insect Horde
which, even as I exult,
is eating its way toward my theology books.

Cimarron Review   *Gary Tapp*

ROSES GONE WILD

Where is my roof that kept out the rain?
Where are my walls that kept out the wind?
Where is my walk that I walked upon?
Where is the hole to show they are gone?
Far away, far away,
Far and far and far away
Wind cries in roses gone wild.

Where is my wife who loved me so long?
Where is the bed which kept us both warm?

Where are our children and how do they live?
Where is the water kept in a sieve?
Far away, far away,
Far and far and far away
Wind cries in roses gone wild.

Where is the money I earned for our bread?
Where is the city I made it all in?
Where is the flag that flew over it all?
Where is an echo ever so small?
Far away, far away,
Far and far and far away
Wind cries in roses gone wild.

New Letters   John Taylor

BUSINESS TRIPS

You are already flying away
when I trace you through the silent house:
stepping in the cold footprints of your shower,
letting the cat in, reheating the coffee.

This time I heard the cab come,
beating sunrise; fragments of your voice,
the driver's; doors slamming—
sounds that eased me into your bedhollow
to wait for the alarm to ring.

Tonight our distance-wearied voices
will string the day's small miseries
on the long shining wires,
count the nights remaining, say goodnight,
leaving the conversation good as new.
Other people are waiting to use these words:
other husbands in bland plastic rooms,
other wives.

The Cape Rock   Laurie Taylor

THE RESURRECTION

That moment now embalmed in decrepitude:
I've chewed it till my teeth split and fell out.
You've wrapped it in potato peels and car pools,
Layered it in fat to keep it sweet.
I know a story of a man who died, finally,
And even in the hospital bed with all those tubes
And red stuff dripping into his heart,
Just at the last gasp and gurgle of the obsolete
    machine,
A little boy
Twinkled in his eyes,

Cried to come out,
And died.

National Forum   *William Edward Taylor*

THE BURIAL

Transferring my ashes from the urn
to a plastic bag, part of me spills
between the keys of the piano
I loved to play. A few
particles
scatter on the rug
and are vacuumed up.

Out of the plane I parachute, confetti.
A speck flies into my wife's eye
and is washed away by a tear. Another is trapped
deep beneath the nail of her ring finger.
She will carry me all her life.

I float down like the season's first snow
on firs around Mt. Hood. A millenium.
I am mud of a robin's nest, silt in the Willamette,
a nucleus of a pearl, in a hailstone
inside a cloud.

The Slackwater Review   *Mark Thalman*

GETTING LOADED

Pulling the last tie rope taut, I pause,
light a cigarette in the lee of my body
and lean against my hay-laden truck:
sun just down, far trees and buildings
black cut-outs. Seven geese fly a wind-
rough vee against flaming clouds. Off south
a freight fills up the Gibbs valley, its rush
cushioned by trees and miles, its gray moan
softer here, warning the crossings. A fox
trots out of the grass fringing the field.
He cocks his head and stands ready for mice,
leaps, urgent muzzle probing; he rises,
proud tail high, and trots off into the brush.
I put out my smoke, crawl into the cab,
lurch slowly out of the field, past the barn
and rusty dump rake, the deserted farm house.

The Cape Rock   *Jim Thomas*

ETUDES

The students groan
Under the heavy burden of remembering Lear.

His tragic flaw, theirs.
Their fate, not quite the same;
They are not killed for sport
And, having not yet committed adequate folly,
They will keep their minds and daughters
But never gain what Lear almost regained
And Gloucester only temporarily lost.

They write,
The answers coming
From heads and pens
And books they have not read
And lectures not attended
Or slept through.
They guess and write too much.
What experience have they had
Of what the author thought?
How equate the happenings
In the book with those ideas
Which they have never had
Because no one ever told them?

A roomful of silence
Like ceasing of bees,
Faces of vacancy
Resplendent in newly-lost knowledge,
As pens trace stains on paper,
The strain.
    The brain
Is predictable; knowledge is not.
Memories seldom fail
Till put to the test—
When they are met with questions
Never before encountered.
Round ruminant room,
Eyes wander to windows
And sometimes to neighboring papers
Pursuing a clue to the truth—
Passing answers.

Educational Studies   *Laurence W. Thomas*

GONE

I saw the fox, his red tail beating
furious and whole. There, on
weedy slopes below this house,
                              nesting,
nursing his sick grey mate. Why
did he make mistakes—out of
                              despairing?
Caring? Was she sick or pregnant?
Thirsting for water in a dry
                              season?

Then the dogs, whose mesalliance
                              with man
drove them with barks and bellows
and quivered tails down the hill,
roused him, shaken, to stand
and turn his wild brown gaze
                              to mine.

Kansas Quarterly   *Joanna Thompson*

ROOFTOP WINTER

There were the starlings hunched against the sky—
black blots crowded, flirting stiffened wings
and shifting feet around the ramparts of
a chimney sighing blacker clouds of smoke.
Heat drew them, pecking for places. The mercury
shrank to thirty below and would not rise.

They said no more than bums around a trash fire.
Ready for everything, they breathed coal smoke
deep and long, all day, because it meant
making tomorrow. Each had learned the language
always right—the survivor's tongue.

Any heat is better than the snow.
There are days when knowing that is enough:
when any more would take up precious room.
To hell with delicate gropings. I hold
whatever offers refuge. Cold is cold.

The Michigan Quarterly Review   *Dwayne Thorpe*

TO MY WIFE ASLEEP

(for Betsy)

Like a spider that leaves its wind-torn web
to weave another in a sheltered place,
you turn your back and abandon my embrace.
It is not for lack of love: we know the grub
that breeds in the sweat of enfolded arms.
Together we squash that worm between our sheets.
Nor is it in fear of what you will meet
when your lonely dreams sound their midnight alarms.
The morning breaks: mist makes dreams take flight.
Now I know why I meet your shoulderblades
and why we then sleep small to small.
You, as I, search for a mother. She is tall,
dark with arms of earth, wide with a womb of shade.

Asleep we are siblings. Our mother's name is Night.

Song   *Edward Tick*

THE PINBALL QUEEN OF SOUTH ILLINOIS ST.

She shifts her pelvis to the tune of muted bells,
hitches and hikes her weight at the low end
of an inclined plane, eyes widened with the weight
of the world rolling down on her. Her skin

picks up colors from distained glass,
windows from a church in low comedy.
Aloof, I reach for popcorn, find my hand
in somebody's glass of beer, hear soft cursing

"jesus crist," and assent. Her fingers push
buttons, move levers, send the world spinning.
She bumps; the machine grinds, clicks in low staccato,
wheels spin, and all the bums howl kow-tow

to see electric demons run a row
of gaudy carillon. She reaches for
a cigarette, abandoned at the edge of the world
too long, and having left her mark on the chrome

and us all, searches softly in her purse
for quarters. To my right, a rough voice
deprecates waste, "goddamnit, too bad that
sonabitch ran out of balls."

The Mississippi Valley Review   *Stephen Tietz*

MY CHILDHOOD'S BEDROOM

This far you have slid
Through the hole in my ceiling.
The firepole is shining brass.

In my childhood's bedroom
All things usable lie horizontal,
All things comfortable are flat.

But I am building a castle
While the house is burning down.
My blocks are years
Growing upward to your eyes.
My alphabet spells love.

Why do you not scream FIRE,
Blow your whistle, grab a blanket,
Let my childhood down your ladder,
Break my rooftop with an axe?

I speak from a tall tower:
You must set the last block for me.
Easy now, my childhood sleeping,
Easy now, my castle weaving,
Let me quickly catch on fire,
Let me tumble at your feet.

Cimarron Review   *Charles Tisdale*

THE LEAGUE OF SELVES

Sighting down the silver barrel,
crosshairs on his temple
I could Kennedy his cranium
or Luther King his eyeballs.
I could RFK his chest
or Lincoln his lung.
Alternatively,
I could Archduke of Sarajevo
him.

There are too many
in the League of Selves
waiting
for the ranks to thin.

Cold shivers
could scarcely halt
my swooping ax
in Mexico,
my pistol shot,
breaking bone in Delhi
near the still-spinning wheel.

It misses the Citroen
speeding to Colombey,
or trafficks with intestines,
planting Wallace in his wheelchair.
At night, stealing in,
I even place dynamite
under the great wooden table
and, watching
panic-music in my eardrums
see Hitler rise
and leave the meeting
before the briefcase bomb
splatters gore,

The company of assassins—
technicians and saints—
crowd to hear my exploits.

"If history books had holes,"
I laugh
with pseudo-insight,
"where names like Ray or Booth appear,
I'd find a different way
to manifest my destiny."

The sudden silver bullet
cuts cartilege,
sings surprise in my chest.

Sun blackens
a hole in the skies,
and one of me,
trigger pulled,
now dies.

The Antioch Review   *Alvin Toffler*

THE BASEMENT WATCH

In the basement beneath my consciousness
you pace your days and nights,
which are all the same down there.
When I built this place
I purposely left out stairs.
Don't try to climb the air!
I have no intention
of letting you up to the house.
Given a moment's lease,
you'd rummage in the bedroom of my life:
check closets, dump drawers, read letters
in rubber bands, steal photos
and books, ask the meaning of this key,
that tie, the burnt spot on the rug.
No, I much prefer you
scavenging through the dust, over the cold
stone, dressed in spider's web and mold,
giving the dampness a lean grace, an
unspeakable easiness as you tap
on the pipes, listen at walls, dream of windows.

I watch your comings and goings through
a pin-hole in the floor, breathless above
your overpowering grasp of reality.

Southwest Review   *Thomas Tolnay*

SLIPPING OUT OF INTENSIVE CARE

I am stuffing this bolster
into my bed to delay the chase.

You will think I'm plugged in
as usual, all systems go,

A sublime conduit—the currents
flow in, the bleeps flash out—

keeping your circuit intact.
Oh, I hear whatever you whisper.

When you mime slyly I can decode
your wince, your raised brow.

Some days you bring grave messages,
such as I've made a false move,

spoken too loudly, my fault, fault,
and why can't I be a good patient?

I shall sign myself out dressed
like a visitor, smiling, holding

flowers, down the grand staircase,
out into traffic, dead or alive.

The Ontario Review   *Florence Trefethen*

MAN ON MOVE DESPITE FAILURES

It is the hottest of days.
I leave the study chained in silence,
suffocating on the air that once inspired me.
The sun crawls very slowly on fiery legs
across the blue infinity
between morning and evening.
Broken bottles glisten in the street before me,
birds chirp, automobiles flash by.
For me there is nothing. My great
and my little failures run beside me
taunting, reminding me
of everything that never happened.
So much is rotting in me unsaid!
What tyrant beats me with this silence,
censors the beauty I have known,
strangles the bird's song, extinguishes spring?
I must rise up, stir up mutinies of words
to overthrow him—or should I sleep?
but emptiness fastens itself
even to my dream: it is everywhere like heat.
The past melts where I try to touch it.
People are looking at me strangely today
because I'm breathing an absurd music
that will not stop.

The New York Smith   *Jeffery Alan Triggs*

BELL WEATHER

Trees file along curbs. Shrub-faces,
    lilac ears listen to dusk
        coming over the lawns.

Indoors, dust weaves its motes among
    coleus and pepper plants.
        Spring slides under the door,

and the phone rings once, its bell hung
    in the heart of dim weather.
        Gray walks from its mousehole

across the rug. Soon a river
of stars will spill overhead—
breach dawn, noon, dusk and fall

into a field of goldenrod
near the blue spruce whose needles
knit and ravel darkness.

Commonweal   *Lewis Turco*

I WANT TO ONE MORNING

I want to one morning
wake up without a thesis
to write, no thoughts on the brain
no long-forgotten footnotes
to articulate someone else's sense
of what I'm piecing together
in this life.

Just imagine, if Ulysses had set
his sights on a Ph.D. and got
bogged down in chapter three
he would not have heard the sirens
sing, always when he loitered
near his ship he'd be looking for
that missing idea that would bring
it all together. One can leave a wife
behind.

I want to one morning
wake to the breeze signalling
from above that slabbed-mountain
slip my arms into my pack
and burst into alpine meadows
till every stream becomes memory
every flower leans my way, no more looking
over the shoulder to wonder
if the thesis has managed this climb.

Event   *Gordon Turner*

NOVEMBER

In the cold
and half light,
I awaken to the sound
of trucks driving through the night
past this rest stop south of Fresno.
I rise, see my breath on the window
and sparrows in the trees outside.

Their black bodies are full and fluffed
against the cold,
as still as the concrete tables standing

empty on the yellow grass beneath the trees.
Beyond in the field a tractor
turns the soil and follows
rows back and forth.

I grip the cold steering wheel
wanting to join the trucks. Lately
I've become accustomed
to the traffic, to the flow I'm in.
The frozen ground, low fog, chill of air
edges me, makes me want to drive
these dark days toward spring.

The Southern Review   *Samuel S. Turner*

25 SPONTANEOUS LINES GREETING THE WORLD

O great humming nymphet & mother & moth &
golden sieve draining vermicelli
in the houses of artists & plumbers & their betters
O Endicott-Johnson shoes gossamer drapes brown-outs
the Bennadetta Sonnets of Gerard Malanga & even
Minimal Art & the Cogitative Platonic Solids of Martin Levin
& Hello out there to Roget's Thesaurus coke sniffers & Ad men
to Freaks & media manipulators newscasters politicians the cities
of Akron Ohio & Pittsburgh hello & yawp! To all of you
prestidigitators on the Johnny Carson Show multiple amputees
the Boston Strangler policemen & thieves alike hookers pimps
the Judges of the Supreme Court Holden Caulfield
Anita O'Day the Shoshonees & hip comedians Allen Funt
Clifford Irving & O frogs O nightingales O Saran Wrap
O marriage between Heaven & Hell the telephone operator
computer analysts rock musicians Buffalo Bill & dwarfs
spaced-out teeny boppers Yves St. Laurent & Nixon
puddle jumpers Aristocrats mailmen boxoffice girls
the Sandman constructors of chile con carne secretaries
stenographers IBM executives the total personnel of IT&T
Sing Sing Bellevue O farmers O ghosts long dead O
Pope Paul the Maharishi Baba Ram Dass Arnold Stang Billy the Kid
& the Rosenbergs Hello Benedict Arnold Rasputin Tito
Charlie the Tuna Rosebud Tchaikowsky Ed Sullivan Bozo the Clown
The Grateful Dead & Amelia Earhart hello to you from me

Street Magazine   *Jim Tyack*

LAST NIGHT THEY HEARD THE WOMAN UPSTAIRS

moaning. They lay in bed
and she did not stop

and she did not stop, and she did not
grow louder.

The husband saw her once, moonfaced
and ample on the stairs.

The wife did not move
her hand along his thigh,

the short hairs springing there.
For a moment she pictured him

not in the bed, not alive
and a scream cracking

like some withered thing from her lips.
Tonight the husband is reading.

The wife bites into a peach.
The woman upstairs

slams a door. The building
takes back its silence like breath.

Last night they heard her
moaning, and they waited

and they thought their skin was visible
through the sheets and the drawn

shade. And the husband said,
She must make love slowly, the way

she climbs the stairs.

Mademoiselle   *Leslie Ullman*

OHIO

1
Rolling along through Ohio,
lapping up Mozart on the radio
(Piano
Concerto No. 21, worn but pure),
having awoken while dawn
was muddying a rainy sky,
I learned what human was:
human was the music,

natural was the static
blotting out arpeggios
with clouds of idiot rage,
exploding, barking, blind.
The stars sit athwart our thoughts
just so.

II
To be fair, though, about that day—
dull sky, scuds of goldenrod,
fields dried flat, the plains hinting
at a tornado,
the choleric sun
a pillowed sort of face upon
which an antic wisp of cirrus
had set a moustache—

at dawn, I remembered all day,
I had parked beneath an overpass
to check my lights, and breathed
the secret green, the rain.
Like hammered melody the empty road
soared east and west. No static. Air.

The American Scholar   *John Updike*

LEAVING MEXICO ONE MORE TIME

Not the branch that taps at the window
Offering a single scarlet pomegranate
Not the grove of green feathers
Not the bird with wings of flame
Not the thin thread of smoke
Not the blue sky clotted with clouds
Not the lion-colored desert
Sleeping under a scratchy blanket
Not the 400-year-old walls
Crumbling at the side of the road
Not the huge sad trees
That stand in black pools of shadow
Not the acrid unmistakeable coffee-smell
Not the clatter of the great bells
Like tumbrils rolling over the cobbles
Nor the heap of yellowing bones
With clumsy knobbed ends
Nor the long twilights, needle-pricked
With sulfur-yellow patterns
Nor images of Espagna
Nor the three tall cypresses
Bending and swaying toward one another
Like black-shawled gossips
Nor the old granny with eyes black as prunes
Nor the withered pod
Nor the dry seed of hunger
Not the simple broom of twigs
Scraping the stones
With a sound older than civilization
Leaving Mexico one more time
Precipitates a sensation
Heavy and cold as a stone.

National Forum   *Constance Urdang*

BLESSING AT KELLENBERGER ROAD

North of Chillicothe
Route 23, divorced and sterile,
Cuts through dewey stubble fields
Which escape its two-pronged monastic thrust

By rippling unconscious to the
Maternal hills.

A few forever farms
With barns gay in their Mail-Pouch midwesterness
Leap on the landscape
And assert their ugly being
To the blank austerity of the road.

I, caught in the mechanical madness
Of the smooth white speed,
Reminded of old ruts and snarls and gutted tires,
Laugh at the bleakness of the fields and farms
And bless the road.

Then suddenly,
Crossing Kinnikinnick Creek—
Erased now, of course, by the concrete zip,
I unprepared meet
Kellenberger Road.

It's gone before I grasp it,
Sucked up in the quenchless throat
Of gushing miles,
Osmosed into the instant milk
Of the white thread behind.

And yet
Unstopping, unable to be stopped,
I feel keen chasing
After me on the rigid bounce.
Like a pebble glancing blithely
Off the left rear mudguard,
Kellenberger Road announces itself.

Ball State University Forum   *Maxine Kent Valian*

BLACK HORSE RUNNING

At ten I saw a black horse running
at twenty it ran toward me
now I am thirty
and the black horse running
is me.

Ball State University Forum   *Noel Maureen Valis*

THE NEW CALF

The calf came two days ago.
I left the plumber standing in the kitchen
when I heard the news
and ran across the yard,
my shoes catching dew from the long grass
in the neighbor's field

where I'd picked daisies and Queen Anne's lace
for my daughter's wedding.

I found him in the trampled place—
sleeping, curled loosely,
his soft face tan and white—
and bent to pat the infant bull
while Abby,
devouring cornstalks
as if it were her last supper,
raised her eyes at me across the wire,
and the farmer pronounced,
in the accent of all his New England ancestors,
If you don't pat the newborn
early and often,
they're apt
to grow up
hostile.

Tendril   *Frances Downing Vaughan*

THE ENIGMATIC TRAVELER

If the whole of Paris is not quite wholly mine
from Place du Tertre down to the Place Bastille,
is it because the travel posters lie?

It is and it is not. A camera
concedes the difference. A painter squints
to part the Quai d'Orsay from what it seems.

Monsieur Mesmer deploys another eye.
The Cirque d'Hiver through his binoculars
of seeing more than what is merely seen

wheels with the cyclists for the sport of it.
But not enough. The mind's Montmartre at night
rounds out the cycle of an underworld

circling the Inferno of its anarchy
to look down there . . . to see, to touch, to know . . .
Not Notre Dame as intricate design.

New Letters   *Byron Vazakas*

SPACE-WANDERER'S HOMECOMING

After eight thousand years among the stars
Nostalgia—suddenly—for August
Tugged me like guilt through half a cosmos
Back to a planet sweet as canebrake,
Where winds have plumes and plumes have throats,
Where pictures
Like 'blue' and 'south' can break your heart with hints.

After a mere eight flickers, nothing changed there
Among the birds, still just as blazing,
Among the lilt of leaves on rivers,
The heartbreak of the south and blue,
The canebrake-sweet of August night;
No change till
I, changeling, asked the natives: 'Oh my people,

'After eight cycles, how is this you greet me?
Where is my horse? Where is my harp?
Why are the drums of goat-skin silent?
Spin my abyss of resin-wine;
Drape me my coat of prophecy;
My name is—.'
Forgot it, I forgot it, the name 'man'.

The Michigan Quarterly Review   *Peter Viereck*

DAUGHTER

There is one grief worse than any other.

When your small feverish throat clogged, and
quit,
I knelt beside the chair on the green rug
and shook you and shook you,
but the only sound was mine shouting you back,
the delicate curls at your temples,
the blue wool blanket,
your face blue,
your jaw clamped against remedy—
how could I put a knife to that white neck?
With you in my lap,
my hands fluttering like flags,
I bend instead over your dead weight
to administer a kiss so urgent, so ruthless,
pumping breath into your stilled body,
counting out the rhythm for how long until
the second birth, the second cry—
oh Jesus that sudden noisy musical inhalation
that leaves me stunned
by your survival.

The Atlantic Monthly   *Ellen Bryant Voigt*

PLACES I HAVE BEEN

Let me tell you where I have walked.
I have entered some dark and grim
Corridors of thought.
I have stepped upon a thorn or two
In the field of my pleasures.
I have been in a place so cold

As to freeze the warmest smile my lips could form.
But then—Oh, then:
I have entered a room wherein the love
Has embraced my very being.
I have entered into that place
Where the light has filled my heart
With that one beautiful instant
Of knowing I AM.
And I have,
Though not often,
But I have,
In a few perfect moments,
Been able to take the hand
Of one or another,
To walk with me and share in the wonder
Of a single star,
Or the beauty of a rainbow.
These places I have known.

Unity   *Joyce M. Volk*

THE SEED OF REALITY

My father used to say:
"The best time of the year,
my son,
is breakfast."

It was his way of
praising God
for the daily miracle
of ever new and glorious beginnings.

This gem of morning brilliance
finds me above the old,
certainly above
egocentricity

and its inclinations
to bisect,
misunderstand and
obliterate.

Dear, dear old man,
thanks
for the seed of
reality.

For the song
of the meadowlark
is always
new.

The Emissary   *Max von Hartmann*

PERSPECTIVE

Old men sit on park benches
leaning on shiny sticks,
leaning into the sun,
shuffling their feet in dry pine needles
and feeding red squirrels
from brown paper bags
telling wrinkled stories
with their freckled hands
Of driving streetcars downhill
on rails of ice
Of trees sliced white
with slippery saws
Of ice cut in blocks
from gray-cloud lakes
Of fields that broke sun-browned men
and black iron plows
Of hobos who swept barns
for sandwiches in waxed paper
Of sunrises colored rusty
by late summer winds
Of sunsets that were silent
in a January woods.

North Country Anvil   *Robert L. Vorpahl*

MAY

In May, the sun climbs
its new trellis of leaves
and the last thread of snow
becomes a stitch of mildew
under the trees. Dandelions
tatter the lawn and the purple
lungs of lilacs sweeten
the bush. The birds come back
as the mud roads dry
and a gown of dust covers
the roadside brush. Between
the first torn cry of a bull-
frog's speech and the beacon
of a firefly, the mosquitoes
start their engines and the grass
lengthens. Twilight crayons
a window and the wind
unwinds its unseen skeins.
At dawn, a woodpecker opens
a sore on the flexed arm
of an elm. Another day
begins.

Kansas Quarterly   *John Stevens Wade*

ELEGY WHILE PRUNING ROSES

What saint strained so much,
Rose on such lopped limbs to a new life?
  —Theodore Roethke

I've weeded their beds, put down manure and bark dust.
Now comes the hard part: theoretically
It has to be done, or they spend their blooming season
In a tangle of flowerless, overambitious arms.
So here go pruning shears in spite of the thorns
That kept off browsers for all the millennia
Before some proto-dreamer decided roses
Were beautiful or smelled their unlikely promise.

Reluctantly I follow the book and stunt them
In the prescribed shapes, but throwing cuttings away
Over the fence to die isn't easy.
They hang onto my gloves and won't let go,
Clutching and backlashing as if fighting
To stay in the garden, but I don't have time or patience
To root them in sand, transplant them, and no room
In an overcrowded plot, even supposing
They could stand my lame midhusbandry.
So into limbo with all these potential saints.

Already the ladybugs, their black-dotted orange
Houses always on fire, are climbing for aphids,
And here come leaf-rollers, thrips and mildew
To have their ways. I've given up poison:
These flowers are on their own for the spring and summer.
But watching the blood-red shoots fade into green
And buds burst to an embarrassing perfection,
I'll cut bouquets of them and remember
The dying branches tumbling downhill together.

Ted, you told me once there were days and days
When you *had* to garden, to get your hands
Down into literal dirt and bury them
Like roots to remind yourself what you might do
Or be next time, with luck. I've searched for that
        mindless
Ripeness and found it. Later, some of these flowers
Will go to the bedside of the woman I love.
The rest are for you, who weren't cut off in your prime
But near the end of a long good growing season
Before your first frost-bitten buds.
You knew where roots belonged, what mysterious roses
Come from and were meant for: thanks,
Apology, praise, celebration, wonder,
And love, in memory of the flourishing dead.

Poetry
                                        David Wagoner

ODE TO THE MUSE ON BEHALF OF A YOUNG POET

Madam, he thinks you've become his lover. He doesn't know
                    You're his landlady,
The keeper of the keys to the front door, the mistress
Of the stairwell, postmistress, indifferent cook, shade-lifter
Veiled by twitching curtains, protectress of thermostats,
                    Handmaiden of dust.

He doesn't see your crowsfeet or cracked smile or the grayness
                    Swept from your temples.
To him, your odor of mothballs is the heady essence
Of the Gardens of Inspiration and your bedridden houseplants
The Garden itself. Look, he has begun to scribble.
                    Grant him your mercy.

If you should tell him he's behind in his rent instead,
                    You may startle him
Out of a year's growth of beard and spirit. Consider
Your reputation, not as a bill-collector, but as the sole
Distributor of Sparks, Flashes, and Sudden Leaps
                    From the Visionary Aether.

His heart's in the right place: in his mouth. If he means
                    Anything, he means well.
If he means nothing to you, why not amuse him for a brief
Lifetime with the benefit of your doubt? What would you be
Without him and his attentions but an empty housekeeper,
                    A closet hostess?

Who else could be more ardent, more flattering? Already
                    He's wondering where you are.
He's inventing enough implausible, brilliant rivals to last you
Forever. He wouldn't dream of asking you to wash
His unmentionable linen or scrub his floor or thaw his dinner.
                    He's starving for *you*.

Blank paper pays you no honor. Using your name in vain
                    Is his only blasphemy.
Go to him now in disguise and comfort him with all
Your charm-filled anger, your dreadful, withering beauty,
Your explosive silences, the consolations of horror,
                    The forgeries of death.

The Atlantic Monthly   *David Wagoner*

AROUND THE BLOCK

                    I will go for a walk before
                    bed, a little stroll to settle
                    the day's upsets. One thing always
                    follows another, but
                    discretely—tree after
                    telephone pole, for instance, or

this series of unlit houses. One moment follows
another,
helplessly, losing its
place instantly to the next. Each frame
fails, leaving behind
an impression of motion.

As for death, at the moment I
think it strangely overrated.

Who now could build
houses like these? who
could afford to? They loom
in the evening of the
East Side, memory-traces
of sometime wealth. Dust
seems forever settling, but
must somehow recirculate.

Once around the block
will do. Porch after porch projects
its columns, seeming one dark and
continuous dwelling. And fear continues,
eternal night shuttering each
source of light. How
remarkable, how remarkably
pleasant, not to be
asleep, still discriminating
dips in the sidewalk, reading
the differences between shadows.

Poetry   *Keith Waldrop*

INSTRUCTIONS FOR A PARK

These apartment acres, good only
for living in, must go. Plant charges
at regular intervals, wherever
ceiling meets floor or flat ridge of floor
meets ceiling.
            Stand back the recommended
distance, hold traffic still as a photo-
graph, the city holding its moment, eased
upon a plunger, a lever, anything
on which to stand and pry the earth.

Allow a lifetime for the air to clear.
Allow twenty years for paint to be done
with cracking, another thirty for lumber
to burrow into the ground and emerge
as tree, twenty-five for brick to crumble
to stone, stone to pebble, pebble to dust.

Then hire dozens of dozers to push
the dust into mounds, the mounds into hills,

hills into mountain. Label the mountain
Erosion, and leave it for another
century.
      Mold your children, your children's
children, the children of the children
great grandchildren bear; convince them
that they are the reason for the past.

If their faces turn red, know that it is
only the wind in the park, the beginnings
of rain or snow. If they grow thirsty,
know that all rivers flow into one, and
that even that one, like a shadow
passing over a park, flows into air.

Shenandoah   *Brad Walker*

PASSAGES
(for F. S., 1949-1978)

Sometimes when a man is old
enough to take his own life
soberly, he takes that life.

(At dawn, the light blue with cold,
I go out past the corncrib
to the chickenrun, gripping
the shotgun; behind a pile
of grainsacks, I make my space
against the weather. Then wait
for the fox to come, or not:
taking the risk a man must
take, I've hung the dead rooster
bloody by the corner post.)

Sometimes when what you wait for
arrives, it's like a river
with a shifting undertow
stirring up silt and trouble.

(I sit there for hours: gun
growing into my hands, eyes
held by the *drip* . . . *drip* slowing
beneath the rooster. Nothing
has come from across the cold
pasture, no leap to trigger
the darkness alight.)

              And sometimes
nothing at all. Then a man
may walk to the river, gun
in hand, to stir up his own
sober trouble. A taking

pains: as though seeing the light.

The Georgia Review   *David Walker*

DELIVER ME, O LORD, FROM MY DAILY BREAD

When paper bags wallow like demons
over the floor in orange dream kitchens
and a legion of groceries nods and winks
on the unrepentant cupboards,
deliver me, then, O Lord, to stones.
Let me not see jam grinning on the face
of whole wheat. Keep cake from rising
on my tongue like morning. May I
despise pizza and beer.
While lemon rings its high bells
and I kneel helpless
in the dark church of chocolate,
Father of slender angels and of the slightly fed,
Deliver me once more from my daily bread.

Cimarron Review   *Jeanne Murray Walker*

GENERATION GAP

I dream my mother
in the image
of those potted plants
that could in forests grow
unstunted
into trees

I dream my mother
dreams me
always moving
long-limbed and confident
beyond her

Yet in my poems
my mother
overruns the narrow edges
of my similes
and when I show her
my persona
she reads it
as a metaphor
for her

Canadian Forum   *Bronwen Wallace*

PUBERTY

I remember not knowing
enough
to reach as far down
as they would allow

                    to the place where
the salty flesh curls,
                            where
    the tight hair clusters
        into wiry tufts.

                I
remember
                    believing
    that if I got inside,
        a fetus would bloom
                            surely
    as fruit
        in a vaguely reptilian dark,
        and I would
                            never again
        be invited to parties.

            So
    I held back, kept
        most of me to myself,
                            which
    is what I wanted anyway:
        to avoid, in that per-
            plexity of flesh, that
                final, awkward easing
    that would declare me
                man and lover,
            water and seed.

Kansas Quarterly   *Jon Wallace*

PRAYER FOR FISH

Twenty below. It is too cold
to talk. Words break in the air.
The tips of my fingers crack and split.
My ice auger and skimmer,
my waxworms and fish bucket
huddle beside me. The wind
clips its swivel to my face.

The fish aren't biting.
I imagine them huddled
around my cold bait, moving slow.
It will take them all day.
I wait with the other ice fishermen,
bent over our holes as in prayer:

Let the fish leave their sleep
and rise up our poles;
let our fingers recover
their delicate grace;
let the patience of walleye and pike

remind us:
all cold things will melt,
all sleeping things wake,
keeping their proper seasons.

Northwest Review   *Ronald Wallace*

BUCKET IN THE WELL

Late afternoon, summer on the prairie,
the porch in shadow and the barn in full, strong light.
A thousand grasshoppers leap
as we walk through the tall grass near the river,
and we, like this water, slow and shallow
this time of year . . .

How I long to lay down in the grass
and sleep through many generations of grasshoppers!
Or climb into the loft—
here is where the cat has her young,
where the tom comes to kill them. Here is where
pigeon eggs roll from nests on the high beams.
Here is where a curious child played secretly with matches.

Here is where I lay me down,
rising only when the first snow blows through the knotholes.
The friendly straw, the horses rustling below,
the everlasting sleep that waits
to be filled, like the bucket
at the bottom of the well.

Sou'wester   *Connie Wanek*

OTHER WOMEN'S CHILDREN

In Wyoming,
plain as far as my eye can see,
there are towns behind mountains,
towns beyond rivers, at the edge
of the range, across peaks
I will never climb

Driving,
I think constantly
of other women's husbands.
Their sleek bodies,
their smiles,
the pressure of their hands
on my back dancing.

In these towns the husbands tend
lawns polished to jade luster.
The houses bloom

like muted flowers, the kitchens
are neat as pins.

I think of the quiet lives
under the elm trees
of every small town
in the midwest:
The bright housedresses.
The clean children
with smooth white knees,
the children who never cry.

The Georgia Review   *Marilyn Nelson Waniek*

CHIRSTOGRAPHIA 35

(a spring bough to Rose)

Not by chance
the cock sparrow
treads his dance,
hen crouched
under him
on the narrow
icy limb.
Love is given
out of wintery
heaven: we,
in our long-wed
limbs, dance
a slow & secret
step, tread
a measure narrow
but deep, find
our branch steep
with glancing light.

Christianity Today   *Eugene Warren*

SWIMMING IN THE PACIFIC

At sunset my foot outreached the mounting Pacific's
Last swirl as tide climbed, and I stood
On the mile-empty beach and the dune-lands. Turned then, and saw,
Beyond knotting fog-clots, how Chinaward now
The sun, a dirty pink smudge, grow larger, smokier,
Flatter. Then sank.

Through sand yet sun-hot, I made to my landmark—
A gray cairn to guard duck pants (not white now), old drawers,
Old sneakers, T-shirt, and my wallet, no treasure.
At dune-foot, I dressed,
Eyes westward, sea graying, one gull at

Great height, but not white-bright, the last
Smudge of sun being gone.

So I stood and I thought how my years, a thin trickle
Of sand-grains—years I could then
Count on fewer than fingers and toes—had led me
Again and again to this lonesome spot where the sea
Might, in mania howl, or calm, lure me out
Till the dunes were profiled in a cloud-pale line, nothing more,
Though the westering sun lured me on.

But beachward by sunset, drawn back
By the suction of years yet to come—
So dressed now, I wandered the sand, drifting on
Toward lights of the city in distance, and pondered
The vague name of Time, that trickled like sand, and was life.

But suppose, after all the sorrow and joy, after all
Love and hate, excitement and roaming, failure, success,
And grains that had long trickled past
And now certainly could not
Be readily counted on fingers and toes—suppose
I should rise from the sea as of old in my nakedness,
Find my cairn, find my clothes, and in gathering fog,
Wander toward the lights of the city of men, what answer at last
Could I give my old questions? Unless,
When the fog closed in
I simply lay down, on the sand supine, and up
Into grayness stared, and staring,

Saw your face, slow, take shape,

Like a dream that all years had moved to.

The American Poetry Review   *Robert Penn Warren*

LESSONS IN HISTORY

How little does history manage to tell?
Did lips of Judas go dry and cold on our Lord's cheek?

Or did tears spring, unwitting, to
His eyes as lips found torch-lit flesh?

What song, in his screechy voice, and joy, did Boone,
At sunset, sing, alone in Kaintuck's Eden wilderness?

Who would not envy Cambron as he uttered his famous word,
At last—at last—fulfilled in identity of pride?

Is it true that your friend was secretly happy when the
Diagnostician admitted, in fact, the growth was malignant?

After the mad Charlotte Corday had done her work,
Did she dip her hands in the water now staining the tub?

And what did Hendrik Hudson see
That last night, alone, as he stared at the Arctic sky?

Or what, at night, is the strange joy with your pain intertwined
As you wander the dark house, your wife not long dead?

What thought had Ann Boleyn as, at last, the axe rose?
Did her parts go moist just before it fell?

And who will ever know how you, at night waking,
See a corner of moonlit meadow, willows, sheen of the whispering
    stream?

And who know, or guess, what, long ago, happened there?

The American Poetry Review   *Robert Penn Warren*

OMALOS

The moon bloats full and white
with spider eggs tonight.
Furred in the moonlight, the fat weed
waits and will welcome moon-sac birth
with broad, thick leaves outspread.
Thistles point.
Rocks sit still.
There is a regularity in the *dangle-dang*
of goat bells, sheep bells, in the hills.
The night world leans.
To sleepers, hunched each into dream
in his stone hut on the plain,
floats downward from rock-jag, wavering,
the baleful laughter of goats.

The Yale Review   *Rosanna Warren*

WHAT IS A SONNET?

What is a sonnet? It is not heart's blood,
Mind's sanity nor index of the soul.
It is not aspiration to the good
Nor an illumination of the whole.
It is not even a feeling in the gut
That makes you clench your teeth with very joy,
Nor from the language does it take the "but"
And substitute what time cannot destroy.

No, it is meter, rhythm, form, tone color,
Assonance, alliteration, rhyme.
You could not find an occupation duller,
A counting-on-the-fingers pantomime.
    So if I lavish my whole life upon it
    And you should ask, I'd say "It's just a sonnet."

Song   *Edward Watkins*

ACROBAT

I walk the tightrope of the heart,
Balancing passion without a net,
Taking chances, calling it art
When it is you I can't forget.
Faintly arises the crowd's applause
As I edge breathless foot by foot:
One misstep, I won't be yours—
So I go careful, I go good.

If life's a circus and I'm an act,
No money on earth could get me where
Imagination becomes a fact
And living is walking on the air:
    Only your smile could bring me to it—
    Clap your hands, and I can do it.

Song   *Edward Watkins*

THE GREATER COUNTRY

This is my country, all this golden plain:
These mountains rising high and purple-blue,
These forests cool and fragrant in the rain,
These meadows silver with the morning dew.
Here I have known the flame of childhood's hour,
The torch of love, the candlelight of toil;
Here I have found a wondrous peace and power
Within a church upon the quiet soil.
This is my country, yet within my heart
I feel a wider kinship, vast and deep;
For I am citizen beyond the chart
Of time and space, and some day, past the sweep
Of earth, my God shall lead me by the hand
To heaven's shining hills, my fatherland.

Pentecostal Evangel   *Grace V. Watkins*

TO J.F.K. 14 YEARS AFTER

Your sculptured lips are sealed
beneath the rushing scene
where Winter lies congealed
over everything.

The empty sky leers
about a silent hive.
Not all your peers
wish you alive,

wish you in deeper peace
than we know here

where children of Cochise
still love every year.

Your coins please crowds
who hoard half dollars,
and gossips stitch shrouds
for your dead and living brothers.

What can lips say true
when truth goes unreported
and news becomes the hue
of privacies unguarded?

Regardless of the fashion
to lower you this year,
I still wish with passion
that you were here.

Poet Lore   *Roger Weaver*

TIDYING UP

On some mad magnificent mornings
I stumble out of sleep
headlong into a sense
of inescapable doom.
Chariots race about my skull
unhindered by laws of nature.
Termites infest my work.
My plans for womankind
are stricken by a steady leak—
battery acid dripping on the canvas
making holes in my picture,
eating away rainbows.
I struggle to instigate order.

I would curl up inside a walnut shell,
drill a very small hole at its tip,
siphon out my dreams
and infest the world with them.
Like fats which do not dissolve,
they ride the watery currents of the world
and cover it.
Harbored in my walnut shell
I would craze the world with my order,
raise the world to my dream.

Nicotine Soup   *Nancy Weber*

YACHTING IN ARKANSAS

I clip coupons from magazines
and travel posters come

in the mail. The beach scenes
I nail to the side of the shed,
to sycamores and fence posts.
I save the Latin women
for the barn. Europe swings
on the corral gate. Those mornings
when the cows rock like buoys
in the fog, I climb aboard
my tractor and sail.

The Chowder Review   *Craig Weeden*

MEMOIR

You again. The ecstatic posture. The victory symbol
around a cigarette, leaning
primeval into the carved
hotel headboard, your wrists without bracelets
enthroned on your knees, while twenty-one stories
above New York, you say that I

don't like sex. The cab
pulls away from the pier. Because the driver
asks how you can leave such a woman, I turn
around again to your wine-
red blouse, and the curve of your chin
shadowed in the sunlit yellow

sky of your hair. I had just come down
with mononucleosis and a new car: in the black
and chrome interior we were delivering
ourselves under the rounded niche of a maple
in the corner lot
of your parents' church when the connection
between the flying buttresses and our encroachment
on the marginal regions—walking toward us,
taking us in, as if we
were even younger and stabbing a puppy—drops
a pencil-written parking ticket
through the slit in the mist.
An elegant old man
in a squash hat and the top half

of a child's head are staring at you
through the plate glass of Budin's
Delicatessen: Kaplansky, daydreamer,
minus a forefinger, steps
from the meat counter pinching
plates of corn beef steaming on the heel. He deals them
across the chrome-rimmed
formica table, wipes his hands,
looking at me in a deadpan, on that bed sheet
of an apron, backtracks
through the sawdust

for our side order of canoe-shaped

dills floating in brine. The wind,
coming down from Canada, hard
off the green ice of Lake Erie,
and swirling in snow,
whips the hat into the cobalt dark,
the door open, and the tracks
into the oblivion we've both been waiting for.

Poetry   *Roger Weingarten*

ART IN AMERICA

Emerson, strolling through the Louvre,
failed to stop before a single painting.
A transparent eyeball, he had in him all
that space, the future, to look after
and, fitting it, a transcendentalism
not to be debased by flyspecked pictures.
Better a man's own eye (and I) or nothing
than alluring, gaudy daubs of others,
especially from such hoary, remote places.
So America, snuffling its fragrant, rare,
untutored air, found its true savant.
And only Whitman shocked him by averring
there were bodies, many bodies, groping,
touching in that mighty, empty space.

The American Poetry Review   *Theodore Weiss*

THE FISHERMAN

(for my father)

Back when I was still trying
to have a boyhood, my father
would take me fishing,
and lie with a book in good
tall grass by the dank Sandusky.

He wasn't fond of fishing.

So whenever he had to rise
and pluck some sorry crappie
from my hook, he would murmur
soft apologies as it struggled
in his hands like live money.

And he always threw it back.

He'd stand there with the sun
in his eyes, and then kneel,
holding his big hands out

> to the river like rusty hooks
> he sometimes dreamed of losing.

The Beloit Poetry Journal   *Will Wells*

WHERE I WALK IN NEBRASKA

Not to the I-80, where
Hiking, even without a hitch,
Is prohibited, the constabulary
Patrols, and only the free-wheeling waterfowl
Carelessly cross in their detours of air.
And not past the edge of the town,
Where development dies down in the dump,
The constabulary patrols, and the ditches
Of landfill smoke with the town's spills.
Here, what I visit within walking distance
Is trees in their sickness and fall:
The brittle-boned cottonwoods,
The blighted elms vomiting leaves;
Or I travel on foot beside roads
With the cattle moving to their death,
And count the road's kills: to lose count
Is not to remember a mile's toll
Of its victims, gaunt tongueless smiles
Of the aging dead, skulls, a half-skull's
Offering of syrup of red mush
Behind a hulled eye. Say my perspective
Is earthbound; say that airborne I might
See it all fairly: the twin minute stars
Of its two sparse cities laid out
In striped fields; or say, farther still,
Seen from Mars, this plain crossed by *canali*
Of concrete reduces its scars to invisibles:
The crawl of mechanical evils, or my least self
Walking out in all weathers to these parts.

Kansas Quarterly   *Nancy G. Westerfield*

THREE CEZANNES

There are three Cezannes
Left in Toronto. Only three.
The filtration plant on Lighthouse Pond
Speaks volumes—with a colour-built severe
Hard stillness where all things to form respond
In harmonies of abstract concrete: sphere
And cube and cone: a seagull-grey expanse
Of lithic sky: of solid water, stroke
By stroke by stroke inlaid: Baroque
Red tiles—concavo waves caught in a trance.

North north-east, across the third-floor roof

Of city hall, you'll find the second: rock
Chipped quarried walls support an ageing steam
Plant: 1920 dormers, tarred, aloof—
Twelve sightless windows way up high. One chalk
White wall. Four white dishevelled
                              shadows steam
From T-square pipes. (Perhaps this one's a fake,
Not quite as monumental as the other two—
And yet it shows the private world he threw
Ours up for: "Analyze. To keep, forsake:
The greatest paintings live *behind* the view.")

Far south of Greenwood Switchyard

                              hangs the third . . .
A strip of horizontal, cold, metallic blue
Cleft by the rigid, tall, red, smokeless stack
Of some abandoned Works down by the lake
—Whose water's blue serene
Invokes the ocean off Toulon, L'Estaque,
Where light has value, weight.
                    Stone-strong, a prayer,
From earth to heaven this red chimney
                              cuts blue air,
A thing more grave and silent than the grave.
—He always set his goals beyond the seen.

Canadian Forum   *George Whipple*

PIGEONS

Pigeons on the roof puzzle me.
Why do they perch so proudly,
these insignificant, unimportant birds?
They primp and prime their plumage
with a patience hard to understand,
and then they strut about with a vanity
incomprehensible to anyone humble as a man.
They peck their food quite daintily,
always, I observe, in proper order,
and even their stools are white.
Their arrogance is their own affair
and, I suppose, to a pigeon, all these airs
represent what's reasonable and right.
Yet I cannot help but wonder why
a pigeon struts when he can fly.

The Cape Rock   *Robert F. Whisler*

RUNNING UNDER STREET LIGHTS

Movement,
Feet hit pavement.

> In, pound, pound;
> Out, pound, pound.
> Breath of life
> Come easy to me.
> Dance, my body!
> In, pound, pound;
> Out, pound, pound.
> Double shadows play,
> One fading,
> One darkening.
> Moment by moment,
> So easy.
> In, pound, pound;
> Out, pound, pound.
> Breathless laughter,
> Slow down the dance.
> Deep breath,
> Filling, filling, full!
> Out and empty again
> To be filled
> To be let go.

The Emissary   *Christy White*

THE HOUSECLEANER

> My mother gathered balls of dust
> from under sofas, tables, chairs;
> bits of paper, single hairs,
> all were gathered in her lust
> for a desperate cleanliness.
> Now I live in tranquil mess,
> safe among my mold and rust,
> storing in my attic head
> all the lint and thread and fuzz
> gathered where the past lies dead
> from the dust my mother was.

The Lyric   *Gail White*

LIKE CHILDREN OF THE SUMMERTIME
PLAYING AT CARDS

> Things never get lost,
> only submerged
> or shuffled into the deck
> like the old maid card
> before the new game starts.
>
> You will not stop writing poetry
> any more than you will
> forget how to ride a bicycle,
> and those who have known the sure

ecstasy of their bodies together
will never lose it—only re-shuffle
it into the deck of crazy cards
to wait for the next big draw.

The Lake Superior Review　　　　*Julie Herrick White*

OF ALL PLANTS, THE TREE

(for Marvin Bell)

Of all plants, the tree is man-sized,
By which to gauge each outdoor thing,
A hedge, a hill, a wooden house.
This is how it figures in my thoughts—
And for its usual sturdiness, like a rafter,
And its shape so much the shape of
A lone person or one rooted within
A leafless winter forest standing
As a stubble along the tops of hills
Deep in snow; the trees a line
For where the sky begins.
　　　　　　　　　　　　Always

I see a tree against the sky,
That larger world, but the air
Circling all among the branches—
That is not the sky,
But a clear and private space
Into which the leaves push out
And fall away.

The Black Warrior Review　　　　*Mary Jane White*

LYRE

The birch-tree trunks are white as plaster casts
And advokat, their leaves, a custard yellow,
Trembling in the wind, bleached enthusiasts,
While skies grow dark as overcast Othello.
A blonde and healthy girl, a soft caress,
Kind enough to love, round enough for lust,
How many years ago we were abed
That night a storm developed from a gust—
And calm as salt, she started to undress,
And numb, I viewed her nakedness,
A body sweet and warm as winter bread?

And wine, the drowsy lovers must have wine
And shadows guttering with candlelight,
And take it for a most propitious sign
A moth has found a refuge from the night;

And afterglow of embering desire
Must keep a second-story window lit,
And comfort any passerby who braves,
For reasons only he can posit,
The icy rain, and high demonic choir
That shrieks through power lines as if a lyre
Could still be why such brutal weather raves.

I've passed that window many times since then,
Rectangle silvered by a summer moon,
Or idle musing of distracted pen
When themes and leaves and images are strewn
Along the grey abandoned avenue
Where rustling birches luminous with rain
Recall one winter's strange delirium;
I've passed, mornings on a windowpane,
As if I looked for evidence those two
Still enjoy that second-story view,
Though lyre's tamed to tintinnabulum.

Prism International   *Patrick White*

DISSONANCE

That single whitethroat, he that lives nearby
Among our poplars, seems to have forgone
The hope of wheat; his song goes reckless, wry
And sour; instead of rising for the sky
In thirds, it droops, no hymn of prospering dawn
But private sundown; past all melodies,
He whistles flat with a chromatic twist
And leaves an earthward music in the trees.
Whether of prophet, fool, or ironist,
That maverick voice, that vowed and obstinate call
Lays chords to come, though yet the notes are wrong
For resolution, and the weeping song,
Insistent on that falling interval,
Keeps the whole woodland echoing to the fall.

Poetry   *Cedric Whitman*

HUMAN GEOGRAPHY

The mother rock is black basalt,
hard, handsome.
Walls are made of it, ancient
synagogues, the house of
Saint Peter's mother-in-law.

Climatic conditions:
a rush of new milk,
brief rains, the slow

grinding of wheat,
disappointments.

Bits of rock fall.
Each passing heel
grinds them. They are whipped
by the chamsin, dried
to fecund dust.

From this my children rose.
They were crops, they were trees.
They will squeeze
greengold liquor from olives
ripening by the black wall.

The Massachusetts Review   *Ruth Whitman*

ON THE LAST PAGE OF THE LAST YELLOW PAD IN
ROME BEFORE TAKING OFF FOR DACCA ON AIR BANGLADESH

Well, you go back then to the central question.
What if you saw, say, Augustus Caesar,
relaxing around a bus stop, reading a paper?
What if you knew that you were awake and sane?
What would you know more than you know already?

You would know that there was life after death.

Or maybe that death doesn't take. What else would you know?
You want to say you would know that God existed.

I would weigh the evidence in his favor.
What could you do with a soul but not a god.
You would assume they have to go together.

It doesn't make any difference what we assume.

Still there's logic though and natural law.

Logic lies and natural law accounts
for the fall to earth of every plane that's fallen.

We've reached the end of the back of the last page.
They're calling the flight.

                              We still have all the margins.

Give it up. We never had the margins.

Suppose you saw, say, Cicero or Catullus?

You've got your ticket. Go get on the plane.

I'm trying to tell you something.

                    I know. I know.

Cimarron Review   *Miller Williams*

LAYING BY

Your crops, old man, are in
the hard red dirt of your father's land.
Scooter plow moves through the
rows of Alabama corn;
you follow it just as he did,
but each terrace is flatter now.
You have no sons to come
hard by, forcing crumbling
furrows to respect the succession
of generations in this labor.
The scrub oaks have overtaken
bottom land cleared by man and mule
forty years ago. Your grandfather
broke it first, but it lay fallow
in his declining years and you
had to work it like new ground.
     And now look—

Now dog days are heavy on the
soil. The August heat is parching
the fat ears like meal in a tin
pan in the oven. But you,
you watch the skies, for the rain
comes in the late afternoon.
You are sure of that.

Southern Exposure　　　　　　　　*Randall Williams*

BRIDESMAID

Stripping the green tissue from the flowers
she is excited, and as she hugs the long stems
before the mirror in the bride's madhouse
she feels herself a flower—a pale, calm rose
undiscovered, beginning slowly to find shape.

In that glass as neutral as real air she sways;
it is a wind whose origin no man has learned
that bends her and teases her formal gown;
it is a light entering through shut windows
that colors her. No madness touches her.

At the ritual—by the slow procession leading
to the heart some say is God's, by the flutter
of words whose wings like hummingbirds' brush
promises from the moist lips of the lovers—
she is nourished, she bows, she is a garden.

Joining after joining, she is the same beauty
fading in the same shadow. This is a formal
enclosure where the gardeners come and go
until she loses count; it is a solemn room
where the windows never break for loneliness.

The kisses of women sustain her. Her hands
waving goodbye become accustomed to the air
as if it were water. The riotous dresses
fill her closets and wait to be used again;
they shoulder one another to be taken first.

Open Places   *Robley Wilson, Jr.*

MY WOMAN

needs no introduction
she is the one with
the scarf that bears
no special attention
she is the one who talks
little and says much
she is the captain's daughter
she lives by the pier and
birds sing in her heart.

her songs are
like a strong anchor
that fill the harbor with
her strength.

she is adam's rib spread
out across the bay
she is an angel of the mud flats
a silk worm boring through
my veins.

my woman needs no introduction.

Second Coming   *A. D. Winans*

JANIS JOPLIN AND THE FOLDING COMPANY

Twenty bracelets and a cackle later,
Janis spins her gut out on my turntable—
resurrects the needle of destruction
that O.D.'d her away from me.
"Summertime" shivers the matched speakers
as the phoenix in feathers
lays her funk on me o, so heavy,
o, so real,
I begin to believe she will crawl thru the
cloth . . . drag the phallic mike to her roughed-
up mouth . . . while her jivey hair
scurries like brown pack rats into the Fillmore
nite. It's JOPLIN!
in pink satin and chains,
stoned on Southern Comfort—phlegming
the floors—grinning in oversized grannies,
hyping the crazies to ball in the aisles;

screeching and beseeching kinky strays
to go "Down On Me" . . . Hippie
queen of smack and bluesrock boogied
her *now* thing, full tilt before and be-
hind the boards; worked her blowsy feet
in hooker's shoes shuffling their action
like a hot deck of Vegas cards: relieved
her gin-mama Self sitting in stopped-up
toilets reading the myths of manic Zelda,
digging their duality. I crowd the shelf
that spills her desperate sound, find
myself weeping dumbly in a rationale of loss
and anger. "Hey sisters . . . hey somebody . . .
give a rousing fuck for Pearl!"

The Rufus   *Bayla Winters*

IN THE LAKE COUNTRY

Above me is the misty English sky
And the soft air is cool against my face;
I see the wooded hills, the lake, and I
Am caught by the enchantment of this place.
There is a sense of Wordsworth lingering here
Where beauty wanders through each glade and glen,
The water mirrors cloudy skies, and clear,
As when idyllic thoughts flowed from his pen.
Along this winding path where arching trees
Make a cathedral aisle of common ground,
He walked, and following a vagrant breeze
Reached the shore line. There at its edge he found
And brought to us, in lyric words that sing,
The daffodils beside the lake in spring.

The Lyric   *Kay Wissinger*

CONSERVATIVE

I was a squanderer once of love and days—
vein after vein, no end to the rich mine—
a spendthrift owner, too well endowed to save
anything of it for a later time.
I had enough stuff in my glittering maze
to stud tiaras and the throats of queens—
generous potentate, I gave and gave—
why not, when so magnificent of means?
Now, though when the source is playing out,
more than half of prodigality
spent, and how much left of it in doubt,
I have to stop and count reality,

my miser fingers fondling every spark
deeper and deeper down, before the dark.

Poet Lore   *Harold Witt*

HER BIRTHDAY

Her birthday—now she's twelve—that little bloody
squinting nothing in a nurse's arms—
maybe there is matter here for study,
year after year going off like alarms
that wake us to the next one—without rest.
Now she can't wait until the slumber party,
gay twisted streamers and her screaming friends,
but soon enough she'll be half past forty.
Today she wishes as she blows the candles
for boys to phone her, for the gift of breasts;
she leans in the wind gripping the ram's horn handles
of her new bike—daughter of our zest—
hair streaming backward in the winter day,
and I watch her as the wheels spin her away.

Poet Lore   *Harold Witt*

FISH

She wishes her eyes did not sting mornings,
that the fish gleaming in the dark river
would not sing to her with his round, soft mouth.
Like bubbles the sound rises, fills the ears,
becomes a soft glove over every sound.

She cannot say it is the wind
because wind never enters the ear so warmly.
The river hardens and only
the center keeps moving,
but the song sings higher.

Sometimes she sees the tail,
a bright fan glimmer,
sometimes the fish hides along the bottom
and will not answer until she turns away.

But always it is the hard eyes she fears
below the song, turning in the wedge of its head
like pieces of clay glittering—
and the mouth gaping, a soft wound.

Colorado Quarterly   *Sandra Witt*

LOOKING AT POWER

1. Nuclear Generating Station, Salem, N.J.

Miles away, the dome
rises over the marsh grass
like a huge, dull moon.
We get as close as the Visitor Center
where a pretty girl hands out "Second Sun" buttons
and comic books that say it's safe:
the happy muskrats and fish don't mind hot water
and "trace amounts of radiation."
An exhibit shows the hard way:
spin a crank and barely light one bulb.
A child shoots a silver raygun
and a chain reaction spreads out forever
on the screen. We get the message:
anyone can split the atom
and heat up toasters clear to Newark.

2. Power Units 1 and 2, Colstrip, Montana

Custer's men carved their names on Medicine Rock,
then died. The Cheyenne knew they would,
and still wedge prayer sticks in the cracks
hoping for rain,
or a job, and peace at home in the trailer.
Twenty miles north, the twin stacks
of the power station's boilers shimmer
in the August heat, strobe lights flashing.
We crouch in the shade of Medicine Rock.
Everything else fits in with no room to spare:
jay, magpie, coyote, even a few men
who stayed long enough to learn the rules.
Now the land's stripped for coal,
then dumped back in the pits like trash.
This is whiteman's land now—
we close wire gates when we leave.

The Beloit Poetry Journal   *Warren Woessner*

GOLDA

One kick
of Cossack's boots
would split the door
my father boarded.
        I killed them

but they sprang alive
in the hoarseness
of curses. They grew
as high as the handsmeasure
of their horses. We
were left bleeding

never to stop. My sister
wept then. I did not weep
but played in the streets waiting
to hear the stamp of their hooves
splattering people
in blood.

     As sure
as the moon's dark menses
they came, played leap-
horse over children
huddled and screaming
     I killed them

but they wouldn't stay dead
only diminished as
they fled
into distance
into the red sky
of Auschwitz, Dachau, Treblinka . . .

Poet Lore   *Adrienne Wolfert*

TOUCHSTONE

My grandmother (Lord, love her jackdaw soul!)
collected things that mattered to a boy,
especially rocks. Nowhere we walked was safe
from her lapidary lusts; she ravished rocks
whose smooths could soothe the hankerings of her
    hands.

Not-quite stones, those that but mocked her touch,
she lodged along the fringes of her hearth
so that winter glows could burnish them at night.
(Old eyes, then dazzled, might trick quicker hands
into fondling, blind with hope, their blemished
    truth.)

What time abrades it also polishes:
my long-gone grandmother, reluctant to dissolve,
has become a gem that blesses now my stream,
whose rememberings ripple-carve her face,
enlightened by the luster they inflict.

The Christian Century   *James Worley*

HAS BEEN

being on the road wasn't so bad

but they started booking me in small clubs
the back rooms of pool halls
little roadhouses in the Adirondacks

I'd have to put on my makeup in the restroom

the mikes would be bad
there'd be no spotlight

usually the pianist was drunk

I'd sing "Melancholy Baby" & some bald geezer
would start singing with me

once this little blonde bitch did a strip
right during "Bill Bailey"

it got so I started tucking a flask of vodka
into my cosmetic case

my waist thickened & my thighs went bad

I couldn't make the high notes anymore

my agent got me on a talk show

I watched it the next day & cried

"That's it, Charlie," I said
"Your shooting star is dead."

Colorado Quarterly   *Alice F. Worsley*

THE TRESTLE BRIDGE

(Cheyenne, Wyoming)

Far off, the rumble of freight trains
through junctions. The moon rides,
aloof and full of herself,
above the cottonwood branches.
In the slough, a beaver pokes its head
through a ripple, slaps its tail,
shatters the moon. Not an echo left
of silver in her trail.
I cross the high train trestle
to the animal shelter at the prairie's edge.
Dogs' eyes stare like inmates'
from the cell blocks; as I walk away,
a wail, claws rake the bars,
chains, like loons' throats, rattle.
On the tracks again, a killdeer shrills
a warning, drags its wing.
I let it fool me from the freight yard nest,
hatchlings in the tufts between oil drums.
Everything's bent on one more breath,
another dive for insects in the evening air,
a branch hacked for fence posts
or a dam. High up, a dark wind starts
in the junipers.
          My life fits its body,

passenger on the outbound car. All I hear,
at the last bridge, by the broken ties,
is that the crossing to the other side is mine.

The American Poetry Review   *Carolyne Wright*

THE COUCH

It was a day for routine maintenance,
a three thousand mile service call
to the psychiatrist, the one I pay,
and he leaned back and yawned
and said that's okay you're okay i'm okay.

More or less. He didn't seem
particularly concerned about my
stomach's resurgence to the fore,
about the tension headaches revisited,
about the nagging narcosis of obsession
as i prick my ex-wife's memory
with startling regularity.

Nope, said the psychiatrist, his beard boun-
cing and his body at ease upon the couch
under the window,
work on those thoughts, my man,
and tell yourself it's two years old
and all over, someday you'll find
those thoughts all gone, give or take.

God, I'm tired, I said.

The Panhandler   *Fred. W. Wright, Jr.*

SHEEP IN THE RAIN

In Burgundy, beyond Auxerre
And all the way down the river to Avallon,
The grass lies thick with sheep
Shorn only a couple of days ago.
They shine all over their plump bodies
In the June mist.

Sheep eat everything
All the way down to the roots.
And maybe that is why
These explorers of the rain
Seem so relaxed in their browsing.
Someone has freed them only a little while
Into the fields, and they have a good life of it
While it lasts.

Burgundian farmers will return
Some morning soon,

And flock the fat sheep down a wall
Into glittering rocks.
Then a boy will go alone back into the grass
And care for the grass.
The farmers are kind to the grass.
They have to be.

Poetry   *James Wright*

THE RATTLESNAKE

(Hell's Canyon, 1978)

He's asleep, or dead, numb with wind
that surprised a whole month.
Coiled on a rock in scrubgrass,
his loops grow angular, circles sinking in
on themselves until he appears to be a rock
merely dreaming of snakes. We prod him
with the long stem of a wildflower. Nothing.
But now the head pulls back, no strike,
no evasive maneuver: he seems only polite.
We keep poking until suddenly the slope erupts
in rattle. He skids off to the brush
and we are smiling. The rattle was pale,
almost skeletal, its thin horror anemic with spring
or sleep. And for a few seconds he is
fully-stretched on the slope, barely a yard long,
a baby. We are grateful—
Not only for his size but for his venom.
He has no idea how he will grow for us
in the miles back home; his head
small as the knuckle on my thumb
will grow to a whole fist, the rich brown
body big as a forearm. But for now
we can walk back down smiling,
for a few yards at least, until
he already begins to grow, and we plant our feet
carefully as cats, the wind picked up
and noisy, his dry music
still singing in our ears.

The Chowder Review   *Robert Wrigley*

OBSERVATION

How the light breaks when it does.
How the eye takes in the light breaking.
How the brain corrects the
                    upside-down image
if that's what it does.

How the mountain's reflection
                    on the lake water
resembles the mountain.
How you become less and less certain.
If you throw a stone, how the
                        water ripples.
How the reflected mountain becomes
                    rippling water only.
How the water becomes smooth again.
How your uncertainty returns if it does so.
How your brain tricks your body
into thinking itself absent.
How water must do just that for stone.

Canadian Forum   *Derk Wynand*

IN A MIST

(Bix Beiderbecke, 1927)

Play it one more time, Bix, so I can cascade down
your waterfall of tears and up again all on my own.

I can tell by the silence of the notes you aren't
hitting that your head's getting funny again from
sitting up all night every night night after night,
banking on bad speak booze to navigate you through
seas of sound on boats that leave but never dock,
at least never long enough to unload your steamy
cargo—a love affair with sound itself and what
it can and cannot do.

Tell me, Bix, jazz darling, legendary refugee from
Cincinnati Oom-Pah-Pah, is there really any difference
(besides time, that is) between your 1920s twenties
and the twenties of Nineteen Now? All that appetizing
ear food, those saucy futuristic chords you cook up
on piano to go, and heat back up on trumpet—where,
if anywhere, will it end up? Better than any physicist,
you already know that time, space, motion, stillness,
distance and nearness are one. What you're deep into
now is the whirling of planets, the whispering of the
hours going by and by and by.

Tell me, doesn't that same lonesome-looking moon still
pull, bringing women around in a cycle as different
from man-made lunacy as bath water from gin? And isn't
what you've always loved and dreamed still as American
as aspirin, or atomic secrets; as American as apple pie
frozen in color on a television screen?

That's the part of the mystery they're going to have to
get a law out against; your secret ingredient, your
mystical spray capable of shattering whole cities and

countrysides while—unlike a neutron bomb—it leaves
listeners intact, craving infinity. Your spirit need
only be there, inside the mystery.

I, they, you, we—we all need your mistiness, Bix.
Play it again please, won't you? Again and again
and again. Life is too long and always too short.

The Beloit Poetry Journal   *Al Young*

THE DOCTOR REBUILDS A HAND

(for Brad Crenshaw)

His hand was a puppet, more wood than flesh.
He had brought the forest back with him: bark, pitch,
the dull leaves and thick hardwood that gave way
to bone and severed nerves throughout his fingers.
There was no pain. He suffered instead the terror
of a man lost in the woods, the dull ache of companions
as they give up the search, wait, and return home.
What creeps in the timber and low brush
crept between his fingers, following the blood spoor.
As I removed splinters from the torn skin
I discovered the landscape of bodies,
the forest's skin and flesh. I felt
the dark pressure of my own blood stiffen within me
and against the red pulp I worked into a hand
using my own as the model. If I could abandon the vanity
of healing, I would enter the forest of wounds myself,
and be delivered, unafraid, from whatever I touched.

Antaeus   *Gary Young*

JUNK

The ruin or the blank that we see when
we look at nature, is in our own eye. —Emerson

Country of desolation between junctions,
Bricks, boards, sidings,
Abandoned truck tires,
The blank at the heart of the ruin.

When the clutch goes,
You look for a gas pump and a garage.
—Only let the eye see more than that,
More than itself in ruins . . .

Creased deep as the dashboard map, a folded acreage
Unfolds in rows of corn, in yields of wheat.
On the hill a kerchief of cloud receding,
And a rainbow's lucent prisms.

Soon farmhouse and haybales appear.
In a circle of sawdust and pinecurls,
A broad back is planing a door.
A hand drops

What he's fixing in the barn to fix your car.
Diapers drift, overalls loft lazily on a line.
Dogs bark at commotions in the corn: cows
Are the commotions, children chasing cows,

A mother and a daughter herding kids,
The mismatch-eyed, the burly-bellied daughter's kids . . .
See the risen bread under her apron!
She is fallow country, fallow as the eye is,

Following her lover to the trysting place,
Where a bashed-in pickup dreams on its hubs,
And the sequent moons of a harrow rust—
He licks his hatchet twice before they kiss.

Linkage, the hand under your car brandishes
The worn-out linkage. You palm it.
A child taps your thigh, points to your fist.
You let him pry your fingers; pinkie, thumb.

He smiles at the prize: it sparkles: junk.

The Seattle Review   *William Zaranka*

RIDDLES AND LIES

Death is asleep.
And in my dream
the earthworm with five hearts
is the hero,
not the moth
who's swallowed up by a flame
or the man who's rusty
in the particulars of love,
or you who make me laugh
with jokes and kisses
and come and go
and go and come again.
Death is asleep.
Though we're buried in the snow
there's still fire and a baby,
a baby on which there crawls
a caterpillar,
a baby that I've held
in my bed and in my body.
Death is asleep.
Feed me salt so I won't die.
Feed me riddles and lies
till a halo shines
bright and still

all around my body.
Feed me the story
about women who scream at men,
and I'll feed you the story
about women who are whispering,
whispering about men
and screaming at babies,
shivering and sweltering
in the sun and the snow.
Make me laugh
about the baby who swallowed
a butterfly,
about the mother who told
a tremendous lie
and was never heard from again,
who was sent to live with the fear
of never-ending emptiness.
Feed me with your words,
feed me snow so
I won't die.
As long as my mind
is still puzzling and hungry.
As long as I continue
to kiss you good-bye.

The Iowa Review   *Christine Zawadiwsky*

INSOMNIA

not fighting it for once
I watch the dawn come against the rooftops
tasting a little loneliness and gall
after the rich sauce, the wine,
the deferent service, crystal, candles
of our anniversary

only with you beside me do I open windows
dare to feel air moving against my skin
for the imaginary burglar I wear flannel
lock up tight, and keep my eyes shut
blinkered on the treadmill of my night thoughts

two years ago on this night in June
lying damp and unfamiliar on the floor
we made love among the leaflets and petitions
we had no place else to go
all we had then is gone
the strangeness, the friendships, the poverty
we have nothing left of that
except each other

light begins to touch the buildings

I lie down again beside you
and map with my lips your warm unconscious form

Dark Horse   *Elizabeth Zelvin*

ZIMMER'S LAST GIG

Listening to hard bop,
I stayed up all night
Just like good times.
I broke the old waxes
After I'd played them:
Out of Nowhere, Mohawk,
Star Eyes, Salt Peanuts,
Confirmation, one-by-one;
Bird, Bean, Bud, Brute, Pres,
All dead, all dead anyway,
As clay around my feet.

Years ago I wanted to
Take Wanda to Birdland,
Certain that the music
Would make her desire me,
That after a few sets
She would give in to
Rhythm and sophistication.
Then we could slip off
Into the wee hours with
Gin, chase, and maryjane,
Check into a downtown pad,
Do some fancy jitterbugging
Between the lilywhites.

But Wanda was no quail.
Bud could have passed
Out over the keys,
Bird could have shot
Up right on stage—
Wanda would have missed
The legends. The band
Could have riffed
All night right by
Her ear, she never
Would have bounced.

Harper's Magazine   *Paul Zimmer*

DARK ROOM

(for M.D.)

I

It was the Autumn of her madness,
developing some residue from the savage within.
She knew the shapes of silence, seasons
of yeasty roots, the wine's thin secret.
We gathered them between us, prudent weeds
rubbing the lumps of prayer; as though silence
held no memory of its own, as though immune.

II

I heard her renounce the empty game, saw
her new name stir from its cold places.
Who knows what secret feasts we shared: thunder
from frail poets, garlands for fatted lambs,
hours from naked water, seven hollow
sea shells gathered at the cheek of a vision,
a black laced spinster with kelp in her gown.

III

And I saw her image move from darkness
into the loneliness she knew and favored.
Her tears, swollen at the neck of hope,
stunned our holy poems, pushed into the shadows
as though something in light might explain us.
It was the hour of inquisition, when darkness
wasn't strange to those who dwelled there.

Southwest Review   *Fredrick Zydek*

Index of Titles

Index of First Lines

Books of Poetry by Contributors

This bibliography is included as an aid for those who wish to locate additional poetry by authors whose work appears in the Anthology. Most of the information was supplied directly by the authors.

A

Aal, Katharyn Machan: *Bird On A Wire.* Privately printed, 1970.
—*The Wind In The Pear Tree.* Privately printed, 1972.
—*The Book Of The Raccoon.* Gehry Press, 1977.
Abbott, Stephen: *Transmuting Gold.* Dancing Rock Press, 1978.
—*Wrecked Hearts.* Dancing Rock Press, 1978.
—*Stretching The Agapé Bra.* Androgyne Press, 1979.
Adcock, Betty: *Walking Out.* Louisiana State University Press, 1975.
Alegria, Claribel: *Anillo De Silencio.* Editorial Botas (Mexico City), 1948.
—*Suite.* Editorial Brigadas Liricas (Mendoza, Argentina), 1951.
—*Vigilias.* Editorial Poesia de America (Mexico City), 1953.
—*Acuario.* Editorial Universitaria (Santiago, Chile), 1955.
—*Huesped De Mi Tiempo.* Editorial Americale (Argentina), 1961.
—*Via Unica.* Editorial Alfa (Montevideo, Uruguay), 1965.
—*Aprendizaje.* Editorial Universitaria (El Salvador), 1970.
—*Pagare A Cobrar.* Editorial Ocnos (Barcelona, Spain), 1973.
—*Sobrevivo.* Editorial Casa de las Americas (Havana, Cuba), 1978.
Aliesan, Jody: *Soul Claiming.* Mulch Press, 1975.
—*as if it will matter.* Seal Press, 1978.
Allen, Dick: *Anon And Various Time Machine Poems.* Delacorte Books, 1971.
—*Regions With No Proper Names.* St. Martin's Press, 1975.
Anderson, Ken: *Permanent Gardens.* Seabolt Press, 1972.
Applewhite, James: *Statues Of The Grass.* University of Georgia Press, 1975.
—*Following Gravity.* University Press of Virginia, 1979.
Ashley, Nova Trimble: *Through An Ocean Of Gold.* Triangle Publishing Co., 1962.
—*Coffee With Nova.* Robbins Printing Co., 1966.
—*Loquacious Mood.* Golden Quill Press, 1970.

—*Haps and Mishaps.* Branden Press, 1973.
—*Hang In There, Mom.* C. R. Gibson Co., 1975.
—*Chin Up, Dad.* C. R. Gibson Co.
Atchity, Kenneth John: *Sleeping With An Elephant: Selected Poems 1965-1976.* Valkyrie Press, 1978.
Aubert, Rosemary: *Two Kinds Of Honey.* Oberon Press, 1977.

B

Baca, Jimmy Santiago: *Rockbottom No. 6.* Sasha Newborn, 1978.
—*Immigrants In Our Own Land.* Louisiana State University Press, 1979.
Bailey, Alice Morrey: *Eden From An Apple Seed.* Utah State Poetry Society, 1971.
Baker, David: *Looking Ahead.* Mid-America Press, 1975.
—*Rivers In The Sea.* Mid-America Press, 1977.
Balazs, Mary: *The Voice Of They Brother's Blood: Poems By Mary Balazs.* Dawn Valley Press, 1976.
—*The Stones Refuse Their Peace.* Seven Woods Press, 1979.
Barnes, Jim: *The Fish On Poteau Mountain.* Cedar Creek Press, 1980.
Barnstone, Willis: *From This White Island.* Twayne Publishers, 1960.
—*A Day In The Country.* Harper & Row, 1971.
—*China Poems.* University of Missouri Press, 1976.
Behm, Richard: *Letters From A Cage & Other Poems.* Raspberry Press, 1976.
—*This Winter Afternoon Of Angels.* sun rise fall-down artpress, 1978.
—*The Book of Moonlight.* Moonlight Publications, 1978.
Bentley, Beth: *Phone Calls From The Dead.* Ohio University Press, 1971.
—*Country Of Resemblances.* Ohio University Press, 1976.
—*Philosophical Investigations.* Sea Pen Press, 1978.
Berg, Sharon: *To A Young Horse.* Borealis Press, 1979.
Berry, Wendell: *The Broken Ground.* Harcourt Brace & Co., 1964.
—*Openings.* Harcourt Brace & Co., 1968.
—*Findings.* Prairie Press, 1969.
—*Farming: A Handbook.* Harcourt Brace Jovano-

vich, 1970.
—*The Country Of Marriage.* Harcourt Brace Jovanovich, 1973.
—*An Eastward Look.* Sand Dollar Press, 1974.
—*Sayings And Doings.* Gnomen Press, 1975.
—*Horses.* Larkspur Press, 1975.
—*To What Listens.* Best Cellar Press, 1975.
—*The Kentucky River: Two Poems.* Larkspur Press, 1976.
—*Clearing.* Harcourt Brace Jovanovich, 1977.
—*Three Memorial Poems.* Sand Dollar Press, 1977.
Black, Charles: *Telescopes And Islands.* Alan Swallow, 1963.
—*Owls Bay In Babylon.* Dustbooks, 1980.
Blackwell, Will H.: *Tides.* Libra Publishers, 1980.
Blessing, Richard: *Winter Constellations.* Ahsahta Press, 1977.
Bottoms, David: *Jamming With The Band At The VFW.* Burnt Hickory Press, 1978.
—*Shooting Rats At The Bibb County Dump.* William Morrow, 1980.
Brand, Millen: *Dry Summer In Providence.* Clarkson Potter, 1966.
—*Local Lives.* Clarkson Potter, 1975.
—*Peace March, Nagasaki to Hiroshima.* Countryman Press, 1980.
Brett, Peter: *Ghost Rhythms.* Blue Cloud Press, 1976.
—*Gallery.* University Press of Virginia, 1978.
—*Borrowing The Sky.* Kastle Press, 1978.
Brodsky, Joseph: *Selected Poems.* Harper & Row/Penguin, 1974.
—*A Part Of Speech.* Farrar, Straus & Giroux, 1979 or 1980.
Brodsky, Louis Daniel: *Trilogy: A Birth Cycle.* Farmington Press, 1974.
—*Monday's Child.* Farmington Press, 1975.
—*The Kingdom Of Gewgaw.* Farmington Press, 1976.
—*Point Of Americas II.* Farmington Press, 1976.
—*Preparing For Incarnations.* Farmington Press, 1976.
—*La Preciosa.* Farmington Press, 1977.
—*Stranded In The Land Of Transients.* Farmington Press, 1978.
—*The Uncelebrated Ceremony Of Pants Factory Fatso.* Farmington Press, 1978.
—*Resume Of A Scapegoat.* Farmington Press, 1979.
Bronk, William: *Silence And Metaphor.* Elizabeth Press, 1975.
—*Finding Losses.* Elizabeth Press, 1976.
—*The Force Of Desire.* Elizabeth Press, 1979.
Brookhouse, Christopher: *Scattered Light.* University of North Carolina Press, 1969.
Broughton, T. Alan: *Adam's Dream.* Northeast/Juniper Press, 1975.
—*In The Face Of Descent.* Carnegie-Mellon University Press, 1975.
—*The Others We Are.* Northeast/Juniper Press, 1979.
—*Far From Home.* Carnegie-Mellon University Press, 1979.
Bruchac, Joseph: *Entering Onondaga.* Cold Mountain Press, 1978.

—*There Are No Trees Inside The Prison.* Blackberry Press, 1978.
—*The Good Message Of Handsome Lake.* Unicorn Press, 1979.
Buckaway, Catherine M.: *The Silver Cuckoo.* Borealis Press.
Buckley, Christopher: *Pentimento.* Bieler Press, 1979.
—*Last Rites.* Ithaca House, 1980.
Burden, Jean: *Naked As The Glass.* October House, 1963.
Burr, Gray: *A Choice Of Attitudes.* Wesleyan University Press, 1969.
Burwell, Rex: *Anti-History.* SmokeRoot Press, 1977.

C

Carlile, Henry: *The Rough-Hewn Table.* University of Missouri Press, 1971.
Carter, Jared: *Early Warning.* Barnwood Press, 1979.
Cherwinski, Joseph: *No Blue Tomorrow.* Kaleidograph Press, 1952.
—*A Land Of Green.* William B. Eerdmans, 1960.
—*Don Quixote With A Rake.* Bruce Humphries, 1964.
—*A Breath Of Snow.* Branden Press, 1969.
—*The Staggering Man.* Branden Press, 1975.
Childers, David C.: *American Dusk.* Buffalo Books, 1977.
Ciardi, John: *From Time To Time.* Twayne Publishers, 1951.
—*Poems New And Selected.* Rutgers University Press, 1955.
—*I Marry You: A Sheaf Of Love Poems.* Rutgers University Press, 1958.
—*Thirty-Nine Poems.* Rutgers University Press, 1959.
—*In The Stoneworks.* Rutgers University Press, 1961.
—*Person To Person.* Rutgers University Press, 1964.
—*This Strangest Everything.* Rutgers University Press, 1966.
—*Lives Of X.* Rutgers University Press, 1971.
—*The Little That Is All.* Rutgers University Press, 1974.
—*Too Gross* (limericks, with Isaac Asimov). W. W. Norton & Co., 1978.
—*For Instance.* W. W. Norton & Co., 1979.
Clampitt, Amy: *Multitudes, Multitudes.* Washington Street Press, 1974.
Clark, Naomi: *Burglaries And Celebrations.* Oyez Press, 1977.
Cochrane, Shirley G.: *Burnsite.* Washington Writers' Publishing House, 1979.
Colby, Joan: *XI Poems.* Interim Books, 1972.
—*Beheading The Children.* Ommatiou Press, 1977.
—*Blue Woman Dancing In The Nerve.* Alembic Press, 1979.
Colquitt, Betsy Feagan: *The Lie And Truth Of The Land.* Thorp Springs Press, 1979.
Cooley, Peter: *The Company Of Strangers.* University of Missouri Press, 1975.
—*The Room Where Summer Ends.* Carnegie-Mellon

University Press, 1979.

Cooperman, Stanley Roy: *The Day Of The Parrot.* University of Nebraska Press, 1968.
  —*The Owl Behind The Door.* McClelland and Stewart, 1968.
  —*Cannibals.* Oberon Press, 1972.

Cotton, John: *Outside The Gates Of Eden.* Taurus Press (England), 1969.
  —*Poetry Introduction 1.* Faber & Faber (England), 1969.
  —*Old Movies And Other Poems.* Chatto & Windus (England), 1971.
  —*The Wilderness.* Priapus Press (England), 1971.
  —*Kilroy Was Here.* Chatto & Windus (England), 1974.
  —*Places.* Priapus Press (England), 1976.
  —*A Berkhamsted Three.* Priapus Press (England), 1978.

Councilman, Emily Sargent: *Bird On A Green Bough: Poems.* South and West, Inc., 1966.

Crow, Mary: *Going Home.* Lynx House, 1979.
  Border. Boa, 1980.

Cutler, Bruce: *The Maker's Name.* Juniper Press, 1980.
  —*The Doctrine Of Selective Depravity.* Juniper Press, 1980.

D

Davenport, Mariana B.: *Storm And Stars.* House of Falmouth, 1963.
  —*The Stone, The Word.* Golden Quill Press, 1973.
  —*The Gift Already Given.* Golden Quill Press, 1979.

De Bolt, William Walter: *Mist From The Earth.* Candor Press, 1969.
  —*Bricks Without Straw.* Candor Press, 1971.
  —*Second Spring.* Candor Press, 1976.

Dennis, Carl: *A House Of My Own.* George Braziller, 1974.
  —*Climbing Down.* George Braziller, 1976.
  —*Signs And Wonders.* Princeton University Press, 1979.

Dey, Richard Morris: *The Bequia Poems.* Offshore Press, 1979.

DiCicco, Pier Giorgio: *We Are The Light Turning.* Thunder City Press, 1976.
  —*The Sad Facts.* Fiddlehead Poetry Books, 1977.
  —*The Circular Dark.* Borealis Press, 1977.
  —*Dancing In The House Of Cards.* Three Trees Press, 1978.
  —*A Burning Patience.* Borealis Press, 1978.
  —*Dolce-Amaro.* Papavero Press, 1978.
  —*The Tough Romance.* McClelland and Stewart, 1979.

Dickey, William: *Of The Festivity* Yale University Press, 1959.
  —*Interpreter's House.* Ohio State University Press, 1964.
  —*Rivers Of The Pacific Northwest.* Two Windows Press, 1969.
  —*More Under Saturn.* Wesleyan University Press, 1971.
  —*The Rainbow Grocery.* University of Massachusetts Press, 1978.

Di Piero, W. S.: *Country Of Survivors.* Rasmussen Publishing Co., 1975.

Ditsky, John: *The Katherine Poems.* Killaly Press, 1975.
  —*Scar Tissue.* Vesta Publications, 1978.

Dobyns, Stephen: *Concurring Beasts.* Atheneum, 1972.
  —*Griffon.* Atheneum, 1976.
  —*Heat Death.* Atheneum, 1980.

Dodd, Wayne: *We Will Wear White Roses.* Best Cellar Press, 1974.
  —*Made In America.* Croissant & Co., 1975.
  —*The General Mule Poems.* Juniper Books, 1980.
  —*The Names You Give It.* Louisiana State University Press, 1980.

Dorn, Alfred: *Wine In Stone.* New Athenaeum Press, 1959.
  —*Flamenco Dancer And Other Poems.* New Orlando Publications, 1959.

DuFault, Peter Kane: *Angel Of Accidence.* Macmillan Co., 1953.
  —*For Some Stringed Instrument.* Macmillan Co., 1957.
  —*On Balance—Selected Poems.* Sagarin Press, 1978.

E

Eaton, Charles Edward: *The Bright Plain.* University of North Carolina Press, 1942.
  —*The Shadow Of The Swimmer.* Fine Editions Press, 1951.
  —*The Greenhouse In The Garden.* Twayne Publishers, 1955.
  —*Countermoves.* Abelard-Schuman, 1962.
  —*On The Edge Of The Knife.* Abelard-Schuman, 1970.
  —*The Man In The Green Chair.* A. S. Barnes and Co., 1977.
  —*Colophon Of The Rover.* A. S. Barnes and Co., 1980.

Ebberts, Ruth N.: *Time Of Grapes.* Prairie Press Books, 1968.
  —*Portraits.* Robbins Printing Co., 1973.

Eberhart, Richard: *Selected Poems.* Oxford University Press, 1951.
  —*Collected Poems, 1930-1960.* Oxford University Press, 1960.
  —*Quarry: New Poems.* Oxford University Press, 1964.
  —*Selected Poems, 1930-1965.* New Directions Publishing Corp., 1966.
  —*Shifts Of Being: Poems.* Oxford University Press, 1968.
  —*Fields Of Grace.* Oxford University Press, 1972.
  —*Poem To Poets.* Penmaen Press, 1975.
  —*Collected Poems, 1930-1976.* Oxford University Press, 1976.
  —*Survivors.* Boa Editions, 1979.

Eberly, Ralph D.: *Moonfire.* Libra Publishers, 1976.

Eddy, Gary: *Waking Up, Late.* Slow Loris Press, 1977.
  —*Borrowing My House From Insects.* Service-berry Press, 1979.

Ellenbogen, George: *Winds Of Unreason.* Contact Press, 1957.

—The Night Unstones. Identity Press, 1971.

Engle, John D., Jr.: *Modern Odyssey.* Golden Quill Press, 1971.

Laugh Lightly. Golden Quill Press, 1974.

—Sea Songs. Branden Press, 1977.

Estes, Laurence E.: *Shadows From Tall Candles.* Merchants Press, 1966.

—Stardust And Silver. Custom Printers (Spokane), 1971.

—Light The Fire And Burn The Wood. Custom Printers (Spokane), 1977.

Evans, Virginia Moran: *When March Sets Free The River.* American Weave Press, 1946.

—In Silence And In Thunder. Kaleidograph Press, 1951.

—Bee In The Wind. Golden Quill Press, 1965.

—Eyes Of The Tiger. Golden Quill Press, 1970.

—To Seek The Sun. Avonelle Assoc., 1977.

F

Falco, Edward: *As A Falling Leaf.* Ainslie House Press, 1973.

—Evocations. sun rise fall down artpress, 1979.

Farber, Norma: *The Hatch.* Charles Scribner's Sons, 1955.

—Look To The Rose. Fandel, 1958.

—A Desparate Thing. Plowshare Press, 1973.

—Household Poems. Hellric Publications, 1975.

—Something Further. Kylix Press, 1979.

—Never Say Ugh! To A Bug. Greenwillow Books, 1979.

Farley, Susan: *Apprentice To Death.* San Marcos Press, 1980.

Finley, C. Stephen: *From Kaspar's Journal.* Alderman Press, 1979.

Francis, Robert: *The Orb Weaver.* Wesleyan University Press, 1960.

—Come Out Into The Sun: Poems New And Selected. University of Massachusetts Press, 1965.

—Like Ghosts Of Eagles. University of Massachusetts Press, 1974.

—Robert Francis: Collected Poems: 1936-1976. University of Massachusetts Press, 1976.

Friebert, Stuart: *Dreaming Of Floods.* Vanderbilt University Press, 1969.

—Up In Bed. Cleveland State University Press, 1975.

—Uncertain Health. Woolmer & Brotherson, Ltd., 1979.

Fried, Elliot: *Poem City.* Rumba Train, 1977.

—Strip Tease. Applezabba, 1979.

Friedlander, Ginny: *The Last Thousand Years.* Charles Street Press, 1979.

Frost, Richard: *The Circus Villains.* Ohio University Press, 1965.

—Getting Drunk With The Birds. Ohio University Press, 1971.

Frumkin, Gene: *Dostoevsky & Other Nature Poems.* Solo Press, 1972.

—The Mystic Writing-Pad. Red Hill Press, 1977.

—Loops. San Marcos Press, 1979.

Funge, Robert: *The Lie The Lamb Knows.* Spoon River Poetry Press, 1979.

G

Galloway, Thomas: *In Lieu Of Reality.* J & C Transcripts, 1975.

—Prison Cells Are Not For Frivolous Thinking. J & C Transcripts, 1977.

Galvin, James: *Everyone Knows Whom The Saved Envy.* Doubleday & Co., 1980.

Garmon, John: *Mornings After The Nativity.* Ball State University English Dept., 1976.

—Llano Sons: 3 From The Southwest (with Tony Clark, Jim Harris). La Prensa, 1976.

Ghiselin, Brewster: *Against The Circle.* E. P. Dutton & Co., 1946.

—The Nets. E. P. Dutton & Co., 1955.

—Country Of The Minotaur. University of Utah Press, 1970.

—Light. Abattoir Editions/Fine Arts Press, 1978.

—Windrose: Poems 1929-1979. University of Utah Press, 1980.

Gildner, Gary: *First Practice.* University of Pittsburgh Press, 1969.

—Digging For Indians. University of Pittsburgh Press, 1971.

—Eight Poems. Terri Bredahl, 1973.

—Nails. University of Pittsburgh Press, 1975.

—Letters From Vicksburg. Unicorn Press, 1977.

—The Runner. University of Pittsburgh Press, 1978.

Glaser, Elton: *Peripheral Vision.* Bits Press, 1980.

Goedicke, Patricia: *Between Oceans.* Harcourt, Brace & World, Inc., 1968.

—For The Four Corners. Ithaca House, 1976.

—The Trail That Turns On Itself. Ithaca House, 1978.

—Crossing The Same River. University of Massachusetts Press, 1980.

—The Dog That Was Barking Yesterday. Lynx House Press, 1980.

Graham, Jorie: *Hybrids Of Plants And Of Ghosts.* Princeton University Press, 1980.

Grapes, Marcus J.: *Seven Is A Frozen Number.* Bombshelter Press, 1967.

—Termination Journal. Bombshelter Press, 1975.

—Breaking On Camera. Bombshelter Press, 1978.

Gregor, Arthur: *A Bed By The Sea.* Doubleday & Co., 1970.

—Selected Poems. Doubleday & Co., 1971.

—The Past Now, New Poems. Doubleday & Co., 1975.

Grossman, Allen: *And The Dew Lay All Night Upon My Branch.* Aleph Press, 1974.

—The Woman On The Bridge Over The Chicago River: A Book Of Poems. New Directions, 1979.

Grossman, Martin: *The Arable Mind.* Blue Mountain Press, 1977.

—Above The Thorn. BkMk Press, 1979.

H

Hajek, Louise E.: *Remembered Music.* Patterson, 1971.

Hall, Joan Joffee: *The Rift Zone.* Curbstone Press, 1978.

Halpern, Daniel: *Traveling On Credit.* Viking Press, 1972.
—*Street Fire.* Viking Press, 1975.
—*Life Among Others.* Viking/Penguin, 1978.
Hamill, Sam: *Petroglyphs.* Three Rivers Press, 1975.
—*The Calling Across Forever.* Copper Canyon Press, 1976.
—*The Book Of Elegiac Geography.* Bookstore Press, 1978.
—*Triada.* Copper Canyon Press, 1978.
Hamilton, Horace E.: *Through The Moongate: Songs For The Foreign Devil.* Dorrance & Co., 1952.
—*The Dry Scratch Of Laurel.* Twayne Publishers, 1953.
—*Before Dark.* Rutgers University Press, 1965.
—*The Cage Of Form.* Dickinson Publishing Co., 1972.
Hammond, Karla M.: *Calendar Wisdom.* Thunder City Press, 1979.
Handy, Nixeon Civille: *Do Not Disturb The Dance.* Creative Aids for Education, 1973.
—*Earth House.* Creative Aids for Education, 1978.
Hanson, Howard G.: *Ageless Maze.* Robert Allen, 1963.
—*Future Coin Or Climber.* John F. Blair, 1967.
Hanzlicek, C. G.: *Living In It.* Stone Wall Press, 1971.
—*A Bird's Companion.* Licklog Press, 1974.
—*Stars.* University of Missouri Press, 1977.
Harmon, William: *Treasury Holiday.* Wesleyan University Press, 1970.
—*Legion: Civic Choruses.* Wesleyan University Press, 1973.
—*The Intussusception of Miss Mary America.* Kayak Press, 1976.
Harris, Michael: *Sparks.* Vehicule Press, 1976.
—*Grace.* Vehicule Press, 1977.
Hartman, Charles O.: *Making A Place.* David Godine, 1980.
Harvey, Gayle Elen: *Between Poems.* Womanchild Press, 1978.
Hawley, Richard A.: *Aspects Of Vision.* Robert Moore, 1976.
Healy, Eloise Klein: *Building Some Changes.* Beyond Baroque Foundation, 1976.
Hearst, James: *Country Men.* Prairie Press, 1937.
—*The Sun At Noon.* Prairie Press, 1943.
—*Man And His Field.* Allan Swallow, Publisher, 1951.
—*Limited View.* Prairie Press, 1962.
—*A Single Focus.* Prairie Press, 1967.
—*Dry Leaves.* Ragnorak Press, 1975.
—*Shaken By Leaf-Fall.* Kylix Press, 1976.
—*Proved By Trial.* Juniper Press, 1977.
—*Landmark.* JiFi Print, 1979.
—*Snake In The Strawberries.* Iowa State University Press, 1979.
Heffernan, Michael: *Booking Passage.* BkMk Press, 1973.
—*A Figure Of Plain Force.* Chowder Chapbooks, 1978.
—*The Cry Of Oliver Hardy.* University of Georgia Press, 1979.
Hicks, John V.: *Now Is A Far Country.* Thistledown Press, 1978.
Hoey, Allen: *First Light In February.* Banjo Press, 1975.

—*Evening In The Antipodes.* Banjo Press, 1977.
—*Relics.* Banjo Press, 1978.
—*Cedar Light.* Street Press, 1979.
—*Naked As My Bones In Transit.* Tamarack Editions, 1979.
Hoffman, Daniel: *The Center Of Attention.* Random House, 1974.
Hollander, Robert: *Walking On Dante.* Pilgrim Press, 1974.
Hollis, Jocelyn: *Chopin And Other Poems.* Fiddlehead Poetry Books, 1972.
—*Bridal Song: The Story Of A Woman's Love.* American Poetry Press, 1979.
—*Vietnam Poems: The War Poems Of Today.* American Poetry Press, 1979.
—*Contemporary Religious Poems For The Modern College Student.* American Poetry Press, 1979.
—*Paradise Lost: A Modern Sequel.* American Poetry Press, 1979.
Hopper, Virginia Shearer: *A Closed Garden.* Boxwood Press, 1966.
Howes, Barbara: *The Undersea Farmer.* Banyan Press, 1948.
—*In The Cold Country.* Bonacio & Saul/Grove Press, 1954.
—*Light And Dark.* Wesleyan University Press, 1959.
—*Looking Up At Leaves.* Alfred A. Knopf, 1966.
—*The Blue Garden.* Wesleyan University Press, 1972.
—*A Private Signal: Poems New & Selected.* Wesleyan University Press, 1977.
Hoyer, Mildred N.: *The Master Key.* Golden Quill Press, 1965.
—*Leaves Of Laughs.* Peacock Press, 1974.
Hummer, T. R.: *Translation Of Light.* Cedar Creek Press, 1976.

I

Ignatow, David: *Poems.* Decker Press, 1948.
—*The Gentle Weight Lifter.* Morris Gallery, 1955.
—*Say Pardon.* Wesleyan University Press, 1962.
—*Figures Of The Human.* Wesleyan University Press, 1964.
—*Earth Hard, Selected Poems.* Rapp and Whiting (London), 1968.
—*Rescue The Dead.* Wesleyan University Press, 1968.
—*Poems: 1934-69.* Wesleyan University Press, 1970.
—*The Notebooks Of David Ignatow.* Swallow Press, 1973.
—*Facing The Tree.* Atlantic/Little, Brown, 1975.
—*The Animal In The Bush.* Slow Loris Press, 1977.
—*Tread The Dark.* Atlantic/Little, Brown, 1978.
—*Sunlight: A Sequence For My Daughter.* Boa Editions, 1979.

J

Jackson, William (Haywood): *An Act Of God.* Samisdat Press, 1979.

Jacobsen, Josephine: *The Human Climate.* Contemporary Poetry, 1962.
—*The Animal Inside & Other Poems.* University of Ohio Press, 1968.
—*The Shade-Seller: New & Selected Poems.* Doubleday & Co., 1974.
Jankola, Beth: *Girl Of The Golden West.* Intermedia, 1977.
—*Jody Said.* Press Gang, 1977.
—*Mirror/Mirror.* Caitlin Press, 1978.
Janowitz, Phyllis: *Rites Of Strangers.* University Press of Virginia, 1978.
Jennings, Kate: *Second Sight.* Iron Mountain Press, 1976.
Johnson, Denis: *The Man Among The Seals.* Stone Wall Press, 1969.
—*Inner Weather.* Graywolf Press, 1976.
Johnson, Michael L.: *Dry Season.* Cottonwood Review Press, 1978.

K

Kammeyer, Virginia Maughan: *Saints Alive!* Bookcraft, Inc., 1970.
—*More Saints Alive!* Far West Publishers, 1979.
Kelley, Shannon Keith: *About In The Dark.* Shaun Higgins, 1978.
Kelly, Dave: *The Night Of The Terrible Ladders.* Hors Commerce Press, 1966.
—*Summer Study.* Runcible Spoon, 1969.
—*Dear Nate.* Runcible Spoon, 1969.
—*All Here Together.* Lillabulero, 1969.
—*Instructions For Viewing A Solar Eclipse.* Wesleyan University Press, 1972.
—*At A Time: A Dance For Voices.* Basilisk Press, 1972.
—*The Flesh-Eating Horse and Other Sagas.* Bartholomews's Cobble, 1976.
—*In These Poems.* Red Hill Press, 1976.
—*Poems In Season.* Texas Portfolio, 1977.
—*Filming Assassinations.* Ithaca House, 1979.
Kennedy, Terry: *Durango.* The Smith, 1979.
Kherdian, David: *On The Death of My Father And Other Poems.* Giligia Press, 1970.
—*Homage To Adana.* Perishable Press, 1970.
—*Looking Over Hills.* Giligia Press, 1972.
—*The Nonny Poems.* Macmillan Publishing Co., 1974.
—*Any Day Of Your Life.* Overlook Press, 1975.
—*Country, Cat: City, Cat.* Four Winds Press, 1978.
—*I Remember Root River.* Overlook Press, 1978.
—*The Farm.* Two Rivers Press, 1979.
Knies, Elizabeth: *Threesome Poems.* Alice James Books, 1976.
—*Streets After Rain.* Alice James Books, 1980.
Kramer, Aaron: *Till The Grass Is Ripe For Dancing.* Harbinger House, 1943.
—*The Glass Mountain.* Beechurst Press, 1946.
—*The Thunder Of The Grass.* International Publishers, 1948.
—*The Golden Trumpet.* International Publishers, 1949.
—*Thru Every Window.* William-Frederick Press, 1950.

—*Denmark Vesey.* Privately printed, 1952.
—*Roll The Forbidden Drums!* Cameron & Kahn, 1954.
—*The Tune Of The Calliope.* Thomas Yoseloff, 1958.
—*Moses.* O'Hare Books, 1962.
—*Henry At The Grating.* Folklore Center, 1968.
—*On The Way To Palermo.* A. S. Barnes & Co., 1973.
—*O Golden Land!* Dowling College Press, 1976.
—*Carousel Parkway.* A. S. Barnes & Co., 1980.
Kroll, Ernest: *Cape Horn And Other Poems.* E. P. Dutton & Co., 1952.
—*The Pause Of The Eye.* E. P. Dutton & Co., 1955.
—*Fifty "Fraxioms."* Abattoir Editions, 1973.
—*Fifteen "Fraxioms."* Putah Creek Press, 1978.
Kunitz, Stanley: *Intellectual Things.* 1930.
—*Passport To The War,* 1944.
—*Selected Poems,* 1928-1958. 1958.
—*The Testing-Tree.* 1971.
—*The Poems Of Stanley Kunitz,* 1928-1978. Atlantic Monthly Press, 1979.
Kuzma, Greg: *Village Journal.* Best Cellar Press, 1978.
—*Adirondacks.* Bear Claw Press, 1978.
—*A Horse Of a Different Color.* Illuminati, 1980.

L

Lattimore, Richard: *Poems.* University of Michigan Press, 1957.
—*Sestina For A Far-Off Summer.* University of Michigan Press, 1962.
—*The Stride Of Time.* University of Michigan Press, 1966.
—*Poems From Three Decades.* Charles Scribner's Sons, 1972.
Lechlitner, Ruth: *Tomorrow's Phoenix.* Alcestis Press, 1937.
—*Only The Years.* James A. Decker.
—*The Shadow Of The Hour.* Prairie Press, 1956.
—*A Changing Season: Selected And New Poems, 1962-1972.* Branden Press.
Le Dressay, Anne: *This Body That I Live In.* Turnstone Press, 1979.
Lefcowitz, Barbara F.: *A Risk of Green.* Gallimaufry Press, 1978.
Le Guin, Ursula K.: *Wild Angels.* Capra Press, 1974.
Lem, Carol: *Searchings.* Vantage Press, 1971.
—*Grassroots.* Peddler Press, 1975.
Lepore, Dominick J.: *The Praise And The Praised.* Bruce Humphries, 1955.
—*Within His Walls.* Branden Press, 1968.
Lietz, Robert: *Running In Place.* L'Epervier Press, 1979.
—*At Park And East Division.* L'Epervier Press, 1980.
Lignell, Kathleen: *The Calamity Jane Poems.* Rosebud Press, 1979.
Lindner, Carl: *Vampire.* Spoon River Poetry Press, 1977.
Lindskoog, Kathryn: *The Gift Of Dreams.* Harper & Row, 1979.
Linthicum, John: *Wrestling With The Angel.* Maya Press (Majorca), 1971.
—*Working The Night.* Spheric House, 1976.

Lipsitz, Lou: *Cold Water.* Wesleyan University Press, 1967.
—*Reflections On Samson.* Kayak Press, 1977.
Locklin, Gerald: *Sunset Beach.* Hors Commerce Press, 1966.
—*POOP, And Other Poems.* MAG Press, 1972.
—*Son Of POOP.* MAG Press, 1973.
—*Toad's Europe.* Venice Poetry Co., 1973.
—*Tarzan And Shane Meet The Toad.* Maelstrom Press, 1975.
—*The Toad Poems.* Venice Poetry Co., 1975.
—*The Criminal Mentality.* Red Hill Press, 1976.
—*Toad's Sabbatical.* Venice Poetry Co., 1977.
—*Frisco Epic.* Maelstrom Press, 1978.
—*Pronouncing Borges.* Wormwood Review, 1978.
Logan, John: *Cycle For Mother Cabrini.* Grove Press, 1955.
—*Ghosts Of The Heart.* University of Chicago Press, 1960.
—*Spring Of The Thief.* Alfred A. Knopf, 1963.
—*Zigzag Walk.* E. P. Dutton & Co., 1969.
—*Anonymous Lover.* Liveright, 1973.
—*Poem In Progress.* Dryad.
London, Jonathan: *In A Season of Birds: Poems For Maureen.* Mudborn Press, 1979.
—*Between The Sun And The Moon.* Lawton Press, 1980.
Long, Virginia: *Song Of America.* Aquarian Truth Press, 1976.
Louthan, Robert: *Shrunken Planets.* Alice James Books, 1980.
Ludvigson, Susan (Susan Bartels): *Step Carefully In Night Grass.* John F. Blair Publisher, 1974.
Luttinger, Abigail: *Good Evening And Other Poems.* Penumbra Press, 1979.
Lutz, Gertrude May: *Song For A New Generation.* Golden Quill Press, 1971.
—*Leis Of Remembrance.* Golden Quill Press, 1975.
—*Time Is The Traveler.* Golden Quill Press, 1975.

M

Maino, Jeannette Gould: *Speeding Into Lost Landscapes.* Privately printed, 1976.
Malarkey, Susannah P.: *Moments In Time.* American Scholar, 1979.
Mangan, Kathy: *Ragged Alphabet.* Rook Press, 1978.
Mannes, Marya: *Subverse (Political Satire In Verse).* George Braziller, 1959.
Marano, Russell: *Poems From A Mountain Ghetto.* Back Fork Books, 1979.
Marcus, Mordecai: *Five Minutes To Noon.* Best Cellar Press, 1971.
—*Return From The Desert.* Newedi Press, 1977.
Mastrolia, Lilyan S.: *Observations From The Back Room.* Privately printed, 1977.
Matthews, William: *Ruining The New Road.* Random House, 1970.
—*Sleek For The Long Flight.* Random House, 1972.
—*Rising And Falling.* Atlantic/Little, Brown, 1979.
Matthias, John: *Bucyrus.* Swallow Press, 1970.
—*Turns.* Swallow Press, 1975.

—*Crossing.* Swallow Press, 1979.
Maura, Sister: *Initiate The Heart.* Macmillan Co., 1946.
—*The Word Is Love.* Macmillan Co., 1958.
—*Bell Sound And Vintage.* Contemporary Poetry, 1966.
—*Walking On Water.* Paulist, 1972.
—*What We Women Know.* Sparrow, 1979.
Maxson, H. A.: *Turning The Wood.* Cedar Creek Press, 1976.
—*Walker In The Storm.* Singing Wind Publications, 1980.
McAleavey, David: *Sterling 403.* Ithaca House, 1971.
—*The Forty Days.* Ithaca House, 1975.
McAnally, Mary: *We Will Make A River.* West End Press, 1979.
—*The Absence Of The Father And The Dance Of The Zygotes.* Cardinal Press, 1979.
McCloskey, Mark: *Goodbye, But Listen: Poems.* Vanderbilt University Press, 1968.
—*The Secret Documents Of America: Poems.* Red Hill Press, 1977.
McCracken, Kathleen: *Reflections.* Fiddlehead Poetry Books, 1978.
—*Into Celebration.* Coach House Press, 1979.
McCurdy, Harold Grier: *A Straw Flute.* Meredith College, 1946.
—*The Chastening Of Narcissus.* John F. Blair, 1970.
McDonald, Walter: *Caliban In Blue.* Texas Tech Press, 1976.
—*One Thing Leads To Another.* Cedar Rock Press, 1978.
McKeown, Tom: *The House Of Water.* Basilisk Press, 1974.
—*Driving To New Mexico.* Sunstone Press, 1974.
—*The Luminous Revolver.* Sumac Press, 1974.
—*Certain Minutes.* Scopcraeft Press, 1978.
McPherson, Sandra: *Elegies For The Hot Season.* Indiana University Press, 1970.
—*Radiation.* Ecco Press, 1973.
—*The Year Of Our Birth.* Ecco Press, 1978.
Meissner, William: *Learning To Breathe Underwater.* Ohio University Press, 1979.
Menebroker, Ann: *It Isn't Everything.* Aldine Society of California, 1968.
—*Three Drums For The Lady.* Second Coming Press, 1972.
—*Slices.* Grande Ronde Press, 1972.
—*If You Are Creative, I Will Vanish.* Zetetic Press, 1973.
—*The Habit Of Wishing* (with Cappello and Smith). Goldermood Press, 1977.
Meyers, Bert: *Early Rain.* Alan Swallow, 1960.
—*The Dark Birds.* Doubleday & Co., 1968.
—*Sunlight On The Wall.* Kayak Books, 1976.
—*The Wild Olive Tree.* West Coast Poetry Review, 1979.
—*Windowsills.* The Common Table, 1979.
Millard, Bob: *Screams From The Bedroom.* Brevity Press, 1977.
Miller, Errol: *Dreams Of The Silvery Night.* R. V. K. Publishing Co., 1975.
—*The Booray Poems.* New York Culture Review

Press, 1976.
—*Morning Star.* Sun Publishing Co., 1979.
Miller, Jane: *Many Junipers, Heartbeats.* Brown University/Copper Beech Press, 1980.
Miller, Jim W.: *Dialogue With A Dead Man.* Georgia University Press, 1974.
—*The Mountains Have Come Closer.* Appalachian Consortium Press, 1979.
Miller, Vassar: *Wage War On Silence.* Wesleyan University Press, 1961.
—*My Bones Being Wiser.* Wesleyan University Press, 1963.
—*Onions And Roses.* Wesleyan University Press, 1968.
—*If I Could Sleep Deeply Enough.* Liveright, 1974.
Mills, Ralph J., Jr.: *Door To The Sun.* Baleen Press, 1974.
—*Night Road/Poems.* Rook Press, 1978.
—*Living With Distance.* Boa Editions, 1979.
Minczeski, John: *The Spiders.* New Rivers Press, 1979.
Miner, Virginia Scott: *Many-Angel River.* Lantern Press, 1938.
—*The Slender Screen.* Pembroke-Country Day Press, 1967.
Minty, Judith: *Lake Songs And Other Fears.* University of Pittsburgh Press, 1974.
—*Yellow Dog Journal.* Center Publications Sumac Poetry Series, 1979.
Moffett, Judith: *Keeping Time.* Louisiana State University Press, 1976.
Moffi, Larry: *10 Poems 10.* Stanboy Press, 1976.
—*Homing In.* Ridge Road Press, 1977.
Moon, Sheila: *Joseph's Son.* Golden Quill Press, 1972.
—*Braver Than That.* Golden Quill Press, 1975.
—*Scarlet Incantations.* Guild for Psychological Studies, 1977.
—*Songs For Wanderers.* Golden Quill Press, 1978.
Morgan, Frederick: *A Book Of Change.* Hudson Review Publications, 1972.
—*Poems Of The Two Worlds.* University of Illinois Press, 1977.
—*The Tarot Of Cornelius Agrippa.* Sagarin Press, 1978.
—*Death Mother And Other Poems.* University of Illinois Press, 1979.
Morris, John N.: *Green Business.* Atheneum Publishers, 1970.
—*The Life Beside This One.* Atheneum Publishers, 1975.
Moss, Stanley: *The Wrong Angel.* Macmillan Co., 1966.
—*Skull Of Adam.* Horizon Press, 1979.
Mott, Michael: *The Cost Of Living.* Adam Books (London), 1957.
—*Tales Of Idiots.* Adam Books (London), 1961.
—*New Exiles.* Adam Books (London), 1961.
—*A Book Of Pictures.* Outposts Publications (London), 1962.
—*Absence Of Unicorns, Presence Of Lions.* Little, Brown, 1976.
—*Counting The Grasses.* Anhinga Press, 1979.
Mueller, Lisel: *The Private Life.* Louisiana State University Press, 1976.
—*Voices From the Forest.* Juniper Press, 1977.

—*The Need To Hold Still.* Louisiana State University Press, 1980.
Mulligan, J. B.: *The Stations Of The Cross.* Samisdat Press, 1979.
Murphey, Joseph Colin: *Trajectories: Twelve Space Poems.* Sam Houston State University Press, 1970.
—*A Return To The Landscape.* Prickly Pear Press, 1979.
Murray, Joan: *Egg Tooth: A Book Of Poems.* Sunbury Press, 1976.
Myers, Jack: *Black Sun Abraxas.* Halcyone Press, 1970.
—*Will It Burn.* Falcon Publishing Co., 1974.
—*The Family War.* L'Epervier Press, 1977.

N

Nathan, Leonard: *Western Reaches.* Talisman Press, 1958.
—*Glad And Sorry Seasons.* Random House, 1963.
—*The Matchmaker's Lament.* Gehenna Press, 1967.
—*The Day The Perfect Speakers Left.* Wesleyan University Press, 1969.
—*Flight Plan.* Cedar Hill Press, 1971.
—*Without Wishing.* Thorp Springs Press, 1973.
—*Returning Your Call.* Princeton University Press, 1975.
—*Coup And Other Poems.* Windflower Press, 1975.
—*The Likeness.* Thorp Springs Press, 1975.
—*The Teachings Of Grandfather Fox.* Ithaca House, 1977.
—*The Lost Distance.* Chowder Chapbooks, 1978.
—*Dear Blood.* University of Pittsburgh Press, 1980.
Nathan, Norman: *Though Night Remain.* Golden Quill Press, 1959.
Nemerov, Howard: *The Collected Poems Of Howard Nemerov.* University of Chicago Press, 1977.
Newell, Mike: *Underground Fires.* Swamp Press, 1976.
Nist, John: *Among The Pyramids And Other Poems.* Northwoods Press, 1977.
—*Love Songs For Marisa.* Northwoods Press, 1978.

O

O'Connor, Martin T.: *The Vicissitudes of Summer.* Bell Publishing, 1979.
Ostriker, Alicia: *Songs.* Holt, Rinehart & Winston, 1969.
—*Once More Out Of Darkness, And Other Poems.* Berkeley Poets' Press, 1974.
—*A Dream Of Springtime: Poems 1970-1978.* Smith/Horizon Press, 1979.
Owen, Sue: *Nursery Rhymes For The Dead.* Ithaca House, 1980.
Ower, John: *Legendary Acts.* University of Georgia Press, 1977.

P

Parham, Robert: *Sending The Children For Song.* Francis Marion Press, 1975.

Pastan, Linda: *A Perfect Circle Of Sun.* Swallow Press, 1971.
—*Aspects Of Eve.* Liveright, 1975.
—*The Five Stages Of Grief.* W. W. Norton, 1978.
Paterson, Evangeline: *The Sky Is Deep Enough.* Starglow Press (Scotland), 1972.
—*Eighteen Poems.* Outposts Unlimited (England), 1974.
—*Whitelight.* Mid-Day Publications (England), 1978.
—*Hard Winter: New And Selected Poems.* Other Poetry Editions (Wales), 1979.
Perlman, Jess: *Looking Glasses.* Branden Press, 1967.
—*This World, This Looking Glass.* South and West, Inc., 1970.
—*Bus To Chapingo.* Branden Press, 1973.
—*Poems Past Eighty.* Dragon's Teeth Press, 1979.
Pflum, Richard: *Moving Into The Light.* Raintree Press, 1975.
—*A Dream Of Salt.* Raintree Press, 1979.
Phillips, Robert: *Inner Weather.* Golden Quill Press, 1966.
—*The Pregnant Man.* Doubleday & Co., 1978.
Pierson, Philip: *See Rock City.* Gallimaufry Press, 1978.
—*Natives.* Chowder Chapbooks, 1979.
Pillin, William: *Dance Without Shoes.* Golden Quill Press, 1956.
—*Pavane For A Fading Memory.* Allan Swallow, 1963.
—*Everything Falling.* Kayak Books, 1971.
—*The Abandoned Music Room.* Kayak Books, 1975.
Pinsker, Sanford: *Still Life And Other Poems.* Greenfield Review Press, 1975.
Pitkin, Anne: *Notes For Continuing The Performance.* Jawbone Press, 1977.
Powers, Jessica: *The Lantern Burns.* Monastine Press, 1939.
—*The Place Of Splendor.* Cosmopolitan Science & Art Service, 1946.
—*The Little Alphabet.* Bruce Publishing Co., 1955.
—*Mountain Sparrow.* Carmel of Reno, 1972.
Privett, Katharine H.: *The Poet-People.* San Marcos Press, 1976.

Q

Quintana, Leroy V.: *Hijo del Pueblo: New Mexico Poems.* Puerto Del Sol Press, 1976.
—*Sangre.* Cenote Press, 1979.

R

Rabb, Lawrence: *Mysteries Of The Horizon.* Doubleday & Co., 1972.
—*The Collector Of Cold Weather.* Ecco Press, 1976.
Raffel, Burton: *Mia Poems.* October House, 1968.
—*Four Humors.* Seagull Publications, 1979.
Rakosi, Carl: *Amulet.* New Directions Publishing Corp., 1967.

—*Ere-Voice.* New Directions Publishing Corp., 1971.
—*Ex Cranium, Night.* Black Sparrow Press, 1975.
Rankin, Paula: *By The Wreckmaster's Cottage.* Carnegie-Mellon University Press, 1977.
Ratti, John: *A Remembered Darkness.* Viking Press, 1969.
—*Memorial Day.* Viking Press, 1974.
Ray, David: *X-Rays, A Book Of Poems.* Cornell University Press, 1965.
—*Dragging The Main And Other Poems.* Cornell University Press, 1968.
—*A Hill In Oklahoma.* BkMk Press, 1972.
—*Gathering Firewood: New And Selected Poems.* Wesleyan University Press, 1974.
—*Enough Of Flying: Poems Inspired By The Ghazals Of Ghalib.* Writers Workshop (India), 1977.
—*The Tramp's Cup.* Chariton Review Press, 1978.
Rector, Liam: *The Weather Gallery.* L'Epervier Press, 1980.
Redl-Hlus, Carolyn D.: *Earthbound.* Borealis Press, 1978.
Reeve, F. D.: *In The Silent Stones.* William Morrow & Co., 1968.
—*The Blue Cat.* Farrar, Straus & Giroux, 1972.
Reiter, Thomas: *River Route.* Cedar Creek Press, 1977.
—*The Zalenka Poems.* Juniper Press, 1981.
Richardson, James: *Reservations.* Princeton University Press, 1977.
Rinaldi, Nicholas: *The Resurrection Of The Snails.* John F. Blair, 1977.
Roberts, Sheila: *Lou's Life And Other Poems.* Bataleur Press (South Africa), 1977.
Rosenberger, Francis Coleman: *One Season Here.* University Press of Virginia, 1976.
—*An Alphabet.* University Press of Virginia, 1978.
Roskolenko, Harry: *Sequence On Violence.* Signal Press, 1938.
—*I Went Into The Country.* James A Decker, 1940.
—*A Second Summary.* National Press (Melbourne, Australia), 1944.
—*Notes From A Journey.* National Press (Melbourne, Australia), 1947.
—*Paris Poems.* Editions Euros (Paris, France), 1950.
—*American Civilization.* National Press (Melbourne, Australia), 1970.
—*Is.* National Press (Melbourne, Australia), 1971.
—*Was.* National Press (Melbourne, Australia), 1976.
—*Baguio Poems.* National Press (Melbourne, Australia), 1976.
—*A Third Summary.* Zone Press, 1979.
Rubin, Larry: *The World's Old Way.* University of Nebraska Press, 1963.
—*Lanced In Light.* Harcourt, Brace & World, 1967.
—*All My Mirrors Lie.* Godine Press, 1975.
Ruth, Fern Pankratz: *Once Summer Came.* Valley Printing Corp., 1968.
Rutsala, Vern: *Laments.* New Rivers Press, 1975.
—*The Journey Begins.* University of Georgia Press, 1976.
—*Paragraphs.* Wesleyan University Press, 1978.
Ryerson, Alice: *Excavation.* Kelsey Street Press, 1979.

S

St. John, David: *Hush*. Houghton Mifflin Co., 1976.
—*The Olive Grove*. W. D. Hoffstadt & Sons, 1979.
—*The Shore*. Houghton Mifflin Co., 1980.
Saner, Reg: *Climbing Into The Roots*. Harper & Row, 1976.
Santos, Sherod: *Elkin Pond*. Porch Publications, 1979.
Sargent, Robert: *Now Is Always The Miraculous Time*. Washington Writers' Publishing House, 1977.
—*A Woman From Memphis*. Word Works, 1979.
Sarton, May: *Plant Dreaming Deep*. W. W. Norton & Co., 1968.
—*Kinds Of Love*. W. W. Norton & Co., 1970.
—*Bridge Of Years*. W. W. Norton & Co., 1971.
—*Grain Of Mustard Seed*. W. W. Norton & Co., 1971.
—*Faithful Are The Wounds*. W. W. Norton & Co., 1972.
—*As We Are Now*. W. W. Norton & Co., 1973.
—*Collected Poems*. W. W. Norton & Co., 1974.
—*Crucial Conversations*. W. W. Norton & Co., 1975.
—*The Small Room*. W. W. Norton & Co., 1976.
—*A Walk Through The Woods*. Harper & Row, 1976.
—*A World of Light*. W. W. Norton & Co., 1976.
—*A Reckoning*. W. W. Norton & Co., 1978.
—*The Fur Person*. W. W. Norton & Co., 1979.
—*A Shower Of Summer Days*. W. W. Norton & Co., 1979.
Saul, George Brandon: *The Cup Of Sand*. Harold Vinal, 1923.
—*Bronze Woman*. Bruce Humphries, 1930.
—*Unimagined Rose*. Hawthorn House, 1937.
—*Only Necessity . . .* Privately printed, 1941.
—*Selected Lyrics*. Decker Press, 1947.
—*October Sheaf*. Prairie Press, 1951.
—*Hound And Unicorn: Collected Verse—Lyrical, Narrative And Dramatic*. Walton Press, 1969.
—*Candlelight Rhymes For Early-To-Beds*. Walton Press, 1970.
—*Postscript . . .* Walton Press, 1971.
—*Skeleton's Progress*. Walton Press, 1971.
—*A Touch Of Acid*. Walton Press, 1971.
—*The Stroke Of Light*. Golden Quill Press, 1974.
—*Adam Unregenerate: Selected Lyrical Poems*. Stemmer House Publishers (McCloud in Canada), 1977.
—*In Borrowed Light*. Parousia Press, 1979.
Scannell, Vernon: *Selected Poems*. Allison & Busby (England), 1971.
—*The Winter Man*. Allison & Busby (England), 1973.
—*The Loving Game*. Robson Books (England), 1975.
Schedler, Gilbert W.: *Waking Before Dawn*. Wampeter Press, 1978.
Schorb, E. M.: *The Poor Boy And Other Poems*. Dragon's Teeth Press, 1975.
Schwabsky, Barry: *The New Lessons*. Tamarisk Press, 1979.
Sears, Peter: *Bike Run*. Raindust Press, 1977.
—*I Want To Be A Crowd*. Breitenbush Publishing Co., 1978.

—*The Lady Who Got Me To Say Solong Mom*. Trask House, 1979.
Sellers, Bettie M.: *Westward From Bald Mountain*. Privately printed, 1974.
—*Spring Onions And Cornbread*. Pelican Publishing Co., 1978.
Shaw, Luci: *Listen To The Green*. Harold Shaw Publishers, 1971.
—*The Risk Of Birth*. Harold Shaw Publishers, 1974.
—*The Secret Trees*. Harold Shaw Publishers, 1976.
Shelton, Richard: *Journal Of Return*. Kayak Press, 1969.
—*The Tattooed Desert*. University of Pittsburgh Press, 1971.
—*Calendar*. Baleen Press, 1972.
—*The Heroes Of Our Time*. Best Cellar Press, 1972.
—*Of All The Dirty Words*. University of Pittsburgh Press, 1972.
—*Among The Stones*. Monument Press, 1973.
—*You Can't Have Everything*. University of Pittsburgh Press, 1975.
—*Chosen Place*. Best Cellar Press, 1975.
—*The Bus To Veracruz*. University of Pittsburgh Press, 1978.
Shepherd, J. Barrie: *Diary Of Daily Prayer*. Augsburg Publishing House, 1975.
Sher, Steven: *Nickelodeon*. Seagull Publications, 1978.
—*Persnickety*. Seven Woods Press, 1979.
Shire, Kent: *First Book Of Stars*. Graceland Printing, 1974.
—*Junior Explorer's Handbook Of Poems Of The Body*. Graceland Printing, 1975.
—*Second Book Of Stars*. Graceland Printing, 1975.
Shuttleworth, Paul: *Refractions*. Impact Press, 1978.
—*Poems To The Memory Of Benny Kid Paret*. Sparrow Press, 1978.
Sklarew, Myra: *In The Basket Of The Blind*. Cherry Valley Editions, 1975.
—*From The Backyard Of The Diaspora*. Dryad Press, 1976.
—*The Science Of Good-Byes*. Jewish Publication Soceity of America, 1980.
Slesinger, Warren: *Field With Figurations*. Cummington Press, 1970.
Smith, Dave: *The Fisherman's Whore*. Ohio University Press, 1974.
—*Cumberland Station*. University of Illinois Press, 1976.
—*Goshawk, Antelope*. University of Illinois Press, 1979.
Smith, R. T.: *Waking Under Snow*. Cold Mountain Review Press, 1975.
—*Good Water*. Banjo Press, 1979.
—*Rural Route*. Banjo Press, 1980.
Smith, Vivian: *Familiar Places*. Angus & Robertson (Australia), 1978.
Soto, Gary: *The Elements Of San Joaquin*. University of Pittsburgh Press, 1977.
—*The Tale Of Sunlight*. University of Pittsburgh Press, 1978.
Southwick, Marcia: *What The Trees Go Into*. Burning Deck Press, 1977.
—*Thaisa*. Singing Wind Publications, 1979.
—*The Leopard's Mouth Is Dry And Cold Inside*

(with Larry Levis). Singing Wind Publications, 1979.

Spacks, Barry: *The Company Of Children.* Doubleday & Co., 1968.
—*Something Human.* Harper's Magazine Press, 1972.
—*Teaching The Penguins How To Fly.* David R. Godine, 1975.
—*Imagining A Unicorn.* University of Georgia Press, 1978.

Speer, Laurel: *The Sitting Duck.* Ommation Press, 1978.
—*A Bit Of Wit.* Gusto Press, 1979.
—*Lovers And Others.* Truedog Press, 1980.
—*The Fire Inside.* Gusto Press, 1980.

Spivack, Kathleen: *Flying Inland.* Doubleday & Co., 1973.
—*The Jane Poems.* Doubleday & Co., 1974.

Stafford, William: *Braided Apart.* Confluence Press, 1976.
—*Stories That Could Be True: New And Collected Poems.* Harper & Row, 1977.
—*Smoke's Way.* Graywolf Press, 1978.

Stanford, Ann: *In Narrow Bound.* Alan Swallow, 1943.
—*The White Bird.* Alan Swallow, 1949.
—*Magellan: A Poem To Be Read By Several Voices.* Talisman Press, 1958.
—*The Weathercock.* Viking Press, 1966.
—*Climbing Up To Light: Eleven Poems.* Magpie Press, 1973.
—*In Mediterranean Air.* Viking Press, 1977.
—*The Descent: Poems.* Viking Press, 1977.

Stange, Ken: *Wolf Cycle.* Nebula Press, 1974.
—*Revenging Language.* Fiddlehead Poetry Books, 1976.
—*Love Is A Grave.* Nebula Press, 1978.
—*Portraits In The Mirror.* Nebula Press, 1978.
—*Nocturnal Rhythms.* Penumbra Press, 1979.
—*Bushed.* York Publishing, 1979.

Stanhope, Rosamund: *So I Looked Down To Camelot.* Scorpion Press (U.K.), 1962.

Stein, Dona: *Children Of The Mafiosi.* West End Press, 1977.

Stern, Gerald: *Rejoicings.* Fiddlehead Poetry Books, 1973.
—*Lucky Life.* Houghton Mifflin Co., 1977.

Stokesbury, Leon: *Often In Different Landscapes.* University of Texas Press, 1976.
—*The Drifting Away Of All We Once Held Essential.* Trilobite Press, 1979.

Stowman, Annette Burr: *Tiger Whiskers.* Privately printed, 1979.

Stripling, Kathryn: *Search Party.* Amicae Press, 1979.

Swaim, Alice Mackenzie: *Crickets Are Crying Autumn.* Pageant Press, 1960.
—*The Gentle Dragon.* Golden Quill Press, 1962.
—*Pennsylvania Profile.* Adams Press, 1966.
—*Beyond My Catnip Garden.* Golden Quill Press, 1970.

Sweeney, Matthew: *Without Shores.* Omens (England), 1978.
—*Empty Trains.* Oasis Books (England), 1978.

Swenson, Karen: *An Attic Of Ideals.* Doubleday & Co., 1974.

Swilky, Jody: *A City Of Fences.* La Huerta Press, 1977.

T

Tagliabue, John: *Poems.* Harper and Brothers, 1959.
—*A Japanese Journal.* Kayak Press, 1966.
—*The Buddha Uproar.* Kayak Press, 1970.
—*The Doorless Door.* Mushinsha/Grossman, 1970.

Taylor, William E.: *Man In The Wind.* Impetus Press, 1960.
—*Down Here With Aphrodite.* South & West, Inc., 1966.
—*Devoirs To Florida.* Olivant, 1968.
—*20 Against Apocalypse.* St. Johns River Press, 1979.

Thompson, Joanna: *Into Dark.* Heidelberg Graphics, 1978.

Tick, Edward: *The Dawn That Bleeds.* High/Coo Press, 1979.

Tietz, Stephen: *The Book Of Trolls And Dragons.* Privately printed, 1973.
—*Isothermal.* Silver-Tongued Devil Press, 1978.

Tolnay, Thomas: *The Magic Whorehouse.* Smith Publishers, 1979.

Turco, Lewis: *Awaken, Bells Falling: Poems 1959-1967.* University of Missouri Press, 1968.
—*The Inhabitant: Poems, With Prints By Thom. Seawell.* Despa Press, 1970.

Turner, Gordon P.: *Each Mouthful Of Forget.* Turnstone Press, 1979.

Tyack, Jim: *A Dozen Letters To Dan Murray In Which Michael McClure Appears.* Laughing Man Press, 1973.
—*The Rented Tuxedo.* Street Press, 1976.

U

Urdang, Constance: *Charades And Celebrations.* October House, 1965.
—*The Picnic In The Cemetery.* George Braziller, 1975.

V

Viereck, Peter: *The Persimmon Tree: New Lyrics & Pastorals.* Xerox University Microfilms, 1965 (reprint).
—*Terror & Decorum.* Greenwood Press, 1972 (reprint).
—*Strike Through The Mask: New Lyrical Poems.* Greenwood Press, 1972 (reprint).
—*The First Morning.* Greenwood Press, 1972 (reprint).
—*New & Selected Poems.* Xerox University Microfilms, 1979 (reprint).

Voigt, Ellen Bryant: *Claiming Kin.* Wesleyan University Press, 1976.

W

Wade, John Stevens: *Some Of My Best Friends Are Trees.* Sparrow Press, 1977.
—*Waterland (A Gathering From Holland).* Holm-gangers Press, 1977.
—*Homecoming.* Icarus Press, 1978.

Wagoner, David: *Collected Poems, 1956-1976.* Indiana University Press, 1976.
—*In Broken Country.* Atlantic/Little, Brown, 1979.

Waldrop, Keith: *A Windmill Near Calvary.* University of Michigan Press, 1968.
—*Poem From Memory.* Treacle Press, 1975.
—*The Garden Of Effort.* Burning Deck, 1975.
—*Windfall Losses.* Pourboire Press, 1977.

Walker, David: *Fathers.* Fragments Publications (New Zealand), 1975.
—*Moving Out.* University Press of Virginia, 1976.

Wallace, Jon: *Dreams & Wakings.* Darian Limited, 1980.

Waniek, Marilyn Nelson: *For The Body.* Louisiana State University Press, 1978.

Warren, Eugene: *Christographia 1-32.* Cauldron Press, 1977.
—*Fishing At Easter.* BkMk Press, 1980.

Warren, Robert Penn: *Eleven Poems On The Same Theme.* New Directions, 1942.
—*Promises: Poems 1954-1956.* Random House, 1957.
—*You, Emperors, And Others: Poems 1957-1960.* Random House, 1960.
—*Selected Poems, New And Old 1923-1966.* Random House, 1966.
—*Incarnations: Poems 1966-1968.* Random House, 1968.
—*Audubon, A Vision.* Random House, 1969.
—*Or Else: Poems 1968-1974.* Random House, 1974.
—*Selected Poems 1923-1975.* Random House, 1976.
—*Now And Then: Poems 1976-1978.* Random House, 1978.
—*Brother To Dragons.* Random House, 1979.
—*Life Is A Fable: Poetry 1978-1980.* Random House, 1980.

Weaver, Roger: *The Orange And Other Poems.* Press-22, 1978.

Weingarten, Roger: *What Are Birds Worth.* Cummington Press/Abattoir Editions, 1975.
—*Ethan Benjamin Boldt.* Alfred A. Knopf, 1975.
—*The Vermont Suicides.* Alfred A. Knopf, 1978.

Weiss, Theodore: *The Catch.* Twayne Poetry Series, 1951.
—*Outlanders.* Macmillan Co., 1960.
—*Gunsight.* New York University Press, 1962.
—*The Medium.* Macmillan Co., 1965.
—*The Last Days And The First.* Macmillan Co., 1968.
—*The World Before Us: Poems,1950-1970.* Macmillan Co., 1970.
—*Fireweeds.* Macmillan Co., 1976.
—*Views & Spectacles.* Chatto & Windus, 1978.
—*Views & Spectacles: New And Selected Shorter Poems.* Macmillan Co., 1979.

White, Gail: *Pandora's Box.* Samisdat Press, 1977.
—*Irreverent Parables.* Border-Mountain Press, 1978.

White, Mary Jane: *The Work Of The Icon Painter.* Osiers Press, 1979.

White, Patrick: *Poems.* Soft Press, 1974.
—*The God In The Rafters.* Borealis Press, 1978.
—*Stations.* Commoner's Books, 1978.

Whitman, Cedric M.: *Orpheus And the Moon Craters.* Middlebury College Press, 1941.
—*Abelard.* Harvard University Press, 1965.

Whitman, Ruth: *The Passion Of Lizzie Borden: New And Selected Poems.* October House, 1973.
—*Permanent Address.* Alice James Books, 1980.

Williams, Miller: *A Circle Of Stone.* Louisiana State University Press, 1964.
—*Recital.* Oceano De Chile, 1965.
—*So Long At The Fair.* E. P. Dutton & Co., Inc., 1968.
—*The Only World There Is.* E. P. Dutton & Co., Inc., 1971.
—*Halfway From Hoxie.* E. P. Dutton & Co., Inc., 1973; Louisiana State University Press, 1976.
—*Why God Permits Evil.* Louisiana State University Press, 1977.

Wilson, Robley, Jr.: *Returning To The Body.* Juniper Press, 1977.

Winters, Bayla: *Tropic Of Mother.* Olivant Press, 1969.
—*bitchpoems.* Olivant Press, 1971.

Witt, Harold: *Family In The Forest.* Porpoise Book Shop, 1956.
—*Superman Unbound.* New Orleans Poetry Journal, 1956.
—*The Death Of Venus.* Golden Quill Press, 1958.
—*Beasts In Clothes.* Macmillan Publishing Co., 1961.
—*Winesburg By The Sea: A Preview.* Hearse Press, 1970.
—*Pop. By 1940: 40,000.* Best Cellar Press, 1971.
—*Now, Swim.* Ashland Poetry Press, 1974.
—*Surprised By Others At Fort Cronkhite.* Sparrow/Vagrom Chap Books, 1975.
—*Winesburg By The Sea.* Thorp Springs Press, 1979.

Witt, Sandra: *Edith And Baby* (with Mark Rae, David Sessions). Freshwater Press, 1971.

Wolfert, Adrienne: *7 Day World.* South and West, Inc., 1962.
—*Natal Fire.* Branden Press, 1975.
—*Discovery Of A Human Fossil.* Lintel, 1979.

Wright, Carolyne: *Stealing The Children.* Ahsahta Press, 1978.

Wrigley, Robert: *The Sinking Of Clay City.* Copper Canyon Press, 1979.

XYZ

Young, Al: *Dancing.* Corinth Books, 1969.
—*The Song Turning Back Into Itself.* Holt, Rinehart & Winston, 1971.
—*Geography Of The Near Past.* Holt, Rinehart & Winston, 1976.

Young, Gary: *Hands.* Illuminati Press, 1979.

Zawadiwsky, Christine: *The World At Large.* Bieler Press, 1978.

Zimmer, Paul: *The Ribs Of Death.* October House, 1967.
—*The Republic Of Many Voices.* October House, 1969.

—*With Wanda: Town And Country Poems.* Dryad Press, 1980.
Zydek, Fredrick: *Lights Along The Missouri.* University of Nebraska Press, 1979.

PART TWO

Yearbook
of American Poetry

The Yearly Record

The following bibliography lists books of and about poetry that were published, copyrighted, officially announced, distributed or that otherwise appeared in the United States and Canada in the year ending October 31, 1979.

(1) COLLECTIONS OF POETRY BY INDIVIDUAL AUTHORS

Abbott, Stephen—*Stretching The Agapé Bra.* Androgyne

Ackerman, Diane—*Wife Of Light.* Morrow

Adamo, Ralph—*The End Of The World: Poems.* Lost Roads

Adoff, Arnold—*Eats: Poems.* Lothrop, Lee & Shepard
—*I Am The Running Girl: Poems.* Harper & Row

Aeschylus—*The Oresteia Of Aeschylus* (translated from Greek by Robert Lowell). Farrar, Straus & Giroux

Ahsen, Akhter—*Manhunt In The Desert: The Epic Dimensions Of Man: An Epic Poem.* Brandon House

Ai—*Killing Floor: Poems.* Houghton Mifflin

Akmajian, Hiag—*Snow Falling From A Bamboo Leaf* (translated from Japanese). Capra

Aldal-Fraide, Patricia Ann—*Reflections Of A Wandering Spirit.* Vantage

Aldan, Daisy—*Between High Tides.* Folder

Aleixandre, Vicente—*A Longing For The Light: Selected Poems Of Vicente Aleixandre* (edited by Lewis Hyde). Harper & Row

Allen, James C. (see listing for Davis, Patricia A.)

Allen, Robert—*The Assumption Of Private Lives.* New Delta

Alonso, Ricardo—*Cimarron.* Wesleyan University

Amichai, Yehuda—*Time.* Harper & Row

Amprimoz, Alexandre—*Selected Poems.* Hounslow

Anania, Michael—*Riversongs.* University of Illinois

Andersdatter, Karla Margaret—*I Don't Know Whether To Laugh Or Cry, 'Cause I Lost The Map To Where I Was Going: Poems.* Second Coming

Anderson, Emily F.—*Lightning's Prophecy.* Privately printed

Anderson, Nat—*My Hand My Only Map.* House of Keys

Andrade, Mario Ildo—*From Deep Within Me.* Dorrance

Anthony, George—*The Road To Deadman Cove: Selected Poems.* Open Places

Applewhite, James—*Following Gravity.* University of Virginia

Aristophanes—*The Knights; Peace; The Birds; The Assemblywomen; Wealth* (translated from Greek by David Barrett, Alan H. Sommerstein). Penguin

Armantrout, Rae—*The Invention Of Hunger.* Tuumba

Asch, Frank—*Country Pie: Poems.* Greenwillow

Ashman, Russell Smith—*Chocoloetry One.* Privately printed

Attia, Zizo—*A Flower Veils The Sun.* Exposition

Atwood, Ann—*Fly With The Wind, Flow With The Water.* Scribner

Auden, W. H.—*Selected Poems* (edited by Edward Mandelson). Vintage

B

Baca, Jimmy Santiago—*Immigrants In Our Own Land: Poems.* Louisiana State University

Bahadur, K. P.—*One Hundred Rural Songs Of India.* Banarsidass

Baker, Houston A., Jr.—*No Matter Where You Travel, You Still Be Black: Poems.* Lotus

Balazs, Mary—*The Stones Refuse Their Peace.* Seven Woods

Ballowe, James—*The Coal Miners.* Spoon River

Baranczak, Stanislaw—*Where Did I Wake Up? The Poetry Of Stanislaw Baranczak* (translated by Frank Kujawinski). Mr. Cogito

Barber, Bob Henry; Webb, Jim—*Mucked.* Hesperus

Baring, Maurice—*The Collected Poems Of Maurice Baring.* AMS (reprint)

Barker, George—*Villa Stellar.* Faber & Faber

Barrett, Eaton Stannard—*All The Talents: The Second Titan War, Or, The Talents Buried Under Portland-Isle; The Talents Run Mad.* Garland (reprint)

Bastian, W. James—*Poetry Of The Young Soldier In World War II.* Dorrance

Beasley, Conger, Jr.—*Over DeSoto's Bones* (edited by Orvis C. Burmaster). Ahsahta

Beining, Guy—*The Ogden Diary.* Zahir

Bellamy, Joe David—*Olympic Gold Medalist.* North American Review

Bely, Andrey—*The First Encounter* (translated from Russian by Gerald Janecek). Princeton University

Berg, Sharon—*To A Young Horse.* Borealis

Berger, Suzanne E.—*These Rooms.* Penmaen

Bernstein, Charles—*Senses Of Responsibility.* Tuumba

Berssenbrugge, Mei-mei—*Random Possessions.* Reed

Bhartrihari; Bilhana—*The Hermit And The Love*

Thief: Sanskrit Poems Of Bhartrihari And Bilhana (translated from sanskrit by Barbara Stoler Miller). Columbia University

Bilhana (see listing for Bhartrihari)

Black, Charles—*Owls Bay In Babylon.* Dustbooks

Bliss, Helen Easton—*Something To Sing About, Something Called Love.* Dorrance

Blotnick, Elihu; Robinson, Barbara—*Mysterious Mr. Blot: In Which We Discover Him.* California Street

Bludau, Lea Viola—*Mosaics From Memories.* Exposition

Bly, Robert—*This Tree Will Be Here For A Thousand Years: Poems.* Harper & Row

Bolle, Kees W. (translator)—*The Bhagavadgita: A New Translation.* University of California

Borenstein, Emily—*Cancer Queen.* Barlenmir House

Bradley, Ardyth—*Inside The Bones Is Flesh.* Ithaca House

Bragg, Miriam Cynthia—*The Incredible Miles.* Exposition

Brand, Shirley—*Remembering You.* Pisces

Brennan, Pegeen—*Release.* Fiddlehead

Brett, Peter—*Borrowing The Sky: 22 Poems.* Kastle

Britton, James S.—*Down The Lonely Road.* Vantage

Brock, Van K.—*Spelunking.* New College
—*Weighing The Penalties.* Burnt Hickory

Brock, Van K.—*Spelunking.* New College—*Weighing The Penalties.* Burnt Hickory

Brodsky, Louis Daniel—*Resume Of A Scapegoat.* Farmington

Bronk, William—*The Force Of Desire.* Elizabeth

Bronte, Charlotte; Bronte, Emily—*Poems By The Bronte Sisters.* Rowman and Littlefield

Bronte, Emily (see listing for Bronte, Charlotte)

Broughton, T. Alan—*The Others We Are.* Northeast/ Juniper
—*Far From Home.* Carnegie-Mellon University

Browne, Joe—*The Ballad Of Newburyport.* Mitchell Price

Browning, Elizabeth Barrett—*Aurora Leigh.* Academy Chicago (reprint)

Bruchac, Joseph—*The Good Message Of Handsome Lake.* Unicorn

Brutus, Dennis—*Stubborn Hope: New Poems, And Selections From China Poems And Strains.* Three Continents

Buckley, Christopher—*Pentimento.* Bieler

Buell, Frederick—*Full Summer.* Wesleyan University

Burns, Robert A.—*Ben Neptune.* Fiddlehead

Burns, Thomas Laborie—*Breaking And Entering.* Privately printed

Bursk, Christopher—*Standing Watch.* Houghton Mifflin

Bush, Barney—*My Horse And A Jukebox.* American Indian Studies Center, UCLA

Byrne, Vincent—*Miracles & Other Poems.* Devin-Adair

C

Caldwell, Justin—*The Sleeping Porch: Poems.* Lost Roads

Caldwell, Ronald C.—*Softly We Lay.* Vantage

Calkin, Ruth Harms—*Lord, I Keep Running Back To You.* Tyndale House

Campbell, John—*Echoes Of My Days.* Sothis

Canan, Janine—*The Hunger.* Oyez

Carroll, Mitchell B.—*A Ring Of Jingles.* Exposition

Carroll, Paul—*New And Selected Poems.* Yellow

Carter, Jared—*Early Warning.* Barnwood

Carter, John Marshall—*A Leap Of Reason.* Henricks
—*Measured Out With Coffee Spoons.* Henricks
—*Flea Flickers.* Leaksville
—*Wampus Cats And Dan River Rimes.* Leaksville

Caswell, Donald—*Watching The Sun Go Down.* Anhinga

Catalano, Gary—*Remembering The Rural Life.* University of Queensland

Catanoy, Nicholas—*The Fiddlehead Republic.* Hounslow

Catullus—*The Poems Of Catullus* (translated from Latin by Frederic Raphael, Kenneth McLeish). Godine

Cavafy, Constantine—*Poems By Constantine Cavafy* (translated by George Khairallah). Privately printed

Ceravolo, Joseph—*Transmigration Solo.* Toothpaste

Chalek, William Dmitri—*Poems, 1968-1978.* Chalek

Chandler, Christine—*Revelations In The Night.* Link

Chandler, Mark K.—*Speaking Of Birds And The River.* Dorrance

Chapin, Henry—*The Constant God.* Bauhan
—*A Celebration.* Bauhan

Chappell, Fred—*Bloodfire.* Louisiana State University
—*Wind Mountain: A Poem.* Louisiana State University

Cheesebro, R. Alan—*Thy And Thee: 100 Meditations, 1975.* Justus

Chenier, Andre—*Andre Chenier, Elegies And Camille* (translated by L. R. Lind). University Press of America

Child, Robin—*Life on A Limb.* Killaly

Chivers, Thomas Holley—*The Path Of Sorrow.* Scholars' Facsimiles

Chriest, Alan J.—*Empty Pieces.* Privately printed

Ciardi, John—*For Instance.* Norton

Clark, Tom—*When Things Get Tough On Easy Street.* Black Sparrow

Coblentz, Stanton Arthur—*Sea Cliffs And Green Ridges: Poems Of The West.* Naturegraph

Cochrane, Shirley—*Burnsite.* Washington Writers

Colby, Joan—*Blue Woman Dancing In The Nerve.* Alembic

Coleman, Lucile—*December Twenty-Fifth.* Edwards

Coleman, Mary Ann—*Disappearances.* Anhinga

Coleman, Wanda—*Mad Dog Black Lady.* Black Sparrow

Coles, Don—*Anniversaries.* Macmillan of Canada

Colligan, Elsa—*The Aerialist.* Barlenmir House

Colquitt, Betsy Feagan—*The Lie And Truth Of The Land.* Thorp Springs

Congdon, Kirby—*Animals.* Kastle

Connors, John—*Caliban.* Vantage

Constandinidou, Loula D.—*The Anthologized Poetry Of Loula D. Constandinidou* (edited by Maria P. Hogan). Exposition

Cooley, Peter—*The Room Where Summer Ends.* Carnegie-Mellon University

Coolidge, Clark—*Own Face.* Angel Hair

Corman, Cid—*Auspices*. Pentagram

Cottle, Joseph—*Alfred, An Epic Poem*. Garland (reprint)

Couzyn, Jeni—*House Of Changes*. Douglas & McIntyre

Cowper, William—*The Unpublished And Uncollected Poems Of William Cowper* (edited by Thomas Wright). Folcroft (reprint)

Cox, Carol—*Woodworking And Places Near By: Poems*. Hanging Loose

Coxe, Louis—*Passage: Selected Poems, 1943-1978*. University of Missouri

Crabbe, George—*Poems* (edited by Adolphus William Ward). AMS (reprint)

Crawford, Emily—*Annals Of A Search For Truth In The Twentieth Century*. Vantage

Crews, Judson—*Never Will Dan Cause No One To*. Holy Terrible

—*Nolo Contendere: New Poems* (edited by J. Whitebird). Wings

Crosbie, John S.—*Crosbie's Book Of Punned Haiku*. Workman

Crow, Mary—*Going Home*. Lynx

Cuadra, Pablo Antonio—*Songs Of Cifar And The Sweet Sea: Selection From The "Songs Of Cifar," 1967-1977* (translated and edited by Grace Schulman, Ann McCarthy de Zavala). Columbia University

Cummings, Edward Estlin—*W*. Liveright

Cunningham, Ralph—*Lovesongs And Others*. Fiddlehead

Curry, David—*Contending To Be The Dream*. New Rivers

Curtis, Walt—*Peckerneck Country*. Mr. Cogito

D

Dacey, Philip—*The Condom Poems*. Ox Head

Dacre, Charlotte—*Hours Of Solitude*. Garland (reprint)

Dalton, Dorothy—*The Moon Rides Witness*. Wolfsong

Dante Alighieri—*Dante's "Rime"* (translated from Italian by Patrick Diehl). Princeton University

Darwin, Erasmus—*The Golden Age; The Temple Of Nature: Or The Origin Of Society*. Garland (reprint)

—*The Botanic Garden*. Garland (reprint)

Davenport, Mariana B.—*The Gift Already Given*. Golden Quill

Davis, Glover—*August Fires*. Abattoir

Davis, Patricia A.; Allen, James C.—*Special Poems*. Privately printed

Dayton, Irene—*In Oxbow Of Time's River*. Windy Row

DeLain, Gene J.—*Words Of A Feather*. Vantage

DelosAnhelis, Ziporah—*On The Eve Of God's 40th Yes*. Karmic

Dennis, Carl—*Signs And Wonders*. Princeton University

Der Hovanessian, Diana—*How To Choose Your Past*. Ararat

DeSanti, Leslie R.—*Am I Too Late?* Dorrance

Dessi, Gigi—*Pressures* (translated by Mario Fratti). Hunter College/Italian Series

Dey, Richard Morris—*The Bequia Poems*. Offshore

Di Cicco, Pier Giorgio—*The Tough Romance*. McClelland and Stewart

Dickey, R. P.—*The Poetic Erotica Of R. P. Dickey*. Phainopepla

Dickson, John—*Victoria Hotel*. Chicago Review

Dlugos, Tim—*Je Suis Ein Americano*. Little Caesar

Dobbs, Charlotte M. (see listing for Salo, Sonja)

Donald, Priscilla—*I Dream Poems*. Vantage

Donicht, Mark—*Seeds To The Wind: Poems, Songs, Meditations*. Whatever

Donnelly, Dorothy—*Kudzu And Other Poems*. Pourboire

Dorko, Dennis A.—*New Dreams To Dream—Here's To Life*. Vantage

Dorn, Edward—*Selected Poems* (edited by Donald Allen). Grey Fox

Dorset, Sixth Earl of (see Sackville, Charles)

Doty, M. R.—*An Alphabet*. Alembic

Dow, Philip—*Paying Back The Sea*. Carnegie-Mellon University

Driscoll, Jack—*The Language Of Bone*. Spring Valley

Duberstein, Helen—*Arrived Safely*. Four Corners

Dubie, Norman—*The City Of Olesha Fruit*. Doubleday

Ducasse, Isidore Lucien—*Maldoror; And Poems* (translated from French by Paul Knight). Penguin

Dudley, Elwood—*This Trivial Harp*. Exposition

Duerden, Richard—*The Air's Nearly Perfect Elasticity*. Tombouctou

Dunn, Douglas—*Barbarians*. Faber & Faber

Dunn, Stephen—*A Circus Of Needs*. Carnegie-Mellon University

Dunster, Mark—*Fasces, Bazaars, Ariosos: 3 Bks Of Poems*. Linden

Dyak, Miriam—*Dying*. New Victoria

Dybek, Stuart—*Brass Knuckles*. University of Pittsburgh

Dyer, Homer L., III—*The Life And Dreams Of You And Me*. Exposition

E

Eberhart, Richard—*Survivors*. Boa

Eddy, Gary—*Borrowing My House From Insects*. Service-berry

Ediger, Max—*A Vietnamese Pilgrimage*. Faith and Life

Edmonds, Willa—*Realistic Reflections In Poetry*. Vantage

Einbond, Bernard Lionel—*The Coming Indoors, And Other Poems*. Tuttle

Elliott, Ebenezer—*The Village Patriarch: Corn Law Rhymes*. Garland (reprint)

Elman, Richard—*Homage To Fats Navarro*. New Rivers

Emanuel, Lynn—*Oblique Light*. Slow Loris

Engdahl, Lee—*Eugene Poems*. Privately printed

Estavan, Lawrence—*How Quaint The Saint*. Creekside

Etter, David—*Alliance, Illinois*. Kylix

—*Central Standard Time*. BkMk

Ewart, Gavin—*All My Little Ones*. Anvil

F

Fagles, Robert—*I, Vincent.* Princeton University

Falco, Edward—*Evocations.* sunrisefalldown artpress

Farallon, Cerise—*The Difference Between.* Vaginal Vegtetun

Farber, Norma—*Never Say Ugh! To A Bug.* Greenwillow
  —*Something Further.* Kylix
  —*Small Wonders: Poems.* Coward, McCann & Geoghegan

Feldman, Alan—*The Happy Genius.* Sun

Feldman, Irving—*New And Selected Poems.* Penguin

Fiebeg, Susan Lynn—*With Every Falling Star.* Vantage

Field, Eugene—*Lullabyland: Songs Of Childhood* (selected by Kenneth Grahame). Shambhala
  —*A Little Book Of Western Verse.* Core Collection (reprint)

Fifer, Ken—*Falling Man.* Ithaca House

Finch, Anne (see listing for Winchilsea, Anne)

Finkel, Donald—*Going Under And Endurance: An Antarctic Idyll.* Atheneum

Finley, C. Stephen—*From Kaspar's Journal.* Alderman

Fisher, T.M.—*ImAges.* Ghost Dance

Flanagan, Robert—*Once You Learn You Never Forget.* Fiddlehead

Flanner, Hildegarde—*The Hearkening Eye.* Ahsahta

Fleming, Geranna—*Starting With Coquille: Poems.* Prescott Street

Flint, Roland—*Say It.* Dryad
  —*And Morning.* Dryad

Florence, Gordon L.—*The Story Of A Song.* Prairie Poet

Follain, Jean—*A World Rich In Anniversaries* (translated by Mary Feeney, William Matthews). Grilled Flowers

Ford, R. A. D.—*Holes In Space.* Hounslow

Foster, Peggy L. (see listing for Spirling, James W.)

Fox, Siv Cedering—*The Blue Horse And Other Night Poems.* Seabury

Fraser, Kathleen—*New Shoes.* Harper & Row

Fratti, Mario—*New Faces.* Hunter College/Italian Series

Friebert, Stuart—*Uncertain Health.* Woolmer & Brotherson

Fried, Elliot—*Strip Tease.* Applezabba

Friedlander, Ginny—*The Last Thousand Years.* Charles Street

Froehlich, John F.—*A Cornocopia Of Thought.* Golden Quill

Frumkin, Gene—*Loops.* San Marcos

Funge, Robert—*The Lie The Lamb Knows.* Spoon River

G

Gallagher, Raymond R.—*The Ballad Of Mich-o-tta-wa.* Dorrance

Gallagher, Tess—*Under Stars.* Graywolf

Garcia Lorca, Federico—*Lament For The Death Of A Bullfighter, And Other Poems In The Original Spanish* (translated from Spanish by A. L. Lloyd). AMS (reprint)
  —*Poems Of Federico Garcia Lorca* (chosen and translated from Spanish by Paul Blackburn). Momo's

Gerber, Dan—*The Chinese Poems: Letters To A Distant Friend.* Sumac

Gershenson, Bernard—*The Neighborhood.* Taurean Horn

Gervais, C. H.—*The Believable Body.* Fiddlehead

Ghigna, Charles—*Divers And Other Poems.* Creekwood

Ghiselin, Brewster—*Light.* Abattoir

Gibbons, Reginald—*Roofs, Voices, Roads.* Quarterly Review of Literature

Gibson, Margaret—*Signs.* Louisiana State University

Gilbert, Kevin—*People Are Legends: Aboriginal Poems.* University of Queensland

Gilbert, Sandra M.—*In The Fourth World: Poems.* University of Alabama

Gilchrist, Ellen—*The Land Surveyor's Daughter.* Lost Roads

Gillespie, Robert—*The Man Chain.* Ithaca House

Gioseffi, Dariela—*Eggs In The Lake.* Boa

Gitin, David—*This Once: New & Selected Poems, 1965-1978.* Blue Wind

Glass, Malcolm—*Bone Love.* University of Florida

Glover, T. R.—*Poets And Puritans.* Folcroft (reprint)

Gold, Doris B.—*Honey In The Lion: Collected Poems.* Biblio

Goldsmith, Oliver—*The Poems Of Oliver Goldsmith.* Scholarly

Goldstein, Laurence—*Altamira.* Abattoir

Gonzalez, David J.—*A Journey To The Third World.* Indigena

Gordon, Jaimy—*The Bend, The Lip, The Kid.* Sun

Gotro, Paul—*Spider In The Sumac.* Fiddlehead

Gould, Robert—*Dream Yourself Flying.* Four Zoas

Grapes, Jack—*Breaking On Camera.* Bombshelter

Gray, May—*In His Hands.* Golden Quill

Greasybear, Charley John—*Songs* (edited by Judson Crews, A. Thomas Trusky). Ahsahta

Greene, Jonathan—*Once A Kingdom Again.* Sand Dollar

Gresseth, G. K.—*A Few Presentation Pieces.* Privately printed

Grieg, Nordahl—*Around The Cape Of Good Hope* (translated by Lars Egede-Niessen). Nordic

Griffis, Clarence Edwin—*As We Live And Learn.* Vantage

Groh, Douglas L.—*I'll Smile Again.* Vantage

Grossman, Allen R.—*The Woman On The Bridge Over The Chicago River: A Book Of Poems.* New Directions

Grossman, Martin—*Above The Thorn.* BkMk

Grue, Lee Meitzen—*French Quarter Poems.* Long Measure

Guillen, Jorge—*Guillen On Guillen: The Poetry And The Poet* (translated from Spanish by Reginald Gibbons, Anthony L. Geist). Princeton University

Gullberg, Hjalmar—*Gentleman, Single, Refined, And Selected Poems, 1937-1959: Poems* (translated from Swedish by Judith Moffett). Louisiana State University

Gunn, Thom—*Selected Poems, 1950-1975.* Farrar, Straus & Giroux

Gupta, Sushil K.—*Song Of Life.* Sverge-Haus

Gustafson, Richard C.—*The Arc From Now.* Iowa State University

H

Hackett, Sabrina—*Shield Me From The Wind.* Vantage

Hadas, Pamela White—*Designing Women.* Knopf

Haddox, Fred Lee—*Mixed Blood, Mixed Emotions.* Vantage

Hall, C. Margaret—*Pearls.* Antietam

Hall, Rodney—*Black Bagatelles.* University of Queensland

Halley, Anne—*The Bearded Mother.* University of Massachusetts

Hamalian, Leo—*Burn After Reading.* Ararat

Hamill, Sam—*Sam Hamill's Triada.* Copper Canyon

Hammond, Karla M.—*Calendar Wisdom.* Thunder City

Han Yu—*Growing Old Alive: Poems* (versions by Kenneth O. Hanson). Copper Canyon

Hanna, Suhail—*Albino Cockroaches.* Woodhix

Hannah-Kendall, Linda—*Nonsense.* M.E.M.

Hanson, Jim—*Reasons For The Sky.* Toothpaste

Harding, Larry—*Genesis Of Love.* Vantage

Harper, Tom—*From The Fog To Apocalypse Street.* Privately printed

Hart, Edward L.—*To Utah.* Brigham Young University

Harteis, Richard—*Fourteen Women.* Three Rivers

Hartman, Geoffrey H.—*Akiba's Children.* Iron Mountain

Hartman, Susan—*Dumb Snow.* University of Florida

Hartnett, Michael—*Poems In English.* Dolmen

Hasansky, Mel—*Limits.* Privately printed

Hass, Robert—*Praise.* Ecco

Hathaway, Baxter—*The Petulant Children.* Ithaca House

Haydu, George—*After The Years.* Waver's Edge

Hayes, Diana—*Moving Inland: Poems 1977-1978.* Fiddlehead

Hayley, William—*The Eulogies Of Howard; Ballads Founded On Anecdotes Relating To Animals; Poems On Serious And Sacred Subjects.* Garland (reprint)

—*An Essay On Sculpture.* Garland (reprint)

Hays, H. R.—*Portraits In Mixed Media.* Survivors' Manual

Hazley, Richard—*A Hive For Bees.* Three Rivers

Head, Gwen—*The Ten Thousandth Night.* University of Pittsburgh

Heaney, Seamus—*Field Work.* Farrar, Straus & Giroux

Hearst, James—*Landmark.* Ji-Fi Print

—*Snake In The Strawberries.* Iowa State University

Heath-Stubbs, John—*The Watchman's Flute.* Carcanet

Heffernan, Michael—*The Cry Of Oliver Hardy.* University of Georgia

Hemphill, Betty—*Third Testament Women: Poems.* Lydian

Henley, Patricia—*Learning To Die.* Three Rivers

Henry, Nathan Lee—*Painting Pictures Of Life With Words.* Vantage

Herring, James W.—*Selected Poems* (edited by James B. Herring). Vantage

Herschel, John—*The Floating World.* New Rivers

Herzele, Margarethe—*Carinthian Love Songs: Poems And Illustrations* (translated from German by Herbert Kuhner). Cross-Cultural Communications

Hesse, Herman—*Hours In The Garden And Other Poems* (translated from German by Rika Lesser). Farrar, Straus & Giroux

Heyen, William—*William Heyen In Print.* Rook

—*Long Island Light: Poems And A Memoir.* Vanguard

Hicks, Linan—*A Rhyme Or Two For Me and You.* Vantage

Hikmet, Nazim—*The Epic Of Sheik Bedreddin* (translated by Randy Blasing, Mutlu Konuk). Persea

—*Things I Didn't Know I Loved* (translated by Randy Blasing, Mutlu Konuk). Persea

Hill, Geoffrey—*Tenebrae.* Houghton Mifflin

Hillert, Margaret—*I'm Special... So Are You!* Hallmark

Hoey, Allen—*Cedar Light.* Street

—*Naked As My Bones In Transit.* Tamarack

Hoffman, Barbara—*Cliffs Of Fall.* Scranton College

Hoffman, George Edward—*This World Is Mine.* Ariel

Hogston, Perry—*Prelude To A Destiny.* Privately printed

Hollander, John—*Blue Wine And Other Poems.* Johns Hopkins University

—*In Place.* Abattoir

Hollis, Jocelyn—*Bridal Song: The Story Of A Woman's Love.* American Poetry Press

—*Vietnam Poems: The War Poems Of Today.* American Poetry Press

—*Contemporary Religious Poems For The Modern College Student.* American Poetry Press

—*Paradise Lost: A Modern Sequel.* American Poetry Press

—*Sex Songs.* American Poetry Press

Holloway, Geoffrey—*All I Can Say.* Anvil

Hong, Sara Klutz—*The Barking Mouse.* Dorrance

Hongo, Garrett Kaoru—*The Buddha Bandits Down Highway 99: Poetry* (with Alan Chong Lau, Lawson Fusao Inada). Buddhahead

Honig, Edwin—*Selected Poems: 1955-1976.* Texas Center for Writers

Howard, Ben—*Father Of Waters: Poems 1965-1976.* Abattoir

Howard, Richard—*Misgivings: Poems.* Atheneum

Howink, Eda—*I Am Just There.* Golden Quill

Huddle, David—*Paper Boy.* University of Pittsburgh

Hueter, Diane—*Kansas: Just Before Sleep.* Cottonwood Review

Huff, Robert—*The Ventriloquist: New And Selected Poems.* University of Virginia

Hugo, Richard—*Selected Poems.* Norton

I

Ignatow, David—*Sunlight: A Sequence For My Daughter.* Boa

Inada, Lawson Fusao (see listing for Hongo, Garrett Kaoru)

Ish, David; Meeker, Lloyd—*The End Of Sorrow.* Word

Itani, Frances—*No Other Lodgings.* Fiddlehead

J

Jackson, Haywood—*An Act Of God.* Samisdat

Jarman, Mark—*North Sea.* Cleveland State University Poetry Center

Jayne, Marian—*Encounters.* Literati

Jeffers, Lance—*Grandsire: Poems.* Lotus

Jenkins, Paul—*Forget The Sky.* L'Epervier

John Paul II (Karol Wojtyla)—*Easter Vigil And Other Poems* (translated from Polish by Jerzy Peterkiewicz). Random House

Johnson, Bobby J.—*Poems From The Asylum.* Dorrance

Johnson, Halvard—*Winter Journey.* New Rivers

Johnson, Howard A. A.—*Windows Of The Mind.* Exposition

Johnson, Kenneth E.—*A Wave Motion.* Privately printed

Johnson, Lionel—*Poetical Works Of Lionel Johnson.* AMS (reprint)

Johnson, Thomas—*The Collapse Of Astronomy: Poems.* Illuminati

Johnston, Martin—*The Sea-Cucumber.* University of Queensland

Jones, John Paul—*Plain Of Dura And Other Poems.* Christopher Publishing House

Jong, Erica—*At The Edge Of The Body.* Holt, Rinehart & Winston

Joselow, Beth—*Gypsies.* Washington Writers

Joyce, James—*Chamber Music, Pomes Penyeach & Occasional Verse: A Facsimile Of Manuscripts, Typescripts & Proofs* (arranged by A. Walton Litz). Garland

Jumper, Will C.—*From Time Remembered.* Foothills

K

Kammeyer, Virginia Maughan—*More Saints Alive!* Far West

Karl, John C.—*Scramblings.* Exposition

Karman, Rita—*Dreams Beyond The Planet Fish.* Karmic

Kaufman, Shirley—*From One Life To Another.* University of Pittsburgh

Kelly, David M.—*Filming Assassinations.* Ithaca House

Kelly, Doris—*Love Lust.* Vantage

Kelly, Robert—*The Book Of Persephone.* Treacle

Kemmet, William—*Riverbank Moss.* Stone Soup

Kemmett, Bill—*The Presence.* White Raven

Kempf, Elizabeth—*Before The Harvest.* Christopher's Books

Kennedy, Richard—*Delta Baby & 2 Sea Songs.* Addison-Wesley

Kennedy, Terry—*Durango.* Smith

Kennedy, X. J.—*The Phantom Ice Cream Man: More Nonsense Verse.* Atheneum

Kenyon, Jane—*From Room To Room.* Alicejames

Keyan, Rostam—*Poetics.* Philosophical Library

Khairallah, George—*Academe: Poems And Epigrams.* Privately printed
—*The Making Of Americans.* Privately printed

Kherdian, David—*The Farm.* Two Rivers

Kiemel, Ann—*I'm Celebrating.* Revell

Kimball, Don—*Driftwood Prayers, Passions And Permissions Promises.* Doubleday

King, Florence Sinclair Arnold—*Random Verse.* Vantage

King, Martha—*Weather.* New Rivers

King, Robert—*Standing Around Outside.* Bloodroot

Kipling, Rudyard—*The Seven Seas.* Longwood (reprint)

Kirby, David—*The Opera Lover.* Anhinga

Kitchen, B. F.—*Garden Motets.* Wind River

Klassen, Jean-Marie—*L'Etoile* (translated from French by Brenda Fleet). Fiddlehead

Klyde—*I Paint With Words . . . Hope You Like My Pictures.* Exposition

Knox, Hugh—*The Queen Of Snakes.* Abattoir

Koch, Kenneth—*The Burning Mystery Of Anna In 1951.* Random House

Kostynuik, Doreen—*Songs Of The Desert.* Vantage

Krauss, Ruth—*Somebody Spilled The Sky.* Greenwillow

Kruscoe, James—*History Of The World.* Bombshelter

Kubach, David—*First Things: Poems.* Holmgangers

Kunitz, Stanley—*The Poems Of Stanley Kunitz; 1928-1978.* Atlantic/Little, Brown

Kuzma, Greg—*Adirondacks.* Bear Claw

L

Lane, Pinkie Gordon—*The Mystic Female.* South and West

Langland, William—*Piers Plowman* (edition of the C-text by Derek Pearsall). University of California

Lansdale, Bruce M.—*Metamorphosis: Or, Why I Love Greece.* Caratzas Bros.

Lapaglia, Janelle Carman—*Sweet Sounds Of Life.* Exposition

Latta, John—*Rubbing Torsos.* Ithaca House

Lau, Alan Chong (see listing for Hongo, Garrett Kaoru)

Lauterbach, Ann—*Many Times, But Then.* University of Texas

Lavin, S. R.—*Let Myself Shine.* Kulchur Foundation

Lawson, Helen—*Women As I Know Them.* Blue Spruce

Lawson, Patrick J.—*Contemporary Thoughts For The Consciously Aware.* Dorrance

Lazard, Naomi—*The Moonlit Upper Deckerina.* Sheep Meadow

Lazaris, Barbara Gunner—*Ankle-Deep In Skyline.* Vantage

Lear, Edward—*The Owl & The Pussycat & Other Nonsense.* Viking
—*The Courtship Of The Yonghy-Bonghy-Bo, And The New Vestments.* Viking

Leax, John—*Reaching Into Silence.* Shaw

Le Dressay, Anne—*This Body That I Live In.* Turnstone

Lee, Laura—*Fireside Poems.* Vantage

Lehman, David—*Day One.* Nobodaddy

L'Engle, Madeleine—*The Weather Of The Heart: Poems.* Shaw

Lenson, David—*Ride The Shadow.* L'Epervier

Levertov, Denise—*Collected Earlier Poems:*

1940-1960. New Directions
—Life In The Forest. New Directions
—Denise Levertov, In Her Own Province (edited by Linda Welshimer Wagner). New Directions
Levi, Peter—*Five Ages.* Anvil
Levin, Steve—*Folly & Wisdom: Love Poems.* APKL
Levine, Philip—*Ashes: Poems New and Old.* Atheneum
—7 Years From Somewhere. Atheneum
Levis, Larry (see Listing for Southwick, Marcia)
Lewandowski, Stephen—*Inside & Out.* Crossing
Lewicki, Krys Val—*Verdigris.* Vantage
Lewis, Clive Staples—*Narrative Poems* (edited by Walter Hooper). Harcourt Brace Jovanovich
Lewis, Janet—*The Ancient Ones.* No Dead Lines
Libbey, Elizabeth—*The Crowd Inside.* Carnegie-Mellon University
Lietz, Robert—*Running In Place.* L'Epervier
Lignell, Kathleen—*The Calamity Jane Poems.* Rosebud
Lindskoog, Kathryn—*The Gift of Dreams.* Harper & Row
Link, William R.—*A Fatherless Country.* Bauhan
Little, Vera—*Tears In My Eyes.* Vantage
Littledale, Freya—*I Was Thinking: Poems.* Greenwillow
Livingston, Jay C.—*Poetics, Prosody & Passion.* Metatron
Livingston, Myra Cohn—*O Sliver Of Liver And Other Poems.* Atheneum
London, Jonathan—*In A Season Of Birds: Poems For Maureen.* Mudborn
Longfellow, Henry Wadsworth—*Paul Revere's Ride.* Dandelion
Lowe, Jonathan F.—*Practical Insanity.* Triton
Lowery, Mike—*Masks Of The Dreamer: Poems.* Wesleyan University
Luttinger, Abigail—*Good Evening And Other Poems.* Penumbra
Lux, Thomas—*Sunday: Poems.* Houghton Mifflin

M

MacDonald, Cynthia—*Transplants.* Braziller
Mace, Charles D., Jr. —*The Spirit Of America.* Vantage
Machado, Antonio—*Selected Poems Of Antonio Machado* (translated by Betty Jean Craige). Louisiana State University
Maclean, Robert—*Selected Poems.* Outland
MacPhee, Rosalind—*Scarecrow.* Fiddlehead
Madgett, Naomi Long—*Exits And Entrances.* Lotus
Magers, Jean Ellen—*Mountain Women.* Seventh Dream/Opus
Magorian, James—*Piano Tuning At Midnight.* Laughing Bear
Maisel, Carolyn—*Witnessing.* L'Epervier
Majors, Barbara Jackson—*Letters From God.* Dorrance
Malanga, Gerard—*100 Years Have Passed.* Little Caesar
—This Will Kill That. Black Sparrow
Malarkey, Susannah P.—*Moments In Time.* American Scholar
Mandelstam, Osip—*Osip Mandelstam: 40 Poems* (translated by Bernard Meares). Persea
Manfred, Freya—*American Roads: A Book Of Poems.* Overlook

Manley, Deborah—*Animals All.* Raintree Children's Books
Marano, Russell—*Poems From A Mountain Ghetto.* Back Fork
Mariah, Paul—*This Light Will Spread: Selected Poems 1960-1975.* Manroot
Marion, Paul F.—*Poems.* Privately printed
Marks, Madge Brace—*From The Heart.* Vantage
Marteau, Robert—*Salamander: Selected Poems Of Robert Marteau* (translated from French by Anne Winters). Princeton University
Masterson, Dan—*On Earth As It Is.* University of Illinois
Matthews, William—*Rising And Falling.* Atlantic/Little, Brown
Matthias, John—*Crossing.* Swallow
Maura, Sister—*What We Women Know.* Sparrow
Mayer, Bernadette—*The Golden Book Of Words.* Angel Hair
Mayes, Frances—*After Such Pleasures.* Seven Woods
Mazzacco, Robert—*Trader.* Knopf
McAnally, Mary—*We Will Make A River.* West End
—The Absence Of The Father And The Dance Of The Zygotes. Cardinal
McBride, Mekeel—*No Ordinary World.* Carnegie-Mellon University
McCarthy, Dermot—*North Shore.* Porcupine's Quill
McCarthy, Eugene J.—*Ground Fog And Night: Poems.* Harcourt Brace Jovanovich
McCarthy, Thomas—*The First Convention.* Dolmen
McCracken, Kathleen—*Into Celebration.* Coach House
McDonald, Walter—*One Thing Leads To Another.* Cedar Rock
McDonough, Kaye—*Zelda.* City Lights
McDowell, Leonora (I am Cree)—*Moccasin Meanderings.* Gusto
McKuen, Rod—*We Touch The Sky.* Simon and Schuster
McWilliams, Peter—*Come Love With Me And Be My Life.* Leo
—Come To My Senses. Leo
—For Lovers & No Others. Leo
—The Hard Stuff: Love. Leo
—I Love Therefore I Am. Leo
—Love . . . An Experience Of. Leo
—Love Is Yes. Leo
Meeker, Lloyd (see listing for Ish, David)
Meissner, William—*Learning To Breath Underwater: Poems.* Ohio University
Merrill, James Ingram—*Mirabell, Books of Number.* Atheneum
Merritt, Robert Amsey—*Appomattox And Other Poems.* Exposition
Merwin, W. S.—*Selected Translations: 1968-1978.* Atheneum
Meyer, Tom—*Staves, Calends, Legends.* Jargon Society
Meyers, Bert—*The Wild Olive Tree.* West Coast Poetry Review
—Windowsills. Common Table
Meynell, Alice Christiana Thompson—*The Poems Of Alice Meynell.* Hyperion (reprint)
Mezey, Robert—*Couplets.* Westigan Review
Mikolowski, Ken—*Little Mysteries: Poems.* Toothpaste
Miller, Errol—*Morning Star.* Sun Pub. Co.

Miller, Jim W.—*The Mountains Have Come Closer.* Appalachian Consortium

Mills, Ralph J., Jr.—*Living With Distance.* Boa

Mills, William—*Stained Glass.* Louisiana State University

Minczeski, John—*The Spiders.* New Rivers

Minty, Judith—*Yellow Dog Journal.* Center

Miranda, Gary—*Listeners At The Breathing Place.* Princeton University

Mitchell, Cynthia—*Playtime.* Collins+World

Mitsui, James Masao—*Crossing The Phantom River.* Graywolf

Mohammed, M. R.—*From The Crucible.* Vantage

Moncure, Jane Belk—*Wishes, Whispers And Secrets.* Child's World

Montale, Eugenio—*The Storm And Other Poems* (translated by Charles Wright). Oberlin College

Montgomery, James—*The West Indies And Other Poems.* Garland (reprint)

Moore, Rosalie—*Year Of The Children: Poems For A Narrative.* Woolmer & Brotherson
—*Of Singles And Doubles.* Woolmer & Brotherson

Moore, T. Sturge—*The Poems Of T. Sturge Moore.* Scholarly (reprint)

Moore, Thomas—*The Poetical Works Of Thomas Moore.* AMS (reprint)

Morgan, Frederick—*Death Mother And Other Poems.* University of Illinois

Morgan, Paula—*Sol's Daughter.* Grosset & Dunlap

Morgan, Robert—*Trunk & Thicket.* L'Epervier

Morse, Samuel French—*The Sequences.* Northeastern University

Moses, Daniel—*Poetic Living: The Mind Of Young America.* Dorrance

Moss, Stanley—*Skull Of Adam.* Horizon

Motier, Donald—*On The Hound And Other Prose-Poems.* Keystone

Mott, Michael—*Counting The Grasses.* Anhinga

Moyles, Lois—*Alleuluia Chorus: New And Selected Poems.* Woolmer & Brotherson

Mulligan, J. B.—*The Stations Of The Cross.* Samisdat

Murphey, Joseph Colin—*A Return To The Landscape.* Prickly Pear

Musgrave, Susan—*A Man To Marry, A Man To Bury.* McClelland and Stewart

Myers, Lisa—*Come—Share My Thoughts.* Dorrance

Myres, R. W.—*Out, Out, Brief Candle.* Exposition

N

Nason, Richard—*A Modern Dunciad.* Smith/New York

Neeld, Judith—*Scripts For A Life In Three Parts.* Stone Country

Nelson, Sharon H.—*Blood Poems.* Fiddlehead

Nelson, Vivian L.—*By Special Request.* Exposition

Nist, John—*Love Songs For Marisa.* Northwoods

Nister, Ernest—*Revolving Pictures: A Reproduction From An Antique Book.* Collins

Nyhart, Nina—*Openers.* Alice James

O

O'Brien, Michael—*To A Dark Moon.* Valkyrie

O'Connor, Martin T.—*The Vicissitudes Of Summer.* Bell

O'Daly, Bill—*The Whale In The Web.* Copper Canyon

O'Grady, Desmond—*The Gododdin* (a version from Welsh). Dolmen

Ó Hehir, Diana—*The Power To Change Geography.* Princeton University

Oles, Carole—*The Loneliness Factor.* Texas Tech

Oliver, Mary Jane—*Twelve Moons.* Little, Brown

Onaatje, Michael—*There's A Trick With A Knife I'm Learning To Do: Poems.* Norton

O'Neill, Catherine—*The Daffodil Farmer.* Washington Writers

Onyeberechi, Sydney—*Africa: Melodies And Thoughts.* Vantage

Oppenheimer, Joel—*Names, Dates & Places.* Saint Andrews

Orlen, Steve—*Permission To Speak.* Wesleyan University

Orlovsky, Peter—*Clean Asshole Poems & Smiling Vegetable Songs.* City Lights

O'Shaughnessy, Arthur—*Poems Of Arthur O'Shaughnessy* (edited by William A. Percy). Greenwood (reprint)

Ostriker, Alicia—*A Dream Of Springtime: Poems 1970-1978.* Smith

Overaker, Harriet Rosling—*And So Onward: A Collection Of Poems.* Vantage

Owen, Lynda Kathleen—*A Woman In The Light.* Vantage

Owens, Rochelle—*The Joe Chronicles, Part 2.* Black Sparrow
—*Shemuel.* New Rivers

P

Paladino, Lyn—*The Horological Tree.* Windy Row

Parcelli, Carlo—*Three Antiphonies.* Proteus

Parry, Barbara M.—*The Philadelphia Man.* Dorrance

Pastor, Lucille E.—*Thoughts Of Old And Life Today.* Dorrance

Payack, Paul J. J.—*Microtales.* Quark

Paz, Octavio—*A Draft Of Shadows, And Other Poems* (edited and translated from Spanish by Eliot Weinberger). New Directions

Peabody, Richard—*I'm In Love With The Morton Salt Girl.* Paycock

Pearson, Ted—*The Blue Table.* Trike

Penniman, Gwendolen Brooks—*Orlando: A Romance Of Italy.* Pegasus

Pere, Vernice Wineera—*Mahanga: Pacific Poems.* Institute for Polynesian Studies

Pereira, Sam—*The Marriage Of The Portuguese.* L'Epervier

Perelman, Bob—*A.K.A.* Tuumba

Perlman, Jess—*Poems Past Eighty.* Dragon's Teeth

Peters, Robert—*The Drowned Man To The Fish.* New Rivers

Petrarch—*Petrarch's Lyric Poems: The "Rime Sparse" And Other Lyrics* (translated and edited by Robert M. Durling). Harvard University

Petti, Gladys—*Dream Catching.* Vantage

Pettit, Rick Alden—*Fragments Of A Lucky Lady.* Vantage

Pflum, Richard—*A Dream Of Salt.* Raintree
Phillips, Frances–*The Celebrated Running Horse Messenger: Poems.* Kelsey Street
Phillips, Michael Joseph—*21 Erotic Haiku For Samantha.* Free University
Piccione, Sandi—*Polar Sun.* Slow Loris
Pierson, Philip—*Natives.* Chowder Chapbooks
Pilinszky, Janos—*Selected Poems* (translated by Ted Hughes, Janos Csokits). Persea
Pinsky, Robert—*An Explanation Of America.* Princeton University
Pobo, Kenneth—*Musings From The Porchlit Sea.* Branden
Poliziano, Angelo—*The "Stanze" Of Angelo Poliziano* (translated by David Quint). University of Massachusetts
Pommy-Vega, Janine—*Journal Of A Hermit &.* Cherry Valley
Ponge, Francis—*The Making Of The Pre* (translated from French by Lee Fahnestock). University of Missouri
Ponsor, Y. R.—*Gawain And The Green Knight: Adventure At Camelot.* Macmillan
Popa, Vasko—*Collected Poems, 1943-1976* (translated from Serbo-Croat by Anne Pennington). Carcanet
Poretz, Doraine—*This Woman In America.* Bombshelter
Potts, Charles—*Rocky Mountain Man.* Smith/New York
Prevert, Jacques—*Words For All Seasons: Collected Poems Of Jacques Prevert.* Unicorn
Price, Darryl—*Dance Until Morning.* My Back Pages
Prince, Frank Templeton—*Collected Poems.* Sheep Meadow
Progoff, Ira—*The White Robed Monk: As An Entrance To Process Meditation.* Dialogue House
Purdy, Al—*Sundance At Dusk.* McClelland and Stewart

Q

Quillen, Ruthellen—*Magdalen.* Sibyl-Child
Quintana, Leroy V.—*Sangre.* Cenote

R

Raffel, Burton—*Four Humors.* Seagull
Ragan, James—*In The Talking Hours.* Eden Hall
Ramke, Bin—*The Difference Between Night And Day.* Yale University
Rapoport, Janis—*Winter Flowers.* Hounslow
Rapp, Florence Dora—*Love In Its Many Aspects.* Vantage
Ratner, Rochelle—*Quarry.* New Rivers
—*Combing The Waves.* Hanging Loose
Ray, David—*The Tramp's Cup.* Chariton Review
Redshaw, Thomas Dillon—*The Floating World.* Aquila Rose
Reed, Clyde Theodore—*Rhythmic Tapestries.* Dorrance
Reh, Lawrence—*If I Could Crown Your Hills With Gold.* Atlantis Rising
Reiss, Edmund—*William Dunbar.* Twayne

Renner, Bruce—*Wakefulness.* L'Epervier
Reyburn, Noel J.—*Thoughts From My Quiet Corner.* Dorrance
Rice, David L.—*Lock This Man Up: Poems.* Lotus
Rice, Helen Steiner—*Everyone Needs Someone: Poems Of Love And Friendship.* Revell
Ridland, John—*In The Shadowless Light.* Abattoir
Riley, Roger D.—*Poetry From Life.* Vantage
Rilke, Rainer Maria—*Duino Elegies* (translated from German by David Young). Norton
—*The Roses & The Windows* (translated from German by A. Poulin). Graywolf
—*Selected Poems Of Rainer Maria Rilke* (translated from German by Robert Bly). Harper & Row
Rimbaud, Arthur—*Illuminations* (translated by Bertrand Mathieu). Boa
Rinder, Walter—*Follow Your Heart.* Celestial Arts
Ritsos, Yannis—*Ritsos In Parenthesis* (translated from Greek by Edmund Keeley). Princeton University
—*Scripture Of The Blind* (translated from Greek by Kimon Friar, Kostas Myrsiades). Ohio State University
Robbins, Martin H.—*A Week Like Summer: And Other Poems Of Love And Family.* X Press
Robinson, Barbara (see listing for Blotnick, Elihu)
Robinson, Barbara B.—*This Fragile Eden: Poems.* Press Pacifica
Rockwell, Tim—*Visions Of Rhyme.* Vantage
Rodgers, Carolyn M.—*The Heart As Ever Green: Poems.* Anchor
Rodney, Janet—*Crystals.* North Atlantic
Ronan, Richard—*Kindred.* Audit/Poetry
Roseliep, Raymond—*A Day In The Life Of Sobi-Shi.* Rook
—*Sailing Bones: Haiku.* Rook
Rosenberger, Francis Coleman—*An Alphabet.* University of Virginia
Roskolenko, Harry—*A Third Summary.* Zone
Ross, Dennis—*The Conservation Of Strangeness: Poems.* Holmgangers
Rossetti, Christina—*The Complete Poems Of Christina Rossetti* (edited by R. W. Crump). Louisiana State University
Rudolph, Lee—*The Country Changes.* Alice James
Ruiz, Juan—*The Book Of True Love* (translated from Old Spanish by Saralyn R. Daly; edited by Anthony N. Zahareas). Pennsylvania State University
Rukeyser, Muriel—*The Collected Poems Of Muriel Rukeyser.* McGraw-Hill
Russell, Patrick M.—*Inside An Inspiration.* Dorrance
Russell, Peter—*Acts of Recognition: Four Visionary Poems.* Golgonooza
Rutsala, Vern—*The New Life.* Trask House
Ryaburn, Carl Bryan—*Tus-Kee-Mah Of The Desert.* Vantage
Ryerson, Alice—*Excavation.* Kelsey Street

S

Sackville, Charles (Sixth Earl of Dorset)—*The Poems Of Charles Sackville, Sixth Earl Of Dorset* (edited by Brice Harris). Garland
Sadoff, Ira—*Palm Reading In Winter.* Houghton Mifflin

Saigyo—*Mirror For The Moon*. New Directions
St. John, David—*The Olive Grove*. Hoffstadt
Salo, Sonja; Dobbs, Charlotte M.—*Notes To A Married Man*. Vantage
Samuelson, Janet—*The Heart's Geographer*. Calliope
Santayana, George—*The Poet's Testament: Poems And Two Plays*. AMS (reprint)
Santos, Sherod—*Elkin Pond*. Porch
Sargent, Robert—*A Woman From Memphis*. Word Works
Sarton, May—*The Fur Person*. Norton
—*A Shower of Summer Days*. Norton
Sasso, Laurence J., Jr.—*Harvesting The Inner Garden*. Greyledge
Saul, George Brandon—*In Borrowed Light*. Parousia
Saxon, Bob—*Beautiful Me*. Privately printed
Scheele, Roy—*Noticing*. Three Sheets
Schjeldahl, Peter—*Since 1964: New And Selected Poems*. Sun
Schwabsky, Barry—*The New Lessons*. Tamarisk
Schwartz, Delmore—*"I Am Cherry Alive," The Little Girl Sang*. Harper & Row
Sears, Peter—*The Lady Who Got Me To Say Solong Mom*. Trask House
Service, Robert—*The Song Of The Campfire*. Dodd, Mead
Shapcott, Thomas W.—*Selected Poems*. University of Queensland
Shapiro, Harvey—*Lauds & Nightsounds*. Sun
Shaw, Luci—*Listen To The Green*. Shaw
—*The Secret Trees*. Shaw.
Sheehan, Thomas F.—*Ah, Devon Unbowed*. Golden Quill
Shelley, Percy Bysshe—*Shelley* (selected by Kathleen Raine). Penguin
Sher, Steven—*Persnickety*. Seven Woods
Sherrill, Jan Mitchell—*Blind Leading The Blind*. New Poets Series
Sherwin, Judith Johnson—*Dead's Good Company*. Countryman
Shevin, David—*The Stop Book*. Konglomerati
Shiplett, Paul D.—*Bags Of Bones*. Broken Whisker
Showers, Jacy—*Sunshine And Shadows: Words Of Love And Loneliness*. Celestial Arts
Shows, Hal Steven—*A Breath For Nothing*. Anhinga
Shuttleworth, Paul—*Poems To The Memory Of Benny Kid Paret*. Sparrow
Silvis, Craig—*Rat Stew*. Houghton Mifflin
Sinopoulos, Takis—*Landscape Of Death: The Selected Poems Of Takis Sinopoulos* (translated from Greek by Kimon Friar). Ohio State University
Skelton, Robin—*Poetic Truth*. Barnes & Noble
Slavitt, David—*Rounding The Horn*. Louisiana State University
Smario, Tom—*Luckynuts And Real People: Poems*. Trask House
Smith, Dave—*Goshawk, Antelope*. University of Illinois
Smith, R. T.—*Good Water*. Banjo
Solan, Miriam—*Seductions*. Barlenmir House
Soos, R., Jr.—*Reality Is A Drunken Feeling!* Realities Library
Sophocles—*Electra; Antigone; Philocletes* (translated from Greek by Kenneth MacLeish). Cambridge University

—*Electra: A Tragedy* (translated from Greek, with notes by Lewis Theobald). AMS (reprint)
Southwick, Marcia—*Thaisa*. Singing Wind
—*The Leopard's Mouth Is Dry And Cold Inside* (with Larry Levis). Singing Wind
Spacks, Barry—*Imagining A Unicorn*. University of Georgia
Speer, Laurel—*A Bit Of Wit: 100 Poems*. Gusto
Spingarn, Lawrence—*The Dark Playground*. Perivale
Spirling, James W.; Foster, Peggy L.—*Some Love And Tears*. Dorrance
Splake, T. Kilgore—*Rest Stop*. Angst
Stadler, John—*Cat At Bat*. Dutton
Stanford, Frank—*You: Poems*. Lost Roads
—*The Singing Knives: Poems*. Lost Roads
Stange, Ken—*Nocturnal Rhythms*. Penumbra
—*Bushed*. York
Stansberger, Richard—*Glass Hat*. Louisiana State University
Starbird, Kaye—*The Covered Bridge House & Other Poems*. Four Winds
Steele, Timothy—*Uncertainties And Rest*. Louisiana State University
Stephens, William—*Standard Forgings: Collected Poems 1919-1950*. Ardis
Stern, Robert—*Spirit Hand*. Konglomerati
Stetser, Virginia M.—*African Palette*. Golden Quill
Stevenson, Robert Louis—*Robert Louis Stevenson's "A Child's Garden Of Verses."* Shambhala
—*Selections From "A Child's Garden Of Verses."* Dandelion
—*"A Child's Garden Of Verses": With Nine Poems Not Published In Prior Editions*. Tuscany
Stewart, Pamela—*The St. Vlas Elegies*. L'Epervier
Stokes, Terry—*Life In These United States: A Travelogue*. St. Luke's
Stokesbury, Leon—*The Drifting Away Of All We Once Held Essential*. Trilobite
Stripling, Kathryn—*Search Party*. Amicae
Studebaker, William—*Everything Goes Without Saying: Poems*. Confluence
Swan, Jon—*A Door To The Forest*. Random House
Swander, Mary—*Succession*. University of Georgia
Swede, George—*A Snowman, Headless*. Fiddlehead
Swenson, Mary—*New & Selected Things Taking Place*. Atlantic/Little, Brown
Syrkin, Marie—*Gleanings: A Diary In Verse*. Rhythms

T

Taggard, Genevieve—*To The Natural World*. Ahsahta
Tanksley, Perry—*Come Share The Joy*. Revell
Tarachow, Michael—*Interlude*. Pentagram
Tate, Allen—*Collected Poems: 1919-1976*. Farrar, Straus & Giroux
Tate, James—*Riven Doggeries*. Ecco
Taube, Herman—*A Chain Of Images: Poetic Notes*. Shulsinger
Taylor, William E.—*20 Against Apocalypse*. St. Johns River
Temme, Mark E.—*Searching For Truth*. Dorrance
Tennessen, Ralph—*Winds Of Hope*. Vantage
Thomas, Edward—*The Collected Poems Of Edward Thomas* (edited by R. George Thomas). Oxford University

Thomas, Richard—*In The Moment.* Avon

Thompson, Francis—*Poems Of Francis Thompson* (edited by Terence L. Connolly). Greenwood (reprint)

Tick, Edward—*The Dawn That Bleeds.* High/Coo

Tilgner, Inez H.—*Moments.* Dorrance

Tolnay, Thomas—*The Magic Whorehouse.* Smith/New York

Tomlinson, Kerry—*Time Payment.* Mudborn

Torbet, Dave—*A Collection Of Works By Our Hero.* Privately printed

Touster, Allison—*Bid Me Welcome.* Golden Quill

Treadwell, Jimmie—*My Victory Or Defeat.* Vantage

Treece, Henry—*How I See Apocalypse.* AMS (reprint)

Turner, Gordon P.—*Each Mouthful Of Forget.* Turnstone

U

Ullman, Leslie—*Natural Histories.* Yale University

Ulrich, Charles Clemens—*Journey Through Life.* Privately printed

V

Valentine, Jean—*The Messenger.* Farrar, Straus & Giroux

Vallejo, Cesar—*Cesar Vallejo: The Complete Posthumous Poetry* (translated by Clayton Eshelman, Jose Rubia Barcia). University of California

Vander Molen, Robert—*Along The River And Other Poems.* New Rivers

Vetrano, Pete—*Voids Of Monday.* Dorrance

Viereck, Peter—*New & Selected Poems.* Xerox University Microfilms (reprint)

Voleman, Victor—*Terrific At Both Ends.* Coach House

W

Wagoner, David—*In Broken Country.* Atlantic/Little, Brown

Wainwright, Jeffrey—*Heart's Desire.* Carcanet

Walcott, Derek—*The Star-Apple Kingdom.* Farrar, Straus & Giroux

Walker, Alice—*Good Night, Willie Lee, I'll See You In The Morning: New Poems.* Dial

Walker, Ashley (see listing for Walker, Taiko)

Walker, Taiko; Walker, Ashley—*Galatea.* Vantage

Wallace, Robert—*Swimmer In The Rain.* Carnegie-Mellon University

Waniek, Marilyn Nelson—*For The Body.* Louisiana State University

Ward, Leo R.—*Irish Portraits And Other Poems.* Fides/Claretian

Warren, Robert Penn—*Brother To Dragons: A Tale In Verse And Voices.* Random House

Washington, Willie, III—*This.* Vantage

Watson, Laura Madrienne—*Blue Rose.* Vantage

Watten, Barrett—*Plasma Parallels "X".* Tuumba

Webb, Jim (see listing for Barber, Bob Henry)

Weber, Florence Hollis—*Singing Words.* Dorrance

Weigl, Bruce—*A Romance.* University of Pittsburgh

Weingarten, Roger—*The Vermont Suicides.* Knopf

Weiss, Ruth—*Single Out.* D'Aurora

Weiss, Theodore—*Views And Spectacles: New And Selected Shorter Poems.* Macmillan

Whatley, John—*Flesh Songs.* Fiddlehead

White, Mary Jane—*The World Of The Icon Painter.* Osiers

Whitman, Walt—*Two Rivulets.* Norwood

Wick, Esther Elizabeth—*In Winter And Other Poems.* Exposition

Wiffen, Jeremiah Holmes—*Julia Alpinula; The Echo Of Antiquity.* Garland (reprint)
—*Poems By Three Friends; Aonian Hours.* Garland (reprint)

Wilbur, Richard—*Opposites.* Harcourt Brace Jovanovich

Wilcox, Patricia—*A Public And Private Hearth: Selected Poems* (edited by Donald Revell). Bellevue

Wild, Peter—*Zuni Butte.* San Pedro
—*Barn Fires.* Floating Island

Williams, Jim—*Symphony No. 1: Words Without Music.* Tortilla

Williams, Jonathan—*Elite/Elate Poems: Selected Poems, 1971-75.* Jargon Society

Wilner, Eleanor—*Maya.* University of Massachusetts

Wilson, Duane—*Selected Works.* Privately printed

Wilson, Keith—*While Dancing Feet Shatter The Earth.* Utah State University

Winchilsea, Anne—*Selected Poems Of Anne Finch, Countess Of Winchilsea.* Ungar

Winn, Howard—*Four Picture Sequence Of Desire And Love.* Front Street

Winner, Robert—*Green In The Body.* Slow Loris

Witt, Harold—*Winesburg By The Sea.* Thorp Springs

Wittlinger, Ellen—*Breakers.* Sheep Meadow

Wojtyla, Karol (see John Paul II)

Wolfe, John—*Rehab And Other Poems.* Nortex

Wolfert, Adrienne—*Discovery Of A Human Fossil.* Lintel

Woods, Elizabeth—*Men.* Fiddlehead

Wordsworth, William—*The Ruined Cottage And The Pedlar* (edited by James Butler). Cornell University

Worsham, Fabian—*The Green Kangaroo.* Anhinga

Wright, C. D.—*Terrorism: Poems.* Lost Roads

Wright, James—*To A Blossoming Pear.* Farrar, Straus & Giroux

Wright, Judith—*The Double Tree.* Houghton Mifflin

Wrigley, Robert—*The Sinking Of Clay City.* Copper Canyon

XYZ

Yeo, Marge—*Something About Silence.* Fiddlehead

Yevtushenko, Yevgeny—*The Face Behind The Face: Poems* (translated from Russian by Arthur Boyars, Simon Franklin). Marek

Young, Gary—*Hands.* Illuminati

Zimroth, Evan—*Giselle Considers Her Future.* Ohio State University

Zink, Donald G.—*The Folksinger.* Vantage

Zolynas, Al—*The New Physics: Poems.* Wesleyan University

Zukofsky, Louis—*"A".* University of California

Zydek, Fredrick—*Lights Along The Missouri.* University of Nebraska

(2) ANTHOLOGIES
(listed alphabetically by title)

A Christmas Feast: An Anthology Of Poems, Sayings, Greetings And Wishes (compiled by Edna Barth). Seabury

A Geography Of Poets (edited by Edward Field). Bantam

A Spot Of Purple Is Deaf (edited by Van K. Brock). Anhinga

The American Mercury Reader: A Selection Of Distinguished Articles, Stories And Poems Published In The American Mercury During The Past Twenty Years (edited by Lawrence E. Spivak, Charles Angoff). AMS (reprint)

An Anthology Of Neo-Latin Poetry (translated and edited by Fred J. Nichols). Yale University

Anthology Of Armenian Poetry (translated from Armenian and edited by Diana der Hovanessian, Marzbed Margossian). Columbia University

Anthology Of Bells: The Bell Collectors' Treasury Of Verses (edited by Dorothy Moody Warren). Exposition

Armenian Poetry, Old And New (compiled and translated by Aram Tolegian). Wayne State University

Brother Songs: A Male Anthology Of Poems About Fathers, Sons, Brothers And Good Friends (edited by Jim Perlman). Holy Cow!

Cafe At St. Marks: The Apalachee Poets (edited by Van K. Brock). Anhinga

Cameos (edited by Felice Newman). Crossing Place

Contemporary Portuguese Poetry: An Anthology In English (selected by Helder Macedo, E. M. de Melo e Castro). Carcanet

Distant Voices: Poetry Of The Preliterate (edited by Denys Thompson). Rowman and Littlefield

Diversity Poems: An Anthology Of Delaware Poems (edited by Jocelyn Hollis, Edward McKinney). American Poetry Press

English And American Surrealist Poetry (edited by Edward B. Germain). Penguin

The Faber Book Of Comic Verse (edited by Michael Roberts). Faber & Faber

The Face Of Poetry: 101 Poets In Two Significant Decades, The '60s And The '70s (edited by LaVerne Harrell Clark, Mary MacArthur). Heidelberg Graphics

Focus: Themes In Literature (partly poetry) (compiled by G. Robert Carlsen, Anthony Tovatt, Patricia O. Tovatt). Webster

Ghost Poems (edited by Daisy Wallace). Holiday House

The Good People Of Gomorrah: A Memphis Miscellany (edited by Gordon Osing). St. Luke's

Happy Christmas (compiled by William Kean Seymour, John Smith) (partly poetry). Westminster

The Heritage Of Vietnamese Poetry: An Anthology (translated and edited by Huynh Sanh Thong). Yale University

Ideas On Wings: A Collection Of Poems From The Christian Science Periodicals (edited by Carol Chapin Lindsey). Christian Science

Kossovo, Heroic Songs Of The Serbs (translated by Helen Rootham). Core (reprint)

The Life: The Lore And Folk Poetry Of The Black Hustler (edited by Dennis Wepman, Ronald B. Newman, Murray B. Binderman). University of Pennsylvania

Lime Tree Prism (edited by Van K. Brock). Privately printed

Men And Boys: An Anthology. Coltsfoot

Merely Players (edited by Lee Bennett Hopkins). Elsevier/Nelson

Metaphysical Lyrics & Poems Of The Seventeenth Century: Donne To Butler (edited by Herbert John Clifford Grierson). Greenwood (reprint)

Modern Catalan Poetry: An Anthology (selected and translated from Catalan by David H. Rosenthal). New Rivers

Modern Japanese Poetry (edited by A. R. Davis; translated by James Kirkup). University of Queensland

Moonjuice 3: An Anthology Of Poems By Santa Cruz Women. Embers

New Directions 37: An International Anthology Of Prose & Poetry (edited by J. Laughlin). New Directions

Northwest Writing: A Collection Of Poetry And Fiction (edited by Roy Carlson). Oregon State University

The Oxford Book Of American Light Verse (chosen and edited by William Harmon). Oxford University

The Penguin Book Of Women Poets (edited by Carol Cosman, Joan Keefe, Kathleen Weaver). Viking

Poems Of Inspiration From The Masters (compiled by

James R. Mills). Revell

Poetry Of Asia: Five Millenniums Of Verse From Thirty-Three Languages (edited by Keith Bosley). Weatherhill

Poetry Hawaii: A Contemporary Anthology (edited by Frank Steward, John Unterecker). University of Hawaii

The Poetry Of Horses (compiled by William Cole). Scribner

The Poetry Of Living Japan: An Anthology With An Introduction (edited by Takamichi Ninomiya, D. J. Enright). Greenwood (reprint)

Poetry For Pleasure: A Choice Of Poetry And Verse On A Variety Of Themes Made By Ian Parsons (edited by Ian Parsons). Norton

The Poets Of Canada (edited by John Robert Colombo). Hurtig

Poets Of The Tamil Anthologies: Ancient Poems Of Love And War (translated by George L. Hart III). Princeton University

Positively Prince Street: An Anthology (edited by Dalton Delan). Positively Prince Street

Pups, Dogs, Foxes And Wolves: Stories, Poems And Verse (selected by Lee Bennett Hopkins). Whitman

Recent Swedish Poetry In Translation (edited by Gunnar Harding, Anselm Hollo). University of Minnesota

Renaissance Latin Verse: An Anthology (edited by Alessandro Perosa, John Sparrow). University of North Carolina

St. Louis Poetry Center: An Anthology, 1946-1976 (edited by Lucy R. Hazelton). Sheba

Silent Voices: Recent American Poems On Nature (edited by Paul Feroe). Ally

Songs Of Gods, Songs Of Humans (translated from Ainu by Donald L. Philippi). Princeton University

The Space Behind The Clock (edited by Van K. Brock). Anhinga

The Stuffed Owl: An Anthology Of Bad Verse (edited by Dominic Bevan Wyndham Lewis). AMS (reprint)

Ten Thousand Leaves: Love Poems From The Manyoshu (translated from Japanese by Harold Wright). Shambhala

30 Kansas Poets (edited by Denise Low). Cottonwood Review

Tilt: An Anthology Of New England Women's Writing And Art. New Victoria

Under The Cherry Tree (poems for children chosen by Cynthia Mitchell). Collins

The Unicorn And The Garden: A Poetry And Prose Anthology From The Textile Museum Poetry & Literature Series (edited by Betty Parry). Word Works

Washington And The Poet (edited by Francis Coleman Rosenberger). University of Virginia

The Wind Has Wings: Poems From Canada (compiled by Mary Alice Downie, Barbara Robertson). Oxford University

Women Working: An Anthology Of Stories And Poems (edited by Nancy Hoffman, Florence Howe). Feminist

(3) BIOGRAPHY AND COMMENT ON SPECIFIC POETS
(listed alphabetically by subject)

Arnold, Matthew— *Matthew Arnold: With An Additional Essay: Matthew Arnold, Poet* (by Lionel Trilling). Harcourt Brace Jovanovich

Ashbery, John— *John Ashbery, An Introduction To The Poetry* (by David Shapiro). Columbia University

Baudelaire, Charles— *Baudelaire, A Self-Portrait: Selected Letters* (edited and translated from French by Lois Boe Hyslop, Francis E. Hyslop, Jr.). Greenwood (reprint)

Blake, William— *Arrows Of Intellect: A Study In William Blake's Gospel Of The Imagination* (by Asloob Ahmad Ansari). R. West (reprint)
—*Blake's Poetry And Designs* (edited by Mary Lynn Johnson, John E. Grant). Norton

Borges, Jorge Luis— *Jorge Luis Borges: A Literary Biography* (by Emir Rodriguez Monegal). Dutton

Bridges, Robert— *In The Classic Mode: The Achievement Of Robert Bridges* (by Donald E. Stanford). University of Delaware

Burns, Robert— *The Burns Country* (by Charles S. Dougall). Folcroft (reprint)

Byron, Lord— *Byron And His Fictions* (by Peter J. Manning). Wayne State University
—*The Byrons And Trevanions* (by Alfred Leslie Rowse). St. Martin's

Char, Rene— *Six French Poets Of Our Time: A Critical And Historical Study* (by Robert W. Greene). Princeton University

Chaucer, Geoffrey— *Chaucer Among The Gods: The Poetics Of Classical Myth* (by John P. McCall). Pennsylvania State University
—*Chaucer And Ovid* (by John M. Fyler). Yale University
—*Companion To Chaucer Studies* (by Beryl Rowland). Oxford University
—*Chaucerian Problems And Perspectives: Essays Presented to Paul E. Beichner, C.S.C.* (edited by Edward Vasta, Zacharias P. Thundy). University of Notre Dame

—*A Chaucer Glossary* (by Norman Davis). Oxford University

Coleridge, Samuel Taylor— *Experience Into Thought: Perspectives In The Coleridge Notebooks* (by Kathleen Coburn). University of Toronto
—*Coleridge's Metaphors Of Being* (by Edward Kessler). Princeton University
—*Coleridge* (by Katharine Cooke). Routledge & Kegan Paul
—*Reading Coleridge: Approaches And Applications* (edited by Walter B. Crawford). Cornell University
—*Coleridge, The Visionary* (by J. B. Beer). Greenwood (reprint)
—*Anima Poeta* (edited by Ernest Hartley Coleridge). Folcroft (reprint)

Cowley, Abraham— *The Poetry Of Abraham Cowley* (by David Trotter). Rowman and Littlefield

Cowper, William— *The Letters And Prose Writings Of William Cowper* (edited by James King, Charles Ryskamp). Oxford University

Crane, Hart—*The Universal Drum: Dance Imagery In The Poetry of Eliot, Crane, Roethke And Williams* (by Audrey T. Rodgers). Pennsylvania State University

Crosby, Caresse— *The Passionate Years* (by Caresse Crosby). Ecco (reprint)

Cummings, E. E.— *Dreams In The Mirror: A biography Of E. E. Cummings* (by Richard S. Kennedy). Liveright
—*E. E. Cummings: An Introduction To The Poetry* (by Rushworth M. Kidder). Columbia University

Dante Alighieri— *Dante Alighieri, The Poet Who Loved St. Francis So Much* (by Alexandre Masseron; translated from French). Franciscan Herald
—*Dante, Poet Of The Desert: History And Allegory In "The Divine Comedy"* (by Giuseppe Mazzotta). Morrow
—*Dante Alighieri* (by Ricardo Quinones). Twayne

Dickinson, Emily— *Lyric Time: Dickinson And The Limits Of Genre* (by Sharon Cameron). Johns Hopkins University
—*The Only Kangaroo Among The Beauty: Emily Dickinson And America* (by Karl Keller). Johns Hopkins University

du Bouchet, Andre— *Six French Poets Of Our Time: A Critical And Historical Study* (by Robert W. Greene). Princeton University

Dunbar, William— *William Dunbar* (by Edmund Reiss). Twayne

Dupin, Jacques— *Six French Poets Of Our Time: A Critical And Historical Study* (by Robert W. Greene). Princeton University

Eliot, George— *The Triptych And The Cross: The Central Myths Of George Eliot's Poetic Imagination* (by Felicia Bonaparte). New York University

Eliot, T. S.— *Leaves Of Quest: A Fundamental Exploration Of Love In The Early Poetry Of T. S. Eliot.* Vantage
—*Thomas Stearns Eliot, Poet* (by Anthony David Moody). Cambridge University
—*The Universal Drum: Dance Imagery In The Poetry Of Eliot, Crane, Roethke And Williams* (by Audrey T. Rodgers). Pennsylvania State University
—*Eliot's Reflective Journey To The Garden* (by Marion Montgomery). Whitson

Emerson, Ralph Waldo— *Emerson's Literary Criticism* (edited by Eric W. Carlson). University of Nebraska

Everson, William— *Benchmark & Blaze: The Emergence Of William Everson* (edited by Lee Bartlett). Scarecrow

Ferlinghetti, Lawrence— *Ferlinghetti, A Biography* (by Neeli Cherkovski). Doubleday

Florit, Eugenio— *The Quest For Harmony: The Dialectics Of Communication In The Poetry Of Eugenio Florit* (by Mirella D'Ambrosio Servodidio). Society of Spanish and Spanish-American Studies

Frost, Robert— *Robert Frost And New England: The Poet As Regionalist* (by John C. Kemp). Princeton University
—*Language And The Poet: Verbal Artistry In Frost, Stevens And Moore* (by Marie Borroff). University of Chicago
—*The Poetry Of Robert Frost* (edited by Edward Connery Lathem). Holt, Rinehart & Winston
—*Robert Frost, A Tribute To The Source* (edited by David Bradley). Holt, Rinehart & Winston

Gogarty, Oliver St. John— *Surpassing Wit: Oliver St. John Gogarty, His Poetry And His Prose* (by James F. Carens). Columbia University

Hallam, Arthur Henry— *The Letters Of Arthur Henry Hallam* (edited by Jack Kolb). Ohio State University

Hesse, Hermann— *Hermann Hesse: The Life Of A Poet Of Crisis* (by Ralph Freedman). Pantheon

Hopkins, Gerard Manley— *Gerard Manley Hopkins: A Biography* (by Paddy Kitchen). Atheneum

Hughes, Ted— *Sylvia Plath And Ted Hughes* (by Margaret Dickie Uroff). University of Illinois

Jeffers, Robinson— *Shining Clarity: God And Man In The Works Of Robinson Jeffers* (by Marlan Beilke). Quintessence

Keats, John— *John Keats* (by W. Jackson Bate). Harvard University
—*Keats, Skepticism, And The Religion Of Beauty* (by Ronald A. Sharp). University of Georgia

Kerouac, Jack— *Talking Poetics From Naropa Institute: Annals Of The Jack Kerouac School Of Disembodied Poetics, Volume Two* (edited by Anne Waldman and Marilyn Webb). Shambhala

Kleist, Heinrich von— *Heinrich Von Kleist: Studies In The Character And Meaning Of His Writings* (by John M. Ellis). University of North Carolina

Lycidas— *Lycidas And The Italian Critics* (by Clay Hunt). Yale University

Lydgate, John— *John Lydgate: A Study In The Culture Of The XVth Century* (by Walter Franz Schirmer; translated by Ann E. Keep). Greenwood (reprint)

MacDonagh, Thomas— *Poets Of The Insurrection* (by C. O'Braonain, G. O'Neill, P. McBrien, A. Clery). AMS (reprint)

MacEntee, John F.— *Poets Of The Insurrection* (by C. O'Braonain, G. O'Neill, P. McBrien, A. Clery). AMS (reprint)

Marvell, Andrew— *Foreshortened Time: Andrew Marvell And Seventeenth Century Revolutions* (by Robert Ian Vere Hodge). Rowman and Littlefield
—*Andrew Marvell: His Life And Writings* (by John Dixon Hunt). Cornell University

Masefield, John— *Letters Of John Masefield To Florence Lamont* (edited by Corliss Lamont, Lansing Lamont). Columbia University

Melville, Herman— *A Concordance To Herman Melville's "Clarel, A Poem And Pilgrimage To The Holy Land"* (edited by Larry Edward Wegener). University Microfilms

Merton, Thomas— *Words And Silence: On The Poetry Of Thomas Merton* (by Therese Lentfoehr). New Directions

Milton, John— *John Milton, Poet Priest And Prophet: A Study Of Divine Vocation In Milton's Poetry And Prose* (by John Spenser Hill). Rowman and Littlefield
—*Milton Studies: Volume XIII* (edited by James D. Dimmonds). University of Pittsburgh
—*Milton And The Art Of Sacred Song* (edited by J. Max Patrick, Roger H. Sundell). University of Wisconsin
—*Milton And His Epic Tradition* (by Joan Webber). University of Washington
—*Visionary Poetics: Milton's Tradition And His Legacy* (by Joseph Anthony Wittreich). Huntington Library
—*Milton And The English Revolution* (by Christopher Hill). Penguin
—*The Harmonious Vision: Studies In Milton's Poetry (by Don Cameron Allen). Octagon (reprint)*
—*John Milton: Poetry* (by David M. Miller). Twayne

Moore, Marianne— *Language And The Poet: Verbal Artistry In Frost, Stevens And Moore* (by Marie Borroff). University of Chicago

Morris, William— *William Morris And His World* (by Ian C. Bradley). Scribner
—*William Morris: His Life And Work* (by Jack Lindsay). Taplinger

Neruda, Pablo— *The Poetry Of Pablo Neruda* (by Rene de Costa). Harvard University
—*Pablo Neruda: All Poets The Poet* (by Salvatore Bizzarro). Scarecrow

Nowlan, Alden— *Poet's Progress: The Development Of Alden Nowlan's Poetry* (by Michael Brian Oliver). Fiddlehead

Olson, Charles— *A Guide To The Maximus Poems Of Charles Olson* (by George F. Butterick). University of California
—*Charles Olson: Call Him Ishmael* (by Paul Christensen). University of Texas

Ovid— *Chaucer And Ovid* (by John M. Fyler). Yale University

Pearse, Padraic H.— *Poets Of The Insurrection* (by C. O'Braonain, G. O'Neill, P. McBrien, A. Clery). AMS (reprint)

Pellicer, Carlos— *Reality And Expression In The Poetry Of Carlos Pellicer* (by George Melnykovich). University of North Carolina

Plath, Sylvia— *Sylvia Plath And Ted Hughes* (by Margaret Dickie Uroff). University of Illinois
—*Sylvia Plath: New Views On The Poetry* (edited by Gary Lane). Johns Hopkins University
—*Sylvia Plath: The Poetry Of Initiation* (by Jon Rosenblatt). University of North Carolina

Pleynet, Marcelin— *Six French Poets Of Our Time: A Critical And Historical Study* (by Robert W. Greene). Princeton University

Plunkett, Joseph M.— *Poets Of The Insurrection* (by C. O'Braonain, G. O'Neill, P. McBrien, A. Clery). AMS (reprint)

Poe, Edgar Allan— *The Rationale Of Deception In Poe* (by David Ketterer). Louisiana State University

Ponge, Francis— *Six French Poets Of Our Time: A Critical And Historical Study* (by Robert W. Greene). Princeton University

Pope, Alexander— *Alexander Pope: The Poet In The Poems* (by Dustin H. Griffin). Princeton University
—*The Art Of Alexander Pope* (edited by Howard Ereskine-Hill, Anne Smith). Barnes & Noble

Pound, Ezra— *End To Torment: A Memoir Of Ezra Pound* (by Hilda Doolittle). New Directions
—*Provence And Pound* (by Peter Makin). University of California
—*Letters To Ibbotson, 1935-1952* (edited by Vittoria I. Mondolfo, Margaret Hurley). National Poetry Foundation

Reverdy, Pierre— *Six French Poets Of Our Time: A Critical And Historical Study* (by Robert W. Greene). Princeton University

Rice, Helen Steiner— *In The Vineyard Of The Lord: My Life Story* (by herself). Revell

Rimbaud, Arthur— *Rimbaud* (by C. Chadwick). Athlone

Rochester, John Wilmot— *Rochester's Poetry* (by David Farley-Hills). Rowman and Littlefield

Roethke, Theodore— *The Universal Drum: Dance Imagery In The Poetry Of Eliot, Crane, Roethke And Williams* (by Audrey T. Rodgers). Pennsylvania State University

Rossetti, Christina— *The Bible And The Poetry Of Christina Rossetti* (edited by Nilda Jimenez). Greenwood

Sandburg, Carl— *Carl Sandburg Remembered* (by William A. Sutton). Scarecrow

Shakespeare, William— *The Poems Of Shakespeare's "Dark Lady"* (by Emilia Lanier). Potter
—*The Fickle Glass: A Study Of Shakespeare's Sonnets* (by Paul Ramsey). AMS

Shelley, Harriet— *Harriet Shelley: Five Long Years* (by Louise Schutz Boas). Greenwood (reprint)

Shelley, Percy Bysshe— *Shelley's "The Triumph Of Life": A Critical Study* (by Donald H. Reiman). Octagon (reprint)
—*New Shelley Letters.* Hyperion (reprint)

Shenstone, William— *The Letters Of William Shenstone* (edited by Marjorie Williams). AMS (reprint)
Sophocles— *Sophocles: An Interpretation* (by R. P. Winnington-Ingram). Cambridge University
Southey, Robert— *Journals Of A Residence In Portugal, 1800-1801, And A Visit To France, 1838* (edited by Adolfo Cabral). Greenwood (reprint)
Spenser, Edmund— *Spenser's Allegory Of Justice In Book Five Of The Faerie Queene* (by T. K. Dunseath). Greenwood (reprint)
 —*Spenser, Selections: With Essays By Hazlitt, Coleridge & Leigh Hunt.* AMS (reprint)
Steere, Richard— *Richard Steere, Colonial Merchant Poet* (by Donald P. Wharton). Pennsylvania State University
Stephens, James— *The Writings Of James Stephens: Variations On A Theme Of Love* (by Patricia McFate). St. Martin's
Stevens, Wallace— *Language And The Poet: Verbal Artistry In Frost, Stevens and Moore* (by Marie Borroff). University of Chicago
Storni, Alfonsina— *Alfonsina Storni* (by Sonia Jones). Twayne
Swinburne, Algernon Charles— *Swinburne: The Poet In His World* (by Donald Thomas). Oxford University

Teasdale, Sara— *Sara Teasdale: Woman & Poet* (by William Drake). Harper & Row
Tennyson, Alfred— *Tennyson And Clio: History In The Major Poems* (by Henry Kozicki). Johns Hopkins University
Thomas, Dylan— *The Religious Sonnets Of Dylan Thomas: A Study In Imagery And Meaning* (by Hyman H. Kleinman). Octagon (reprint)
 —*Dylan Thomas* (by Paul Ferris). Penguin

Verlaine, Paul— *Confessions Of A Poet* (translated from French by Joanna Richardson). Hyperion (reprint)
Virgil— *Virgil's Poem Of The Earth: Studies In The "Georgics"* (by Michael C. J. Putnam). Princeton University
 —*Darkness Visible: A Study Of Virgil's "Aeneid"* (by W. R. Johnson). University of California

Welch, Lew— *Genesis Angels: The Saga Of Lew Welch And The Beat Generation* (by Aram Saroyan). Morrow
Whitman, Walt— *The American Quest For A Supreme Fiction: Whitman's Legacy In The Personal Epic* (by James Edwin Miller, Jr.). University of Chicago
Williams, William Carlos— *The Universal Drum: Dance Imagery In The Poetry Of Eliot, Crane, Roethke And Williams* (by Audrey T. Rodgers). Pennsylvania State University
 —*William Carlos Williams' Paterson* (by Margaret Glynne Lloyd). Fairleigh Dickinson University
Wordsworth, William— *Romantic Paradox: An Essay On The Poetry Of Wordsworth* (by Colin Campbell Clarke). Greenwood (reprint)
 —*Wordsworth And The Literature Of Travel* (by Charles Norton Coe). Octagon
 —*The Written Spirit: Thematic And Rhetorical Structure In Wordsworth's "The Prelude"* (By Karl R. Johnson). Salzburg University
 —*"The Prelude," 1799, 1805, 1850: Authoritative Texts, Context And Reception, Recent Critical Essays* (edited by Jonathan Wordsworth, M. H. Abrams, Stephen Gill). Norton

Yeats, William Butler— *Yeats At Work* (edited by Curtis B. Bradford). Ecco
 —*The Whole Mystery Of Art: Pattern Into Poetry In The Work Of W. B. Yeats* (by Giorgio Melchiori). Greenwood (reprint)
 —*Yeats, The Poetics Of The Self* (by David Lynch). University of Chicago
 —*Yeats, The Man And The Mask* (by Richard Ellmann). Norton (reprint)
Young, Andrew— *Andrew Young, Remembrance & Homage* (compiled by Leslie Norris). Tidal

(4) COMMENT AND CRITICISM
(listed alphabetically by author)

Altieri, Charles— *Enlarging The Temple: New Directions In American Poetry During The 1960s.* Bucknell University

Barbe, William— *Famous Poems Explained: Helps To Reading With The Understanding: With Biographical Notes Of The Authors Represented.* Folcroft (reprint)
Blessington, Francis C.— *Paradise Lost And The Classical Epic.* Routledge & K. Paul
Bloom, Harold; De Man, P.; Derrida, J.; Hartman, G. H.; Miller, J. H.— *Deconstruction And Criticism.* Seabury
Brault, Gerard J.— *The Song Of Roland: An Analytical Edition* (Vols. I, II). Pennsylvania State University

Bronowski, Jacob— *The Poet's Defence.* Hyperion (reprint)
Brown, E. K.— *Responses And Evaluations: Essays On Canada* (contains material on poetry) (edited by Davis Staines). McClelland and Stewart
Browning, Robert M.— *German Poetry In The Age Of The Enlightenment, From Brockes To Klopstock.* Pennsylvania State University

Chisholm, Alan Rowland— *Towards Herodiade: A Literary Genealogy.* AMS (reprint)
Cosman, Anna— *How To Read And Write Poetry.* Watts

Davenport, W. A.— *The Art Of The Gawain-Poet.* Athlone

De Beaugrande, Robert— *Factors In A Theory Of Poetic Translating.* Van Gorcum

De Man, P. (see listing for Bloom, Harold)

Derrida, J. (see listing for Bloom, Harold)

Dessner, Lawrence Jay— *How To Write A Poem.* New York University

Eberhart, Richard— *Of Poetry And Poets.* University of Illinois

Egudu, R. N.— *Modern African Poetry And The African Predicament.* Barnes & Noble

Fehrman, Carl— *Poetic Creation: Inspiration Or Craft* (translated by Karin Petherick). University of Minnesota

Feldman, Ruth; Swann, Brian (editors)— *Italian Poetry Today: Currents And Trends.* New Rivers

Forrest-Thomson, Veronica— *Poetic Artifice: A Theory Of Twentieth-Century Poetry.* St. Martin's

Ghorsen, Kristine A. (see listing for Reardon, Joan)

Gibbons, Reginald (editor)— *The Poet's Work: 29 Masters Of 20th Century Poetry On The Origins And Practice Of Their Art.* Houghton Mifflin

Gilbert, Sandra M; Gubar, Susan (editors)— *Shakespeare's Sisters: Feminist Essays On Women Poets.* Indiana University

Greenfield, Concetta Carestia— *Humanist And Scholastic Poetics.* Bucknell University

Gross, Harvey (editor)— *The Structure Of Verse.* Ecco

Gubar, Susan (see listing for Gilbert, Sandra M.)

Hartman, G. H. (see listing for Bloom, Harold)

Hayley, William— *Ode, Inscribed To John Howard; An Essay On Painting; The Triumphs Of Temper; An Essay On Epic Poetry.* Garland (reprint)

Highet, Gilbert— *Poets In A Landscape.* Greenwood (reprint)

Hobsbaum, Philip— *Tradition And Experiment In English Poetry.* Rowman and Littlefield

Hollis, Jocelyn— *How To Write: A Guidebook And Workbook For Students Of Creative Writing Of Poetry.* American Poetry Press

Howard, Helen Addison— *American Indian Poetry.* Twayne

Hugo, Richard— *The Triggering Town: Lectures And Essays On Poetry And Writing.* Norton

Hungerland, Isabel— *Poetic Discourse.* AMS (reprint)

Jackson, A. V. Williams— *Early Persian Poetry: From The Beginnings Down To The Time Of Firdausi.* Longwood (reprint)

Jaffa, Herbert C.— *Modern Australian Poetry, 1920-1970: A Guide To Information Sources.* Gale Research

Jerome, Judson— *The Poet And The Poem.* Writer's Digest

Johnson, Charles F.— *Forms Of English Poetry.* Folcroft (reprint)

Keller, John Esten— *Pious Brief Narrative In Medieval Castilian & Galican Verse: From Berceo To Alfonso X.* University of Kentucky

Kennedy, X. J. (compiler)— *Literature: An Introduction To Fiction, Poetry And Drama* (contains material on poetry). Little, Brown

Kramer, Samuel Noah— *From The Poetry Of Sumer: Creation, Glorification, Adoration.* University of California

Lawler, Justus George— *Celestial Pantomime: Poetic Structures Of Transcendence.* Yale University

Lee, Peter H.— *Celebration Of Continuity: Themes In Classic East Asian Poetry.* Harvard University

Lerner, Arthur (editor)— *Poetry In The Therapeutic Experience.* Pergamon

Lewalski, Barbara Kiefer— *Protestant Poetics And The Seventeenth-Century Religious Lyric.* Princeton University

Lindsay, Jack— *Song Of A Falling World: Culture During The Break-up Of The Roman Empire.* Hyperion (reprint)

Maresca, Thomas E.— *Three English Epics: Studies Of "Troilus And Criseyde," "The Faerie Queene" And "Paradise Lost."* University of Nebraska

Maynadier, Howard— *The Arthur Of The English Poets.* Octagon

Miller, J. H. (see listing for Bloom, Harold)

Miner, Earl Roy— *Japanese Linked Poetry: An Account With Translations Of Renga And Haikai Sequences.* Princeton University

Molesworth, Charles— *The Fierce Embrace: A Study Of Contemporary American Poetry.* University of Missouri

Morris, Cyril Brian— *A Generation Of Spanish Poets.* Cambridge University

Nagy, Gregory— *The Best Of The Achaeans: Concepts Of The Hero In Archaic Greek Poetry.* Johns Hopkins University

Parker, Patricia A.— *Inescapable Romance: Studies In The Poetics Of A Mode.* Princeton University

Perkins, David— *A History Of Modern Poetry.* Harvard University

Peters, Robert— *The Great American Poetry Bake-Off.* Scarecrow

Peterson, Houston— *Poet To Poet: A Treasury Of Golden Criticism.* Granger (reprint)

Quintana, Ricardo; Whitley, Alvin (editors)— *English Poetry Of The Mid And Late Eighteenth Century: An Historical Analogy.* Greenwood (reprint)

Ransom, John Crowe— *The New Criticism.* Greenwood (reprint)

Raw, Barbara C.— *The Art And Background Of Old English Poetry.* Arnold

Reardon, Joan; Ghorsen, Kristine A.— *Poetry By American Women, 1900-1945.* Scarecrow

Reed, Ishmael (project director)— *Calafia, The California Poetry.* Y'Bird

Rubin, Louis D., Jr.— *The Wary Fugitives: Four Poets And The South.* Louisiana State University

Salustri, C. A.— *Roman Satirical Poems And Their Translation* (translated from Italian by Grant

Showerman). Greenwood (reprint)

Segre, Cesare— *Structures And Time: Narration, Poetry, Models* (translated from Italian by John Meddemmen). University of Chicago

Sikes, E. E.— *The Greek View Of Poetry*. Hyperion (reprint)

—*Roman Poetry*. Hyperion (reprint)

Simpson, David— *Irony And Authority In Romantic Poetry*. Rowman and Littlefield

Skelton, Robin— *Poetic Truth*. Barnes & Noble

Smith, A. J. M.— *On Poetry And Poets*. McClelland and Stewart

Snyder, Gary— *He Who Hunted Birds In His Father's Village: The Dimensions Of A Haida Myth*. Grey Fox

Spender, Stephen— *The Thirties And After: Poetry, Politics, People*. Vintage

Storey, Mark— *Poetry And Humor From Cowper To Clough*. Rowman and Littlefield

Swann, Brian (see listing for Feldman, Ruth)

Taylor, Anya— *Magic And English Romanticism*. University of Georgia

Thomas, J. W.— *Medieval German Lyric Verse In English Translation*. AMS (reprint)

Turner, James G.— *The Politics Of Landscape: Rural Scenery And Society In English Poetry, 1630-1660*. Harvard University

Vernon, John— *Poetry And The Body*. University of Illinois

Volborth, J. Ivaloo— *Thunder-root: Traditional And Contemporary Native American Verse*. American Indian Studies Center

Waldman, Anne; Webb, Marilyn (editors)— *Talking Poetics From Naropa Institute*. Random House

Wasserman, Earl Reeves— *The Subtler Language: Critical Readings Of Neoclassic And Romantic Poems*. Greenwood (reprint)

Webb, Marilyn (see listing for Waldman, Anne)

Book Publishers Publishing Poetry

Following is a directory of publishers in the United States and Canada who issued at least one book of poetry during the year ending October 31, 1979; it is based upon publishers represented in Section 1 of The Yearly Record *in this volume. Not included are those specializing in reprints.*

A

APKL Publications, Woodstock, NY 12498
Abattoir Editions, University of Nebraska, Cleary House, P.O. Box 688, Omaha, NE 68101
Addison-Wesley Publishing Co., Inc., Jacob Way, Reading, PA 01867
Ahsahta Press, Boise State University, English Dept., Boise, ID 83725
Alembic Press, 1744 Slaterville Rd., Ithaca, NY 14850
Alice James Books, 138 Mt. Auburn St., Cambridge, MA 02138
American Indian Studies Center, University of California, Los Angeles, CA 90024
American Poetry Press, 565 Fifth Ave., New York, NY 10017
American Scholar Publications, Inc., 777 Third Ave., New York, NY 10017
Amicae Press, P.O. Box 489, Cullowhee, NC 28723
Anchor Press/Doubleday, Garden City, NY 11530; 245 Park Ave., New York, NY 10017
Androgyne Press, 930 Shields, San Francisco, CA 94132
Angel Hair Books, P.O. Box 718, Lenox, MA 01240
Angst Productions, Battle Creek, MI
Anhinga Press, Tallahasee, FL
Antietam Press, P.O. Box 62, Boonsboro, MD 21713
Anvil Press Poetry, P.O. Box 37, Millville, MN 55957
Appalachian Consortium Press, Boone, NC 28608
Applezabba Press, 333 Orizaba, Long Beach, CA 90814
Aquila Rose, St. Paul, MN
Ararat Press, 628 Second Ave., New York, NY 10016
Ardis Publishers, 2901 Heatherway Dr., Ann Arbor, MI 48104
Ariel Press, P.O. Box 9183, Berkeley, CA 94709
Atheneum Publishers, 122 E. 42nd St., New York, NY 10017
Atlantic/Little, Brown, 34 Beacon St., Boston, MA 02106
Atlantis Rising, 308 Eureka St., San Francisco, CA 94114
Audit/Poetry, Buffalo, NY
Avon Books, 959 Eighth Ave., New York, NY 10019

B

Banjo Press, P.O. Box 455, Potsdam, NY 13676
Barlenmir House Publishers, 413 City Island Ave., New York, NY 10064
Barnes & Noble Books, 10 E. 53rd St., New York, NY 10022
Barnwood Press, R.R. 2, Box 11C, Daleville, IN 47334
William L. Bauhan Publishers, Old Country Rd., Dublin, NH 03444
Bear Claw Press, 215 Bucholz Court, Ann Arbor, MI 48104
Bellevue Press, 60 Schubert St., Binghamton, NY 13905
BkMk Press, 8700 W. 63rd St., Shawnee Mission, KS 66202
Black Sparrow Press, P.O. Box 3993, Santa Barbara, CA 93105
Bloodroot, P.O. Box 891, Grand Forks, ND 58201
Blue Wind Press, P.O. Box 7175, Berkeley, CA 94707
Boa Editions, 92 Park Ave., Brockport, NY 14420

Bombshelter Press, 1092 Loma Dr., Hermosa Beach, CA 90254
Borealis Press, 9 Ashburn Dr., Ottawa, Ont. K2E 6N4, Canada
Branden Press, Inc., 221 Columbus Ave., Boston, MA 02116
Brandon House, Inc., P.O. Box 240, Bronx, NY 10471
George Braziller, Inc., 1 Park Ave., New York, NY 10016
Brigham Young University Press, 209 University Press Bldg., Provo, UT 84602
Broken Whisker Studio, 4225 Seeley, P.O. Box 54, Downers Grove, IL 60515
Buddhahead Press, Mountain View, CA
Burnt Hickory Press, Austell, GA 30001

C

California Street Books, Berkeley, CA
Calliope Press, P.O. Box 4255, Overland Park, KS 66204
Cambridge University Press, 32 E. 57th St., New York, NY 10022
Capra Press, P.O. Box 2068, Santa Barbara, CA 93120
Caratzas Bros. Publishers, 246 Pelham Rd., New Rochelle, NY 10805
Cardinal Press, Inc., 4707 S. Madison Ave., Tulsa, OK 74105
Carnegie-Mellon University Press, Pittsburgh, PA 15213
Cedar Rock Press, 1121 Madeline, New Braunfels, TX 78130
Celestial Arts Publishing Co., 231 Adrian Rd., Millbrae, CA 94030
Center Publications, 905 S. Normandie Ave., Los Angeles, CA 90006
Chariton Review Press, Northeast Missouri State University, Kirksville, MO 63501
Charles Street Press, P.O. Box 4692, Baltimore, MD 21212
Cherry Valley Editions, P.O. Box 303, Cherry Valley, NY 13320
Chicago Review Press, University of Chicago, Faculty Exchange Box C, Chicago, IL 60637
Child's World, 1556 Weatherstone Lane, Elgin, IL 60120
Chowder Chapbooks, P.O. Box 33, Wollaston, MA 02170
Christopher Publishing House, 53 Billings Rd., North Quincy, MA 02171
Christopher's Books, P.O. Box 2457, Santa Barbara, CA 93120
City Lights Books, Inc., 261 Columbus Ave., San Francisco, CA 94133
Cleveland State University Poetry Center, Cleveland, OH 44115
Coach House Press, 401 Huron St., Toronto, Ont. M5S 2G5, Canada
Collins+World Publishers, 2080 W. 117th St., Cleveland, OH 44111
Columbia University Press, 136 S. Broadway, Irvington, NY 10533
Confluence Press, Inc., Art Center, Lewis & Clark Campus, Lewiston, ID 83501
Copper Canyon Press, P.O. Box 271, Port Townsend, WA 98368
Cornell University Press, 124 Roberts Place, Ithaca, NY 14850
Cottonwood Review, Box J, Kansas Union, University of Kansas, Lawrence, KS 66044
Countryman Press, Inc., Taftsville, VT 05073
Coward, McCann & Geoghegan, Inc., 200 Madison Ave., New York, NY 10016
Creekside Press, Birmingham, AL
Cross-Cultural Communications, 239 Wynsum Ave., Merrick, NY 11566
The Crossing Press, 17 W. Main St., Trumansburg, NY 14886

D

Dandelion Press, New York, NY
D'Aurora Press, Mill Valley, CA 94941
Devin-Adair Co., Inc., 143 Sound Beach Ave., Old Greenwich, CT 06870
Dial Press, 1 Dag Hammarskjold Plaza, New York, NY 10017
Dialogue House Library, 45 W. 10th St., New York, NY 10011
Dodd, Mead & Co., Inc., 79 Madison Ave., New York, NY 10016
Dorrance & Co., Inc., 35 Cricket Terrace, Ardmore, PA 19003
Doubleday & Co., Inc., Garden City, NY 11530; 245 Park Ave., New York, NY 10017
Douglas & McIntyre, Ltd., 1875 Welch St., North Vancouver, B.C. V7P 1B7, Canada
Dragon's Teeth Press, El Dorado National Forest, Georgetown, CA 95634
Dryad Press, Inc., P.O. Box 1656, Washington, DC 20013
Dustbooks, P.O. Box 100, Paradise, CA 95969
E. P. Dutton & Co., Inc., 201 Park Ave., S., New York, NY 10003

E

Ecco Press, 1 W. 30th St., New York, NY 10001
Eden Hall Press, Los Angeles, CA
G. E. Edwards, Lawton, OK 73501
Elizabeth Press, 103 Van Etten Blvd., New Rochelle, NY 10804
Exposition Press, Inc., 900 S. Oyster Bay Rd., Hicksville, NY 11801

F

Faber & Faber, Inc., 22 S. Broadway, Salem, NH 03079
Faith and Life Press, 724 Main St., Newton, KS 67114
Far West Publishers, Lynnwood, WA 98036
Farmington Press, Farmington, MO 63640
Farrar, Straus & Giroux, Inc., 19 W. Union Square, New York, NY 10003
Fiddlehead Poetry Books, The Observatory, University of New Brunswick, Fredericton, N.B. E3B 5A3, Canada
Fides/Claretian, P.O. Box F, Notre Dame, IN 46556
Floating Island Publications, P.O. Box 516, Point Reyes Station, CA 94956
Folder Editions, 10326 68th Rd., #A63, Forest Hills, NY 11375
Foothills Press, El Dorado Hills, CA 95630
Four Winds Press, 50 W. 44th St., New York, NY 10035
Four Zoas Press, P.O. Box 461, Ware, MA 01082
Free University Press, 526 E. 52nd St., Indianapolis, IN 46205
Front Street Publishers, 129 Front St., Rm. 301, New York, NY 10005

G

Chost Dance Press, 6009 W. 101st Place, Shawnee Mission, KS 66207
Godine Press, 306 Dartmouth St., Boston, MA 02116
Golden Quill Press, Inc., Francestown, NH 03043
Graywolf Press, P.O. Box 142, Port Townsend, WA 98368
Greenwillow Books, 105 Madison Ave., New York, NY 10016
Grey Fox Press, P.O. Box 159, Bolinas, CA 94924
Greyledge Press, Smithfield, RI 02917
Grilled Flowers Press, P.O. Box 809, Iowa City, IA 52240
Grosset & Dunlap, Inc., 51 Madison Ave., New York, NY 10010
Gusto Press, 2960 Philip Ave., Bronx, NY 10465

H

Hallmark Publishing, 25th & McGee, Kansas City, MO 64141
Hanging Loose Press, 231 Wyckoff St., Brooklyn, NY 11217
Harcourt Brace Jovanovich, Inc., 757 Third Ave., New York, NY 10017
Harper & Row Publishers, Inc., 10 E. 53rd St., New York, NY 10022
Harvard University Press, 79 Garden St., Cambridge, MA 02138
Thom Henricks Associates, c/o Delcon Corp., Harlan Star Route, P.O. Box 323, Eddyville, OR 97343
Hesperus Press, Williamson, NY 14589
High/Coo Press, 26-11 Hilltop Dr., West Lafayette, IN 47906
W. D. Hoffstadt & Sons, 606 Ulster St., Syracuse, NY 13204
Holmgangers Press, 22 Arith Lane, Alamo, CA 94507
Holt, Rinehart & Winston, Inc., 383 Madison Ave., New York, NY 10017
Holy Terrible Editions, Albuquerque, NM
Horizon Press, 156 Fifth Ave., New York, NY 10010
Hounslow Press, 124 Parkview, Toronto, Ont., Canada
Houghton Mifflin Co., 2 Beacon St., Boston, MA 02107
House of Keys, P.O. Box 7952, Atlanta, GA 30357
Hunter College Press, 695 Park Ave., New York, NY 10021

I

Illuminati Press, 1147 S. Robertson Blvd., Los Angeles, CA 90035
Indigena Publications, Venice, CA 90291
Institute for Polynesian Studies, Laie, HI 96762
Iowa State University Press, S. State Ave., Ames, IA 50010
Iron Mountain Press, P.O. Box D, Emory, VA 24327
Ithaca House, 108 N. Plain St., Ithaca, NY 14850

J

Jargon Society, P.O. Box 106, Frankfort, KY 40602
Johns Hopkins University Press, Baltimore, MD 21218
Justus Publications, San Diego, CA

K

Karmic Revenge Laundry Shop Press, P.O. Box 14, Guttenberg, NJ 07093
Kastle Press, 170 Broadway, New York, NY 10038
Kelsey Street Press, 2824 Kelsey St., Berkeley, CA 94705
Keystone Press, Harrisburg, PA
Killaly Press, 764 Dalkeith Ave., London, Ont. N5X 1R8, Canada
Alfred A. Knopf, Inc., 201 E. 50th St., New York, NY 10022
Konglomerati Press, 5719 S. 29th Ave., Gulfport, FL 33707
Kulchur Foundation, 888 Park Ave., New York, NY 10021
Kylix Press, 1485 Maywood, Ann Arbor, MI 48103

L

Laughing Bear Press, P.O. Box 14, Woodinville, WA 98072
Leo Press, Allen Park, MI 48101
L'Epervier Press, 1219 E. Laurel, Fort Collins, CO 80521
Linden Publishers, 27 W. 11th St., New York, NY 10011
Link Limited Press, Chicago, IL
Literati Press, Freeport, NY 11520
Little, Brown & Co., 34 Beacon St., Boston, MA 02106
Little Caesar Press, 3373 Overland Ave., #2, Los Angeles, CA 90034
Liveright Publishing Corp., 500 Fifth Ave., New York, NY 10036
Long Measure Press, P.O. Box 1618, Chalmette Meraux, LA 70075
Lost Roads Publishers, P.O. Box 210, Fayetteville, AR 72701
Lothrop, Lee & Shephard Co., 105 Madison Ave., New York, NY 10016
Lotus Press, P.O. Box 21607, College Park Sta., Detroit, MI 48221
Louisiana State University Press, University Sta., Baton Rouge, LA 70803
Lydian Press, Kaneohe, HI 96744
Lynx House Press, P.O. Box 800, Amherst, MA 01002

M

MEM Press, Kokomo, IN 46901
Macmillan Publishing Co., Inc., 866 Third Ave., New York, NY 10022
Macmillan Co. of Canada, Ltd., 70 Bond St., Toronto, Ont. M5B 1X3, Canada
Manroot, P. O. Box 982, South San Francisco, CA 94080
Richard Marek Publishers, Inc., 200 Madison Ave., New York, NY 10016
McClelland and Stewart, Ltd., 25 Hollinger Rd., Toronto, Ont. M4B 3G2, Canada
McGraw-Hill Book Co., 1221 Ave. of the Americas, New York, NY 10020
Metatron, Milwaukee, WI
Mr. Cogito Press, Pacific University, P.O. Box 627, Forest Grove, OR 97116
Momo's Press, P.O. Box 14061, San Francisco, CA 94114

William Morrow & Co., Inc., 105 Madison Ave., New York, NY 10016
Mudborn Press, 209 W. De la Guerra, Santa Barbara, CA 93101

N

Naturegraph Publishers, Inc., Indian Creek Rd., P.O. Box 1075, Happy Camp, CA 96039
New College Press, 5700 N. Trail, Sarasota, FL 33580
New Delta, La Salle, Que., Canada
New Directions Publishing Corp., 333 Ave. of the Americas, New York, NY 10014
New Poets Series, 541 Piccadilly Rd., Baltimore, MD 21204
New Rivers Press, 1602 Selby Ave., St. Paul, MN 55104
New Victoria Publishers, Inc., 7 Bank St., Lebanon, NH 03766
No Dead Lines, 241 Bonita, Portola Valley, CA 94025
Nobodaddy Press, 100 College Hill Rd., Clinton, NY 13323
Nordic Books, P.O. Box 1941, Philadelphia, PA 19105
Nortex Press, P.O. Box 120, Quanah, TX 79252
North American Review Press, University of Northern Iowa, Cedar Falls, IA 50613
North Atlantic Books, 456 Hudson St., Oakland, CA 94618
Northeast/Juniper Books, 1310 Shorewood Dr., La Crosse, WI 54601
Northeastern University Press, 360 Huntington Ave., Boston, MA 02115
Northwoods Press, Inc., R.D. 1, Meadows of Dan, VA 24120
W. W. Norton & Co., Inc., 500 Fifth Ave., New York, NY 10036
Norwood Editions, P.O. Box 38, Norwood, PA 19074

O

Oberlin College Press, Oberlin, OH 44074
Offshore Press, Westport Point, MA 02791
Ohio State University Press, 2070 Neil Ave., Columbus, OH 43210
Ohio University Press, 56 E. Union St., Athens, OH 45701
Open Places, c/o Stephens College, P.O. Box 2085, Columbia, MO 65201
Osiers Press, 204 W. Main St., Decorah, IA 52101
Outland Press, Lewisville, PA 19351
Overlook Press, 625 Madison Ave., New York, NY 10022
Ox Head Press, 414 N. 6th St., Marshall, MN 56258
Oxford University Press, 200 Madison Ave., New York, NY 10016; 70 Wynford Dr., Toronto, Ont., Canada
Oyez, P.O. Box 5134, Berkeley, CA 94705

P

Parousia Press, P.O. Box 500, Storrs, CT 06268
Paycock Press, 5202 Fordyce Place, Bethesda, MD 20014
Pegasus Publications, Saratoga, CA 95070
Penguin Books, Inc., 625 Madison Ave., New York, NY 10022
Pennsylvania State University Press, 215 Wagner Bldg., University Park, PA 16802
Pentagram Press, P.O. Box 11609, Milwaukee, WI 53211
Penumbra Press, Moonbeam, Ont., Canada
Perivale Press, 13830 Erwin St., Van Nuys, CA 91401
Persea Books, Inc., P.O. Box 804, Madison Square Sta., New York, NY 10010
Phainopepla Press, Tucson, AZ
Philosophical Library, Inc., 15 E. 40th St., New York, NY 10016
Pisces Press, Wellton, AZ 85356
Porch Publications, c/o James Cervantes, Arizona State University, Dept. of English, Tempe, AZ 85281
Porcupine's Quill, Erin, Ont., Canada
Pourboire Press, P.O. Box 315, Woods Hole, MA 02543
Prairie Poet Books, P.O. Box 35, Charleston, IL 61920
Prescott Street Press, 407 Postal Bldg., Portland, OR 97204
Press Pacifica, P.O. Box 47, Kailua, HI 96734
Prickly Pear Press, 2132 Edwin St., Fort Worth, TX 76110

Princeton University Press, 41 William St., Princeton, NJ 08540
Proteus Press, 1004 N. Jefferson St., Arlington, VA 22205

Q

Quarterly Review of Literature, 26 Haslet Ave., Princeton, NJ 08540

R

Raintree Children's Books, 205 W. Highland Ave., Milwaukee, WI 53203
Raintree Press, 4043 Morningside Dr., Bloomington, IN 47401
Random House, Inc., 201 E. 50th St., New York, NY 10022
Realities Library, 2480 Escalonia Court, San Jose, CA 95121
I. Reed Books, New York, NY
Fleming H. Revell Co., 184 Central Ave., Old Tappan, NJ 07675
Rhythms Press, Santa Barbara, CA
Rook Press, P.O. Box 144, Ruffs Dale, PA 15679
Rosebud Press, Berkeley, CA
Rowman and Littlefield, Inc., 81 Adams Dr., Totowa, NJ 07512

S

Saint Andrews Press, Saint Andrews Presbyterian College, Laurinburg, NC 28352
St. John's River Press, Orange City, FL 32763
St. Luke's Press, 1407 Union Ave., Ste. 401, Memphis, TN 38104
St. Martin's Press, 175 Fifth Ave., New York, NY 10010
Samisdat Press, P.O. Box 231, Richford, VT 05476
San Marcos Press, P.O. Box 53, Cerrillos, NM 87010
San Pedro Press, R.R. 1, Box 220, St. David, AZ 85630
Sand Dollar Books, 1222 Solano Ave., Albany, CA 94706
Charles Scribner's Sons, 597 Fifth Ave., New York, NY 10017
Seabury Press, Inc., 815 Second Ave., New York, NY 10017
Seagull Publications, Inc., 1736 E. 53rd St., Brooklyn, NY 11234
Second Coming Press, P.O. Box 31249, San Francisco, CA 94131
Service-berry Press, Milwaukee, WI
Seven Woods Press, P.O. Box 32, New York, NY 10014
Seventh Dream/Opus, Catonsville, MD 21228
Shambhala Publications, Inc., 1123 Spruce St., P.O. Box 271, Boulder, CO 80302
Harold Shaw Publishers, 388 Gundersen Dr., P.O. Box 567, Wheaton, IL 60187
Sheep Meadow Press, 145 Central Park West, New York, NY 10023
Shulsinger Bros., Inc., 121 W. 17th St., New York, NY 10011
Sibyl-Child Press, Inc., c/o Stapen, 6906 W. Park Dr., Hyattsville, MD 20783
Simon & Schuster, Inc., 630 Fifth Ave., New York, NY 10020
Singing Wind Press, 4164 W. Pine, St. Louis, MO 63108
Slow Loris Press, 923 Highview St., Pittsburgh, PA 15206
The Smith Publishers (New York/London), 5 Beekman St., New York, NY 10038
Sothis & Co. Publishing, P.O. Box 1166, Del Mar, CA 92014
South and West, Inc., P.O. Box 446, Fort Smith, AR 72901
Sparrow Press, c/o Vagrom Publications, 103 Waldron St., West Lafayette, IN 47906
Spoon River Poetry Press, P.O. Box 1443, Peoria, IL 61655
Spring Valley Press, P.O. Box 306, Langley, WA 98260
Stone Country Press, 20 Lorraine Rd., Madison, NJ 07940
Stone Soup Press, P.O. Box 83, Santa Cruz, CA 95063
Street Press, P.O. Box 555, Port Jefferson, NY 11777
Sumac Press, P.O. Box 39, Fremont, MI 49412
Sun Publishing Co., P.O. Box 4383, Albuquerque, NM 87106
sun rise fall down artpress, 838A Wisconsin St., Oshkosh, WI 54901
Sverge-Haus Publishers, 11 Indian Spring Rd., Milton, MA 02186
Swallow Press, Inc., 811 W. Junior Terrace, Chicago, IL 60613

T

Tamarisk Press, 188 Forest Ave., Ramsey, NJ 07446
Taurean Horn Press, P.O. Box 14726, San Francisco, CA 94114
Texas Center for Writers Press, P.O. Box 19876, Dallas, TX 75219
Texas Tech Press, Lubbock, TX 79409
Thorp Springs Press, 3414 Robinson Ave., Austin, TX 78722
Three Continents Press, 1346 Connecticut Ave., NW, Ste. 1131, Washington, DC 20036
Three Rivers Press, Carnegie-Mellon University, P.O. Box 21, Pittsburgh, PA 15213
Three Sheets Press, Lincoln, NE
Thunder City Press, P.O. Box 11126, Birmingham, AL 35202
Tombouctou Books, P.O. Box 265, Bolinas, CA 94924
Toothpaste Press, 626 E. Main St., P.O. Box 546, West Branch, IA 52358
Tortilla Press, South Pasadena, CA 91030
Trask House Books, Inc., 2754 SE 27th Ave., Portland, OR 97202
Treacle Press, 437 Springtown Rd., New Paltz, NY 12561
Trike, P.O. Box 7322, Pismo Beach, CA 93449
Triton Press, Boulder Creek, CA 95006
Turnstone Press, St. John's College, University of Manitoba, Winnipeg, Man. R3T 2M5, Canada
C. E. Tuttle Co., Rutland, VT 05701
Tuscany Alley, San Francisco, CA
Tuumba Press, 2639 Russell St., Berkeley, CA 94705
Twayne Publishers, Inc., c/o G. K. Hall & Co., 70 Lincoln St., Boston, MA 02111
Tyndale House Publishers, 336 Gundersen Dr., Wheaton, IL 60187

U

Frederick Ungar Publishing Co., 250 Park Ave., S., New York, NY 10003
Unicorn Press, P.O. Box 3307, Greensboro, NC 27402
University of Alabama Press, Drawer 2877, University, AL 35486
University of California Press, 2223 Fulton St., Berkeley, CA 94720
University Presses of Florida, 15 NW 15th St., Gainesville, FL 32661
University of Georgia Press, Waddell Hall, Athens, GA 30602
University of Illinois Press, Urbana, IL 61801
University of Massachusetts Press, P.O. Box 429, Amherst, MA 01002
University of Missouri Press, 107 Swallow Hall, Columbia, MO 65201
University of Nebraska Press, 901 N. 17th St., Lincoln, NE 68588
University of Pittsburgh Press, 127 N. Bellefield Ave., Pittsburgh, PA 15260
University Press of America, 4710 SE Auth Place, Washington, DC 20023
University of Texas Press, P.O. Box 7819, Austin, TX 78712
University Press of Virginia, P.O. Box 3608, University Sta., Charlottesville, VA 22903
Utah State University Press, UMC 05, Logan, UT 84322

V

Vaginal Vegtetun Editions, Albuquerque, NM
Valkyrie Press, Inc., 2135 1st St., S., St. Petersburg, FL 33712
Vanguard Press, Inc., 424 Madison Ave., New York, NY 10017
Vantage Press, Inc., 516 W. 34th St., New York, NY 10001
Viking Press, Inc., 625 Madison Ave., New York, NY 10022
Vintage Books, 201 E. 50th St., New York, NY 10022

W

Washington Writers' Publishing House, P.O. Box 50068, Washington, DC 20006
Waver's Edge Press, Bayside, NY 11364
Wesleyan University Press, 55 High St., Middletown, CT 06457
West Coast Poetry Review, 1335 Dartmouth Dr., Reno, NV 89509
West End Press, P.O. Box 697, Cambridge, MA 02139

Westigan Review Press, University of Utah, Dept. of English, Salt Lake City, UT 84112
Whatever Publishing, Berkeley, CA
White Raven, Boston, MA
Windy Row Press, 43 Grove St., Peterborough, NH 03458
Wings Press, R. 2, Box 325, Belfast, ME 04915
Wolfsong, P.O. Box 252, Iola, WI 54945
Woodhix Press, Seattle, WA
Woolmer & Brotherson, Ltd., Gladstone Hollow, Andes, NY 13731
The Word, San Francisco, CA
Word Works, Inc., P.O. Box 4054, Washington, DC 20015
Workman Publishing Co., Inc., 231 E. 51st St., New York, NY 10022

X

X Press Publishers, Manchester, MA 01944

Y

Yale University Press, 302 Temple St., New Haven, CT 06511
Yellow Press, Inc., 2394 Blue Island, Chicago, IL 60608
York Publishing, 653 The Queensway, Toronto, Ont., Canada

Z

Zahir, P.O. Box 715, Newburyport, MA 01950
Zone Press, P.O. Box 194, Bay Sta., Brooklyn, NY 11235

Magazines Publishing Poetry

*The following United States and Canadian periodicals publish
original poetry on a regular basis.*

A

A.M.E. Review, 468 Lincoln Dr., NW, Atlanta, GA 30318

A.S.F.A. Poetry Quarterly, Alabama School of Fine Arts, 800 8th Ave., W., Box A-16, Birmingham Southern College, Birmingham, AL 35204

ASPO Newsletter, P.O. Box 6112, Albany, CA 94706

A Different Drummer—The Poets Journal, P.O. Box 487x, Toms River, NJ 08753

A Shout In The Street: A Journal Of Literary And Visual Art, English Dept., Queens College, Flushing, NY 11367

Abba, A Journal of Prayer, P.O. Box 8516, Austin, TX 78712

Abbey, 5011-2 Green Mountain Circle, Columbia, MD 21044

Absinthe, Indian Tree Press, Barryville, NY 12719

Abyss, P.O. Box C, Somerville, MA 02143

Acceptance, 230 San Juan, Venice, CA 90291

Acid Switch, 716 Clement Ave., Charlotte, NC 28204

Adirondack Almanack, Box 11-A, RD 2, Corinth, NY 12822

Adventures In Poetry Magazine, 3915 SW Military Dr., San Antonio, TX 78211

Advisory Board Record, P.O. Box 2066 or 2204, Chapel Hill, NC 27514

Aeolian-Harp, 1395 James St., Burton, MI 48529

Aero Sun-Times, 435 Stapleton Bldg., Billings, MT 59101

After-Image, P.O. Box 10144, Towson, MD 21204

Against The Wall, P.O. Box 444, Westfield, NJ 07091

The Agni Review, P.O. Box 349, Cambridge, MA 02138

Ahsahta, Boise State University, Dept. of English, Boise, ID 83725

Akwesasne Notes, Mohawk Nation, Roosevelt, NY 13683

Albatross, P.O. Box 2046, Central Sta., East Orange, NJ 07019

Albireo Quarterly P.O. Box 4345, Albuquerque, NM 87106

The Alchemist, Box 123, LaSalle, P.Q., Canada

Alcheringa: Ethnopoetics, 745 Commonwealth Ave., Boston, MA 02215

Aldebaran, Roger Williams College, Bristol, RI 02809

Alembic, 1744 Slaterville Rd., Ithaca, NY 14850

Aleph, 7319 Willow Ave., Takoma Park, MD 20012

Alive! For Young Teens, P.O. Box 179, St. Louis, MO 63166

All-Time Favorite Poetry, P.O. Box 2057, North Babylon, NY 11703

Alpha, P.O. Box 1269, Wolfville, N.S. BOP 1X0, Canada

The Altadena Review, P.O. Box 212, Altadena, CA 91001

The Alternative Press, 3090 Copeland Rd., Grindstone City, MI 48467

Alternative Sources of Energy Magazine, Rt. 2, Box 90A, Milaca, MN 56353

America, 106 W. 56th St., New York, NY 10019

The American Atheist, 4408 Medical Pkwy., Austin, TX 78756

American Dane Magazine, Box 31748, Omaha, NE 68131

American Jewish Times-Outlook, P.O. Box 10674, Charlotte, NC 28234

American Poetry League Magazine, 3925 SW Military Dr., San Antonio, TX 78211

American Poetry Review, 1616 Walnut St., Rm. 405, Philadelphia, PA 19103

The American Scholar, 1811 Q St., NW, Washington, DC 20009

The American Zionist, 4 E. 34th St., New York, NY 10016

Androgyne, 930 Shields, San Francisco, CA 94132

Anemone, Journal of Poetry And Related Arts, 550 Alta Vista Way, Laguna Beach, CA 92651

Anima, 1053 Wilson Ave., Chambersburg, PA 17201

Ann Arbor Review, Washtenaw Community College, Ann Arbor, MI 48106

Annals Of Saint De Beaupre, Basilica of St. Anne, Quebec, P.Q. GOA 3C0, Canada

Another Chicago Magazine, 1742 W. Touhy, Chicago, IL 60626

Antaeus, 1 W. 30th St., New York, NY 10001

Anthos, P.O. Box 4789, Sta. E., Ottawa, Ont. K1S 5H9, Canada

The Antigonish Review, St. Francis Xavier University, Antigonish, Nova Scotia B2G, 1C0, Canada

Antioch Review, P.O. Box 148, Yellow Springs, OH 45387

Apalachee Quarterly, P.O. Box 20106, Tallahassee, FL 32304

Applecart, 12201 N. Woodcrest Dr., Dunlap, IL 61525

Aquila, Box 174-B, Petersburg, PA 16669

Ararat, 628 Second Ave., New York, NY 10016

The Ardent Saboteur: A Journal of Amnemonics, 716 Clement Ave., Charlotte, NC 28204

Ariel, University of Calgary, Calgary, Alta. T2N 1N4,

Canada

Arizona Quarterly, University of Arizona, Tucson, AZ 85721

The Ark River Review, c/o A. G. Sobin, Box 14, Wichita State University, Wichita, KS 67208

Artaud's Elbow, P.O. Box 1139, Berkeley, CA 94701

As Is, 6302 Owen Pl., Bethesda, MD 20034

Ascent, English Dept., University of Illinois, Urbana, IL 61801

The Asia Mail, P.O. Box 1044, Alexandria, VA 22313

Aspect, 13 Robinson St., Somerville, MA 02145

Aspen Anthology, P.O. Box 3185, Aspen, CO 81611

Aspire, 1819 E. 14th Ave., Denver, CO 80218

Ataraxia, 291 Pine St., Madison, GA 30650

The Atlantic Advocate, Gleaner Bldg., Phoenix Square, Fredericton, N.B. E3B 5A2, Canada

The Atlantic Monthly, 8 Arlington St., Boston, MA 02116

Atlantis, Box 294, Acadia University, Wolfville, N.S., Canada

Attention Please, 708 Inglewood Dr., Broderick, CA 95605

August Derleth Society Newsletter, 61 Teecomwas Dr., Uncasville, CT 06382

Auntie Bellum, P.O. Box 3473, Columbia, SC 29230

B

Bachy, 11317 Santa Monica Blvd., Los Angeles, CA 90025

Back Country, P.O. Box 83, Elkins, WV 26241

Back Door, P.O. Box 481, Athens, OH 45701

Back Roads. P.O. Box 543, Cotati, CA 94928

Ball State University Forum, Ball State University, Muncie, IN 47306

Barataria, P.O. Box 15060, New Orleans, LA 70175

Barbeque Planet, 2513-B Ashwood Ave., Nashville, TN 37212

Bardic Echoes, 1036 Emerald Ave., NE, Grand Rapids, MI 49503

The Beehive, 201 8th Ave., S., Nashville, TN 37203

The Bellingham Review, 412 N. State St., Bellingham, WA 98225

Beloit Poetry Journal, P.O. Box 2, Beloit, WI 53511

Bennington Review, Bennington College, Bennington, VT 05201

Berkeley Barb, P.O. Box 1247, Berkeley, CA 94701

Berkeley Monthly, 2275 Shattuck Ave., Berkeley, CA 94704

Berkeley Poetry Review, c/o Office of Student Activities, 103 Sproul Hall, University of California, Berkeley, CA 94720

Berkeley Poets Cooperative, P.O. Box 459, Berkeley, CA 94701

Best Friends, 29 Montclaire, NE, Albuquerque, NM 87108

Best in Poetry, P.O. Box 2057, North Babylon, NY 11703

Best Poets Of The 20th Century, Drawer J, Babylon, NY 11702

Beyond Baroque, 681 Venice Blvd., Venice, CA 90291

Big Moon, P.O. Box 4731, Modesto, CA 95350

Bird Effort, 25 Mudford Ave., Easthampton, NY 11937

Birthstone, 1319 6th Ave., San Francisco, CA 94122

Bits, c/o Dept. of English, Case Western Reserve University, Cleveland, OH 44106

Bitterroot, Blythebourne Sta., P.O. Box 51, Brooklyn, NY 11219

Bittersweet, 777 Brice St., Lebanon, MO 65536

Black American Literature Forum, Indiana State University, Parsons Hall 237, Terre Haute, IN 47809

The Black Cat, c/o Richard Morgan, English Dept., P.O. Box 22990A, East Tennessee State University, Johnson City, TN 37601

Black Forum, P.O. Box 1090, Bronx, NY 10451

Black Graphics International, P.O. Box 732, Detroit, MI 48206

Black Maria, 815 W. Wrightwood, Chicago, IL 60614

Black Moss, RR 1, Coatsworth, Ont., Canada

The Black Scholar, P.O. Box 908, Sausalito, CA 94965

The Black Warrior Review, University of Alabama, P.O. Box 2936, University, AL 35486

Blackberry, P.O. Box 4757, Albuquerque, NM 81706

Bleb/The Ark, P.O. Box 322, Times Square Sta., New York, NY 10036

Blind Alley, P.O. Box 1296, Edinburg, TX 78539

Bloodroot, P.O. Box 891, Grand Forks, ND 58201

Blue Buildings, 661 34th St., Des Moines, IA 50312

Blue Moon News, c/o English Dept., University of Arizona, Tucson, AZ 85721

Blue Pig, 23 Cedar St., Northampton, MA 01060

Blue Ridge Review, P.O. Box 1425, Charlottesville, VA 22902

Blue Unicorn, 22 Avon Rd., Kensington, CA 94707

The Body Politic-Gay Liberation Journal, P.O. Box 7289, Sta. A, Toronto, Ont. M5W 1X9, Canada

Bombast Poetry Review, P.O. Box 3752, Modesto, CA 95352

Bonsai: A Quarterly of Haiku, P.O. Box 7211, Phoenix, AZ 85011

Books In Canada, 366 Adelaide St., E., Toronto, Ont., Canada

The Boston Phoenix, 100 Massachusetts Ave., Boston, MA 02115

Boston University Journal, 704 Commonwealth Ave., Boston, MA 02215

Both Sides Now, 1232 Laura St., P.O. Box 13079, Jacksonville, FL 32206

Bottomfish Magazine, 21250 Stevens Creek, Cupertino, CA 95014

Boundary 2, State University of New York, Binghamton, NY 13901

Box 749 Magazine, P.O. Box 749, Old Chelsea Sta., New York, NY 10011

Boxcar, 1001-B Guerrero, San Francisco, CA 94110

Boxspring, Hampshire College, Amherst, MA 01002

Branching Out, P.O. Box 4098, Edmonton, Alta T6E 4T1, Canada

Breakthrough! 2015 S. Broadway, Little Rock, AR 72206

Bridge Magazine, P.O. Box 477, New York, NY 10013

Brilliant Corners: A Magazine Of The Arts, 1372 W. Estes, #2N, Chicago, IL 60626

Buckeye Farm News, 245 N. High St., Columbus, OH 43216

Buckle, English Dept., State University, 1300 Elmwood Ave., Buffalo, NY 14222

0B9, Canada

The Emissary, P.O. Box 328, Loveland, CO 80537

En Passant Poetry Quarterly, 1906 Brant Rd., Wilmington, DE 19810

Encore: A Quarterly Of Verse And Poetic Arts, 1121 Major Ave., NW, Albuquerque, NM 87107

Enduring World Adult Teacher, 6401 The Paseo, Kansas City, MO 64131

Endymion, 562 West End Ave., Apt. 6A, New York, NY 10024

Epoch: A Magazine Of Contemporary Literature, 245 Goldwin Smith Hall, Cornell University, Ithaca, NY 14853

Epos, Dept. of English, Troy State University, Troy, AL 36081

Etc: A Review of General Semantics, University of Wyoming, Laramie, WY 82070

Eureka Review, Dept. of English, University of Cincinnati, Cincinnati, OH 45221

Euterpe, 417 W. 56th St., New York, NY 10019

Evangel, 999 College Ave., Winona Lake, IN 46590

The Evangelical Beacon, 1515 E. 66th St., Minneapolis, MN 55423

Event, Douglas College, P.O. Box 2503, New Westminster, B.C. V3L 5B2, Canada

Exile, Box 546, Downsview, Ont., Canada

Exit, 50 Inglewood Dr., Rochester, NY 14619

Expanding Horizons (for older poets only), 93-05 68th Ave., Forest Hills, NY 11375

Expressive Arts Review, P.O. Box 444, Brentwood, NY 11717

F

Face-To-Face, 201 8th Ave., S., Nashville, TN 37202

The Falcon, Mansfield State College, Mansfield, PA 16933

Fantasy Crossroads, P.O. Box 12428, Shawnee Mission, KS 66212

Far West, 2949 Century Pl., Costa Mesa, CA 92626

Farm Wife News, 733 N. Van Buren, Milwaukee, WI 53202

The Fault, 33513 6th St., Union City, CA 94587

Feminist Studies, c/o Women's Studies Program, University of Maryland, College Park, MD 20742

The Fiddlehead, The Observatory, University of New Brunswick, Fredericton, N.B. E3B 5A3, Canada

Field, Rice Hall, Oberlin College, Oberlin, OH 44074

Fifth Sun, 1134-B Chelsea Ave., Santa Monica, CA 90403

Film Culture, G.P.O. Box 1499, New York, NY 10001

Firelands Arts Review, Firelands Campus, Huron, OH 44839

First World: An International Journal Of Black Thought, 1580 Avon Ave., S.W., Atlanta, GA 30311

Fit, 524 Linden Rd., University Park, PA 16802

Florida Fiesta, P.O. Box 820, Boca Raton, FL 33432

Floral Underawl Gazette, P.O. Box 2066 or 2204, Chapel Hill, NC 27514

Focus: A Journal For Gay Women, Room 323, 419 Boylston St., Boston, MA 02116

Focus/Midwest, 928a N. McKnight, St. Louis, MO 63132

Folio, 2207 Shattuck Ave., Berkeley, CA 94704

Follies, P.O. Box 5231, Pasadena, CA 91107

The Foolkiller: A Journal Of Popular People's Culture, 2 W. 39th St., Kansas City, MO 64111

The Foothill Quarterly, 12345 El Monte Rd., Los Altos Hills, CA 94022

Footprint Magazine, 150 W. Summit St., Somerville, NJ 08876

Forge, 47 Murray St., New York, NY 10007

Forum On The Jewish People, Zionism and Israel, 515 Park Ave., New York, NY 10022

4 Elements, 504 Inverness Ct., St. Simons Island, GA 31522

Four Quarters, La Salle College, Olney Ave. at 20th St., Philadelphia, PA 19141

Fragments, P.O. Box 1128, Los Alamitos, CA 90720

Free Lance: A Magazine Of Poetry And Prose, 6005 Grand Ave., Cleveland, OH 44104

The Friend, 50 East North Temple, Salt Lake City, UT 84150

Friday Forum (Of The Jewish Exponent), 226 S. 16th St., Philadelphia, PA 19102

The Front, P.O. Box 1355, Kingston, Ont. K7L 5C6, Canada

Front Street Trolley, 2125 Acklen Ave., Nashville, TN 37212

Frontiers: A Journal Of Women Studies, Hillside Court 104, University of Colorado, Boulder, CO 80309

Frozen Waffles, 321 N. Indiana, Bloomington, IN 47401

The Further Range, 27 Oval Rd., Milburn, NJ 07041

G

G.P.U. News, P.O. Box 92203, Milwaukee, WI 53202

Galileo, 339 Newbury St., Boston, MA 02115

Gargoyle, 160 Boylston St., No. 3, Jamaica Plain, MA 02130

Gay Sunshine: A Journal Of Gay Liberation, P.O. Box 40397, San Francisco, CA 94140

Gay Tide, P.O. Box 14638, Sta. A, Vancouver, B.C. V5L 1X5, Canada

The Georgia Review, University of Georgia, Athens, GA 30602

Gesar-Buddhist Perspectives, 5856 Doyle St., Emeryville, CA 94608

Ghost Dance: The International Quarterly Of Experimental Poetry, 526 Forest, East Lansing, MI 48823

Glassworks, P.O. Box 163, Rosebank Sta., Staten Island, NY 10305

Gnostica Magazine, Box 3383, St. Paul, MN 55165

Golf Magazine, 380 Madison Avenue, New York, NY 10017

The Goliards, 3515 18th St., Bellingham, WA 98225

Good Housekeeping, 959 Eighth Ave., New York, NY 10019

Gourmet, 777 Third Ave., New York, NY 10017

Graffiti, English Dept., Box 418, Lenoir Rhyne College, Hickory, NC 28601

Graham House Review, Box 489, Englewood, NJ 07631

The Gramercy Review, P.O. Box 15362, Los Angeles, CA 90015

Granite, P.O. Box 1367, Southampton, NY 11968

Grass Roots Forum, P.O. Box 472, San Gabriel, CA 91778

Gravida, P.O. Box 76, Hartsdale, NY 10530

Gray Day, 2830 Napier Ave., Macon, GA 31204

Great Circumpolar Bear Cult, P.O. Box 468, Ashland, WI 54806

The Great Lakes Review, Northeastern Illinois University, Chicago, IL 60625

Great River Review, 211 W. Wabasha, Winona, MN 55987

Green Mountain Quarterly, 460 N. Main St., Oshkosh, WI 54901

Green River Review, SVSC Box 56, University Center, MI 48710

The Greenfield Review, P.O. Box 80, Greenfield Center, NY 12833

Greenhouse Review, 126 Escalona Dr., Santa Cruz, CA 95060

Green's Magazine, P.O. Box 313, Detroit, MI 48231

Greensboro Review, Dept. of English, North Carolina University, Greensboro, NC 27412

Grist, 195 Lakeview Ave., Cambridge, MA 02138

Grit, 208 W. Third St., Williamsport, PA 17701

Grub Street, P.O. Box 91, Bellmore, NY 11710

Guide, 6856 Eastern Ave., Washington, DC 20012

H

Hampden-Sydney Poetry Review, P.O. Box 126, Hampden-Sydney, VA 23943

Hand Book, 184 NW Broadway, Columbus, OH 43214

Hang Gliding, P.O. Box 66306, 11312½ Venice Blvd., Los Angeles, CA 90066

Hanging Loose, 231 Wyckoff St., Brooklyn, NY 11217

Happiness Holding Tank, 1790 Grand River, Okemos, MI 48864

Happy Times, 3558 S. Jefferson Ave., St. Louis, MO 63118

Hard Pressed, P.O. Box 161915, Sacramento, CA 95816

Harlequin, 240 Duncan Mill Rd., Don Mills, Ont. M3B 1Z4, Canada

Harmony, M.U.B. Rm. 153, University of New Hampshire, Durham, NH 03824

Harper's Magazine, 2 Park Ave., Room 1809, New York, NY 10016

The Harvard Advocate, 21 South St., Cambridge, MA 02138

Harvest, P.O. Box 78, Farmington, CT 06032

Harvest Quarterly, 907 Santa Barbara St., Santa Barbara, CA 93101

Hawaii Review, Dept. of English, University of Hawaii, Honolulu, HI 96822

Heirs, 657 Mission St., San Francisco, CA 94105

The Herald, SPO 11, Asbury Theological Seminary, Wilmore, KY 40390

Heresies: A Feminist Publication On Art And Politics, 225 Lafayette St., Rm. 1008, New York, NY 10013

Hh Magazine, 5355 Walkley, No. 40, Montreal, P.Q., Canada

Higginson Journal Of Poetry, 4508 38th St., Brentwood, MD 20722

High/Coo: A Quarterly Of Short Poetry, 26-11 Hilltop Dr., West Lafayette, IN 47906

Hills, 1220 Folsom, San Francisco, CA 94183

Hiram Poetry Review, P.O. Box 162, Hiram, OH 44234

His, 5206 Main St., Downers Grove, IL 60515

Hodmandod, 610 35th Ave., San Francisco, CA 94121

The Hollins Critic, P.O. Box 9538, Hollins College, VA 24020

Hollow Spring Review Of Poetry, P.O. Box 76, Berkshire, MA 01224

Horseman: The Magazine Of Western Riding, 5314 Bingle Rd., Houston, TX 77092

Hot Water Review, 42 W. Washington Lane, Philadelphia, PA 19144

Houston Scene Magazine, 3600 Yoakum, Houston, TX 77006

The Hudson Review, 65 E. 55th St., New York, NY 10022

Huerfano, P.O. Box 49155, University Sta., Tucson, AZ 85717

The Humanist, 923 Kensington Ave., Buffalo, NY 14215

Humanist In Canada, P.O. Box 157, Victoria, B.C. V8W 2M6, Canada

Humpty Dumpty's Magazine, 52 Vanderbilt Ave., New York, NY 10017

Huron Review, 423 S. Franklin Ave., Flint, MI 48503

Hyperion: A Poetry Journal, c/o Hogan/Chase Park 2-D, Chapel Hill, NC 27514

I

Icarus, P.O. Box 8, Riderwood, MD 21139

Iconomatrix, P.O. Box 2, Postal Sta. A, Fredericton, N.B. E3B 4Y2, Canada

Ideals, 11315 Watertown Plank Rd., Milwaukee, WI 53201

Identity, 420 Madison Ave., New York, NY 10017

Illuminations, 1900 9th St., No. 8, Berkeley, CA 94710

Illyrian Revue, P.O. Box 450, Saddle Brook, NJ 07662

Image Magazine, P.O. Box 28048, St. Louis, MO 63119

Images, English Dept., Wright State University, Dayton, OH 45435

Impact: An International Quarterly Of Contemporary Poetry, P.O. Box 61297, Sunnyvale, CA 94088

Impressions, P.O. Box 5, Sta. B, Toronto, Ont. M5T 2T2, Canada

Impulse, P.O. Box 901, Sta. Q, Toronto, Ont., Canada

In A Nutshell, P.O. Box 22248, Sacramento, CA 95822

In Stride (poems about running, bicycling, raquetball, kayaking, etc.), 407 Jasmine Ave., Corona del Mar, CA 92625

In Touch, P.O. Box 2000, Marion, IN 46952

Indiana Writes, 321 Goodbody Hall, Bloomington, IN 47401

Inlet, Virginia Wesleyan College, Norfolk, VA 23502

Insight, 6856 Eastern Ave., Washington, DC 20012

Insight: A Quarterly Of Gay Catholic Opinion, P.O. Box 5110, Grand Central Sta., New York, NY 10017

The Insurgent Sociologist Magazine, c/o Dept. of Sociology, University of Oregon, Eugene, OR 97403

Integrity: Gay Episcopal Forum, 701 Orange St., No. 6, Fort Valley, GA 31030

Interaction, 3558 S. Jefferson, St. Louis, MO 63118

Intermedia, P.O. Box 31-464, San Francisco, CA 94131

Intermedia, Century Club Educational Arts Project, 10508 W. Pico Blvd., Los Angeles, CA 90026

The International New Age Newsletter, P.O. Box 1137, Harrison, AR 72601

International Poetry Review, SVSC Box 56, University Center, MI 48710

The International University Poetry Quarterly, 501 E. Armour Blvd., Kansas City, MO 64109

Interstate, P.O. Box 7068, University Sta., Austin, TX 78712

Intrepid, P.O. Box 1423, Buffalo, NY 14214

Intro, P.O. Box 501, Sta. S, Toronto, Ont. M5M 3L8, Canada

Invisible City, 6 San Gabriel Dr., Fairfax, CA 94930

The Iowa Review, EPB 321, University of Iowa, Iowa City, IA 53342

Ironwood, P.O. Box 40907, Tucson, AZ 85717

It's Our World, 800 Allegheny Ave., Pittsburgh, PA 15233

J

Jacksonville Poetry Quarterly, 5340 Weller Ave., Jacksonville, FL 32211

Jam To-day, P.O. Box 249, Northfield, VT 05663

Japanophile, P.O. Box 223, Okemos, MI 48864

Jeopardy, Western Washington University, Humanities 346, Bellingham, WA 98225

The Jewish Spectator, P.O. Box 2016, Santa Monica, CA 90406

"Joint" Conference (material written by prison inmates), P.O. Box 19332, Washington, DC 20036

Journal Of The Hellenic Diaspora, 461 Eighth Ave., New York, NY 10001

Journal Of Irish Literature, P.O. Box 361, Newark, DE 19711

Journal Of New Jersey Poets, English Dept., Fairleigh Dickinson University, 285 Madison Ave., Madison, NJ 07940

Journal Of Reading: The Reading Teacher, 600 Barksdale Rd., Newark, DE 19711

Journal Of World Education, 530 E. 86th St., New York, NY 10028

Jubilee (Canadian material only), 332 Minnic St., Wingham, Ont. NOG 2W0, Canada

Juice, 5402 Ygnacio, Oakland, CA 94601

K

Kaldron, 441 N. 6th St., Grover City, CA 93433

Kansas Quarterly, Denison Hall, Kansas State University, Manhattan, KS 66506

Karaki, 831 Kelvin St., Coquitlam, B.C., Canada

Karamu, English Dept., Eastern Illinois University, Charleston, IL 61920

Kayak, 325 Ocean View, Santa Cruz, CA 95062

The Kenyon Review, Kenyon College, Gambier, OH 43022

The Kindergartner, 201 Eighth Ave., S., Nashville, TN 37202

Konglomerati, 5719 29th Ave., S., Gulfport, FL 33707

Kosmos, 130 Eureka, San Francisco, CA 94114

Kudzu, P.O. Box 865, Cayce, SC 29033

Kuksu: Journal Of Backcountry Writing, P.O. Box 980, Alleghany Star Route, Nevada City, CA 95959

L

La-Bas: A Newsletter Of Experimental Poetry & Poetics, P.O. Box 431, College Park, MD 20740

The Ladder, P.O. Box 5025, Washington Sta., Reno, NV 89503

Lady-Unique-Inclination-Of-The-Night, P.O. Box 803, New Brunswick, NJ 08903

The Lake Superior Review, P.O. Box 724, Ironwood, MI 49938

Lakes & Prairies: A Journal Of Writings, P.O. Box A-3454, Chicago, IL 60690

The Lamb, 2352 Rice Blvd., Houston, TX 7705

Language, 464 Amsterdam Ave., New York, N.Y. 10024

Laomedon Review, 3359 Mississauga Rd., Mississauga, Ont. L5L 1C6, Canada

Lapis Lazuli: An International Quarterly, 712 NW 4th St., Corvallis OR 97330

Latin-American Literary Review, Dept. of Modern Languages, Carnegie-Mellon University, Pittsburgh, PA 15213

Laughing Bear, P.O. Box 14, Woodinville, WA 98072

The Laurel Review, West Virginia Wesleyan College, Buckhannon, WV 26201

Leatherneck, P.O. Box 1775, Quantico, VA 22134

The Lesbian Tide, 8855 Cattaragus Ave., Los Angeles, CA 90034

Lesbian Voices, 330 S. 3rd, Suite B, San Jose, CA 95112

Letters, P.O. Box 82, Stonington, ME 04681

Liberation, 186 Hampshire St., Cambridge, MA 02139

Life And Health, 6856 Eastern Ave., NW, Washington, DC 20012

Light: A Poetry Review, P.O. Box 1298, Stuyvesant Sta., New York, NY 10009

The Limberlost Review, c/o Dept. of English, Idaho State University, Pocatello, ID 83209

Listen Magazine, 6830 Laurel St., NW, Washington, DC 20012

The Literary Monitor, 1070 Noriega Ave., No. 7, Sunnyvale, CA 94086

Literary Review, Fairleigh Dickinson University, 285 Madison Ave., Madison, NJ 07940

The Little Around Journal, P.O. Box 541, Mentone, IN 46539

Little Caesar, 3373 Overland Ave., No. 2, Los Angeles, CA 90034

The Little Magazine, P.O. Box 207, Cathedral Sta.,

New York, NY 10025

The Little Review, English Dept., Marshall University, Huntington, WV 25701

Live, 1445 Boonville Ave., Springfield, MO 65802

The Living Wilderness, 1901 Pennsylvania Ave., NW, Washington, DC 20006

Logos Journal, 201 Church St., Plainfield, NJ 07060

Long Island Review, 360 W. 21st St., New York, NY 10011

Long Pond Review, English Dept., Suffolk Community College, Selden, NY 11784

Look Quick, P.O. Box 4434, Boulder, CO 80306

The Lookout, 15 State St., New York, NY 10004

Loon, P.O. Box 11633, Santa Rosa, CA 95406

Lost And Found Times, 137 Leland Ave., Columbus, OH 43214

Lowlands Review, 8204 Maple, No. 1, New Orleans, LA 70118

Lucille, 5 Kern Ramble, Austin, TX 78722

Lunch, 220 Montross Ave., Rutherford, NJ 07070

The Lutheran Journal, 7317 Cahill Rd., Edina, MN 55435

The Lutheran Standard, 426 S. 5th St., Minneapolis, MN 55415

Lutheran Women, 2900 Queen Lane, Philadelphia, PA 19129

The Lyric, 307 Dunton Dr., SW, Blacksburg, VA 24060

M

Mademoiselle, 350 Madison Ave., New York, NY 10017

Madrona, 4730 Latona, NE, Seattle, WA 98105

Maelstrom Review, P.O. Box 4261, Long Beach, CA 90804

Maine Edition, 22 Bridge St., Topsham, ME 04086

Maine Magazine, P.O. Box 494, Ellsworth, ME 04605

The Mainstreeter, Dept. of English, University of Wisconsin, Stevens Point, WI 54481

Makara, 1101 Commercial Dr., Vancouver, B.C. V5L 3X1, Canada

The Malahat Review, P.O. Box 1700, Victoria, B.C. V8W 2Y2, Canada

Mamashee, R. R. 1, Inwood, Ont. NON 1KO, Canada

Many Smokes, P.O. Box 9167, Spokane, WA 99209

The Massachusetts Review, Memorial Hall, University of Massachusetts, Amherst, MA 01002

Mati, 5548 N. Sawyer, Chicago, IL 60625

Mature Living, 127 9th Ave., N., Nashville, TN 37234

Maybe Mombasa, c/o Ralph La Charity, #701-LAMC, San Francisco, CA 94129

Mazagine, Pima College, 2202 W. Anklam Rd., Tucson, AZ 85709

The Mennonite, 600 Shaftesbury Blvd., Winnipeg, Man. R3P 0M4, Canada

Merlin Papers, P.O. Box 5602, San Jose, CA 95150

The Message Magazine, P.O. Box 59, Nashville, TN 37202

Metamorphosis, Rumford, ME 04276

Miami Magazine, 3361 SW Third Ave., Miami, FL 33145

Michigan Quarterly Review, 3032 Rackham Bldg., University of Michigan, Ann Arbor, MI 48109

The Mickle Street Review, 330 Mickle St., Camden, NJ 08103

Micromegas, 84 High Point Dr., Amherst, MA 01002

The Midatlantic Review, P.O. Box 398, Baldwin Place, NY 10505

Midstream, 515 Park Ave., New York, NY 10022

Midwest Chaparral, 5508 Osage, Kansas City, KS 66106

The Midwest Quarterly, Pittsburg State University, Pittsburg, KS 66762

Mikrokosmos, Box 14, Dept. of English, Wichita State University, Wichita, KS 67208

Milk Quarterly, 2394 Blue Island Ave., Chicago, IL 60608

Milkweed Chronicle, P.O. Box 24303, Edmina, MN 55424

The Mill, P.O. Box 996, Adelphi, MD 20783

Mill Street Journal, P.O. Box 10562, Eugene, OR 97401

Mini Review, P.O. Box 4261, Long Beach, CA 90804

The Minnesota Review, P.O. Box 211, Bloomington, IN 47401

Minotaur, 2131 Shelter Island Dr., San Diego, CA 92106

The Miraculous Medal, 475 E. Chelten Ave., Philadelphia, PA 19144

The Mississippi Mud, 3125 SE Van Water, Portland, OR 97202

Mississippi Review, Center for Writers, University of Southern Mississippi, P.O. Box 37, Southern Sta., Hattiesburg, MS 39401

Mississippi Valley Review, Dept. of English, Western Illinois University, Macomb, IL 61455

The Missouri Review, Dept. of English, 231 Arts & Science, University of Missouri, Columbia, MO 65211

Mr. Cogito, Box 627, Pacific University, Forest Grove, OR 97116

Mix, 1300 Elmwood Ave., Buffalo, NY 14222

Mixed Breed, 1275 N. Swinton Ave., Delray Beach, FL 33444

Modern Bride, 1 Park Ave., New York, NY 10017

Modern Haiku, 260 Vista Marina, San Clemente, CA 92672

Modern Liturgy, P.O. Box 444, Saratoga, CA 95070

Modern Maturity, 215 Long Beach Blvd., Long Beach, CA 90801

The Modern Woodmen, 1701 1st Ave., Rock Island, IL 61201

The Modularist Review, 65-45 Yellowstone Blvd., Forest Hills, NY 11375

Moment Magazine (Jewish oriented), 462 Boylston St., Suite 301, Boston, MA 02116

Montemora, P.O. Box 336, Cooper Sta., New York, NY 10003

Moondance, 720 Shotwell, Memphis, TN 38111

Moons And Lion Tailes, P.O. Box 8434, Lake St. Sta., Minneapolis, MN 55408

The Moosehead Review, P.O. Box 287, Waterville, P.Q., Canada

Mother's Manual Magazine, 176 Cleveland Dr., Croton-on-Hudson, NY 10520

Mountain Gazette, 2025 York St., Denver, CO 80205

Mountain Review, P.O. Box 660, Whitesburg, KY 41858

Mountain Summer, "Glen Antrim," Sewanee, TN 37375

The Mountain Thought Review, 612 E. Georgia, No. 8, Gunnison, CO 81230

Moving Out, Wayne State University, 4866 3rd, Detroit, MI 48202

Ms. Magazine, 370 Lexington Ave., New York, NY 10017

Mundus Artium: A Journal Of International Literature And The Arts, University of Texas, Box 688, Richardson, TX 75080

N

Nantucket Review, P.O. Box 1444, Nantucket, MA 02554

Natchez Trace Literary Review, P.O. Box 6945, Jackson, MS 39212

The Nation, 333 Ave. of the Americas, New York, NY 10014

National Forum, Box 19420A, East Tennessee University, Johnson City, TN 37601

Nebula, 970 Copeland St., North Bay, Ont. P1B 3E4, Canada

New America: A Review, Humanities Rm. 324, University of New Mexico, Albuquerque, NM 87131

New Boston Review, 77 Sacramento St., Somerville, MA 02143

New Catholic World, 1865 Broadway, New York, NY 10023

New Collage Magazine, 5700 North Trail, Sarasota, FL 33580

New Directions, Dept. of Human Relations and Publications, Howard University, Washington, DC 20059

New Directions For Women, 223 Old Hook Rd., Westwood, NJ 07675

New Earth Review, P.O. Box 83, Murfreesboro, NC 27855

The New Earth Review, 58 St. Marks Pl., New York, NY 10003

New England Review, P.O. Box 170, Hanover, NH 03755

New England Senior Citizen/Senior American News, 470 Boston Post Rd, Weston, MA 02193

The New Era, 50 E. North Temple, Salt Lake City, UT 84150

The New Infinity Review, P.O. Box 412, South Point, OH 45680

New Jersey Poetry Monthly, P.O. Box 824, Saddle Brook, NJ 07662

The New Kent Quarterly, 239 Student Center, Kent State University, Kent, OH 44240

The New Laurel Review, P.O. Box 1083, Chalmette, LA 70044

New Letters, University of Missouri, 5346 Charlotte, Kansas City, MO 64110

New Literature & Ideology, P.O. Box 727, Adelaide Sta., Toronto, Ont., Canada

The New Moon, 2147 Oakland Dr., Kalamazoo, MI 49008

New Orleans Review, Loyola University, New Orleans, LA 70118

The New Renaissance, 9 Heath Rd., Arlington, MA 02174

The New Republic, 1220 19th St., NW, Washington, DC 20036

New Voices, P.O. Box 308, Clintondale, NY 12515

New World Journal, 2845 Buena Vista Way, Berkeley, CA 94708

New York Arts Journal, 560 Riverside Dr., New York, NY 10027

The New York Culture Review, 128 E. 4th St., New York, NY 10003

New York Quarterly, P.O. Box 2415, Grand Central Sta., New York, NY 10017

The New York Smith, 5 Beekman St., New York, NY 10038

The New Yorker, 25 W. 43rd St., New York, NY 10036

NeWest ReView, 11441 84th St., Edmonton, Alta. T5B 3B5, Canada

Neworld, 1308 S. New Hampshire Ave., Los Angeles, CA 90006

Newsart, 5 Beekman St., New York, NY 10038

The Niagara Magazine, 195 Hicks St., Apt. 3B, Brooklyn, NY 11201

Nicotine Soup, P.O. Box 22613, San Francisco, CA 94122

Nimrod, University of Tulsa, 600 S. College, Tulsa, OK 74104

Nit And Wit, 1908 W. Oakdale, Chicago, Ill. 60657

Nitty-Gritty, 331 W. Bonneville, Pasco, WA 99301

North American Mentor Magazine, 1745 Madison St., Fennimore, WI 53809

The North American Review, University of Northern Iowa, Cedar Falls, IA 50613

The North Carolina Review, 3329 Granville Dr., Raleigh, NC 27609

North Coast Poetry, P.O. Box 56, East Machias, ME 04630

North Country, Dept. of English, University of North Dakota, Grand Forks, ND 58201

North Country Anvil, P.O. Box 37, Millville, MN 55957

North Stone Review, P.O. Box 14098, University Sta., Minneapolis, MN 55414

Northeast, 1310 Shorewood Dr., LaCrosse, WI 54601

Northeast Journal, P.O. Box 235, Annex Sta., Providence, RI 02901

Northern Light, University of Manitoba, 605 Fletcher Argue Bldg., Winnipeg, Man. R3J 2E4, Canada

Northern New England Review, P.O. Box 825, Franklin Pierce College, Rindge, NH 03461

Northwest America, P.O. Box 9365, Boise, ID 83707

Northwest Review, 369 P.L.C., University of Oregon, Eugene, OR 97405

Northwoods Journal, R.D. No. 1, Meadows of Dan, VA 24120

Nostoc, 101 Nehoiden Rd., Waban, MA 02168

Not Man Apart, 124 Spear St., San Francisco, CA 94105

The Notebook & Other Reviews, P.O. Box 180, Birmingham, MI 48012

Nous: A Journal of Arts And Ideas, 716 Clement Ave.,

Charlotte, NC 28204

Nursery Days, 201 8th Ave., S., Nashville, TN 37202

O

Obsidian: Black Literature In Review, 10 Georges Pl., Fredonia, NY 14063

The Ohio Journal, Dept. of English, Ohio State University, 164 W. 17th Ave., Columbus, OH 43210

Ohio Motorist, P.O. Box 6150, Cleveland, OH 44101

The Ohio Review, Ellis Hall, Ohio University, Athens, OH 45701

Oink! 7021 Sheridan, Chicago, IL 60626

Omega, 145 E. Main St., Cambridge, NY 12816

On The Line, 616 Walnut Ave., Scottdale, PA 15683

Ontario Review, 6000 Riverside Dr., E., Windsor, Ont. N8S 1B6, Canada

Open Places, Box 2085, Stephens College, Columbia, MO 65201

Opinion, P.O. Box 1885, Rockford, IL 61110

The Orchard, 500 26th Ave., Santa Cruz, CA 95062

Oregon Times Magazine, 1000 SW 3rd Ave., Portland, OR 97204

Origins, P.O. Box 5072, Sta. E, Hamilton, Ont. L8S 4K9, Canada

Osiris, P.O. Box 297, Deerfield, MA 01342

Other Press Poetry Review, 2503 Douglas College, New Westminster, B.C., Canada

Our Family, Box 249, Battleford, Sask. SOM OEO, Canada

Our Little Friend; Primary Treasure, 1350 Villa St., Mountain View, CA 94042

Out There Magazine, 552 25th Ave., San Francisco, CA 94121

Oxymoron: Journal Of Convulsive Beauty, P.O. Box 3424, Charlottesville, VA 22903

P

Pacific Northwest Review Of Books, P.O. Box 21566, Seattle, WA 98111

Pacific Poetry And Fiction Review, English Office, San Diego State University, San Diego, CA 92182

The Pacifica Review, P.O. Box 1034, Pacifica, CA 94044

Padan Aram, 52 Dunster St., Harvard University, Cambridge, MA 02138

Paintbrush, Dept. of English, Northeastern University, Boston, MA 02115

Painted Bride Quarterly, 527 South St., Philadelphia, PA 19147

Pan American Review, 1101 Tori Lane, Edinburg, TX 78539

Panache, P.O. Box 77, Sunderland, MA 01375

The Panhandler, Writers Workshop, English Dept., University of West Florida, Pensacola, FL 32504

Panjandrum Poetry Journal, 99 Sanchez St., San Francisco, CA 94114

The Paris Review, 45-39 171st Place, Flushing, NY 11358

Parnassus: Poetry In Review, 205 W. 89th St., New York, NY 10024

Partisan Review, Boston University, 128 Bay State Rd., Boston, MA 02215

Pass-Age: A Futures Journal, 431 S. 45th St., Philadelphia, PA 19104

The Passage, 40 Pleasant St., Portsmouth, NH 03801

Paunch, 123 Woodward Ave., Buffalo, NY 14214

The Pawn Review, P.O. Box 29250, Dallas, TX 75229

Pebble, 118 S. Boswell, Crete, NE 68333

Pembroke Magazine, P.O. Box 756, Pembroke, NC 28372

The Pen Woman Magazine, 1300 17th St., NW, Washington, DC 20036

Pennsylvania Black Observer, P.O. Box 72, Reading, PA 19603

The Penny Dreadful, Dept. of English, Bowling Green State University, Bowling Green, OH 43403

Pentecostal Evangel, 1445 Boonville, Springfield, MO 65802

Pequod, P.O. Box 491, Forest Knolls, CA 94933

Periodical Of Art In Nebraska, University of Nebraska at Omaha, P.A.N., U.N.O., Annex 21, Box 688, Omaha, NE 68101

Permafrost Magazine, University of Alaska, Fairbanks, AK 99701

Perspectives, English Dept., West Virginia University, Morgantown, WV 26506

Phantasm, P.O. Box 3404, Chico, CA 95927

Phoebe, 4400 University Dr., Fairfax, VA 22030

The Phoenix, Morning Star Farm, RFD, Haydenville, MA 01039

Photo Insight, Suite 2, 91-24 168th St., Jamaica, NY 11432

Pierian Spring, Brandon University Press, Brandon, Man. R7A 6A9, Canada

Pigiron, P.O. Box 237, Youngstown, OH 44501

The Pikestaff Forum, P.O. Box 127, Normal, IL 61761

Pivot, 221 S. Barnard, State College, PA 16801

Plainswoman, P.O. Box 8027, Grand Forks, ND 58202

Plexus, 2600 Dwight Way, 209, Berkeley, CA 94704

Ploughshares, P.O. Box 529, Cambridge, MA 02139

Plum, 549 W. 113th St., New York, NY 10025

Plumbers Ink, 780 Amana St., No. 1606, Honolulu, HI 96814

Poem, P.O. Box 1247, West Sta., Huntsville, AL 35807

Poet, 208 W. Latimer Ave., Campbell, CA 95008

The Poet, 2314 W. 6th St., Mishawaka, IN 46544

Poet & Critic, English Dept., Iowa State University, 203 Ross Hall, Ames, IA 50011

Poet Lore, 4000 Albemarle St., NW, Suite 504, Washington, DC 20016

Poet Papers, P.O. Box 528, Topanga, CA 90290

The Poetic Hardware Press, 1815 Riverside Dr., 4K, New York, NY 10034

Poetry, 601 S. Morgan St., P.O. Box 4348, Chicago, IL 60680

Poetry Canada Poesie, P.O. Box 1280, Sta. "A," Toronto, Ont. M5W 1G7, Canada

Poetry Canada Review, P.O. Box 277, Sta. "F," Toronto, Ont. M4Y 2L7, Canada

Poetry &, P.O. Box A3298, Chicago, IL 60690

The Poetry Memo Of Brentwood, 783 Old Hickory Blvd., Brentwood, TN 37027

The Poetry Miscellany, P.O. Box 165, Signal Mountain, TN 37377

Poetry Newsletter, Dept. of English, Temple University, Philadelphia, PA 19122

Poetry Northwest, 4045 Brooklyn, NE, University of Washington, Seattle, WA 98195

Poetry Northwest Magazine, The Oregonian, Portland, OR 97201

Poetry Now, 3118 K St., Eureka, CA 95501

Poetry Society of America Bulletin, 15 Gramercy Park, New York, NY 10003

Poetry Texas, Div. of Humanities, College of the Mainland, Texas City, TX 77590

Poetry Toronto Newsletter, 224 St. George St., Apt. 709, Toronto, Ont. M5R 2N9, Canada

Poetry Venture, 2135-49 1st Ave. S., St. Petersburg, FL 33712

Poetry View, 1125 Valley Rd., Menasha, WI 54952

Poetry-Windsor-Poesie, P.O. Box 7186, Sandwich P.O., Windsor, Ont. N9C 3Z1, Canada

Poets' League Of Greater Cleveland Newsletter, P.O. Box 6055, Cleveland, OH 44101

Poets On, P.O. Box 255, Chaplin, CT 06235

Point Of Contact, 110 Bleecker St., 16B, New York, NY 10012

Pontchartrain Review, P.O. Box 1065, Chalmette, LA 70044

Porch, 1422 37th Ave., Seattle, WA 98122

Portland Review, P.O. Box 751, Portland, OR 97207

Prairie Schooner, 201 Andrews Hall, University of Nebraska, Lincoln, NE 68588

Praxis: A Journal Of Radical Perspectives On The Arts, P.O. Box 207, Goleta, CA 93017

Prelude To Fantasy, Rt. 3, Box 193, Richland Center, WI 53703

Present Tense (Jewish oriented), 165 E. 56th St., New York, NY 10022

Pre-Vue, P.O. Box 20768, Billings, MT 59104

Primavera, Ida Noyes Hall, University of Chicago, Chicago, IL 60637

Primipara (contributors restricted to Wisconsin residents), P.O. Box 171, Oconto, WI 54153

Prism International, Dept. of Creative Writing, University of British Columbia, Vancouver, B.C. V6T 1W5, Canada

Progressive Labor Magazine, GPO Box 808, Brooklyn, NY 11201

Proteus, 1004 N. Jefferson St., Arlington, VA 22205

Provincetown Poets, 216 Bradford St., Provincetown, MA 02657

Puddingstone, P.O. Box 8800, University Sta., Knoxville, TN 37916

Puerto Del Sol, P.O. Box 3E, Las Cruces, NM 88003

Pulp, c/o Sage, 720 Greenwich St., 4H, New York, NY 10014

Pulp: Fiction & Poetry, P.O. Box 243, Narragansett, RI 02882

Purpose, 616 Walnut Ave., Scottdale, PA 15683

Q

Quarry, P.O. Box 1061, Kingston, Ont. K7L 4Y5, Canada

Quarry West, College V, University of California, Santa Cruz, CA 95064

Quarterly Review Of Literature, 26 Haslet Ave., Princeton, NJ 08540

Quarterly West, 312 Olpin Union, University of Utah, Salt Lake City, UT 84112

Queen, 40 S. Saxon Ave., Bay Shore, NY 11706

Queen's Quarterly: A Canadian Review, Queen's University, Kingston, Ont. K7L 3N6, Canada

Quest, 1133 Ave. of the Americas, New York, NY 10036

Quest: A Feminist Quarterly, P.O. Box 8843, Washington, DC 20003

Quoin, 1226 W. Talmage, Springfield, MO 65803

R

R.T.: A Journal Of Radical Therapy, P.O. Box 89, West Somerville, MA 02144

Raccoon, 561 Ellsworth, Apt. 1, Memphis, TN 38111

The Rag, 850 Reynard St., SE, Grand Rapids, MI 49507

Rainbow, American Baptist Board of Educational Ministries, Valley Forge, PA 19481

Raintree, 4043 Morningside Dr., Bloomington, IN 47401

Ram: The Letter Box, 430 4th St., Brooklyn, NY 11215

Realities Library, 2480 Escaloma Court, San Jose, CA 95121

Reconstructionist, 432 Park Ave., S., New York, NY 10016

Red Cedar Review, 325 Morrill, Dept. of English, Michigan State University, East Lansing, MI 48824

Red Fox Review, Mohegan Community College, Norwich, CT 06360

Red M(irage) P.O. Box 1539 G.P.O., Brooklyn, NY 11202

Red Weather, P.O. Box 1104, Eau Claire, WI 54701

The Remington Review, 505 Westfield Ave., Elizabeth, NJ 07208

Response: A Contemporary Jewish Review, 523 W. 113th St., New York, NY 10025

Review, Center for Inter-American Relations, 680 Park Ave., New York, NY 10021

Revista Chicano-Riquena, Indiana University Northwest, 3400 Broadway, Gary, IN 46408

Revista/Review Interamericana, G.P.O. Box 3255, San Juan, PR 00936

Rhino, 77 Lakewood Pl., Highland Park, IL 60035

Rikka, P.O. Box 6031, Sta. A, Toronto, Ont. M5W 1P4, Canada

Ripples, 718 Watersedge, Ann Arbor, MI 48105

River Styx, 7420 Cornell Ave., St. Louis, MO 63130

Riversedge, P.O. Box 1547, Edinburg, TX 78539

Riverside Quarterly, P.O. Box 14451, University Sta., Gainesville, FL 32604

Road Apple Review, 3263 Shorewood Dr., Oshkosh, WI 54901

Road/House, 99 W. 9th St., Belvidere, IL 61008

Rockbottom, 209 W. De La Guerra, Santa Barbara, CA 93101

Rocky Mountain Review, P.O. Box 1848, Durango,

CO 81301

The Romantist, 3610 Meadowbrook Ave., Nashville, TN 37205

Roof Magazine, 300 Bowery, New York, NY 10012

Room Magazine, P.O. Box 40610, San Francisco, CA 94140

Room Of One's Own (Feminist), 1918 Waterloo St., Vancouver, B.C. V6R 3G6, Canada

Round Notes, P.O. Box N, Boulder Creek, CA 95006

Roundtable, 170 S. Hobart, Los Angeles, CA 90004

Rufus, P.O. Box 16, Pasadena, CA 91102

Ruhtra, P.O. Box 12, Boyes Hot Springs, CA 95416

Rune, 81 St. Mary's St., Box 299, Michael's College, Toronto, Ont. M5S 1J4, Canada

Rural Electric Missourian, 2722 E. McCarty St., Jefferson City, MO 65101

S

Sackbut Review, 2513 E. Webster, Milwaukee, WI 53211

Sagebloom, P.O. Box 79464, Houston, TX 77079

St. Andrews Review, St. Andrews College, Laurinberg, NC 28352

St. Joseph's Messenger & Advocate Of The Blind, St. Joseph's Home, P.O. Box 288, Jersey City, NJ 07303

Saint Louis Literary Supplement, 3523 Itaska St., St. Louis, MO 63111

Salmagundi, Skidmore College, Saratoga Springs, NY 12866

Salome: A Literary Dance Magazine, 5548 N. Sawyer, Chicago, IL 60625

Salt, 1119 13th Ave., NW, Moose Jaw, Sask. S6H 4N5, Canada

The Salt Cedar, Route 3, Box 652, Fort Collins, CO 80521

Salt Lick Press, P.O. Box 1064, Quincy, IL 62301

Salthouse, 1562 Jones Dr., Ann Arbor, MI 48105

Sam Houston Literary Review, English Dept., Sam Houston State University, Huntsville, TX 77340

Samisdat, P.O. Box 231, Richford, VT 05476

San Jose Studies, San Jose State University, San Jose, CA 95192

San Marcos Review, P.O. Box 4368, Albuquerque, NM 87106

Sandlapper: The Magazine Of South Carolina, P.O. Box 1668, Columbia, SC 29202

Sandscript, P.O. Box 333, Cummaquid, MA 02637

The Saturday Evening Post, 1100 Waterway Blvd., Indianapolis, IN 46202

Scandinavian Review, 127 E. 73rd St., New York, NY 10021

Scholia Satyrica, Dept. of English, University of South Florida, Tampa, FL 33620

Scimitar And Song, P.O. Box 151, Edgewater, MD 21037

Scope, 426 S. Fifth St., Minneapolis, MN 55415

The Seattle Review, Padelford Hall GN-30, University of Washington, Seattle, WA 98195

Second Coming, P.O. Box 31249, San Francisco, CA 94131

Second Growth, Dept. of English, East Tennessee State University, Johnson City, TN 37601

The Second Wave, P.O. Box 344, Cambridge A., Cambridge, MA 02139

Secrets, Macfadden Women's Group, 205 E. 42nd St., New York, NY 10017

The Seeker Newsletter, P.O. Box 7601, San Diego, CA 92107

Seems, Dept. of English, University of Northern Iowa, Cedar Falls, IA 50613

Seneca Review, Hobart & William Smith Colleges, Geneva, NY 14456

Sequoia, Storke Publications Bldg., Stanford, CA 94305

Seriatum: A Journal Of Ectopia, 122 Carmel, El Cerrito, CA 94530

Serpent's Egg, P. O. Drawer 2850, La Jolla, CA 92038

Seven, 115 S. Hudson, Oklahoma City, OK 73102

Seven Stars Poetry, P.O. Box 33512, San Diego, CA 92103

Seventeen, 850 Third Ave., New York, NY 10022

Sewanee Review, University of the South, Sewanee, TN 37375

Shabda Poetry Journal, 217 W. Julian St., San Jose, CA 95110

Shakespeare Newsletter, University of Illinois, Chicago Circle, Chicago, IL 60680

Shameless Hussy Review, P.O. Box 424, San Lorenzo, CA 94580

Shantih, P.O. Box 125, Bay Ridge Sta., Brooklyn, N.Y. 11220

Shelly's, 6560 Tower St., Ravenna, OH 44266

Shenandoah, P.O. Box 722, Lexington, VA 24450

Sibyl-Child: A Woman's Arts & Culture Journal, P.O. Box 1773, Hyattsville, MD 20783

Silver Vain, P.O. Box 2366, Park City, UT 84060

Sisters Today, St. John's Abbey, Collegeville, MD 56321

Skywriting, 511 Campbell St., Kalamazoo, MI 49007

Slackwater Review, Confluence Press, Lewis-Clark Campus, Lewiston, ID 83501

Slick Press, 5336 S. Drexel, Chicago, IL 60615

Slit Wrist, 333 E. 30th St., New York, NY 10016

The Slough, 184 Q St. (2), University of Utah, Salt Lake City, UT 84103

Slow Loris Reader, 923 Highview St., Pittsburgh, PA 15206

The Small Farm, P.O. Box 563, Jefferson City, TN 37760

Small Moon, 52½ Dimick St., Somerville, MA 02143

The Small Pond Magazine of Literature, 10 Overland Dr., Stratford, CT 06497

The Smith, 5 Beekman St., New York, NY 10038

The Smudge, P.O. Box 19276, Detroit, MI 48219

Snakeroots, Pratt Institute, Liberal Arts & Sciences, Brooklyn, NY 11205

Snowy Egret, 205 S. Ninth St., Williamsburg, KY 40769

So & So, 1730 Carleton, Berkeley, CA 94703

The Socialist Republic, P.O. Box 80, Madison Square Sta., New York, NY 10010

Solana (women writers only), 5712 Pennsylvania, St. Louis, MO 63111

The Sole Proprietor, 2770 NW 32nd Ave., Miami, FL 33142

Soma-Haoma, P.O. Box 649, Dennis, MA 02638

Some, 309 W. 104th St., Apt. 9D, New York, NY 10025

Some Friends, P.O. Box 6395, Tyler, TX 75701

Song, 808 Illinois, Stevens Point, WI 54481

So's Your Old Lady, 3149 Fremont Ave., S., Minneapolis, MN 55408

Soulbook, P.O. Box 61213, Los Angeles, CA 90059

Soundings/East, English Dept., Salem State College, Salem, MA 01970

Source, Queens Council on the Arts, 161-04 Jamaica Ave., New York, NY 11432

South Atlantic Quarterly, P.O. Box 6697, College Sta., Durham, NC 27708

South Carolina Review, English Dept., Clemson University, Clemson, SC 29631

South Dakota Review, Box 111, University Exchange, Vermillion, SD 57069

South Shore, P.O. Box 95, Au Train, MI 49806

South & West, P.O. Box 446, Fort Smith, AR 72901

Southern Erotique, P.O. Box 2303, Baton Rouge, LA 70821

Southern Exposure, P.O. Box 230, Chapel Hill, NC 27514

Southern Fried Turnip Greens, P.O. Box 5003, Greensboro, NC 27403

Southern Humanities Review, 9090 Haley Center, Auburn University, Auburn, AL 36830

Southern Poetry Review, Dept. of English, University of North Carolina, UNCC Sta., Charlotte, NC 28223

The Southern Review, Drawer D, University Sta., Baton Rouge, LA 70893

Southwest Review, Southern Methodist University, Dalls, TX 75275

Sou'wester, Dept. of English, Southern Illinois University, Edwardsville, IL 62025

Speak Out, P.O. Box 737, Stamford, CT 06904

The Spirit, 601 Market St., St. Genevieve, MO 63670

The Spirit That Moves Us, P.O. Box 1585, Iowa City, IA 52240

The Spoon River Quarterly, Bradley University, Peoria, IL 61606

Spring Rain Press, P.O. Box 15319, Seattle, WA 98115

The Squatchberry Journal, Box 205, Geraldton, Ont. POT 1MO, Canada

Star West, P.O. Box 731, Sausalito, CA 94965

Stardancer, P.O. Box 128, Athens, OH 45701

Star-Web Paper, All This & Less Publishers, La Mesilla, NM 88046

Starwind, P.O. Box 3346, Columbus, OH 43210

Stone Country, 20 Lorraine Rd., Madison, NJ 07940

Stone Mountain Review, 857 N. Broadway, Massapequa, NY 11758

Stonecloud, 1906 Parnell Ave., Los Angeles, CA 90025

Stony Hills, P.O. Box 715, Newburyport, MA 01950

Story Friends, 616 Walnut Ave., Scottdale, PA 15683

Street Cries, 33 Edi Ave., Plainview, NY 11803

Street Magazine, P.O. Box 555, Port Jefferson, NY 11777

The Student, 127 9th Ave., N., Nashville, TN 37234

Studies In Poetry: A Graduate Journal, Dept. of English, Texas Tech University, Lubbock, TX 79409

Stuffed Crocodile, 764 Dalkeith Ave., London, Ont. N5X 1R8, Canada

Sun, 456 Riverside Dr., 5B, New York, NY 10027

The Sun: A Magazine Of Ideas, 412 W. Rosemary St., Chapel Hill, NC 27514

Sun & Moon: A Journal Of Literature And Art, 4330 Hartwick Rd., No. 418, College Park, MD 20740

Sun Tracks: An American Indian Literary Magazine, Dept. of English, University of Arizona, Tucson, AZ 85721

Sunbury, P.O. Box 274, Jerome Ave. Sta., Bronx, NY 10468

Sunday Digest, 850 N. Grove Ave., Elgin, IL 60120

Sunshine, P.O. Box J, Babylon, NY 11702

The Sunstone Review, P.O. Box 2321, Santa Fe, NM 87501

Surfside Poetry Review, P.O. Box 289, Surfside, CA 90743

Survivor, 50 Inglewood Dr., Rochester, NY 14619

Swallowing The Poison, P.O. Box 911, W. T. Sta., Canyon, TX 79016

T

Tailings, Hancock, MI 49930

Tamarack, P.O. Box 455, Potsdam, NY 13676

Tamarisk, 188 Forest Ave., Ramsey, NJ 07446

Tar River Poetry, Dept. of English, East Carolina University, Austin Bldg., Greenville, NC 27834

Tawte: Texas Artists And Thinkers In Exile, 2311-C Woolsey, Berkeley, CA 94705

Teens Today, 6401 The Paseo, Kansas City, MO 64131

Telephone, P.O. Box 672, Old Chelsea Sta., New York, NY 10011

10 Point 5, P.O. Box 124, Eugene, OR 97440

Tendril, P.O. Box 512, Green Harbor, MA 02041

The Texas Arts Journal, P.O. Box 7458, Dallas, TX 75209

Texas Country Magazine, P.O. Box 966, Alief, TX 77411

The Texas Methodist/United Methodist Reporter, P.O. Box 1076, Dallas, TX 75221

Texas Quarterly, P.O. Box 7517, University Sta., Austin, TX 78712

Text, 552 Broadway (6th Flr.), New York, NY 10012

Third Eye, 250 Mill St., Williamsville, NY 14221

13th Moon, P.O. Box 3, Inwood Sta., New York, NY 10034

This, 326 Connecticut St., San Francisco, CA 94107

Thistle: A Magazine Of Contemporary Writing, P.O. Box 144, Ruffs Dale, PA 15679

Thoreau Journal Quarterly, 304 English-Math Bldg., University of Maine, Orono, ME 04473

Thought: The Quarterly Of Fordham University, Box L, Fordham University, Bronx, NY 10458

Three Cent Pulp, P.O. Box 48806, Sta. Bental, Vancouver, B.C., Canada

Three Rivers Poetry Journal, P.O. Box 21, Carnegie-Mellon University, Pittsburgh, PA 15213

Three Sisters, P.O. Box 969, Hoya Sta., Washington, DC 20057

Thunder Mountain Review, P.O. Box 11126, Birmingham, AL 35202

Tightrope, 300 Main St., Oneonta, NY 13820

Tinderbox, 334 Molasses Lane, Mt. Pleasant (Charleston), SC 29464

Titmouse, 720 W. 19th Ave., Vancouver, B.C., Canada

Total Lifestyle: The Magazine Of Natural Living, P.O. Box 1137, Harrison, AR 72601

Touch, P.O. Box 7244, Grand Rapids, MI 49510

Touchstone, Drawer 42331, Houston, TX 77042

Town And Country Journal, 101½ Mill St., Coudersport, PA 16915

Tracks: A Journal Of Artists' Writings, P.O. Box 557, Old Chelsea Sta., New York, NY 10011

Translation, 307A Mathematics, Columbia University, New York, NY 10027

Trellis, P.O. Box 656, Morgantown, WV 26505

Triquarterly, Northwestern University, University Hall 101, Evanston, IL 60201

Truck, 1645 Portland Ave., St. Paul, MN 55104

True Experience, Macfadden Women's Group, 205 E. 42nd St., New York, NY 10017

True Romance, Macfadden Women's Group, 205 E. 42nd St., New York, NY 10017

Two Steps In, P.O. Box 11425-A, Palo Alto, CA 94301

U

US1 Worksheets, 21 Lake Dr., Roosevelt, NJ 08555

UT Review, University of Tampa, Tampa, FL 33606

Ululatus, P.O. Box 397, Fort Smith, AR 72902

Umbral: A Quarterly of Spectual Poetry, 2330 Irving St., Denver, CO 80211

Unicorn, 4501 N. Charles St., Baltimore, MD 21210

Unicorn: A Miscellaneous Journal, 345 Harvard St., 3B, Cambridge, MA 02138

Unity Magazine, Unity Village, MO 64065

University Of Windsor Review, University of Windsor, Windsor, Ont. N9B 3P4, Canada

The Unlimited, 1806 Bonita, Berkeley, CA 94709

Unmuzzled Ox, P.O. Box 840, Canal St. Sta., New York, NY 10013

The Unrealist, P.O. Box 53, Prince, WV 25907

The Unspeakable Visions Of The Individual, P.O. Box 439, California, PA 15419

Upcountry: The Magazine Of New England Living, 33 Eagle St., Pittsfield, MA 01201

Uroboros, 111 N. 10th St., Olean, NY 14760

Urthkin, P.O. Box 67485, Los Angeles, CA 90067

Uzzano, P.O. Box 169, Mount Carroll, IL 61053

V

Vagabond, 1610 N. Water, Ellensburg, WA 98926

Valhalla 5, 1719 13th Ave., S., Birmingham, AL 35205

Valley Views Magazine, P.O. Box 39096, Solon, OH 44139

Vanderbilt Poetry Review, c/o Rochester Routes, 50 Inglewood Dr., Rochester, NY 14619

Vanguard, 229 College St., Toronto, Ont. M5T 1R4, Canada

Vantage Point, Centre College, Danville, KY 40422

Vector Magazine, c/o Ball State News, Ball State University, Muncie, IN 47306

Velvet Wings, 1228 Oxford St., Berkeley, CA 94709

Victimology: An International Journal, P.O. Box 39045, Washington, DC 20016

View From The Silver Bridge, 1928 Nunns Rd., Campbell River, B.C. V9W 1H2, Canada

Village Idiot, 209 W. De la Guerra, Santa Barbara, CA 93101

The Villager, 135 Midland Ave., Bronxville, NY 10708

The Vine, 201 Eighth Ave., S., Nashville, TN 37203

The Virginia Quarterly Review, 1 West Range, Charlottesville, VA 22903

Vista, P.O. Box 2000, Marion, IN 46952

Voices International, 1115 Gillette Dr., Little Rock, AR 72207

W

The Walrus Said, P.O. Box 5904, St. Louis, MO 63134

Waluna: The Soho Review, 72 Wooster St., New York, NY 10012

Wascana Review, University of Regina, Regina, Sask., Canada

Washington Review, P.O. Box 50132, Washington, DC 20004

The Washingtonian Magazine, 1828 L St., NW, Washington, DC 20036

Washout Review, P.O. Box 2752, Schenectady, NY 12309

Waters Journal Of The Arts, Box 19341, Cincinnati, OH 45219

Waves, Room 357, Stong College, York University, 4700 Keele St., Downsview, Ont. M3J 1P3, Canada

Wayside Quarterly, P.O. Box 475, Cottonwood, AZ 86326

Webster Review, Webster College, Webster Groves, MO 63119

Wee Wisdom, Unity Village, MO 64065

Weekly Bible Reader, 8121 Hamilton Ave., Cincinnati, OH 45231

Weid: The Sensibility Revue, P.O. Box 1409, Homestead, FL 33030

West Branch, Dept. of English, Bucknell University, Lewisburg, PA 17837

West Coast Poetry Review, 1335 Dartmouth Dr., Reno, NV 89509

West Coast Review, English Dept., Simon Fraser University, Burnaby, B.C. V5A 1S6, Canada

West End Magazine, P.O. Box 354, Jerome Ave. Sta., Bronx, NY 10468

Westbere Review, 2504 E. 4th St., Tulsa, OK 74104

The Westerly Review, 229 Post Rd., Westerly, RI 02891

The Western Critic, P.O. Box 591, Boise, ID 83701

Western Humanities Review, University of Utah, Salt Lake City, UT 84112

The Western Reserve Magazine, P.O. Box 243, Garrettsville, OH 44231

Westways, P.O. Box 2890, Terminal Annex, Los Angeles, CA 90051

Whetstone, P.O. Box 226, Bisbee, AZ 85603

Whiskey Island Quarterly, University Center, Rm. 7, Cleveland State University, Cleveland, OH 44115

White Mule, 2710 E. 98th Ave., Tampa, FL 33612

Wild Fennel, 2510 48th St., Bellingham, WA 98225

Willmore City, P.O. Box 1601, Carlsbad, CA 92008

Win Magazine, 503 Atlantic Ave., 5th Flr., Brooklyn, NY 11217

Wind, P.O. Box 2000, Marion, IN 46952

Wind Literary Journal, RFD Rt. 1, Box 809K, Pikeville, KY 41501

The Windless Orchard, Indiana University, English Dept., Fort Wayne, IN 46805

Window, 7005 Westmoreland Ave., Takoma Park, MD 20012

Wip, c/o English Dept., Box 1852, Brown University, Providence, RI 02912

Wisconsin Review, Box 245, Dempsey Hall, University of Oshkosh, Oshkosh, WI 54901

Wolfsong, P.O. Box 252, Iola, WI 54945

Woman Spirit (women contributors only), P.O. Box 263, Wolf Creek, OR 97497

Women: A Journal of Liberation (women contributors only), 3028 Greenmount Ave., Baltimore, MD 21218

Women Talking, Women Listening, P.O. Box 2414, Dublin, CA 94566

Women's Circle Home Cooking, P.O. Box 338, Chester, MA 01011

Wonder Time, 6401 The Paseo, Kansas City, MO 64131

The Woodstock Review, 27 Oriole Dr., Woodstock, NY 12498

Word Garden, 225 Norton St., Long Beach, CA 90805

Working Cultures, 2039 New Hampshire Ave., NW (#702), Washington, DC 20009

World Literature Today, 630 Parrington Oval, Room 110, Norman, OK 73019

World Of Poetry, 2431 Stockton Blvd., Sacramento, CA 95817

The World Of Rodeo, P.O. Box 660, Billings, MT 59103

The Wormwood Review, P.O. Box 8840, Stockton, CA 95204

Wow, American Baptist Board of Educational Ministries, Valley Forge, PA 19481

Writ, 2 Sussex Ave., Toronto, Ont. M5S 1J5, Canada

Writers In Residence, P.O. Box 393, Tiffin, OH 44883

Writing, 9231 Molly Woods Ave., La Mesa, CA 92041

X

X: A Journal Of The Arts, P.O. Box 2648, Harrisburg, PA 17105

Xanadu, Box 773, Hunington, NY 11743

Y

The Yale Literary Magazine, Box 243-A, Yale Station, New Haven, CT 06520

The Yale Review, 1902A Yale Sta., New Haven, CT 06520

Yankee, Dublin, NH 03444

Yellow Brick Road, P.O. Box 40814, Tucson, AZ 85717

Young Judean, 817 Broadway, New York, NY 10003

Young World, P.O. Box 567B, Indianapolis, IN 46206

Youth Alive! 1445 Boonville Ave., Springfield, MO 65802

Z

Z, Poets Corner, Calais, VT 05648

Zahir, P.O. Box 715, Newburyport, MA 01950

Zeugma, 25 Jeanette Ave., Belmont, MA 02178

Zone, P.O. Box 194, Bay Sta., Brooklyn, NY 11235

Poetry Associations, Organizations and Clubs

This directory lists organizations in the United States and Canada devoted to poetry. An asterisk (*) denotes affiliation with the National Federation of State Poetry Societies.

ALABAMA
Alabama State Poetry Society*, c/o Dr. Frances T. Carter, 2561 Rocky Ridge Rd., Birmingham, AL 35243

ARIZONA
Arizona State Poetry Society*, c/o Florence W. Otter, 16622 Lakeforest Dr., Sun City, AZ 85351
First Friday Poets, c/o Changing Hands Bookstore, 414 Mill Ave., Tempe, AZ 85281
University of Arizona Poetry Center, c/o Lois Shelton, 1086 N. Highland, Tucson, AZ 85721

ARKANSAS
Poets Roundtable of Arkansas*, c/o Opal Jane O'Neal, 421 Dell, Hot Springs, AR 71901

CALIFORNIA
Alchemedias Poets Circle, c/o Stephanie Buffington, 1005 Buena Vista St., South Pasadena, CA 91030
California Federation of Chaparral Poets, 1422 Ashland Ave., Claremont, CA 91711
California Poetry Reading Circuit, c/o James McMichael, University of California, Dept. of English, Irvine, CA 92664
California Poets-in-the-Schools, c/o J. O. Simon, San Francisco State University, 1600 Holloway (HLL Bldg.), San Francisco, CA 94132
California State Poetry Society*, c/o Ward Fulcher, 2925 Roanoke Court, Bakersfield, CA 93306
College of San Mateo Poetry Center, c/o Jean Pumphrey, 1700 W. Hillsdale Blvd., San Mateo, CA 94402
The Grand Piano Poetry Readings, c/o Steve Benson and Carla Harryman, 1607 Haight St., San Francisco, CA 94117
Intersection Poets and Writers Series, c/o Jim Hartz, 756 Union St., San Francisco, CA 94133
New College Modern American Poetry and Poetics Program, c/o Louis Patler, 777 Valencia St., San Francisco, CA 94110
The Poetry Center, San Francisco State University, 1600 Holloway Ave., San Francisco, CA 94132
Poetry Organization for Women, P.O. Box 2414, Dublin, CA 94566
The Poets Place, c/o Beverly Michaels-Cohn, Hyperion Theatre, 1835 Hyperion Ave., Los Angeles, CA 90027
World Poetry Society, c/o E. A. Falkowski, 208 W. Latimer Ave., Campbell, CA 95008
Yuki Teikei Haiku Society, c/o Haiku Journal, Kiyoshi Tokutomi, 1020 S. 8th St., San Jose, CA 95112

COLORADO
Poetry Society of Colorado*, c/o Vera M. Graham, 2235 Newport St., Denver, CO 80207

CONNECTICUT
Connecticut Poetry Circuit, c/o Jean Maynard, The Honors College, Wesleyan University, Middletown, CT 06457
Connecticut Poetry Society*, c/o Ben Brodinsky, P.O. Box 44, Old Saybrook, CT 06476

DELAWARE
First State Writers*, c/o E. Jean Lanyon, 4 E. Cleveland Ave., Newark, DE 19711

DISTRICT OF COLUMBIA
Ascension Poetry Reading Series, c/o E. Ethelbert Miller, Howard University, P.O. Box 441, Washington, DC 20059
Federal Poets of Washington, D.C.*, c/o Betty Wollaston, 5321 Willard Ave., Chevy Chase, MD 20015

FLORIDA
Florida State Poet's Association*, c/o Robert DeWitt, P.O. Box 608, Green Cove Springs, FL 32043
National Poetry Day Committee, 1110 N. Venetian Dr., Miami Beach, FL 33139

GEORGIA
Atlanta Poetry Society, c/o Robert Manns, 1105-E N. Jamestown Rd., Decatur, GA 30033
Georgia State Poetry Society*, c/o Edward Davin Vickers, P.O. Box 8129, Atlanta, GA 30306
Poetry at Callanwolde, c/o Gene Ellis, 980 Briarcliff Rd., NE, Atlanta, GA 30306

HAWAII
Hawaii Writers Club*, c/o Louise Martin, 1634 Makiki St., Honolulu, HI 96822

IDAHO
Idaho Poets-in-the-Schools, c/o Keith Browning, Lewis & Clark State College, Dept. of English, Lewiston, ID 83501
Idaho State Poetry Society*, c/o Margaret Ward Dodson, 3883 Northbridge Way, Boise, ID 83706

ILLINOIS
Apocalypse Poetry Association, c/o Rose Lesniak, Creative Writing Center, 3307 Bryn Mawr, Chicago, IL 60625
Illinois State Poetry Society*, c/o Dr. Edwin B. Doran, Rte. 3, Box 47, Eureka, IL 61530
Modern Poetry Association, 1228 N. Dearborn Pkwy., Chicago, IL 60610
The Poetry Center, c/o Paul Hoover, Museum of Contemporary Art, 237 E. Ontario, Chicago, IL 60611

INDIANA
Indiana State Federation of Poetry Clubs*, c/o Kay Kinamon, Rte. 3, Alexandria, IN 46001
Poets' Study Club of Terre Haute, 826 S. Center St., Terre Haute, IN 47807

IOWA
Ellsworth Poetry Project, c/o Daniel M. McGuiness, Ellsworth College, 1100 College Ave., Iowa Falls, IA 50126
Iowa Poetry Association*, c/o Will C. Jumper, 111 Lynn Ave., Apt. 408, Ames, IA 50010

KENTUCKY
Kentucky State Poetry Society*, c/o Carolyn Fuqua, 3310 Cox Mill Rd., Hopkinsville, KY 42240

LOUISIANA
Louisiana State Poetry Society*, c/o Bernice Larson Webb, 159 Whittington Dr., Lafayette, LA 70503
New Orleans Poetry Forum, c/o Garland Strother, 76 Marcia Dr., Luling, LA 70070

MAINE
Maine Poetry and Writers Guild*, c/o Patricia R. King, P.O. Box 2573, South Portland, ME 04106

MARYLAND
Howard County Poetry and Literature Society, c/o Ellen C. Kennedy, 10446 Waterfowl Terrace, Columbia, MD 21044
Maryland State Poetry Society*, c/o B. Floyd Flickinger, 300 St. Dunstans Rd., Baltimore, MD 21212

MASSACHUSETTS
Blacksmith House Poetry Program, c/o Gail Mazur, 5 Walnut Ave., Cambridge, MA 02140
Massachusetts State Poetry Society*, c/o Jeanette Maes, 64 Harrison Ave., Lynn, MA 01905
New England Poetry Club, c/o Diana Der Hovanessian, 2 Farrar St., Cambridge, MA 02138

MICHIGAN
Miles Modern Poetry Committee, c/o Steve Tudor, Wayne State University, Dept. of English, Detroit, MI 48202
Poetry Resource Center, c/o Lori Eason, Thomas Jefferson College/Grand Valley State Colleges, Lake Huron Hall, Allendale, MI 49401
Poetry Society of Michigan*, c/o Joyce S. Giroux, 825 Cherry Ave., Big Rapids, MI 49307
Rhyme Space and West Park Poetry Series, c/o Carolyn Holmes Gregory, 709 W. Huron, Ann Arbor, MI 48103

MINNESOTA
Hungry Mind Poetry Series, c/o Jim Sitter, Hungry Mind Bookstore, 1648 Grand Ave., St. Paul, MN 55105
University Poets' Exchange of Minnesota, c/o William Elliott, Bemidji State University, Dept. of English, Bemidji, MN 56601

MISSISSIPPI
Mississippi State Poetry Society*, c/o Charlene V. Barr, 943 Carlisle St., Jackson, MS 39202

MISSOURI
American Poets Series and Poetry Programs, c/o Gloria Goodfriend, Jewish Community Center of Kansas City, 8201 Holmes Rd., Kansas City, MO 64131
St. Louis Poetry Center, c/o Leslie Konnyu, 5410 Kerth Rd., St. Louis, MO 63128

NEBRASKA
Nebraska Poets' Association*, c/o Maurice Jay, 604 S. 22nd St., 1119, Omaha, NE 68102

NEVADA
Nevada Poetry Society*, c/o Sister Margaret McCarran, McCarran Ranch, via Sparks, NV 89431

NEW HAMPSHIRE
The Frost Place, c/o Donald Sheehan, Ridge Rd., Box 74, Franconia, NH 03580
Poetry Society of New Hampshire*, c/o Sharon Clarke Jones, Daniel Plummer Rd., Goffstown, NH 03045

NEW JERSEY

Kilmer House Poetry Center, c/o Robert Truscott, 88 Guilden St., New Brunswick, NJ 08901
New Jersey Poetry Society*, c/o Vivian M. Meyer, 6 Park Ave., Mine Hill, Dover, NJ 07801
Poets & Writers of New Jersey, P.O. Box 852, Upper Montclair, NJ 07043
Walt Whitman International Poetry Center, c/o Frederick W. Missimer, 2nd and Cooper Sts., Camden, NJ 08102

NEW MEXICO

National Federation of State Poetry Societies, c/o Alice Briley, 1121 Major Ave., Albuquerque, NM 87107
New Mexico State Poetry Society*, c/o Ruth Roberts, 1810 Morningrise Place, SE, Albuquerque, NM 87108

NEW YORK

Academy of American Poets, 1078 Madison Ave., New York, NY 10028
Bronx Poets and Writers Alliance, 5800 Arlington Ave., Bronx, NY 10471
Columbia Street Poets, c/o Emilie Glen, 77 Barrow St., New York, NY 10014
Haiku Society of America, Japan House, 333 E. 47th St., New York, NY 10017
Ithaca Community Poets, c/o Katharyn Machan Aal, 431-B E. Seneca St., Ithaca, NY 14850
New York Poetry Forum*, c/o Dorothea Neale, 3064 Albany Crescent, Apt. 54, Bronx, NY 10463
New York State Poets-in-the-Schools, c/o Myra Klahr, 24 N. Greeley Ave., Chappaqua, NY 10514
Noho for the Arts Poetry Forum, c/o Palmer Hasty, 542 La Guardia Place, New York, NY 10012
Nuyorican Poet's Cafe, c/o Miguel Algarin, 524 E. 6th St., New York, NY 10003
Outriders Poetry Program, c/o Max A. Wickert, 182 Colvin Ave., Buffalo, NY 14216
Poetry Center, c/o Grace Schulman, 92nd St. YM-YWHA, 1395 Lexington Ave., New York, NY 10028
Poetry Society of America, 15 Gramercy Park, New York, NY 10003
Poets Union, c/o Lester Von Losberg, Jr., 315 Sixth Ave., Brooklyn, NY 11215
Poets & Writers, Inc., 201 W. 54th St., New York, NY 10019
C. W. Post Poetry Center, Dept. of English, C. W. Post Center, Long Island University, Greenvale, NY 11548
Rochester Poetry Central, c/o Jim LaVilla-Havelin, 322 Brooks Ave., Rochester, NY 14619
Rochester Poetry Society, c/o Dale Davis, 155 S. Main St., Fairport, NY 14450
St. Mark's Poetry Project, c/o Maureen Owen or Paul Violi, Second Ave. and 10th St., New York, NY 10003
Shelley Society of New York, c/o Annette B. Feldmann, 144-20 41st Ave., Apt. 322, Flushing, NY 11355

NORTH CAROLINA

North Carolina Poetry Society*, c/o Margaret Boothe Baddour, 125 Pineridge Lane, Goldsboro, NC 27530

OHIO

Cleveland State University Poetry Center, c/o Alberta T. Turner, Euclid at 24th St., Cleveland, OH 44115
Kenyon Poetry Society, c/o George C. Nelson, Kenyon College, Gambier, OH 43022
Ohio Poetry Day Committee, c/o Evan Lodge, 1506 Prospect Rd., Hudson, OH 44236
Poetry Circuit of Ohio, c/o R. W. Daniel, P.O. Box 247, Gambier, OH 43022
Poets League of Greater Cleveland, P.O. Box 6055, Cleveland, OH 44101
Toledo Poets Center, c/o Joze Lipman, UH—507-C, University of Toledo, Toledo, OH 43606
Verse Writers' Guild of Ohio*, c/o Amy Jo Zook, 3520 State Rte. 56, Mechanicsburg, OH 43044
Yellow Pages Poets, c/o Jack Roth, P.O. Box 8041, Columbus, OH 43201

OKLAHOMA

Poetry Society of Oklahoma*, c/o Helen Downing, 2309 NW 47th, Oklahoma City, OK 73112

OREGON

Oregon State Poetry Association*, c/o Patricia Banta, Echo Bend Rd., Roseburg, OR 97470
Western World Haiku Society, 40102 NE 130th Place, Portland, OR 97230

PENNSYLVANIA

Homewood Poetry Forum, Inner City Services, Homewood Branch, Carnegie Library, 7101 Hamilton Ave., Pittsburgh, PA 15206
International Poetry Forum, c/o Dr. Samuel Hazo, 4400 Forbes Ave., Pittsburgh, PA 15213
Pennsylvania Poetry Society*, c/o Cecilia Parsons Miller, 264 Walton St., Lemoyne, PA 17043
Y Poetry Center/Workshop, c/o Anne-Sue Hirshorn, YM-YWHA Branch of JYC, Broad and Pine Sts., Philadelphia, PA 19147

RHODE ISLAND

Rhode Island State Poetry Society*, c/o Robert Hazlett, 91 Fatima Dr., Bristol, RI 02809

SOUTH DAKOTA

South Dakota State Poetry Society*, c/o Mrs. Murray Stevens, 909 E. 34th St., Sioux Falls, SD 57105

TENNESSEE

Poetry Society of Tennessee*, c/o Chester Rider, 254 Buena Vista, Memphis, TN 38112
Tennessee Poetry Circuit, c/o Paul Ramsey, University of Tennessee, Chattanooga, TN 37405

TEXAS
American Poetry League, 3915 SW Military Dr., San Antonio, TX 79601
Hyde Park Poets, c/o Albert Huffstickler, 609 E. 45th St., Austin, TX 78751
Poetry Society of Texas*, c/o Pat Stodgill, 1424 Highland Rd., Dallas, TX 75218
Stella Woodall Poetry Society, 3915 SW Military Dr., San Antonio, TX 79601

UTAH
Utah State Poetry Society*, c/o Maxine Jennings, 3985 Orchard Dr., Ogden, UT 84403

VIRGINIA
Pause for Poetry, c/o Margaret T. Rudd, 6925 Columbia Pike, Annandale, VA 22003

WASHINGTON
Poetry League of America, 5603 239th Place, SW, Mountain Terrace, WA 98043

WEST VIRGINIA
Morgantown Poetry Society, 673 Bellaire Dr., Morgantown, WV 26505
West Virginia Poetry Society*, c/o Dr. Kathleen Rousseau, 239 Hoffman St., Morgantown, WV 26505

WISCONSIN
Wisconsin Fellowship of Poets*, c/o Marjorie Nienstaedt, 809 Dorr Ave., Rhinelander, WI 54501

WYOMING
Poetry Programs of Wyoming, c/o David J. Fraher, P.O. Box 3033, Casper, WY 82602
Poets of Wyoming Writers*, c/o Charles Popovich, 1311 LaClede, Sheridan, WY 82801

CANADA
League of Canadian Poets, 175 Carlton, Toronto, Ont. M5A 2K3

Awards and Prizes for Poetry /
The 1979 Winners

For the purpose of this list, 1979 winners are those announced during the calendar year 1979; they are arranged alphabetically by name of sponsor.

Academy of American Poets
1078 Madison Ave.
New York, NY 10028
  The Fellowship: May Swenson.
  Walt Whitman Award: David Bottoms, for "Shooting Rats At The Bibb County Dump."
  Lamont Poetry Selection: "Sunrise," by Frederick Seidel.

American Academy and Institute of Arts and Letters
633 W. 155th St.
New York, NY 10032
  Gold Medal for Poetry: Archibald MacLeish.
  Awards in Literature (to poets): John N. Morris, Philip Schultz, Dave Smith.

American Poetry Review
1616 Walnut St., Rm. 405
Philadelphia, PA 19103
  American Poetry Review Prizes: First—Derek Walcott, for "Star-Apple Kingdom And Other Poems"; Second—Tess Gallagher, for "Open Fire Near A Shed And Other Poems."

Arizona State Poetry Society
Dorothy Greenlee, Contest Chairman
4805 S. Birch
Tempe, AZ 85282
  Traditional Award: First—Harry Wood, for "On Seeing Madame Pogany's Hand By Brancusi"; Second—Harry Wood, for "Emily Dickinson"; Third—Regina Brault, for "Rime De Plume."
  Free Verse Award: First—Eunice de Chazeau, for "Woman With Plastic Bag Gathering Shells"; Second—Regina Brault, for "Lazaretto Sketch"; Third—Tom Morris, for "Soldier's Monument."
  Southwest Award: First—Harry Wood, for "Immortal Skeletons"; Second—Diane Chapman, for "Dog Fox"; Third—Shirley VanCleef, for "Coyote."
  Arizona Award: First—Dorothy Greenlee, for "The Alchemy of Desert Sun"; Second—Marybeth Martin, for "Who Lights A Candle To See The Sun?"; Third—Truth Mary Fowler, for "Daily Death."
  Haiku Award: First—Florence Otter, for Abandoned Depot"; Second—Nida Ingram, for "Twilight Deepens, Yet . . ."; Third—Louise Somers Winder, for "The New Calendar."
  Dramatic Monolog Award: First—Bai Heifferon, for "The Ancient Ones"; Second—Harry Wood, for "The Rest Is Silence"; Third—Lois Hayna, for "In Answer To Your Query."
  Sonnet Award: First—Beatrice Rundle, for "Death In The Morn"; Second—Agnes Gray Ronald, for "A Fantasy For Sarah, 5"; Third—Esther Lieper, for "Putting Up Storm Windows."
  Cinquain Award: First—Diane Chapman, for "Transitions"; Second—LeRoy Meagher, for "April Mourning"; Third—Violette Newton, for "So Close To Time."
  Humor Award: First—Diane Chapman, for "In Praise Of Heroic Couplets"; Second—Frank Rodocker, for "Send Me"; Third—Dorothy Lykes, for "Grand Canyon."
  General (Youth) Award: First—Terri Chernov, for "And A Man Just Can't"; Second—Frank Stafford, for "Cure For Stage Fright"; Third—Lenore Brancato, for "Bona Fide Bozo."

Associated Writing Programs
Florida International University
English Dept.
Tamiami Trail
Miami, FL 33199
  Series for Contemporary Poetry: Jeanne Larsen, for "James Cook In Search Of Terra Incognita."

Association of American Publishers
1 Park Ave.
New York, NY 10017
  National Book Award (poetry): James Merrill, for "Mirabell: Books Of Number."

Bitterroot Magazine
Blythebourne Sta., P.O. Box 51
Brooklyn, NY 11219
  Gustave Kaitz Awards: First—Annabel Thomas, for "The Sound Of Wings"; Second—Fran Thomas, for "Saying"; Third—Lois Beebe Hayna, for "Unremembered Time, Forgotten Place."
  William Kushner Awards: First—Anne Wittels, for "Teach Me To Love"; Second—Frank Sims, for "Ode To A Black Woman"; Third—Dorothy M. Bechhold, for "There Is Bafflement Here."
  Albert Tallman Awards: First—Marie Hayes Grime, for "Night Hours"; Second—Christopher Humble, for "Old Retainers"; Third—Gerard John Conforti, for "Alone."

Black Warrior Review
P.O. Box 2936
University, AL 35486

Black Warrior Literary Award: First—Anne Cherner, for six "Place Poems"; Second—William Doreski, for seven poems from "Half Of The Map."

California Federation of Chaparral Poets
1422 Ashland Ave.
Claremont, CA 91711
Theme Poem: Marylu Terral Jeans, for "High Country."
Maud O'Neil Memorial Contest: First—Claire J. Baker, for "The Rocking Horse"; Second—Gertrude May Lutz, for "Windward Isles"; Third—Mabelle A. Lyon, for "Cold Night."
Dramatic Monologue: First—Nelle Fertig, for "His Last Duchess"; Second—Norma Calderone, for "Taste Of Heaven"; Third—Virginia Russ, for "I Am A Man."
Sonnet: First—Norma Calderone, for "A Gift For All Seasons"; Second—Pegasus Buchanan, for "The Young Rebels"; Third—Jessie Ruhl Miller, for "Chirp Me A Poem."
8 Lines or Less: First—Jeanne Bonnette, for "Summer Cinquain"; Second—Ernestine Hoff Emrick, for "I Head For Home"; Third—Ruth M. Hammond, for "A Snake In Every Garden."
Free Verse: First—Ina Ladd Brown, for "Journey"; Second—Joyce Odam, for "The Horse"; Third—Thelma Murphy, for "Father."
Nature—Canals, Creeks, Rivers: First—Vivian Breck, for "Song Of The Carmel River"; Second—Ruth Gibbs Zwall, for "I Have Followed The River"; Third—Dennis Wheeler, for "More 'Life On The Mississippi'."
Light or Humorous Verse: First—Edgar Bledsoe, for "Of Rhymes And Roses"; Second—Nelle Fertig, for "Surprise!"; Third—Anona McConaghy, for "A Day Gone Wrong."
Poems About California: First—Ruth Gibbs Zwall, for "Redwood Forest"; Second—Nelle Fertig, for "Miracle Of Pacific Grove"; Third—Leah Briggs, for "His Claim, A Desert Spring."
Narrative/Ballad: First—Helen Young, for "Ballad Of The Tree-Cutting Man"; Second—Barbara Meyn, for "The Ballad Of Elderberry"; third—Virginia Russ, for "The Laughter Of Red Angus."
Archie Rosenhouse Memorial Award: Mary M. Pronovost, for "When Days Are Steel."
Junior High Serious: First—Angela Broadus, for "The Last Leaf"; Second—Yvonne Galbreath, for "Brown"; Third—Julie Noah, for "Who Am I You Wanted To Know?"
Junior High Light or Humorous: First—Tiffany Booth, for "Magic Word"; Second—Sheila Donnelly, for "Stuck In The Woods On A Muddy Night"; Third—Vicky Yates, for "The Tiny Fly."
Senior High Serious: First—Jackie Johnston, for "Foresight"; Second—Katie Bjork, for "The Brass Rubbing"; Third—Scott Hamilton, for "Second Mate Whaler."
Senior High Light or Humorous: First—Kevin Foerstler, for "For The Ride"; Second—Tania Ansley, for "Windowshopping For Tomorrow's Dreams"; Third—Lori Nakamura, for "A Strange Planet."
California (High School): First—Michael D. Rankins, for "The Real California"; Second—Sue Troli, for "Dreamers State"; Third—Gloria Heilman, for "Old California."
Christmas: First—Stella Worley, for "Beggar Woman's View"; Second—Joyce McDavid Douglas, for "Synthetic Christmas"; Third—Elna Forsell Pawson, for "Similarity."

Callanwolde Arts Center
980 Briarcliff Rd., NE
Atlanta, GA 30306
Poets' and Writers' Workshop Poetry Award: Nancy Powell, for "Night Feeding"; Ron Hendricks, for "The Exchange."

Canada Council
P.O. Box 1047
Ottawa, Ont. K1P 5V8, Canada
Governor General's Literary Award (poetry): English language—Patrick Lane, for "Poems New And Selected"; French language—Gilbert Langevin, for "Mon Refuge Est Un Volcan."

Canadian Authors Association
24 Ryerson Ave.
Toronto, Ont. M5T 2P3, Canada
Canadian Authors Association Award (poetry): Andrew Suknaski, for "The Ghosts Call You Poor."

Canadian Authors Association
Edmonton Branch
c/o Mrs. June Fritch
13104-136 Ave.
Edmonton, Alta. T5L 4B3
Canada
Alberta Poetry Contest—
Jessie Drummond Boyd Prize: MaryBeth Aksenchuk, for "dust and rain."
Alberta Scouten Memorial Award: Michael Garland Coleman, for "Sphinx At Gizeh."
Georgia May Cook Sonnet Award: Dorothy Harrington MacAulay, for "Boat Family."
Special Class: Jean Reinhardt, for "Taxco."
Sonnet Class: Phyllis Brown, for "Yacht Race"; Gill Foss, for "Storm Warning: British Virgin Islands"; Patricia G. Armstrong, for "The Widower."
Short Poem Class: Norma West Linder, for "Refugees"; Douglas G. Banham, for "Glencoe"; Michael Kortsen, for "Pastoral Interlude."
Humorous Verse Class: Luetta Trehas, for "Year Of The Child"; Eileen Burnett, for "Retrospect"; Ellamae Gunn, for "Soup Of The Day: Chicken."
Juvenile Poems Class: Wanda Morgan, for "Not Today"; Shawna Downey, for "Old Stove"; Bernadette Andrea, for "The Night."

Carolina Quarterly
Greenlaw Hall 066A
University of North Carolina
Chapel Hill, NC 27514
Contest in Fiction and Poetry (poetry winners): First—Paul Jones, for "Native American Revolutionaries"; Second—Jim Daniels, for "Work Shoes #2"; Third—Kathryn Stripling, for "Lullabye."

Casa de las Americas
Havana, Cuba
First Prize for Poetry (Anglophone Caribbean Category): Andrew Salkey, for a collection of poems

about Chile.

Cedar Rock Magazine
1121 Madeline
New Braunfels, TX 78130
    Joseph P. Slomovich Memorial Awards: First—
    Nicholas Rinaldi, for "The Window"; Second—
    John Nist, for "Hometown Remembered"; Third—
    Teresa Anderson, for "Song To Be Sung To No
    One"; Fourth—Lawrence Murphy, for "We Should
    Love Lorca"; Fifth—Susan Strayer Deal, for "When
    He Moved."

Columbia University
Advisory Board on Pulitzer Prizes
New York, NY 10027
    Pulitzer Prize in Poetry: Robert Penn Warren, for
    "Now And Then: Poems—1976-1978."

Commonwealth Club of California
681 Market St.
San Francisco, CA 94105
    Silver Literary Medal Award (poetry): Sheila
    Moon, for "Songs For Wanderers."

The Crossroads Magazine
2014 Palo Alto
Carrollton, TX 75006
    Viola Hayes Parsons Awards: Grand Prize—A. R.
    Nooncaster, for "June Blow-Out"; Second—Sandra
    Little, for "Snow Day (No School)"; Third
    —LaVonne Smith, for "Seatown, Revisited."
    Leroy Memorial Awards: Grand Prize—Dorothylee
    Chapman, for "Legend Of The Eagle Dance."
    Judge 1: First—Dawn Godes, for "The Luck O'
    The Irish"; Second—James W. Proctor, for "I Can't
    Unwish The Night"; Third—Alice Morrey Bailey,
    for "It Laughs To Me." Judge 2: First—Janis
    Wyburn, for "caring"; Second—Vivian Smallwood,
    for "Room 207"; Third—Allyn LeHew, for "Dog-
    gerel For A Cat." Judge 3: First—Patricia Conrad
    Bowen, for "A Footnote To The Hunting Of Wild
    Ducks"; Second—Jack Fenwick, for "At The Grave
    Of The Great God Pan"; Third—Louise Hajek, for
    "Almost Deserted."

Great Lakes Colleges Association
220 Collingwood, Suite 240
Ann Arbor, MI 48103
    New Writer's Award (poetry): Leslie Ullman, for
    "Natural Histories"; Honorable Mention—Carole
    Oles, for "The Loneliness Factor."

Gusto Magazine
2960 Philip Ave.
Bronx, NY 10465
    Best Poem: First—Ruth Wildes Schuler; Second—
    Anne Ormand; Third—Magny L. Jensen; Honorable
    Mentions—Dawna Maydak Andrejcak, Tony Curtis,
    M. M. Hanna, Eda Howink, Frona Lane.
    Best Haiku/Senryu: First—Jim Handlin; Second—
    George Swede; Third—Gloria H. Proscal; Honorable
    Mentions—Joyce Walker Currier, Ruth O. Maun-
    ders, Barbara McCoy, Raymond Roseliep, Robert
    W. Thurber.

Houghton Mifflin Company
666 Third Ave.
New York, NY 10017

Houghton Mifflin New Poetry Series: Tom Lux,
for "Sunday."

Illinois Arts Council
111 N. Wabash Ave.
Chicago, IL 60602
    Annual Literary Awards (for poetry): Michael
    Brown, for "Miss Brooks"; Dan Campion, for
    "Night Flying"; Elizabeth Libbey, for "Juana Bau-
    tista Lucero"; Ralph J. Mills, Jr., for "Mid-Aug-
    ust"; Bob Bensen, for "Arthur's Seat, Edinburgh";
    G. E. Murray, for "In Memory Of A Coastal Nov-
    ember"; Netta Gillespie, for "Seated In A Chinese
    Painting, He Speaks"; James Ballowe, for "Sur-
    vival"; Neil Lukatch, for "Farm Couple, Belgium,
    1914"; Lisel Mueller, for "The Artist's Model, Ca.
    1912"; Lucien Stryk, for "Cherries."

Image Magazine
P.O. Box 28048
St. Louis, MO 63119
    Anthony J. Summers Memorial Poetry Award:
    First—Graham Sykes, for "The Bells Are Ringing
    For John Donne"; Second—Laurel Speer, for "The
    Dying Have Sad Eyes."

International Platform Association
2564 Berkshire Rd.
Cleveland Heights, OH 44106
    Carl Sandburg Award: William Meredith.

Islands and Continents
P.O. Box 25
Setauket, NY 11733
    Translation Award: Eleni Fourtouni, for "Contem-
    porary Greek Women Poets."

**Jewish Book Council of National Jewish Welfare
Board**
15 E. 26th St.
New York, NY 10010
    *Harry and Florence Kovner Memorial Award for
    Poetry:* Moishe Steingart, for "In Droisen Fun Der
    Velt."

The Lyric
307 Dunton Dr., SW
Blacksburg, VA 24060
    Lyric Memorial Prize: Dennis McDermott, for
    "Which Robin In The Night."
    Nathan Haskell Dole Prize: Grace P. Simpson, for
    "Two For Cordelia."
    Roberts Memorial Prize: Anne Barlow, for "Sep-
    tember Sonnet."
    Leitch Memorial Prize: Marguerite Enlow Barze,
    for "One Clear Call."
    Virginia Prize: John Robert Quinn, for "Being."
    New England Prize: Jess Perlman, for "Lines For
    New Walls."
    Panola Prize: Robert Lee Brothers, for "Lady At
    High Noon."
    Fluvanna Prize: Annette Patton Cornell, for
    "Strange Estate."
    Quarterly Prizes: Winter—Margaret Secrist, for
    "Hawk At The Feeder"; Spring—George S. Bas-
    com, for "Horatio On Hamlet"; Summer—Elsie
    Kurz, for "The Blind Child"; Fall—Gwendolyn

Niles, for "Rites Of Passage."

Collegiate Poetry Contest: First—Stephen Lang, for "Paperweight"; Second—Bonnie Heltibrand, for "Gather Ye Rosebuds"; Third—William Ender, for "The Perfect People"; Honorable Mention—Robert Bess, for "Gathrite's Pride," John Bill, for "Answer To Housman," Brian Richard Plant, for "A Question Of Love," Susan Porter, for "Family Bible," Jane Oliensis, for "Rain," and Jane Sullivan, for "A Renaissance Sonnet."

Mademoiselle Magazine
350 Madison Ave.
New York, NY 10017
College Poetry Competition: First Prizes—Amy Boesky, for "North Of Grayling," and Tan Lin, for "Regret—The Dead Man Speaks To His Wife"; Honorable Mentions—Wendy Laura Frisch, for "Letters To The Tormentor VII," Jean Kane, for "Liners," Lynn Wardley, for "In New Fain," and Harte Valerie Weiner, for "Dr. Hermione And I."

Mr. Cogito Press
Pacific University, P.O. Box 267
Forest Grove, OR 97116
2nd Pacific Northwest Translation Award: Grazio Falzon, for poems from the Maltese of Mario Azzopardi.

Modern Language Association of America
62 Fifth Ave.
New York, NY 10011
James Russell Lowell Prize (this year awarded for a book on poetry): Andrew Welsh, for "Roots Of Lyric: Primitive Poetry And Modern Poetics."

National Federation of State Poetry Societies
Amy Jo Zook, Contest Chairman
3520 State Rte. 56
Mechanicsburg, OH 43044
NFSPS Grand Prize: First—Alice Morrey Bailey, for "The Black Knight"; Second—Sue Scalf, for "What You Were"; Third—M. Michael Black, for "Tutankhamen."
Agnes C. Brothers Pathway of Life Award: First—Millicent Allen, for "The House That Love Built"; Second—Marcella Siegel, for "Summer Is For Popsicles"; Third—Virginia Blanck Moore, for "To A Son."
Mason Sonnet Award: First—LeRoy Burke Meagher, for "Room 203, Sunshine Manor"; Second—Myrtle Marmaduke, for "The Only"; Third—Violette Newton, for "Where Beauty's Advocate."
John A. Lubbe Memorial Award: First—Sally McCluskey, for "Isaac Bashevis Singer: Shosha"; Second—M. Michael Black, for "Continuum"; Third—Jeri McCormick, for "To Belong."
Alabama State Poetry Society Award: First—Erin Wells, for "Sanctuary"; Second—Lael W. Hill, for "Under Late Leaves"; Third—Ida Fasel, for "Gardening."
Indiana Award: First—Georgette Perry, for "Persephone"; Second—Vonna Adrian, for "All That Now Remains"; Third—Marion Buchman, for "The Find."
Random Rhyme Award: First—Anna Nash Yar-

brough, for "The Prude"; Second—Flora G. Ardito, for "Farewell And Smile"; Third—Selma Youngdahl, for "Where Is It Now?"
Arkansas Award: First—Norma Calderone, for "To Ruth On The Eve Of Suicide"; Second—LeRoy Burke Meagher, for "Gift Of Seasons"; Third—A. T. Kemper, for "Confrontation."
Florida State Poets Association Award: First—Violette Newton, for "Burdocks' Is Gone"; Second—Maggie Smith, for "Osceola's Kate Maroon"; Third—Eve Braden Hatchett, for "Love Letter From A Blue Eyed Gingerbread Boy."
Oklahoma State Poetry Society Award: First—Vesta P. Crawford, for "One Who Claimed The Wilderness"; Second—Marilyn Eynon Scott, for "Planet Of The Heart"; Third—Geraldine R. Pratt, for "Somehow, We Fly."
New York Poetry Forum Award: First—Helen B. Harary, for "To A Blind Man At A Poetry Reading"; Second—Pete Lee, for "Hawkins Revisited"; Third—Aileen R. Jaffa, for "Triptych Of Emily."
Our American Indian Heritage Award: First—M. Michael Black, for "Sun Dancer"; Second—Opal Jane O'Neal, for "Acculturation Complete"; Third—Louise Morris Kelley, for "Hozhoni."
South Dakota Poetry Society Award: First—Sally McCluskey, for "Will Eddy"; Second—Daley Rushton, for "Bison Bison"; Third—Riley N. Kelly, for "Lovers' Leap."
Manningham Award: First—Ulrich Troubetzkoy, for "Out Of The Many"; Second—Ida Fasel, for "Once More, Lest We Forget"; Third—Lee Highbridge, for "Security Blanket."
Poet Laureate Emeritus of Louisiana Award: First—Carlee Swann, for "Apple Basket"; Second—Barbara Leavell Smith, for "Mirrors"; Third—Elsbeth Liebowitz, for "Touch."
Humorous Poetry Award: First—Helen Stallcup, for "Gardening News"; Second—Judith A. Powell, for "The Chambered Mortgagor"; Third—Florence Wahl Otter, for "You Were Expecting Welcome Wagon?"
Olive H. McHugh Memorial Award: First—Verna Lee Hindegardner, for "The Eagle Screams"; Second—Julia Hurd Strong, for "The Question"; Third—Evelyn Corry Appelbee, for "A Ray Of Light."
Bible Award: First—Betty W. Madsen, for "John At Easter"; Second—Ida Fasel, for "Joseph"; Third—Pat Lantay, for "Nativity."
Clement Hoyt Memorial Haiku Award: First—Alberta Babcock, for Haiku; Second—Raymond McCarty, for Haiku; Third—Cecilia Parsons Miller, for Haiku.
Beymorlin Sonnet Award: First—Carlee Swann, for "The Poet Converses With A Mouse"; Second—Kitty Yeager, for "Dream Companion"; Third—Vonnie Thomas, for "Blind Climber."
Evans Spencer Wall Memorial Award: First—Violette Newton, for "On Style"; Second—Sister Helene, for "Bernstein In Concert"; Third—Jack E. Murphy, for "Emily Dickinson."
Gertrude Saucier Historical Award: First—Pearl Hand Cockrell, for "Sadat-Begin, A Beginning?";

Second—Norma Calderone, for "The Song: America's Own"; Third—Mary C. Ferris, for "Oliver Gainbridge Reports To The National Geographic Society."

Gertrude Saucier Lyric Award: First—Mary Logan Sweet, for "Niobe"; Second—Sharon E. Rusbuldt, for "Box Of Crayolas"; Third—Elizabeth Shafer, for "In The Hollow Of The Hills."

Betty Miller Davis Memorial Award: First—Maria Illo, for "Tree Spirit"; Second—Beatrice M. Land, for "The Vagabonds"; Third—Annette Burr Stowman, for "I'm Trying To Tell You."

Crossroads Award: First—Jaye Giammarino, for "A Time For Healing"; Second—Susan Zivich, for "The Miracle"; Third—Bettie M. Sellers, for "A Silence When The Rest Have Left The Room."

Youth Award: First—Renee Gardikes, for "The Cycle Of Life"; Second—Gregory A. White, for "The World Inside"; Third—Laura Beth Margolis, for "Party."

NFSPS Patriotism Award: First—Robert G. Vessey, for "Who Speaks For America?"; Second—Norma Calderone, for "Operation Homecoming"; Third—Blanche N. Skeans, for "Patriotism."

Poetry Society of Texas Award: First—Opal Jane O'Neal, for "Fourth Floor Ward"; Second—Shirley Handley, for "Las Vegas Bitters"; Third—Bryanne Nanfito, for "A Matter Of Math."

Eunice Pond Laselle Memorial Award: First—Kitty Yeager, for "Ruie Taylor: Pied Piper Poet"; Second—Gretelle Suzanne LeGron, for "A Silent Thunder"; Third—Myrtle Marmaduke, for "Poet And Pedestrian."

Mary Ellen Riddell No. Eighty-One Award: First—Glenna Holloway, for "Birthday At The State Fair"; Second—Norma Calderone, for "Act III"; Third—Patricia S. Grimm, for "Della In The Hall."

NFSPS Modern Award: First—Marjorie Knott Hause, for "Rocks"; Second—Jack Fenwick, for "The Holy Place"; Third—Maxine Jennings, for "Children Going Home From School."

NFSPS Traditional Award: First—Raymond Henri, for "The End Of The Battle"; Second—Pauline Durrett Robertson, for "What I Did Last Summer"; Third—Helen Bryant, for "Fossil Bones At Olduvai."

Arizona State Poetry Society Award: First—Mildred Crabtree Speer, for "Beyond The Tree Line"; Second—Norma Calderone, for "The Colored Glass Of Passion"; Third—Violette Newton, for "Scattered Through My Life, Your Poems."

Maryland Award: First—Will Pollard, for "In The Self Poem The Metaphor Moves In Circles Of Unborn Light"; Second—Sandra Basner Shrigley, for "My Daughter"; Third—Marion Brimm Rewey, for "A Release Of Ravens."

Spoon River Award: First—Sally McClusky, for "The Woman Who Hated Housework"; Second—Beatrice Meyer, for "Worth A Thousand Words"; Third—Helen Elaine Ray, for "Sylvia Plath."

Louisiana State Poetry Society Award: First—Bettie M. Sellers, for "Bluegrass Interval"; Second—Suzie Siegel, for "Maybe When Spring Comes"; Third—Lois Marie Harrod, for "The Artist Returns To His Frescoed Wall."

Utah State Award: First—Vivian Smallwood, for "Night Watchman"; Second—Helena C. Defenbaugh, for "This Froth Of Spring"; Third—Shel McDonald, for "Envy Of A Sort."

Wichita Falls Texas Poetry Society Award: First—LeRoy Burke Meagher, for "When Silence Wintered"; Second—Carol Hamilton, for "Eagle Feather"; Third—Bai Heifferon, for "The Rainmaker."

Wisconsin Poetry Award: First—Glenna Holloway, for "Before A Poet Knows What She Is"; Second—Edward Davin Vickers, for "Poets' Train"; Third—Evelyn Hunt, for "Eden Revisited."

Verse Writers Guild of Ohio Award: First—M. Michael Black, for "Song Of The Buffalo Wind"; Second—Joy Gresham Hagstrom, for "Haunted Land"; Third—Byranne Nanfito, for "Shrink."

Poet Laureate of Texas Award: First—Carol Hamilton, for "A Secret"; Second—Margaret Rose Champion, for "seascape"; Third—Marion Brimm Rewey, for "Savage."

Music Award: First—Alice Briley, for "The Source Of Music"; Second—Gertrude Ryder Bennett, for "Radio Musicians"; Third—Marguerite Arthur Brewster, for "Where The Flute-Bird Calls."

Mary Lee Hite Memorial Folklore Award: First—Sally McCluskey, for "The Ghostly Regiment"; Second—Norma Calderone, for "The Crow Girl"; Third—Elsie S. Lindgren, for "Hear How The Stones Cry Out."

John Greenbank Memorial Award: First—James MacWhinney, for "A Kid's Garden 1979"; Second—Claudia Watson Stewart, for "A Federal Case"; Third—Beatrice Branch, for "At The Beach."

Ida Ruth Voss Memorial Award: First—Mildred Crabtree, for "The Testimonial"; Second—Fan Benno, for "Speech Therapist"; Third—stevan-adele Morley, for "In That Remembered Season."

Leona Lloyd Memorial Award: First—Leith I. terMeulen, for "Pockets"; Second—Lois Marie Harrod, for "Celandine"; Third—Michael R. Acton, for "New England Beach At Night."

Oregon State Poetry Association Award: First—Marion Brimm Rewey, for "The Crows In Snow"; Second—Helen Dressling Corliss, for "From End To Beginnings"; Third—Gwen Casilli, for "Romanesque."

National Magazine Awards Foundation
1240 Bay St., Suite 300
Toronto, Ont. M5R 2A7
Canada

du Maurier Awards for Poetry: Gold—Sean Virgo, for "Deathwatch On Skidegate Narrows" (*Malahat Review*); Silver—George Faludy, for "Death Of A Chleuch Dancer" (*Canadian Forum*); Honorable Mentions—Brian Fawcett, for "Ten Island Poems" (*Capilano Review*), and Margaret Atwood, for "Night Visits, Torture, Elegies, Bread, Beginnings" (*Canadian Forum*).

National Poetry Series
284 Fifth Ave.
New York, NY 10001

National Poetry Series (winning manuscripts): "Collected Poems," by Sterling A. Brown; "Any Body's Song," by Joseph Langland; "Denizens," by Ronald Perry; "Silks," by Roberta Spear; "Folly River," by Wendy Salinger.

New England Poetry Club
2 Farrar St.
Cambridge, MA 02138
  Golden Rose Award: John Updike, for the poetry in "The Coup," for "Tossing And Turning," and for his translations.

New Hope Foundation
430 Park Ave.
New York, NY 10022
  Lenore Marshall Poetry Prize: Hayden Carruth, for "Brothers, I Loved You All."

New Letters Magazine
University of Missouri-Kansas City
Kansas City, MO 64110
  William Carlos Williams Prize for Poetry: Gary Thompson, for three poems in Fall/78 issue.

New Mexico State Poetry Society
c/o Ruth C. Roberts
1810 Morningrise Place, SE
Albuquerque, NM 87108
  New Mexico State Poetry Society Contest: (Rhymed Lyric) First—Virginia Moran Evans, for "There Will Be Daffodils"; Second—Regina Murray Brault, for "From Hand To Hand"; Third—Helena C. Defenbaugh, for "No Need For Spring"/(Free Verse) First—Caroline Patterson, for "Grandmother, I Found The Doll"; Second—Dorothy Foltz-Gray, for "Perfume"; Third—Gloria Bruckner, for "Ann Sexton"/(General) First—Lois Beebe Hayna, for "Moment Of The Butterfly"; Second—Harry B. Sheftel, for "HomoLogous"; Third—Vera Whitmer, for "Glass Gril"/(Humorous) First—Alice Briley, for "A Man's Best Friend, Friend, Friend"; Second—Ben Sweeney, for "Wall To Wall"; Third—Mary Abbot, for "Sage Advice."

New York Quarterly
80 8th Ave.
New York, NY 10011
  Poetry Day Award: Muriel Rukeyser.

New York University
Dept. of English
19 University Pl., Room 200
New York, NY 10003
  Thomas Wolfe Memorial Prize: First—William Elmore; Second—Eric Mathern; Third—Nancy L. Provine and Kathryn Petras.

Nimrod Magazine
University of Tulsa
Tulsa, OK 74104
  Pablo Neruda Prize for Poetry: First—Carol Haralson, for "Watching For Deer" and "How To Grow Roses"; Second—William Carpenter, for "The Yacht: A Meditation On Form."

Alfred B. Nobel Foundation
Nobel House
Sturegatan 14
11436 Stockholm, Sweden
  Nobel Prize for Literature (this year awarded to a poet): Odysseus Elytis.

North American Mentor Magazine
P.O. Drawer 69
Fennimore, WI 53809
  Annual Poetry Contest: First—Edna Meudt, for "Plain Chant For A Tree"; Second—Merrill G. Christophersen, for "The Heron."

North Carolina Literary and Historical Association
109 E. Jones St.
Raleigh, NC 27611
  Roanoke-Chowan Poetry Cup: Fred Chappell, for "Bloodfire."

Ohio Poetry Day Association
c/o Evan Lodge
1506 Prospect Rd.
Hudson, OH 44236
  Poet of the Year: Novella Humphrey Davis.
  Special Award: First—Michael Scanlon, for "The Rainmaker"; Second—Dalene Workman Stull, for "Stolen Cello"; Third—Anthony R. Mendenhall, for "Never Again!"

P.E.N. American Center
47 Fifth Ave.
New York, NY 10003
  P.E.N. Translation Prize: Charles Wright, for "The Storm And Other Poems," by Eugenio Montale.

Poetry Magazine
601 S. Morgan St.
Chicago, IL 60680
  Levinson Prize: Philip Levine, for poems in Sept./79 issue.
  Oscar Blumenthal Prize: Lynne Lawner, for poems in Aug./79 issue.
  Eunice Tietjens Memorial Prize: Robert Morgan, for poems in Nov./78 issue.
  Bess Hokin Prize: Robert Beverley Ray, for his work in June/79 issue.
  Jacob Glatstein Memorial Prize: Anne Winters, for translation of Marteau in April/79 issue.
  English-Speaking Union Prize: John Ashbery, for poems in July/79 issue.

Poetry Society of America
15 Gramercy Park
New York, NY 10003
  Bernice Ames Memorial Award: Alice McIntyre.
  Gordon Barber Memorial Award: Geraldine C. Little.
  Melville Cane Award: Andrew Welsh.
  Gertrude B. Claytor Award: Isabel Nathaniel.
  Gustav Davidson Memorial Award: Ulrich Troubetzkoy, Richard Frost (award shared).
  Mary Carolyn Davies Award: Ulrich Troubetzkoy.
  Emily Dickinson Award: Mildred Nash.
  Consuelo Ford Memorial Award: Joan LaBombard.
  Cecil Hemley Award: Geraldine C. Little.
  Elias Lieberman Student Poetry Award: Catherine Talmadge.
  John Masefield Memorial Award: G. N. Gabbard.
  Lucille Medwick Memorial Award: Gary Miranda.
  Alfred Kreymborg Memorial Award: Elizabeth Spires.
  Poetry Society of America First Prize: Alfred

Dorn.
Poetry Society of America Second Prize: Grace Morton.
Shelley Memorial Award: Hayden Carruth.
Celia B. Wagner Memorial Award: Ona Siporin.
William Carlos Williams Award: Back Roads Press, for "Teachings," by David Fisher.

Poetry Press
P.O. Box 736
Pittsburg, TX 75686
Poetry Press Poetry Contest: First—Cora Chapman Arthur, for "Stonehenge"; Second—Ardella B. Renn, for "Afterglow"; Third—Robert Erwin, for "Icarus."

Poetry Society of Oklahoma
c/o Clara Laster, Contest Chairman
204 E. 45th Pl.
Tulsa, OK 74105
Agnew Award: Clara Laster, for "Near The Port Of Joppa."
Capps Award: Clara Laster, for "Youthful Skier."
Clay Award: Clara Laster, for "My Heart's Country."
Kolbe Award: Clara Laster, for "Signature."
Anonymous Award: Gretelle Suzanne LeGron, for "Merry-Go-Round."
McRill Award: Gretelle Suzanne LeGron, for "Sweet Singer."
Thomason Award: Gretelle Suzanne LeGron, for "Sleeping Beauty."
Bennett Award: Winona Nation, for "To My Father."
Smith Award: Winona Nation, for "For No Reason At All."
Poetry Society of Oklahoma Award: Jim Skaggs, for "Refuge."
Green Award: Jim Skaggs, for "Aunt Alice."
Stealey Award: Marj Bennett, for "Father's Hands."
Hill Award: William Dean Williams, for "Possession."
Oliver Award: Jerald James Daly, for "Childhood, Remembering An Old Man."
Poet Laureate Award: Kathleen Peace, for "Three Notes Of Lavender."
Doughery Award: Kathleen Peace, for "Morning Song."
Johnson Award: Carol Hamilton, for "Desert Awakening."
Nonmember Award: Alice Mackenzie Swaim, for "Always A Father Sea."
Donors Award: Lois Beebe Hayne, for "Before The Butterfly."
Laster Award: Dorothy Colvert, for "The Long Wait."
Lucy Award: Robert Carson, for "The Urge."
McMahan Award: Lee Highbridge, for "Winding River."

Poets of the Foothills Art Center
809 15th St.
Golden, CO 80401
Poetry Chapbook Contest: Diane Furtney, for "Destination Rooms And Other Poems"; Runners-up—Joe D. Milosch, E. R. Nelson, Randall Schroth and Bonnie Hearn.

Poets' Roundtable of Arkansas
c/o Opal Jane O'Neal
421 Dell
Hot Springs, AR 71901
Arkansas Poetry Day Awards—
Sybil Nash Abrams Award: First—Verna Lee Hinegardner.
Rosa Zagnoni Marinoni Award: First—Opal Jane O'Neal; Second—Bonnie Lee Reynolds; Third—Lisa Ross.
Bernie Babcock Memorial Award: First—Marguerite B. Palmer; Second—Diane Taylor; Third—Ida Crane Walker.
Brownie Award: First—Verna Lee Hinegardner; Second—Dorothy B. Wiley; Third—Sister Mary Ricarda McGuire.
Fort Smith Southwest Times Record Award: First—Doll Gardner; Second—Jack E. Murphy; Third—Virginia Long.
Arkansas Gazette Foundation Award: First—Don Jones; Second—Opal Jane O'Neal; Third—Evelyn Tooley Hunt.
Roundtable Poets of Fort Smith Award: First—Verna Lee Hinegardner; Second—Helene Stallcup; Third—Ruth N. Ebberts.
Dr. Perry Crane Walker Memorial Award: First—Betty Fraser; Second—James W. Proctor; Third—Marnelle Robertson.
Roundtable Poets of Hot Springs Award: First—Viola Jacobson Berg; Second—Marnelle Robertson; Third—Vonnie Thomas.
Iris O'Neal Bowen Memorial Award: First—Viola Jacobson Berg; Second—Ann Ganschow; Third—Betty Fraser.
Siloam Springs Branch, Dr. Lily Peter Award: First—May Gray; Second—Kitty Yeager; Third—Diane Taylor.
Daves-Gipson-Larocco Award: First—May Gray; Second—Kitty Yeager; Third—James W. Proctor.
Clara B. Kennan Memorial Award: First—Lois Beebe Hayna; Second—Jeanie Carter; Third—Maggie Smith.
Marion Petefish Francis Award: First—Opal Jane O'Neal; Second—Helene Stallcup; Third—Ninagene Tillery.
Betty Fraser Award: First—Frances Sydnor Tehie; Second—LeRoy Burke Meagher; Third—Dorothy Ellen Meuser.
Pierson Mettler Memorial Award: First—Viola Jacobson Berg; Second—Doryes Daves; Third—Sister Mary Ricarda McGuire.
Searcy Award: First—Viola Jacobson Berg; Second—Anna Nash Yarbrough; Third—Verna Lee Hinegardner.
Etheree Award: First—Geneva I. Crook; Second—Jaye Giammarino; Third—Ida Crane Walker.
May Strate Memorial Award: First—Virginia Bridges Smith; Second—Opal Jane O'Neal; Third—Jeanie Carter.
Neva Jay Award: First—Verna Lee Hinegardner; Second—Jean M. Wyness; Third—Clara Gehron Willis.
Doriece Award: Betty Fraser, Nola Baber Green, Peggy Vining, James W. Proctor, and Helene Stall-

cup.

Arkansas Bank and Trust Co. Student Award:
First—Allison Lassieur; Second—Pam Crossley;
Third—Suzanne Tanner.

Luncheon Award: First—Verna Lee Hinegardner;
Second—Valeria Browne Thornton; Third—Doryes
Daves.

Arkansas Award of Merit: Lucille T. Babcock.

Portland Review
P.O. Box 751
Portland, OR 97207

Branford P. Millar Memorial Awards (poetry): $50
Award—James Den Boer, for "Appaloosa Mule";
$25 Award—Dave Smith, for "Southern History,"
and David Ignatow, for "Above Everything"; $50
Student Award—Patricia Ware, for "The Taped
Alternative: At The Fillmore"; $25 Student
Award—Verlena Orr Richardson, for "Notes With-
out Envelopes," and Marcie Goldsby, for "Stopping
By The Side Of The Road."

Post Poetry Center
C. W. Post Center
Long Island University
Greenvale, NY 11548

Winthrop Palmer Poetry Prize: Glenn Schmidt, for
"Separation."

Alumni Association Awards: First—Edward But-
scher, for "From The Back Porch"; Second—Bar-
bara-Jo Howard, for "Persephone"; Honorable
Mention—Susan Patt, for "Warm Sunday"; Facul-
ty—Barbara Kunat, for "Shadows," and William
Fahey, for "An Equestrian Statue"; Staff—Marcia
Eppstein, for "Summer Funeral."

Post Library Association Community Award:
First—Charles Fishman, for "March Weather";
Second—Susan Astor, for "The Big Top Folds Over
The Big Apple," and A. O. Howell, for "The
Moons Of Saturn"; Honorable Mention—Sarah
Singer, for "Power Failure," Patti Renner-Tana, for
"Eros And Civilization," and Nancy Sheridan, for
"If God Had Me . . ."

Floyd And Dorothy Lyon Award: Laura Vecsey,
for "time"; Honorable Mention—Ann Vigo, for
"Eucharist," and Marissa Martino, for "Centen-
nial."

Post Poetry Center Junior High Award: Corinna
Vecsey, for "You Are A Faithful Lover . . ."

Prairie Schooner Magazine
201 Andrews Hall
University of Nebraska-Lincoln
Lincoln, NE 68588

Prairie Schooner Prize for Poetry: Ted Kooser, for
four poems in Fall/78 issue.

Primipara Magazine
P.O. Box 371
Oconto, WI 54153

Annual Poetry Contest: First—Martha Mihalyi, for
"Anniversary"; Second—Patty Barnes, for "Woman
In The Morning"; Third—Martha Mihalyi, for
"Crossing Over."

Pteranodon Magazine
P.O. Box 229
Bourbonnais, IL 60914

First Pteranodon Poetry Contest: First—Nancy G.

Westerfield, for "Minute Discoveries"; Second—
Nancy G. Westerfield, for "Crossing—Arms";
Third—Ralph D. Eberly, for "Decades."

Second Pteranodon Poetry Contest: First—Eddie-
Lou Cole, for "I, Imagist"; Second—Howard D.
Koenig, for "The Rock Island Line"; Third—
Marguerite Brewster, for "The Measure of My
Days."

Third Pteranodon Poetry Contest: First—Esther M.
Leiper, for "Shaman"; Second—Joseph R. Shaffer,
for "Oh, Absolom!"; Third—Joyce Sandeen John-
son, for "River Catch."

Pulitzer Prize (see Columbia University)

Religious Arts Guild
25 Beacon St.
Boston, MA 02108

Dorothy Rosenberg Annual Poetry Award: First—
Elizabeth R. Hennefrund, for "Reference";
Second—Rose Rosberg, for "The Burning-Glass";
Honorable Mention—Patricia C. Groth, for
"Rachel's Mother," Jeanne Lohmann, for "Prepar-
ing To Go," Betty Lowry, for "Spanish Doors,"
Bea Sandler, for "Yarzheit," Alice Mackenzie
Swaim, for "Beginnings," and Sue Walker, for
"Gliderman."

San Francisco Foundation
425 California St.
San Francisco, CA 94104

James D. Phelan Literary Award (this year awarded
to a poet): Roberta Spear, for "Silks."

Seven Magazine
115 S. Hudson
Oklahoma City, OK 73102

Jesse Stuart Contest: First—Maryon Wood Harper,
for "Death On A Small Hill"; Second—Gregor Roy,
for "Barabbas," and Maxine R. Jennings, for "A
Soliloquy At The Airport"; Third—Rose King, for
"Black Boy On A Garbage Truck"; Honorable
Mentions: Emma Crobaugh, for "Cold Frost On
His Plow," and Charlotte Mann, for "Season's
End."

Southwest Review
Southern Methodist University
Dallas, TX 75275

Elizabeth Matchett Stover Memorial Award: Neva
Johnson Herrington, for "Blue Stone."

Spiritual Celebration Magazine
P.O. Box 431645
South Miami, FL 33143

Dorothy St. Clair Poetry Prize: Margaret Honton,
for "Fenced By An Unrelenting Wind."

Stanford University
Creative Writing Center
Dept. of English
Stanford, CA 94305

Wallace E. Stegner Fellowships (in poetry): David
Leedy; David Weissmann.

Syracuse University
Dept. of English
Syracuse, NY 13210

Delmar Schwartz Poetry Prize: Gael Sweeney;
George Jevremovic.

Loring Williams Award: Joe-Ann McLaughlin.
Whiffin Poetry Prize: Steven Pisano.

Triton College
2000 Fifth Ave.
River Grove, IL 60171
All Nations Poetry Contest: Discovery—Susan Astor, for "Physics Fantasia"; Claire Baker, for "Hiking Alone"; Henri Cole, for Sestina For A Sister"; Nina Dorfman, for "Some Fantasies In Search Of A Life"; Pat Gray, for "Midwinter Sauna"; Michael Holstein, for "Fishing For Poems"; Suzan Jarmoc, for "Khieh"; David Koenig, for "Gravel Bones-Waltz Time"; Carol Kanar, for "Van Gogh Among The Groceries"; Janet McCann, for "The Pack Of Dogs." Defeat—Susan Baumann, for "The Loss"; Susan Deal, for "In This Stark Place"; Ronald Gillette, for "Flatlands"; Alice Kennedy, for "Biography"; Caroline H. Knowles, for "The Hawk To Her Young"; Janet Krauss, for "Initiations"; David McKain, for "Caleb"; Janet McCann, for "Old Maid"; Melanie Richards, for "Coming Home"; Lynn Shoemaker, for "Three War Stories." Victory—Naomi Chase, for "Wirococha, The Jaguar"; Gay Davidson, for ''Homer''; Nina Dorfman, for "Indigines: Diptych"; William Harrold, for "A Piece Of Censored Film"; Robert Hoover, for "The Long Stemmed Success"; John Kotsakis, for "On The Centennial Celebration"; David McKain, for "Sunday School Lesson"; Lido Musique, for "Villet's Lament"; Stephen Roberts, for "A Dream Of Desire In Western New York"; C. Schaack, for "Wakefield."

University of Massachusetts Press
P.O. Box 429
Amherst, MA 01102
Juniper Prize: Eleanor Wilner, for "maya."

University of Missouri-Kansas City
Dept. of English
Kansas City, MO 64110
Barbara Storck Poetry Award: Jim Howard, for "Song Of The Resident Voyeur."

University of Missouri Press
107 Swallow Hall
Columbia, MO 65211
Devins Award: G. E. Murray, for "Repairs."

Virginia Quarterly Review
1 West Range
Charlottesville, VA 22903
Emily Clark Balch Award for Poetry: Connie Martin, for "Wood Work"; Honorable Mention—Tomas Transtromer (Samuel Charters, translator), for "Schubertiana."

Water Mark Press
175 East Shore Rd.
Huntington Bay, NY 11743
Water Mark Poets of North America First Book Award: Michael Blumenthal, for "Sympathetic Magic."

Webster Review
Webster College
Webster Groves, OH 63119
Webster Review Prizes (poetry): First—Marsha Peterson, for "The Wooden Coat," "Mime, To While Away," "Sledge Diary," and "Young Couple: Version Of An Etching By Kaethe Kollwitz"; Second—Robert Lee Mahon, for "Portraits Of Helen."
Webster Review Prizes (poetry translation): First Prize—Cecilia Liang, for "Twelve Folk Poems" (from the Chinese); Charles Guenther, for "The Crucifixion" (by Cocteau) (from the French).

Wilory Farm
Quemado, TX 78877
Wilory Farm Poetry Contest: First—Barbara Sears McRae, for "For The Fat Woman At The Laundromat"; Second—Linda Buchanan, for "Chamoix"; Third—E. F. Jennings, for "Ode To The Six O'Clock Newsperson."

Writer's Digest
9933 Alliance Rd.
Cincinnati, OH 45242
Writing Competition (First Prize, poetry): Julia Evatt, for "Exchange."

Yale University Library
Box 1603A, Yale Sta.
New Haven, CT 06520
Bollingen Prize in Poetry: M. S. Merwin.

Yale University Press
92A, Yale Sta.
New Haven, CT 06520
Yale Series of Younger Poets: William Virgil Davis, for "One Way To Reconstruct The Scene."

Yankee Magazine
c/o Jean Burden, Poetry Editor
Dublin, NH 03444
Yankee Awards: First—Gene Frumkin, for "Apocalyptic"; Second—Janet Lewis, for "Snail Garden" and Francis Golffing, for "Frame Of Late September"; Honorable Mention—Ruth Moose, for "The Well."

Yuki Teikei Haiku Society of the U.S.A. and Canada
c/o Haiku Journal
Kiyoshi Tokutomi
1020 S. 8th St.
San Jose, CA 95112
Shugyo Award (Grand Prize): Jerald T. Ball.
Yuki Teikei Haiku Society Award: First—Beth Martin Haas; Second—Louise Somers Winder; Third—Raymond Roseliep.
Haiku Journal Award: First—Edwin A. Falkowski; Second—James Hargan; Third—Joan Couzens Sauer.
Golden State Sanwa Bank Award: First—Thelma Murphy; Second—Miriam Sinclair; Third—George Swede.
Sumitomo Bank Award: Brett Brady.
California First Bank Award: Catherine Gumm McCord.

Acknowledgements

The publisher expresses appreciation to the authors represented in this anthology for graciously permitting the inclusion of their poetry.

In addition, credit has been given to all magazines where material in this volume was originally published, with their names appearing after each respective poem.

In individual instances where authors, magazines or publishers required special acknowledgments or credit lines for copyrights they control, such recognition is hereby given as follows:

"Green Pastures," by Dick Allen, first appeared in *Poetry*. © 1979 by The Modern Poetry Association. Reprinted by permission of the Editor of *Poetry*.

"God is Here," by Charles Angoff, is reprinted from *The Literary Review* (Fall, 1979, Vol. 23, No. 1), published by Fairleigh Dickinson University, Madison, NJ 07940.

"Old Man," by Philip Booth, first appeared in *The American Poetry Review*, © 1978 by Philip Booth and reprinted by permission of Philip Booth.

"To His Love in Middle-Age," by Edwin Brock, first appeared in *Poetry*. © 1979 by The Modern Poetry Association. Reprinted by permission of the Editor of *Poetry*.

"The Letters Of Summer," by Christopher Buckley, first appeared in *Poetry*. © 1979 by The Modern Poetry Association. Reprinted by permission of the Editor of *Poetry*.

"The Measuring," by Jared Carter, was first published in *Sou'wester*, © by the Board of Trustees of Southern Illinois University at Edwardsville.

"No White Birds Sing," by John Ciardi, first appeared in *Poetry*. © 1979 by The Modern Poetry Association. Reprinted by permission of the Editor of *Poetry*.

"Last Rites," by David Citino, is reprinted from *The Literary Review* (Spring, 1979, Vol. 22, No. 3), published by Fairleigh Dickinson University, Madison, NJ 07940.

"On Disadvantages Of Central Heating," by Amy Clampitt, first appeared in *The Atlantic Monthly*. © 1979 by The Atlantic Monthly Company, Boston, Mass. Reprinted with permission.

"The Other," by Peter Cooley, first appeared in *The New Yorker*, and is reprinted by permission; © 1979, The New Yorker Magazine, Inc.

"Fragments," by John Cotton, first appeared in *Poetry*. © 1979 by The Modern Poetry Association. Reprinted by permission of the Editor of *Poetry*.

"Flying West, October," by Marky Daniel, originally appeared in *Poetry Northwest*, © by the University of Washington.

"Why Write Poetry," by Pamela Oberson Davis, first appeared in *Pulp* (Vol. 3, Nos. 2-3). Reprinted with permission.

"Fog 9/76," by Richard Morris Dey, first appeared in *Poetry*. © 1979 by The Modern Poetry Association. Reprinted by permission of the Editor of *Poetry*.

"Cathedrals," by W. S. Doxey, first appeared in *The Atlantic Monthly*. © 1978 by The Atlantic Monthly Company, Boston, Mass. Reprinted with permission.

"Experiential Religion," by Travis Du Priest, was first published in *Kentucky Poetry Review* and reprinted in *The Christian Century* and *Contemporary Quarterly*.

"Not Being Wise," by Virginia Elson, is reprinted from *The Literary Review* (Spring, 1979; Vol. 22, No. 3), published by Fairleigh Dickinson University, Madison, NJ 07940.

"Dancer: Four Poems," by Paul Engle, first appeared in *Poetry*. © 1979 by The Modern Poetry Association. Reprinted by permission of the Editor of *Poetry*.

"How To Own Land," by Susan Farley, appeared originally in *The Broadside Series*, published by San Marcos Press.

"After Grave Deliberation," by Elizabeth Flynn, is reprinted from *The Literary Review* (Spring, 1979, Vol. 22, No. 3), published by Fairleigh Dickinson University, Madison, NJ 07940.

"Arachne," by Richard Foerster, is reprinted by permission of the author, all rights reserved.

"Another Cross," by Stephen Gardner, first appeared in *Stone Country*, Vol. 6, No. 2, 1979.

"Meridian," by Brewster Ghiselin, is from his book, *Light*, published by Harry Duncan, Abbatoir Editions, 1978, and also appeared in *The Western Humanities Review*. © by Brewster Ghiselin.

"My Father After Work," by Gary Gildner, is from his collection, *The Runner*, published by University of Pittsburgh Press, and also appeared in *Poetry Northwest*. © 1978 by Gary Gildner. Reprinted by permission of the author.

"One More Time," by Patricia Goedicke, first appeared in *Three Rivers Poetry Journal*, © by Three Rivers Press. The poem is also to be included in the author's book, *Crossing The Same River* (University of Massachusetts Press).

"To Paul Eluard" is taken from *Hybrids of Plants and of Ghosts*, by Jorie Graham, published by Princeton University Press, and is copyrighted © 1980 by Princeton University Press. Reprinted by permission of Princeton University Press.

"Gnostics On Trial," by Linda Gregg, was originally published in *The Kenyon Review*, Vol. I, No. 3 (Summer, 1979). Copyright © Kenyon College.

"The Ritual," by Joy Gwillim, first appeared in *Poetry*. © 1979 by The Modern Poetry Association. Reprinted by permission of the Editor of *Poetry*.

"Not To March," by Kris Hackleman, reprinted from *Insight*, a Christian youth magazine published by Seventh-day Adventists, © 1979, Review and Herald Publishing Association, Washington, D. C. 20012.

"As Rocks Rooted," by Howard G. Hanson, first appeared in *Arizona Quarterly*. Reprinted by permission.

"The Ice Castle," by Michael Harris, first appeared in *The Atlantic Monthly*. © 1979 by The Atlantic Monthly Company, Boston, Mass. Reprinted with permission.

"Hard Way To Learn," by James Hearst, first appeared in *Poetry*. © 1979 by The Modern Poetry Association. Reprinted by permission of the Editor of *Poetry*.

"Two Weeks After An April Frost," by Steven Helmling, is reprinted by permission from *The Hudson Review*, Vol. XXXI, No. 3 (Autumn, 1978). Copyright © 1978 by Steven Helmling.

"The Glassblower," by Andrea Herling, first appeared in *Christianity Today*. © 1979 by *Christianity Today*. Reprinted with permission.

"Himself," by Daniel Hoffman, is reprinted by permission from *The Hudson Review*, Vol. XXXI, No. 2 (Summer, 1978). Copyright © 1978 by Daniel Hoffman.

"Indulgences," by Michael Hogan, first appeared in *National Forum*. © 1979 by Michael Hogan. Reprinted by permission of Michael Hogan.

"Family Portrait," by Rebecca Hood-Adams, first appeared in *Delta Scene*. Reprinted by permission of *Delta Scene*, owner of copyright.

"Mill At Romesdal," by Richard Hugo, first appeared in *Poetry*. © 1979 by The Modern Poetry Association. Reprinted by permission of the Editor of *Poetry*.

"The Wait," by Phyllis Janowitz, first appeared in *The Atlantic Monthly*. © 1978 by The Atlantic Monthly Company, Boston, Mass. Reprinted with permission.

"The Boarding," by Denis Johnson, first appeared in *Poetry*. © 1979 by The Modern Poetry Association. Reprinted by permission of the Editor of *Poetry*.

"Tango," by Elena Jordana, first appeared in *Review*, published by the Center for Inter-American Relations. Reprinted by permission of the Center for Inter-American Relations.

"The Stammerers," by Margaret Kent, first appeared in *Poetry*. © 1979 by The Modern Poetry Association. Reprinted by permission of the Editor of *Poetry*.

"Circles," by Elizabeth Knies, is reprinted by permission from *The Hudson Review*, Vol. XXXI, No. 3 (Autumn, 1978). Copyright © 1978 by Elizabeth Knies.

"Western Ways," by Richard Lattimore, first appeared in *Poetry*. © 1979 by The Modern Poetry Association. Reprinted by permission of the Editor of *Poetry*.

"The Mind Is Still," by Ursula K. Le Guin, was originally published in *The Kenyon Review*, Vol. I, No. 4 (Fall, 1979). Copyright © 1979 Kenyon College. Also Copyright © 1979 by Ursula K. Le Guin. Reprinted by permission of the author and her agent, Virginia Kidd.

"The Library," by John Logan, first appeared in *Poetry*. © 1979 by the Modern Poetry Association. Reprinted by permission of the Editor of *Poetry*.

"Driving: Driven," by David McAleavey, first appeared in *Poetry*. © 1979 by The Modern Poetry Association. Reprinted by permission of the Editor of *Poetry*.

"Going To Press," by Judith Moffett, first appeared in *Poetry*. © 1979 by The Modern Poetry Association. Reprinted by permission of the Editor of *Poetry*.

"The Argument," by Jane P. Moreland, first appeared in *Poetry*. © 1979 by The Modern Poetry Association. Reprinted by permission of the Editor of *Poetry*.

"Meadow Grass," by Michael Mott, first appeared in *Poetry*. © 1979 by The Modern Poetry

Association. Reprinted by permission of the Editor of *Poetry.*

"Playing Catch," by Keith Moul, first appeared in *Pig Iron Magazine,* No. 5, March 1979. Reprinted by permission.

"Lost Objects," by Diana Ó Hehir, first appeared in *Poetry.* © 1979 by The Modern Poetry Association. Reprinted by permission of the Editor of *Poetry.*

"Anxiety About Dying," by Alicia Ostriker, first appeared in *Poetry.* © 1979 by The Modern Poetry Association. Reprinted by permission of the Editor of *Poetry.*

"Missouri Town," by John Palen, originally appeared in *Poetry Northwest,* © 1978 by the University of Washington.

"When At Night," by Mark Perlberg, first appeared in *Poetry.* © 1979 by The Modern Poetry Association. Reprinted by permission of the Editor of *Poetry.*

"Creation Myths," by Burton Raffel, first appeared in *The Michigan Quarterly Review.* Copyright 1979 The University of Michigan. Reprinted with permission.

"Postscript, On A Name," by Stephen Ratcliffe, first appeared in *Poetry.* © 1979 by The Modern Poetry Association. Reprinted by permission of the Editor of *Poetry.*

"Less Is More," by Vern Rutsala, first appeared in *Poetry.* © 1979 by The Modern Poetry Association. Reprinted by permission of the Editor of *Poetry.*

"The Avenues," by David St. John, first appeared in *Poetry.* © 1979 by The Modern Poetry Association. Reprinted by permission of the Editor of *Poetry.*

"England," by Mary Jo Salter, first appeared in *The Atlantic Monthly.* © 1978 by The Atlantic Monthly Company, Boston, Mass. Reprinted with permission.

"Country Landscape," by Sherod Santos, first appeared in *Poetry.* © 1979 by The Modern Poetry Association. Reprinted by permission of the Editor of *Poetry.*

"Fragment Of A Pastoral," by Barry Schwabsky, first appeared in *Poetry.* © 1979 by The Modern Poetry Association. Reprinted by permission of the Editor of *Poetry.*

"Bent Tree," by Peter Serchuk, is reprinted by permission from *The Hudson Review,* Vol. XXXI, No. 2 (Summer, 1978). Copyright © 1978 by Peter Serchuk.

"Judas, Peter," by Luci Shaw, © 1979 by Luci Shaw. Harold Shaw Publishers, Wheaton, IL 60187. Used by permission.

"The Deer," by Laurie Sheck, first appeared in *Poetry.* © 1979 by The Modern Poetry Association. Reprinted by permission of the Editor of *Poetry.*

"How To Amuse A Stone," by Richard Shelton, first appeared in *Poetry.* © 1979 by The Modern Poetry Association. Reprinted by permission of the Editor of *Poetry.*

"Poem Of The Mother," by Myra Sklarew, first appeared in *Quest / 79.* Reprinted with permission.

"The Roundhouse Voices," by Dave Smith, first appeared in *The New Yorker* and is included in his book, *Goshawk, Antelope,* published by University of Illinois Press. © 1979 by Dave Smith. Reprinted with permission of Dave Smith and University of Illinois Press.

"Epitaph Of A Stripper," by William Jay Smith © 1979 by William Jay Smith. Reprinted by permission of William Jay Smith.

"Initial Response," by Katherine Soniat, first appeared in *The American Scholar,* published by United Chapters of Phi Beta Kappa. Reprinted by permission of Katherine Soniat.

"Owning A Dead Man," by Marcia Southwick, first appeared in *Poetry.* © 1979 by The Modern Poetry Association. Reprinted by permission of the Editor of *Poetry.*

"The Orchard," by Michael Spence, first appeared in *Jam To-Day,* No. 7. Copyright © by *Jam To-Day.* Reprinted by permission.

"The Center of the Garden," by Ann Stanford, first appeared in *The Atlantic Monthly.* © 1978 by The Atlantic Monthly Company, Boston, Mass. Reprinted with permission.

"Circumstance," by Laurie Stroblas, first appeared in *Pulp* (Vol. 3, Nos. 2-3). © by Laurie Stroblas. Reprinted with permission.

"The League Of Selves," by Alvin Tofler © 1979 by Alvin Tofler. Reprinted by permission of Alvin Tofler.

"Daughter," by Ellen Bryant Voigt, first appeared in *The Atlantic Monthly.* © 1979 by The Atlantic Monthly Company, Boston, Mass. Reprinted with permission.

"Ode To The Muse On Behalf Of A Young Poet," by David Wagoner, first appeared in *The Atlantic Monthly.* © 1979 by The Atlantic Monthly Company. Reprinted with permission.

"Being Herded Past The Prison's Honor Farm," by David Wagoner, first appeared in *Poetry.* © 1979 by The Modern Poetry Association. Reprinted by permission of the Editor of *Poetry.*

"Around The Block," by Keith Waldrop, first appeared in *Poetry*. © 1979 by The Modern Poetry Association. Reprinted by permission of the Editor of *Poetry*.

"Instructions For A Park," by Brad Walker, is © 1979 by Washington and Lee University, reprinted from *Shenandoah: The Washington & Lee University Review*, with the permission of the Editor.

"Christographia 35," by Eugene Warren, first appeared in *Christianity Today*. © 1979 by *Christianity Today*. Reprinted with permission.

"Memoir," by Roger Weingarten, first appeared in *Poetry*. © 1979 by The Modern Poetry Association. Reprinted by permission of the Editor of *Poetry*.

"Of All Plants, The Tree," by Mary Jane White, is from the author's book, *The Work Of The Icon Painter*, to be published by Osiers Press.

"Dissonance," by Cedric Whitman, first appeared in *Poetry*. © 1979 by The Modern Poetry Association. Reprinted by permission of the Editor of *Poetry*.

"On The Last Page Of The Last Yellow Legal Pad in Rome Before Taking Off For Dacca on Air Bangladesh," by Miller Williams © 1979 by Miller Williams.

"Sheep In The Rain," by James Wright, first appeared in *Poetry*. © 1979 by The Modern Poetry Association. Reprinted by permission of the Editor of *Poetry*.

"In A Mist," by Al Young © 1978 by Al Young. Reprinted by permission of the author.

The following poems were first published in Ball State University *Forum*: "Humiliation Revisited," by Nora Trimble Ashley; "Tides," by Will H. Blackwell; "Unplanned Design," by Neal Bowers; "Buffalo," by Louis Daniel Brodsky; "Remembering Apple Time," by John T. Hitchner; "Black Horse Running," by Noel Maureen Valis. Reprinted by permission of Ball State University *Forum*, holder of international copyright.

The following poems were first published in *Cimarron Review*: "The Insect Shuffle Method," by Gary Tapp; "My Childhood's Bedroom," by Charles Tisdale; "Deliver Me, O Lord, From My Daily Bread," by Jeanne Murray Walker. Reprinted with permission of Board of Regents for Oklahoma State University, copyright owner of *Cimarron Review*.

The following poems first appeared in *The Iowa Review*, published by The University of Iowa: "Ashes," by Philip Levine; "Lullaby," by Sue Owen; "Eagle Squadron," by Vern Rutsala. Reprinted with permission of The University of Iowa and the respective authors.

The following poems are reprinted from *The Massachusetts Review*, © 1979 The Massachusetts Review, Inc.: "My Relatives For The Most," by Frederick B. Hudson; "The Wedding," by Sandra Kohler; "Sonnet to Seabrook," by David Ray; "Human Geography," by Ruth Whitman.

The following poems first appeared in *Neworld*: "What I Did Last Summer," by Ron Ikan; "How Night Falls In The Courtyard," by Christine Rimmer; "Mirror Images," by Laura Speer. Reprinted by permission of *Neworld: The Multi-Cultural Magazine of the Arts*.

The following poems first appeared in *Ploughshares*, © 1979 by Ploughshares, Inc., and reprinted with permission: "Hunting With My Father," by Tom Absher; "Elegy For My Father," by Robert Louthan; "Love Poem," by Susan Irene Rea. Reprinted by permission of Ploughshares, Inc. and by the individual authors.

The following poems first appeared in *Prairie Schooner*: "Holding On," by Richard Jackson; "The Homes," by Anne Pitkin; "In The Season Of Wolves And Names," by Mariève Rugo; "Morning," by Marjorie Saiser. © 1979 by The University of Nebraska Press.

The following poems first appeared in *Primavera*: "Your Woods," by Margaret Holley; "Shopping," by Jane Chance Nitzche; "The Death Watchers," by Alice Ryerson. © 1979 by *Primavera*.

"The Band," in Carl Dennis' *Signs and Wonders*, copyright © 1979 by Princeton University Press (pp. 68/69). Reprinted by permission of Princeton University Press.

The following poems first appeared in *The Yale Review*: "Late Autumn Walk," by J. D. McClatchy; "Early Morning Of Another World," by Tom McKeown; "Wake," by Elizabeth Spires; "Omalos," by Rosanna Warren. © Yale University. Reprinted by permission.

The following poems first appeared in *Yankee*: "The Blue Church," by Peter Balakian; "Absence," by Jeannette Barnes; "Welcome To This House," by Faye George; "Lament Of A Last Letter," by Janet E. Harrison; "Dragon Lesson," by James Hearst; "There Is Good News," by Josephine Jacobsen; "The Beasts Of Boston," by Betty Lowry; "Neighbors," by Charles Malam; "New England Greenhouse," by Rennie McQuilkin; "Breakfast," by Robin Shectman; "Three Things," by May Sarton; "Circa 1814," by David Staudt. Reprinted by permission of Yankee, Inc., and by the individual authors.